Hannah Bartha/13

W9-BJO-615

MATHPOWER™ *Seven*

Authors

George Knill, B.Sc., M.S.Ed.
Hamilton, Ontario

Dino Dottori, B.Sc., M.S.Ed.
North Bay, Ontario

Eileen Collins, B.A., M.Ed.
Hamilton, Ontario

Jan Cornwall, B.A.
Scarborough, Ontario

Reviewers

Mary Crowley
Halifax, Nova Scotia

Terry Clifford
Winnipeg, Manitoba

Judith Lambie
Saskatoon, Saskatchewan

Bob Michie
Calgary, Alberta

McGraw-Hill Ryerson Limited

Toronto Montreal New York Auckland Bogotá Caracas
Lisbon London Madrid Mexico Milan New Delhi Paris
San Juan Singapore Sydney Tokyo

Copyright © McGraw-Hill Ryerson Limited, 1993.
All rights reserved. No part of this publication may be reproduced or transmitted in any form or by any means, or stored in a data base or retrieval system, without the prior written permission of McGraw-Hill Ryerson Limited.

ISBN 0-07-549888-X

1 2 3 4 5 6 7 8 9 10 TRI 2 1 0 9 8 7 6 5 4 3

Printed and bound in Canada

Care has been taken to trace ownership of copyright material contained in this text. The publishers will gladly accept any information that will enable them to rectify any reference or credit in subsequent editions.

Canadian Cataloguing in Publication Data

Main entry under title:

Mathpower™ 7

Includes index.

ISBN 0-07-549888-X

1. Mathematics. I. Knill, George, date— .

QA107.M387 1992 510 C92-095348-4

Executive Editor: Michael Webb
Editors: Jean Ford and Bonnie Di Malta
Senior Supervising Editor: Carol Altilia
Cover and Interior Design: Pronk&Associates
Electronic Assembly: Pronk&Associates
Cover Illustration: Doug Martin

This book was manufactured in Canada using acid-free and recycled paper.

CONTENTS

USING MATHPOWER™ 7 x

A Problem Solving Model xii

Exploring Math xiii

Problem Solving xiii
Communication xiv
Reasoning xv
Connections xvi
Number and Number Relationships xvii
Number Systems and Number Theory xviii
Computation and Estimation xix
Patterns and Functions xx
Algebra xxi
Statistics xxii
Probability xxiii
Geometry xxiv
Measurement xxv

CHAPTER 1
Number Connections 1

GETTING STARTED
Mathematics of a Pencil 2
Warm Up, *Mental Math* 3
1.1 Choosing a Calculation Method 4
LEARNING TOGETHER
Comparing and Ordering Numbers 6
1.2 Place Value 8
1.3 Rounding Numbers: *Mental Math* 10
LEARNING TOGETHER
Exploring Mental Math 12
1.4 Problem Solving: Look for a Pattern 14
1.5 Estimating Sums and Differences: *Mental Math* 16
1.6 Adding and Subtracting Numbers 18
1.7 Problem Solving: Guess and Check 20
1.8 Multiplying by Powers of Ten: *Mental Math* 22
1.9 Using Powers of Ten: *Mental Math* 23
1.10 Estimating Products: *Mental Math* 24
1.11 Multiplying Numbers 26
1.12 Dividing by Powers of Ten: *Mental Math* 28
1.13 Estimating Quotients: *Mental Math* 30
TECHNOLOGY
The Computerized Home 31
1.14 Short Division 32
1.15 Dividing Numbers 34
1.16 Problem Solving: Make an Assumption 36
1.17 Order of Operations 38
CONNECTING MATH AND CANADIAN HISTORY
On What Day Did It Happen? 40
Review 42
Group Decision Making: Making a Television Commercial 43
Chapter Check 44
Problem Solving: Using the Strategies 45

Dog→

CHAPTER 2
Number Theory 47

GETTING STARTED
The Hundred Chart 48
Mental Math 49

LEARNING TOGETHER
Divisibility Tests 50

2.1 Factors and Divisibility 52
2.2 Problem Solving: Work Backward 54
2.3 Prime and Composite Numbers 56
2.4 Prime Factors 58
2.5 Problem Solving: Draw a Diagram or Flow Chart 60

TECHNOLOGY
How Computers Calculate 62

CONNECTING MATH AND LOGICAL REASONING
Three-Dimensional Tick-Tack-Toe 63

2.6 Greatest Common Factor 64
2.7 Lowest Common Multiple 66
2.8 Exponents 68
2.9 Problem Solving: Use a Data Bank 70
2.10 More About Order of Operations 72
2.11 Problem Solving: Solve a Simpler Problem 74

Review 76
Group Decision Making: Researching Media Careers 77
Chapter Check 78
Problem Solving: Using the Strategies 79

CHAPTER 3
Geometry 81

GETTING STARTED
Tangrams 82
Mental Math 83

LEARNING TOGETHER
Geometry Around Us 84

3.1 The Language of Geometry 86
3.2 Angles 88
3.3 Classifying Angles 90
3.4 Problem Solving: Sequence the Operations 92
3.5 Lines: Intersecting, Perpendicular, and Parallel 94

CONNECTING MATH AND GEOGRAPHY
Colouring Maps 96

3.6 Classifying Triangles 98
3.7 The Sum of the Interior Angles in a Triangle 100
3.8 Problem Solving: Use a Table 102
3.9 Polygons 104

TECHNOLOGY
Making Tracks with LOGO 106

3.10 Congruent Figures 108

LEARNING TOGETHER
Lines of Symmetry 110

3.11 Problem Solving: Identify the Extra Information 112

Review 114
Group Decision Making: Making Primary/Junior Math Games 115
Chapter Check 116
Problem Solving: Using the Strategies 117

CHAPTER 4
Perimeter and Area 119

GETTING STARTED
Data Bank:
Travelling Around Canada 120
Decimal Skills, *Mental Math* 121

LEARNING TOGETHER
Estimating and Measuring Length 122

4.1 Perimeter 124
4.2 Perimeters of Special Figures 126
4.3 Circumference 128
4.4 Working with Perimeter 130
4.5 Problem Solving:
Find the Missing Information 132

LEARNING TOGETHER
Estimating and Measuring Area 134

LEARNING TOGETHER
Relating Perimeter and Area 136

4.6 Area of a Rectangle and Square 138
4.7 Areas of Figures 140
4.8 Area of a Parallelogram 142
4.9 Problem Solving:
Use a Formula 144
4.10 Area of a Triangle 146

TECHNOLOGY
How Computer Programs Work 148

TECHNOLOGY
Programming Formulas in BASIC 149

4.11 Working with Area 150

CONNECTING MATH AND ENGLISH
Lewis Carroll 152

4.12 Problem Solving:
Use Logical Reasoning 154

Review 156

Group Decision Making:
Researching Travel Industry Careers 157

Chapter Check 158

Problem Solving:
Using the Strategies 159

Cumulative Review, Chapters 1 - 4 160

CHAPTER 5
Fractions 163

GETTING STARTED
Fractions 164
Tangrams, *Mental Math* 165

5.1 The Meaning of Fractions 166
5.2 Equivalent Fractions 168
5.3 Improper Fractions and
Mixed Numbers 170
5.4 Comparing and Ordering Fractions 172
5.5 Estimating Sums and Differences
with Fractions 174
5.6 Adding Fractions 176
5.7 Subtracting Fractions 178
5.8 Adding and Subtracting
Mixed Numbers 180

LEARNING TOGETHER
Multiplying Fractions 182

TECHNOLOGY
Programming Computer
Games in BASIC 183

5.9 Multiplying Fractions 184
5.10 Reciprocals: *Mental Math* 186
LEARNING TOGETHER
Dividing Fractions 187
5.11 Dividing Fractions 188
5.12 Multiplying and Dividing Mixed Numbers 190
5.13 Decimals and Fractions 192
5.14 Order of Operations with Fractions 194
CONNECTING MATH AND TIME
The Sundial 195
Review 196
Group Decision Making: Designing a Cross Number Puzzle 197
Chapter Check 198
Problem Solving: Using the Strategies 199

CHAPTER 6
Ratio and Rate 201

GETTING STARTED
Finding Patterns 202
Warm Up, *Mental Math* 203
6.1 Ratio 204
6.2 Equivalent Ratios 206
6.3 Solving Proportions 208
TECHNOLOGY
Technology on the Job 210
TECHNOLOGY
Pattern Power from Calculators 211
6.4 Similar Triangles 212

6.5 Scale Drawings 214
6.6 Maps and Scales 216
CONNECTING MATH AND GEOGRAPHY
Terry Fox and the Marathon of Hope 218
LEARNING TOGETHER
Rates 220
6.7 Rates 222
6.8 Unit Pricing 224
Review 226
Group Decision Making: Designing a Classroom of the Future 227
Chapter Check 228
Problem Solving: Using the Strategies 229

CHAPTER 7
Percent 231

GETTING STARTED
Parts of 100, Advertising 232
Decimals and Fractions, *Mental Math* 233
LEARNING TOGETHER
Percents 234
7.1 Percent 236
7.2 Fractions and Decimals as Percents 238
7.3 Percents as Fractions and Decimals 240
7.4 Finding a Percent of a Number 242
7.5 Estimating with Percent: *Mental Math* 244

7.6 Finding the Percent 246
TECHNOLOGY
The Arts 248
TECHNOLOGY
More Pattern Power from Calculators 249
7.7 Percents Greater Than 100% 250
7.8 Simple Interest 251
7.9 Discount and Sale Price 252
7.10 Goods and Services Tax (GST) 253
7.11 Provincial Sales Tax (PST) 254
7.12 Commission 255
CONNECTING MATH AND THE ENVIRONMENT
The Shrinking World of the Grizzly 256
Review 258
Group Decision Making:
Researching Community Service Careers 259
Chapter Check 260
Problem Solving:
Using the Strategies 261

CHAPTER 8
Three-Dimensional Geometry 263

GETTING STARTED
Models in Three Dimensions 264
Polygons and Lines of Symmetry, *Mental Math* 265
8.1 Three-Dimensional Figures 266
8.2 Identifying and Classifying Polyhedra 268
8.3 Solids, Shells, and Skeletons 270
8.4 Planes of Symmetry 271
TECHNOLOGY
Designing with LOGO 272
8.5 Nets of Polyhedra 274
8.6 Surface Area 276
8.7 Regular Polyhedra: The Platonic Solids 278
8.8 Perspective of Objects 280
LEARNING TOGETHER
Estimating and Measuring Volume 282
8.9 Volumes of Prisms 284
LEARNING TOGETHER
Estimating and Measuring Mass 286
LEARNING TOGETHER
Estimating and Measuring Capacity 287
8.10 Volume, Capacity, and Mass 288
CONNECTING MATH AND SCIENCE
Geometry in Nature 290
Review 292
Group Decision Making:
Volunteering in the Community 293
Chapter Check 294
Problem Solving:
Using the Strategies 295
Cumulative Review, Chapters 5 - 8 296

CHAPTER 9
Statistics 299

GETTING STARTED
Testing Computer Games 300
Math Skills for Statistics, *Mental Math* 301
9.1 Collecting Data 302
LEARNING TOGETHER
Collecting Data 304
9.2 Using a Sample to Make Predictions 306
9.3 Reading and Drawing Pictographs 308
9.4 Reading Bar Graphs and Broken-Line Graphs 310
9.5 Drawing Bar Graphs 312
9.6 Drawing Broken-Line Graphs 314
9.7 Reading Circle Graphs 316
9.8 Drawing Circle Graphs 318
TECHNOLOGY
Computer Databases 320

9.9 The Mean or Average 322
9.10 The Median and the Mode 324
9.11 Stem-and-Leaf Plots 326
LEARNING TOGETHER
Misleading Graphs 328
9.12 Possible Outcomes 330
9.13 Probability 332
CONNECTING MATH AND LOGIC
The Game Show 334
The Dinosaur Museum 335
Review 336
Group Decision Making:
Researching Health Careers 337
Chapter Check 338
Problem Solving:
Using the Strategies 339

CHAPTER 10
Integers 341

GETTING STARTED
A Number Jigsaw, A Lock 342
Warm Up, *Mental Math* 343
10.1 Integers 344
10.2 Comparing and Ordering Integers 346 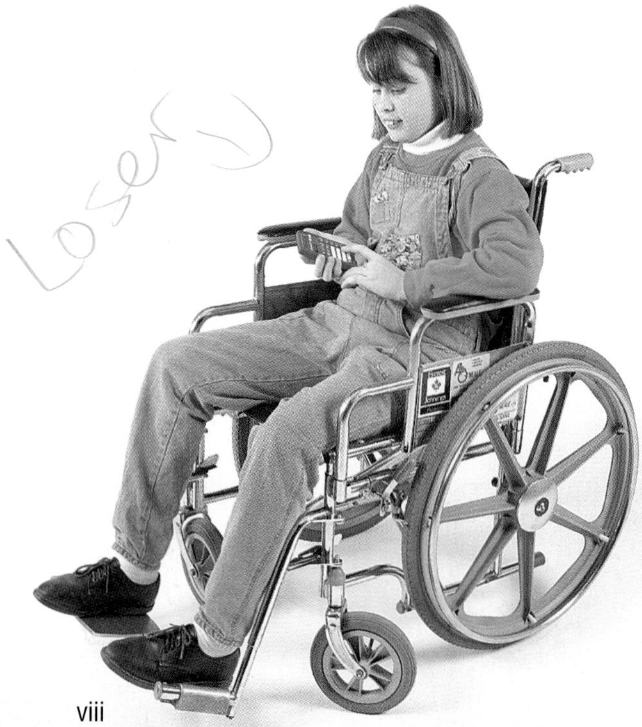
LEARNING TOGETHER
Investigating Integers 348
10.3 Adding Integers 350
10.4 Subtracting Integers 352
CONNECTING MATH AND LOGIC
Codes and Cyphers 354
10.5 Multiplying Integers 356
10.6 Dividing Integers 358
TECHNOLOGY
Integers on a Calculator 360
Review 362
Group Decision Making:
Planning a Vacation 363
Chapter Check 364
Problem Solving:
Using the Strategies 365

CHAPTER 11
Algebra 367

GETTING STARTED
Number Tiles 368
Warm Up, *Mental Math* 369
11.1 Variables in Expressions 370
11.2 Words and Symbols 372
11.3 Solving Equations 374
LEARNING TOGETHER
See-Saw Math 376
11.4 Solving Equations by Subtraction 377
11.5 Solving Equations by Addition 378
11.6 Solving Equations by Division 379
11.7 Solving Equations by Multiplication 380
11.8 Solving Equations in Two Steps 381
11.9 Writing and Reading Equations 382
11.10 Using Equations to Solve Problems 384
11.11 Inequalities 386
11.12 Tables of Values 388
TECHNOLOGY
Computer Spreadsheets 390
11.13 Ordered Pairs 392
11.14 The Coordinate Plane 394
11.15 Graphing Ordered Pairs 396
CONNECTING MATH AND LANGUAGE
Braille 398

Review 400

Group Decision Making: Researching Business Careers 401

Chapter Check 402

Problem Solving: Using the Strategies 403

CHAPTER 12 Transformations 405

GETTING STARTED
- Dominoes 406
- Polyominoes, *Mental Math* 407

LEARNING TOGETHER
- Slides, Flips, and Turns 408

LEARNING TOGETHER
- Tessellations 410

12.1 Translations 412

12.2 Reflections 414

12.3 Rotations 416

TECHNOLOGY
- Transformations in Computer Graphics 418

12.4 Lines of Symmetry 420

12.5 Rotational Symmetry 422

LEARNING TOGETHER
- Enlargements and Reductions 424

LEARNING TOGETHER
- Distortions 425

CONNECTING MATH AND SCIENCE
- Sending Messages into Space 426

Review 428

Group Decision Making: Saving the Environment 429

Chapter Check 430

Problem Solving: Using the Strategies 431

Cumulative Review, Chapters 9 - 12 432

CHAPTER 13 Geometric Constructions 435

GETTING STARTED
- Construction Patterns 436
- *Mental Math* 437

13.1 Constructing Congruent Line Segments and Angles 438

13.2 Constructing Bisectors 440

13.3 Constructing Perpendiculars 442

13.4 Constructing Parallel Lines 444

TECHNOLOGY
- Computer Assisted Design 446

13.5 Constructing Polygons 448

CONNECTING MATH AND ENGINEERING
- Paper Airplanes 450

Review 452

Group Decision Making: Organizing a Career Day 453

Chapter Check 454

Problem Solving: Using the Strategies 455

Data Bank 456

Glossary 465

Index 473

USING MATHPOWER™ 7

Each chapter contains a number of sections.
In a typical section, you find the following features.

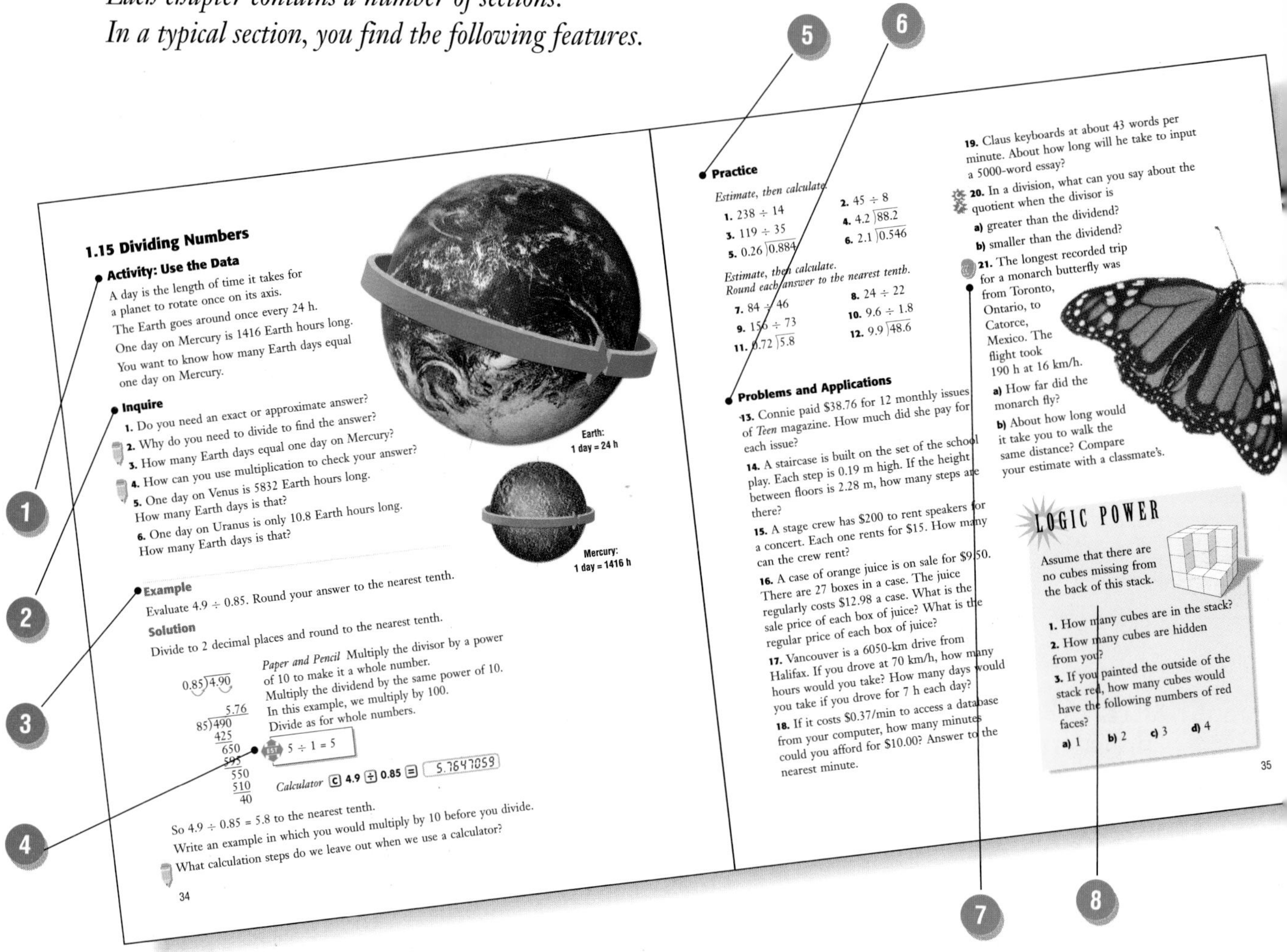

5 6

1.15 Dividing Numbers

Activity: Use the Data

A day is the length of time it takes for a planet to rotate once on its axis.
The Earth goes around once every 24 h.
One day on Mercury is 1416 Earth hours long.
You want to know how many Earth days equal one day on Mercury.

Earth:
1 day = 24 h

Mercury:
1 day = 1416 h

Inquire

1. Do you need an exact or approximate answer?
2. Why do you need to divide to find the answer?
3. How many Earth days equal one day on Mercury?
4. How can you use multiplication to check your answer?
5. One day on Venus is 5832 Earth hours long. How many Earth days is that?
6. One day on Uranus is only 10.8 Earth hours long. How many Earth days is that?

Example

Evaluate 4.9 ÷ 0.85. Round your answer to the nearest tenth.

Solution

Divide to 2 decimal places and round to the nearest tenth.

$0.85\overline{)4.90}$

Paper and Pencil Multiply the divisor by a power of 10 to make it a whole number.
Multiply the dividend by the same power of 10.
In this example, we multiply by 100.
Divide as for whole numbers.

$$\begin{array}{r} 5.76 \\ 85\overline{)490} \\ 425 \\ \hline 650 \\ 595 \\ \hline 550 \\ 510 \\ \hline 40 \end{array}$$

EST 5 ÷ 1 = 5

Calculator C 4.9 ÷ 0.85 = 5.7647059

So 4.9 ÷ 0.85 ≐ 5.8 to the nearest tenth.
Write an example in which you would multiply by 10 before you divide.
What calculation steps do we leave out when we use a calculator?

34

Practice

Estimate, then calculate.

1. 238 ÷ 14
2. 45 ÷ 8
3. 119 ÷ 35
4. $4.2\overline{)88.2}$
5. $0.26\overline{)0.884}$
6. $2.1\overline{)0.546}$

Estimate, then calculate. Round each answer to the nearest tenth.

7. 84 ÷ 46
8. 24 ÷ 22
9. 156 ÷ 73
10. 9.6 ÷ 1.8
11. $0.72\overline{)5.8}$
12. $9.9\overline{)48.6}$

Problems and Applications

13. Connie paid $38.76 for 12 monthly issues of *Teen* magazine. How much did she pay for each issue?
14. A staircase is built on the set of the school play. Each step is 0.19 m high. If the height between floors is 2.28 m, how many steps are there?
15. A stage crew has $200 to rent speakers for a concert. Each one rents for $15. How many can the crew rent?
16. A case of orange juice is on sale for $9.50. There are 27 boxes in a case. The juice regularly costs $12.98 a case. What is the sale price of each box of juice? What is the regular price of each box of juice?
17. Vancouver is a 6050-km drive from Halifax. If you drove at 70 km/h, how many hours would you take? How many days would you take if you drove for 7 h each day?
18. If it costs $0.37/min to access a database from your computer, how many minutes could you afford for $10.00? Answer to the nearest minute.
19. Claus keyboards at about 43 words per minute. About how long will he take to input a 5000-word essay?
20. In a division, what can you say about the quotient when the divisor is
a) greater than the dividend?
b) smaller than the dividend?
21. The longest recorded trip for a monarch butterfly was from Toronto, Ontario, to Catorce, Mexico. The flight took 190 h at 16 km/h.
a) How far did the monarch fly?
b) About how long would it take you to walk the same distance? Compare your estimate with a classmate's.

LOGIC POWER

Assume that there are no cubes missing from the back of this stack.

1. How many cubes are in the stack?
2. How many cubes are hidden from you?
3. If you painted the outside of the stack red, how many cubes would have the following numbers of red faces?
a) 1 b) 2 c) 3 d) 4

35

1 2 3 4 7 8

1

You start with an activity to generate your own learning.

The inquire questions help you learn from the activity.

The example shows you how to use what you have learned.

The EST logo in a solution indicates an estimate.

These questions let you practise what you have learned.

These questions let you apply and extend what you have learned.

These logos indicate special kinds of questions.

The pencil logo tells you that you will be writing about math.

The critical thinking logo indicates that you will need to think carefully before you answer a question.

The working together logo shows you opportunities for working with a classmate or in a larger group.

The power questions are challenging and fun. They encourage you to reason mathematically.

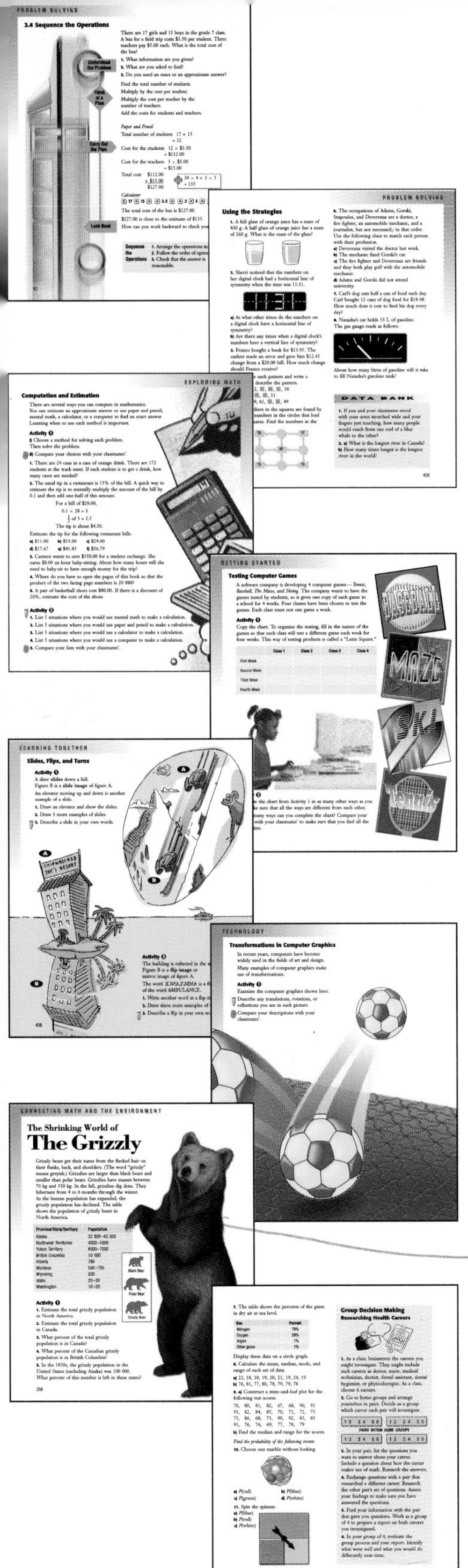

In the first 4 chapters of the book, there are 13 P[…] SOLVING sections that help you to use different […] ing strategies.

At or near the end of each chapter is a page h[…] SOLVING: Using the Strategies. To solve the […] page, you use the strategies you have studied. In all cha[…] except chapter 1, this page ends with DATA BANK questions. To solve them, you need to look up information in the Data Bank on pages 456 to 463.

There are 13 EXPLORING MATH pages before chapter 1. The activities on these pages let you explore 13 mathematical standards that will be essential for citizens of the twenty-first century.

A GETTING STARTED section begins each chapter. This section reviews, in a fun way, what you should know before you work on the chapter. Each GETTING STARTED section includes a set of Mental Math questions.

In LEARNING TOGETHER sections, you learn by completing activities with your classmates.

The TECHNOLOGY sections show you some uses of technology and how you can apply technology to solve problems.

Some sections are headed CONNECTING MATH AND.... In these sections, you apply math to other subject areas, such as geography, history, language, science, and the environment.

Each chapter includes sets of questions called REVIEW and CHAPTER CHECK, so that you can test your progress.

At the end of each review is a column headed GROUP DECISION MAKING. Here, you work with your classmates to research careers and do other projects.

Chapters 4, 8, and 12 end with sets of questions headed CUMULATIVE REVIEW. These three reviews cover the work you did in chapters 1-4, 5-8, and 9-12.

The GLOSSARY on pages 465 to 471 helps you to understand mathematical terms.

Problem Solving Model

The world is full of mathematical problems. Just think of all the problems you solve in day-to-day living. Whatever career you choose, you will have to solve problems in order to make decisions. *MATHPOWER*™ 7 will help you to develop the skills you need to solve problems.

George Polya was one of the world's best problem solvers. The problem solving model used in this book has been adapted from a model developed by George Polya.

The problem solving model includes the following 4 stages.

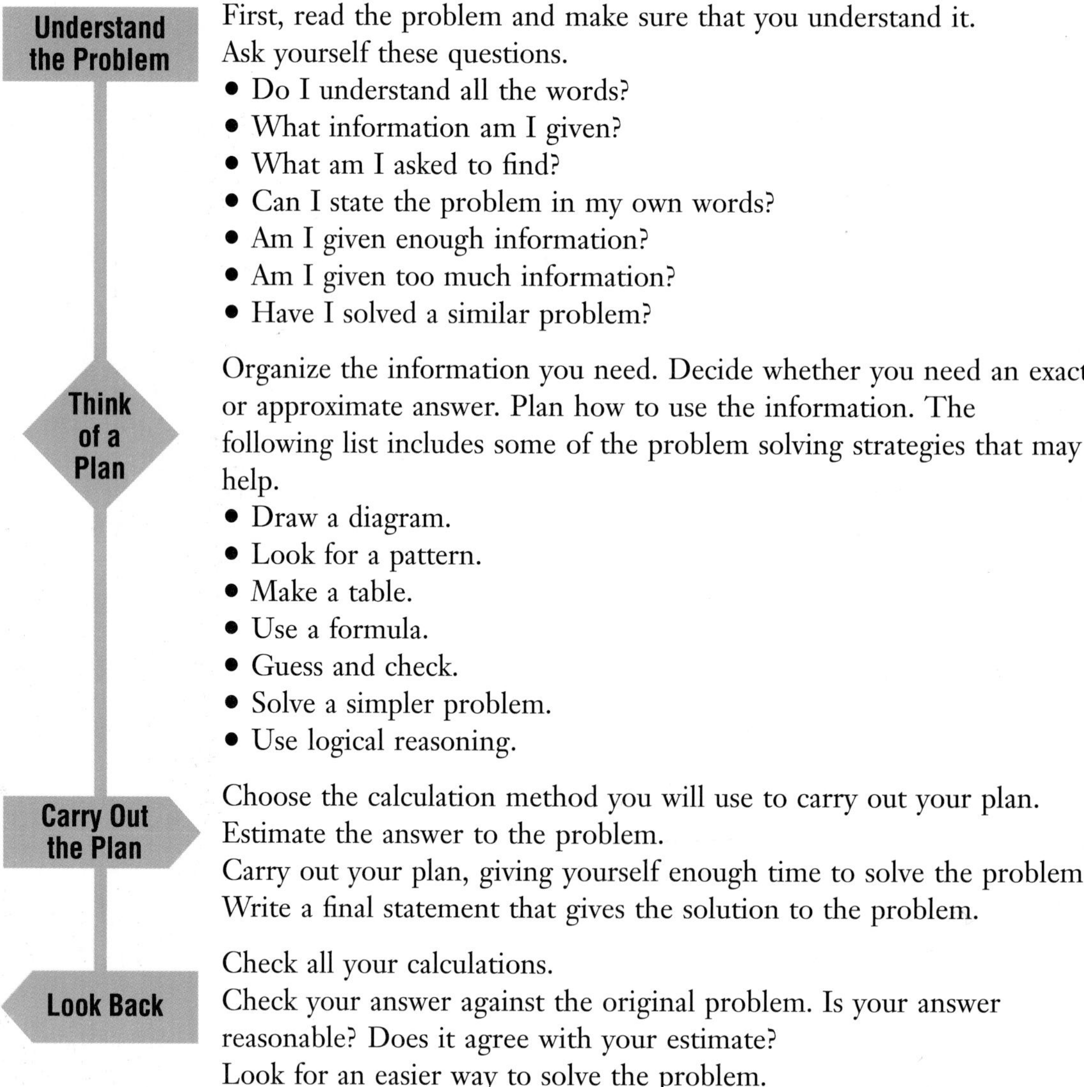

First, read the problem and make sure that you understand it. Ask yourself these questions.

- Do I understand all the words?
- What information am I given?
- What am I asked to find?
- Can I state the problem in my own words?
- Am I given enough information?
- Am I given too much information?
- Have I solved a similar problem?

Organize the information you need. Decide whether you need an exact or approximate answer. Plan how to use the information. The following list includes some of the problem solving strategies that may help.

- Draw a diagram.
- Look for a pattern.
- Make a table.
- Use a formula.
- Guess and check.
- Solve a simpler problem.
- Use logical reasoning.

Choose the calculation method you will use to carry out your plan.
Estimate the answer to the problem.
Carry out your plan, giving yourself enough time to solve the problem.
Write a final statement that gives the solution to the problem.

Check all your calculations.
Check your answer against the original problem. Is your answer reasonable? Does it agree with your estimate?
Look for an easier way to solve the problem.

Problem Solving

Mathematics gives you the power to solve problems. Strong problem solving skills will help you to tackle the world.

Activity

Solve the following problems. In each case, write a short description of your method. Compare your solutions and your methods with your classmates'.

1. It is three o'clock in the afternoon. How many times will the hands of the watch cross in the next 12 h?

2. a) Use the digits 2, 3, 4, 5, and 6 to form a 3-digit number and a 2-digit number so that their product is as large as possible.

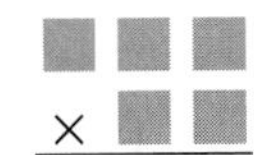

b) Place the digits so that the product is as small as possible.

3. You must take a dog, a cat, and a mouse across a river in a boat so small it will only take one across at a time. You cannot leave the dog and cat alone because the dog will scare off the cat. You cannot leave the cat and mouse alone because the cat will scare off the mouse. How do you get them all across the river?

4. a) Use markers or coins to make the triangle.

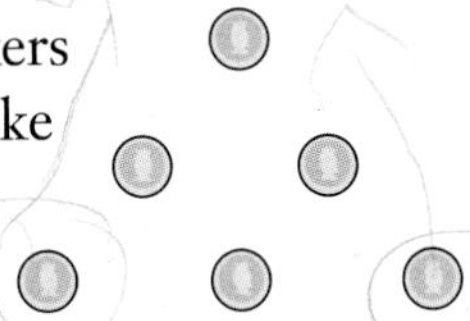

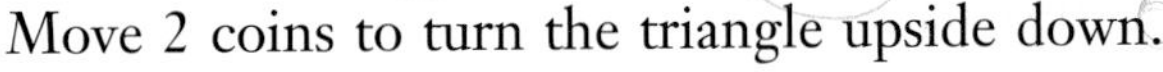

Move 2 coins to turn the triangle upside down.

b) Move 3 coins to turn this triangle upside down.

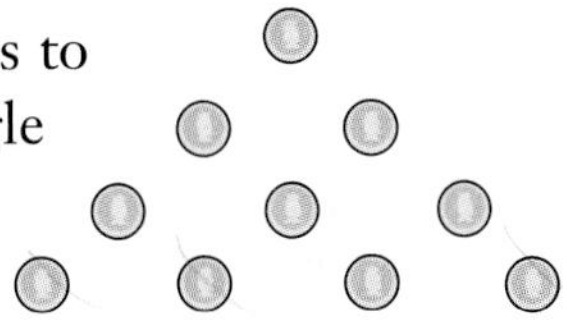

c) What is the smallest number of moves you would need to turn a 15-coin triangle upside down?

Communication

Mathematics is a language that helps you communicate your ideas clearly.

Activity ❶

This puzzle shows how you can communicate in mathematics using words, pictures, or symbols.

1. Examine the following table.

Words	Pictures	Symbols
Think of a number.	♥	n
Add three.	♥♦♦♦	$n + 3$
Multiply by two.	♥♥♦♦♦♦♦♦	$2 \times n + 6$
Subtract four.	♥♥♦♦	$2 \times n + 2$
Divide by two.	♥♦	$n + 1$
Subtract your original number.	♦	1

2. Describe why this number puzzle always gives the same result.

3. Change the words in the chart so that the answer is 3.

Activity ❷

A magazine surveyed teenagers to determine the number of hours they spent listening to music each week.

1. Predict the national average and give your reasons.

2. Share your predictions with your group. What does the group predict the national average to be? Write a summary of the group discussion.

3. In your group, decide how a national survey could be taken. Where would you look for the results of such a survey?

4. Design and conduct a class survey to determine the number of hours students listen to music each week. Prepare a written report. Compare the results of the survey with your predictions. Describe why there are differences.

Reasoning

Reasoning is what you do when you think your way through a problem. The ability to reason logically is a skill that you can improve with practice.

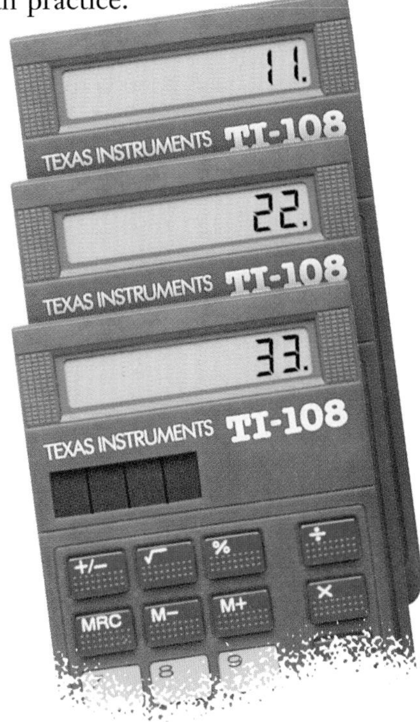

Activity ❶

Use a calculator to do the first three multiplications in each question. Then identify the pattern and complete the table without a calculator.

1.
$99 \times 11 =$ ■
$99 \times 22 =$ ■
$99 \times 33 =$ ■
$99 \times 44 =$ ■
$99 \times 55 =$ ■
$99 \times 66 =$ ■
$99 \times 77 =$ ■
$99 \times 88 =$ ■
$99 \times 99 =$ ■

2.
$99 \times 111 =$ ■
$99 \times 222 =$ ■
$99 \times 333 =$ ■
$99 \times 444 =$ ■
$99 \times 555 =$ ■
$99 \times 666 =$ ■
$99 \times 777 =$ ■
$99 \times 888 =$ ■
$99 \times 999 =$ ■

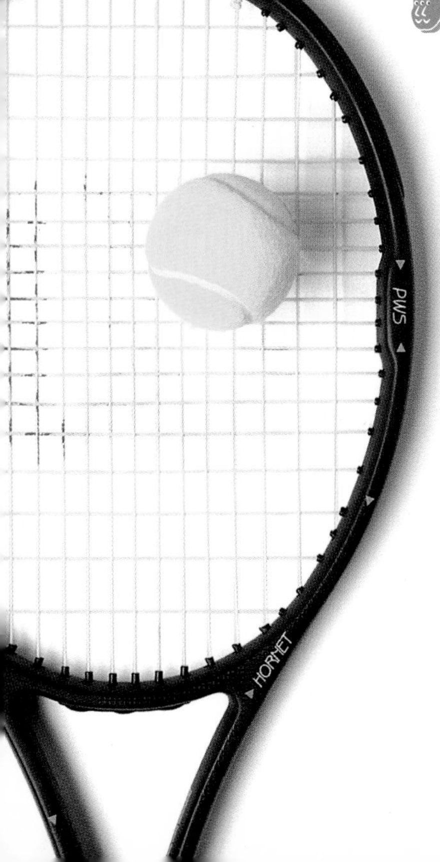

Activity ❷

Solve each problem. Compare your solution and your method with your classmates'.

1. If ▲▲▲ balances ●●●●●

and ★ balances ●●▲

will ▲▲▲▲ balance ★●●● ?

2. Three women, Carol, Janine, and Sue and their husbands, Mark, Ravi, and Evan, were playing tennis. In a doubles match, Mark partnered Ravi's wife and Carol's husband partnered Janine. Evan sat out with his sister. Who is married to whom?

Activity ❸

Determine each pattern and find the next 3 numbers.

1. 8, 6, 13, 11, 18, ■, ■, ■

2. 1, 2, 4, 7, 11, ■, ■, ■

3. 1, 2, 3, 5, 8, 13, ■, ■, ■

4. 1, 4, 9, 16, ■, ■, ■

Connections

Mathematical thinking can be found in many other areas such as art, music, and science.

A type of art called *Op Art* can be created using a ruler, coloured pencils or pens, and compasses.

Activity ❶

Decide how large you want your design to be. Draw horizontal lines the same distance apart.

Draw some dividing lines.

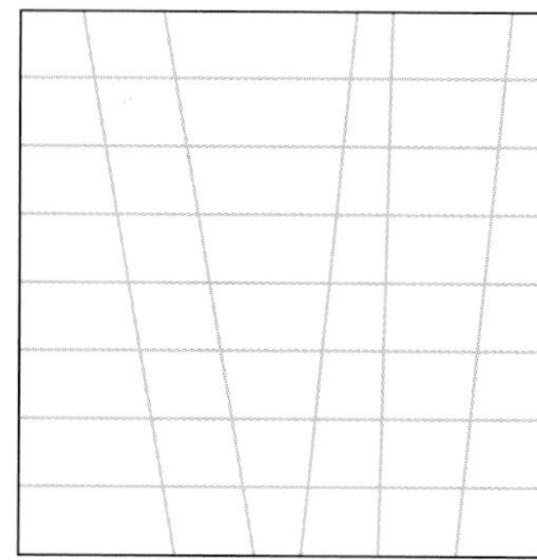

Choose 2 colours for your design. Colour every other shape a different colour.

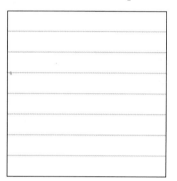

What geometric shapes do you see in the finished design?

Activity ❷

Repeat Activity 1 using intersecting lines as the dividing lines.

What geometric shapes do you see in this design?

Activity ❸

Here is another design. What geometric shapes do you see in this design?

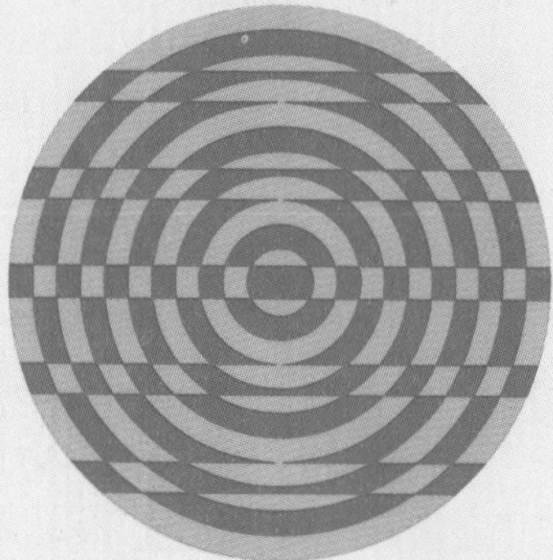

Make your own design using circles and straight lines.

Number and Number Relationships

When you think of mathematics, you think of numbers. Numbers are a very important part of everyday life. Having good number sense helps you solve many problems.

Activity ❶

1. How many seconds are there in a day? a week? a year?

2. How old are you in seconds?

3. If you had a billion dollars and you spent one dollar every second, how many years would it take you to spend it all?

Activity ❷

The fastest bird on land is the ostrich. It can run as fast as 80 km/h. Use your research skills to help answer the following questions.

1. How long would it take an ostrich to run from Halifax to Vancouver if it did not have to stop?

2. How long would it take an ostrich to run to the moon?

3. How long would it take an ostrich to run to the sun?

Activity ❸

The graph shows the precipitation in Winnipeg and Toronto for one year.

1. In which months did Toronto have less precipitation than Winnipeg?

2. Which city had more precipitation in the year?

3. If your group was planning to visit both cities, when would you visit each city? List the reasons in a report.

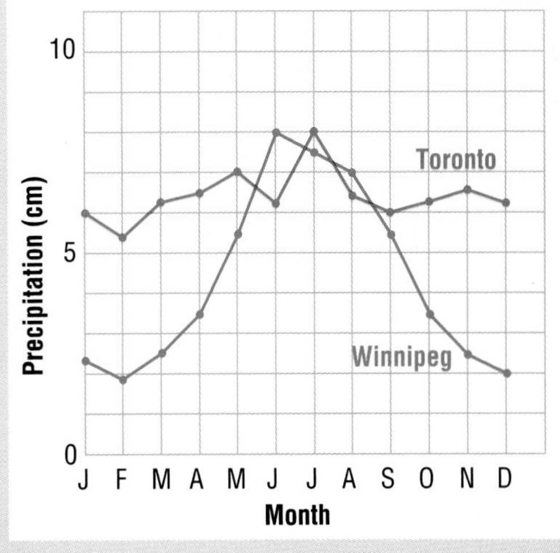

Number Systems and Number Theory

Knowing number systems and number theory lets you explore ideas that are interesting and useful.

Activity ❶

Obtain a supply of 25 square tiles.

Seven tiles will make only one rectangle.

7 is a prime number.

Eight tiles will make two rectangles.

8 is a composite number.

1. Which numbers will divide evenly into 7? into 8?

2. Build rectangles using your set of tiles.
Record your results in the table.

Number of Tiles	Number of Rectangles	Prime or Composite	Even or Odd	Divisors
1				
2				
3				
•				
•				
•				
25				

3. Which number of the 25 tiles allows you to build the greatest number of rectangles?

4. Describe any patterns you identify in your table.

5. Compare these patterns with those found by other members of your group.

Activity ❷

1. The number 12 has 1, 2, 3, 4, 6, and 12 as factors.

a) Find 5 numbers that have exactly 3 factors.

b) Find 5 numbers that have exactly 4 factors.

c) Find 5 numbers that have exactly 5 factors.

2. List the factors of each of the following numbers.

a) 2 **b)** 3 **c)** 5 **d)** 7 **e)** 11

3. List the factors of each of the following numbers.

a) 4 **b)** 9 **c)** 16 **d)** 25 **b)** 36

4. Decide in your group what kind of numbers have exactly 2 factors.

Computation and Estimation

There are several ways you can compute in mathematics. You can estimate an approximate answer or use paper and pencil, mental math, a calculator, or a computer to find an exact answer. Learning when to use each method is important.

Activity ❶

Choose a method for solving each problem. Then solve the problem. Compare your choices with your classmates'.

1. There are 24 cans in a case of orange drink. There are 172 students at the track meet. If each student is to get a drink, how many cases are needed?

2. The usual tip in a restaurant is 15% of the bill. A quick way to estimate the tip is to mentally multiply the amount of the bill by 0.1 and then add one-half of this amount.

For a bill of $28.00, estimate as follows.

$$0.1 \times 30 = 3$$

$$\frac{1}{2} \text{ of } 3 = 1.5$$

The tip is about $4.50.

Estimate the tip for the following restaurant bills.

a) $11.00 **b)** $35.00 **c)** $24.00

d) $17.67 **e)** $41.85 **f)** $56.79

3. Carmen wants to save $350.00 for a student exchange. She earns $8.00 an hour baby-sitting. About how many hours will she need to baby-sit to have enough money for the trip?

4. Where do you have to open this book so that the product of the two facing page numbers is 20 880?

5. A pair of basketball shoes costs $80.00. If there is a discount of 20%, find the cost of the shoes.

Activity ❷

1. List 5 situations where you would use mental math to make a calculation.

2. List 5 situations where you would use paper and pencil to make a calculation.

3. List 5 situations where you would use a calculator to make a calculation.

4. List 5 situations where you would use a computer to make a calculation.

5. Compare your lists with your classmates'.

Patterns and Functions

Mathematics involves the study of patterns. The ability to recognize patterns is an important problem solving skill.

Activity ❶

Everywhere we look, there are patterns.
Describe the patterns you see in each picture.

© 1938 M.C. Escher/Cordon Art Baarn-Holland

plowed field | building | artwork | leaves | tiled surface | corn

Activity ❷

A town of 1200 people has a "fan-out" system for emergencies. In an emergency, the mayor phones two people. In the next minute, each of these people phones two other people. The pattern continues until all 1200 people are contacted.

1. Complete the table to determine how many minutes it takes for all 1200 people to be contacted.

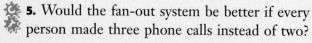

People Called	2	4	
Total People Called	2	6	
Time Needed (in minutes)	0	1	

2. How many people could be contacted in 15 min?

3. How long would the fan-out system take to contact everyone in your class?

4. What do you think is the largest community in which a fan-out system would work?

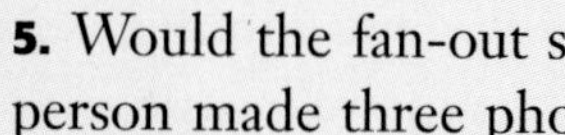

5. Would the fan-out system be better if every person made three phone calls instead of two?

Algebra

Algebra is the part of mathematics that uses letters and numbers to communicate ideas.

Activity 1

The perimeter of the tile figure is 14 units. Let us call this perimeter p.

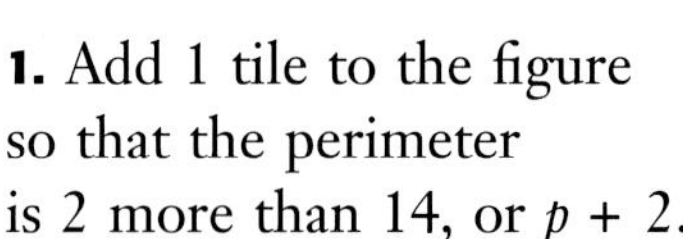

1. Add 1 tile to the figure so that the perimeter is 2 more than 14, or $p + 2$. Draw a diagram of your answer.

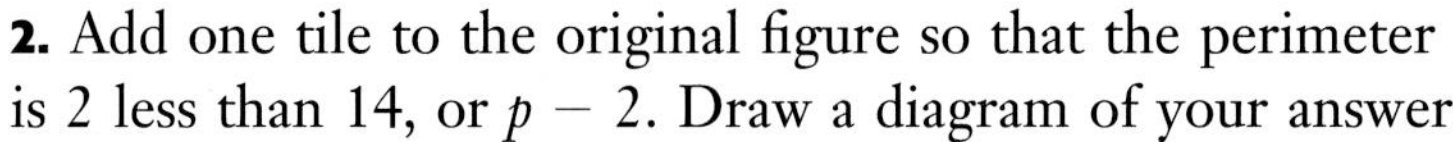

2. Add one tile to the original figure so that the perimeter is 2 less than 14, or $p - 2$. Draw a diagram of your answer.

3. Add two tiles to the original figure so that the perimeter is 4 more than 14, or $p + 4$. Draw a diagram of your answer.

Activity 2

1. Find the value of the letter to make each statement true.

a) $n + 5 = 12$ **b)** $x - 8 = 4$ **c)** $7 + t = 15$

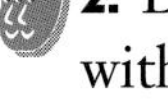

2. Describe the method you used in each case and compare with a classmate's method.

Activity 3

1. The rectangle has a perimeter of 24 units.

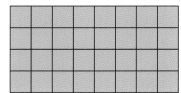

Using the same number of tiles, how many other rectangles can you make that have a perimeter of 24 units?

2. Use square tiles to draw as many rectangles as you can that have a perimeter of 36 units. Which rectangle has the largest area?

3. Compare your findings with a classmate's.

Activity 4

1. What is the value of one tile if two tiles plus 10 is 20?

2. What is the value of one tile if three tiles minus 4 is 8?

Statistics

In statistics, we take data and process it. How we collect and organize the data depends on the information we want.

Activity

In taking a survey, the people you choose to ask can make a difference in the results.

1. Determine the number of hours and minutes you are in class each day.

2. In your group, decide whether you think that each of the following groups of people regard this time as too long, too short, or just right.

a) parents **b)** students **c)** teachers

3. Survey people's opinions of how long a student should be in class each day. Ask 10 parents, 10 students, and 10 teachers. Tell the person how many hours you are in school each day. Ask the following question.

Is the time students spend in class too long, too short, or just right?

Record your data in a table.

Use a tally system.

/ means 1, /// means 3, ~~////~~ means 5, ~~////~~ /// means 8.

4. Use your data to answer the following questions.

a) What fraction of the parents think the time students spend in class is too short?

b) What fraction of the students think the time students spend in class is just right?

c) What fraction of the teachers think the time students spend in class is too long?

5. How did the results of the survey compare with what your group expected. Suggest 3 reasons why parents, students, and teachers might have different opinions of how long a student should be in class.

Probability

Probability tells you how likely something is to happen.

There is a 20% chance of rain.

What is the chance it will not rain?

The chance of rolling a 3 with one die is 1 in 6.

What is the chance of rolling a 3 or a 4?

We find the answers to many questions like these through probability.

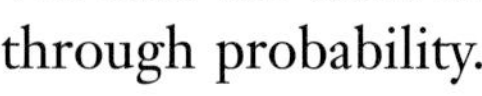

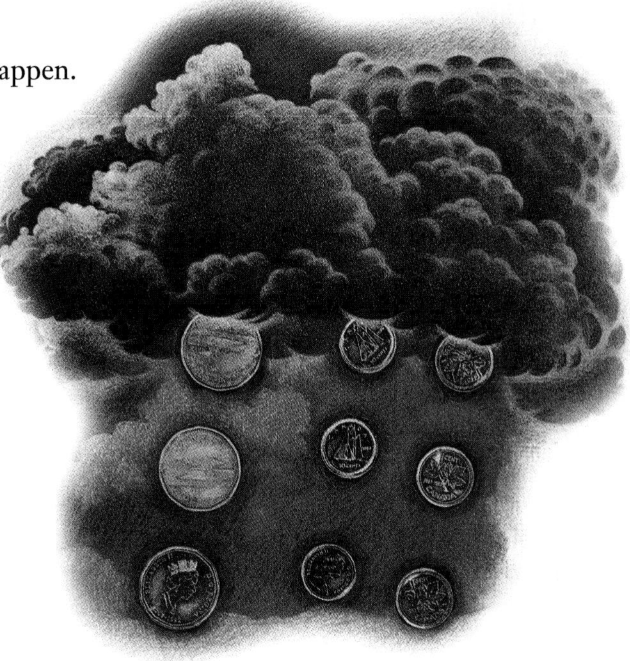

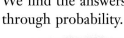

Activity

Work with a classmate.

Call one person Player A and the other person Player B.

Obtain 3 different coins, such as a penny, a dollar, and a dime.

Take turns tossing the 3 coins.

Player A wins if 2 heads or 2 tails are tossed.

Player B wins if 3 heads or 3 tails are tossed.

Repeat the game several times.

1. In how many different ways can the 3 coins land?

2. In how many ways can Player A win?

3. In how many ways can Player B win?

4. Is the game fair? Explain.

Geometry

Knowledge of geometry will help you to represent and make sense of the world around you. Geometric models can be used to help you solve problems.

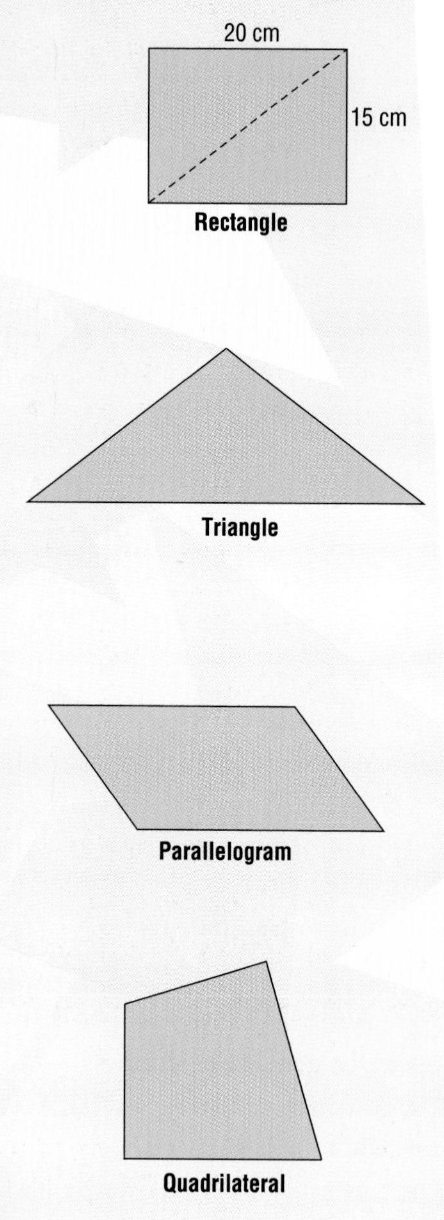

Activity

1. Cut out a rectangle 15 cm by 20 cm. Cut the rectangle along one diagonal to make two triangles.

2. a) Arrange the two triangles to make a large triangle.

b) Make a diagram of the large triangle.

c) How many different triangles can you make?

d) Describe the kinds of triangles that can be formed and find the perimeter of each.

3. a) Arrange the two triangles to make a parallelogram.

b) Make a diagram of the parallelogram.

c) How many different parallelograms can you make?

d) Decide whether all of the parallelograms have the same perimeter.

4. a) Arrange the two triangles to make a quadrilateral that is not a rectangle and not a parallelogram.

b) Make a diagram and find the perimeter.

5. Compare the perimeters of all the shapes you made. Which perimeter is the shortest?

Measurement

Wherever you go, you will usually find measurement. It is used in areas such as architecture, art, science, map reading, sports, cooking, and shopping.

Questions like 'how long?' and 'how much?' will always need answers.

Activity ❶

1. List 10 examples that show measurement being used in sports.

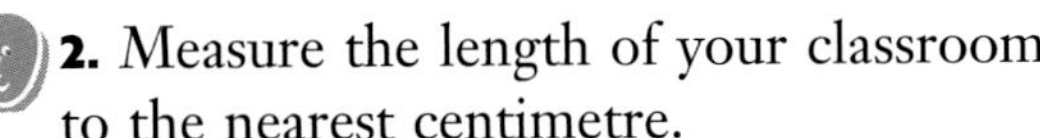

2. Measure the length of your classroom to the nearest centimetre.
   Record your answer and the results of your classmates.
   Explain why some lengths are different from others.
3. List 5 professions where you must measure length very accurately.
4. List 5 professions where measuring time accurately is very important.

Activity ❷

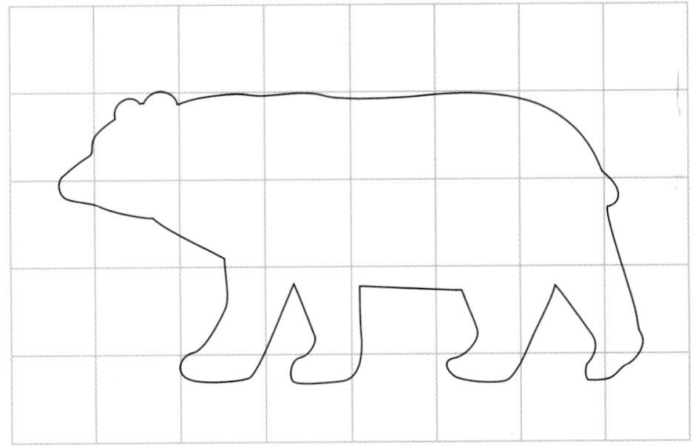

1. The area of each square on the grid is 1 cm^2. Count squares to estimate the area of the shape.
2. Trace your hand on centimetre grid paper and estimate its area.
3. Repeat with your other hand. Is the area of both hands the same?

Planet	Distance (millions of kilometres)
Mercury	60
Venus	110
Earth	150
Mars	230
Jupiter	800
Saturn	1400
Uranus	2900
Neptune	4500
Pluto	6000

Activity ❸

The table gives approximate distances of the planets from the sun in millions of kilometres. Make a scale model of our solar system.

You may want to use the hall or gymnasium.

CHAPTER 1

Number Connections

The *Pioneer 10* spacecraft is carrying a plaque like this one to the nearest stars. It is an attempt to communicate with other life forms.

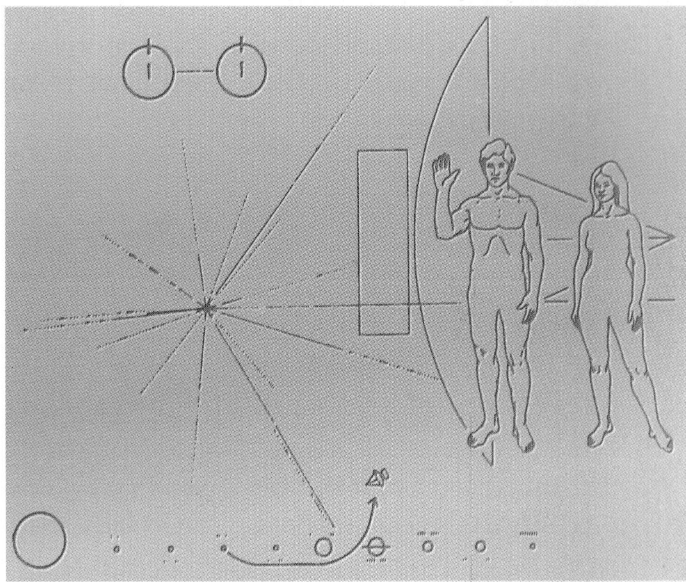

Describe what the plaque shows about us and the Earth.

How many numbers did you use in your description?

Design a plaque of your own that you could send into space to tell others about life on Earth.

Mathematics of a Pencil

It is hard to imagine the world without pencils. The pencil with a round lead was invented in 1879. Before that, the lead was square. Actually, the "lead" in a pencil is not really lead. It is a mixture of graphite and clay. It is probably called "lead" because graphite was once called "black lead."

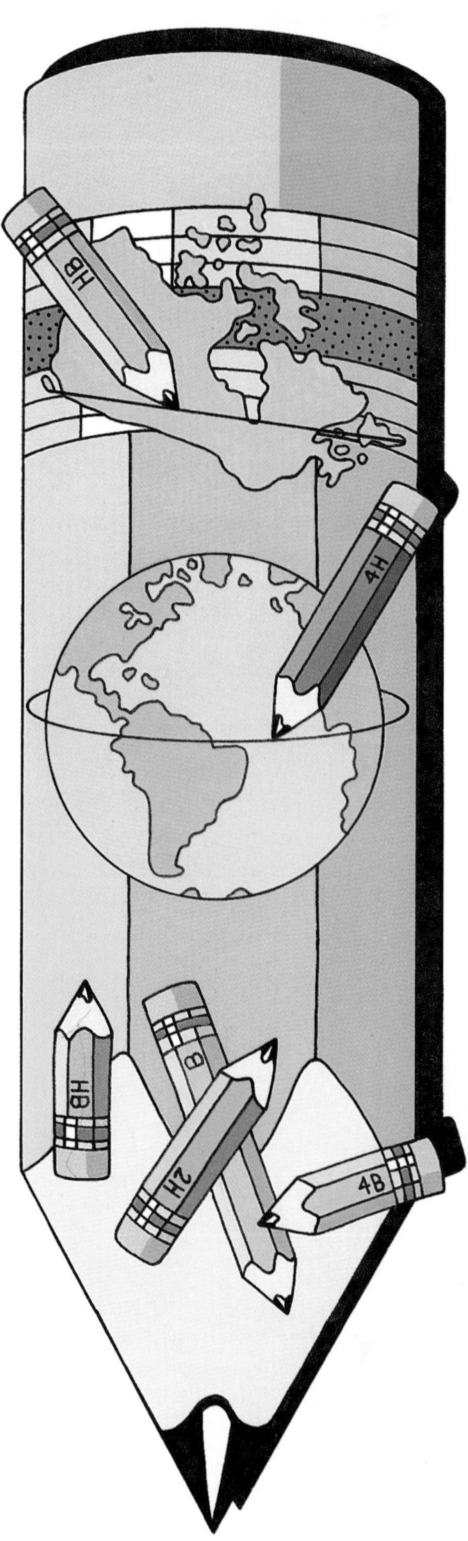

Activity ❶

1. You can make about 4000 check marks with a pencil before sharpening it.
You can sharpen a pencil about 17 times.
How many check marks can you make with one pencil?

2. A pencil can write about 45 000 words. The average word has 4.5 letters. How many letters can a pencil write?

3. St. John's, Newfoundland, is 7775 km from Victoria, British Columbia. A pencil can draw a line about 56 km long. How many pencils would you need to draw a line across Canada?

Activity ❷

1. Canadians buy about two hundred fifty million (250 000 000) pencils a year. If each pencil can draw a 56-km line, how long a line could a year's supply draw?

2. The moon is 384 000 km away. How many lines could a year's supply of pencils draw from the Earth to the moon?

3. The distance around the Earth's equator is about 40 000 km. If you laid a year's supply of pencils end to end, would they circle the Earth?

Activity ❸

1. What do you think is the most popular colour of pencil? Compare your idea with your classmates'.

2. One of the materials used to make pencils is called tragacanth. Research what it is and where it comes from.

3. How many years ago was the pencil with the round lead invented?

4. Most pencils have letters and numbers on them, like **HB**, **B**, and **2H**. Research what they mean.

Warm Up

1. Copy the figure. Place the numbers from 1 to 7 in the circles, so that the sum of the numbers in each of the two rows, two diagonals, and one column is 12.

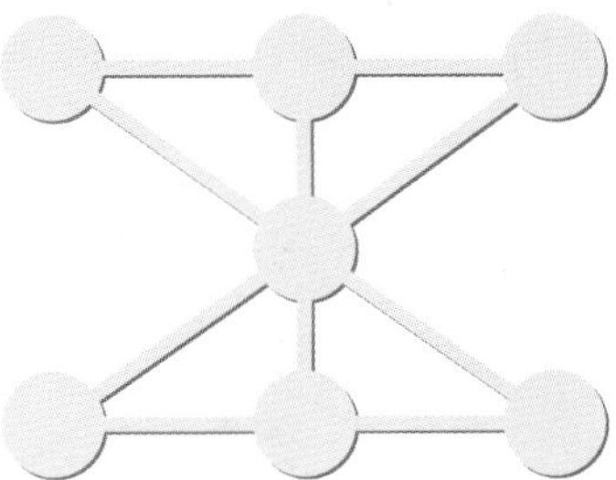

2. How many times will you see the digit 8 in the numbers from 1 to 100?

3. Fill in the blanks to make the statement true.

4. The names of the first three whole numbers are: one, two, and three. The letters are not in alphabetical order in any of these names. Find the smallest whole number whose name has the letters in alphabetical order.

5. List all the different ways you can make change for a dollar.

6. Write any number on a piece of paper. Fold the paper in half and stand on it. Your teacher will tell you what is on the paper.

Mental Math

Calculate.

1. 15 + 12 **2.** 24 + 11 **3.** 22 + 37 **4.** 14 + 15 **5.** 20 + 43 **6.** 27 + 50

Calculate.

7. 20 − 13 **8.** 30 − 21 **9.** 40 − 22 **10.** 50 − 33 **11.** 22 − 11 **12.** 34 − 13

Calculate.

13. 9×7 **14.** 9×8 **15.** 8×6 **16.** 9×12 **17.** 8×12

18. 12×7 **19.** 9×9 **20.** 7×8 **21.** 12×6 **22.** 12×11

Calculate.

23. $63 \div 9$ **24.** $72 \div 8$ **25.** $81 \div 9$ **26.** $90 \div 10$ **27.** $72 \div 6$ **28.** $96 \div 8$

29. $132 \div 11$ **30.** $108 \div 9$ **31.** $200 \div 10$ **32.** $150 \div 10$ **33.** $80 \div 8$ **34.** $56 \div 7$

1.1 Choosing a Calculation Method

Colleen Evans is a park warden. She often uses mathematics. She answers many questions that involve numbers. Sometimes, Colleen gives an **exact** answer. Other times, she gives an **approximate** answer.

Activity: Study the Statements

Colleen told a newspaper reporter:

"The park had 2 fires in July."

"There are about 3000 deer in the park."

"There are 23 people who work at the park."

Inquire

1. Which of the numbers are exact? How do you know?
2. Which are approximate? How do you know?

Colleen sometimes needs to calculate an answer. After she decides whether to be exact or approximate, she chooses a **calculation method** to work out the answer. There are several methods to choose from.

Method	Example
• **Estimating** or making an **educated guess** gives an approximate answer. We also estimate to check that calculated answers make sense.	The campers' canoe races start at 11:30. It takes 40 min to walk to the lake. We should leave at about 10:45.
• **Calculators** give exact answers. They can also help you estimate.	The camping trip will cost $785.75. There are 7 of us, so we owe $112.25 each.
• **Paper and pencil** can help you to calculate exact answers and to estimate.	There are 131 campsites. We have weeded 76. We have 55 more campsites to weed. $131 - 76 = 55$
• For some calculations you can use **mental math** to work out exact answers in your head. You can also estimate mentally.	We have 19 empty campsites and 24 cars at the gate. Five will not get in.
• A **computer** gives exact answers. Computers save time in calculations that must be done over and over again.	We will spend $ 7855.13 each month on salaries for park employees.

Problems and Applications

State whether you need an exact answer or an approximate answer.

1. You are the captain of a commercial airplane. What time will you arrive in Vancouver?

2. How long will it take you to cut the lawn?

3. How many buses will you need for a school trip?

4. You are timing a runner in the Olympic marathon. How long does she take?

5. You are the student council treasurer. How much money is in the bank?

6. You are buying hot dogs to sell at the baseball tournament. How many should you buy?

7. How much money will you need to go to college?

8. How much does your employer owe you after you work for 10 hours on the weekend?

Choose a calculation method for each of the following problems.

9. How many litres of paint will you need to paint your room?

10. You are asked to count the cars passing in front of the school between 08:15 and 09:00 on Monday.

11. You have your passbook updated at the bank. You want to check the bank's accuracy.

12. Eighty-one students will attend the class party. Sixty-three of them need a bus. This will cost $8.75 each. Food will cost $7.15 per student. What is the total cost?

13. You are responsible for calculating the landing time of the space shuttle.

14. You keep score at a basketball game.

Choose and record a method for each calculation. Evaluate each expression.

15. $200 \div 5$

16. $375 + 125$

17. $456 - 106$

18. $3922 \div 73$

19. 123×10

20. $31 - 5 - 6$

21. 456×33

22. $100 + 250 - 75$

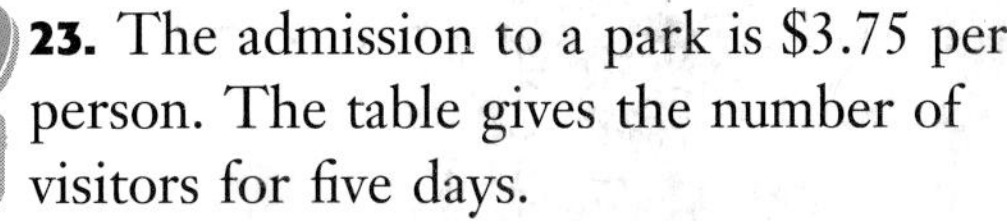

23. The admission to a park is $3.75 per person. The table gives the number of visitors for five days.

Day	Visitors
Wednesday	132
Thursday	221
Friday	372
Saturday	456
Sunday	401

Write two questions using these data. One should need an exact answer and the other an approximate answer. Have a classmate answer your questions.

LOGIC POWER

If you turn a right-handed glove inside out, will you get a right-handed glove or a left-handed glove?

Comparing and Ordering Numbers

Activity 1

1. Look at the 3 lines. Estimate which is longest and which is shortest.

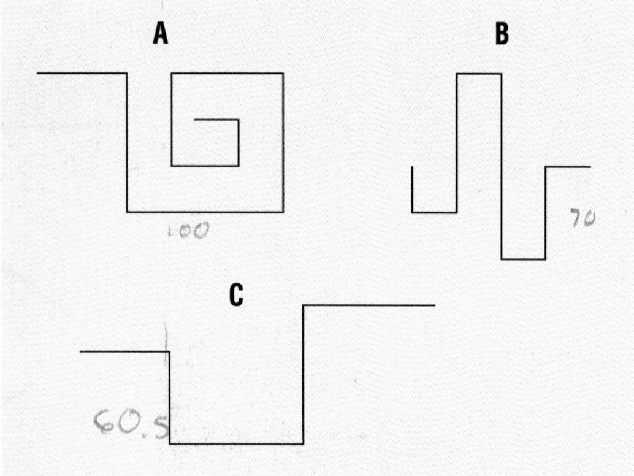

2. Measure the lines. Order them from longest to shortest.
How close was your estimate?

Activity 2

The table gives the heights, lengths, and masses of several animals.

Animal	Height (m)	Length (m)	Mass (kg)
Grizzly bear	2.83	2.64	336
Polar bear	1.41	2.63	410
Caribou	1.34	1.74	214
Hippopotamus	1.52	4.29	3750
Lion	1.17	2.13	205
Orangutan	1.53	1.46	58
Rhinoceros	1.61	3.28	3000

1. List the animals in order from tallest to shortest.

2. List the animals in order from longest to shortest.

3. List the animals in order from heaviest to lightest.

Activity 3

1. Without measuring, list the 4 men in order from tallest to shortest.

2. Measure the heights of the 4 men.
Compare your findings with your predicted order of heights.

Activity ❹

The table gives the winning times for the gold medal winners in downhill skiing at the Winter Olympics.

Year	Women's Downhill	Time
1968	Pall (Austria)	1:40.87
1972	Nadig (Switzerland)	1:36.68
1976	Mittermaier (West Germany)	1:46.16
1980	Moser-Pröll (Austria)	1:37.52
1984	Figini (Switzerland)	1:13.36
1988	Kiehl (West Germany)	1:25.86
1992	Lee-Gartner (Canada)	1:52.55

Year	Men's Downhill	Time
1968	Killy (France)	1:59.85
1972	Russi (Switzerland)	1:51.43
1976	Klammer (Austria)	1:45.73
1980	Stock (Austria)	1:45.50
1984	Johnson (USA)	1:45.59
1988	Zurbriggen (Switzerland)	1:59.63
1992	Ortlieb (Austria)	1:50.37

1. Order the women's times from longest to shortest.

2. Order the men's times from longest to shortest.

3. Do we know that the skiers with the longest times were the slowest? Explain.

Activity ❺

Write three numbers between each pair of numbers.

1. 126, 131 **2.** 5.28, 5.32 **3.** 89, 91

4. 1.2, 1.4 **5.** 0.07, 0.09 **6.** 1000, 1001

Activity ❻

Use an almanac or some other source to choose the 10 cities in the world with the greatest populations. Order them from highest population to lowest population.

1.2 Place Value

Activity: Review Our Number System

In the decimal system, the value of a digit in a number depends on its place in the number.

The digit **3** has a **different value** in each of the following numbers.

1**3**48	7**3**1	61**3**	7.**3**	0.8**3**
3 hundreds	**3 tens**	**3 ones**	**3 tenths**	**3 hundredths**
or 300	or 30	or 3	or 0.3	or 0.03

Inquire

1. How many times greater than 0.03 is 3?

2. How many times smaller than 300 is 0.3?

Suppose that you could walk to the moon. You would take about 548 570 000 steps. The walk would take about 8.59 years non-stop. A *place value table* can help you read and write numbers like these.

Trillions			Billions			Millions			Thousands			Ones						
Hundred	Ten	One	Hundred	Ten	One	Hundred	Ten	One	Hundred	Ten	One	Hundred	Ten	One		Tenths	Hundredths	Thousandths
						5	4	8	5	7	0	0	0	0	.			
														8	.	5	9	

We would read 548 570 000 as:

five hundred forty-eight million five hundred seventy thousand

We would read 8.59 as:

eight and fifty-nine hundredths ← Read "and" for the decimal

The digits for large numbers, such as 548 570 000, are separated into groups of three by spaces. The groups of three are called **periods.**

The number 548 570 000 is in **standard form.** The **expanded form** of this number shows the total value of each digit.

$$500\ 000\ 000 + 40\ 000\ 000 + 8\ 000\ 000 + 500\ 000 + 70\ 000$$
$$= 5 \times 100\ 000\ 000 + 4 \times 10\ 000\ 000 + 8 \times 1\ 000\ 000 + 5 \times 100\ 000 + 7 \times 10\ 000$$

The number 8.59 is in standard form. In expanded form, it is:

$$8 + 0.5 + 0.09$$
$$= 8 + 5 \times 0.1 + 9 \times 0.01$$

Practice

Read each number to a classmate. Have your classmate write down the number. Switch roles and repeat.

1. 2340 **2.** 769

3. 25.6 **4.** 300.45

5. 2 000 000 000 **6.** 203 203

7. 1 230 000 **8.** 45.796

A calculator display does not show the spaces between periods. Write each number using spaces.

9. 3156920 **10.** 45631.52

11. 573182463 **12.** 74810000

13. 84333.33 **14.** 383469.101

Write the total value of the underlined digit in each number.

15. 23$\underline{7}$4.56 **16.** 1$\underline{2}$0 581

17. 567.2$\underline{9}$ **18.** 3$\underline{4}$ 678 900

19. 561$\underline{2}$ **20.** 0.23$\underline{4}$

Write each number in standard form.

21. six thousand one hundred twelve

22. thirty-one and fifty-seven hundredths

23. four hundred thirty-three thousand

24. seven and forty-one hundredths

25. two hundred eighteen thousandths

26. seventy-three billion

Write in standard form.

27. 3000 + 200 + 70 + 6

28. 40 000 + 5000 + 800 + 50 + 2

29. $8 \times 1 + 6 \times 0.1 + 9 \times 0.01$

30. $4 \times 1000 + 7 \times 100 + 9 \times 10 + 1$

31. $3 \times 10 + 4 \times 0.01 + 2 \times 0.001$

Write in expanded form.

32. 4567 **33.** 7.021 **34.** 12 400

35. 3407.5 **36.** 762 010 **37.** 450.27

Problems and Applications

In questions 38–42, write each number in words.

38. Asteroids are small planets between the orbits of Mars and Jupiter. Asteroid 2917 is named after Canadian astronomer Helen Sawyer Hogg. The asteroids named after the Beatles are 4147 (Lennon), 4148 (McCartney), 4149 (Harrison), and 4150 (Starr).

39. The oldest known rocks were found in the Northwest Territories near Yellowknife. Their age was estimated at 3 962 000 000 years.

40. There are 0.002 police officers for every person in Canada.

• **41.** The painting *Sunflowers* by Vincent van Gogh sold for $39 921 750.

42. The Helena's hummingbird has a mass of 1.985 g.

43. Why might a magazine article about baseball use "4 million fans" instead of "4 000 000 fans"?

44. On a cheque for thirty thousand dollars, would you write the number as 30000 or 30 000? Explain. Find out how large numbers are written on cheques.

45. Form a group with 2 or 3 of your classmates. Create a short story using 6 of the following numbers.

0.5, 3, 5.67, 13.72, 123, 287,

600, 8001, 45 600, 999 999

Read your story to the rest of the class.

NUMBER POWER

The final score in a soccer game was 3–3. How many possible half-time scores were there?

1.3 Rounding Numbers: Mental Math

Activity: Apply the Example

When the television commentator said the leader in the Canadian Grand Prix motor race had 4 laps to go, she was using an *exact* number.

There were 50 350 tickets sold for the race.
The commentator announced:
"There are about 50 000 spectators here today."
This time, she did not need to be exact.
She used an *approximate* number.
To do this, she *rounded*.

50 350 is between 50 000 and 51 000.

50 350 is closer to 50 000, so 50 350 rounds to 50 000.

50 350

50 000 — 50 500 — 51 000

Inquire

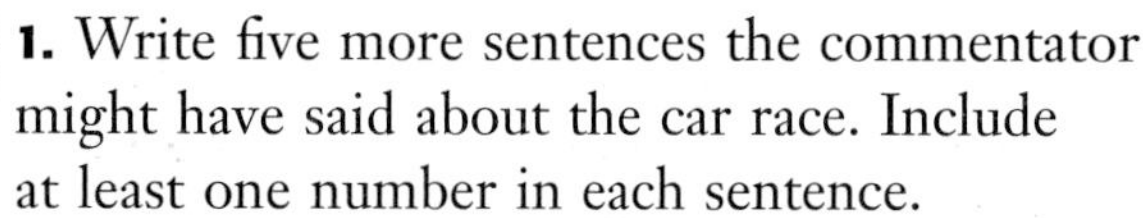

1. Write five more sentences the commentator might have said about the car race. Include at least one number in each sentence.

2. In which sentences did you use rounded numbers? Explain why.

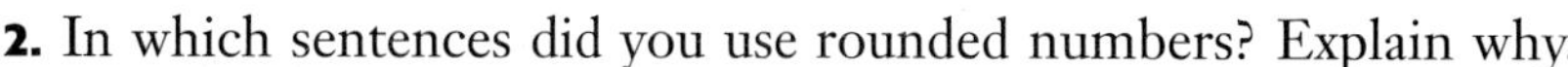

When you round, if the digit to the right of the place you are rounding is 5 or more, **round up**.

Example 1

Round 2634 to the nearest thousand.

Solution

2634 → 3000

The digit to the right of the thousands place is 6.
6 is greater than 5, so round up. Add 1 to the 2.

Example 2

Round 2.359 to the nearest tenth.

Solution

2.359 → 2.4

The digit to the right of the tenths place is 5, so round up. Add 1 to the 3.

If the digit to the right of the place you are rounding is less than 5, **round down**.

Example 3

Round 426 to the nearest hundred.

Solution

426 → 400

The digit to the right of the hundreds place is 2.
2 is less than 5, so round down. Do not change the 4.

Practice

Round the red number to one end of the line.

1. 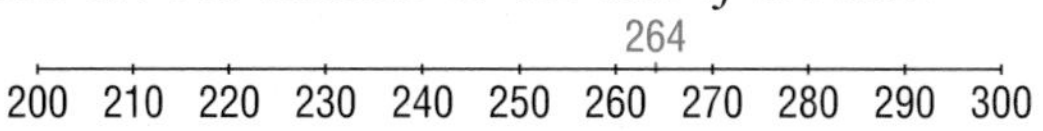

2. 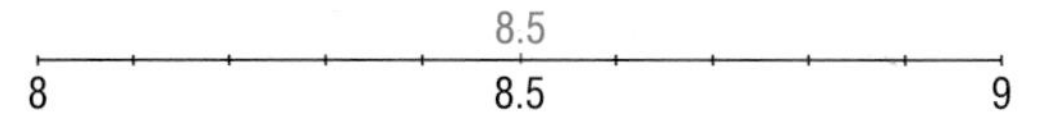

3. 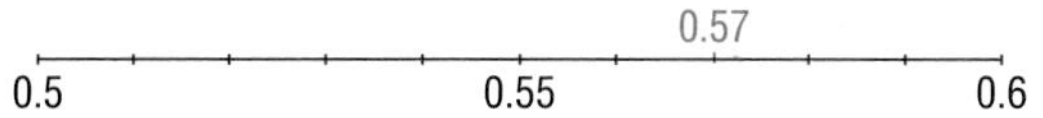

4. 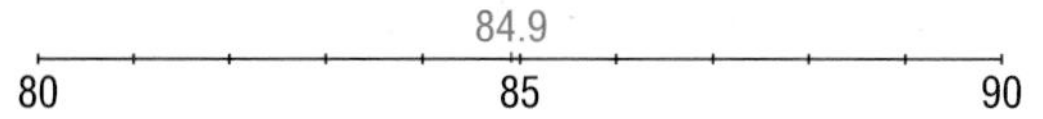

Round to the nearest ten.

5. 26 **6.** 142 **7.** 201

8. 1265 **9.** 374 **10.** 505

Round to the nearest hundred.

11. 862 **12.** 942 **13.** 658

14. 2432 **15.** 957 **16.** 4669

Round to the nearest thousand.

17. 3417 **18.** 6814 **19.** 39 600

20. 43 578 **21.** 57 209 **22.** 24 560

Round to the nearest ten thousand.

23. 34 456 **24.** 68 900 **25.** 85 200

26. 203 000 **27.** 707 000 **28.** 605 111

Round to the stated place value.

29. 450 000, hundred thousand

30. 36 400 000, million

31. 7 900 000, million

32. 45 000 000, ten million

33. 23 600 000 000, billion

Round to the nearest tenth.

34. 0.46 **35.** 2.525 **36.** 76.55

37. 0.066 **38.** 13.233 **39.** 1.057

Round to the nearest hundredth.

40. 0.567 **41.** 1.202 **42.** 56.785

43. 3.406 **44.** 33.335 **45.** 0.452

Round to the nearest thousandth.

46. 0.3472 **47.** 7.8065 **48.** 66.5678

What digits can you replace ■ with so that

49. 8■5 rounds to 900?

50. 3■66 rounds to 3000?

51. 1.7■6 rounds to 1.8?

52. 21.54■ rounds to 21.54?

Problems and Applications

53. You are a late night disc jockey for radio station CING. One of your jobs is to rewrite and read the latest news. Rewrite the following news stories with a classmate. Use exact or rounded numbers.

- Tonight, 12 532 fans watched the Cobras beat the Pythons 8 to 1. Attendance at Python games is up 50% over last year.
- Yesterday, Raisa, the zoo's popular tiger, gave birth to three cubs. Their masses were 4.1 kg, 4.2 kg, and 5.4 kg.
- The broadway show *Dancing Fool* has had 731 performances and ticket sales of $1 235 678.50.
- The rock group *Telescope* will play here on May 12, 22 days from now. This will be the third stop on a 34-city tour lasting 43 days. Tickets will cost $27.50. *Telescope's* latest recording has sold 380 000 copies.

54. a) The sign on the inside of an elevator states how many people it can hold. The number is an **underestimate** because it is deliberately low. Why?

b) Work with a classmate and describe 3 situations in which you would underestimate.

c) Describe 3 situations in which you would **overestimate**, that is, estimate too high.

Exploring Mental Math

Instead of using a calculator or paper and pencil, it is sometimes easier and quicker to do math problems mentally. A few strategies can help.

Activity ❶

Adding

Change the order.

$$33 + 46 + 67$$
$$= \underbrace{33 + 67} + 46$$
$$= \underbrace{100 + 46}$$
$$= 146$$

Break up one or two numbers.

$$43 + 88$$
$$= 40 + 3 + 80 + 8$$
$$= \underbrace{40 + 80} + \underbrace{3 + 8}$$
$$= \underbrace{120 \quad + \quad 11}$$
$$= 131$$

Change the problem.

$$54 + 97$$
$$= \underbrace{54 + 100} - 3$$
$$= \underbrace{154 - 3}$$
$$= 151$$

Work with a classmate. Both do each question mentally. Before completing the next question, share the strategy you used.

1. 14 + 25 + 36
2. 35 + 38
3. 21 + 47 + 19
4. 56 + 99
5. 20 + 40 + 60
6. 22 + 65 + 18 + 15
7. 32 + 18 + 10
8. 47 + 45
9. 21 + 33 + 9 + 7

Activity ❷

Subtracting

Break up one of the numbers.

$$84 - 29$$
$$= \underbrace{84 - 20} - 9$$
$$= \underbrace{64 - 9}$$
$$= 53$$

Change the problem.

$$245 - 193$$
$$= \underbrace{245 - 200} + 7$$
$$= \underbrace{45 + 7}$$
$$= 52$$

Work with a classmate. Both do each question mentally. Before completing the next question, share the strategy you used.

1. 90 − 37
2. 156 − 95
3. 87 − 28
4. 234 − 192
5. 73 − 56
6. 456 − 280
7. 78 − 66
8. 123 − 96
9. 56 − 23

Activity ❸

Multiplying

Change the order.

$2 \times 13 \times 5$

$= \underbrace{2 \times 5} \times 13$

$= \underbrace{10 \times 13}$

$= 130$

Break up one of the numbers.

3×46

$= \underbrace{3 \times 40} + \underbrace{3 \times 6}$

$= \underbrace{120 + 18}$

$= 138$

Work with a classmate. Both do each question mentally. Before completing the next question, share the strategy you used.

1. $2 \times 12 \times 5$
2. 3×65
3. 37×4
4. $4 \times 14 \times 5$
5. 7×16
6. 16×12
7. $2 \times 9 \times 15$
8. $3 \times 0 \times 8$
9. 103×4

Activity ❹

Properties of Operations

1. Does the order in which you add numbers matter? Support your answer with an example.

2. If you change the order of the numbers in a subtraction question, do you change the result? Support your answer with an example.

3. Does the order in which you multiply numbers matter? Support your answer with an example.

4. If you change the order of the numbers in a division question, do you change the result? Support your answer with an example.

Activity ❺

Work with a classmate. Both do each question mentally. Before completing the next question, share the strategy you used.

1. $67 + 18 + 13$
2. $74 - 39$
3. $6 \times 7 \times 5$
4. $38 + 41$
5. $86 - 46$
6. $11 \times 9 \times 0$
7. 6×36
8. 210×5
9. $14 + 39 + 21 + 16$

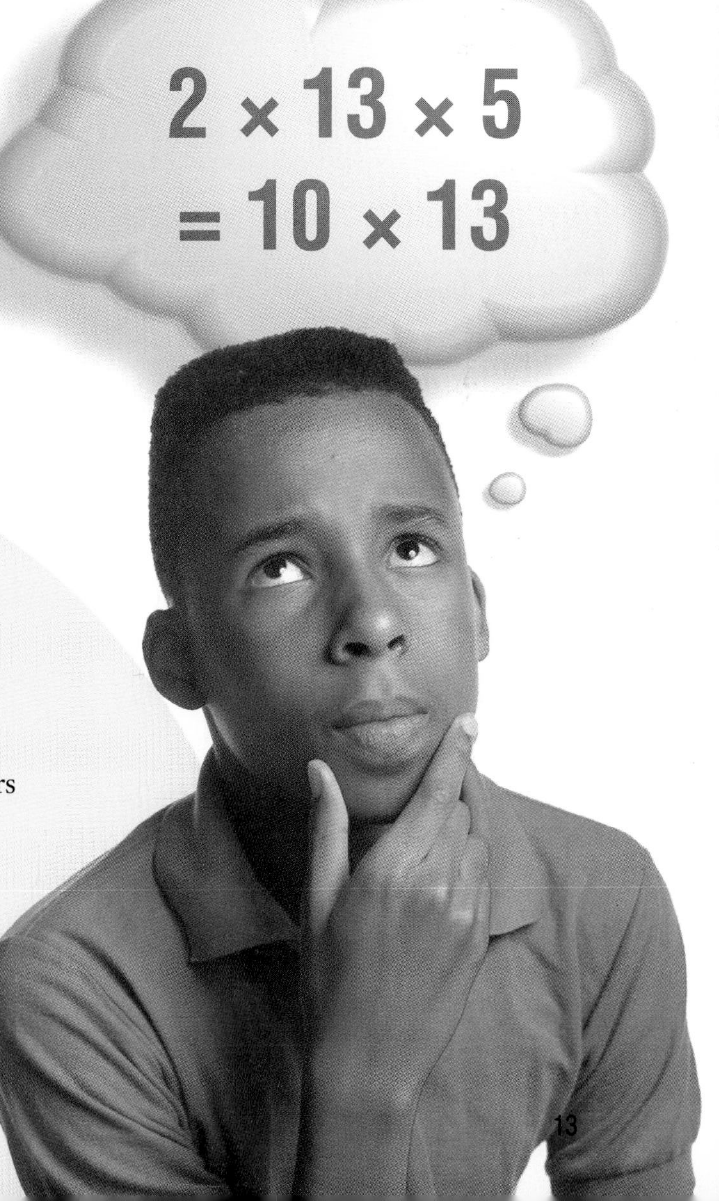

1.4 Look For A Pattern

The first diagram shows the chairs around a square table.
The second diagram shows an extra table and more chairs.
The pattern continues until there are 12 tables in a row.
How many chairs are in the 12th diagram?

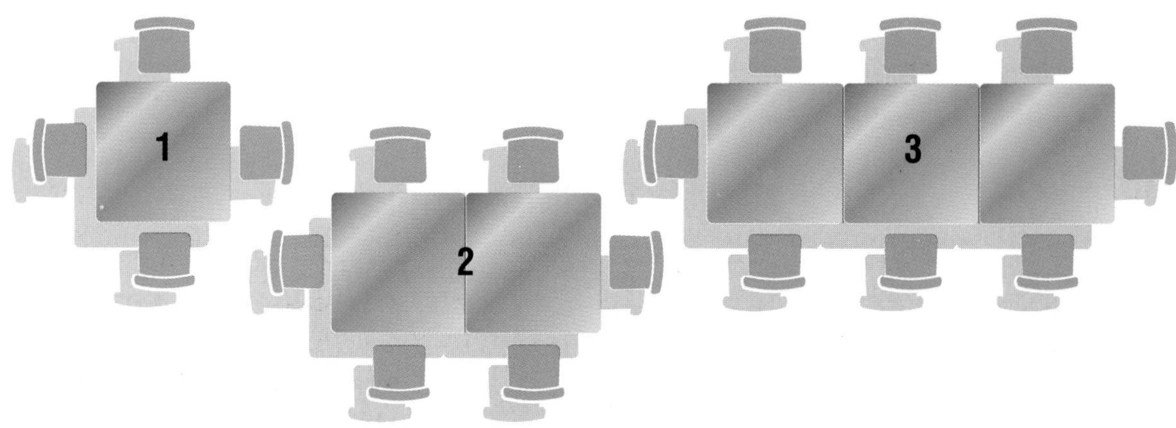

Understand the Problem

1. How many chairs are in the 1st diagram?
2. How many chairs are in the 2nd diagram?
3. How many chairs are added to the 1st diagram to make the 2nd?
4. How many chairs are added to the 2nd diagram to make the 3rd?
5. How many chairs are added to the 1st diagram to make the 3rd?

Think of a Plan

The pattern starts with 4 chairs.
You add 2 chairs when you go from one diagram to the next.
To make the 2nd diagram, you add 2 chairs to the 1st.
To make the 3rd, you add 2×2 or 4 chairs to the 1st.
To make the 4th, you add 2×3 or 6 chairs to the 1st.

Carry Out the Plan

To make the 12th diagram, you add 11×2 or 22 chairs to the 1st.

$$\begin{aligned} 4 + 11 \times 2 &= 4 + 22 \\ &= 26 \end{aligned}$$

There are 26 chairs in the 12th diagram.

Look Back

Does the answer seem reasonable?
Is there another way to solve the problem?

Look for a Pattern	1. Use the given information to find a pattern. 2. Use the pattern to solve the problem. 3. Check that the answer is reasonable.

Problems and Applications

1. Draw the next two flowers.

2. How many toothpicks are in the 12th diagram?

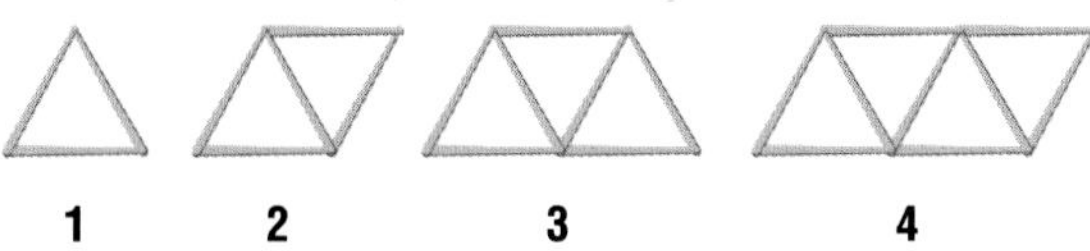

3. With one cut, you can cut a piece of wood into two pieces. With two cuts, you get three pieces. How many pieces will you get with 45 cuts?

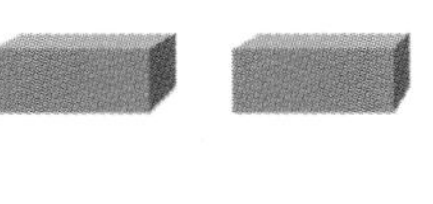

Look for a pattern, then name the next 3 numbers in each sequence below.

4. 2, 8, 14,...

5. 4, 5, 7, 10, 14,...

6. 71, 62, 53, 44,...

7. 5000, 500, 50,...

8. 4, 12, 36,...

Determine and state each pattern. Copy and complete each table.

9.

5	8
4	7
7	10
6	
9	

10.

7	6
9	8
4	3
8	
5	

11.

2	6
4	12
5	15
6	
7	

12.

10	5
12	6
8	4
6	
4	

13. How many cubes are in the 15th pattern?

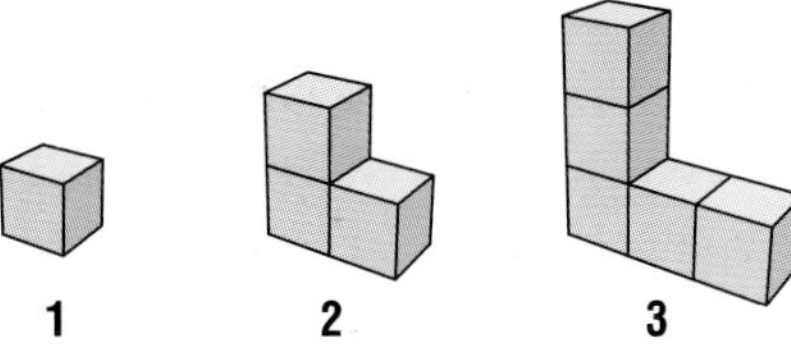

14. Find the next 3 figures.

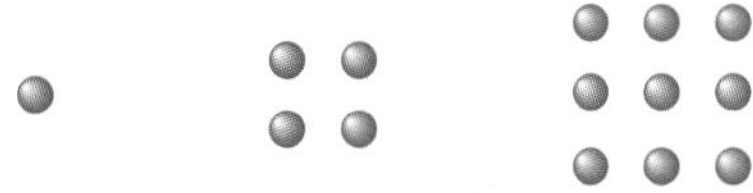

15. In a flu epidemic, medical health officers find 5 cases the first day, 12 cases the second day, 26 cases the third day, and 54 cases the fourth day. If this pattern continues, on what day will they find 1000 cases?

16. Seven people are at a party. Each person shakes hands with each of the others. What is the total number of handshakes? Act out the scene with your classmates.

17. Make up a pattern and use it to write a problem. Have a classmate solve the problem.

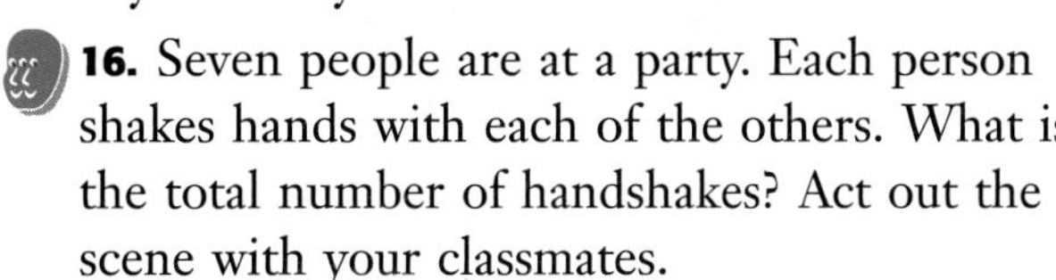

PATTERN POWER

The statements 5 ★ 1 = 16 and 4 ★ 2 = 14 are true when ★ means "triple the first number and add the second."

State what ■ and ▲ mean, then complete the last two statements in each pattern.

6 ■ 2 = 10	3 ▲ 2 = 12
5 ■ 7 = 19	5 ▲ 3 = 30
2 ■ 6 = 14	4 ▲ 1 = 8
3 ■ 5 = 13	3 ▲ 6 = 36
4 ■ 6 = ?	2 ▲ 5 = ?
8 ■ 3 = ?	6 ▲ 2 = ?

1.5 Estimating Sums and Differences: Mental Math

Activity: Study the Example

Carol Li and Mark Edwards did a science project on the whooping crane. The whooping crane is the tallest bird in North America. It is an endangered species. In 1941, there were only 15 wild birds. Their numbers have increased since. The birds spend the summer in Wood Buffalo National Park, Alberta. The map shows the route they take to their winter home in Texas. Carol and Mark used different ways of estimating the distance the birds fly.

Carol estimated a distance of 3000 km. Mark estimated about 3200 km.

Carol		Mark	
1250 →	1000	1250 →	1300
630 →	1000	630 →	600
390 →	0	390 →	400
940 →	+ 1000	940 →	+ 900
	3000		3200

Inquire

1. How did Carol round the numbers?
2. How did Mark round the numbers?

3. What is the advantage of rounding Carol's way?
4. What is the advantage of rounding Mark's way?

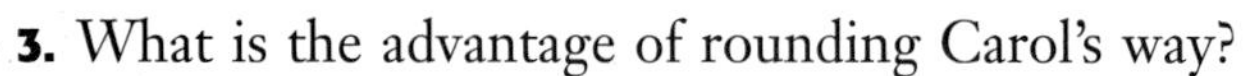

We often estimate sums and differences using rounding.

Example

Estimate 5.78 − 0.328.

Solution

Round each number and subtract mentally.
Estimates may vary with the place value you choose for rounding.

Round to the greatest place value of the greatest number.		Round to the greatest place value of the smallest number.		Round to the greatest place value of each number.	
5.78 →	6	5.78 →	5.8	5.78 →	6.0
−0.328 →	− 0	−0.328 →	− 0.3	−0.328 →	− 0.3
	6		5.5		5.7

Find out the height of a whooping crane.
Estimate the difference between its height and your own.

Practice

Estimate each sum.

1. 71 + 68 + 43

2. 5.67 + 9.01 + 5.55

3. 4500 + 2341 + 6798

4. 556 + 678 + 719 + 443

5. 12.5 + 23.5 + 46.7 + 67.6

6. 34 890 + 62 000 + 79 111 + 11 233

7. 567 + 891 + 402 + 103

8. 5678 + 2005 + 5670 + 9812

Estimate each difference.

9. 872 − 235

10. 36.78 − 15.67

11. 591 − 401

12. 34 567 − 22 314

13. 56 788 − 18 979

14. 7.89 − 4.71

15. 2356 − 986

16. 45.7 − 9.72

Problems and Applications

The following are receipts from a grocery store. Estimate each total mentally. State whether you think you have made an overestimate (more than the total) or an underestimate (less than the total).

17. $6.78, 1.33, 7.89

18. $8.95, 4.66, 0.87

19. $7.02, 3.33, 0.98

20. $2.06, 5.61, 1.81

21. $6.78, 3.15, 6.49, 2.61

22. $5.79, 4.48, 0.88, 9.22

23. On Saturday morning, Elise sold 145 tapes, 113 CDs, and 87 videos. Estimate the total number of items sold that morning.

24. When Maria started her vacation, the odometer on her car read

26847.8

When she returned, the odometer showed

30384.4

Approximately how far did Maria drive?

25. Estimate the difference between the number of student textbooks in your classroom and the number of students in the class.

26. Estimate the total amount of time the students in your class spend on homework on the weekend.

27. a) Estimate the number of students in each grade in your school.

b) Estimate the total number of students in your school.

c) Compare your estimate with your classmates'. Describe how you obtained your estimate.

28. You have $200 to spend on clothes. You want the following items. The prices listed include all taxes.

Item	Price
Sneakers	$75
Sweat shirt	$56
Jeans	$43
Jacket	$92

Estimate whether you can afford all the items. If not, what is the least expensive item you can leave out to afford the other three? Explain your reasoning.

1.6 Adding and Subtracting Numbers

Activity: Interpret the Map

Fansaway Tours offers baseball fans a bus trip. You book a tour from Niagara Falls, with stops for baseball games in Toronto, Detroit, and Cleveland. The distances are given on the map. You want to know the the total distance you will travel.

Inquire

1. Do you need an exact or approximate answer?

2. Estimate the distance you will travel.

3. Choose a calculation method and calculate the distance you will travel.

4. Is your estimate close to your calculated value?

Example

Another tour leaves from Niagara Falls for games in Toronto and Montreal. The bus then returns to Niagara Falls. At the start of the trip, the odometer on the bus reads 47 681.4 km. At the end, it reads 49 024.1 km. How far was the trip?

Solution

To find the difference, we *subtract.*

Paper and Pencil	*Estimate (by rounding to the nearest 1000)*		
49 024.1	49 024.1	⟶	49 000
– 47 681.4	– 47 681.4	⟶	– 48 000
1 342.7			1 000

Calculator **C** **49024.1** **–** **47681.4** **=** 1342.7

The trip was 1342.7 km.

Why did we round to the nearest thousand and not the nearest ten thousand to estimate?

Why did we not round to the nearest 100 to estimate?

Practice

Add.

1. 567 + 879 **2.** 56.7 + 98.9

3. 34 698 + 4545 **4.** 1.23 + 8.79

5. 678.9 + 88.85 **6.** 457 678 + 23 940

Subtract.

7. 876 − 435 **8.** 3005 − 789

9. 45.7 − 21.6 **10.** 67.2 − 34.65

11. 8.23 − 5.613 **12.** 4193 − 458.1

Calculate.

13. 4560 + 700 + 7123

14. 23.47 − 9.87

15. 103 + 306 + 402 − 701

16. 129.08 + 332.2 + 2.32 + 40.05

Find ■ .

17. ■ = 5467 + 136

18. ■ = 34.21 − 8.93

19. ■ = 101 + 234 + 12

20. 23.4 + 89.1 + 20.1 = ■

Find the missing numbers.

21.	**22.**	**23.**	**24.**
567	4510	459	6581
+ ■	+ ■	− ■	− ■
983	7613	132	3002

Problems and Applications

25. The odometer on the Chan car reads 234 787.8 km. The odometer on the Bean car reads 198 450.9 km. How much farther have the Chans driven?

26. A baker has 4.5 kg of sugar. He uses 1.85 kg in one recipe and 2.2 kg in another. Does he have enough sugar left to bake a cake that needs 0.55 kg?

27. Saturn is 1 425 000 000 km from the sun. Uranus is 4 497 000 000 km from the sun. How much farther from the sun is Uranus?

28. Three classes from Centennial school went to the museum. The total cost was $408.50. Teachers had collected $42.75, $61.50, and $90.25 from the students. How much more was needed?

29. A train arrived at Bay Street station with 1203 people on board. At the station, 236 people got on the train and 197 got off. How many were on board when it left the station?

30. In 1984, Sylvie Bernier won an Olympic gold medal for Canada in springboard diving by scoring 530.70 points. Four years later, Min Gao from China won the gold by scoring 580.23 points. Who had the higher score? How much higher was it?

31. The East Side Boys and Girls Club spent $784.79 for a television, $456.50 for a sofa, and $276.98 for an entertainment centre. How much was spent altogether?

32. Write a problem that uses addition or subtraction and the values $94.67, $256.23, and $456.80. Ask a classmate to solve your problem.

WORD POWER

Change the first word to the second word by changing one letter at time. Each time you change a letter, you must form a real word. Write down the words you form and compare with a classmate.

F A N

___

___

A I R

1.7 Guess and Check

Lydia scored 5 more points than Martina in the basketball game. Together, they scored 29 points. How many points did each of them score?

Understand the Problem

1. What facts are given?
2. What must you find?

Think of a Plan

Guess Martina's score.

Add 5 to Martina's score to get Lydia's score.

Add Martina's and Lydia's scores to see if they make 29.

If they do not, make another guess at Martina's score.

Carry Out the Plan

GUESS | CHECK

Martina's Score	Lydia's Score	Total Score	Is the total 29?
5	5 + 5 = 10	5 + 10 = 15	Too small
8	8 + 5 = 13	8 + 13 = 21	Too small
13	13 + 5 = 18	13 + 18 = 31	Too large
12	12 + 5 = 17	12 + 17 = 29	29 = 29

Checks!

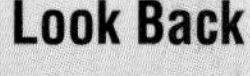

Lydia scored 17 points and Martina scored 12 points.

Look Back

Check: 17 is 5 more than 12.
12 + 17 = 29

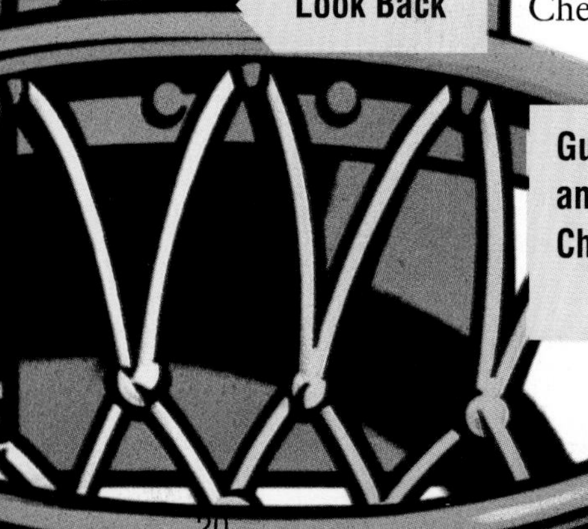

Guess and Check

1. Guess an answer that fits one of the facts.
2. Check the answer against the other facts.
3. If necessary, adjust your guess.
4. Check again.

Problems and Applications

Find the whole numbers in questions 1–5.

1. The sum of two numbers is 9.
Their product is 20.

2. The sum of two numbers is 12.
One number is 4 more than the other.

3. One number is 5 times another.
Their sum is 18.

4. The product of two consecutive numbers is 702.

5. The sum of two numbers is 18.
The difference between them is 2.

Solve.

6. Moro has 95¢ in nickels and dimes. He has 13 coins. How many of each does he have?

7. There are 7 more boys than girls in a class of 23. How many of each are there?

8. Matthew lives 7 km closer to the school than Berthe. They live a total of 31 km from the school. How far does each live from the school?

9. On the target, the sum of the points for A and B is 7. The sum for B and C is 12. The product of the points for A and C is 24. Find the points for A, B, and C.

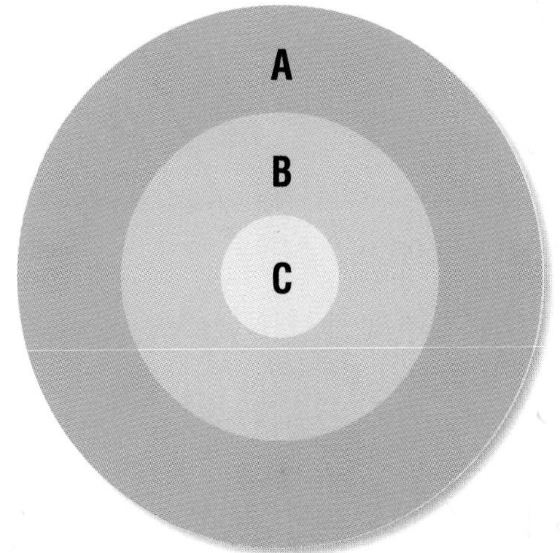

10. José has $51 in $2 and $5 bills. He has 15 bills. How many of each does he have?

11. A sports coat has twice as many small buttons as large buttons. It takes 600 buttons to make 100 coats. How many of each size of button are on each coat?

12. Merle bought a tape and a CD for $27.45. The CD cost $8.45 more than the tape. What was the price of each?

13. A team picture and frame cost $59.85. The frame cost twice as much as the picture. What did the picture cost?

14. A riding school has horses and trainers. Barbara counted 50 heads and 164 feet there. How many horses are there?

15. Bruce scored 11 points more than Charles in basketball. They scored a total of 61 points. How many points did Bruce score?

LOGIC POWER

Examine the map. Use your knowledge of geography to decide which province this area is in. Find the area on a complete map.

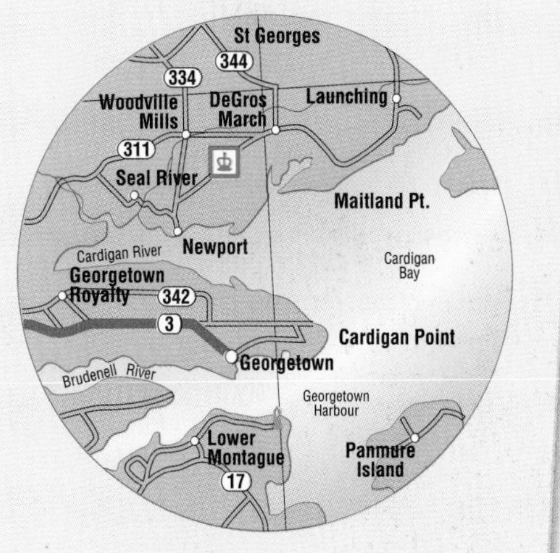

1.8 Multiplying by Powers of Ten: Mental Math

Activity: Look for a Pattern

Examine the following products of numbers multiplied by 10 and 0.1.

3600 × 10 = 36 000	8650 × 0.1 = 865
360 × 10 = 3600	865 × 0.1 = 86.5
36 × 10 = 360	86.5 × 0.1 = 8.65
3.6 × 10 = 36	8.65 × 0.1 = 0.865
0.36 × 10 = 3.6	0.865 × 0.1 = 0.0865

Inquire

1. Describe the pattern you see when you multiply by 10.

2. Write the rule for multiplying by 10.

3. Describe the pattern you see when you multiply by 0.1.

4. Write the rule for multiplying by 0.1.

Practice

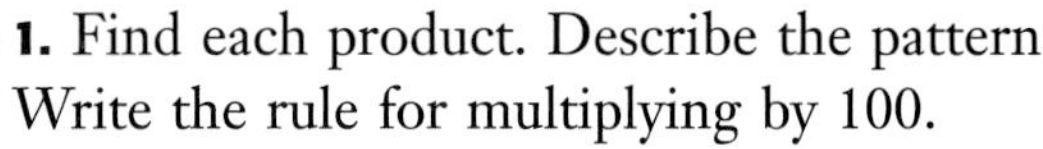

1. Find each product. Describe the pattern. Write the rule for multiplying by 100.

100 × 350 =	679 × 100 =
100 × 35 =	67.9 × 100 =
100 × 3.5 =	6.79 × 100 =
100 × 0.35 =	0.679 × 100 =

2. Multiply. Describe the pattern. Write the rule for multiplying by 1000.

1000 × 350 =	679 × 1000 =
1000 × 35 =	67.9 × 1000 =
1000 × 3.5 =	6.79 × 1000 =
1000 × 0.35 =	0.679 × 1000 =

3. Multiply. Describe the pattern. Write the rule for multiplying by 0.01.

0.01 × 3400 =	7000 × 0.01 =
0.01 × 340 =	700 × 0.01 =
0.01 × 34 =	70 × 0.01 =
0.01 × 3.4 =	7 × 0.01 =

4. Find each product. Describe the pattern. Write the rule for multiplying by 0.001.

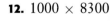

0.001 × 3400 =	7000 × 0.001 =
0.001 × 340 =	700 × 0.001 =
0.001 × 34 =	70 × 0.001 =
0.001 × 3.4 =	7 × 0.001 =

Multiply the following mentally.

5. 234 × 100

6. 0.01 × 29

7. 300 × 0.1

8. 45.7 × 1000

9. 10 × 4.3

10. 0.001 × 600

11. 0.1 × 56.3

12. 1000 × 8300

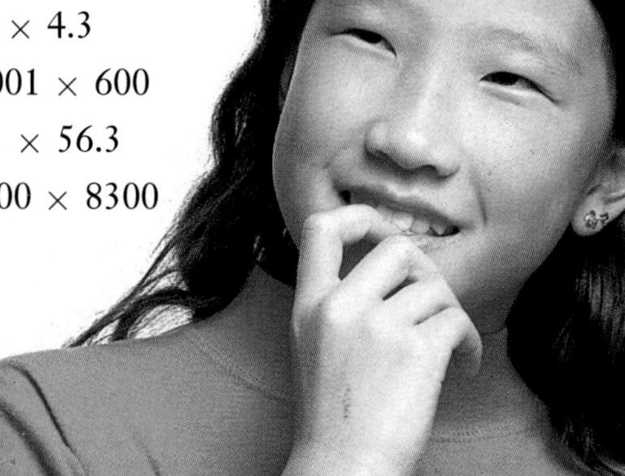

1.9 Using Powers of Ten: Mental Math

3600
360

Activity: Look For A Pattern

Compare the results of multiplying:

by 10 and by 30	by 100 and by 300	by 1000 and by 3000
$2 \times 10 = 20$	$2 \times 100 = 200$	$2 \times 1000 = 2000$
$2 \times 30 = 60$	$2 \times 300 = 600$	$2 \times 3000 = 6000$

by 0.1 and 0.4	by 0.01 and 0.04	by 0.001 and 0.004
$7 \times 0.1 = 0.7$	$7 \times 0.01 = 0.07$	$7 \times 0.001 = 0.007$
$7 \times 0.4 = 2.8$	$7 \times 0.04 = 0.28$	$7 \times 0.004 = 0.028$

Inquire

1. Describe the patterns you see when you multiply by multiples of 10, 100, and 1000.

2. Describe the patterns you see when you multiply by multiples of 0.1, 0.01, and 0.001.

Practice

Multiply.

1. 3×400 **2.** 7×600 **3.** 9×6000
4. 2×800 **5.** 700×5 **6.** 9000×8
7. 60×3 **8.** 300×9 **9.** 5000×8

Multiply.

10. 6×0.3 **11.** 8×0.04 **12.** 5×0.007
13. 3×0.2 **14.** 0.6×8 **15.** 0.02×9
16. 0.002×8 **17.** 0.05×7 **18.** 9×0.7

Multiply.

19. 0.008×20 **20.** 30×800
21. 0.6×5000 **22.** 900×50
23. 600×0.02 **24.** 20×7000
25. 500×0.6 **26.** 8000×0.2
27. 10×0.07 **28.** 40×0.03

Problems and Applications

29. Sandra earned $20 an hour as a tour guide. Last month she worked 80 hours. How much did she earn?

30. The school choir has 50 members. School blazers cost $80 each. How much will it cost to buy blazers for the choir?

31. About 0.7 of your body mass is water. Armin has a mass of 60 kg. What is the mass of water in his body? What is the mass of water in your body?

32. An ant can lift an object that is 50 times its body mass. If you were as strong as an ant, how much could you lift? Would you win a medal in the Olympics? Could you pick up a small car?

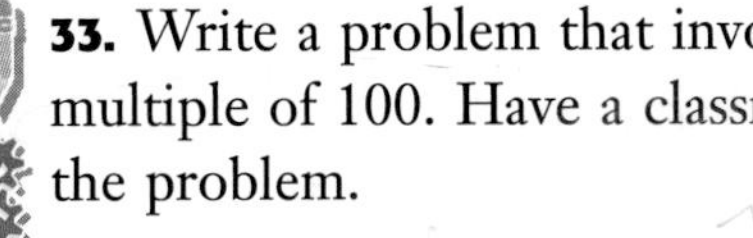

33. Write a problem that involves a multiple of 100. Have a classmate solve the problem.

1.10 Estimating Products: Mental Math

Activity: Study the Information

On February 23, 1909, at Baddeck Bay in Nova Scotia, J.A.D. McCurdy made the first airplane flight in Canada. He flew the *Silver Dart* for 44 s at a speed of 18.2 m/s.

Inquire

1. About how far did the *Silver Dart* fly in 1 s?
2. About how far did it fly in 10 s?
3. About how far did it fly in 44 s?
4. Compare your estimates with your classmates'.

Written in different units, the speed of the *Silver Dart* was only about 65 km/h. Modern passenger aircraft fly over 10 times faster.

Example

A passenger aircraft takes 3.9 h to fly from Toronto to Edmonton at 690 km/h. About how far does it fly?

Solution

Estimate 690×3.9.

Round to the greatest place value of each number and multiply mentally.

$$\begin{array}{rcr} 690 & \longrightarrow & 700 \\ \times 3.9 & \longrightarrow & \times 4 \\ \hline & & 2800 \end{array}$$

The plane flies about 2800 km.

When estimating with decimals less than **1**, look for numbers that are close to **1** or to **0.5**.

Example

Estimate.

a) 0.89×7.6

b) 0.547×10.8

Solution

a) To estimate 0.89×7.6,
think $\mathbf{1} \times 7.6 = 7.6$
or think $\mathbf{1} \times 8 = 8$

b) To estimate 0.547×10.8,
think $\mathbf{0.5} \times 10.8 = 5.4$
or think $\mathbf{0.5} \times 10 = 5$

Practice

Estimate.

1. 56 × 345
2. 47.8 × 8.4
3. 3200 × 17
4. 99 × 33
5. 6.7 × 88
6. 592 × 2

Estimate.

7. 47 × 128
8. 88.2 × 67.1
9. 33 × 99
10. 4500 × 23.6
11. 1000 × 67.99
12. 0.67 × 400

Work with a partner. Choose the best estimate, a), b), or c), of each product. Then use your calculator to find the exact answer. Compare the exact answer with your estimate.

13. 83 × 7 **a)** 630 **b)** 560 **c)** 720

14. 54 × 29 **a)** 1800 **b)** 1000 **c)** 1500

15. 421 × 26 **a)** 12 000 **b)** 8000 **c)** 15 000

16. 389 × 6 **a)** 1800 **b)** 1200 **c)** 2400

17. 15.6 × 49 **a)** 400 **b)** 1000 **c)** 750

18. 258.6 × 4.1 **a)** 1200 **b)** 800 **c)** 1000

Look for numbers close to 1 or 0.5. Estimate each product.

19. 0.89 × 51
20. 1.08 × 37
21. 0.46 × 33
22. 14.7 × 0.62
23. 0.93 × 371
24. 460 × 0.38
25. 345.8 × 1.2
26. 0.41 × 0.86

Estimate each product.

27. 317 × 48
28. 756 × 21
29. 43 × 66
30. 45.6 × 19.8
31. 234.6 × 8.5
32. 8.77 × 4.21
33. 657 × 8.9
34. 123 × 404
35. 86.9 × 301

Estimate each product.

36. 2300 × 456
37. 567 × 5601
38. 0.67 × 6089
39. 76 000 × 0.92
40. 8901 × 0.39
41. 56.8 × 49.3

Problems and Applications

42. Carla drove at 85 km/h from 08:30 to 10:45. Estimate the distance she drove.

43. Thirty-three students went to the art gallery. The tickets cost $5.75 each. Estimate the total cost.

44. When you sleep, you breathe about 7.5 L of air each minute. About how much air do you breathe in seven hours of sleep? About how much air did you breathe last night?

45. Kadeem's mass was 3.41 kg at birth. His mother read that his mass should be about 21.6 times greater when he is full grown. About how heavy will Kadeem be?

NUMBER POWER

The marking **8** × **30** is engraved on Sarah's binoculars. Use your research skills to answer the following.

a) What does the **8** mean?

b) What does the × mean?

c) What does the **30** mean?

1.11 Multiplying Numbers

Activity: Study the Information

People who do stunts for movies and television belong to ACTRA, the Alliance for Canadian Cinema, Television, and Radio Artists. One year, the ACTRA pay rate for stunt people was \$392.25 a day. A movie production company hired Terry Lee for 6 days. Terry wanted to work out his earnings.

Inquire

1. Did Terry need an exact answer or an estimate?

2. What calculation method would you have used?

3. How much did Terry earn in 6 days?

Example

For difficult stunts, a stunt person asks for more money. Terry earned an extra \$375.50 an hour for a car chase scene. The scene took 3.5 h to shoot. How much extra did Terry earn?

Solution

To find the answer, you multiply.

Calculator C 375.50 × 3.5 = 1314.25

Paper and Pencil

375.50	← 2 decimal places
× 3.5	← 1 decimal place
187750	
112650	
1314.250	← 3 decimal places

EST

375.50	→	400
× 3.5	→	× 4
		1600

The answer is close to the estimate. Terry earned \$1314.25 extra.

Some students can multiply whole numbers but not decimals. Write them some instructions for multiplying decimals.

Practice

Estimate, then multiply.

1. 75×6
2. 64×0.9
3. 4.06×7
4. 739×6

Estimate, then multiply.

5. 2.7×5.2
6. 56×76
7. 6.9×81
8. 29×0.38

Estimate, then multiply.

9. 211×2.3
10. 456×0.62
11. 5.02×15
12. 6.72×33
13. 0.46×54
14. 890×0.5

Estimate, then multiply.

15. 67.2×0.48
16. 45.7×1.2
17. 307×97

Estimate, then multiply. Round each answer to the nearest tenth.

18. 6.76×8.4
19. 67.2×0.48
20. 1.52×0.6

Problems and Applications

21. Thirty-two students each deliver 60 flyers to advertize the school garage sale. How many flyers are delivered?

22. A survey shows that people watch 19 hours and 38 minutes of television each week. How many minutes is that in one year?

23. Every hour, about 3 000 000 meteors enter the Earth's atmosphere. About how many enter in the month of April?

24. Your heart is a hard-working muscle. It beats about 70 times a minute. About how many times does it beat in a day?

25. A season ticket for the ballet costs \$199.50. If 1023 season tickets are sold, what is the value of the tickets sold?

26. Audio tape goes through a tape player at a rate of 8.64 cm each second.

a) Calculate the length of a 60-minute tape.

b) Calculate the length of a 90-minute tape.

27. In a math contest, students earn 1.25 points for a correct answer and lose 0.5 points for an incorrect answer. Calculate the score for each team after 20 questions.

Eagles: 15 correct   Bears: 12 correct
Owls: 18 correct   Tigers: 14 correct

Find the value of each ■ .

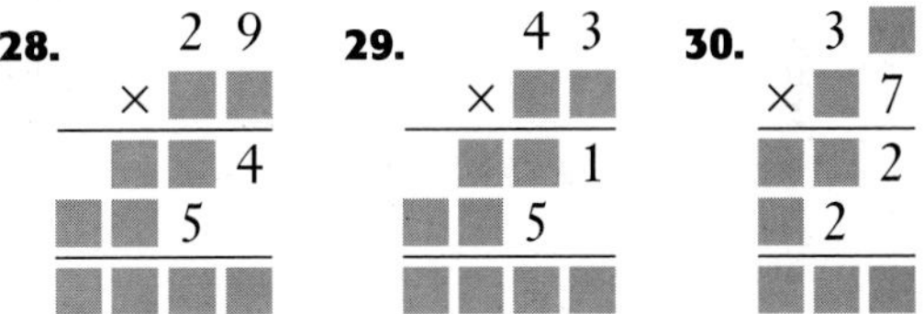

CALCULATOR POWER

Some calculators display up to 8 digits. What do you do when the answer is larger than 8 digits?

Here is a way to multiply 12 342 × 46 678 using place value.

```
   12 000 + 342
 × 46 000 + 678
        231 876  ←  342 × 678
      8 136 000  ←  12 × 678
     15 732 000
  + 552 000 000
    576 099 876
```

then add the zeros

1. Describe the steps.

Use the method to multiply.

2. 23 467 × 55 799

3. 457 121 × 56 789

4. 498 666 × 831 222

1.12 Dividing by Powers of Ten: Mental Math

Activity: Look for a Pattern

Examine the quotients.

365 ÷ 10 = 36.5	8970 ÷ 10 = 897
365 ÷ 100 = 3.65	8970 ÷ 100 = 89.7
365 ÷ 1000 = 0.365	8970 ÷ 1000 = 8.97

Inquire

1. Describe the pattern you see.

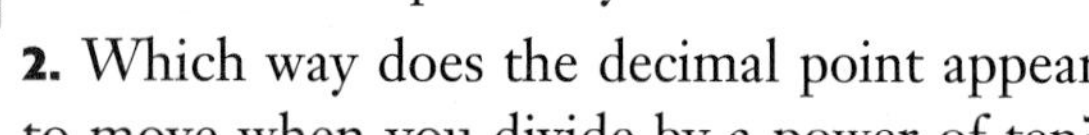
2. Which way does the decimal point appear to move when you divide by a power of ten?

3. Write a rule for dividing by powers of ten.

Some powers of ten can be written as decimals less than 1. Examples are 0.1, 0.01, and 0.001.

Use your calculator to find the quotients.

365 ÷ 0.1 =	8970 ÷ 0.1 =
365 ÷ 0.01 =	8970 ÷ 0.01 =
365 ÷ 0.001 =	8970 ÷ 0.001 =

Work with a classmate to describe the pattern.

Which way does the decimal point appear to move when you divide by a decimal power of ten?

Write a rule for dividing by decimal powers of ten.

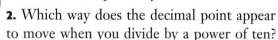

Practice

Divide by 10.

1. 65 **2.** 243 **3.** 807
4. 2.5 **5.** 0.18 **6.** 13.2
7. 115.7 **8.** 2.653 **9.** 72.94

Divide by 100.

10. 26 **11.** 571 **12.** 8429
13. 15.8 **14.** 73.9 **15.** 136.5
16. 6.737 **17.** 89.425 **18.** 0.856

Divide by 1000.

19. 75 **20.** 829 **21.** 1534
22. 20.83 **23.** 46.2 **24.** 91.06
25. 631.4 **26.** 789.6 **27.** 5392

Divide by 0.1.

28. 53 **29.** 658 **30.** 746
31. 8.6 **32.** 9.2 **33.** 37.4
34. 22.5 **35.** 48.36 **36.** 158.9

Divide by 0.01.

37. 84 **38.** 392 **39.** 587

40. 19.16 **41.** 38.52 **42.** 7.903

43. 118.2 **44.** 506.8 **45.** 0.238

Divide by 0.001.

46. 29 **47.** 436 **48.** 9645

49. 4.7 **50.** 8.06 **51.** 64.29

52. 35.64 **53.** 731.5 **54.** 0.375

Simplify.

55. 28×0.01 **56.** 64×100

57. 926×0.001 **58.** 0.54×0.1

59. 12.05×10 **60.** 841.7×1000

61. 2.63×0.01 **62.** 5.78×100

63. 7.602×0.001 **64.** 18.09×1000

Problems and Applications

65. Remi paid $56.00 for 100 pencils. How much was each pencil?

66. A lacrosse team bought 1000 oatmeal cookies for $350.00 and sold them for $500.00. For each cookie, determine the following.

a) the cost **b)** the selling price

c) the profit

67. Calculate.

a) 65×10
$65 \div 0.1$

b) 12.5×100
$12.5 \div 0.01$

c) 7.2×1000
$7.2 \div 0.001$

d) 46×0.1
$46 \div 10$

e) 812×0.01
$812 \div 100$

f) 3915×0.001
$3915 \div 1000$

Make a statement about the results. Multiply and divide other numbers by powers of ten to check your statement.

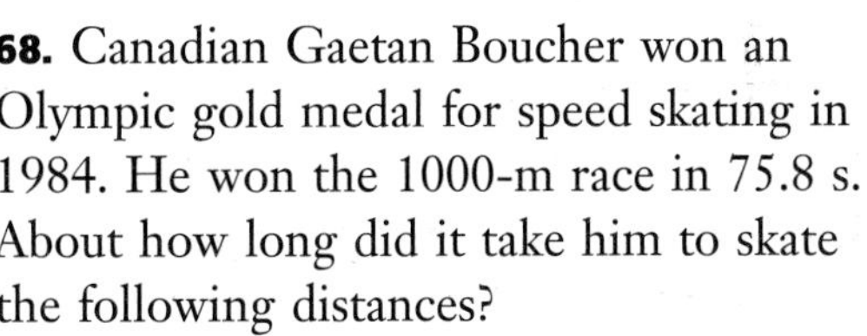

68. Canadian Gaetan Boucher won an Olympic gold medal for speed skating in 1984. He won the 1000-m race in 75.8 s. About how long did it take him to skate the following distances?

a) 1 m **b)** 10 m **c)** 100 m

PATTERN POWER

Find the pattern. Write the last four answers without multiplying.

$2.5 \times 2.5 = 6.25$ $6.5 \times 6.5 =$

$3.5 \times 3.5 = 12.25$ $7.5 \times 7.5 =$

$4.5 \times 4.5 = 20.25$ $8.5 \times 8.5 =$

$5.5 \times 5.5 = 30.25$ $9.5 \times 9.5 =$

1.13 Estimating Quotients: Mental Math

Activity: Study the Example

Ron saw two brands of soup at 8 for \$4.29 and 6 for \$3.65. He did these mental calculations to decide the better buy.

\$4.00 ÷ 8 = 50¢ $\qquad$ \$3.60 ÷ 6 = 60¢

Inquire

1. Why did Ron round \$4.29 to \$4.00?

2. Why did Ron round \$3.65 to \$3.60?

3. Discuss why the rounded numbers were chosen in the following estimates.

29.2 ÷ 7	219.4 ÷ 28	97.59 ÷ 13.6	18.5 ÷ 0.82
28 ÷ 7	210 ÷ 30	96 ÷ 12	18.5 ÷ 1
= 4	= 7	= 8	= 18.5

Practice

Round the dividend to be a multiple of the divisor. Estimate the quotient.

1. $\frac{48.5}{7}$ **2.** $\frac{16.9}{9}$ **3.** $\frac{58.2}{4}$

4. $\frac{113.25}{11}$ **5.** $\frac{153.6}{8}$ **6.** $\frac{309.48}{3}$

7. $\frac{276.3}{9}$ **8.** $\frac{571.96}{7}$ **9.** $\frac{418.51}{5}$

10. $\frac{612.4}{12}$ **11.** $\frac{191.87}{6}$ **12.** $\frac{26.9}{4}$

Estimate the quotient.

13. 18.4 ÷ 7.9 **14.** 26.3 ÷ 4.7

15. 82.6 ÷ 9.4 **16.** 201 ÷ 6.3

17. 117 ÷ 8.5 **18.** 347 ÷ 5.9

19. 48.29 ÷ 7.6 **20.** 516.8 ÷ 9.7

21. 86.03 ÷ 2.7 **22.** 117.3 ÷ 4.1

Problems and Applications

23. Charron earned \$225.25 for working 26.5 h on a construction site. Estimate her hourly pay.

24. Mr. Novak has 20 m of felt to make string puppets for his drama class. Each puppet takes 2.65 m. How many puppets can he make?

25. Baharah ordered 4 CDs from a music club. The total bill, including taxes and delivery, was \$60.42. The taxes and delivery charge totalled \$10.66. How much was each CD?

Estimate the cost of 1 kg of each food from the prices given.

26. 3.6 kg of apples cost \$6.80.

27. 2.8 kg beans cost \$7.17.

28. 4.5 kg potatoes cost \$3.48.

29. 8.2 kg bananas cost \$8.84.

The Computerized Home

In the future, many homes will have built-in computers. One computer program might monitor and water the house plants. Another might turn the lights on and off as you move from one room to another.

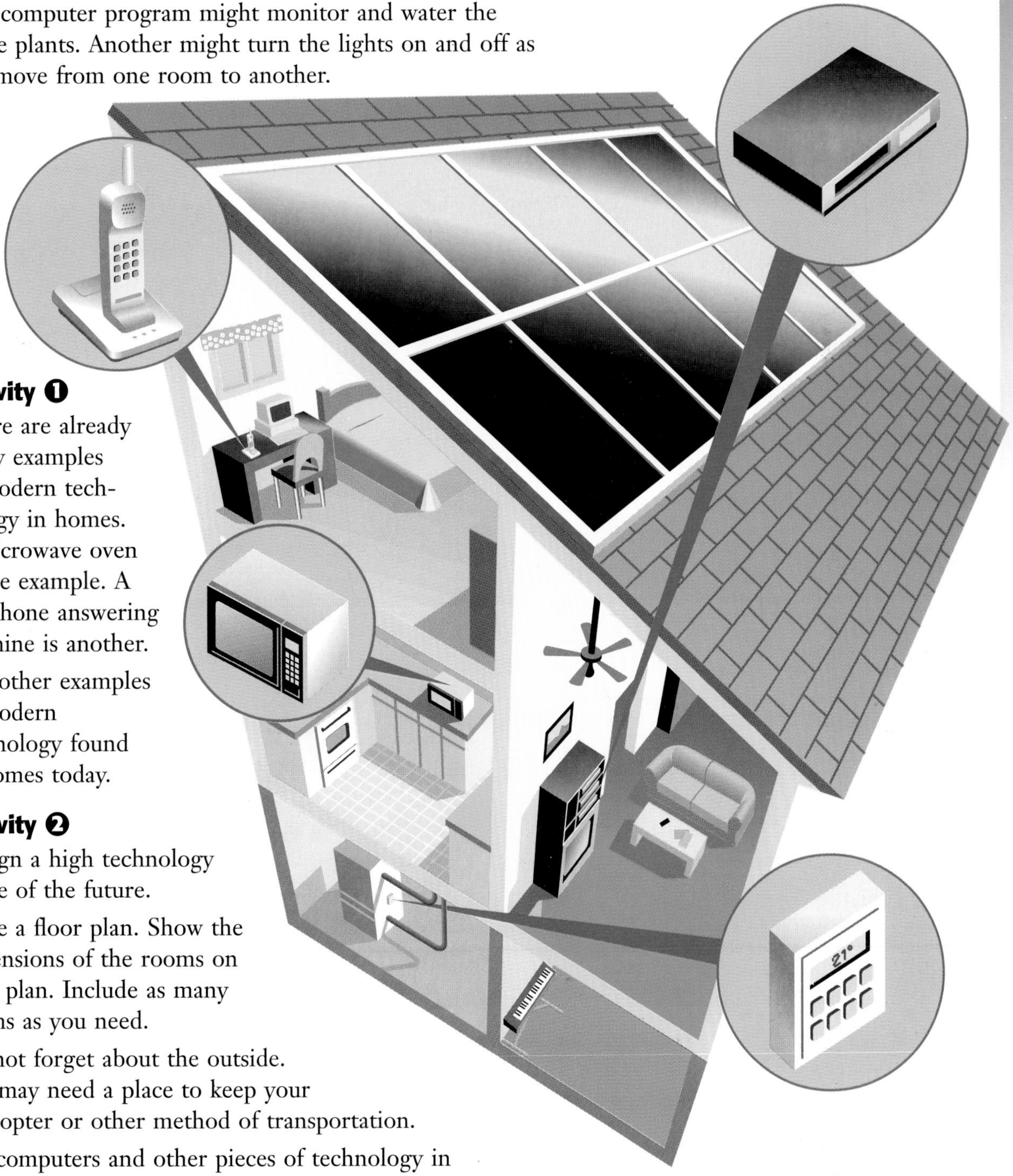

Activity ❶

There are already many examples of modern technology in homes. A microwave oven is one example. A telephone answering machine is another.

List other examples of modern technology found in homes today.

Activity ❷

Design a high technology home of the future.

Make a floor plan. Show the dimensions of the rooms on your plan. Include as many rooms as you need.

Do not forget about the outside. You may need a place to keep your helicopter or other method of transportation.

Put computers and other pieces of technology in and around the home and describe what they would do.

1.14 Short Division

Activity: Study the Example

Some students had $200 to decorate the gym for Children of the World Week. They wanted to know how many flags they could rent at $7.00 each and how much money would be left.

They divided using short division.

$200 \div 7$ → $7\overline{)200}$ → $7\overline{)2{0}^{6}0}$ with 2 above → $7\overline{)2{0}^{6}0}$ with 28 R4 above

7 > 2

7 < 20
20 ÷ 7 = 2 R6

7 < 60
60 ÷ 7 = 8 R4

They could rent 28 flags and have $4.00 left.

The students found some decorative stickers at $0.05 each. How many stickers could they buy with the money they had left?

$4 \div 0.05$ → $0.05\overline{)4}$ → $0.05\overline{)400}$ → $5\overline{)400}$ with 80 above

$0.05 \times 100 = 5$
$4 \times 100 = 400$

They could buy 80 stickers.

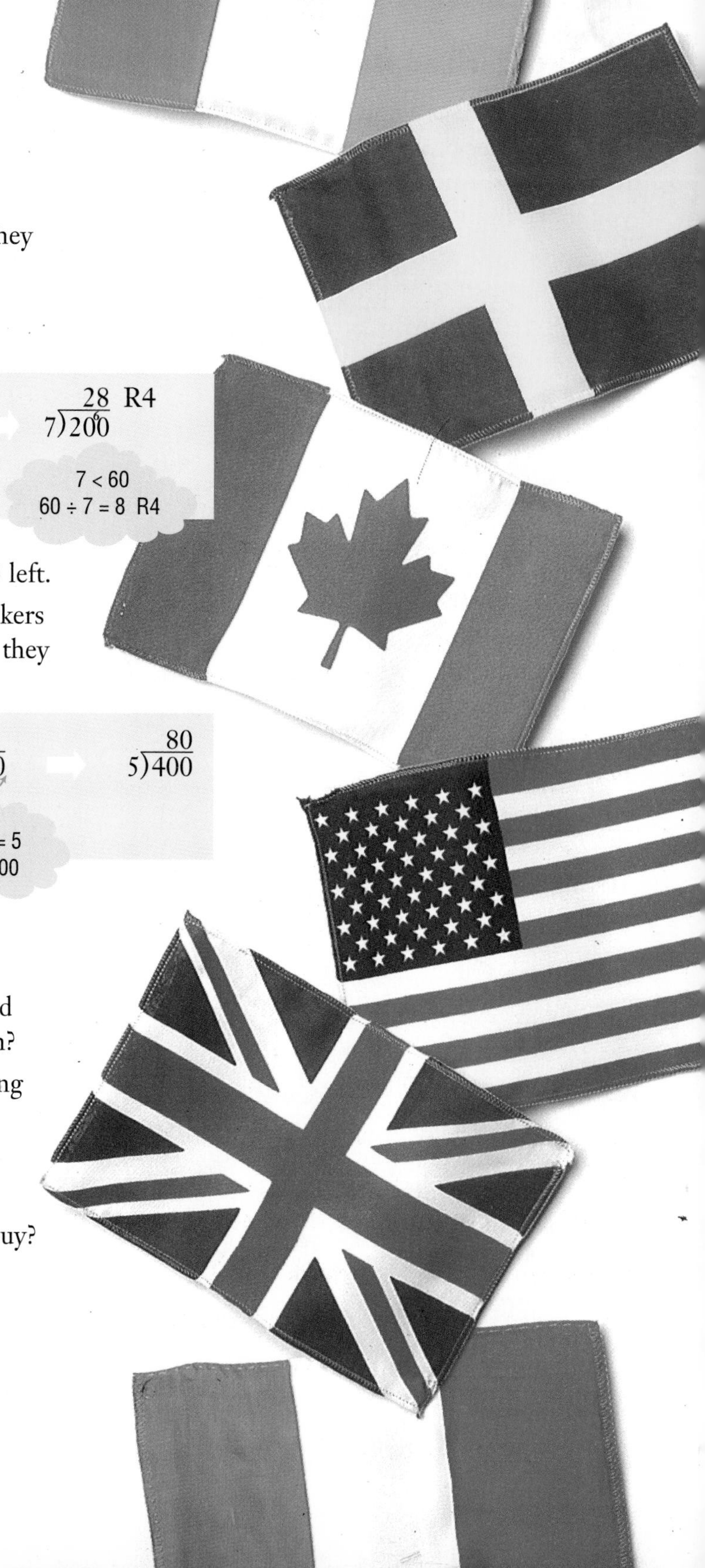

Inquire

1. Why were the divisor and the dividend multiplied by 100 in the decimal division?

2. How could you check the answers using

a) estimation?

b) multiplication?

3. If the students decided to rent only 26 flags, how many stickers could they buy?

Practice

Divide using short division.

1. $5\overline{)465}$ **2.** $3\overline{)396}$ **3.** $4\overline{)288}$

4. $7\overline{)427}$ **5.** $7\overline{)224}$ **6.** $6\overline{)258}$

Divide using short division. State the remainder.

7. $366 \div 7$ **8.** $346 \div 9$ **9.** $331 \div 4$

10. $534 \div 8$ **11.** $1588 \div 5$ **12.** $4371 \div 6$

Estimate, then divide.

13. $19.58 \div 2$ **14.** $44.96 \div 4$

15. $128.05 \div 5$ **16.** $74.4 \div 6$

17. $281.6 \div 8$ **18.** $103.23 \div 9$

Rewrite each question with the divisor as a whole number.

19. $0.5\overline{)35}$ **20.** $1.2\overline{)144}$ **21.** $0.07\overline{)63}$

22. $\frac{1.44}{0.06}$ **23.** $\frac{0.72}{0.9}$ **24.** $\frac{4.2}{0.007}$

Study the example, then copy and complete each question.

$$\frac{7.5}{1.5}\frac{\times 10}{\times 10} = \frac{75}{15} = 5$$

25. $\frac{8.4}{0.2}\frac{\times \blacksquare}{\times \blacksquare} = \blacksquare$ **26.** $\frac{0.56}{0.7}\frac{\times \blacksquare}{\times \blacksquare} = \blacksquare$

27. $\frac{240}{0.06}\frac{\times \blacksquare}{\times \blacksquare} = \blacksquare$ **28.** $\frac{81}{0.9}\frac{\times \blacksquare}{\times \blacksquare} = \blacksquare$

Estimate, then divide.

29. $0.15 \div 0.3$ **30.** $2.8 \div 0.7$

31. $67.2 \div 0.06$ **32.** $0.3285 \div 0.009$

33. $3.428 \div 0.004$ **34.** $493 \div 0.05$

35. $59.28 \div 0.8$ **36.** $0.2552 \div 0.04$

37. $0.861 \div 0.007$ **38.** $11.36 \div 0.002$

Problems and Applications

39. A plane flew 2456 km in 4 h. How far did it fly in one hour?

40. The Greenfield Zoo has been open for 1948 consecutive days.

a) How many full weeks is this?

b) How many more days are needed to make another full week?

41. A school van holds 9 students. The van took 30 students to a track meet. How many trips were needed?

42. In a diving competition, Zaleena had 134.4 points after 4 dives. She scored 35.7 points on one dive. Her scores on the other three dives were equal. How many points did she score on each of these three dives?

43. A box contains 0.475 kg of cereal. A recommended serving is 0.03 kg.

a) How many full servings are in the box?

b) If Marsha eats 0.05 kg in each serving, how many full servings are in the box?

NUMBER POWER

Division by Zero

We can think of $24 \div 6$ as a repeated subtraction.

$$24 - 6 - 6 - 6 - 6 = 0$$

As 6 can be subtracted from 24 four times, we can write the following division statement.

$$24 \div 6 = 4$$

Write each of the following as a repeated subtraction, then write the division statement.

1. $12 \div 3$ **2.** $5 \div 1$ **3.** $3 \div 0.5$

4. Can you write $4 \div 0$ as a repeated subtraction? Explain.

5. Is it possible to divide by zero?

1.15 Dividing Numbers

Activity: Use the Data

A day is the length of time it takes for a planet to rotate once on its axis.

The Earth goes around once every 24 h.

One day on Mercury is 1416 Earth hours long.

You want to know how many Earth days equal one day on Mercury.

Earth:
1 day = 24 h

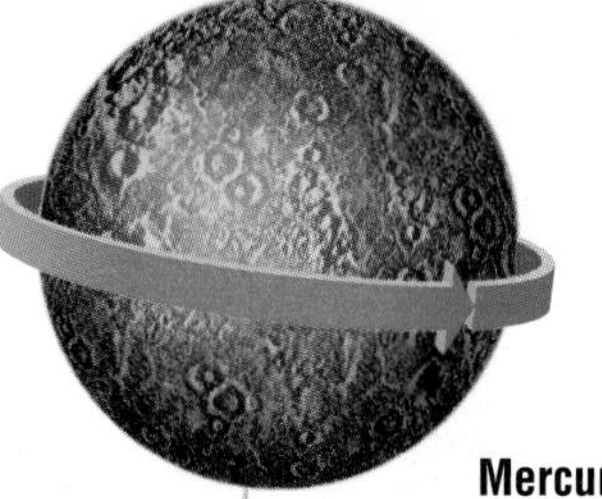

Mercury:
1 day = 1416 h

Inquire

1. Do you need an exact or approximate answer?
2. Why do you need to divide to find the answer?
3. How many Earth days equal one day on Mercury?
4. How can you use multiplication to check your answer?
5. One day on Venus is 5832 Earth hours long. How many Earth days is that?
6. One day on Uranus is only 10.8 Earth hours long. How many Earth days is that?

Example

Evaluate $4.9 \div 0.85$. Round your answer to the nearest tenth.

Solution

Divide to 2 decimal places and round to the nearest tenth.

$$0.85\overline{)4.90}$$

$$\begin{array}{r} 5.76 \\ 85\overline{)490} \\ \underline{425} \\ 650 \\ \underline{595} \\ 550 \\ \underline{510} \\ 40 \end{array}$$

Paper and Pencil Multiply the divisor by a power of 10 to make it a whole number.
Multiply the dividend by the same power of 10.
In this example, we multiply by 100.
Divide as for whole numbers.

EST $5 \div 1 = 5$

Calculator C 4.9 ÷ 0.85 = 5.7647059

So $4.9 \div 0.85 = 5.8$ to the nearest tenth.

Write an example in which you would multiply by 10 before you divide.

What calculation steps do we leave out when we use a calculator?

Practice

Estimate, then calculate.

1. $238 \div 14$

2. $45 \div 8$

3. $119 \div 35$

4. $4.2\overline{)88.2}$

5. $0.26\overline{)0.884}$

6. $2.1\overline{)0.546}$

Estimate, then calculate.
Round each answer to the nearest tenth.

7. $84 \div 46$

8. $24 \div 22$

9. $156 \div 73$

10. $9.6 \div 1.8$

11. $0.72\overline{)5.8}$

12. $9.9\overline{)48.6}$

Problems and Applications

13. Connie paid $38.76 for 12 monthly issues of *Teen* magazine. How much did she pay for each issue?

14. A staircase is built on the set of the school play. Each step is 0.19 m high. If the height between floors is 2.28 m, how many steps are there?

15. A stage crew has $200 to rent speakers for a concert. Each one rents for $15. How many can the crew rent?

16. A case of orange juice is on sale for $9.50. There are 27 boxes in a case. The juice regularly costs $12.98 a case. What is the sale price of each box of juice? What is the regular price of each box of juice?

17. Vancouver is a 6050-km drive from Halifax. If you drove at 70 km/h, how many hours would you take? How many days would you take if you drove for 7 h each day?

18. If it costs $0.37/min to access a database from your computer, how many minutes could you afford for $10.00? Answer to the nearest minute.

19. Claus keyboards at about 43 words per minute. About how long will he take to input a 5000-word essay?

20. In a division, what can you say about the quotient when the divisor is

a) greater than the dividend?

b) smaller than the dividend?

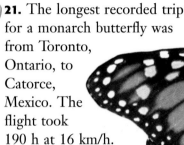

21. The longest recorded trip for a monarch butterfly was from Toronto, Ontario, to Catorce, Mexico. The flight took 190 h at 16 km/h.

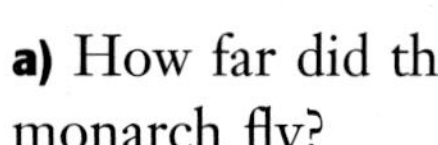

a) How far did the monarch fly?

b) About how long would it take you to walk the same distance? Compare your estimate with a classmate's.

LOGIC POWER

Assume that there are no cubes missing from the back of this stack.

1. How many cubes are in the stack?

2. How many cubes are hidden from you?

3. If you painted the outside of the stack red, how many cubes would have the following numbers of red faces?

a) 1 **b)** 2 **c)** 3 **d)** 4

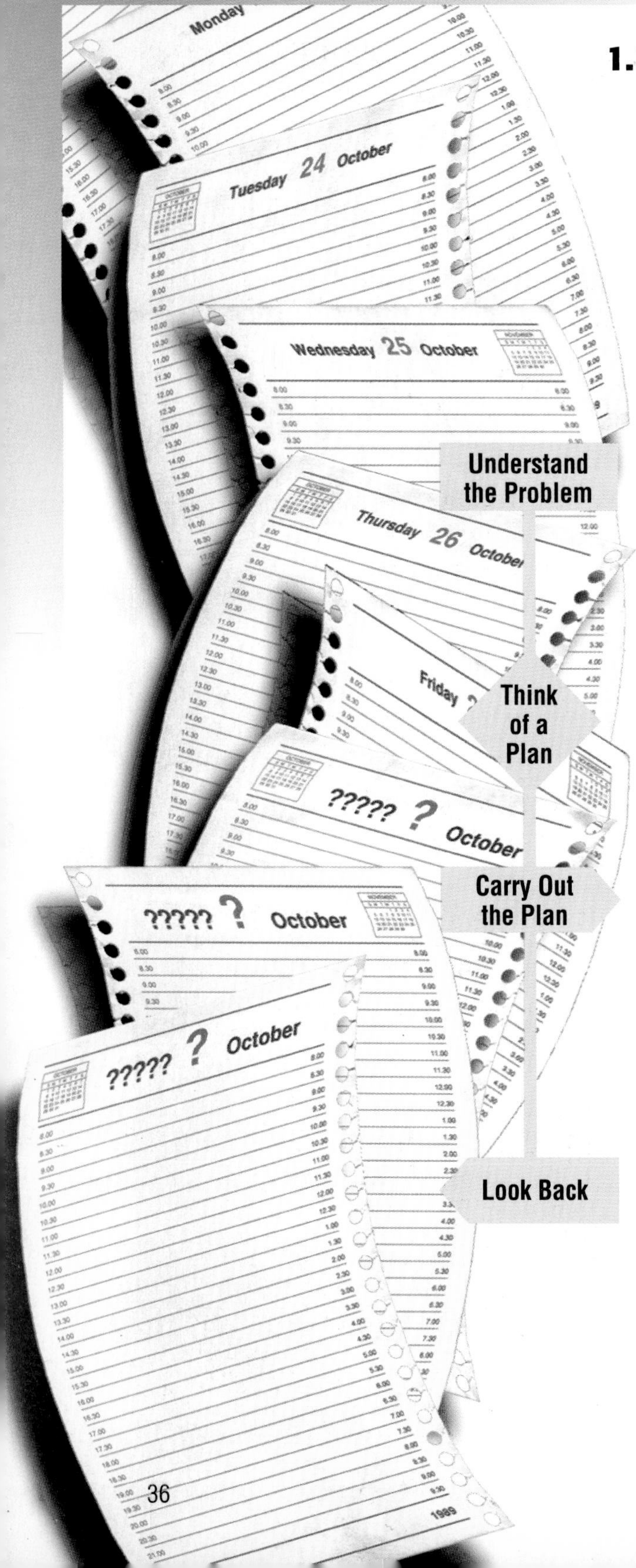

1.16 Make an Assumption

When you **make an assumption** about something, you take it for granted. You suppose it is true. People make the assumption that the sun will come up every morning. To solve some problems, you must make assumptions.

Janine has saved \$30.00 for a new bicycle. It costs \$220.00. Janine cuts lawns for a week and earns \$21.50. If she cuts lawns for 9 weeks, will she be able to buy the bicycle?

Understand the Problem

1. What information are you given?

2. What are you asked to find?

Think of a Plan

Make an assumption. Assume that Janine will earn \$21.50 each week by cutting lawns. Add the amount she earns to the amount she has already saved.

Compare her total amount of money to the cost of the bicycle.

Use a calculator.

Carry Out the Plan

Money from cutting lawns = 9 × \$21.50
= \$193.50
Savings = \$30.00
Total = \$223.50

If Janine earns \$21.50 a week for 9 weeks, she will have \$3.50 more than she needs to buy the bicycle.

Look Back

Does the answer seem reasonable? How could you use division to find the amount Janine should earn each week? What could prevent Janine from earning enough money? What could Janine do to make sure she has enough?

Make an Assumption
1. Make a reasonable assumption.
2. Solve the problem.
3. Check that the answer is reasonable.

Problems and Applications

Determine the pattern, make an assumption, then list the next 3 terms.

1. 1, 6, 11, 16, ■, ■, ■

2. 30, 29, 27, 24, ■, ■, ■

3. 3, 6, 12, 24, ■, ■, ■

4. In one week, Roberto earns $23.00 from babysitting. How much will he earn in a year? What assumptions have you made?

5. The zoo is 200 km from the school. The school bus can travel at 80 km/h. How long will the journey take? What assumptions have you made?

6. Susan scores 12 points in her first basketball game. How many points will she score in 13 games? What assumptions have you made?

7. Without studying, Shara scored 70 on a math test. She spent half an hour studying for the next test and scored 80. For how long should she study to get 100 on a test? What assumptions have you made? What mark would Shara get if she studied for 3 h?

8. Caroline is president of the student council. She asks 20 grade 7 students if they will buy school sweat shirts. Ten say they will. There are 600 students in the school.

a) How many sweat shirts can the student council expect to sell? What assumptions have you made?

b) Do you agree with Caroline's way of finding out how many students will buy sweat shirts?

c) How would you find out the number of students who will buy sweat shirts?

9. Michel learned that, in the 1904 Olympic Games, the men's 100-m dash was run in 11 s. Sixty years later, in 1964, it was run in 10 s. Michel figured that, in the year 2024, it would be run in 9 s.

a) What assumptions did Michel make?

b) Use Michel's assumptions to predict when the 100-m dash will be run in 0 s.

c) What is wrong with Michel's assumptions?

10. Frank planned a barbecue for his scout patrol. There were 12 members, including Frank. He bought 24 hot dogs for $7.58, 24 hot dog rolls for $3.58, 12 hamburger patties for $6.19, 12 hamburger buns for $1.79, and 24 cans of pop for $0.50 a can. How much did Frank spend? What assumptions did he make?

NUMBER POWER

Place the numbers 1 to 8 in the circles so that the sum of each side is the same. Is there more than one answer?

1.17 Order of Operations

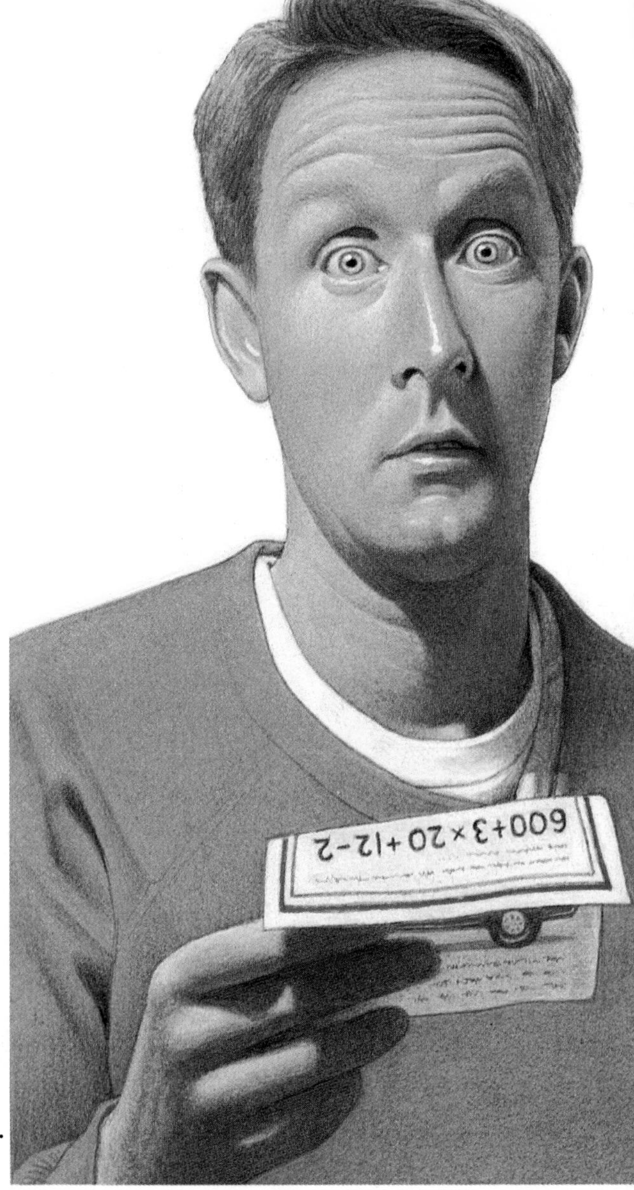

Activity: Solve the Problem

The **Reduce Impaired Driving Everywhere** program, or R.I.D.E. program, started in 1977. One year, all the motorists who were stopped were given a booklet of valuable coupons. One coupon was an entry form for a draw to win a new car. The form included the following statement.

Before being declared a winner, the selected entrant must answer this skill testing question.

$$600 + 3 \times 20 + 12 - 2$$

Inquire

1. Evaluate the expression in more than one way to answer the skill testing question. Do not make any errors in arithmetic.

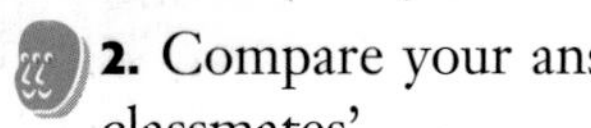

2. Compare your answers with your classmates'.

To make sure we get one correct answer for an expression, we use the following rules. They are called the **order of operations**.

Order of Operations

- Do calculations in brackets first.
- Change "of" to $\times$.
- Divide and multiply in order from left to right.
- Add and subtract in order from left to right.

Example 1

Simplify $15 \div (7 - 4) \times 6$

Solution

$= 15 \div \underbrace{(7 - 4)} \times 6$

$= \underbrace{15 \div 3} \times 6$

$= \underbrace{5 \times 6}$

$= 30$

Example 2

Simplify $\frac{1}{2}$ of $8.4 + 9.1 - 3.6$

Solution

$= \underbrace{\tfrac{1}{2} \text{ of } 8.4} + 9.1 - 3.6$

$= \underbrace{4.2 + 9.1} - 3.6$

$= \underbrace{13.3 - 3.6}$

$= 9.7$

Some calculators *automatically* follow the order of operations. These calculators are said to use **algebraic logic**.

For other calculators, you must apply the order of operations by entering numbers and operations in the right order.

To test your calculator, enter the following.

C 12 ÷ 2 + 6 × 3

If you get the correct answer, 24, your calculator uses algebraic logic.

If your answer is 36, your calculator does not use algebraic logic.

What is wrong with the way this answer is calculated?

Practice

Calculate.

1. $5 + 7 - 4$

2. $20 \div 5 + 3$

3. $13 - 2 - 3$

4. $8 + 4 \div 2$

5. $24 \div 6 - 1$

6. $15 - 4 \times 2$

7. $10 \div 2 \times 5$

8. $4 \times 7 - 10$

9. $30 \div 6 + 11$

10. $8 \times 4 \div 2$

11. $\frac{1}{2}$ of $8 + 6 - 2$

12. $5 + \frac{1}{3}$ of $1.5 - 3$

Simplify.

13. $(7 - 5) \times 3.4$

14. $12 \div (4.9 + 1.1)$

15. $(3 + 4) \times 5.6$

16. $4.3 \times (10 - 7)$

17. $3.6 \div (8 + 4)$

18. $(8 + 7) - 11$

19. $7 \times (8 - 5)$

20. $20.4 \div (8 \div 2)$

21. $\frac{1}{4}$ of $(10.8 - 2.2)$

22. $\frac{1}{3}$ of $15.9 - 3.7$

Calculate.

23. $5 \times 3 + 8 \times 4$

24. $8 \times 7 - 4 \times 3.4$

25. $(5 + 3 + 2) \times 6$

26. $3 \times 9 + 10 \div 5$

27. $\frac{1}{2}$ of $16.8 - 2.3 \times 0$

28. $16.8 \div 4 - 9.9 \div 3$

Problems and Applications

29. A hockey team gets 2 points for a win and 1 point for a tie. There are four teams in the Western League, the Eagles, Falcons, Hawks, and Cardinals. Each team plays 25 games. The Eagles win 15 and tie 3. The Cardinals win 6 and lose 14. The Hawks win 13 and lose 8. The Falcons win 9 and tie 2. Prepare a standings chart for the league. Order the teams from most points to least points.

Team	Won	Tied	Lost	Points

NUMBER POWER

This expression for the number 1 uses four 4s.

$$\frac{4 \times 4}{4 \times 4}$$

So does another: $(4 + 4) \div (4 + 4)$

Work with a classmate and use four 4s to write expressions for the numbers 2, 3, 4, 5, 6, 7, 8, and 9.

On What Day Did It Happen?

On January 22, 1992, Dr. Roberta Bondar became the first Canadian woman in space. She flew aboard the space shuttle *Columbia*. On what day of the week did she take off?

One way to find the day is to use a perpetual calendar. You can also use mathematics. Here are the 8 steps.

1. Write the date. **January 22, 1992**

2. Divide the last two digits of the year by 4. If there is a remainder, drop it. Use just the quotient, in this case **23**, in the next step.

$$4\overline{)92} = 23$$

3. Add the code number for the month to the quotient.

Code Numbers					
January	1	February	4	March	4
April	0	May	2	June	5
July	0	August	3	September	6
October	1	November	4	December	6

For leap years, use January = 0 and February = 3.

As 1992 was a leap year, we add 0.

$$23 + 0 = 23$$

4. Add the date of the month to the number found in Step 3.

$$23 + 22 = 45$$

5. Add the last two digits of the year, **92**, to the number found in Step 4.

$$45 + 92 = 137$$

6. For dates in the 1700s, add 4 to step 5.

For dates in the 1800s, add 2 to step 5.

For dates in the 1900s, add 0 to step 5.

For dates in the 2000s, add 6 to step 5.

For dates in the 2100s, add 4 to step 5.

$$137 + 0 = 137$$

7. Divide the number from step 6 by **7**. Drop the quotient and use the remainder, **4**, to find the day of the week in step 8.

$$7\overline{)137} = 19$$
$$137 - 7 = 67,\quad 67 - 63 = 4$$

8. The day of the week is found in the chart.

A remainder of

1 = Sunday	5 = Thursday
2 = Monday	6 = Friday
3 = Tuesday	0 = Saturday
4 = Wednesday	

Roberta Bondar went into space on a Wednesday.

Activity ❶

Each picture shows an event. On what day did each event happen?

James Naismith, who was born in Almonte, Ontario, invented basketball in 1891. He used peach baskets and a soccer ball. The first game took place on December 12, 1891.

Alexander Graham Bell, the inventor of the telephone, received the world's first telephone call over outdoor wires on August 10, 1876. The call went from Brantford to Paris, Ontario, a distance of 13 km.

On February 15, 1965, Canada got a new flag.

On September 9, 1954, Canadian Marilyn Bell became the first person to swim across Lake Ontario. She swam from Youngstown, New York, to Toronto, Ontario, in 21 h. Over 100 000 people watched as she arrived in Toronto.

Activity ❷

From your birthdate, work out the day of the week on which you were born.

Review

State whether you need an exact answer or an approximate answer.

1. How long will it take you to shovel snow off the sidewalk?

2. At what time does the football game start?

3. You get a part-time job. How much will you make an hour?

4. How much spending money should you take to camp for a month?

Write each number in words.

5. 34 500 **6.** 703.246 **7.** 76 080 000

Write each number in expanded form.

8. 23 000 **9.** 456.81 **10.** 23 100 000 000

Write each number in standard form.

11. $2 \times 10 + 7 \times 1 + 3 \times 0.1 + 8 \times 0.01$

12. $6 \times 1000 + 3 \times 100 + 4 \times 10 + 9 \times 1$

Round to the nearest ten and to the nearest hundred.

13. 55 **14.** 842 **15.** 234.5 **16.** 6573

Round to the nearest thousand and to the nearest ten thousand.

17. 8500 **18.** 23 666 **19.** 111 444

Round to the given place value.

20. 7.064 nearest tenth

21. 15.609 nearest one

22. 23.7482 nearest thousandth

23. 3.9107 nearest hundredth

Estimate, then calculate.

24. $342 + 897 + 3456$

25. $5.76 + 18.98 + 0.67$

26. $3210 + 4369 + 789 + 5560$

27. $2.34 + 67.8 + 54.33$

Estimate, then calculate.

28. $401 - 234$ **29.** $67.8 - 24.98$

30. $7800 - 5678$ **31.** $0.678 - 0.301$

Find the product mentally.

32. $5 \times 3 \times 100$ **33.** $30 \times 30 \times 30$

Estimate, then calculate.

34. 2.32×0.88 **35.** 311×54 **36.** 84×21 **37.** 561×0.03

Find the quotient mentally.

38. $\frac{3600}{60}$ **39.** $\frac{300\ 000}{5000}$ **40.** $\frac{6400}{800}$

Divide. Use short division.

41. $7\overline{)364}$ **42.** $6\overline{)324}$ **43.** $3\overline{)1569}$

Divide. Use short division and state the remainder.

44. $5\overline{)764}$ **45.** $8\overline{)2018}$ **46.** $7\overline{)1689}$

Estimate, then calculate.

47. $42\overline{)882}$ **48.** $\frac{26.32}{4.7}$ **49.** $\frac{3.328}{0.64}$

50. The table gives the number of different species for several kinds of birds. Arrange the numbers in order from greatest to smallest.

Bird	Species
Pigeons	271
Owls	146
Parrots, cockatoos	330
Pheasants	265
Cuckoos	128

51. The Jensens paid \$269.75 for a hotel, \$47.60 for gas, and \$283.48 for food on a trip. Estimate the total cost.

Estimate the cost of each purchase.

52. 8 oranges at \$0.71 each

53. 5 boxes of dog treats at \$4.89 a box

54. 6 cans of meat at \$5.78 each

55. 3 paperback books at \$6.95 each

56. Yonge Street, which begins in Toronto, Ontario, is the longest street in the world. At first, the street was 54.71 km long. It is now 1896.24 km long. How much longer is Yonge Street now than it was at first?

57. The Wongs' car uses 10.4 L of gasoline every 100 km. How much gas does it need for a trip of 3500 km?
About how much would the gas cost today?

58. There are about 16 000 000 thunderstorms a year. Estimate how many thunderstorms there are each day. What assumption did you make?

59. How many toothpicks are in the tenth diagram?

1st 2nd 3rd

60. The first known living things on Earth were cells that floated on water 3.2 billion years ago.

a) Write this number in standard form.

b) Write this number in expanded form.

61. The first Olympics were held in 776 B.C. How many years ago was that?

62. Canada has 3 002 000 km of road, the second highest amount of any country in the world. Canada also has 67 066 km of railway track, the third highest amount of any country in the world. Estimate how many kilometres of road there are for each kilometre of railway track.

Calculate.

63. $7 \times 4 + 5 \times 9$

64. $8 \times 6 - 6 \div 3$

65. $0.555 \times 100 \div 0.5$

66. $42 \div 7 - 5 + 8$

67. $(9 + 6) \div 5 + 14$

68. $4.6 + \frac{1}{2}$ of $8.84 - 3.1$

69. $\frac{5.6 + 24.4}{0.6}$

70. $(13 - 7) \div (11 - 9)$

Group Decision Making

Making a Television Commercial

People often solve problems by working together. Here are some rules that help groups work effectively.

a) Contribute ideas by speaking quietly.

b) Encourage others to participate and listen to them carefully.

c) Respect the opinions of others.

d) Ask for help from the teacher only when everyone in your group has the same difficulty.

In this activity, each group will write and act out a 30-second television commercial. All group members will take part in the commercial.

1. Meet as a group and choose 3 or 4 products you would like to make commercials about.

2. Meet as a class and list all the choices on the chalkboard. As a class, decide which product each group will work on.

3. Prepare your commercial in your group.

4. Act out your commercial for the class.

5. Meet as a group to evaluate how well your group worked together. Describe how you used math in preparing your commercial.

6. Meet as a class to discuss the group process.

Chapter Check

State whether you need an exact answer or an approximate answer.

1. How long will it take you to cut the lawn?

2. How much bus fare do you need to get to the library?

Write each number in words.

3. 3460 **4.** 607 321 **5.** 78.903

6. Arrange the numbers in order from smallest to largest.

345.6, 346.1, 345.2, 346, 345.5, 345.2

Write in standard form.

7. $7 \times 10 + 5 \times 1 + 8 \times 0.1 + 4 \times 0.001$

8. $5 \times 1000 + 8 \times 100 + 6 \times 1 + 2 \times 0.01$

9. $3 \times 100\,000 + 2 \times 1000 + 4 \times 0.001$

Write each number in expanded form.

10. 53 102 **11.** 6.895

Estimate, then calculate.

12. $4567 + 978 + 2900$

13. $56.78 + 8.99 + 13.06$

14. $3005 - 1456$

15. $123.6 - 5.677$

Estimate, then calculate.

16. $\begin{array}{r} 56 \\ \times 48 \\ \hline \end{array}$ **17.** $\begin{array}{r} 5.62 \\ \times 0.77 \\ \hline \end{array}$ **18.** $\begin{array}{r} 1.04 \\ \times 32 \\ \hline \end{array}$

Divide. Use short division.

19. $6\overline{)744}$ **20.** $5\overline{)89.2}$ **21.** $4\overline{)34.84}$

Estimate, then calculate.

22. $23\overline{)276}$ **23.** $4.5\overline{)4.95}$ **24.** $51\overline{)2600}$

25. The school minibus holds 19 passengers. There are 162 band members. How many trips will the minibus have to make to take the band to the park?

26. Liam rents 3 videos for $5.99 during the week. On the weekend, he pays $2.45 for each one. How much does Liam save by renting 3 movies during the week?

27. Determine the pattern and find the next three numbers.

1, 3, 6, 10, ■, ■, ■

28. Canada ranks sixth in the world for the number of visitors it has each year. Canada has about 12 180 000 visitors each year. Estimate how many visitors that is each week. What assumption did you make?

Calculate.

29. $9 + 4 \times 5$ **30.** $12 - 8 \div 4$

31. $6 \times (9 - 2) + 4$

32. $\frac{1}{2}$ of $10 - 1 + 5$

©1991 Tribune Media Services, Inc. All Rights Reserved

Reprinted by permission: Tribune Media Services

Using the Strategies

1. Frank earned $25.00 from babysitting last week. He is saving to buy a $160.00 jacket. How many more weeks will he need to babysit to afford the jacket? What assumptions have you made?

Describe the pattern and complete the table.

2.

7	9	12	15	17	?	?
13	15	18	?	?	32	41

3.

1.2	3.1	2.5	0.3	?	?	4.7
2.8	4.7	4.1	?	1.7	5.1	?

4.

3.6	2.7	5.4	?	?	4.8	9.9
1.2	0.9	1.8	2.2	0.5	?	?

5.

3	5	7	8	10	?	?
12	20	28	?	?	44	80

6. Susan asked ten grade 7 students if they would go to a school dance for students in grades 6, 7, and 8. Eight students said they would. There are 150 students in grades 6, 7, and 8. How many will attend the dance? What assumptions have you made?

7. One number is 7 more than another number. The sum of the two numbers is 45. What are the numbers?

8. Determine the pattern and write the next 3 rows.

$1 \times 9 + 2 = 11$
$12 \times 9 + 3 = 111$
$123 \times 9 + 4 = 1111$

9. At a campsite, the logs are piled in triangles.

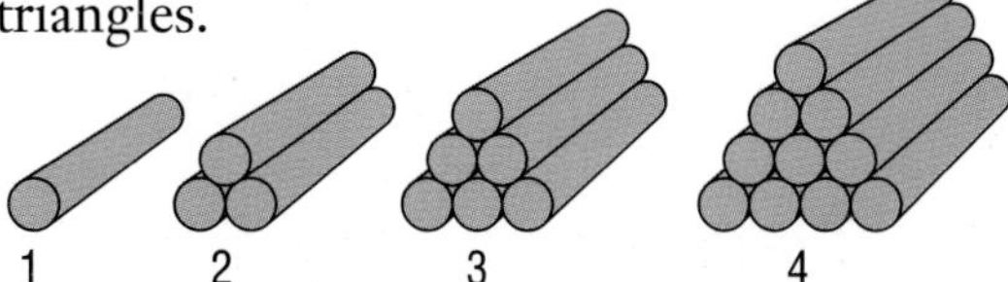

How many logs are in the tenth pile?

10. Zahia has $2.25 in dimes and quarters. She has 12 coins. How many dimes and how many quarters does she have?

11. If you multiply a certain number by 7 then add 15, the result is 71. What is the number?

Look for a pattern and write the next 3 numbers.

12. 81, 80, 78, 75, 71, 66, ■, ■, ■

13. 70.4, 35.2, 17.6, 8.8, ■, ■, ■

14. 1.3, 1.5, 1.8, 2.2, ■, ■, ■

15. 3, 6, 12, 24, ■, ■, ■

16. In the last 12 days, 4800 people have taken the day-long rafting trip through the Wild River Rapids. Each day, 25 rafts were used. How many people does one raft hold? What assumptions have you made?

17. Mario runs for 20 min in the morning as part of his fitness program. How many hours will he run in a year? What assumptions have you made?

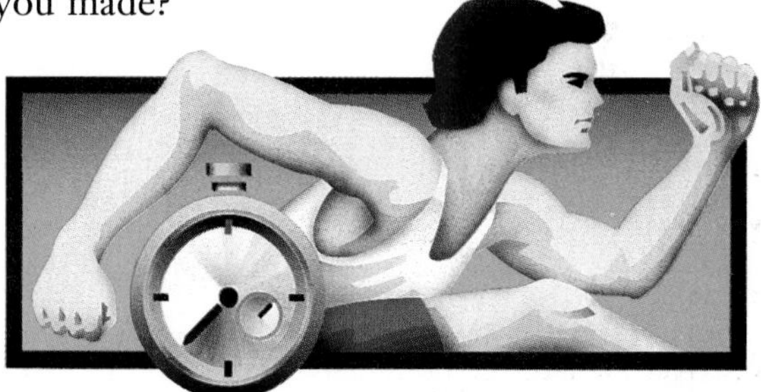

18. Copy the figures. Place the numbers from 1 to 7 in the circles so that the sum of each row or column of 3 numbers is the same. How many different ways can you find?

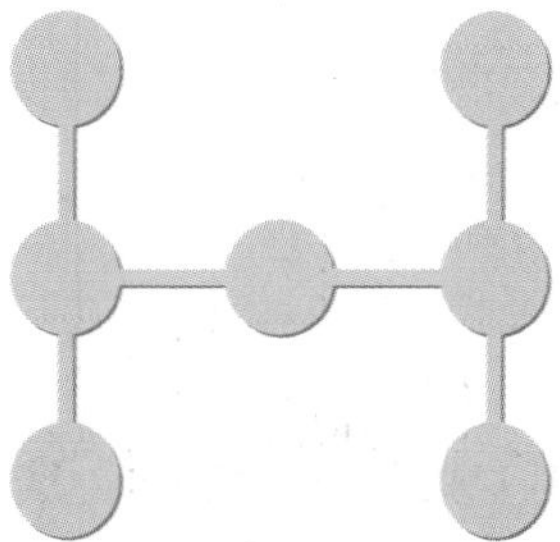

CHAPTER 2

Number Theory

With your back turned, ask a classmate to roll three dice and add the faces.

Keeping your back turned, ask your classmate to pick up one die and add the number on the bottom of the die to the total.

Keeping your back turned, ask your classmate to roll this die and add the number on top to the total to give a final value.

Turn around and say that you have no way of knowing which die was rolled for a second time.

Add the three faces that you see. Add 7 to this total, and tell your classmate what the final value was.

Try this activity a few times.

Explain how it works.

The Hundred Chart

1	2	3	4	5	6	7	8	9	10
11	12	13	14	15	16	17	18	19	20
21	22	23	24	25	26	27	28	29	30
31	32	33	34	35	36	37	38	39	40
41	42	43	44	45	46	47	48	49	50
51	52	53	54	55	56	57	58	59	60
61	62	63	64	65	66	67	68	69	70
71	72	73	74	75	76	77	78	79	80
81	82	83	84	85	86	87	88	89	90
91	92	93	94	95	96	97	98	99	100

Examine the hundred chart.

1. Which digit is used the most?

2. Which digit is used the least?

Copy the following table.

Row	1	2	3
Sum			

3. Add the numbers in each of the first three rows of the hundred chart. Complete the table.

4. What is the difference between the sums of row 1 and row 2? row 2 and row 3?

5. Predict the difference between the sums of other pairs of adjacent rows.

6. Explain the difference you found in questions 4 and 5.

Copy the following table.

Column	1	2	3
Sum			

7. Add the numbers in each of the first three columns of the hundred chart. Complete the table.

8. What is the difference between the sums of column 1 and column 2? column 2 and column 3?

9. Predict the difference between the sums of other pairs of adjacent columns.

10. Explain the difference you found in questions 8 and 9.

Examine the numbers along both diagonals, of the hundred chart.

11. What is the difference between adjacent numbers on the diagonal from the top left to the bottom right?

12. What is the difference between adjacent numbers on the diagonal from the top right to the bottom left?

13. Describe other patterns among the numbers on each diagonal.

Choose three consecutive numbers in any row.

14. What is their sum?

15. What is the middle number times three?

16. Compare your answers to questions 14 and 15.

17. Predict whether you will see the same result as in question 16 for three consecutive numbers

a) on any row.

b) in any column.

c) on either diagonal.

18. Test your predictions from question 17.

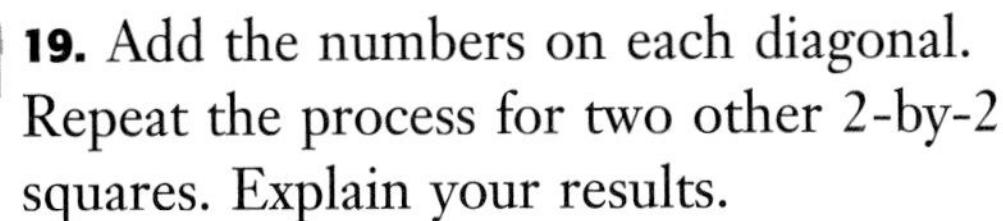

Select 4 numbers in a 2-by-2 square on the hundred chart.

19. Add the numbers on each diagonal. Repeat the process for two other 2-by-2 squares. Explain your results.

20. Predict whether you will see the same result in 3-by-3 squares. Test your prediction.

21. Repeat the process for 4-by-4 squares.

Select 9 numbers in a 3-by-3 square on the hundred chart.

22. Add the numbers.

23. Multiply the middle number in the square by 9. Compare the product to your answer in question 22.

24. Repeat for another square of 9 numbers. Explain your results.

Select 25 numbers in a 5-by-5 square on the hundred chart.

25. Add the numbers.

26. Multiply the middle number in the square by 25. Compare the product to your answer in question 25.

27. Repeat for another square of 25 numbers. Explain your results.

28. Predict whether you will see the same result in a square of 49 numbers. Test your prediction.

Mental Math

Add.

1. $8 + 8 + 8$ **2.** $4 + 4 + 4 + 4$
3. $6 + 6 + 6 + 6$ **4.** $9 + 9 + 9$
5. $7 + 7 + 7$ **6.** $24 + 8$
7. $63 + 9$ **8.** $48 + 6$
9. $49 + 7$ **10.** $56 + 8$

Subtract.

11. $36 - 9$ **12.** $42 - 6$ **13.** $64 - 8$
14. $45 - 9$ **15.** $28 - 7$ **16.** $30 - 6$
17. $63 - 7$ **18.** $42 - 3$ **19.** $32 - 4$

Calculate.

20. $21 - 7 + 14$ **21.** $24 + 6 - 12$
22. $36 + 9 - 18$ **23.** $48 - 8 + 16$
24. $28 - 4 + 12$ **25.** $33 + 3 - 9$
26. $42 + 7 - 21$ **27.** $72 - 9 + 18$

Multiply.

28. 9×8 **29.** 7×9 **30.** 6×7
31. 9×6 **32.** 7×80 **33.** 50×9
34. 40×6 **35.** 7×60 **36.** 9×70

Divide.

37. $45 \div 9$ **38.** $72 \div 8$ **39.** $63 \div 7$
40. $56 \div 7$ **41.** $32 \div 8$ **42.** $180 \div 9$
43. $480 \div 6$ **44.** $280 \div 4$ **45.** $360 \div 9$

Calculate.

46. 25×2 **47.** $25 + 25$
48. $250 \div 5$ **49.** $63 - 9$
50. $72 + 8$ **51.** $800 \div 8$
52. $12 \times 4 \div 6$ **53.** $36 \div 6 \times 3$
54. $8 \times 4 \div 2$ **55.** $6 \times 4 \div 8$

Divisibility Tests

If one number divided by a second number gives a remainder of zero, then the first number is **divisible** by the second.

Even numbers, which end in 0, 2, 4, 6, or 8, are all divisible by 2. So, when we check whether a number is even, we carry out a **divisibility test** for 2.

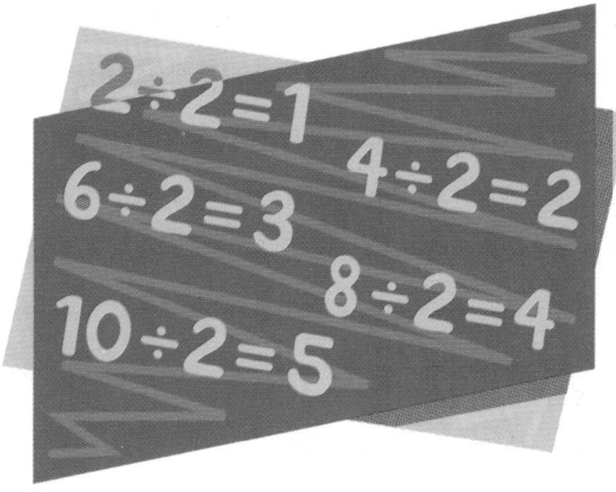

Activity ❶

1. Use your calculator to find which of the following are divisible by 3.

630   1701   960   1412   954

2354   4251   763   885

2. Add the digits in each number that is divisible by 3.

3. What number are all these sums divisible by?

4. Write the divisibility test for 3.

5. Use your test to predict whether each of the following is divisible by 3.

324   69   136   4131   102

6313   62 160   5241   28 312   7038

6. Write 6 numbers that are divisible by 3. Do not use numbers from this page.

Activity ❷

1. Use your calculator to find which of the following are divisible by 4.

324   630   7168   3354   976

894   6528   480   2616

2. In each number divisible by 4, record the pair of digits in the ones and tens places.

3. What number are all these pairs of digits divisible by?

4. Write the divisibility test for 4.

5. Use your test to predict whether each of the following is divisible by 4.

84   248   742   6082   35 636

6. Write 6 numbers that are divisible by 4. Do not use numbers from this page.

7. Are all numbers that are divisible by 2 also divisible by 4? If not, give an example. Explain your answer.

8. Are all numbers that are divisible by 4 also divisible by 2? If not, give an example. Explain your answer.

Activity ❸

1. Use your calculator to find which of the following are divisible by 6.

876 789 4230 888 8433

9243 936 6732 543

2. Use the divisibility tests for 2 and 3 to find the numbers above that are divisible by both 2 and 3. What is the pattern?

3. Write the divisibility test for 6.

4. Use your test to predict whether each of the following is divisible by 6.

84 856 124 7614 2154

5166 23 742 4914 25 623 7254

5. Write 4 numbers that are divisible by 6. Do not use numbers from this page.

Activity ❹

1. Use your calculator to find which of the following are divisible by 8.

168 124 128

2168 3124 4128

42 168 53 124 74 128

2. In each number divisible by 8, what are the digits in the ones, tens, and hundreds places?

3. What number are all these sets of three digits divisible by?

4. Write the divisibility test for 8.

5. Use your test to predict whether each of the following is divisible by 8.

604 1824 912 8436 5346

12 506 23 760 8724 24 266 3628

6. Write 4 numbers that are divisible by 8. Do not use numbers from this page.

Activity ❺

1. Use your calculator to find which of the following are divisible by 9.

270 216 300 4572 2613

8424 711 409 6444

2. Add the digits in each number divisible by 9.

3. Write the divisibility test for 9.

4. Use your test to predict whether each of the following is divisible by 9.

108 234 181 315 5130

8361 70 245 702 2015 5409

5. Write 5 numbers that are divisible by 9. Do not use numbers from this page.

2.1 Factors and Divisibility

Activity: Solve the Problem

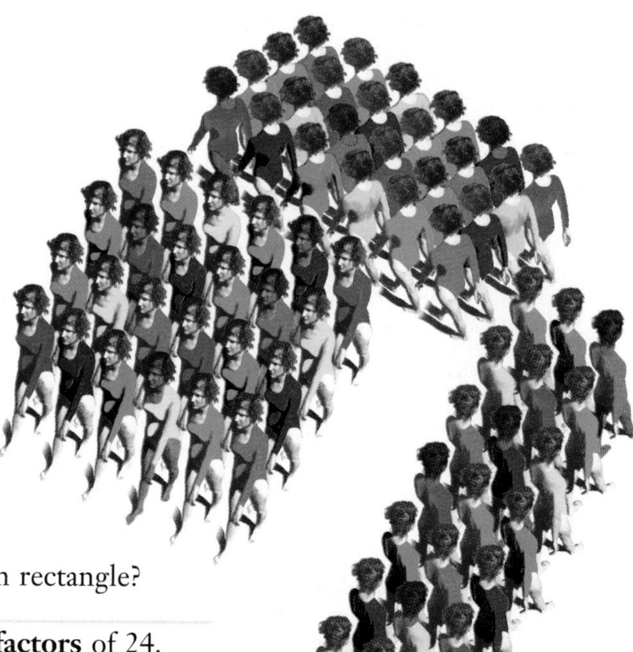

Twenty-four gymnasts plan for a Canada Day parade. They want to march in rows and columns to form a rectangle. They want to know the number of formations they can use.

Inquire

1. Use 24 square tiles to build as many rectangles as possible. Copy and complete the chart. (The first line is completed for you.)

Rows	Columns	Dimensions
1	24	1×24

2. How many formations can the gymnasts use?

3. What is the product of the dimensions of each rectangle?

The numbers 1, 2, 3, 4, 6, 8, 12, and 24 are all **factors** of 24.

Because $6 \times 4 = 24$, 6 is a factor of 24.

You can also say that 6 is a factor of 24 because 6 divides 24 evenly.

Why is 4 also a factor of 24?

Example

Fifty marchers play the bagpipes. They march in rows of 6. How many full rows are there?

Solution

$$6\overline{)50}\quad 8R2$$

There are 8 full rows of 6.

(The other 2 marchers may have a row to themselves.)

Because 6 does not divide 50 evenly, 6 is not a factor of 50.

Divisibility Rules

The divisibility rules help you to find factors.

A number is divisible by:

2 if it ends in 0, 2, 4, 6, or 8.

3 if the sum of the digits is divisible by 3.

4 if the last two digits are divisible by 4.

5 if it ends in 0 or 5.

6 if it is divisible by 2 and 3.

8 if the last three digits are divisible by 8.

9 if the sum of the digits is divisible by 9.

10 if it ends in 0.

Practice

State the missing factor.

1. 10 × ■ = 80 **2.** ■ × 8 = 32
3. ■ × 9 = 54 **4.** 40 × ■ = 160
5. 6 × ■ = 18 **6.** ■ × 7 = 56

Use factors to complete each of the following. There may be more than one solution.

7. ■ × ■ = 63 **8.** ■ × ■ = 32
9. ■ × ■ = 60 **10.** ■ × ■ = 48
11. ■ × ■ = 40 **12.** ■ × ■ = 54

13. The products 1 × 12, 2 × 6, and 3 × 4 are all 12. List the factors of 12 in order from smallest to largest.

14. The products 1 × 30, 2 × 15, 3 × 10, and 6 × 5 are all 30. List the factors of 30 in order from smallest to largest.

Which numbers have 3 as a factor?

15. 16 **16.** 27 **17.** 18 **18.** 53
19. 30 **20.** 41 **21.** 48 **22.** 57

Which numbers have 8 as a factor?

23. 12 **24.** 24 **25.** 30 **26.** 48
27. 68 **28.** 72 **29.** 84 **30.** 96

List all the factors of each number.

31. 16 **32.** 18 **33.** 24 **34.** 30
35. 32 **36.** 36 **37.** 49 **38.** 50
39. 60 **40.** 72 **41.** 75 **42.** 80

Express each number as a product of 2 factors in all the ways you can. Make a class list of the answers.

43. 9 **44.** 15 **45.** 23 **46.** 51
47. 8 **48.** 13 **49.** 29 **50.** 42
51. 45 **52.** 63 **53.** 52 **54.** 38

State the missing factors. Do not use 1. Work together to find as many solutions as possible.

55. 9 × ■ × ■ = 180
56. 6 × ■ × ■ = 150
57. ■ × ■ × ■ = 80
58. 4 × ■ × 6 = 72
59. 36 × ■ × ■ = 360
60. 50 × ■ × ■ = 2400
61. 81 × 3 × ■ = 972
62. 13 × ■ × ■ = 390
63. 14 × 5 × ■ = 420
64. 16 × ■ × ■ = 640
65. 30 × ■ × ■ = 1080
66. ■ × 7 × ■ = 280
67. ■ × 6 × ■ = 204
68. 9 × ■ × ■ = 576

Problems and Applications

69. Space Patrol ride tickets are numbered 1 to 300. Tickets whose numbers are factors of 300 give a free ride. Which tickets give a free ride?

70. Draw the different rectangular patios Sheila can build by placing 45 square slabs side by side.

71. Akeesh's age is an odd number less than 30 but greater than 20. The number has only 3 factors. How old is Akeesh?

72. Mr. Barbaza made a tray 27 cm by 36 cm. He covered it exactly with the largest possible square tiles.

a) What size was each tile?

b) How many tiles did he use?

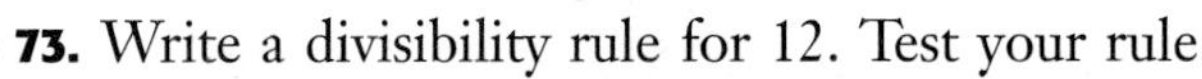

73. Write a divisibility rule for 12. Test your rule.

74. A number is greater than 50 but less than 100. It has exactly 5 factors. What is the number? Compare with a classmate. How do your solutions differ?

2.2 Work Backward

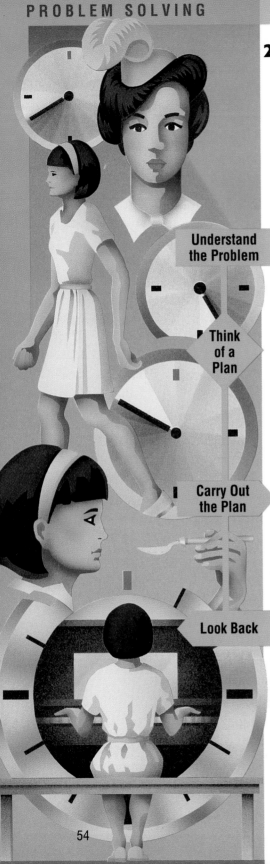

The school play starts at 19:30. Cheryl must be at school 50 min before the start of the play to put on her costume and make-up. It takes Cheryl 15 min to walk to school. She needs 35 min to eat supper before she leaves. She has to practise the piano for 30 min before supper.

At what time should Cheryl start to practise to be on time for the play?

Understand the Problem

1. What information are you given?
2. How much time is needed for each activity?
3. What are you asked to find?
4. Do you need an exact or approximate answer?

Think of a Plan

Start at 19:30 and work backward.

You normally add times to work out a final time from an initial time. Working backward requires the opposite operation. Subtract the time for each activity until you get to the time Cheryl should start to practise the piano.

Carry Out the Plan

Play starts	19:30
Make-up/Costume	50
Arrive at school	18:40
Walk to school	15
Leave for school	18:25
Eat supper	35
Start supper	17:50
Practise piano	30
Start to practise	17:20

Cheryl should start to practise at 17:20.

Look Back

Is the answer reasonable? Can you think of another way to solve the problem?

When you work backward, remember to use the opposite operation from when you work forward. For example, a number multiplied by 5 is 15. So 15 divided by 5 gives the number, which is 3.

Work Backward

1. Start with what you know.
2. Work backward to get the answer.
3. Check that the answer is reasonable.

Problems and Applications

Work backward to find the unknown number.

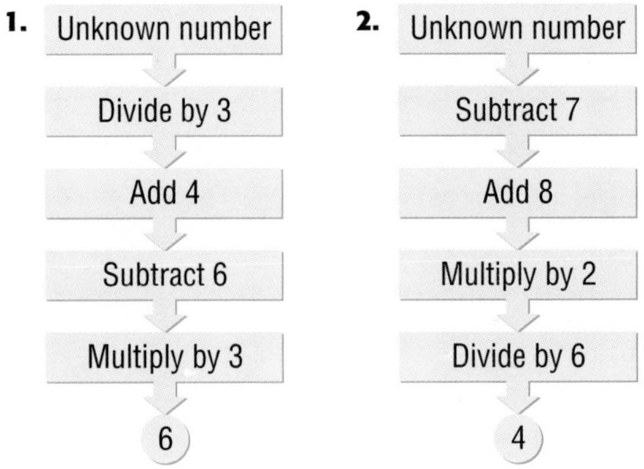

3. Your plane leaves at 07:15. It takes 45 min to get to the airport. You must get to the airport at least 20 min before the plane leaves. What is the latest time you should leave for the airport?

4. Yanmei has some sample problems to practise for a math contest. On Monday, she gets 8 more problems. On Tuesday, she gets another 5. On Wednesday, Yanmei hands in 10 problems. On Thursday, she gets 7 more problems. On Friday, she has 30 problems. How many problems did she have at the beginning of the week?

5. A bus leaves Merrivale Station. Seven people get off at Bells' Corners. Eight get on at Richmond Station. Five get off at Orleans Station, and 17 get on at Express Station. There are 24 people now on the bus. How many were on the bus when it left Merrivale Station?

6. Paula will run a 15-km race on June 12. She plans to run a 15-km practice on June 10 and to rest on June 11. Paula will start training with a 5-km run and will then increase the distance by 1 km each day. On what date should she start training to reach 15 km on June 10?

7. The school craft sale is on Friday, December 19. Each school day, the class can make 7 items for the sale. They want 100 items for the sale. On what date should work begin?

8. Maia got her allowance on Friday. She spent $2 on bus tickets and half of the rest on a movie and a drink. She then bought a T-shirt for $8 and had $12 left. What was Maia's allowance?

9. Bob Itsumie bought 50 L of gasoline for his fishing boat. He also bought 1 L of oil for $2.95 and bait for $5.50. His total bill was $40.95. What was the cost per litre of gasoline?

10. Lou Johnson plays professional basketball. Last season, Lou scored 24 three-point shots, 52 two-point shots, and 18 one-point foul shots. At the end of the season, Lou's career points totalled 728. How many career points did he have before the season began?

11. The play starts at 20:00. You need 25 min to get to the theatre. You should arrive at the theatre 20 min before the play starts. You plan to eat dinner before the play. You should allow 45 min for that. Before you leave home, you need to study for 50 min for a math test. What is the latest time at which you should start to study?

LOGIC POWER

Ann, Wayne, and Kali are friends. One is a teacher, one is a plumber, and one sells cars. The plumber, who lives next door to Wayne, takes Kali to lunch. As they enter the restaurant, they see the teacher get on a bus. Which one of them sells cars?

2.3 Prime and Composite Numbers

Activity: Complete the Table

Work with a classmate. List the factors of each number from 1 to 24.

Number	Factors
1	1
2	1, 2
3	1, 3
4	1, 2, 4
.	
.	
.	
23	
24	

Inquire

1. Which numbers have exactly two factors?
2. Which numbers have more than two factors?
3. Look up the definition of **prime number** in the glossary.
4. Which numbers from 1 to 24 are prime?
5. Numbers that are not prime are called **composite numbers**. Write your own definition of composite numbers.
6. Which numbers from 1 to 24 are composite?

We can use the number of factors to decide whether a whole number is prime or composite.

Example 1

Is 12 a composite number?

Solution

A composite number is a whole number with more than two factors. The factors of 12 are 1, 2, 3, 4, 6, and 12.
So, 12 is a composite number.

Example 2

Is 7 a prime number?

Solution

A prime number is a whole number with exactly 2 factors, 1 and the number itself. The factors of 7 are 1 and 7.
So, 7 is a prime number.

Why is the number 1 neither prime nor composite?
What is the only even number that is prime?

Practice

1. State the prime numbers.

7	9	11	16
20	21	23	41
51	29	49	33

2. State the composite numbers.

18	31	45	50
37	42	57	83
80	69	55	63

Draw as many rectangles as you can to represent these prime and composite numbers.

3. 8 **4.** 9 **5.** 7 **6.** 12

7. 10 **8.** 24 **9.** 13 **10.** 25

Problems and Applications

11. How many prime numbers are between 20 and 40?

12. The numbers 29 and 31 are called **twin primes** because they differ by 2. List all twin primes less than 100.

13. In a hockey game played before 16 845 fans, the score was 8–7. There were 26 penalties, and 17 players earned 40 points. The game was played on December 19. List all the numbers given in the game summary. Write "prime" or "composite" beside each number.

14. Find the pattern, write the next 5 numbers, and identify those that are prime.

11, 13, 17, 23, ….

15. Find the difference between the smallest even prime number and the smallest odd composite number.

16. Every even number greater than 2 can be written as the sum of two prime numbers.

$$14 = 11 + 3$$
$$\text{or } 14 = 7 + 7$$

Write each even number from 40 to 80 as the sum of 2 prime numbers.

17. The mathematician Christian Goldbach said that every odd number greater than 7 can be written as the sum of 3 prime numbers.

$$15 = 5 + 5 + 5$$
$$\text{or } 15 = 3 + 5 + 7$$
$$\text{or } 15 = 2 + 2 + 11$$

Write each of the following as the sum of 3 prime numbers.

a) 19 **b)** 43 **c)** 27 **d)** 53

18. Solve this riddle.

"My family has an even number of children, a prime number of pets, an odd number of cars, and a house with a composite number of bedrooms. The total of the unknown numbers is 10. What are the numbers?"

19. Make up your own riddle. Include the words "odd," "even," "prime," and "composite." Have a classmate solve the riddle.

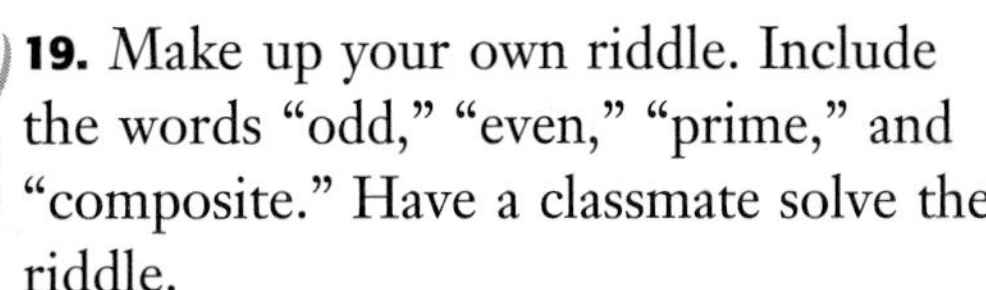

The number 6 is called a **perfect number**, because its factors, not counting 6, add up to 6.

$$1 + 2 + 3 = 6$$

Find the next perfect number. It is smaller than 35.

2.4 Prime Factors

We know that $3 \times 5 = 15$. So 3 and 5 are factors of 15. But 3 and 5 are also prime numbers. We call 3 and 5 the **prime factors** of 15.

We can write every composite number as the product of prime factors. This process is called the **prime factorization** of the number.

Activity: Study the Process

A **factor tree** helps us to find prime factors. Study these factor trees for the prime factorization of 48 and 120.

48
12 × 4
3 × 4 × 2 × 2
3 × 2 × 2 × 2 × 2

120
10 × 12
2 × 5 × 4 × 3
2 × 5 × 2 × 2 × 3

Inquire

1. Describe how a factor tree works.

2. Use other factor trees to find the prime factors of 48 and 120.

3. Do the prime factors of a number depend on the factor tree you choose?

We can also use division to find prime factors.

Example

Use division to write 24 as the product of prime factors.

Solution

Divide by prime numbers in increasing order. Start with 2.

$\begin{array}{r}12\\2\overline{)24}\end{array}$ $\quad\begin{array}{r}6\\2\overline{)12}\end{array}$ $\quad\begin{array}{r}3\\2\overline{)6}\end{array}$

When 2 no longer divides evenly, divide by the next prime number that divides evenly.

$\begin{array}{r}1\\3\overline{)3}\end{array}$

Stop when the quotient is 1.
So, $24 = 2 \times 2 \times 2 \times 3$.

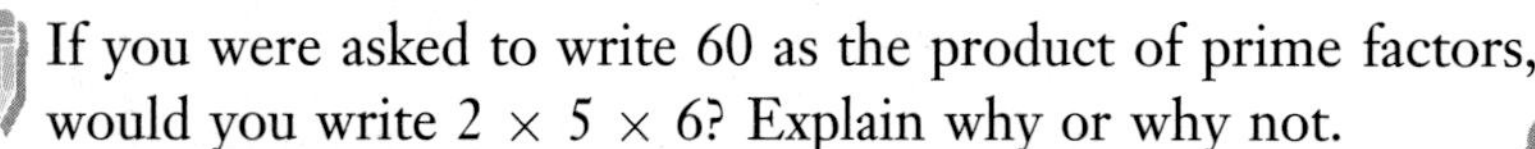

If you were asked to write 60 as the product of prime factors, would you write $2 \times 5 \times 6$? Explain why or why not.

Practice

Copy and complete each factor tree.

1.

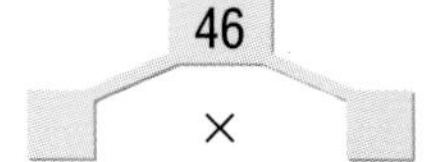

2.

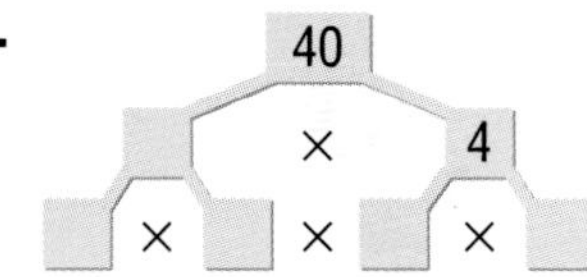

3.

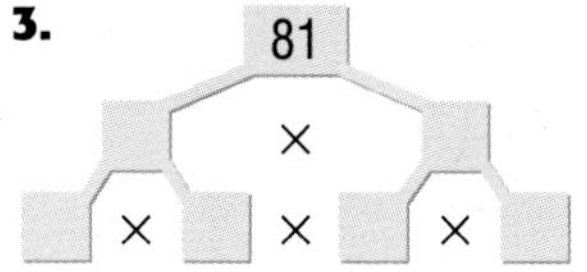

4.

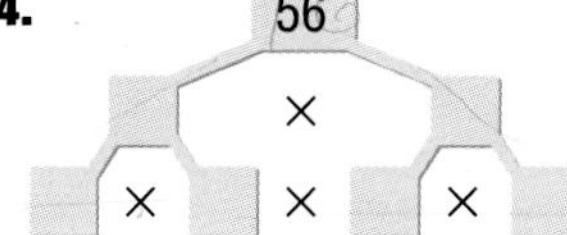

5.

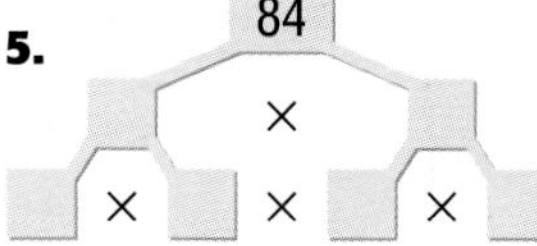

Write as the product of prime factors.

6. 16 **7.** 42 **8.** 63

9. 45 **10.** 66 **11.** 70

12. 100 **13.** 160 **14.** 132

15. 125 **16.** 225 **17.** 270

Draw 2 different factor trees for each number.

18. 30 **19.** 48

20. 36 **21.** 60

Problems and Applications

22. A number's prime factors are 2, 3, and 5. State 3 other factors of the number.

23. One factor of a number is 15. State two other factors of the number.

24. A number divisible by 6 and 10 has 3 prime factors. What is the number?

Complete each factor tree.

25.

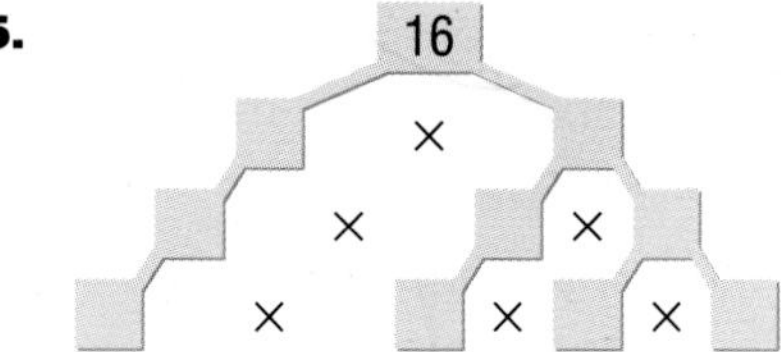

26.

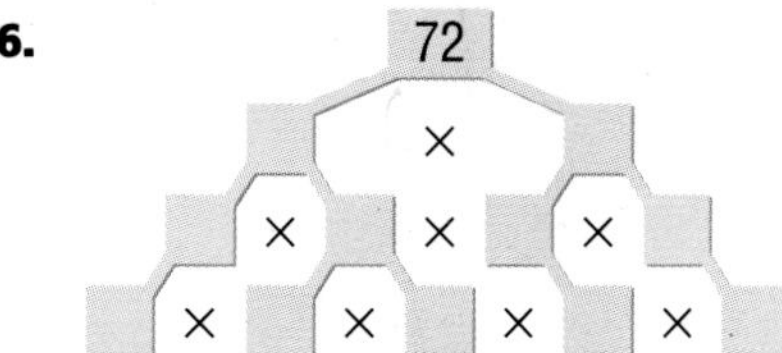

27.

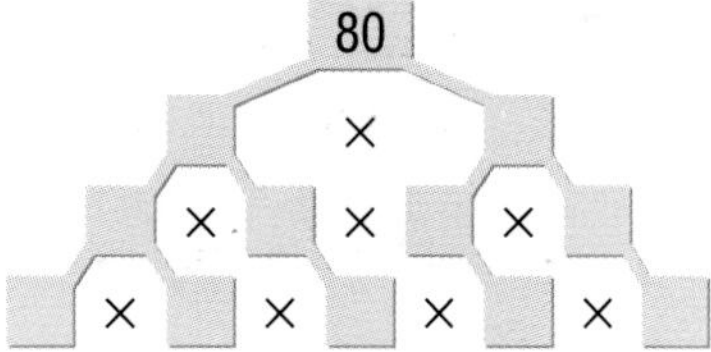

28. What is the smallest number that has 4 different prime factors?

WORD POWER

Write at least four words of 3 letters or more using the letters of the word PRIME. Compare your words with your classmates'. How many different words do you have altogether?

2.5 Draw a Diagram or Flow Chart

A veterinarian needs a square holding pen, 9 m by 9 m, for large animals. She designs it with fence posts 3 m apart. She plans a 1.5 m wide gate for one corner. The gate requires an extra post. How many posts does she need for the pen?

Understand the Problem

1. What information are you given?
2. What are you asked to find?
3. Do you need an exact or approximate answer?

Think of a Plan

Draw a diagram and count the number of posts.

Carry Out the Plan

She needs 13 fence posts.

Look Back

Check the diagram against the information given. Does the answer seem reasonable?

A flow chart can show the process used to solve a problem. The flow chart shows how to play against a computer at guessing a number between 1 and 100. Try this strategy with a classmate who plays the role of the computer.

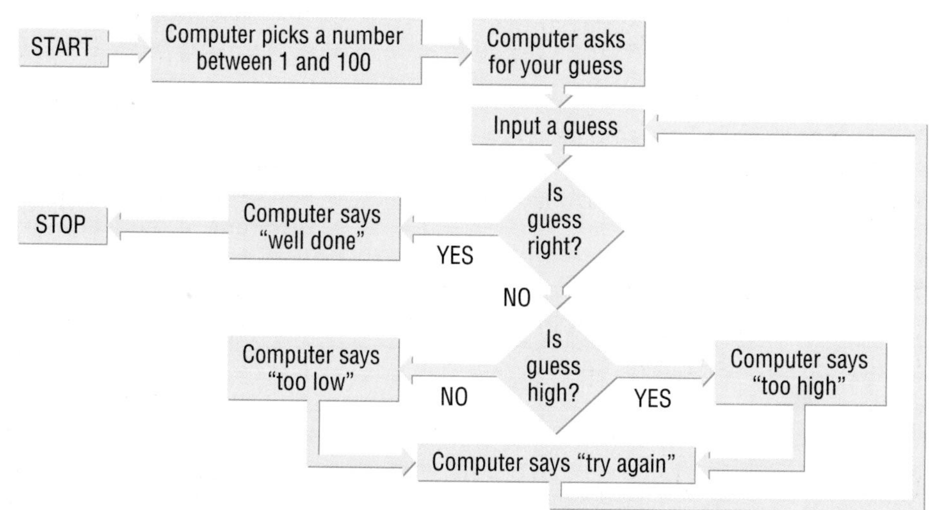
START
Computer picks a number between 1 and 100
Computer asks for your guess
Input a guess
Is guess right?
YES
Computer says "well done"
STOP
NO
Is guess high?
NO
Computer says "too low"
YES
Computer says "too high"
Computer says "try again"

Draw a Diagram or Flow Chart

1. Organize the given information in a diagram or flow chart.
2. Read the needed information from the diagram or flow chart.
3. Check that the answer is reasonable.

Problems and Applications

Put the instructions for Questions 1 and 2 in the right order.

1. To make a telephone call:
Dial the number.
Get the busy signal.
Insert the coin.
Lift the receiver.
Get the coin back.
Lift the receiver again.
Hang up the receiver.
Have the conversation.
Redial the number.
Hang up the receiver again.
Re-insert the coin.

2. To rent a movie from a video store:
Leave the store.
Select the movie.
Watch the movie.
Show your card.
Pay for the movie.
Return the movie.
Enter the store.
Go home.
Line up at the desk.

3. Calgary is 4973 km from Halifax. Montreal is 1249 km from Halifax. Montreal is between Calgary and Halifax. How far is Calgary from Montreal?

4. The heights of Armin, Bob, and Carl add to 498 cm. Armin is 21 cm taller than Bob. Carl is 36 cm taller than Bob. How tall is Armin?

5. A number is multiplied by 3, then divided by 5, then has 16 added, then has 12 subtracted to give a final answer. Draw a flow chart and use it to find the answer when the number has each of the following values.

a) 20 **b)** 100 **c)** 55

6. The signpost shows the distances to four places along a trail.

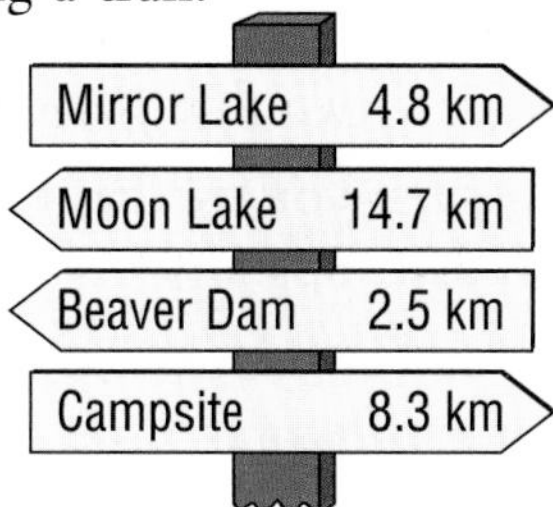

a) How far is Mirror Lake from Moon Lake?
b) How far is Moon Lake from Beaver Dam?
c) How far is the Campsite from Mirror Lake?

7. Using only 3 cuts, what is the largest number of pieces you can get from a round pie?

8. Jatinder's team picture is 20 cm by 25 cm. The frame adds a 5-cm border. What are the outside dimensions of the frame?

9. You need to build a 146 cm wide picket gate. Pickets are 10 cm wide. You want them 7 cm apart. How many pickets do you need?

Draw a flow chart to show the steps in each of the following. Compare your flow chart with a friend's.

10. You get ready for school in the morning.

11. You open a combination lock.

12. You lock a bicycle to a parking meter.

LOGIC POWER

Examine the map. Use your knowledge of geography to decide which province this area is in. Then find the area on a complete map.

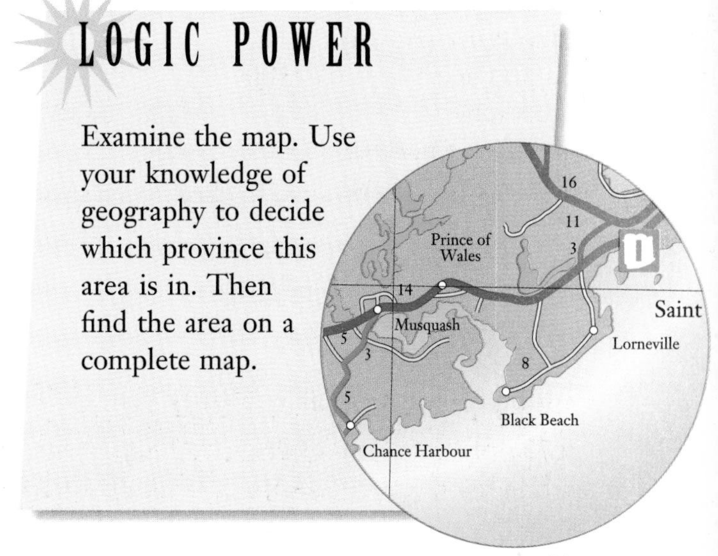

How Computers Calculate

We think that computers are very complex, yet they know only two things: **on** and **off**.

The number system you use has ten digits.
0, 1, 2, 3, 4, 5, 6, 7, 8, and 9

A computer's number system has only two digits, 1 and 0, which correspond to on and off. Since this system uses only two digits, it is called a **binary system**.

The table gives the first few binary numbers. Look for the pattern.

Decimal Number	Binary Number
0	0
1	1
2	10
3	11
4	100
5	101
6	110
7	111
8	1000

Activity ❶

Make a table of the first 32 binary numbers.

Activity ❷

Add. Use your table to check your answers.

a) 110 + 111

b) 1111 + 1100

c) 1101 + 11 + 1011

d) 101 + 10101 + 11 + 100

Activity ❸

Subtract. Use your table to check your answers.

a) 1100 − 111

b) 10111 − 1010

c) 11011 − 101

d) 11111 − 10001

Activity ❹

Multiply. Use your table to check your answers.

a) 101 × 10

b) 1001 × 11

c) 110 × 101

d) 1000 × 100

Three-Dimensional Tick-Tack-Toe

These are the playing grids for three-dimensional tick-tack-toe.

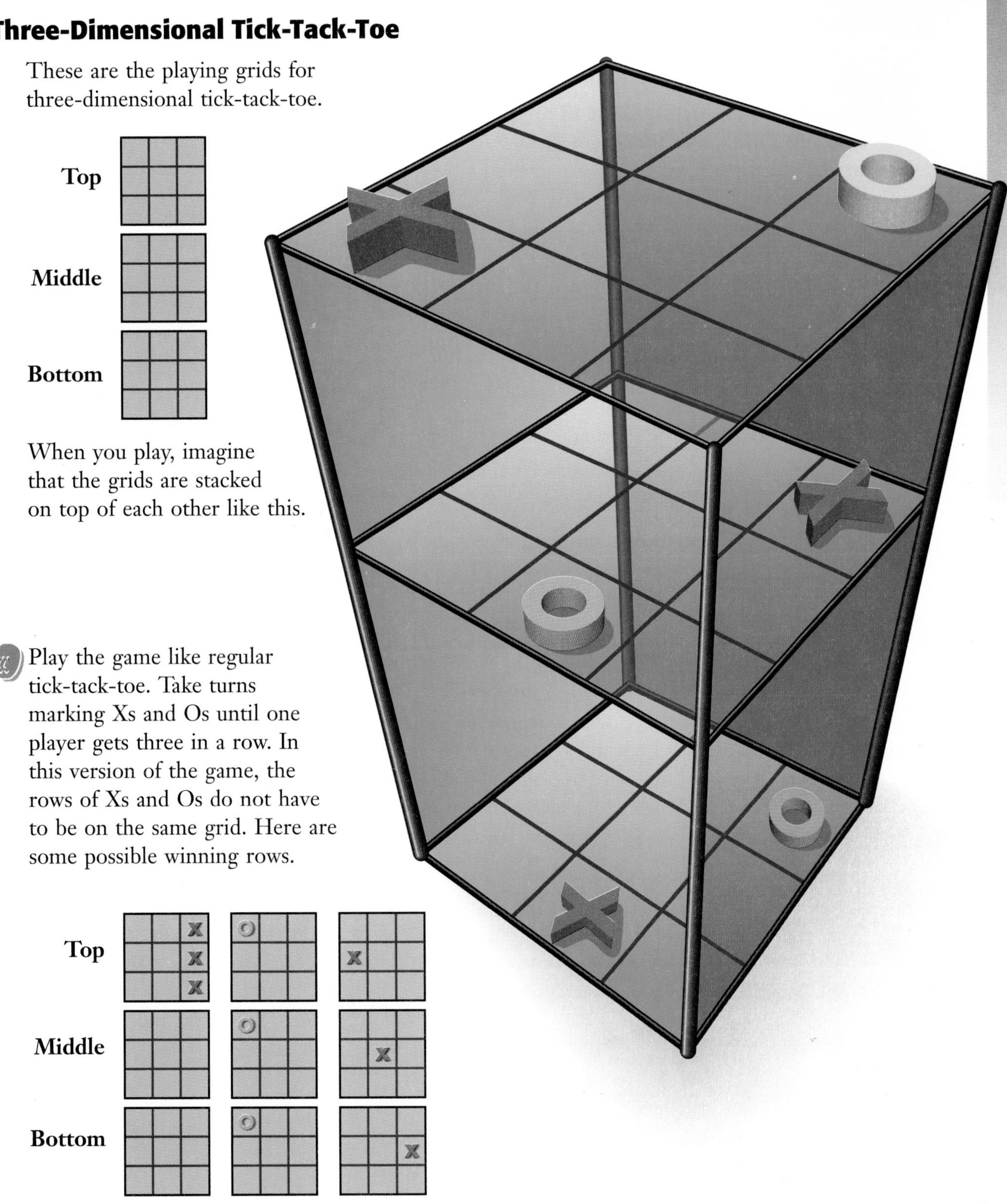

When you play, imagine that the grids are stacked on top of each other like this.

Play the game like regular tick-tack-toe. Take turns marking Xs and Os until one player gets three in a row. In this version of the game, the rows of Xs and Os do not have to be on the same grid. Here are some possible winning rows.

2.6 Greatest Common Factor

Activity: Analyze the Problem

A friend tells you that Melissa spent \$30 on baseball tickets and that Charlie spent \$75. You also know that since their seats are in the same section, their tickets cost the same. You have \$18 and want to know if you can afford to go to the game with them. So you work out the most a ticket could cost.

Inquire

1. What are the factors of 30?
2. What are the factors of 75?
3. What factors do 30 and 75 have in common?
4. What is the largest factor they have in common?
5. What is the most that one ticket could cost?
6. Can you afford to go to the game?

The largest factor that two or more numbers have in common is called the **greatest common factor** (GCF).

Example

Twenty-four grade 6 students, 48 grade 7 students, and 36 grade 8 students sign up for a dodgeball tournament. The organizers keep the grades separate and form teams with equal numbers of players. What is the greatest number of players on each team?

Solution 1

List the factors.

48: 1, 2, 3, 4, 6, 8, 12, 16, 24, 48
24: 1, 2, 3, 4, 6, 8, 12, 24
36: 1, 2, 3, 4, 6, 9, 12, 18, 36
GCF = 12

Solution 2

Write as products of prime factors.

$48 = 2 \times 2 \times 2 \times 2 \times 3$
$24 = 2 \times 2 \times 2 \times 3$
$36 = 2 \times 2 \times 3 \times 3$

Multiply the common factors.

$\text{GCF} = 2 \times 2 \times 3$
$= 12$

The greatest number of players on each team is 12.

What would the answer be if 4 more grade 8 students signed up?

Practice

List the common factors of each pair of numbers.

1. 8, 12 **2.** 6, 15 **3.** 8, 10

4. 6, 24 **5.** 14, 28 **6.** 18, 24

7. 4, 12 **8.** 12, 42 **9.** 24, 20

Find the greatest common factor.

10. 8, 24 **11.** 48, 32 **12.** 18, 45

13. 20, 30 **14.** 42, 60 **15.** 21, 63

16. 25, 75 **17.** 12, 20 **18.** 28, 42

19. 13, 21 **20.** 44, 52 **21.** 41, 25

Find the greatest common factor.

22. 15, 45, 60 **23.** 24, 30, 90

24. 32, 72, 64 **25.** 42, 63, 28

26. 27, 75, 120 **27.** 24, 42, 54

28. 54, 81, 48 **29.** 24, 56, 48

Problems and Applications

30. Linda built a games board in industrial arts class. The top was a rectangle 60 cm by 48 cm. What was the largest size of identical felt squares she could use to cover the top exactly?

31. What are the smallest 3 different numbers with a greatest common factor of 45?

32. Franz has a rectangular piece of wood 45 cm by 75 cm. What are the largest identical squares Franz can make by cutting the wood? What assumptions have you made?

33. What is the greatest common factor of two prime numbers? Why?

34. The GCF of 6 and two other numbers is 6. What must be true about the other two numbers? Explain.

Euclid, a Greek mathematician, had another way of finding the greatest common factor of two numbers.

To find the GCF of 25 and 60, he

a) *divided the larger number by the smaller number;*

$$\begin{array}{r} 2 \\ 25\overline{)60} \\ \underline{50} \\ 10 \end{array}$$

b) *divided the divisor by the remainder, repeating until the remainder was zero;*

$$\begin{array}{r} 2 \\ 10\overline{)25} \\ \underline{20} \\ 5 \end{array} \qquad \begin{array}{r} 2 \\ 5\overline{)10} \\ \underline{10} \\ 0 \end{array}$$

c) *chose the final divisor as the GCF.*
The GCF of 25 and 60 is 5.

Use the above method to find the GCF of the following.

35. 54, 60 **36.** 36, 99 **37.** 80, 200

WORD POWER

Write a three letter word using letters that appear in both WORD and POWER.

What is the meaning of your word?

Compare with your classmates. Are you all thinking of the same word and the same meaning?

2.7 Lowest Common Multiple

Activity: Solve the Problem

A group of students buys flowers to decorate the gym for graduation. The market flower stall sells roses in bunches of 6 and carnations in bunches of 4. The students want to know the smallest number of flowers they can buy to have the same number of each kind.

Inquire

1. List the first 4 multiples of 4.
2. List the first 4 multiples of 6.
3. What is the smallest number that is a multiple of both 4 and 6?
4. To have the same number of each kind of flower, what is the smallest number that students can buy?
5. If roses came in bunches of 12 and carnations in bunches of 8, what would the smallest number be?

The **lowest common multiple** (LCM) of a set of numbers is the smallest number that is a multiple of each number in the set.

Example

These are the door prizes at a school dance.

every 10th student → a button
every 15th student → a fruit drink
every 20th student → a straw hat

Which student is the first to get all three prizes?

Solution 1

List the multiples of each number.
Find the smallest number that is in every list.

buttons: 10, 20, 30, 40, 50, **60,** 70, 80
drinks: 15, 30, 45, **60,** 75, 90
hats: 20, 40, **60,** 80

Solution 2

Write each number as the product of prime factors. Find the smallest number that contains all the prime factors of each number.

buttons: $10 = 2 \times 5$
drinks: $15 = 5 \times 3$
hats: $20 = 2 \times 5 \times 2$

$2 \times 5 \times 3 \times 2 = 60$

The lowest common multiple is 60. So, the 60th student gets all 3 door prizes.

Practice

List the next 3 multiples.

1. 2, 4, 6,... **2.** 3, 6, 9,...

3. 15, 30, 45,... **4.** 7, 14, 21,...

5. 12, 24, 36,... **6.** 16, 32, 48,...

7. 9, 18, 27,... **8.** 100, 200, 300,...

Use multiples to find the LCM.

9. 3, 5 **10.** 4, 6 **11.** 3, 7 **12.** 4, 5

13. 6, 9 **14.** 6, 10 **15.** 8, 6 **16.** 5, 2

Use prime factors to find the LCM.

17. 4, 9 **18.** 10, 8 **19.** 6, 4 **20.** 9, 4

21. 6, 3 **22.** 12, 8 **23.** 8, 9 **24.** 7, 8

Find the LCM.

25. 3, 4, 2 **26.** 4, 3, 6 **27.** 2, 5, 3

Problems and Applications

28. A school cafeteria serves fish every 4th school day and spaghetti every 6th school day. Both fish and spaghetti were served on Monday. On which day of the week will they both be served again? What assumptions have you made?

29. Marigolds are sold in flats of 6 plants, and snapdragons in flats of 8 plants. Antonio wants to buy the same number of each plant. What is the smallest number of each he can buy?

30. Every 2nd customer at the opening of the Landing Restaurant gets a free hat. Every 5th customer gets a free coffee mug. Every 10th customer gets a free meal. Which customer is first to get all three?

31. Three sets of neon lights are turned on at the same time. The first set blinks every 5 s, the second every 4 s, and the third every 6 s. How often do all three sets blink at the same time?

32. The LCM of a number and 12 is 24. What is the number?

33. Two ferry boats sail between Merryland and Dream Island. One boat takes 4 h for the round trip. The other takes 5 h. They both leave Merryland at 06:00 on October 8. When will they next dock at Merryland together? Explain your solution.

34. "The LCM of two prime numbers is always the product of the numbers." Is this statement true? How do you know?

CALCULATOR POWER

To find the LCM of two numbers, divide the smaller number into multiples of the larger number until you get a whole number quotient. Find the LCM of 12 and 15 as shown.

$15 \div 12 = 1.25$
$30 \div 12 = 2.5$
$45 \div 12 = 3.75$
$60 \div 12 = 4$

The LCM is 60.

Use this method and your calculator to find the LCM of the following.

1. 32, 18 **2.** 30, 85 **3.** 35, 25

4. Adapt the method to find the LCM of 3 numbers. First try 5, 10, and 14. Check that your method works for other sets of 3 numbers. Describe your method.

2.8 Exponents

Bryan Adams' *Reckless* sold more than 1 000 000 copies in Canada. The number 1 000 000 is in standard form. It can also be written as repeated multiplication.

$10 \times 10 \times 10 \times 10 \times 10 \times 10$

A shorter way to write this is in **exponential form** as 10^6.

Activity: Complete the Table

Copy and complete this table.

Repeated Multiplication	Exponential Form
$4 \times 4 \times 4$	4^3
$3 \times 3 \times 3 \times 3$	
$6 \times 6 \times 6 \times 6$	
$7 \times 7 \times 7 \times 7 \times 7 \times 7$	
$9 \times 9 \times 9 \times 9 \times 9 \times 9 \times 9$	

Inquire

1. What does the small raised number mean in 4^3?
2. What is 10^8 as repeated multiplication and in standard form?
3. What is the value of 1^4?
4. What is the value of 3^1?

The product 4×4 can be written as 4^2. We call 4^2 a **power** of 4.

power → 4^2 ← exponent
base

This power is four to the exponent two, or four squared. The **base**, 4, is the number we multiply. The **exponent**, 2, is the number of times we multiply the base.

The power 4^3 is four to the exponent 3, or four cubed.

4^3	=	$4 \times 4 \times 4$	=	64
exponential form		repeated multiplication		standard form

Example

Express 64 as a power of 2.

Solution

Write the number in standard form. 64

Write the base, 2, as many times as it multiplies to equal 64. $= 2 \times 2 \times 2 \times 2 \times 2 \times 2$

Write the power. $= 2^6$

So, $64 = 2^6$.

Practice

Write the exponent.

1. 4^5 **2.** 10^5 **3.** 7^3 **4.** 9^2

5. 2^9 **6.** 25^{11} **7.** 20^8 **8.** 8^6

Write the base.

9. 4^2 **10.** 3^5 **11.** 10^5 **12.** 5^3

13. 6^3 **14.** 2^{12} **15.** 6^{16} **16.** 7^4

Write as repeated multiplication.

17. 5^2 **18.** 10^5 **19.** 12^6 **20.** 20^3

21. 8^3 **22.** 9^7 **23.** 2^3 **24.** 4^5

Write in exponential form.

25. $2 \times 2 \times 2 \times 2 \times 2 \times 2$

26. $10 \times 10 \times 10 \times 10 \times 10 \times 10 \times 10$

27. $5 \times 5 \times 5 \times 5 \times 5$

28. $3 \times 3 \times 3 \times 3 \times 3 \times 3 \times 3 \times 3 \times 3$

29. 6×6

30. $9 \times 9 \times 9 \times 9$

Write as a power of 10.

31. 100 **32.** 10 000

33. 10 **34.** 1000

35. 1 000 000 **36.** 100 000

37. 10 000 000 **38.** 10 000 000 000

Write in standard form.

39. $3 \times 3 \times 3$ **40.** $8 \times 8 \times 8$

41. $6 \times 6 \times 6 \times 6$ **42.** $5 \times 5 \times 5$

43. 2×2 **44.** $4 \times 4 \times 4 \times 4$

Write in standard form.

45. 2^4 **46.** 3^2 **47.** 4^5 **48.** 8^3

49. 9^3 **50.** 7^4 **51.** 5^5 **52.** 8^4

53. 6^3 **54.** 2^{10} **55.** 3^4 **56.** 4^4

Copy and complete the table.

	Power	Base	Exponent	Standard Form
57.	3^5	?	?	243
58.	?	10	4	?
59.	2^6	2	?	?
60.	4^3	?	?	64
61.	$?^3$	?	?	125

Problems and Applications

Write the powers in order from smallest to largest.

62. 3^4, 4^3, 2^5, 5^2 **63.** 8^3, 5^4, 6^3, 4^6

Evaluate.

64. 3.1^2 **65.** 1.2^3 **66.** 5.6^2

67. 8.5^2 **68.** 2.4^3 **69.** 1.5^4

70. Use the numbers 2, 4, 5, 8, and 10 once each in a number sentence to make a result of 0. Use one number as an exponent. You can use any of the operations $+$, $-$, $\times$, or $\div$.

71. Since $2 + 2 = 4 = 2^2$, does $2 + 2 + 2 = 2^3$? Explain your answer.

72. Which is greater, 3^2 or 2^3? Explain.

CALCULATOR POWER

Some calculators have an exponent key, [Y^x].

To calculate 2^3, press [C] 2 [Y^x] 3 [=]

The display is [8].

1. Describe a way to use a calculator without a [Y^x] key to evaluate powers.

Evaluate using your calculator.

2. 5^3 **3.** 3^5 **4.** 2^8

5. 3^4 **6.** 10^6 **7.** 12^4

2.9 Use A Data Bank

Sometimes, the information you need to solve a problem is missing. You need to look it up. Some sources of information are books, newspapers, magazines, and computer data bases.

The Beaumonts will drive from Regina to Saint John in the summer. They plan to drive about 800 km each day. How many days will the trip take?

Understand the Problem

1. What information are you given?

2. What information do you need?

3. Where could you find the missing information?

4. Do you need an exact or approximate answer?

Think of a Plan

Find the driving distance from Regina to Saint John. You could use an atlas, an almanac, a tourist information service, or a road map.

To practise locating information, use the Data Bank on pages 456 to 463 of this book.

Round the driving distance from Regina to Saint John to the nearest 1000 km. Divide by 800 to get the approximate number of days.

Carry Out the Plan

The chart entitled "Canadian Driving Distances Between Cities" gives the driving distance from Regina to Saint John as 3919 km.

The number of days for the trip suggests an approximate answer, so round 3919 km to 4000 km. To find the number of days, divide 4000 by 800.

$$\frac{4000}{800} = 5$$

The trip will take the Beaumonts 5 days.

Look Back

Check: $5 \times 800 = 4000$

Does the answer seem reasonable?

Use a Data Bank

1. Find the missing information.
2. Use the information to solve the problem.
3. Check that the answer is reasonable.

Problems and Applications

Use the Data Bank on pages 456 to 463 of this book to solve the problems. For each problem, state the title of the chart, list, or map that contains the missing information.

1. The Lee family is going to drive from Toronto to Vancouver. They plan to visit tourist attractions on the way. They will drive about 500 km each day. How many days will the trip take?

2. Francine lives in Halifax. Her best friend, Sabrina, lives in Victoria. If Francine phones Sabrina from Halifax at 09:00 on Saturday, what time is it in Victoria?

3. How much longer is the Amazon River than the Mackenzie River?

4. Which distance is longer, the flying distance from St. John's to Victoria or the length of the Nile River?

5. How much closer to the sun is Earth than the planet Jupiter?

6. Which of the sun's planets has the most moons? Which of the planets have no moons?

7. Which whale is longer, a killer whale or a gray whale?

8. How much farther is the driving distance from Ottawa to Calgary than the flying distance?

9. The temperature outside is –7°C. The wind speed is 40 km/h. What is the wind chill temperature?

10. How much deeper is Lake Superior than Lake Ontario?

11. Use information from the Data Bank to create 3 problems for your classmates to solve. Have the answers ready so they can check their results.

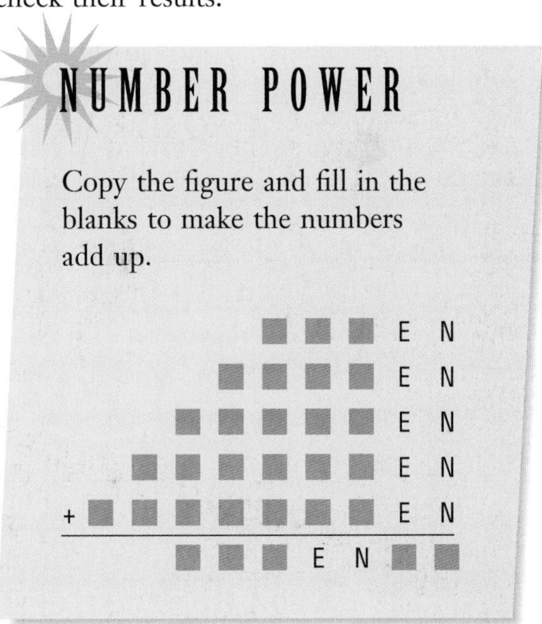

NUMBER POWER

Copy the figure and fill in the blanks to make the numbers add up.

2.10 More About Order of Operations

Activity: Describe the Steps

Paul won a computer as first prize in a contest.
He had to answer this skill-testing question.

$$9^2 - (5 - 2)^2 + 4 = \blacksquare$$

Inquire

1. In what order would you do the calculations?

2. Calculate the answer and compare with a classmate.

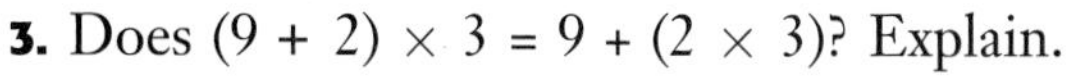

3. Does $(9 + 2) \times 3 = 9 + (2 \times 3)$? Explain.

4. "Half of \$4 and \$6" can have two meanings.
Write an expression to show each meaning.
Which amount of money would you rather have? Explain.

When evaluating expressions, we use the order of operations.

Order of Operations

1. Do operations in **brackets** first. — B

2. Evaluate **exponents**. — E

3. Do **divisions** and **multiplications** in the order they appear, from left to right. — D M

4. Do **additions** and **subtractions** in the order they appear, from left to right. — A S

BEDMAS will help you remember the order.

Example 1

Evaluate $(4 + 2)^2 - 5$.

Solution

$$\begin{aligned} &(4 + 2)^2 - 5 && \text{brackets} \\ &= 6^2 - 5 && \text{exponents} \\ &= 36 - 5 && \text{subtract} \\ &= 31 \end{aligned}$$

Example 2

Evaluate $3^2 \div 3 + 2 \times (12 - 10)^2$.

Solution

$$\begin{aligned} &3^2 \div 3 + 2 \times (12 - 10)^2 \\ &= 3^2 \div 3 + 2 \times (2)^2 \\ &= 9 \div 3 + 2 \times 4 \\ &= 3 + 8 \\ &= 11 \end{aligned}$$

Practice

Evaluate.

1. $10^2 - 25$
2. $10^2 + 64$
3. $8^2 - 36$
4. $12 + 5^2 - 36$
5. $3^2 + 4^2 - 5^2$
6. $5^2 + 13$
7. $3^2 - 4$
8. $7^2 - 2$

Evaluate.

9. $2^3 + 5 \times 4$
10. $6^2 + 5 - 3^3$
11. $8^3 - 3^2 - 2^2$
12. $(6^3 + 3) - 4^2$
13. $(7 - 3)^2 + 6 \times 9$
14. $4^2 \times 3^3 + 15$
15. $1^4 + 99$
16. $6^2 \div 3 \times 2$

Calculate.

17. $(18 - 4)^2 \div 2$
18. $9^2 + (8 \times 9 \div 18)$
19. $(4^2 - 6)^2 \div 4$
20. $5 \times 3^3 - (3 \times 4)$
21. $10^5 - 10^4$
22. $5 \times 2^3 + 6 - 3^2$

Problems and Applications

Replace each ● with >, <, or = to make each statement true.

23. 3^2 ● 5^2
24. 2^3 ● 3^2
25. 10^2 ● 5^4
26. 4^3 ● $5 + 6^2$
27. 8^2 ● 2×3^4
28. 9^2 ● $4 + 3^2 - 2$

Replace each ● with >, <, or = to make each statement true.

29. $(10 - 5)^2$ ● $(3 - 1)^3$
30. $5 \times (2^2 + 3^2)$ ● $3 \times (5^2 - 4^2)$
31. $8^2 \times (3^2 + 1)$ ● $3^2 \times (8^2 + 1)$

Use brackets to make each statement true.

32. $2 + 1 \times 4 - 1 = 9$
33. $20 \div 4 + 1 - 2 = 2$
34. $9 - 3 + 5 = 1$
35. $3 \times 5 + 4 = 27$

The numbers 4, 9, 16, and 25 are perfect squares.

2×2 (or 2^2) $= 4$ $\quad$ 3×3 (or 3^2) $= 9$

4×4 (or 4^2) $= 16$ $\quad$ 5×5 (or 5^2) $= 25$

Some numbers that are not perfect squares can be written as the sum of a perfect square and a prime number.

$39 = 6^2 + 3$ or $39 = 4^2 + 23$

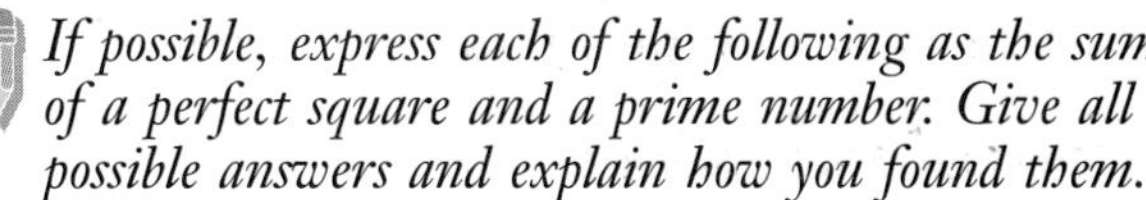

If possible, express each of the following as the sum of a perfect square and a prime number. Give all possible answers and explain how you found them.

36. 21
37. 28
38. 52
39. 68
40. 13
41. 20

NUMBER POWER

You can use the order of operations and four 3s to write an expression for 10.

$3 \times 3 + 3 \div 3 = 10$

a) Work with a classmate and use four 3s to write expressions for the numbers from 0 to 9.

b) Find other numbers you can make using four 3s and challenge your classmates to make the expressions.

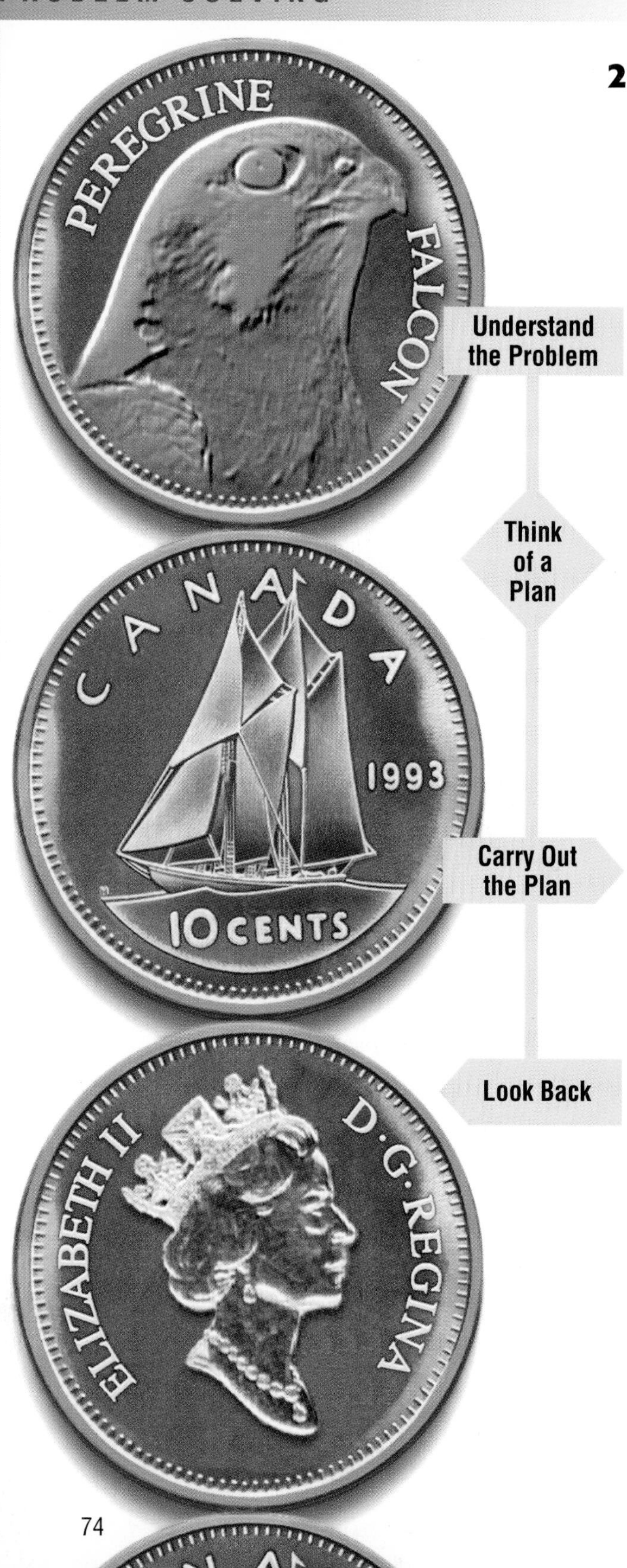

2.11 Solve a Simpler Problem

Leon and Gemma raise funds to help save peregrine falcons. They want to collect a kilometre of dimes placed end to end. If they do, how much will they raise?

Understand the Problem

1. What facts are given?

2. In your own words, state what you must find.

Think of a Plan

Placing dimes end to end for 1 km takes too long. Look for a simpler problem to solve.

You could find how many dimes are in 1 m and multiply by 1000 to get the number of dimes in 1 km.

Then multiply the number of dimes in 1 km by \$0.10 to find the amount of money.

Carry Out the Plan

The number of dimes end to end in 1 m is 55.5. The number of dimes end to end in 1 km is

$1000 \times 55.5 = 55\ 500$

The value of 55 500 dimes is

$\$0.10 \times 55\ 500 = \$5550.00$

Leon and Gemma will raise \$5550.00.

Look Back

Does the answer seem reasonable?

Is there another way to solve the problem?

Discuss and try some other methods.

Solve a Simpler Problem

1. Break the problem into smaller problems that can be solved more easily.
2. Solve the problem.
3. Check that the answer is reasonable.

Problems and Applications

1. A rectangular field is 240 m long and 130 m wide.

A fence is constructed around the field. Fence posts are 2 m apart. How many posts are used?

2. Describe how you would estimate the number of listings in the white pages of your telephone book.

3. Cans of vegetables are stacked for display in a grocery store as shown.

How many cans would be in the display if there were 12 rows of cans?

4. Using only a ruler for measurement, find the thickness of a page of this book. Write a description of your method.

5. How many times does your heart beat in one year?

6. How thick is a dime?

7. How many $1 coins stack 1 m high?

8. Take a paper clip. How many of these clips make a 5-m chain?

9. Sixty-four people enter a squash tournament. Players are eliminated after 1 loss. There are no ties. How many games are played in the tournament?

10. The distance from Calgary to Montreal along the Trans Canada Highway is 3743 km. How many students would it take to form a human chain from Calgary to Montreal along the Highway? What assumptions have you made?

11. Booths in a flea market are numbered from 1 to 150. How many booth numbers contain at least one 3?

12. How long would it take you to complete a 25-km walkathon?

13. A pizza stand offers 4 choices of toppings. How many different 2-topping pizzas could it make?

14. There is an airport in each of the following cities.

How many direct air routes are needed to connect every airport to the other five?

15. How many steps do you take to walk 1 km? Compare your solution with other students'. How are they different?

LOGIC POWER

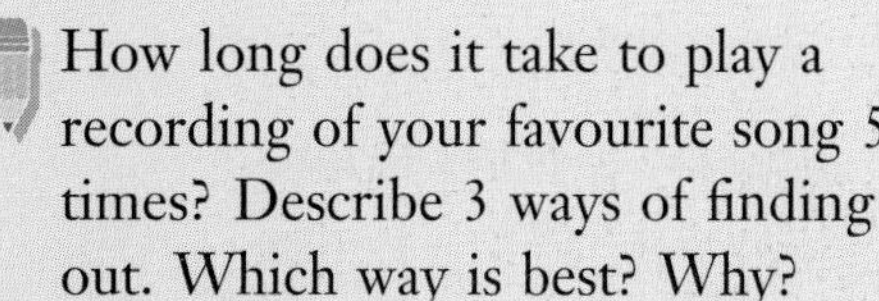

How long does it take to play a recording of your favourite song 5 times? Describe 3 ways of finding out. Which way is best? Why?

Review

1. Which are divisible by 2 and 3?

42 144 398 81 156

2. Which are divisible by 6?

96 432 1092 844 157

3. Which are divisible by 4?

6294 372 4298 9404 1654

4. Which are divisible by 8?

4168 2228 808 216 5608

5. Which are divisible by 9?

979 1017 5526 4102 656

6. Write a four-digit number divisible by 2 and 4.

7. Write a five-digit number divisible by 2 but not 4.

Use factors to complete the following. Give all possible answers.

8. ■ × ■ = 30 **9.** ■ × ■ = 28

10. ■ × ■ = 72 **11.** ■ × ■ = 64

List all factors of each number.

12. 40 **13.** 56 **14.** 64 **15.** 100

Is each number prime or composite?

16. 3 **17.** 18 **18.** 34 **19.** 141

20. 168 **21.** 37 **22.** 80 **23.** 85

List the prime numbers between each of the following.

24. 10 and 20 **25.** 70 and 90

26. Write the only even prime number.

27. Is the number 1 prime or composite? Explain your answer.

Write as a product of prime factors.

28. 18 **29.** 35 **30.** 42

Copy and complete each factor tree.

31.

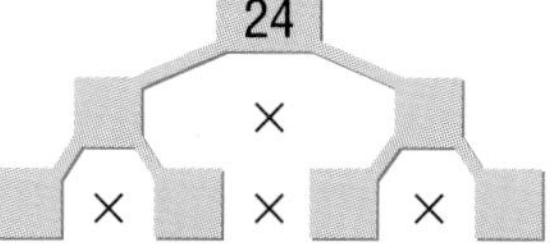

32.

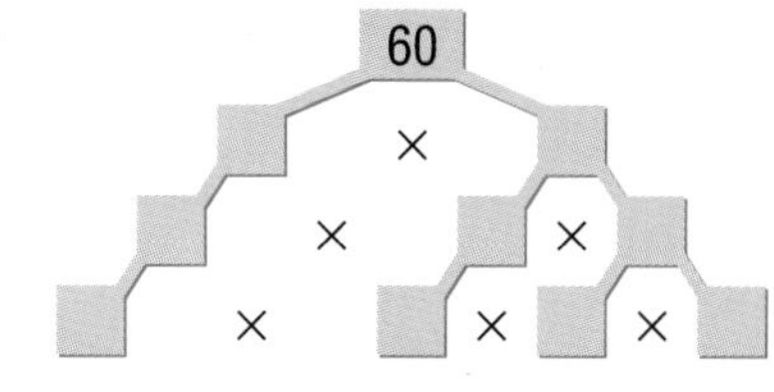

33.

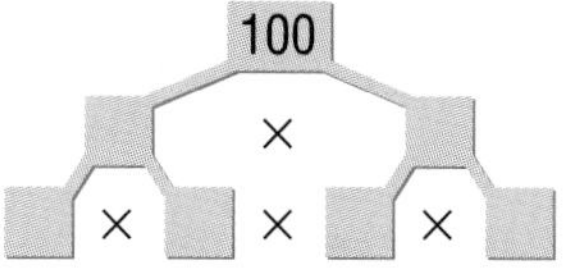

Draw two different factor trees for each number.

34. 40 **35.** 18

List the common factors of each pair.

36. 12, 15 **37.** 12, 30 **38.** 30, 36

Find the greatest common factor of each pair.

39. 6, 8 **40.** 10, 15 **41.** 14, 21

42. 12, 15 **43.** 7, 11 **44.** 8, 12

Find the greatest common factor of each set.

45. 4, 8, 16 **46.** 6, 9, 15

47. 20, 32, 44 **48.** 10, 15, 20

Find the lowest common multiple of each pair.

49. 3, 4 **50.** 5, 10 **51.** 2, 3

52. 6, 8 **53.** 8, 12 **54.** 4, 7

Find the lowest common multiple of each set.

55. 2, 3, 4 **56.** 4, 8, 6 **57.** 5, 10, 15

58. A menu includes soup every fourth day and fruit salad every sixth day. Both are served on Monday, October 31. When will they next be served together?

Write in standard form.

59. $5 \times 5 \times 5 \times 5 \times 5 \times 5 \times 5$

60. $2 \times 2 \times 2 \times 2 \times 2 \times 2$

61. $9 \times 9 \times 9$

62. $10 \times 10 \times 10 \times 10$

Write in standard form.

63. 3^4 **64.** 10^6 **65.** 2^8 **66.** 20^3

Write in order from smallest to largest.

67. $2^5, 5^2, 3^4$

68. $10^3, 3^5, 5^3$

69. $4^3, 3^4, 2^6$

70. $1^5, 5^1, 10^1$

Evaluate.

71. $5^3 - 75$

72. $8^2 + 64$

73. $7^2 - 45$

74. $3^3 - 25 + 2^3$

Evaluate.

75. $10^3 - 5^4$

76. $2 \times 3^2 - 2^4$

77. 5×10^2

78. $5^3 - 5^2$

79. What are the prime factors that all multiples of 10 have in common?

80. Which will form more different rectangular shapes, a set of 10 square tiles or a set of 12 square tiles? Draw diagrams to show your answer.

81. The Marshalls want to tile their kitchen floor. The floor is a rectangle that measures 6 m by 3 m. The tiles are squares that measure 30 cm by 30 cm. How many tiles do they need?

82. A rectangular field measures 200 m by 100 m. A fence is put around the field. The fence posts are 2 m apart. How many posts are used?

83. Winnipeg is 2232 km from Vancouver. Regina is 571 km from Winnipeg. Regina is between Winnipeg and Vancouver. How far is Regina from Vancouver?

Group Decision Making

Researching Media Careers

1. As a class, choose six careers that involve radio, television, or newspapers. You may choose careers like disc jockey, news broadcaster, reporter, camera operator, computer operator, make-up artist, salesperson, or advertising writer. Number the careers from 1 to 6.

2. Go to *home groups* of 6 students. Give each home group member a different career to research.

1 2 3 4 5 6 | 1 2 3 4 5 6

Home Groups

1 2 3 4 5 6 | 1 2 3 4 5 6

3. Form an *expert group* of 4 with students who have the same career as you to research. In your group, research the career. As a group, focus on the formal education needed, what the job is like, and how math is used on the job.

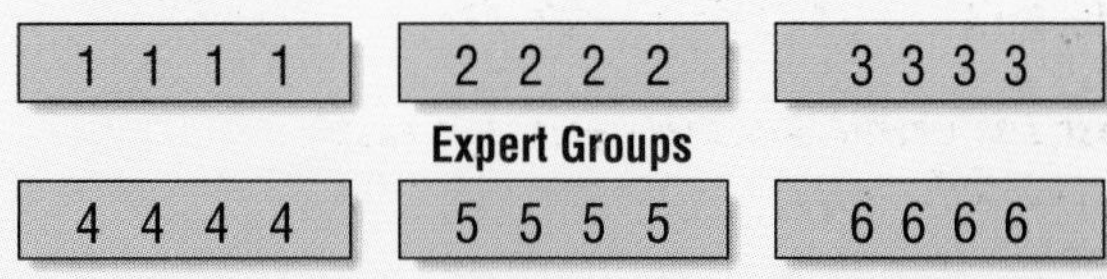

4. Return to your home group and describe what you learned in your expert group. As a group, prepare a report on the 6 careers. The report can be written, acted out, or presented as a video, on a poster, or in any other appropriate form.

Chapter Check

Questions 1 – 3 deal with these numbers.

93	42	114
51	81	216
186	498	1232

1. Which are divisible by 2 and 3?

2. Which are divisible by 3 and 9?

3. Which are divisible by 6?

List all the factors for each of the following.

4. 48 **5.** 81 **6.** 121 **7.** 96 **8.** 150

9. List the composite numbers between 30 and 40.

10. List the prime numbers between 50 and 60.

Draw a factor tree for each of the following.

11. 20 **12.** 54 **13.** 75

Write as a product of prime factors.

14. 18 **15.** 28 **16.** 35 **17.** 44 **18.** 50

Find the greatest common factor of each set.

19. 8, 12 **20.** 8, 16 **21.** 6, 12, 18

Find the lowest common multiple of each set.

22. 2, 3 **23.** 3, 4 **24.** 5, 2

Write as a power of 10.

25. 1000 **26.** 10 000

27. 1 000 000 **28.** 100 000 000

Write in standard form.

29. 2^5 **30.** 12^2

31. $6 \times 6 \times 6$ **32.** $2 \times 2 \times 2 \times 2 \times 2$

Evaluate.

33. $2^5 - 5^2$ **34.** $10^3 - 1$ **35.** $3 \times (9^2 + 9)$

36. Jacques counts aloud by 4s and Jean-Pierre by 6s. Write the first two numbers that they will both say.

37. Which will form more different rectangular shapes, a set of 12 square tiles or a set of 15 square tiles? Draw diagrams to illustrate your answer.

38. Every third person entering a ball park gets a free pennant. Every fifth person gets a free cap. Which person is the first to get a free pennant and a free cap?

39. In how many different ways can a penny, a nickel, a dime, and a quarter be arranged in a straight line if the dime must always be last on the right?

40. Sixty-four teams have entered a slow pitch baseball tournament. A team is eliminated after one loss. How many games must be played to determine a winner?

©1992 Tribune Media Services, Inc.
All Rights Reserved

Reprinted by permission: Tribune Media Services

Using the Strategies

1. How many whole numbers greater than 0 and less than 140 do not contain the digit 5?

2. If you multiply a certain number by 15 and then add 38, the result is 158. What is the number?

3. The train leaves at 11:00. It will take you 5 min to buy your ticket at the station. It will take 24 min to get from the school to the station. You will need 5 min to get your books from your locker before you leave the school. At what time should you be excused from class so that you can catch the train?

4. The figure has alternating red and white squares in each row. The first four rows are shown. All rows begin and end with a white square. How many red squares are in the 40th row?

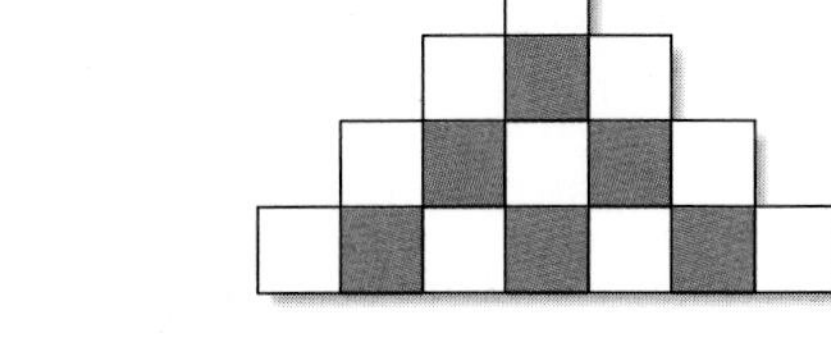

5. It is 240 km from the school to the swim meet. The bus can travel at 60 km/h. How long will it take to get to the meet? What assumptions have you made?

6. The diagrams show 2 ways in which 4 stamps may be attached. Draw 10 other ways in which they may be attached. Stamps must attach along at least one side.

7. Write 100 as the sum of two prime numbers.

8. Summit Hill is 37 km from Border Lake. Redding Downs is 11 km from Border Lake. Malcolm travelled from Summit Hill to Border Lake to Redding Downs and back to Summit Hill. He travelled 82 km. How far is Redding Downs from Summit Hill?

9. Last year, Wei could square a number and get her age. Next year, Wei will be able to cube a number and get her age. How old is she?

10. What do the numbers in the rectangle have in common?

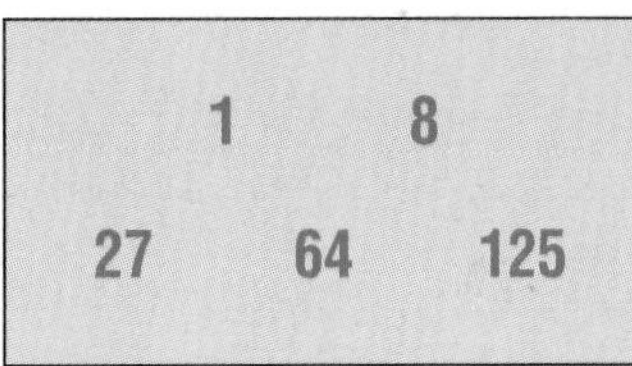

11. Jerry, Roberto, Imelda, and Sylvia held a tennis tournament. They all played each other once. How many matches were played in the tournament?

12. A magazine costs $4.67. If Helene gives the clerk a $10.00 bill and two pennies, how much change should she receive?

DATA BANK

1. How long will it take a raft to float down the Amazon River at 3 km/h?

2. About how many times bigger than Lake Erie is Lake Superior?

3. If the temperature outside is –9°C and the wind speed is 40 km/h, what is the wind chill temperature?

CHAPTER 3

Geometry

The summer is a wonderful time to look at the stars. One way to map the sky is to use groups of stars called constellations. They form pictures of humans and animals. Most of them come from the myths of the Greeks and Romans.

The star map shows the constellations of summer. List all the geometric shapes you see in the star map. State the constellation that each shape appears in.

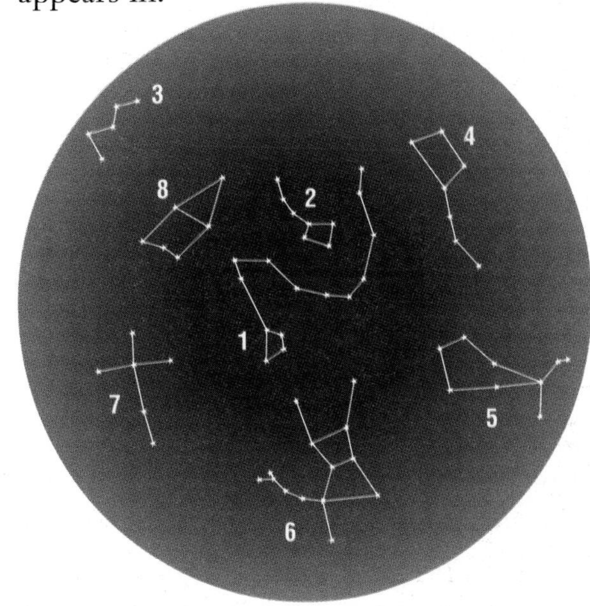

1. Draco	**2.** Ursa Minor
3. Cassiopeia	**4.** Ursa Major
5. Bootes	**6.** Hercules
7. Cygnus	**8.** Cepheus

Tangrams

This 7-piece puzzle from China is called a **tangram**. It is a square cut into 7 geometric shapes. Each shape is called a **tan**.

We have labelled the tans with letters.

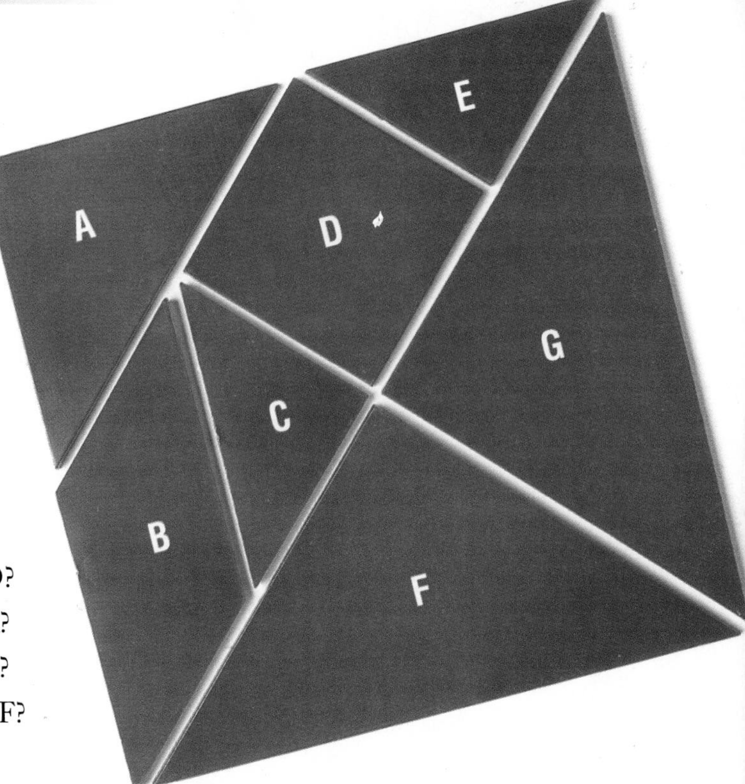

Activity ❶

1. Make the 7 tans out of stiff cardboard or use a plastic tangram set.

2. Identify each tan as a triangle, square, or parallelogram.

3. Which tan exactly matches tan F?

4. Which two tans together match tan D?

5. Which two tans together match tan A?

6. Which two tans together match tan B?

7. Which three tans together match tan F?

Activity ❷

Complete the area sentences.

1. tan A + tan B + tan C + tan D + tan E = tan ■ + tan ■

2. tan F + tan G − tan A = tan ■ + tan ■ + tan ■ + tan ■

3. tan C + tan D + tan E = tan ■

4. tan A + tan C + tan E = tan ■

5. tan A − tan E = tan ■

6. tan F − tan C − tan E = tan ■

7. tan C + tan D = tan ■ + tan ■

Activity ❸

Construct as many of the following figures as you can with up to 7 tans.

1. Squares　**2.** Triangles

3. Rectangles　**4.** Parallelograms

5. Trapezoids

Sketch your solutions in a large chart set up like this one. Be careful! It is impossible to complete all sections of the chart.

Activity ❹

Use the 7 tans to construct each of the following figures.

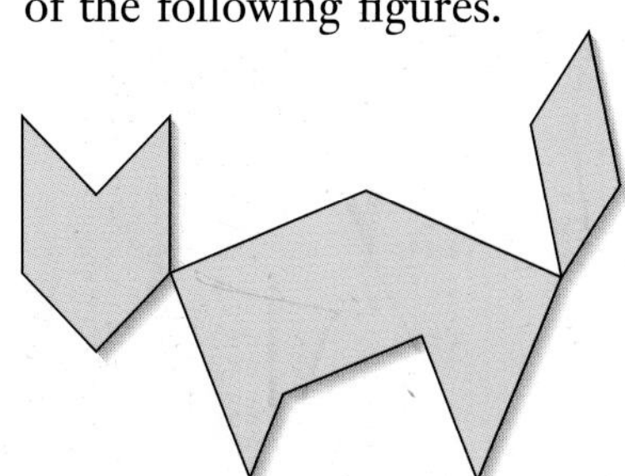

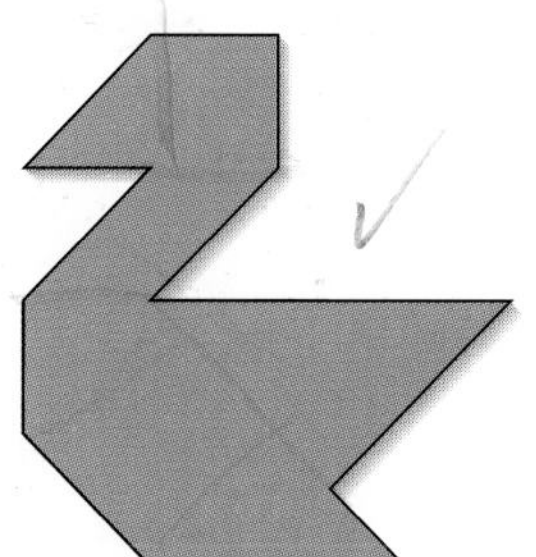

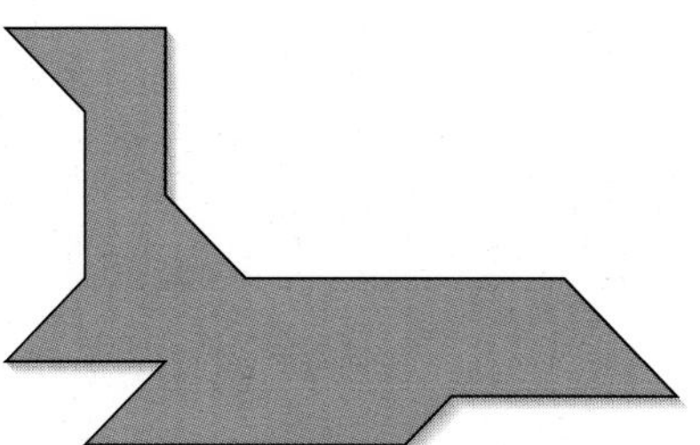

Mental Math

Add.

1. 150 + 25 **2.** 250 + 25 **3.** 225 + 25 + 25 **4.** 225 + 50

5. 250 + 25 + 50 **6.** 325 + 25 + 50 **7.** 400 + 25 + 75 **8.** 450 + 75 + 75

Subtract.

9. 175 − 25 **10.** 225 − 50 **11.** 150 − 75 **12.** 200 − 75

13. 300 − 25 **14.** 200 − 50 − 25 **15.** 175 − 50 − 50 **16.** 150 − 25 − 50

Calculate.

17. 150 + 75 − 25 **18.** 200 − 50 + 25 **19.** 50 + 75 − 100 **20.** 225 + 50 − 25

21. 250 − 50 + 25 **22.** 25 + 50 − 25 **23.** 75 + 75 − 25 **24.** 125 − 75 + 50

Multiply.

25. 3 × 25 **26.** 25 × 4 **27.** 6 × 50 **28.** 8 × 25 **29.** 75 × 3

30. 150 × 2 **31.** 9 × 25 **32.** 5 × 50 **33.** 25 × 7 **34.** 75 × 6

Divide.

35. 75 ÷ 3 **36.** 150 ÷ 50 **37.** 125 ÷ 5 **38.** 200 ÷ 8 **39.** 175 ÷ 7

40. 200 ÷ 4 **41.** 125 ÷ 25 **42.** 250 ÷ 10 **43.** 225 ÷ 9 **44.** 150 ÷ 6

Geometry Around Us

Activity ❶

The designs of houses and apartment buildings contain many geometric shapes.

1. List the shapes you see in the pictures.
2. List the shapes you see on the outside of the building you live in.
3. Use at least 4 geometric shapes to design the outside of a house.
4. Write a short description of your design.
5. Share your design with the rest of the class.

Activity ❷

Many toys contain geometric shapes.

1. List the shapes you see in the pictures.
2. Use geometic shapes to design a toy for someone to ride.
3. Describe your toy to other students.

Activity ❸

Office buildings and bridges contain geometric shapes.

1. List the shapes you see in the pictures.

2. Use geometric shapes to design two office buildings linked by an overhead walkway.

3. Make a poster to show the different buildings designed in your class.

3.1 The Language of Geometry

The terms that we use in geometry have definite meanings. Here are 5 of the most common terms.

1. Points identify a position.
They are represented by **dots**.
Point B is written as B.

2. Lines are made up of a set of points. A line goes on forever in *both* directions.
Line CD is written as $\overleftrightarrow{CD}$.

3. A **ray** is a part of a line with one endpoint. A ray begins at the endpoint and goes on forever in *one* direction.
Ray EF is written as $\overrightarrow{EF}$.

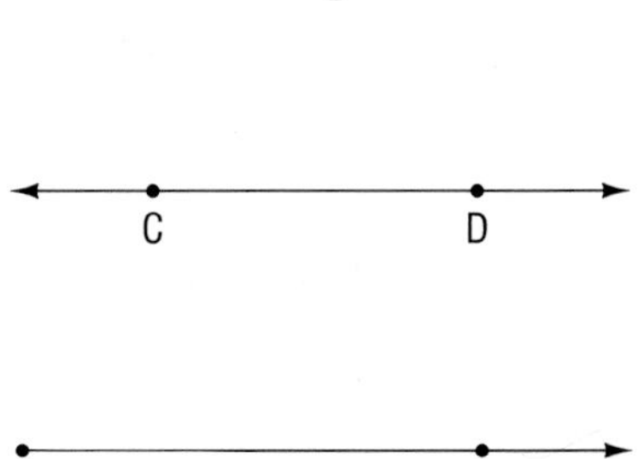

4. A **line segment** is part of a line with 2 endpoints.
Line Segment XY is written as $\overline{XY}$ or just XY.

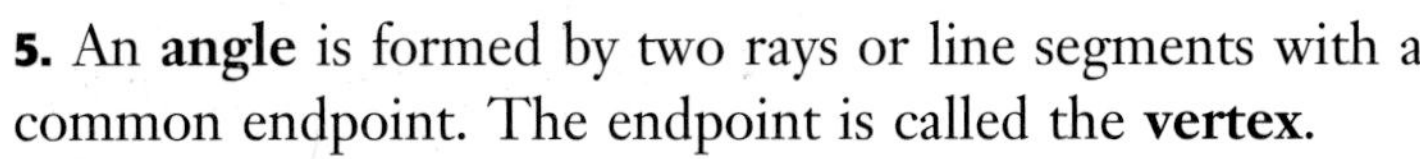

5. An **angle** is formed by two rays or line segments with a common endpoint. The endpoint is called the **vertex.**
Angle RST is written as ∠RST or ∠TSR.

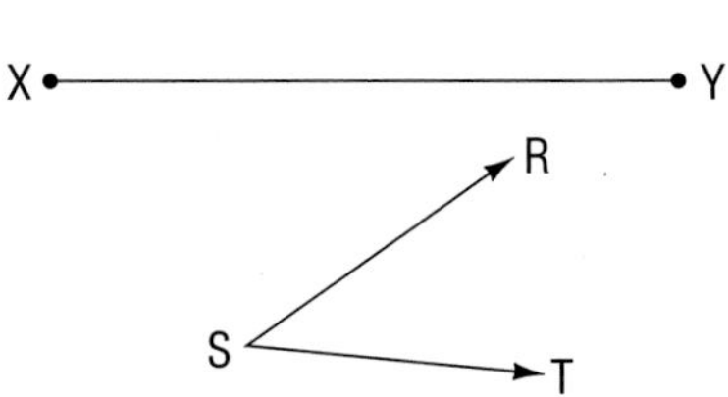

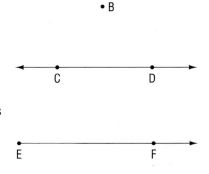

The middle letter represents the vertex.
We can write ∠RST in short form as ∠S.

Activity: Use the Definitions

Look at the picture. It shows a section of a geodesic dome.

Inquire

1. Which of the above geometric figures do you see in the picture?

2. Why do we use two arrows when we draw a line?

3. Why do we use one arrow when we draw a ray?

4. Name the geometric figure suggested by each of the following.

a) the edge of your book

b) a flashlight beam

c) the corner of a desk top

d) the centre of a desk top

e) a star in the sky

f) a sunbeam

5. Are ∠ABC and ∠ACB alternative ways of writing the same angle? Explain.

Practice

1. The names and symbols in the following lists do not match. Rewrite the lists so that the names and symbols match.

Point B	$\overleftrightarrow{AB}$
Ray EA	$\overline{AB}$
Line segment AB	$\angle PQR$
Line AB	B
Angle PQR	$\overrightarrow{EA}$

Write the name and symbol for each of the following figures.

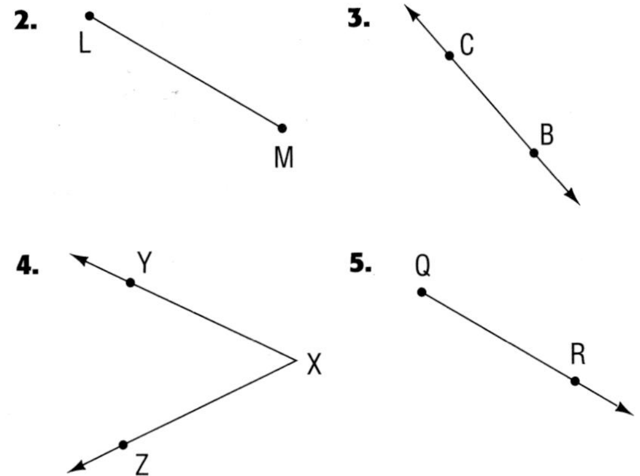

Problems and Applications

6. Estimate, then measure the length of each line segment. Copy and complete the chart.

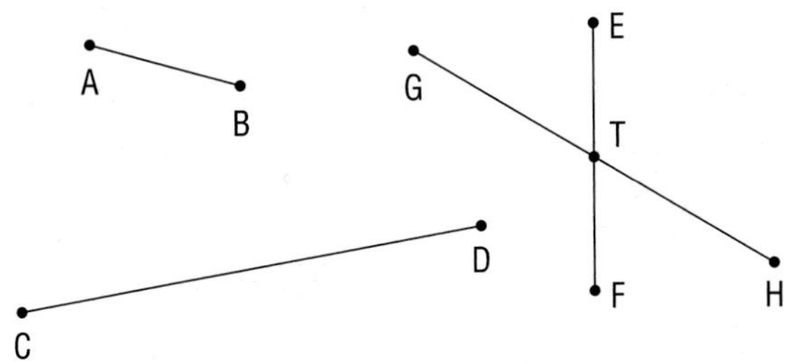

Line Segment	Estimate	Measure	Difference

From the diagram, give the symbols of the following.

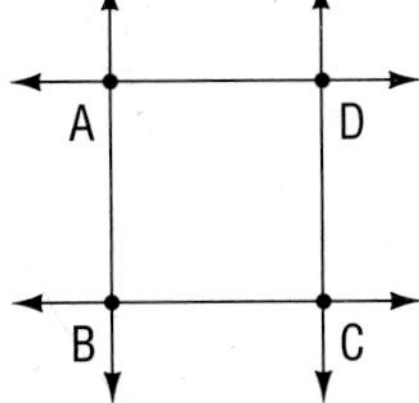

7. 4 points

8. 4 line segments

9. 4 lines

10. 8 rays

11. 4 angles

Use the figure to give the symbols of the following.

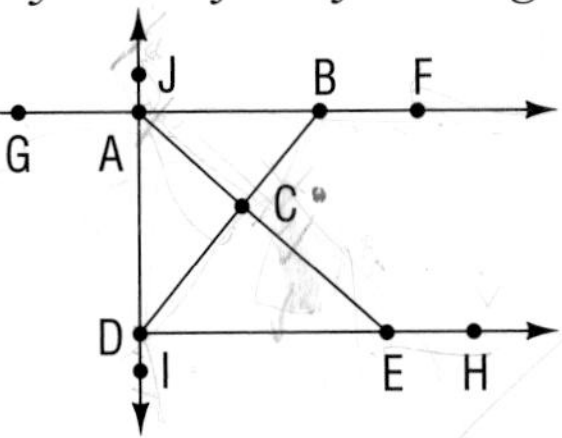

12. 6 points

13. 8 line segments

14. 2 lines

15. 8 angles

16. 3 rays

17. Copy and complete the following chart.

2 Points	3 Points	4 Points	5 Points	6 Points
1 line	3 lines	__ lines	__ lines	__ lines

What is the pattern?

Predict the number of lines with 10 points.

Share your solution with your group.

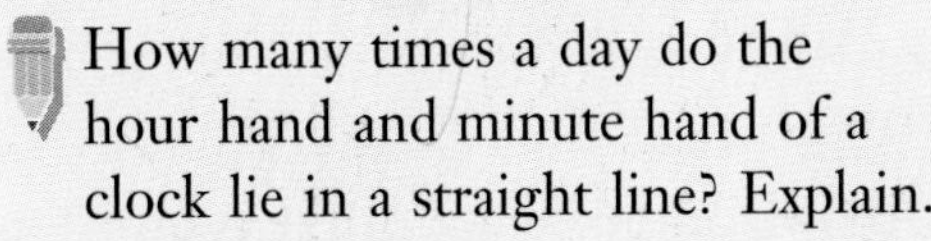

LOGIC POWER

How many times a day do the hour hand and minute hand of a clock lie in a straight line? Explain.

3.2 Angles

Activity: Learn from the Picture

George Ferris built the first ferris wheel in 1893 for the Chicago World's Fair. The wheel had 36 gondolas, each holding 60 people. The arms of a ferris wheel make angles. We measure angles in **degrees**, symbol °. Passengers on a ferris wheel ride around the outside of a circle. There are 360° in a circle.

Inquire

1. How many degrees would you have moved from A to B on the ferris wheel?

2. How many degrees would you have moved from A to C?

3. How many degrees were there between adjacent gondola arms on the ferris wheel?

4. If a ferris wheel has 12 arms, how many degrees are there between adjacent arms?

We measure angles with a **protractor**. This usually has an inner scale and an outer scale. The scale we use depends on how we place the protractor on the angle.

Example 1

What is the measure of ∠XYZ?

Solution

Place the centre of the protractor on vertex Y.

$\overrightarrow{YZ}$ crosses 0° on the outer scale. $\overrightarrow{YX}$ crosses 70° on the outer scale. So ∠XYZ = 70°.

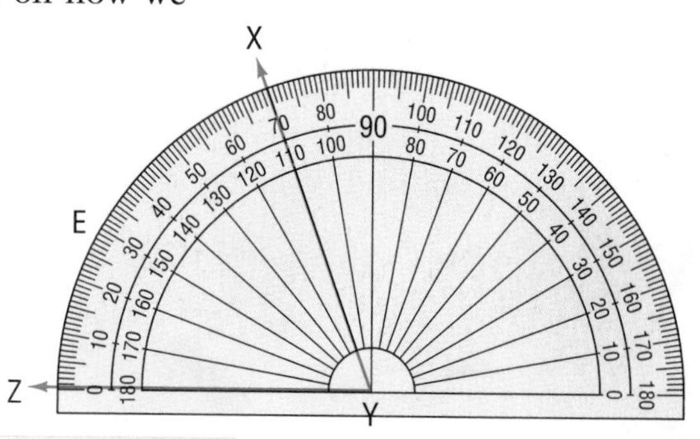

We can also use a protractor to construct angles.

Example 2

Draw ∠ABC = 155°.

Solution

Draw AB. Place the centre of the protractor on B and line up BA with 0° on the inner scale. Mark C at 155° on the inner scale. Join BC. We have drawn ∠ABC = 155°.

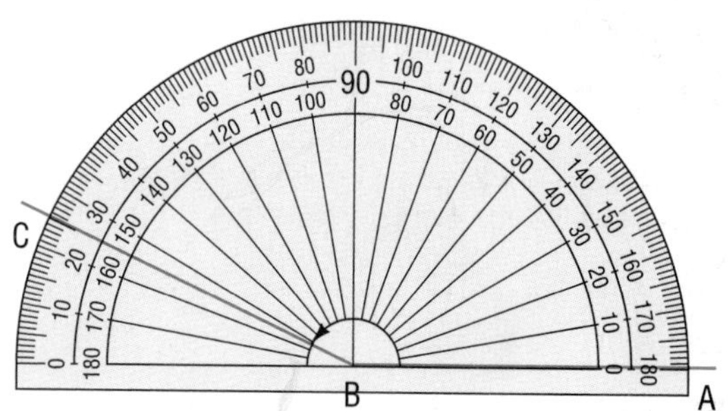

Practice

Name each angle in two ways.

1. **2.**

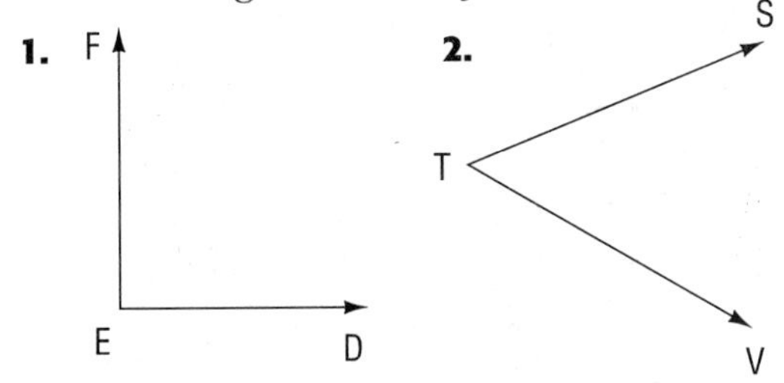

3. **4.**

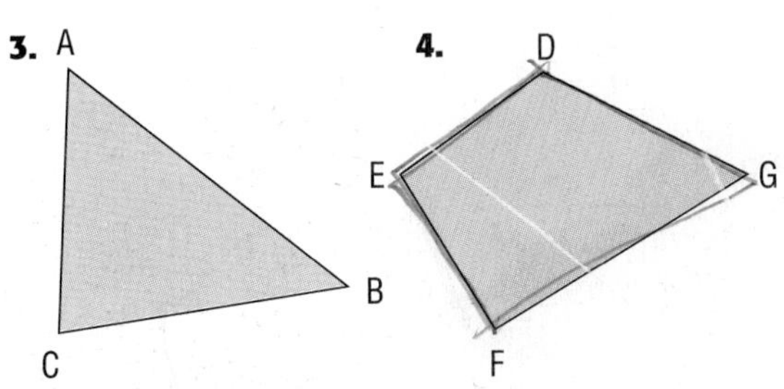

State the measure of each angle in 5–13.

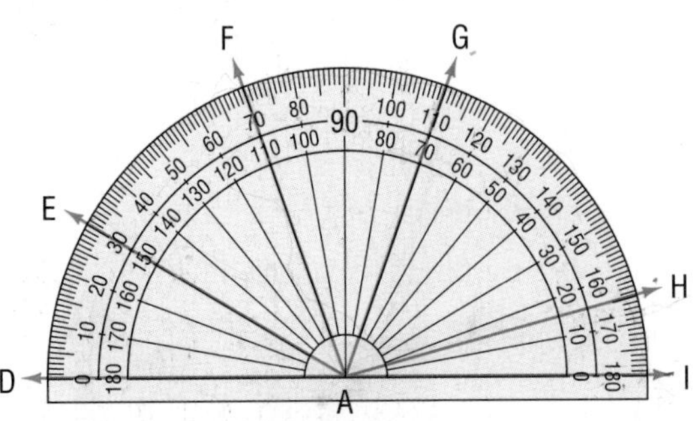

5. ∠DAE	**6.** ∠HAG	**7.** ∠EAH
8. ∠DAG	**9.** ∠GAE	**10.** ∠EAF
11. ∠IAH	**12.** ∠DAH	**13.** ∠FAI

Draw angles with the following measures. Label and name each angle.

14. 60°	**15.** 45°	**16.** 100°
17. 10°	**18.** 165°	**19.** 70°
20. 130°	**21.** 90°	**22.** 32°

Problems and Applications

Estimate the measure of each angle. Measure the angle with a protractor. Copy and complete the chart.

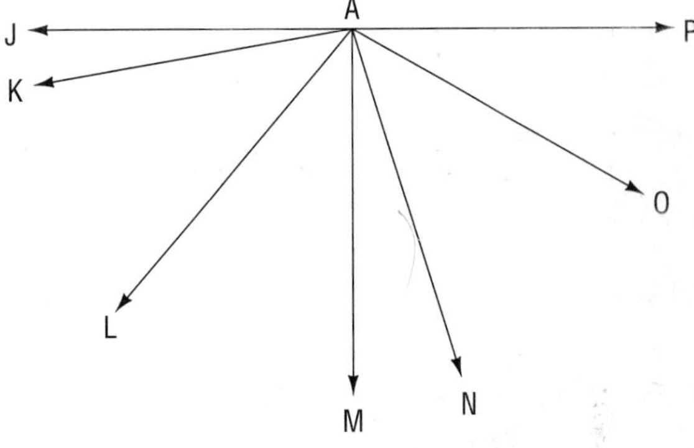

23. ∠PAO	**24.** ∠NAP	**25.** ∠KAO
26. ∠JAK	**27.** ∠MAO	**28.** ∠JAL
29. ∠KAM	**30.** ∠LAM	**31.** ∠OAL

Angle	Estimate	Measure	Difference

32. Draw ∠MLS = 70°. Draw a point, W, between LM and LS to make ∠MLW = ∠WLS. What is the measure of ∠MLW? of ∠WLS?

33. Suppose you face north and turn counterclockwise by 120°, then by another 200°, and then by another 40°. Which way do you face afterwards? Explain.

34. How would you use a protractor to draw an angle of 210°? of 330°? Explain.

LOGIC POWER

How many times a day do the minute hand and hour hand of a clock make an angle of 90°? Explain.

3.3 Classifying Angles

We name angles according to their sizes.

An **acute angle** measures less than 90°.

A **right angle** measures 90°.

An **obtuse angle** measures between 90° and 180°.

A **straight angle** measures 180°.

A **reflex angle** measures between 180° and 360°.

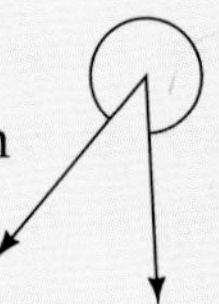

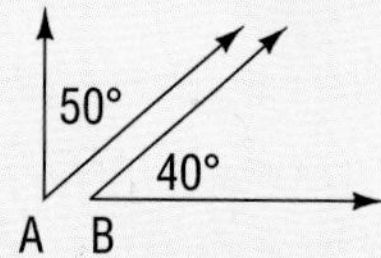

Two angles whose sum is 90° are called **complementary angles.**

∠A and ∠B are complementary angles.

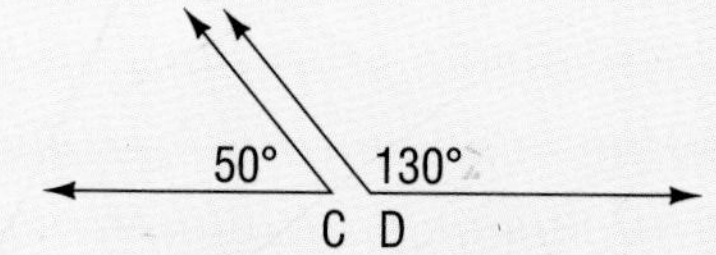

Two angles whose sum is 180° are called **supplementary angles.**

∠C and ∠D are supplementary angles.

Activity: Use the Definitions

Look at the picture. It shows Alexander Graham Bell's home in Brantford, Ontario.

Inquire

1. List the types of angles you see in the picture.

2. If you see any angles that are complementary, describe where they are.

3. If you see any angles that are supplementary, describe where they are.

4. Is it possible for two angles to be supplementary if one of them is a straight angle? Explain.

5. If two equal angles are complementary, what is the measure of each angle? Explain.

Example

∠ABC = 41°.

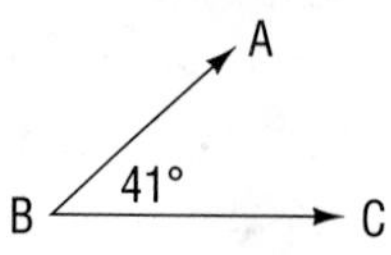

Find the measure of the angle that is

a) complementary to ∠ABC.

b) supplementary to ∠ABC.

Solution

a) 90° − 41° = 49°

The complementary angle measures 49°.

b) 180° − 41° = 139°

The supplementary angle measures 139°.

Practice

Classify each angle as acute, right, obtuse, straight, or reflex.

1. 53°	**2.** 7°	**3.** 90°	**4.** 425°
5. 180°	**6.** 79°	**7.** 167°	**8.** 37°
9. 13°	**10.** 299°	**11.** 115°	**12.** 151°
13. 72°	**14.** 190°	**15.** 315°	**16.** 179°

Classify each angle as acute, right, obtuse, straight, or reflex.

17.

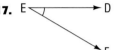

18.

19.

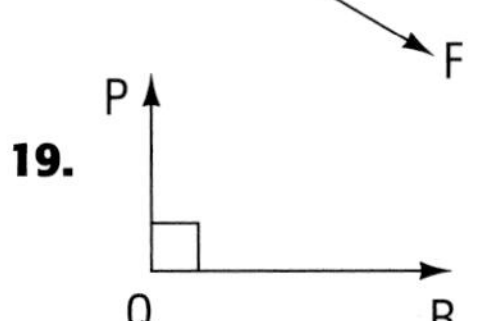

20. L M N

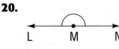

21.

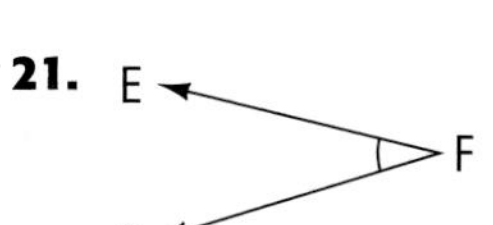

22.

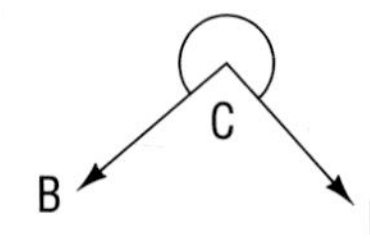

Problems and Applications

For each of the following angles, draw the complementary angle and state its measure.

23. 60°	**24.** 45°	**25.** 84°
26. 72°	**27.** 54°	**28.** 17°

For each of the following angles, draw the supplementary angle and state its measure.

29. 50°	**30.** 130°	**31.** 35°
32. 144°	**33.** 68°	**34.** 104°

Determine the missing measures.

35.

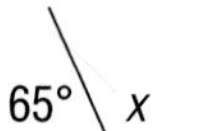

36.

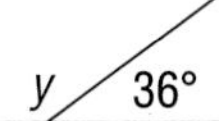

37.

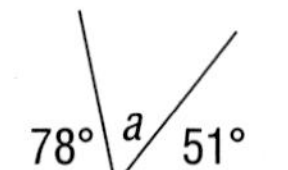

38.

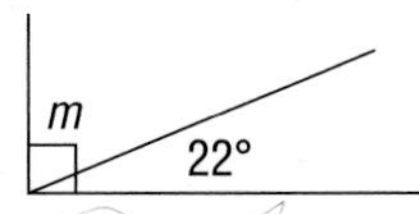

39. Draw a 75° angle.

a) Draw the complementary angle and state its measure.

b) Draw the supplementary angle and state its measure.

c) Is the supplement of an acute angle always greater than its complement? Explain.

d) What type of angle is the supplement of an acute angle?

e) What type of angle is the complement of an acute angle?

Examine the picture of the compass, then answer questions 40–43.

40. If you turn 90° clockwise from north, which way will you face?

41. If you face northwest and turn 180°, which way will you face?

42. If you turn 135° counterclockwise from south, which way will you face?

43. You decide to turn 225° clockwise from north. A friend says that you could face the same way by turning a smaller angle from north. What is the smaller angle and which way do you turn? Which way will you face afterwards?

NUMBER POWER

A group of students each bought the same item at a variety store. The total cost before taxes was \$56.29. How many students were in the group?

3.4 Sequence the Operations

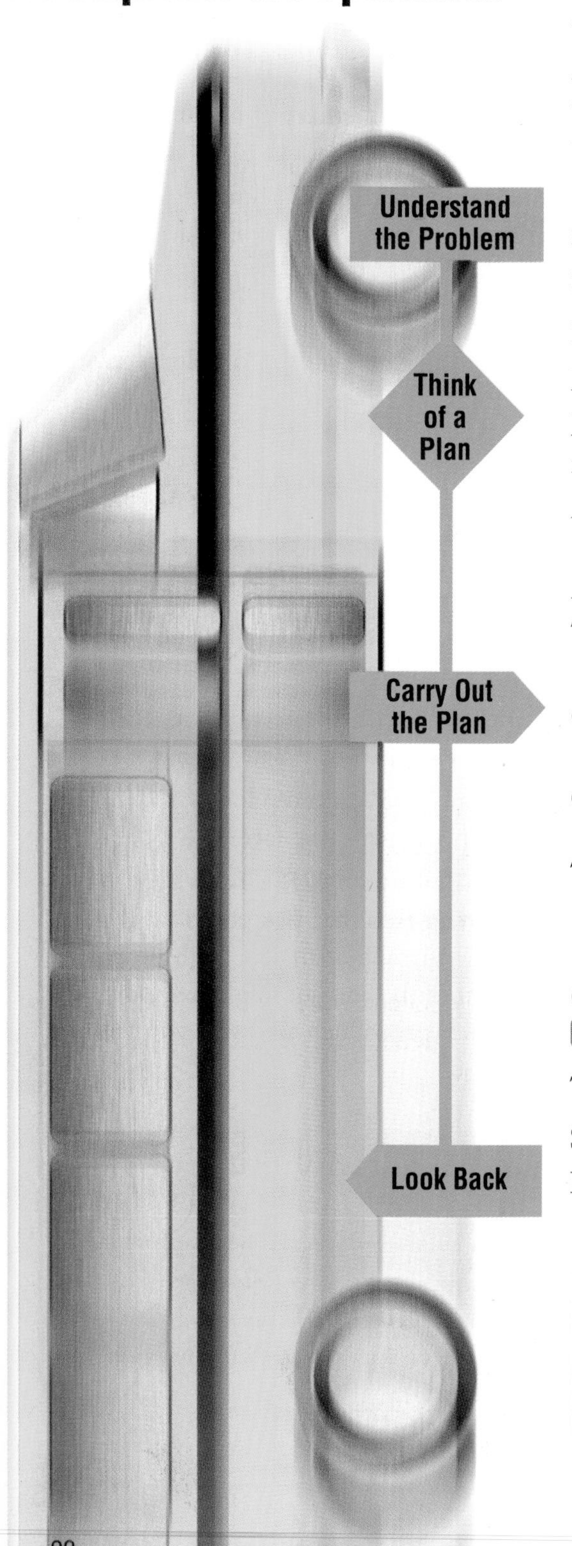

There are 17 girls and 15 boys in the grade 7 class. A bus for a field trip costs \$3.50 per student. Three teachers pay \$5.00 each. What is the total cost of the bus?

1. What information are you given?

2. What are you asked to find?

3. Do you need an exact or an approximate answer?

Find the total number of students.

Multiply by the cost per student.

Multiply the cost per teacher by the number of teachers.

Add the costs for students and teachers.

Paper and Pencil

Total number of students 17 + 15
= 32

Cost for the students 32 × \$3.50
= \$112.00

Cost for the teachers 3 × \$5.00
= \$15.00

Total cost \$112.00
+ \$15.00
\$127.00

EST: 30 × 4 + 3 × 5
= 135

Calculator

C 17 + 15 = × 3.5 = + 3 × 5 = 127

The total cost of the bus is \$127.00.

\$127.00 is close to the estimate of \$135.

How can you work backward to check your answer?

Sequence the Operations

1. Arrange the operations in order.
2. Follow the order of operations.
3. Check that the answer is reasonable.

Problems and Applications

1. Jack had $20.00. He paid $13.50 for a haircut and $2.00 for bus fare. How much does he have left?

2. Bolts cost 7¢ each, and nuts cost 5¢ each. Washers are 3 for 10¢. Find the cost of 30 nuts, 30 bolts, and 30 washers.

3. The blue course at the cross-country ski club is 5.8 km long. The red course is 10.3 km long. Mark skied the blue course 15 times. Katerina skied the red course 15 times. How much farther did Katerina ski?

4. Mohamed bought 3 notebooks at $2.35 each and 3 pens at $1.98 each. How much did he spend?

5. There are 12 players on the school basketball team. Uniforms cost $59.95 each, including socks. Shoes are $79.50 a pair. What is the cost of uniforms and shoes for the team?

6. The population of St. John's, Newfoundland, was 86 600 in 1976. It fell by 2800 by 1981. Between 1981 and 1986, the population increased by 12 400. What was the population of St. John's in 1986?

7. One tonne (1 t) is 1000 kg. How many grams are there in 1 t?

8. The sunniest city in Canada is Saskatoon, which averages about 6.7 h of sunshine a day. About how many hours a month is that? What assumptions have you made?

9. Mr. Atarius paid $12.00 for 3 h of babysitting. What would 7 h of babysitting cost?

10. Helen Lam's car travels 6.5 km on 1 L of gasoline. The gas tank holds 56 L. How far can she drive on one tank of gas?

11. Sondra earns $12.50/h and works 36 h each week. If she gets a raise of $0.75/h, how much more does she earn in 4 weeks?

12. Bob and Lina do the same part-time job. Last week, Lina worked 1 h longer than Bob. Bob earned $93.00, and Lina earned $100.75. How much do they each earn per hour?

13. A baggage handler at an airport earns $14.00/h for the first 40 h worked in a week. For each extra hour, the handler gets 1.5 times as much. What does the handler earn for working 50 h in a week?

14. Volunteers raise money for charity by selling bags of peanuts. The nuts cost $220.00 and sell for $550.00. Four charities share the profit equally. How much does each one get?

15. Write a problem in which operations must be sequenced. Have a classmate solve your problem.

WORD POWER

Change the word SEE to the word FAR by changing one letter at a time. Each time you change a letter, you must form a real word. Write down all the words you form and compare with a classmate.

3.5 Lines: Intersecting, Perpendicular, and Parallel

The diagram shows the runways at Lester B. Pearson International Airport. Three pairs of runways are **intersecting**, which means that they cross each other. Two runways are **parallel**. This means that they would never cross each other, even if they went on forever.

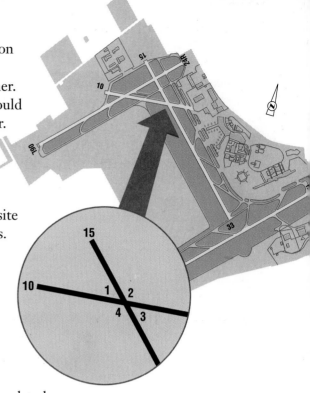

Activity: Investigate Intersecting Lines

Draw runways 10 and 15 as two intersecting lines, as shown. When two lines intersect, pairs of **opposite angles** are formed. ∠1 and ∠3 are opposite angles. So are ∠2 and ∠4. Measure the four angles.

Inquire

1. How are ∠1 and ∠3 related?

2. How are ∠2 and ∠4 related?

3. Draw two intersecting lines of your own. Measure and compare the opposite angles.

4. Compare your results with your classmates'.

5. Write a statement about how opposite angles are related.

6. Two lines that intersect at right angles are called **perpendicular** lines. Draw runways 06L and 15 as two perpendicular lines. What is the measure of the opposite angles?

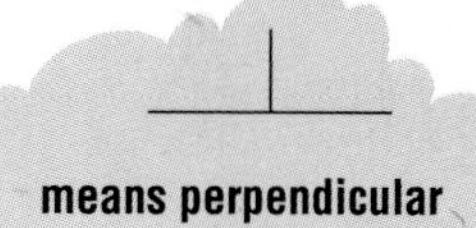

Activity: Investigate Parallel Lines

Draw the parallel lines by using both sides of a ruler. Draw the line that intersects both parallel lines. This line is called a **transversal**. Label the angles as shown. Measure the eight angles.

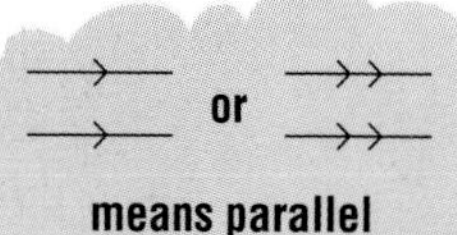

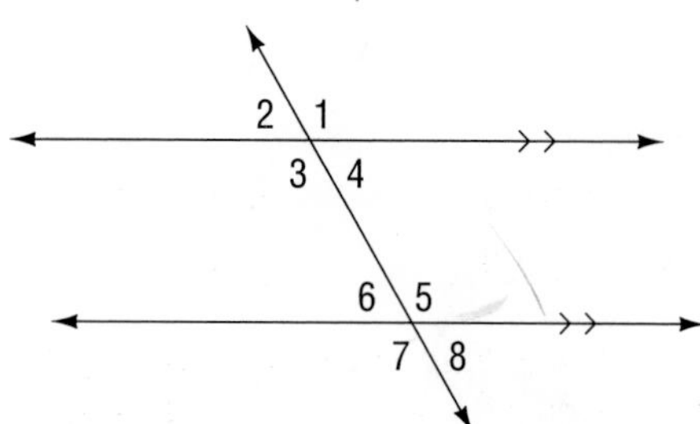

Inquire

1. How are angles 1, 3, 5, and 7 related?

2. How are angles 2, 4, 6, and 8 related?

3. What is the sum of angles 4 and 5?

4. What is the sum of angles 3 and 6?

5. Repeat the activity for two other parallel lines and a different transversal.

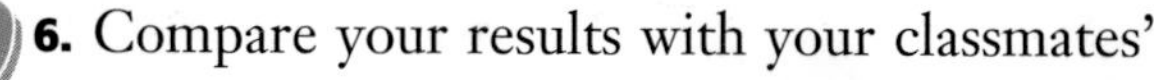

6. Compare your results with your classmates'.

7. Write a statement about how the angles are related when a transversal crosses two parallel lines.

Practice

Use the diagram to complete questions 1–3.

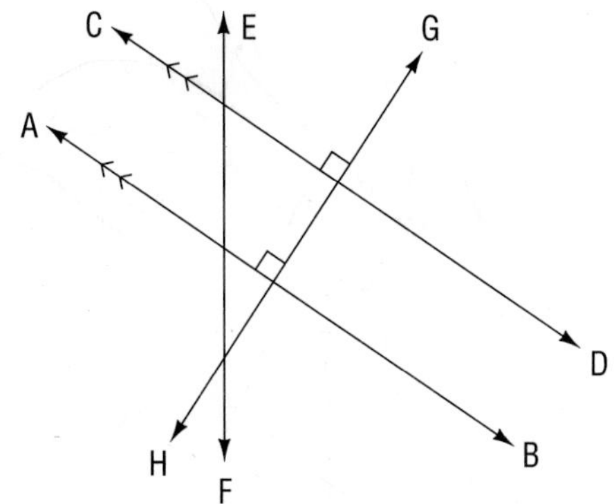

1. Name five pairs of intersecting lines.
2. Name two pairs of perpendicular lines.
3. Name one pair of parallel lines.

Use the following diagram to identify each pair of lines as intersecting, perpendicular, or parallel.

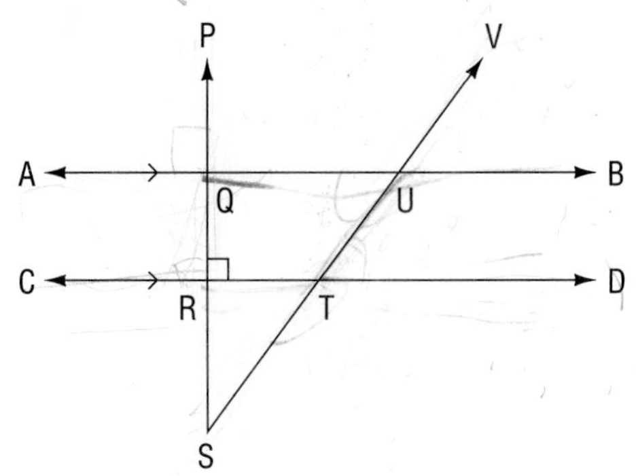

4. AB and PR
5. SP and SV
6. CD and SV
7. AB and CD
8. SP and CD
9. TV and AB

Use the same diagram as in questions 4–9 to state how the following angle measures are related.

10. ∠VUB and ∠QUT
11. ∠VUB and ∠UTD
12. ∠STD and ∠TUB
13. ∠RTU and ∠STD
14. ∠UTD and ∠TUB
15. ∠CRQ and ∠TRQ
16. ∠CRQ and ∠SRT
17. ∠PQB and ∠QRD

Problems and Applications

Determine angle measures x, y, and z.

18.

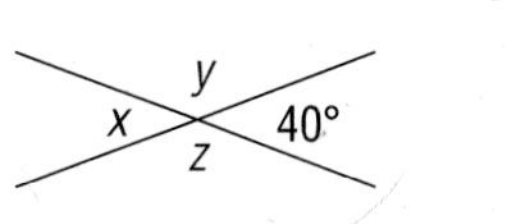

19.

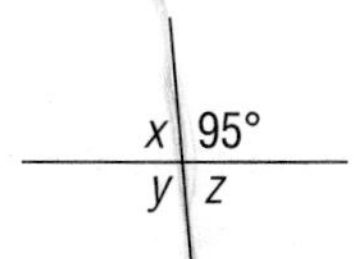

Determine angle measures w, x, y, and z.

20.

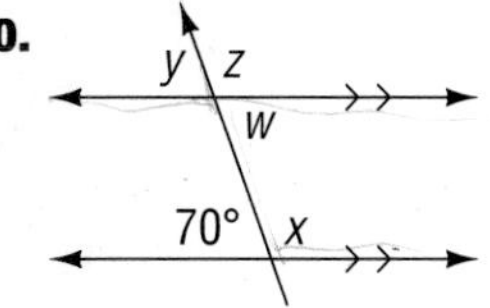

21.

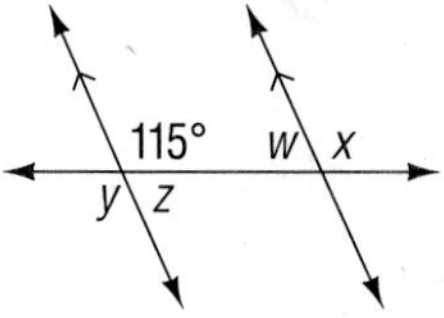

22. Are two lines that are both perpendicular to the same line always parallel to each other? Explain.

23. Trains travel along parallel rails. Sketch how the rails appear as you look along them into the distance. In your sketch, do the rails seem parallel? Explain.

Sketch 4 lines so that they intersect in the following number of points. Compare your sketches with a classmate's.

24. 0	**25.** 1	**26.** 3
27. 4	**28.** 5	**29.** 6

PATTERN POWER

The product 23 × 96 = 2208.
Reverse the digits: 32 × 69 = 2208.

a) Multiply 48 × 21 and the reversed digits.

b) Describe the pattern in the pairs of digits.

c) Find another pair of two-digit numbers with the same property.

Colouring Maps

How many colours do you need to colour the countries on a map? This problem has fascinated mathematicians and geographers for years.

To colour a map correctly, you must use different colours for any two countries that share a border.

Map 1 is coloured correctly. Map 2 is not, because countries A and B share a border and should have different colours.

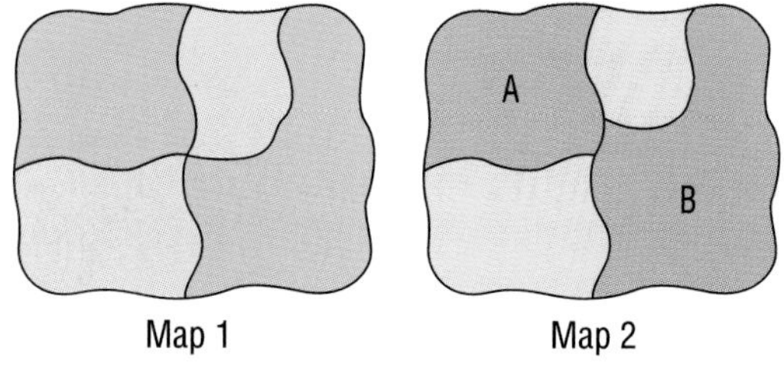

Map 1 Map 2

Activity ❶

1. Copy these straight line maps into your notebook.

2. Colour each map using as few colours as possible. Make sure that regions with shared borders have different colours.

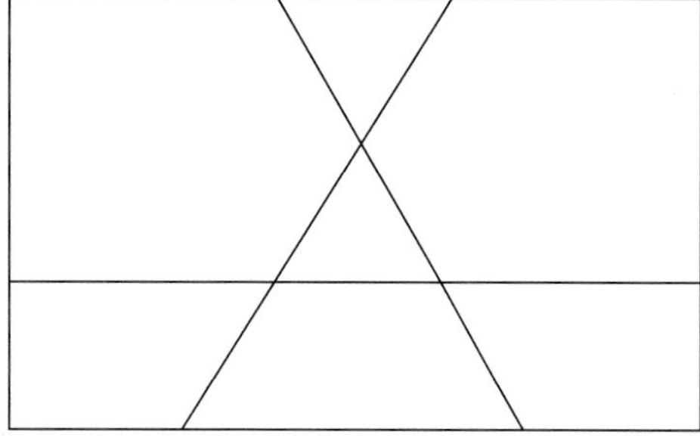

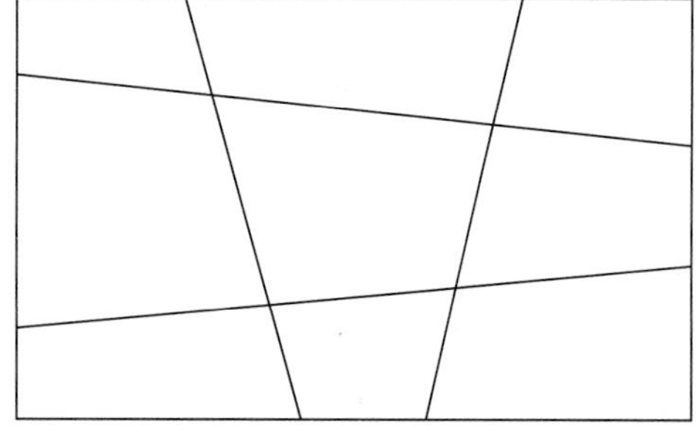

Activity ❷

1. Make up some straight line maps of your own and colour them with as few colours as possible.

2. If you use as few colours as possible, what is the greatest number of colours you ever need for a straight line map.

3. Compare your answer with your classmates'.

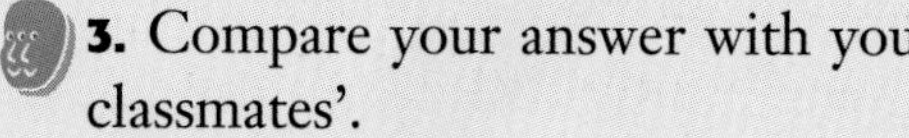

Activity ❸

1. Copy these maps into your notebook.

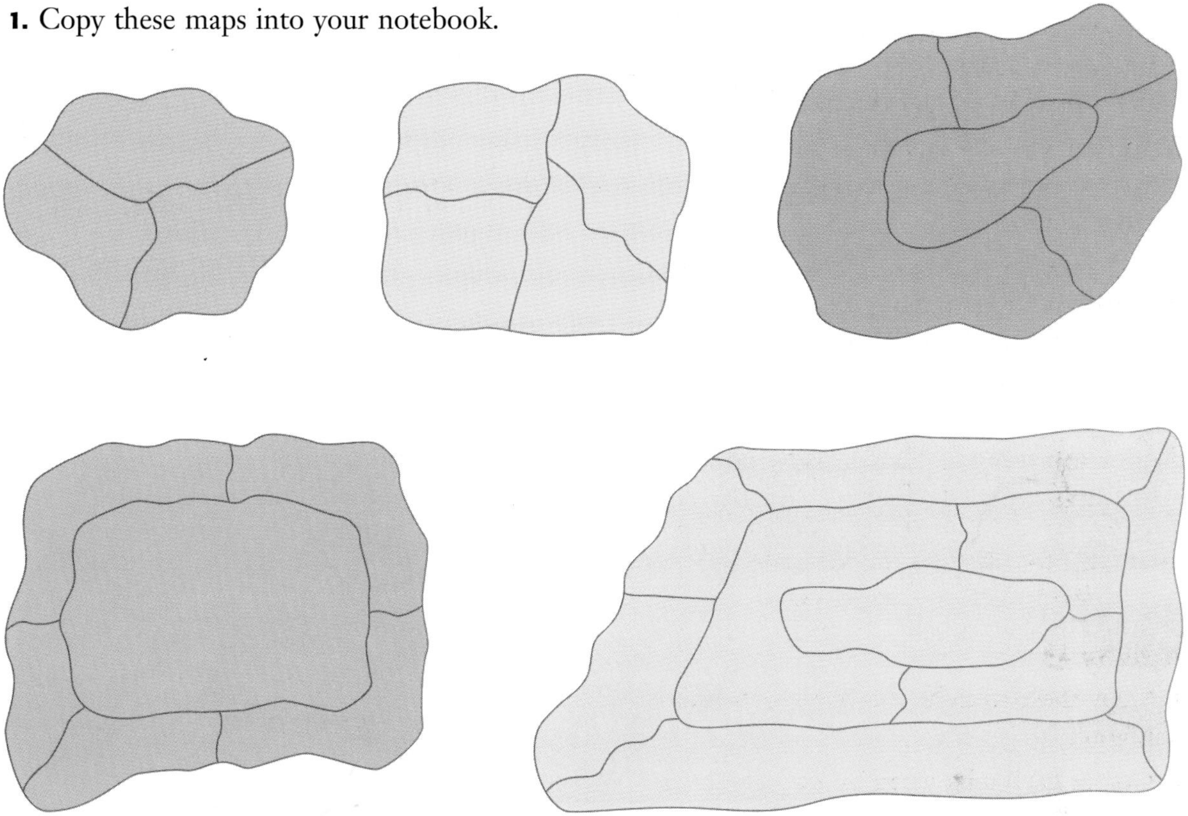

2. Colour each map using as few colours as possible. Make sure that regions that share borders have different colours.

3. What do you think is the smallest number of colours needed to colour all the maps in an atlas?

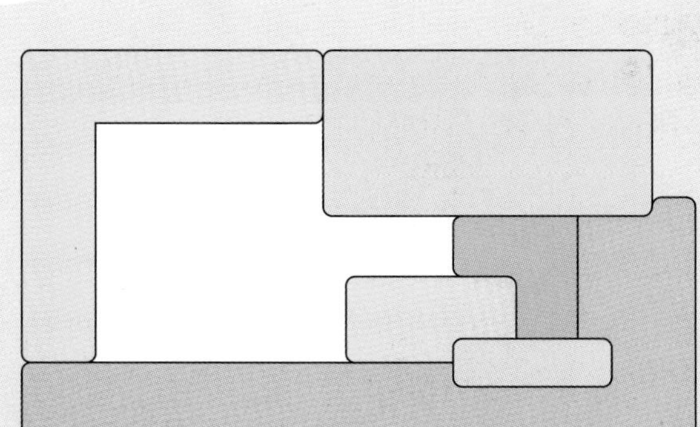

Activity ❹

One area of this map has not been coloured. Four colours have already been used, and it seems that we need a fifth colour to complete the map.

1. Copy the map into your notebook, but omit the present colours.

2. Colour the map with only four colours.

3. Compare your method with your classmates'.

3.6 Classifying Triangles

A triangle has three sides and three angles. The point where two sides meet is a **vertex**. The symbol △ replaces the word "triangle" in the name of the figure.

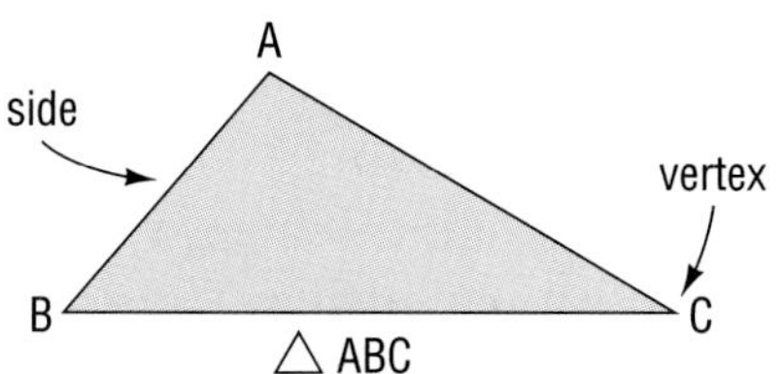

We classify triangles by the measures of their angles.

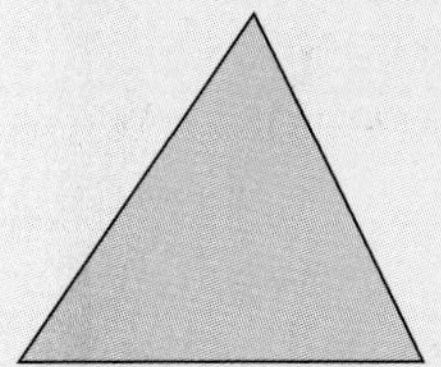

An **acute triangle** has three acute angles.

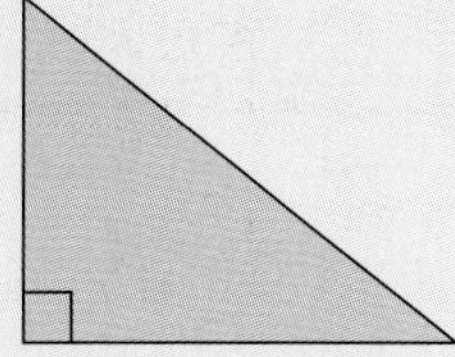

A **right triangle** has one right angle.

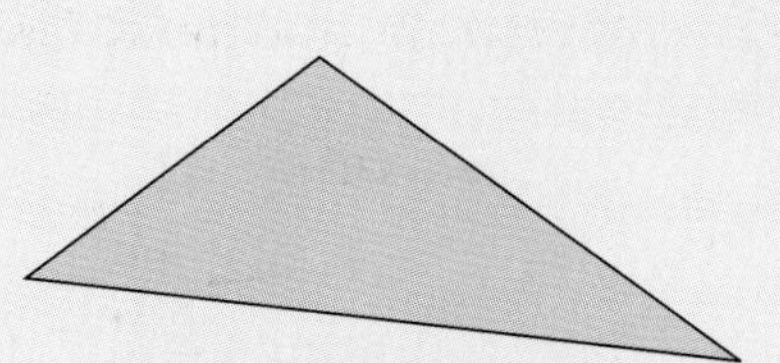

An **obtuse triangle** has one obtuse angle.

We also classify triangles by the lengths of their sides.

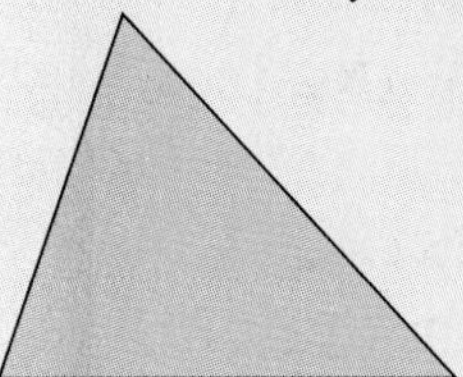

A **scalene triangle** has no sides of equal length.

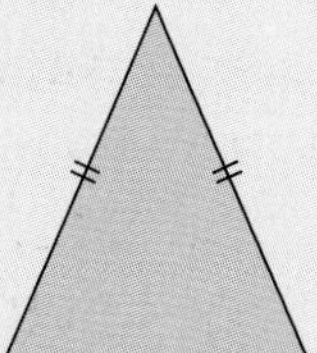

An **isosceles triangle** has two sides of equal length.

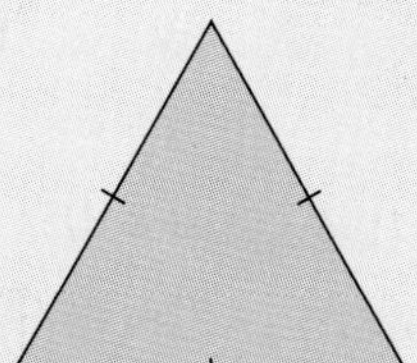

An **equilateral triangle** has three sides of equal length.

Activity: Use the Definitions

Look at the picture. It shows a power transmission tower.

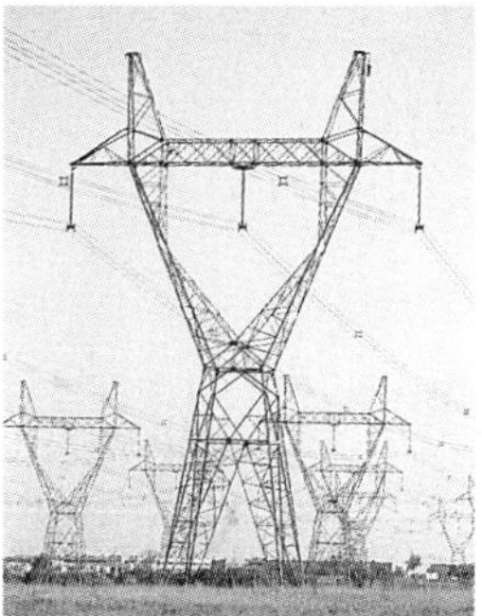

Inquire

1. List the types of triangles you see in the picture.

2. Copy the chart and try to draw an example of each triangle in each space.

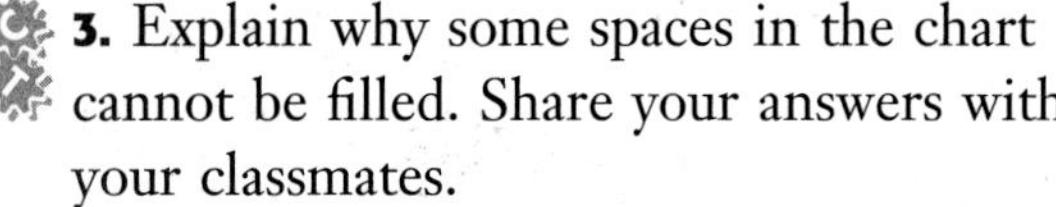

3. Explain why some spaces in the chart cannot be filled. Share your answers with your classmates.

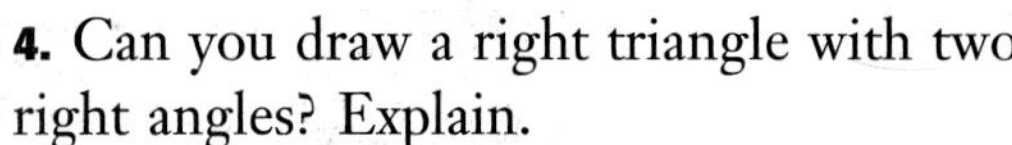

4. Can you draw a right triangle with two right angles? Explain.

	Scalene	Isosceles	Equilateral
Acute			
Right			
Obtuse			

Practice

Name all triangles in each diagram.

1.

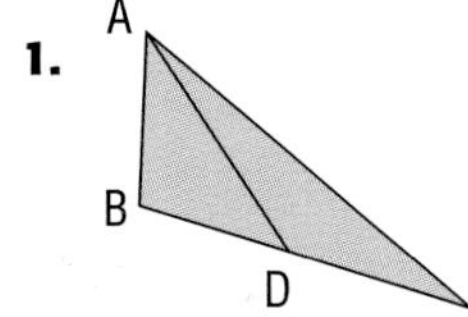

2.

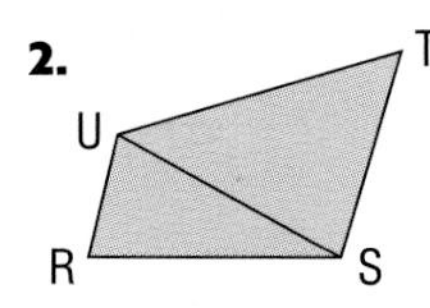

Classify each triangle as equilateral, isosceles, or scalene.

3.

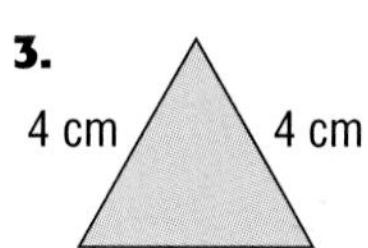

4.

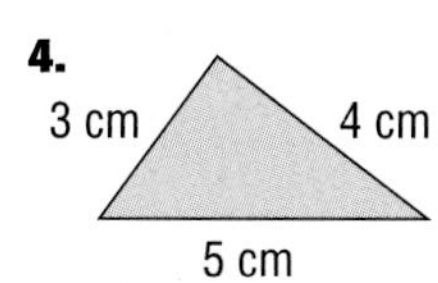

5.

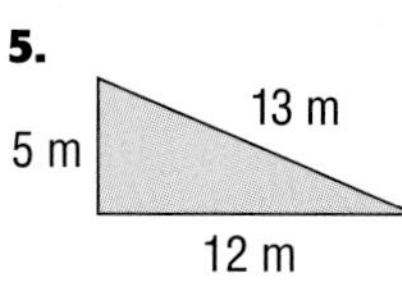

6.

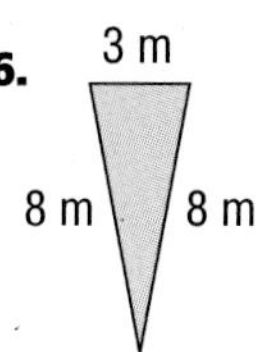

Classify each triangle as acute, right, or obtuse.

7.

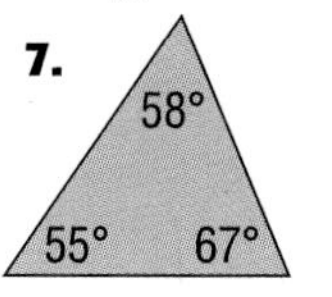

8.

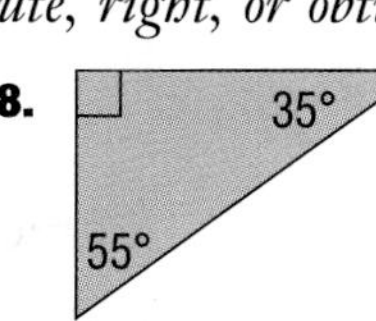

9.

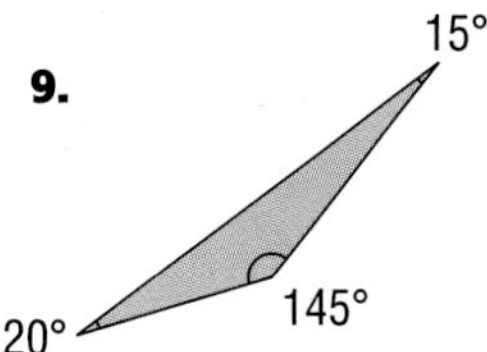

10.

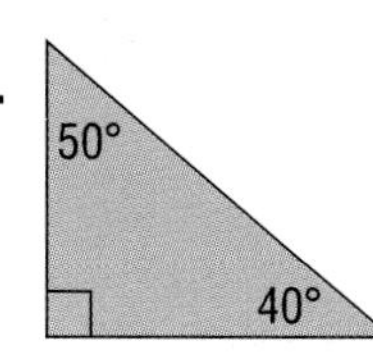

Classify each triangle in two ways.

11.

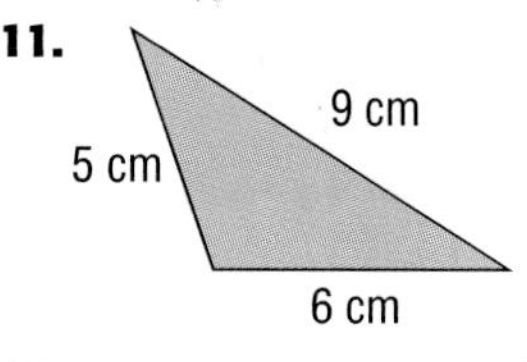

12.

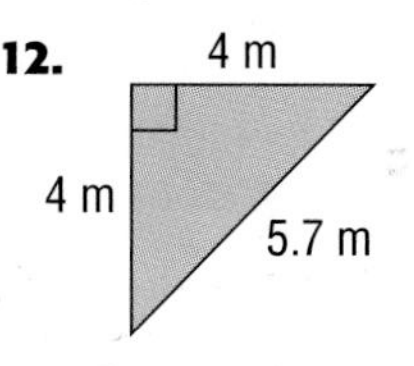

13.

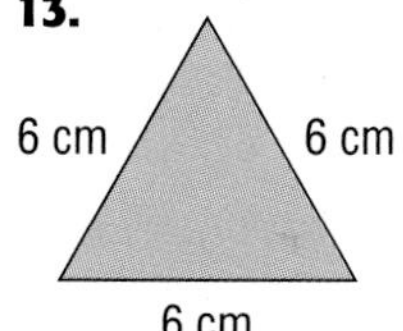

14.

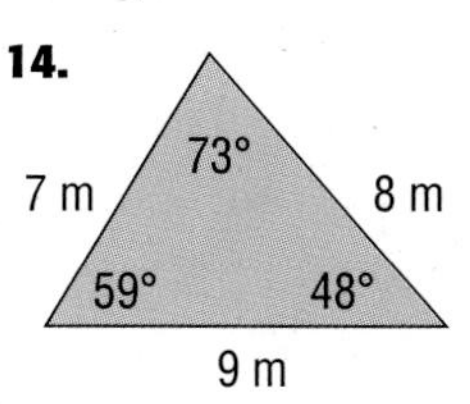

Problems and Applications

Use the diagram for each triangle in 15–18.

a) *Estimate the length of each side.*

b) *Measure each side.*

c) *Classify the triangle.*

15. **16.** **17.** **18.**

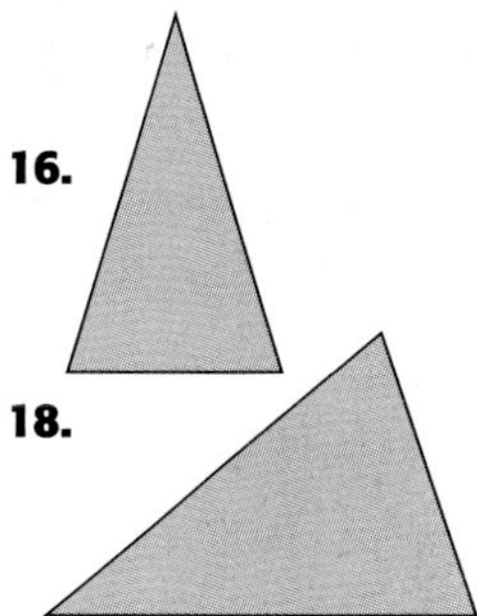

Complete a)–c) for each triangle in 19–22.

a) *Make a rough sketch.*

b) *Draw the triangle using a ruler and protractor.*

c) *Classify the triangle.*

19. $\triangle ABC$ with $\angle A = 90°$, AB = 10 cm, and AC = 10 cm.

20. $\triangle DEF$ with each side 11 cm.

21. $\triangle LMN$ with $\angle M = 90°$, LM = 6 cm, and MN = 8 cm.

22. $\triangle PQR$ with $\angle P = 55°$, PQ = 9 cm, and PR = 9 cm.

In questions 23–26, is each statement always true, sometimes true, or never true?

23. An acute triangle is scalene.

24. A right triangle is isosceles.

25. An obtuse triangle is isosceles.

26. A right triangle is obtuse.

27. The flag of Newfoundland and Labrador includes triangles. Look up the flags of other provinces and countries. Sketch the ones that include triangles. Classify the triangles.

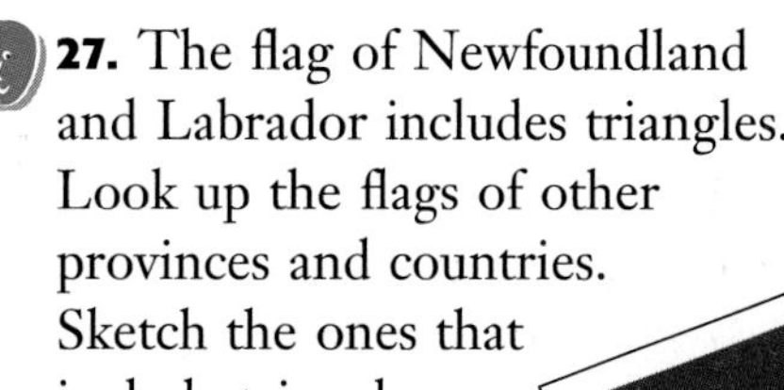

3.7 The Sum of the Interior Angles in a Triangle

Activity: Explore the Triangle

Draw an acute triangle on cardboard and cut it out.

Colour each angle a different colour.

Tear the angles off of the triangle and line them up as shown.

Inquire

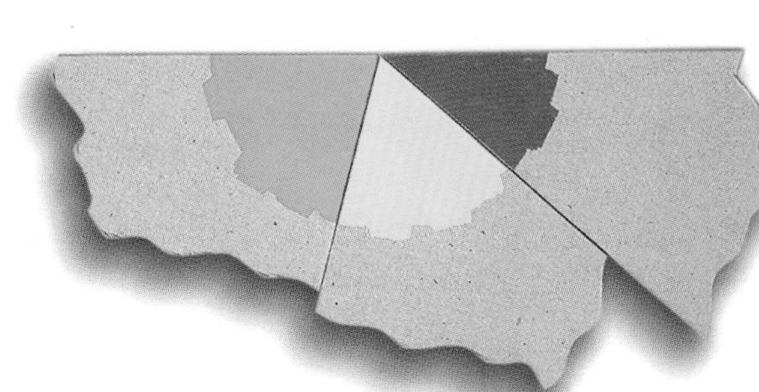

1. What kind of angle do the three angles make? What is the measure of this kind of angle?

2. Repeat the activity for an obtuse triangle.

3. Repeat the activity for a right triangle.

4. Draw four large triangles of different shapes. Measure the interior angles of each triangle and complete the chart.

Sketch of Triangle	∠A	∠B	∠C	Sum of the 3 Angles

5. Write a statement about the sum of the interior angles of a triangle.

If you know the measures of two angles in a triangle, you can calculate the measure of the third.

Example

Calculate the measure of ∠A.

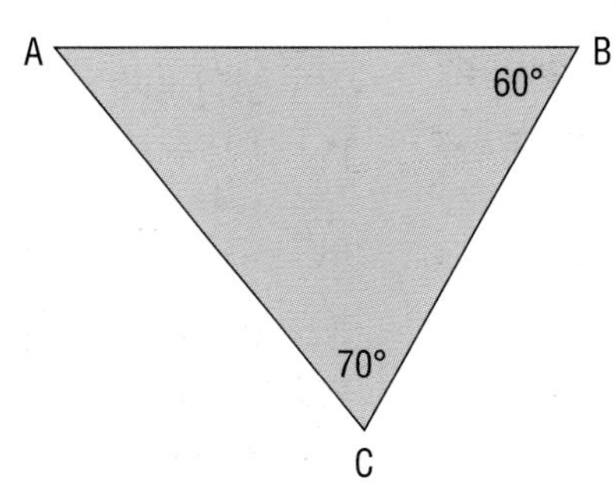

Solution

$$\angle A + \angle B + \angle C = 180^\circ$$
$$\angle A + 60^\circ + 70^\circ = 180^\circ$$
$$\angle A + 130^\circ = 180^\circ$$
$$\angle A = 50^\circ$$

Practice

Determine x.

1.

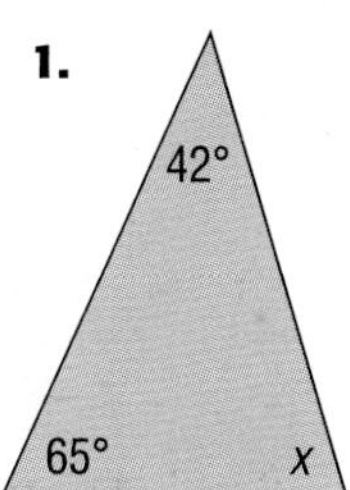

2.

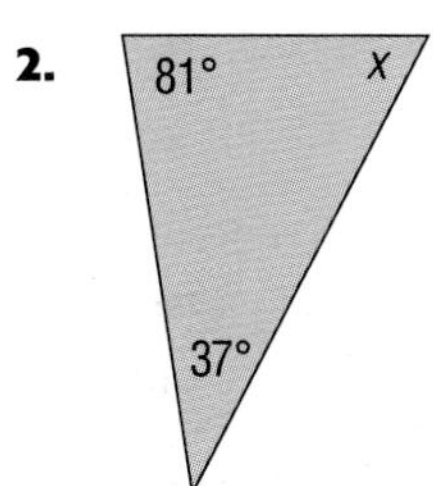

3.

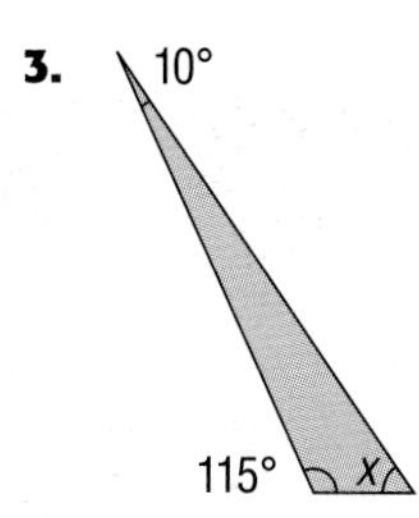

4.

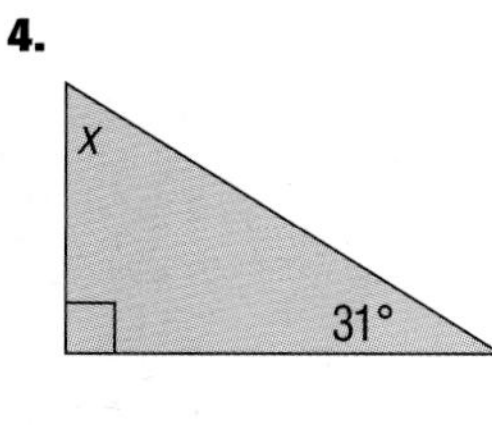

5. **6.**

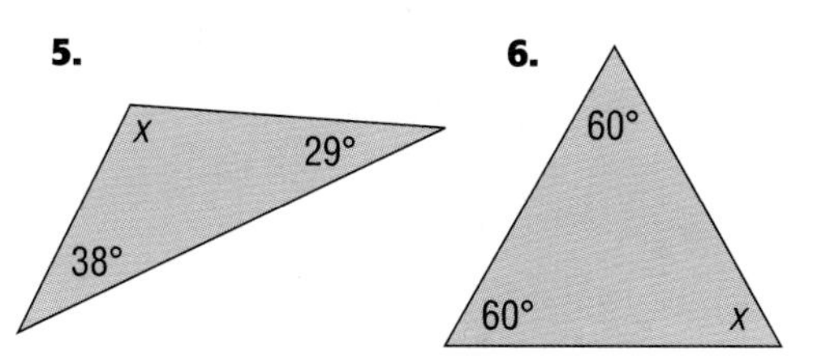

Problems and Applications

7. The measures of two angles in a triangle are 68° and 77°. Find the measure of the third angle.

8. What are the measures of the angles in an equilateral triangle?

9. One angle in a triangle is 56°. The other two angles are equal. Find their measures.

10. Explain why a right triangle must have two acute angles.

11. Explain why an obtuse triangle cannot have a right angle.

12. What is the smallest number of acute angles in any triangle? Explain.

13. You can draw one diagonal from one vertex in a quadrilateral (a four-sided figure).

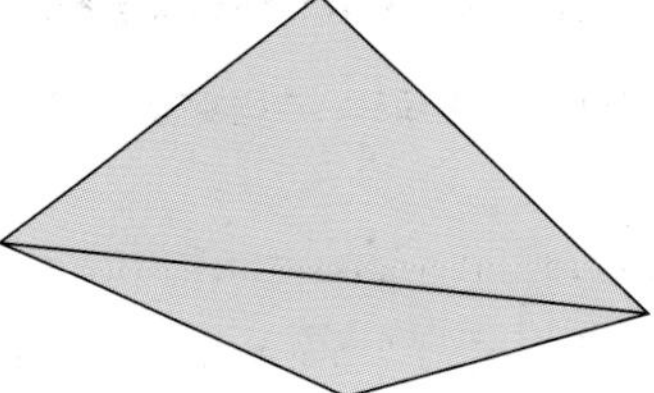

a) How many triangles are formed?
b) What is the sum of the angles in each triangle?
c) What is the sum of the angles of a quadrilateral?

14. a) How many diagonals can you draw from one vertex in a pentagon (a five-sided figure)?

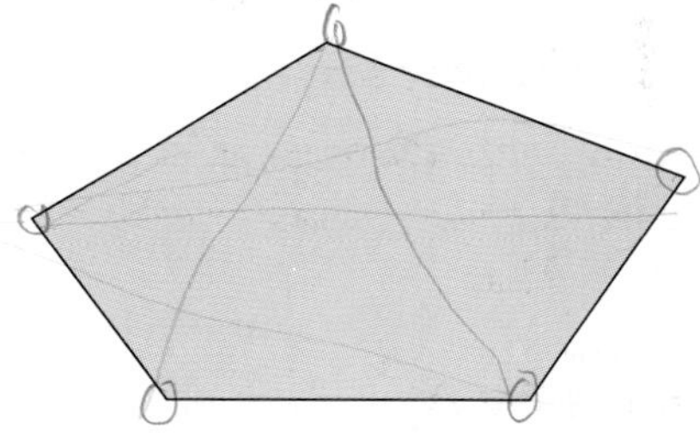

b) How many triangles are formed?
c) What is the sum of the angles of a pentagon?

15. a) How many diagonals can you draw from one vertex in a hexagon (a six-sided figure)?
b) How many triangles are formed?
c) What is the sum of the angles of a hexagon?

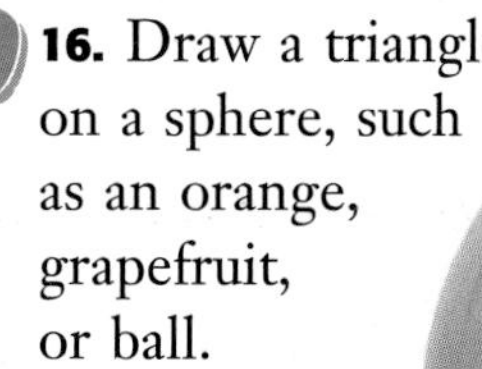

16. Draw a triangle on a sphere, such as an orange, grapefruit, or ball.

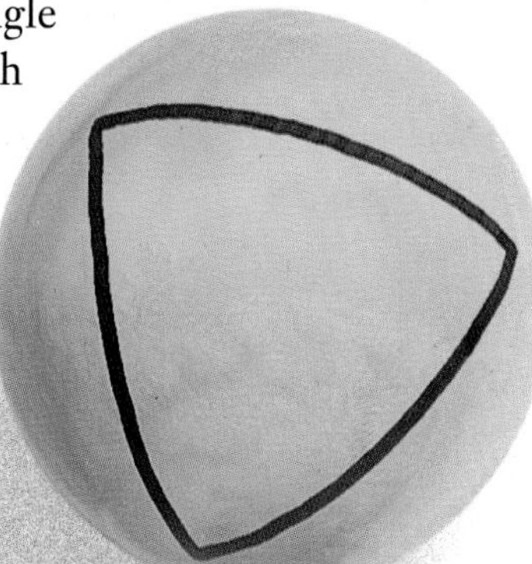

a) Measure the angles and find their sum.
b) Could you draw this triangle on a piece of paper? Explain.

3.8 Use a Table

Janos and Iris operate a food stall.

They offer a Soup and Sandwich Special on weekends.

One weekend, they charged $4.00 for each special and sold 300. Their receipts were $4.00 × 300 = $1200.

The next weekend, they dropped the price by 25¢ to $3.75. Their sales increased by 25 to 325.

In fact, every time they dropped the price by 25¢, sales went up by 25.

What should Janos and Iris charge for the special to get the greatest receipts?

Understand the Problem

1. What information are you given?
2. What are you asked to find?
3. Do you need an exact or an approximate answer?

Think of a Plan

Set up a table that shows the price of the special and the number sold over several weekends.

Use a calculator to find the receipts for each weekend.

Examine the table to find the price that gives the greatest receipts.

Carry Out the Plan

Price	Number Sold	Receipts
$4.00	300	$4.00 × 300 = $1200.00
$3.75	325	$3.75 × 325 = $1218.75
$3.50	350	$3.50 × 350 = $1225.00
$3.25	375	$3.25 × 375 = $1218.75
$3.00	400	$3.00 × 400 = $1200.00

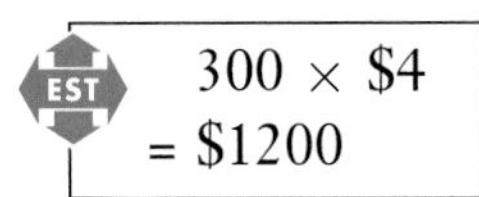

Look Back

The price of $3.50 for the special gives the greatest receipts, $1225.00. The receipts are close to the estimate of $1200.00. How could you use division to check your answer?

Use a Table

1. Organize the given information in a table.
2. Complete the table with the results of your calculations.
3. Find the answer from the table.
4. Check that your answer is reasonable.

Problems and Applications

Use the following table of top speeds on land to answer questions 1–5.

Animal	Top Speed (km/h)
Cheetah	110
Antelope	95
Jackrabbit	70
Ostrich	50
Human	45

1. Name the fastest animal in the table.

2. How many animals in the table are faster than humans?

3. Which animals can run more than twice as fast as humans?

4. Which animals can run more than twice as fast as an ostrich?

5. How much faster than an antelope is a cheetah?

Use the following table to answer questions 6–9. It shows the average growth pattern for North American males from birth to when they are full grown.

Age (years)	Average Height (cm)
0 (birth)	51
2	88
4	103
8	130
12	150
16	173
18	176

6. Determine whether the increase in height is the same from ages 4 to 8 as it is from ages 8 to 12.

7. At what age is the height half of the full-grown height?

8. Between what ages is growth fastest?

9. Between what ages is growth slowest?

10. In a summer at the beach, Jeanine expects to sell 1200 bags of shells at $2.00 per bag. She expects to sell an extra 200 bags each time she lowers the price by 20¢. What should she charge per bag to get the greatest receipts?

11. A company uses two machines to make the boards and wheels for skateboards. One machine makes 32 boards in 1 h. The other makes 160 wheels in 1 h. The board machine is turned on 2 h before the wheel machine. How many hours after the board machine starts will there be 4 wheels for every board?

12. Gary walks 6 km in 1 h. Allain walks 8 km in 1 h. Allain starts 2 h after Gary and walks along the same trail in the same direction. For how long will Allain walk before catching up to Gary?

13. Write a problem whose solution includes the following values. Have a classmate solve your problem.

Price	Number Sold
$20.00	120
$22.00	110
$24.00	100
$26.00	90

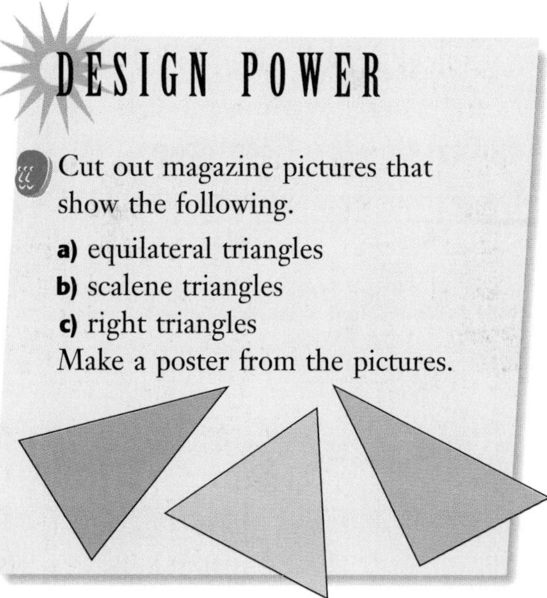

DESIGN POWER

Cut out magazine pictures that show the following.

a) equilateral triangles
b) scalene triangles
c) right triangles

Make a poster from the pictures.

3.9 Polygons

A **polygon**, is a closed figure formed by 3 or more line segments.

We name polygons according to the number of sides they have.

Sides	Name of Polygon
3	Triangle
4	Quadrilateral
5	Pentagon
6	Hexagon
7	Heptagon
8	Octagon
9	Nonagon
10	Decagon

In a **regular polygon**, all sides and all angles are equal.

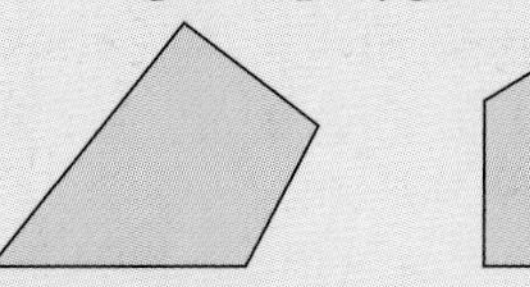
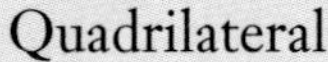
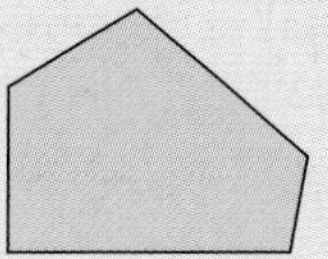
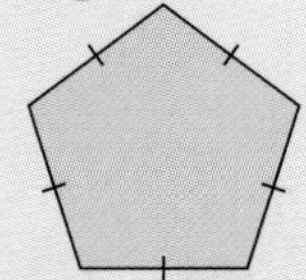
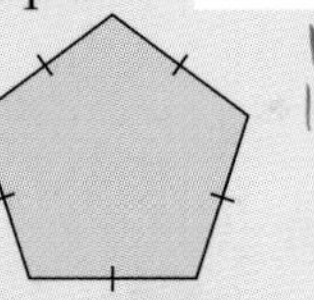
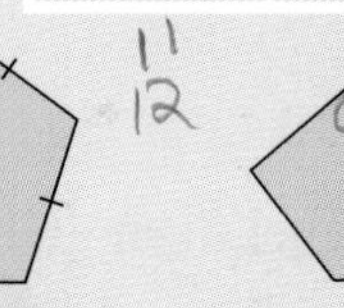

Quadrilateral Pentagon Regular Pentagon Hexagon

Some quadrilaterals have special names.

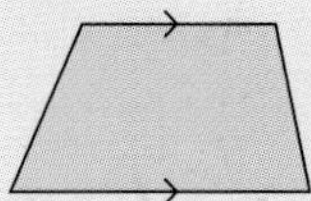
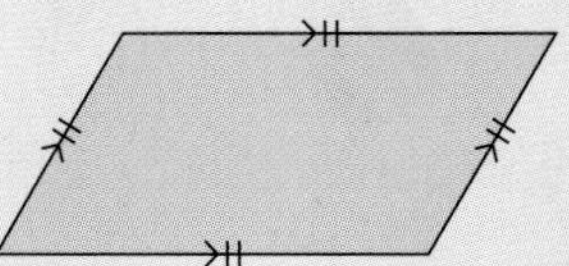

A **trapezoid** is a quadrilateral with exactly two parallel sides.

A **parallelogram** is a quadrilateral with opposite sides parallel and equal in length.

Some parallelograms have special names.

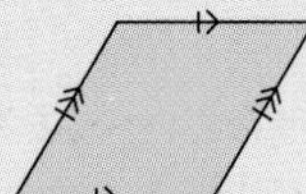
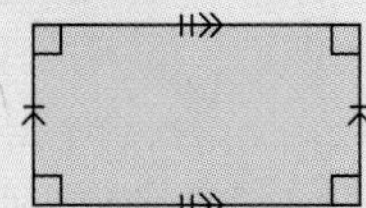
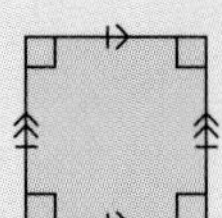

A **rhombus** is a parallelogram with 4 equal sides.

A **rectangle** is a parallelogram with 4 right angles.

A **square** is a parallelogram with 4 right angles and 4 equal sides.

Activity: Use the Definitions

Look at the picture. It shows the National Gallery of Canada.

Inquire

1. List the types of polygons you see in the picture.
2. What is another name for a regular quadrilateral?
3. Is every square a rhombus? Explain.
4. Is a rhombus a regular polygon? Explain.
5. Is a rectangle a trapezoid? Explain.
6. Is every parallelogram a rectangle? Explain.
7. Is every rectangle a parallelogram? Explain.

Practice

Is each figure a quadrilateral? If not, explain why not.

1. 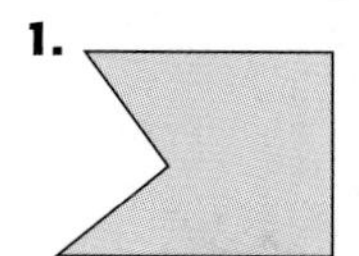 **2.** 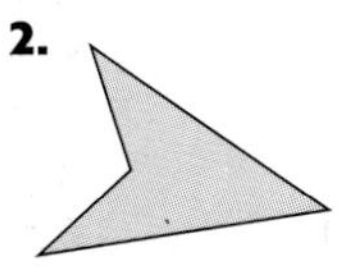 **3.** 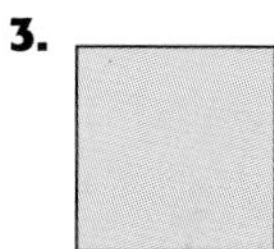

4. 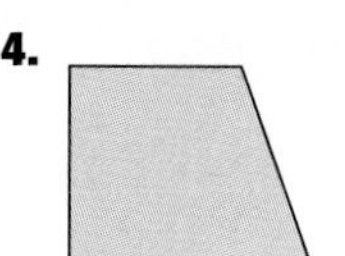 **5.** 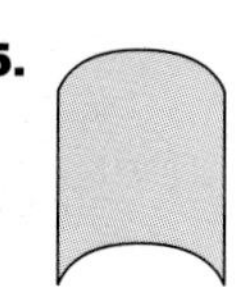 **6.** 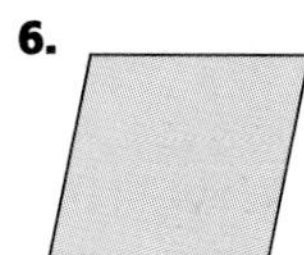

Name each of the following polygons and state whether it is regular or not.

7. 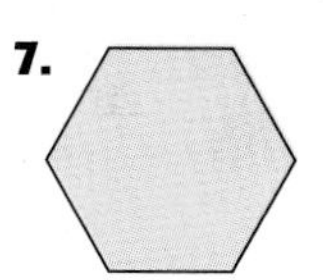 **8.** 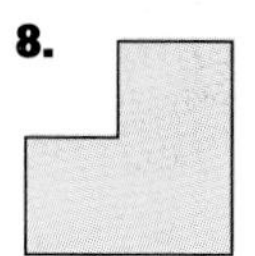 **9.** 

10. 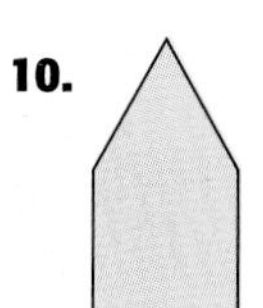 **11.** 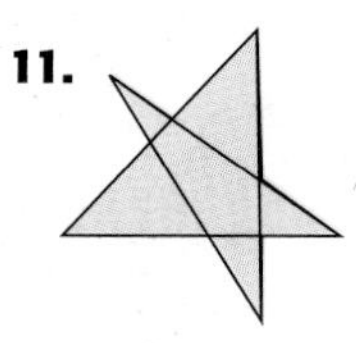 **12.** 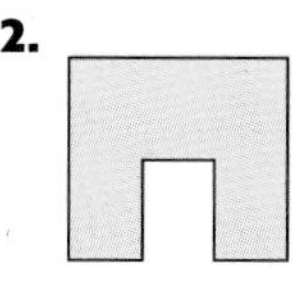

Problems and Applications

Identify the polygons in the signs.

13. 

14. 

15. 

16. 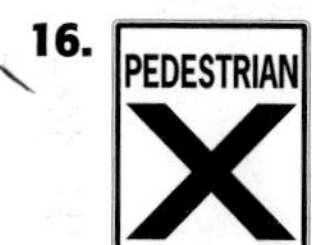

17. 

18. 

Identify the regular polygons in the symbols.

19. **20.** 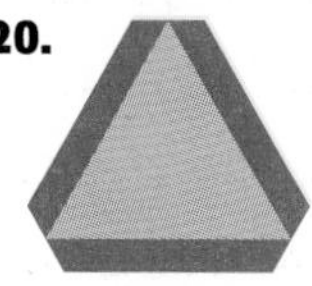 **21.** 

22. If a regular pentagon has the same perimeter as a regular decagon, which figure has the longer sides? Explain.

23. A diagonal joins two vertices in a polygon. A quadrilateral has two diagonals.

Polygon	Sides	Diagonals
Triangle	3	0
Quadrilateral	4	2
Pentagon		
Hexagon		
Heptagon		
Octagon		

a) Copy and complete the chart.

b) What is the pattern?

c) How many diagonals does a decagon have?

d) How many diagonals does a hendecagon (11 sides) have?

e) How many diagonals does a dodecagon (12 sides) have?

In questions 24–27, decide if each statement is always true, sometimes true, or never true.

24. A polygon with equal sides is regular.

25. A parallelogram is a rhombus.

26. A decagon has twice as many sides as a pentagon.

27. A parallelogram is a trapezoid.

28. List the polygons in your classroom and where you see them. Compare your list with a classmate's.

PATTERN POWER

How many different-sized squares can you make on a 5 by 5 geoboard?

Making Tracks with LOGO

In the LOGO computer program, a turtle draws on the screen.

Here are some LOGO commands:

Command	What the turtle does
FD	Moves forward
FD 40	Moves forward 40 units
BK	Moves backward
RT	Turns right a number of degrees
RT 90	Turns right 90°
LT	Turns left a number of degrees
PU	Does not draw a line (Pen Up)
PD	Draws a line (Pen Down)
HOME	Goes to the centre of the screen

For the turtle to draw the picture you want, the commands must be in the right order.

This program draws a square whose sides are 60 units long.

```
TO SQUARE
FD 60
RT 90
FD 60
RT 90
FD 60
RT 90
FD 60
RT 90
END
```

This command puts the turtle back where it started. (points to the final RT 90)

In the program above, the commands
FD 60 and **RT 90**
were repeated 4 times.

We could have used LOGO's repeat command instead.

```
TO SQUARE
REPEAT 4[FD 60 RT 90]
END
```

REPEAT 4 tells the computer to repeat the instructions in the brackets 4 times.

To save this program, hold down the Ctrl key and the C key.

The computer will answer with **SQUARE DEFINED**.

Now, when you enter the command **SQUARE**,
the computer draws your square.

Activity ❶

Draw what the turtle will draw with these commands. Use 1 cm for every 10 turtle units.

1. FD 70
   LT 90
   FD 90
   LT 90
   FD 70
   LT 90
   FD 90
   LT 90
   END

2. RT 60
   FD 80
   RT 120
   FD 80
   RT 120
   FD 80
   RT 60
   END

3. RT 60
   FD 50
   RT 30
   FD 80
   RT 150
   FD 50
   RT 30
   FD 80
   RT 90
   END

Activity ❷

Draw what the turtle will draw with these commands. Use 1 cm for every 10 turtle units.

1. REPEAT 4[FD 50 LT 90]
2. REPEAT 3[FD 60 RT 120]
3. REPEAT 6[FD 70 LT 60]
4. REPEAT 5[FD 80 RT 72]
5. REPEAT 8[FD 70 LT 45]
6. REPEAT 10[FD 50 LT 36]

Activity ❸

Write a program to draw each of the following figures.

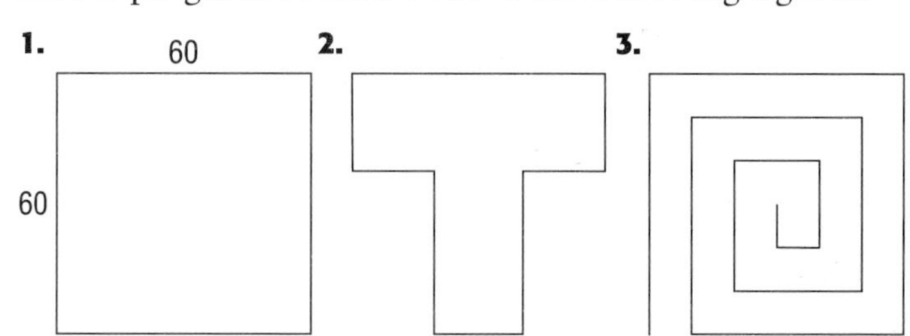

Activity ❹

Draw your own figure, then work out the program that draws it.

3.10 Congruent Figures

The two red rectangles on the Canadian flag are identical. They are examples of **congruent figures**. They have the same size and shape.

Activity: Use Tracing Paper

Trace each triangle on the left. Use your tracings to find a triangle on the right that is congruent to each triangle on the left.

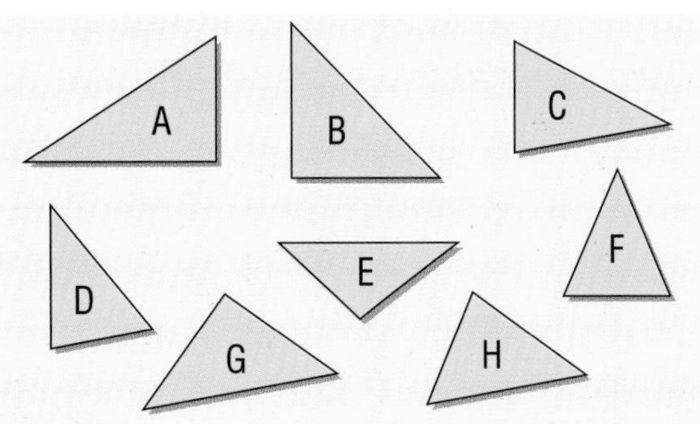

Inquire

1. Which pairs of triangles are congruent?

2. Are all equilateral triangles congruent? Explain.
3. Can an obtuse triangle and a right triangle be congruent? Explain.
4. Are two squares with equal sides congruent? Explain.

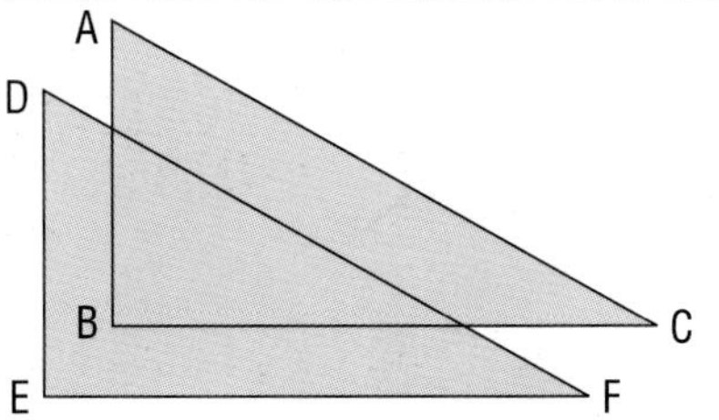

Look at the triangles to the right. A tracing of △ABC fits exactly on △DEF. △ABC has exactly the same size and shape as △DEF. So △ABC is congruent to △DEF.

The **corresponding parts** of congruent figures are equal. We use marks on the figures to show the sides of equal length and the angles of equal measure.

Example

List and mark the corresponding parts in △ABC and △DEF.

Solution

Sides: AB = DE
BC = EF
AC = DF

Angles: ∠A = ∠D
∠B = ∠E
∠C = ∠F

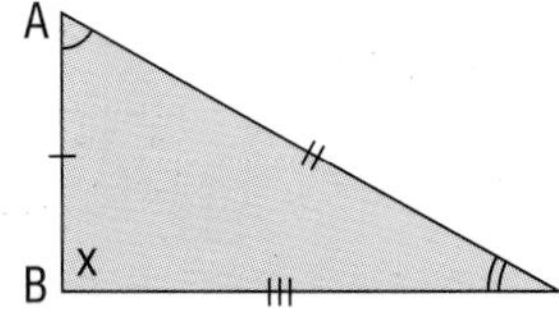

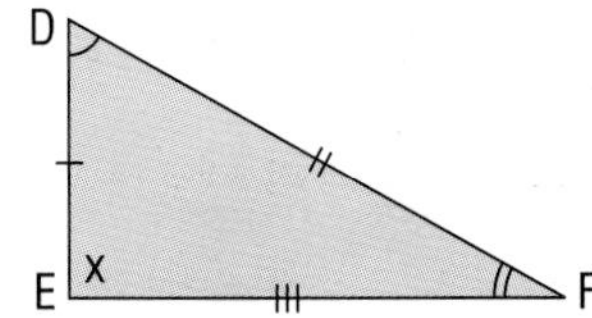

Practice

1. Identify the pairs of congruent triangles by tracing or measuring.

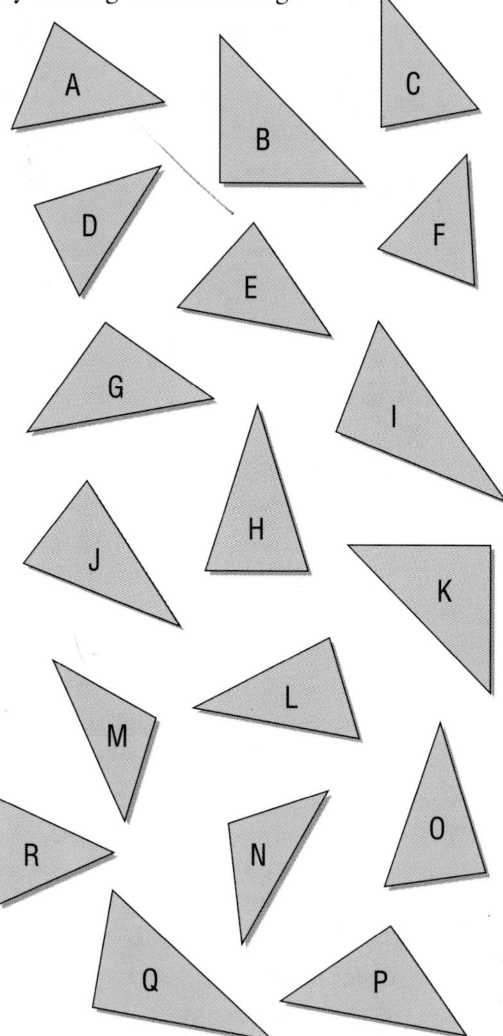

2. The triangles are congruent. Match the equal parts.

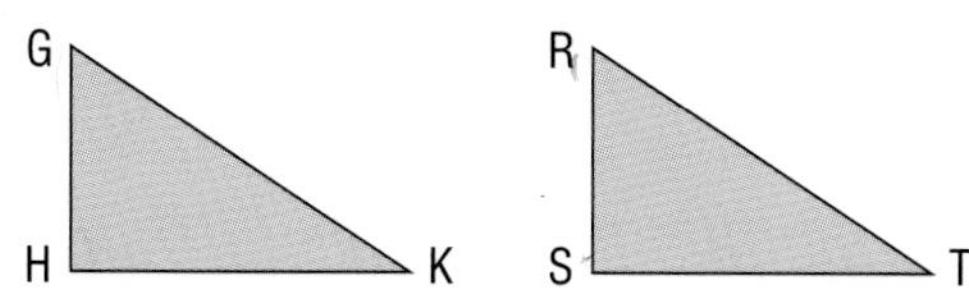

a) GH = ? **b)** HK = ? **c)** GK = ?

d) ∠G = ? **e)** ∠H = ? **f)** ∠K = ?

Problems and Applications

3. The triangles are congruent. Match the equal parts.

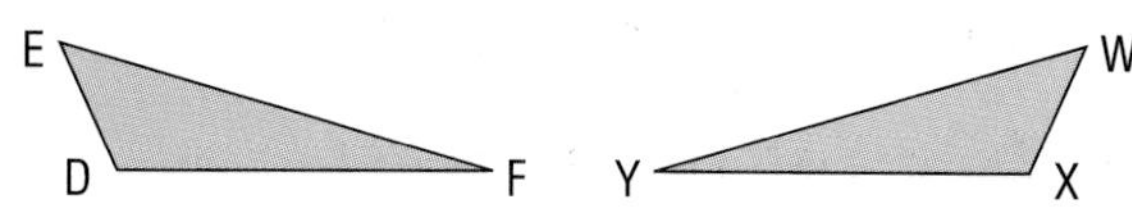

a) DF = ? **b)** WX = ? **c)** WY = ?

d) D = ? **e)** Y = ? **f)** W = ?

Name the corresponding parts of each pair of congruent figures.

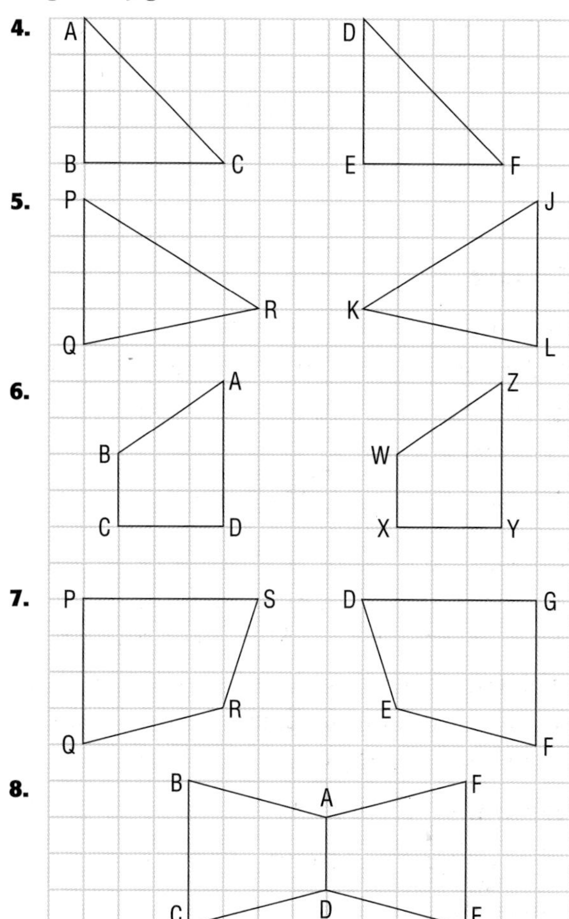

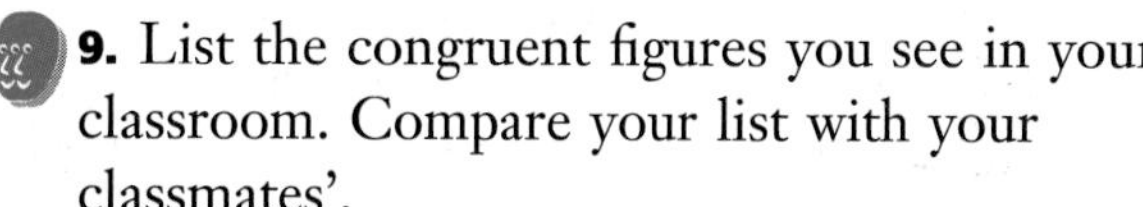

9. List the congruent figures you see in your classroom. Compare your list with your classmates'.

Lines of Symmetry

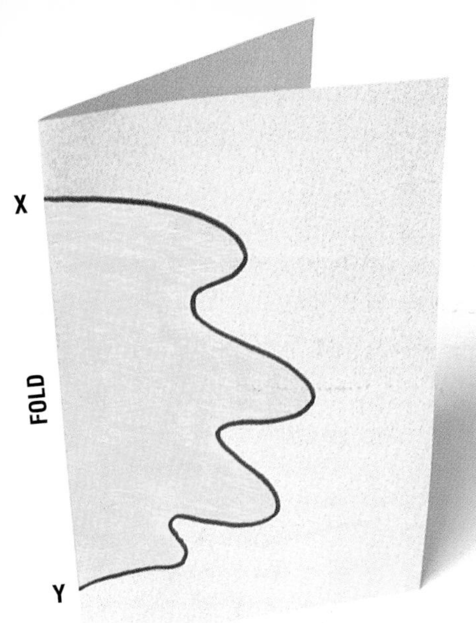

Activity ❶

1. Fold a piece of paper in half.
Draw the curved line from X to Y.
Cut along the curved line from X to Y.
Unfold the figure you cut out.

2. The fold line through the figure is called a **line of symmetry**. Describe what the line of symmetry does to the figure.

3. Repeat the activity by drawing a different line from X to Y on another sheet of paper. Does the line of symmetry do the same to this figure?

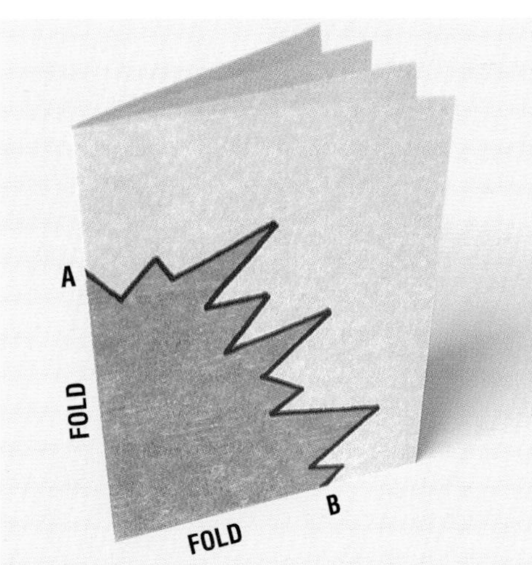

Activity ❷

1. Fold a piece of paper twice (into quarters).
Draw the jagged line from A to B.
Cut along the jagged line and unfold the figure.

2. How many lines of symmetry does this figure have?

3. Repeat the activity by drawing a different line from A to B on another sheet of paper. Do you see the same number of lines of symmetry?

Activity ❸

1. Fold a piece of paper three times, so that all the folds go through one point.
Draw the crooked line from P to Q.
Cut along the crooked line and unfold the figure.

2. How many lines of symmetry does this figure have?

3. Repeat the activity by drawing a different line from P to Q on another sheet of paper.
Do you see the same number of lines of symmetry?

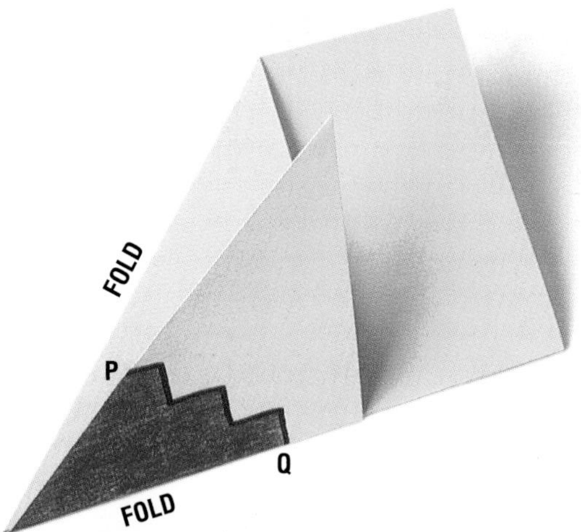

Activity ❹

If a triangle can be folded into two congruent parts, the fold line is a line of symmetry.

1. Draw a scalene, an isosceles, and an equilateral triangle as shown on the right.

2. Cut out each triangle.

3. Use folding or a MIRA to determine how many lines of symmetry each triangle has.

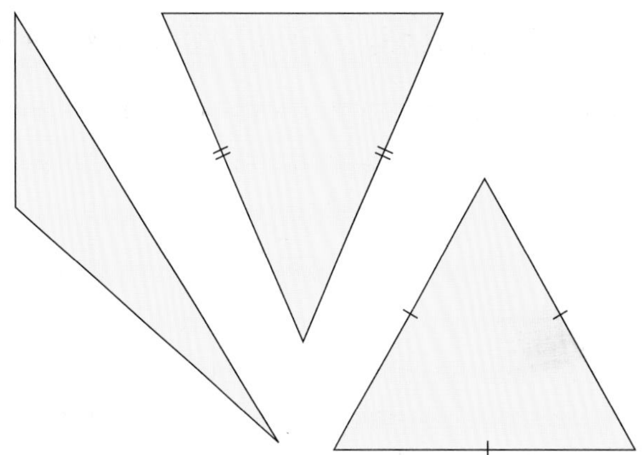

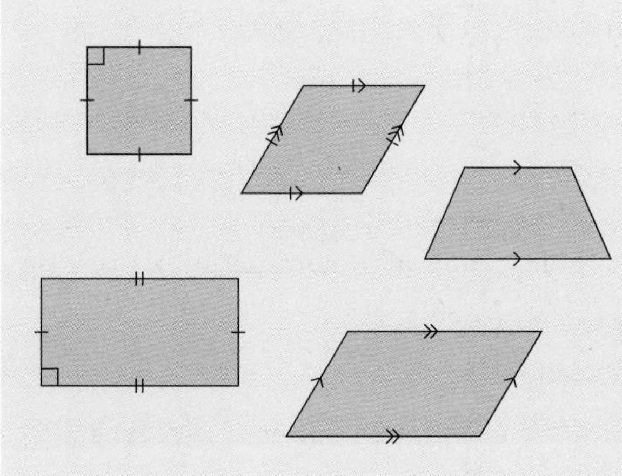

Activity ❺

If a quadrilateral can be folded into two congruent parts, the fold line is a line of symmetry.

1. Draw a square, a rectangle, a parallelogram, a trapezoid, and a rhombus as shown on the left.

2. Cut out each quadrilateral.

3. Use folding or a MIRA to determine how many lines of symmetry each quadrilateral has.

Activity ❻

How many lines of symmetry do you see in each of the following designs?

1. Canadian flag

2. Yield sign

3. Stop sign

Activity ❼

Make a poster of logos from magazine ads. Make sure that each logo has at least one line of symmetry.

3.11 Identify the Extra Information

A problem may contain more information than you need. In many cases, extra information is distracting. Decide what information you need and then eliminate the extra information.

At the beginning of 1992 there were 295 Members of Parliament (MPs) in the House of Commons in Ottawa. The table shows the number of MPs elected from each province or territory. How many MPs were elected from the Atlantic Provinces?

Province or Territory	Number of MPs	Province or Territory	Number of MPs
Alberta	26	Nova Scotia	11
British Columbia	32	Ontario	99
Manitoba	14	Prince Edward Island	4
New Brunswick	10	Quebec	75
Newfoundland and Labrador	7	Saskatchewan	14
Northwest Territories	2	Yukon	1

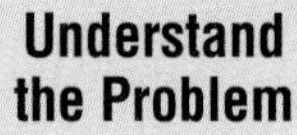

1. What information are you given?
2. What are you asked to find?
3. Do you need an exact or approximate answer?
4. What information is unnecessary?

Think of a Plan

The four Atlantic Provinces are New Brunswick, Newfoundland and Labrador, Nova Scotia, and Prince Edward Island.

We do not need the information about the other provinces or territories.

Add the numbers of MPs from the Atlantic Provinces.

Carry Out the Plan

Number of MPs = 10 + 7 + 11 + 4
= 32

So, 32 MPs are elected from the Atlantic Provinces.

Look Back

How could you use subtraction to check your answer?

Identify the Extra Information

1. List the given facts.
2. Decide which information is needed.
3. Eliminate the extra information.
4. Complete the calculation.
5. Check that your answer is reasonable.

Problems and Applications

Identify the extra information in questions 1–3. Do not solve each problem.

1. The four longest rivers in Canada are:

Mackenzie 4241 km	Yukon 3185 km
St. Lawrence 3058 km	Nelson 2575 km

How much longer is the Yukon than the Nelson?

2. In 1971, the population of Canada was 21 568 000. In 1981, it was 24 343 000. How many years apart were these population figures determined?

3. The areas of the largest lakes in Canada are:

Lake Superior	82 100 km^2
Lake Huron	59 600 km^2
Great Bear Lake	31 328 km^2
Great Slave Lake	28 568 km^2
Lake Erie	25 700 km^2
Lake Winnipeg	24 387 km^2
Lake Ontario	18 960 km^2

What is the total area of the lakes that lie on the Canadian border?

In questions 4–10, solve the problem.

4. It takes the planet Mercury 88 days to complete one revolution around the sun. The Earth takes 365.25 days. Mars takes 687 days. How many complete revolutions will Mercury make in the time that Mars takes for one revolution?

5. The tallest tree is a California redwood, which is 112 m high. The tallest Douglas fir is 92 m high. The tallest bamboo has a height of 37 m. How much taller than the Douglas fir is the California redwood?

6. The human body normally has a temperature of 37.0°C. The hummingbird's body temperature is 3.1°C higher, while the blue whale's body temperature is 1.5°C lower. What is the body temperature of the hummingbird?

7. A golf ball has a mass of 45.9 g. The mass of a baseball is from 141.7 g to 148.8 g. The mass of a softball is from 177.2 g to 198.4 g. A cloth bag has a mass of 8.5 g. What is the greatest possible mass of a cloth bag containing a golf ball, a baseball, and a softball?

8. The five largest islands in the world are:

Baffin Island	507 451 km^2
Borneo	728 260 km^2
Greenland	2 184 000 km^2
Madagascar	589 311 km^2
New Guinea	795 000 km^2

List the three largest islands from largest to smallest.

9. Canada is one of the least crowded countries. On average, there are only 2.8 people in every square kilometre. Hong Kong is 2000 times more crowded than Canada. Monaco is 5000 times more crowded than Canada. How many people are there for each square kilometre in Monaco?

10. The tallest office buildings in three Canadian cities are:

Calgary	Canada Trust Tower	216 m
Edmonton	Manulife Place	146 m
Vancouver	Royal Centre	140 m

How many times taller than the Royal Centre is the Canada Trust Tower? Round your answer to the nearest tenth.

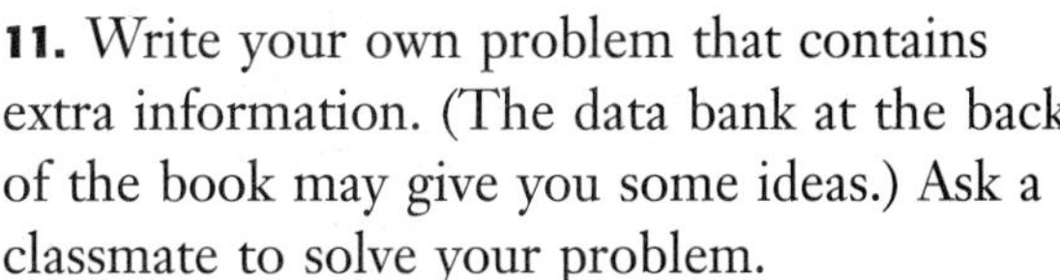

11. Write your own problem that contains extra information. (The data bank at the back of the book may give you some ideas.) Ask a classmate to solve your problem.

Review

Use the diagram to name the figures in questions 1–4.

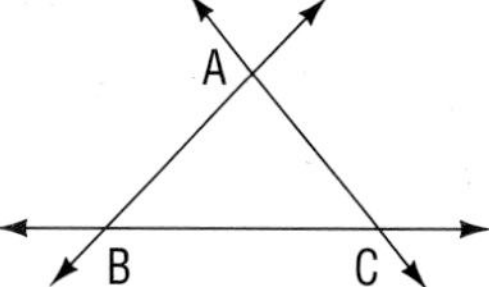

1. 3 lines **2.** 3 line segments

3. 6 rays **4.** 3 angles

Describe the difference between the following.

5. A line and a line segment

6. A line and a ray

Classify the following angles as acute, right, straight, obtuse, or reflex.

7.

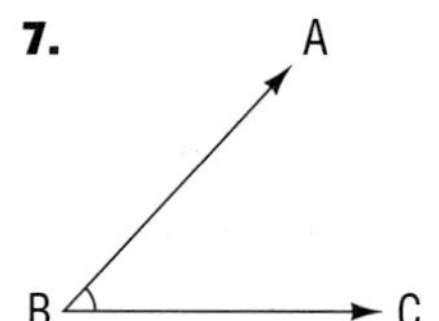

8.

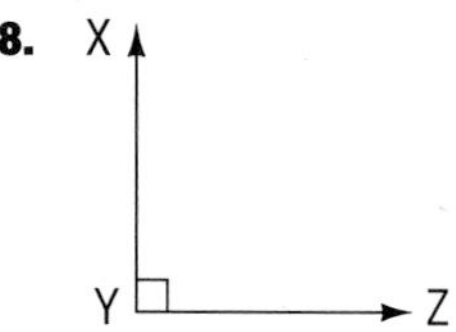

9.

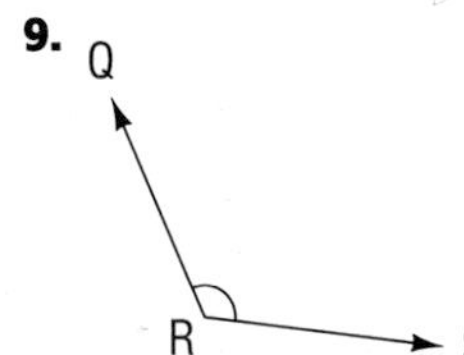

10.

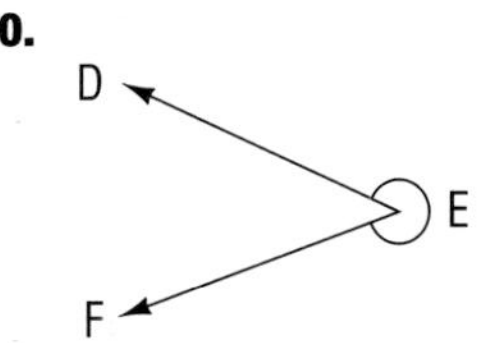

State the measure of each angle.

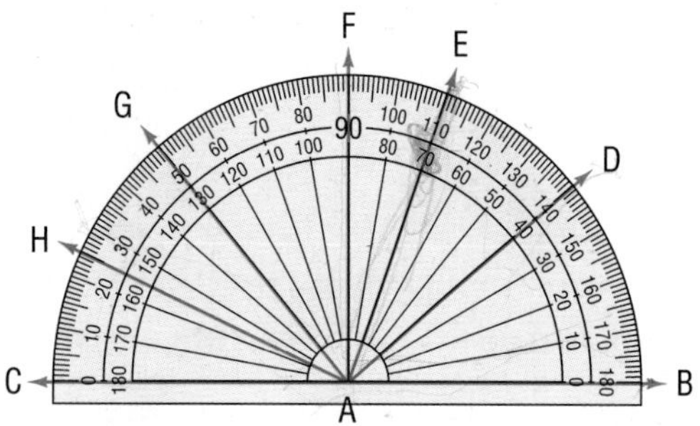

11. ∠HAC **12.** ∠DAB **13.** ∠EAB

14. ∠FAB **15.** ∠GAC **16.** ∠HAB

17. ∠DAC **18.** ∠GAB **19.** ∠EAC

Use a protractor to draw angles with the following measures.

20. 90° **21.** 35° **22.** 120° **23.** 64°

Find the missing angle measures.

24.

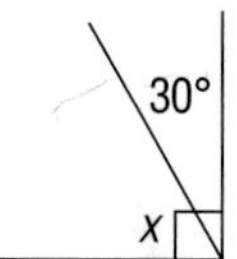

25.

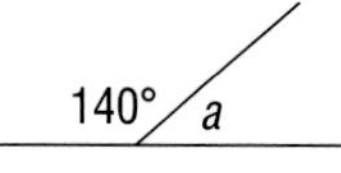

26.

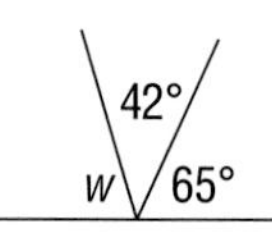

27.

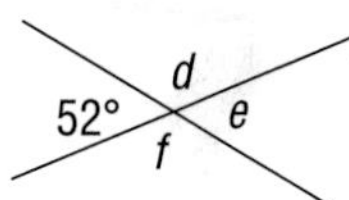

28.

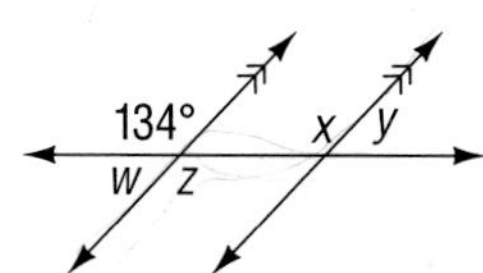

29.

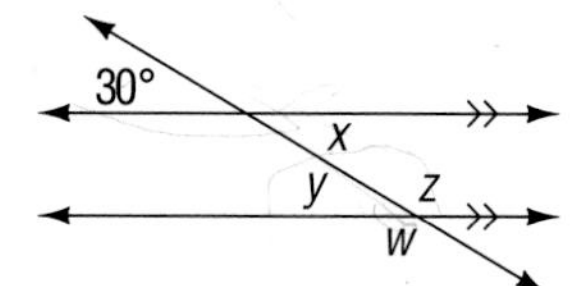

Classify each triangle as equilateral, isosceles, or scalene.

30.

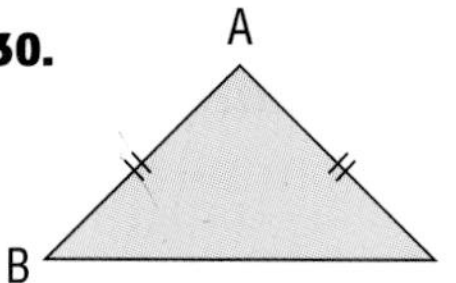

31.

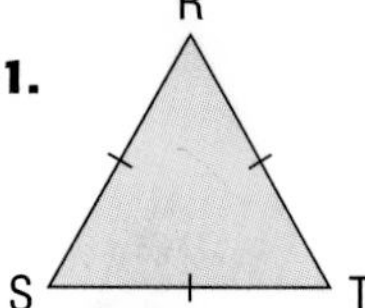

32.

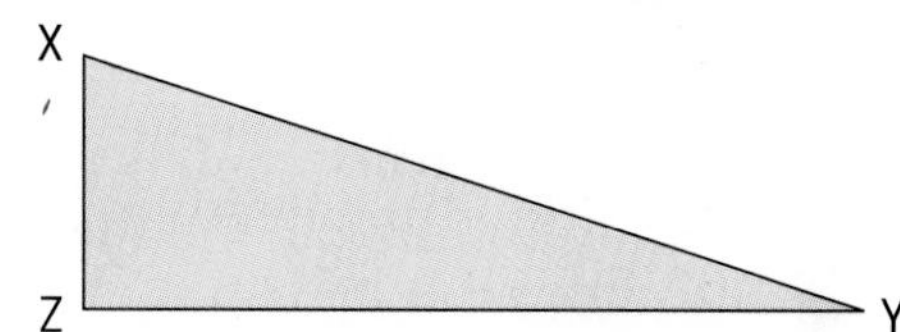

Name the following quadrilaterals.

33.

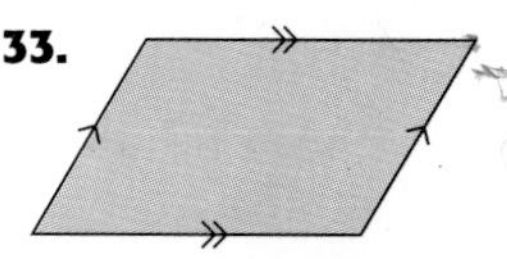
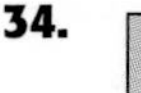

34.

35.

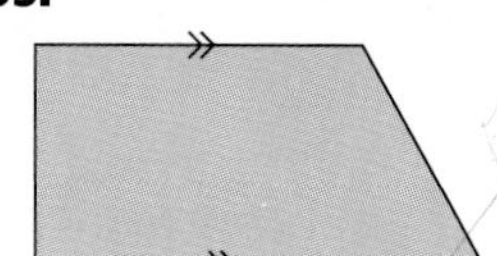

36.

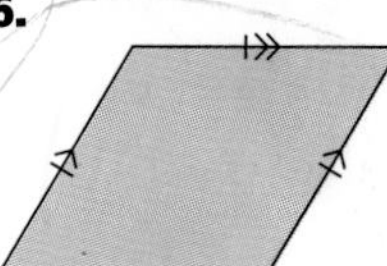

Name the polygons. State whether they are regular or not.

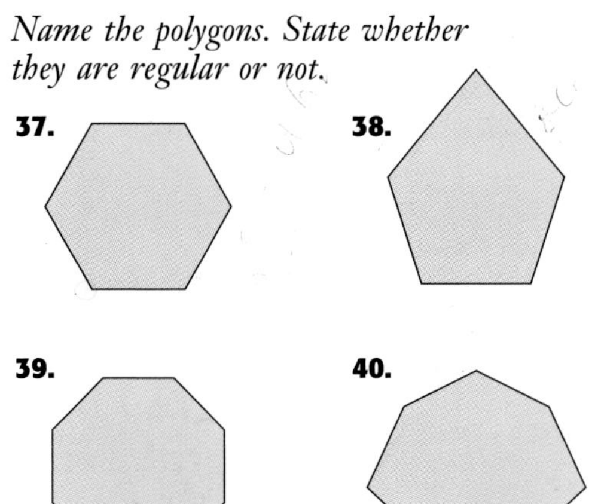

Find the missing angle measures.

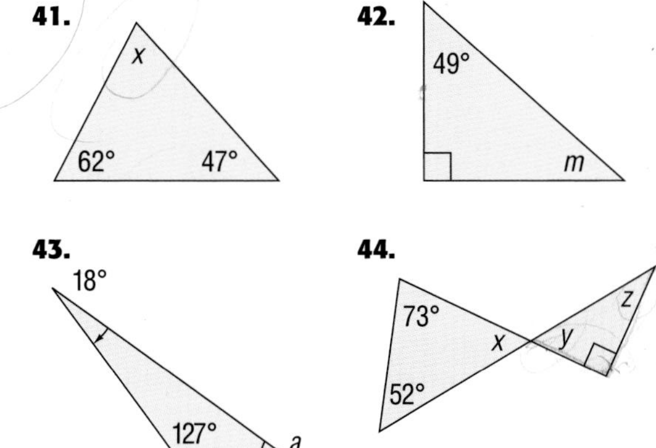

Name the corresponding parts of each pair of congruent triangles.

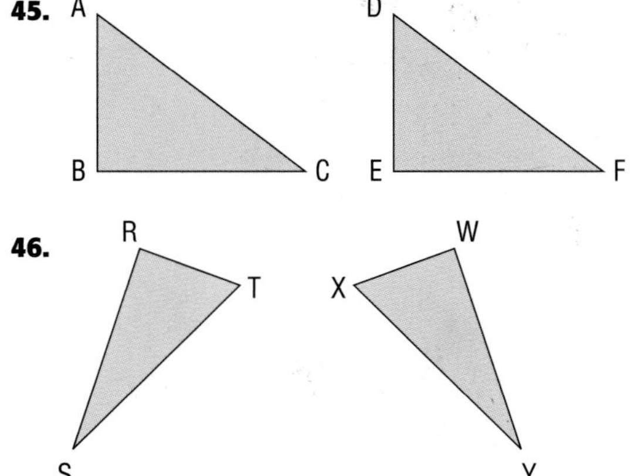

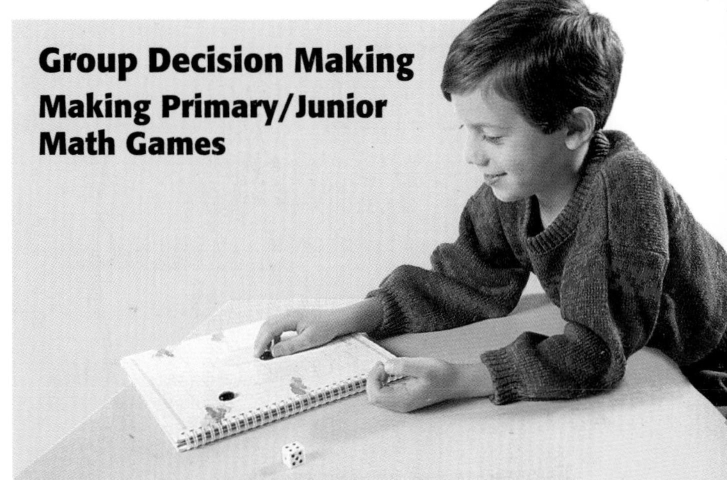

Group Decision Making

Making Primary/Junior Math Games

You are going to make a math game for students in one of the grades in the primary or junior divisions.

1. Decide as a class whether different groups will make a game for the same grade or for different grades. If you choose different grades, decide which grade each group will have.

2. Have one member of your group meet with the teacher of the chosen grade. Ask the teacher what math the students are learning. Report to the other members of your group.

3. Research the games already available to students at the chosen grade level. Suggest ideas about the kind of game you want to make.

4. Decide as a group on the type of game and on the math you want to include.

5. Make the game and test it with the students it was made for.

6. Ask the students who play the game how they like it. Have their teacher evaluate the game.

7. Prepare a report for the class. Include a demonstration of the game.

Chapter Check

Use the diagram to name 4 of each of the following.

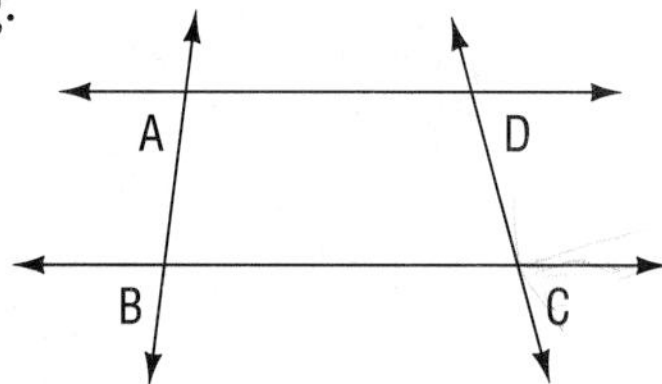

1. lines
2. line segments
3. rays
4. angles

Determine the missing measures.

5.

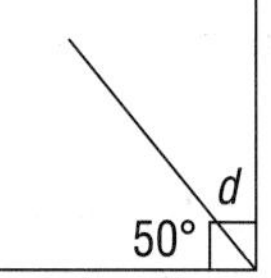

6.

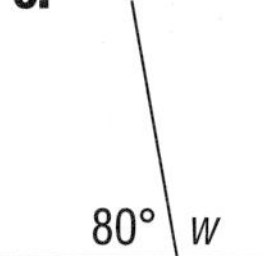

7.

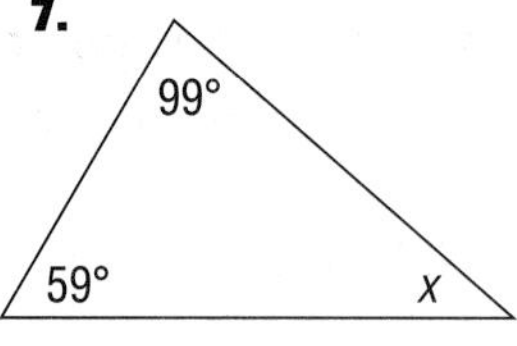

8.

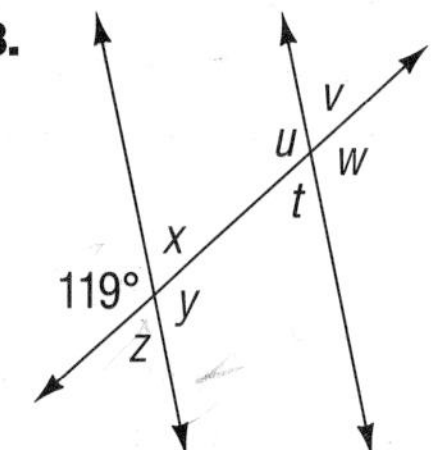

Name the quadrilaterals.

9.

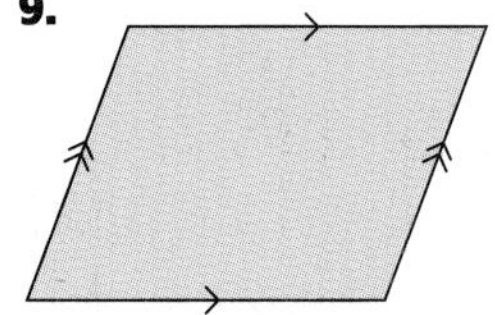

10.

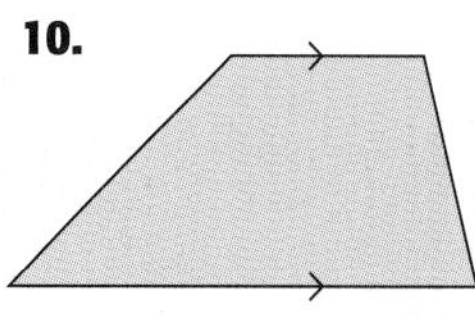

11.

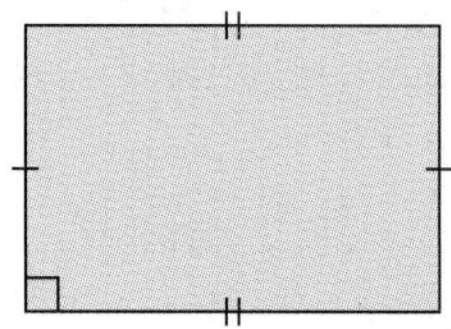

12.

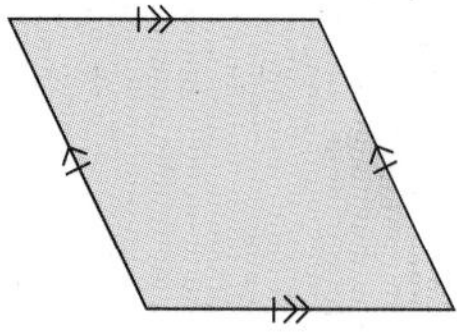

Name each polygon and state whether it is regular or not.

13.

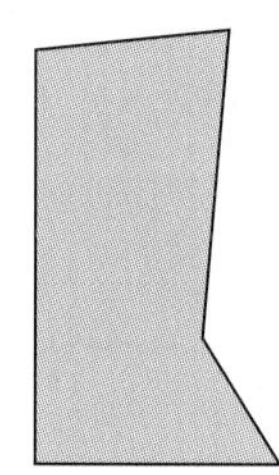

14.

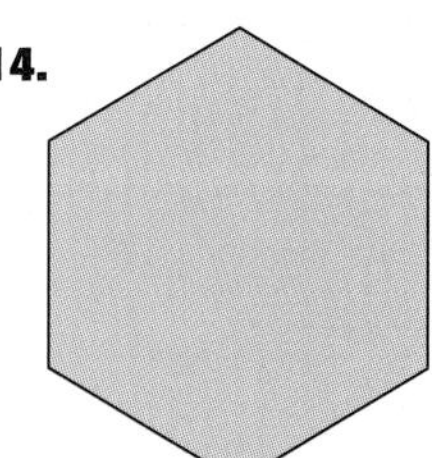

15.

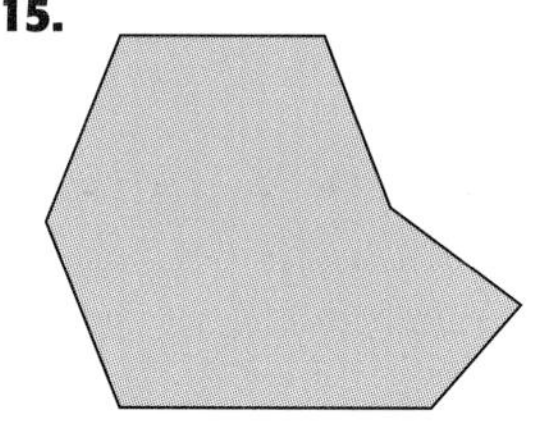

16.

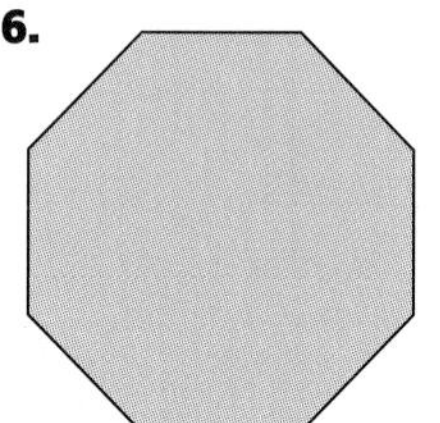

Classify each triangle in two ways.

17.

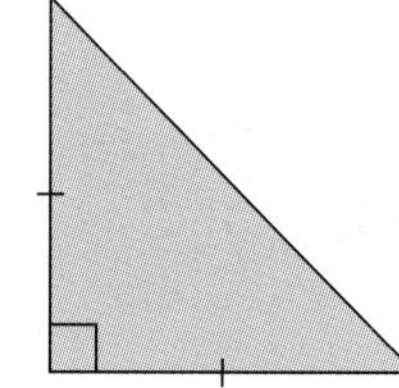

18.

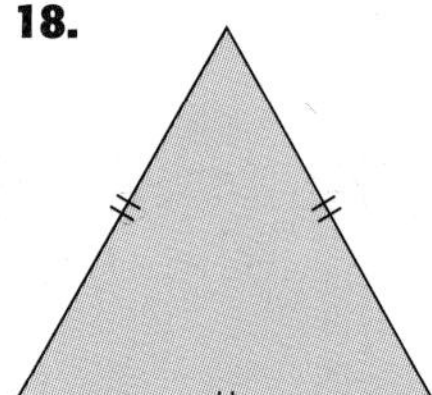

19.

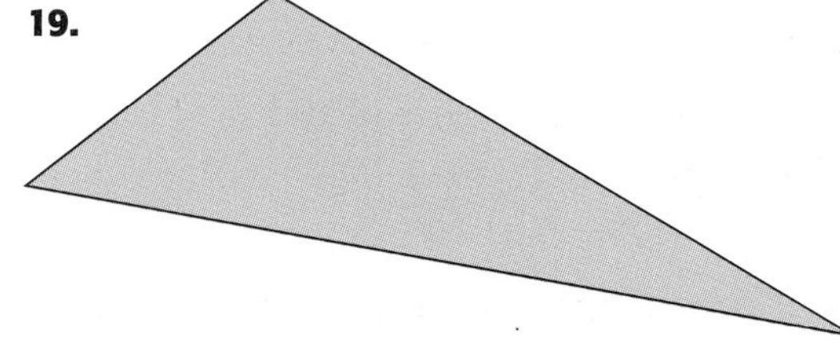

20. The following triangles are congruent. Name the corresponding parts.

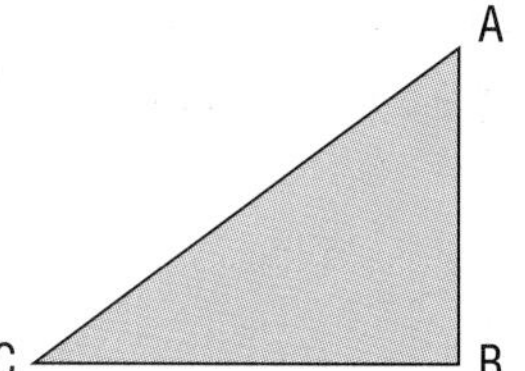

Using the Strategies

1. The two figures are made up of congruent squares. The perimeter of the first figure is 24 cm. What is the perimeter of the second?

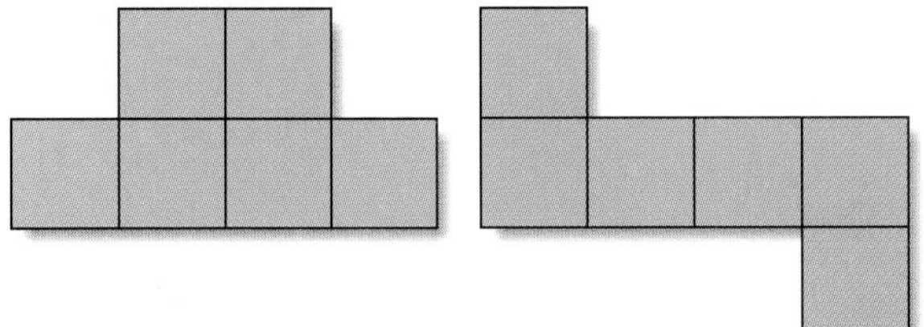

2. The yellow car is already parked. Three other cars will park in the three spaces.

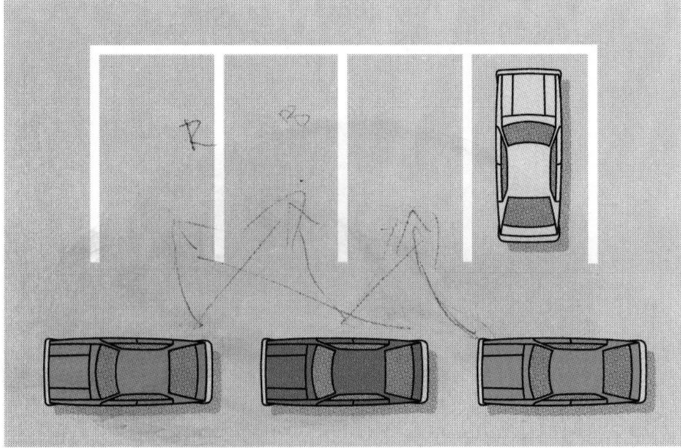

One possible order of colours is red-green-blue-yellow. How many other orders are there if the yellow car does not move?

3. In how many ways can you divide 9 books into 3 groups so that there is an odd number of books in each group?

4. Write 100 as the sum of 3 prime numbers.

5. Sam worked 3 h at a car wash and earned \$5.15/h. Then he pumped gas for 4.5 h at \$5.90/h. How much did Sam earn?

6. What time will it be 2347 h from now?

7. The annual Teachers' Challenge Run is a 15-km event. Charles runs 1 km in 5 min. Mario runs 1 km in 5.5 min. If they start at the same time, how much sooner does Charles finish?

8. The target is used in a game in which each player throws 3 bean bags.

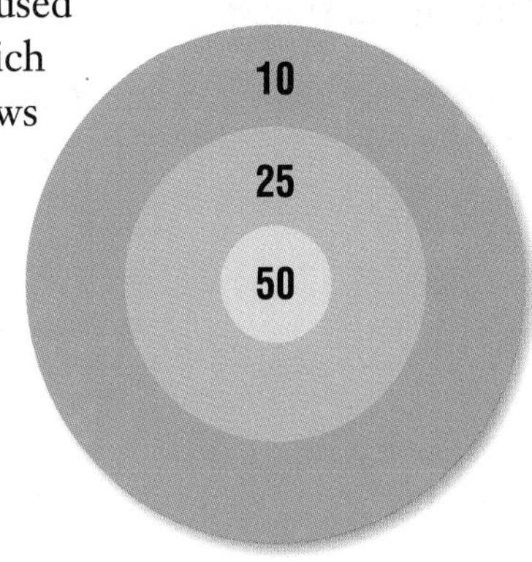

a) If all 3 bean bags land on the target, how many possible totals are there?

b) If one bean bag misses the target, how many possible totals are there?

9. A camp is in the shape of a square of side 10 km. Allan entered the camp from the middle of the north side. He walked 3 km due south, then 2 km due west. Then he walked another 5 km due south. At this point, how far was he from the eastern edge of the camp?

10. Anitha's plane leaves at 09:35. She must be at the airport an hour and a half before take-off. The trip to the airport takes 55 min. She needs 35 min to pack. At what time should she start packing?

DATA BANK

1. How much farther from the sun is Jupiter than Mercury?

2. Paula in Paris, France, called her friend in Vancouver. When she called, it was 07:00 on a Monday in Paris. What was the time and the day in Vancouver?

CHAPTER 4

Perimeter and Area

Pentominoes are made up of 5 squares joined at their edges. Two of the 12 different pentominoes are shown. Use squares of the same size to draw the other 10.

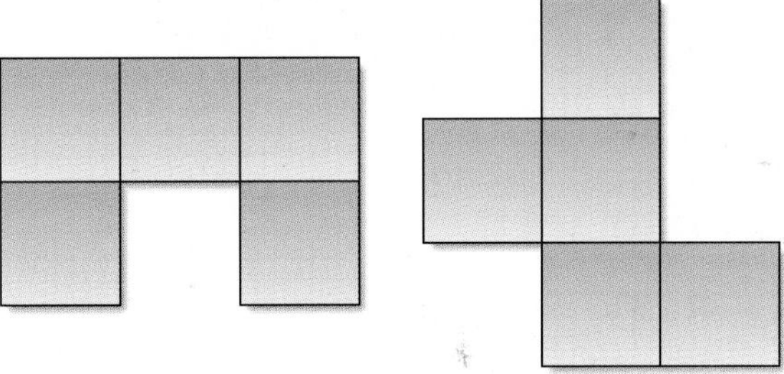

Each of your pentominoes contains 5 identical squares, so all your pentominoes cover the same amount of surface. But is the distance around all your pentominoes the same? Explain.

Describe a common situation in which you need to know the distance around something.

Data Bank: Travelling Around Canada

Use the Data Bank at the back of the book for these activities.

Activity ❶

Calculate the difference in the driving distance and the flying distance between each pair of cities.

1. Halifax and Toronto
2. Toronto and Edmonton
3. Winnipeg and Vancouver
4. Montreal and Calgary
5. St. John's and Calgary
6. Regina and Saskatoon

Activity ❷

A round trip begins and ends at the same place. For each round trip, estimate the driving distance to the nearest 100 km.

1. Montreal → Toronto → Montreal
2. Vancouver → Winnipeg → Edmonton → Vancouver
3. Whitehorse → Regina → Whitehorse
4. Quebec City → Ottawa → Quebec City
5. Montreal → Saskatoon → Montreal
6. Victoria → Whitehorse → Calgary → Victoria

Activity ❸

Calculate the flying distance for each round trip.

1. Regina → Vancouver → Regina
2. Charlottetown → Toronto → Charlottetown
3. Windsor → Toronto → Windsor
4. Toronto → Calgary → Montreal → Toronto
5. Montreal → St. John's → Halifax → Montreal

Activity ❹

At an average of 70 km/h, how long does each drive take?

1. Toronto to Ottawa
2. Vancouver to Edmonton
3. Halifax to Saint John
4. Montreal to Winnipeg
5. St. John's to Victoria

Activity ❺

Refer to the map of Canada.

1. List the provinces from largest to smallest by area.
2. Check your list against the Data Bank.

Decimal Skills

Write in standard form.

1. $4 \times 100 + 3 \times 10 + 2 \times 1 + 5 \times 0.1$

2. $9 \times 10 + 4 \times 0.1 + 6 \times 0.01$

3. $8 \times 100 + 5 \times 1 + 7 \times 0.1 + 9 \times 0.001$

4. $5 \times 1000 + 8 \times 100 + 4 \times 0.01$

Round to the indicated place value.

5. 15.613 to the nearest tenth

6. 208.49 to the nearest one

7. 119.238 to the nearest hundredth

8. 342.16 to the nearest ten

9. 573.88 to the nearest hundred

Estimate, then calculate.

10. $52.8 + 4.96 + 73.57$

11. $116.2 - 58.46$

12. $401.33 - 157.08$

13. $63.6 + 25.88 + 9.3$ **14.** 14.6×3.2

15. $28.26 \div 4.5$

Estimate, then calculate.

16. $2 \times 7.8 + 2 \times 4.5$ **17.** $2 \times 13.4 + 2 \times 8.9$

18. 6×2.8 **19.** 4×9.6

20. 8×11.9 **21.** $2 \times 6.7 + 2 \times 5.2$

Simplify.

22. $15.4 \times 2.3 + 6.7 \times 4$

23. $3.5 \times 1.9 - 2.4 \times 1.6$

24. $12.2 \times 9.6 - 10.5 \times 8.8$

25. $32.1 \times 15 + 16.3 \times 12$

26. $25 \times 8.4 + 8.7 \times 11.5$

Complete each statement.

27. 3500 m = ■ km **28.** 5 cm = ■ mm

29. 250 cm = ■ m **30.** 1.5 km = ■ m

31. 400 mm = ■ cm **32.** 2.8 m = ■ cm

Mental Math

Add.

1. $6 + 7$ **2.** $13 + 8$ **3.** $9 + 5$

4. $4 + 19$ **5.** $15 + 16$ **6.** $12 + 19$

Subtract.

7. $10 - 3$ **8.** $30 - 8$ **9.** $15 - 7$

10. $16 - 9$ **11.** $20 - 14$ **12.** $21 - 12$

Multiply.

13. 6×8 **14.** 9×7 **15.** 4×6

16. 7×12 **17.** 5×11 **18.** 3×8

State the quotient and remainder.

19. $13 \div 4$ **20.** $47 \div 5$ **21.** $75 \div 8$

22. $50 \div 7$ **23.** $23 \div 2$ **24.** $58 \div 6$

Calculate.

25. $5 \times 8 + 3$ **26.** $3 \times 6 + 9$

27. $2 \times 7 + 8$ **28.** $9 \times 6 + 4$

Calculate.

29. $8 \times 3 - 6$ **30.** $5 \times 6 - 2$

31. $9 \times 6 - 4$ **32.** $7 \times 3 - 8$

Calculate.

33. $36 \div 10$ **34.** 25×100

35. $415 \div 100$ **36.** 76×10

37. $206 \div 10$ **38.** 1.5×1000

39. 5.2×10 **40.** $3.8 \div 10$

Simplify.

41. 9^2 **42.** 2^3 **43.** $5^2 - 10$

44. $6^2 + 4$ **45.** $4^2 + 2^2$ **46.** $7^2 - 3^2$

Estimating and Measuring Length

Using the lengths of familiar objects as references helps us to make better estimates.

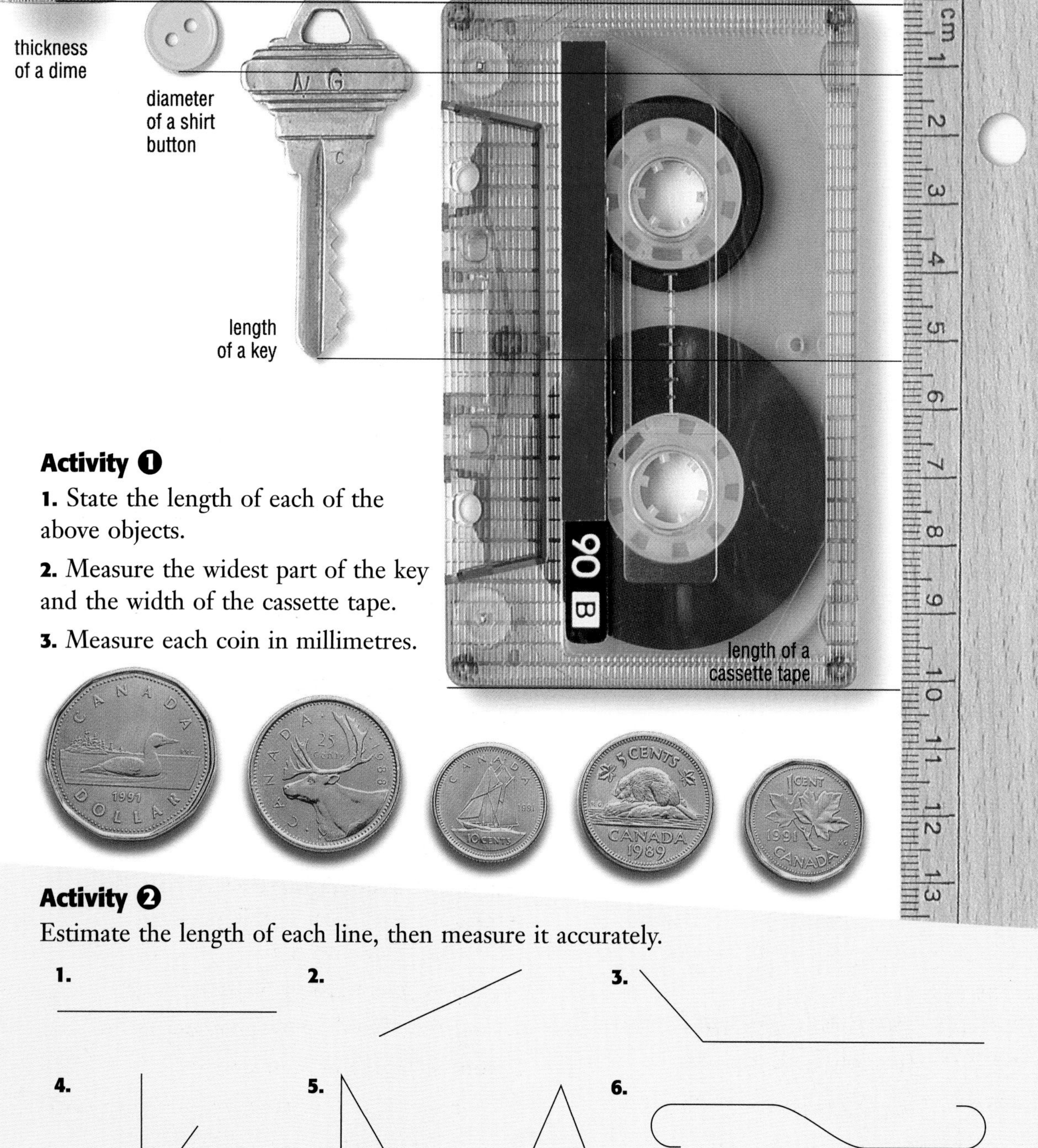

Activity ❶

1. State the length of each of the above objects.

2. Measure the widest part of the key and the width of the cassette tape.

3. Measure each coin in millimetres.

Activity ❷

Estimate the length of each line, then measure it accurately.

1.

2.

3.

4.

5.

6.

Activity ❸

A single bed is about 1 m wide. Estimate whether each of the following measurements is greater than or less than 1 m. Check by measuring with a partner.

1. height of a door
2. width of a school desk
3. distance around a garbage can
4. length of your normal step
5. width of your school's entrance
6. height of the chalk ledge

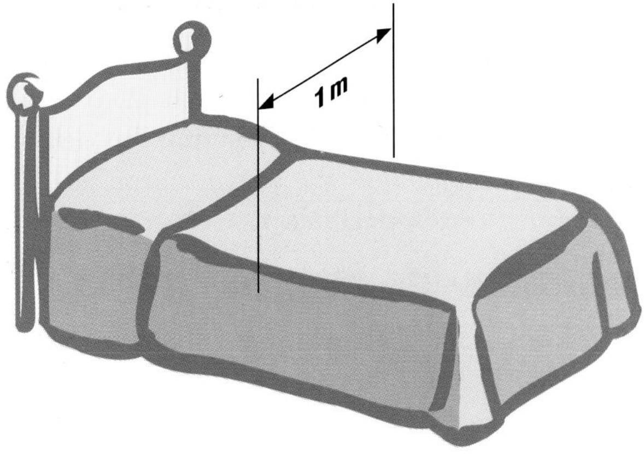

Activity ❹

Find an object or distance that you estimate to have each length. Check by measuring.

1. 22 cm	**2.** 14 cm	**3.** 65 cm	**4.** 6 m
5. 30 cm	**6.** 120 cm	**7.** 10 cm	**8.** 3.5 m

Units of Length
1 km = 1000 m
1 m = 100 cm
1 m = 1000 mm
1 cm = 10 mm

Activity ❺

State the best unit of length to complete each statement.

1. The radio battery is 48 ■ long.
2. The desk is 72 ■ high.
3. The football field is 0.4 ■ around.
4. The calculator is 6 ■ wide.
5. The McKinleys travelled 165 ■ .
6. The coffee cup is 24 ■ around.
7. The flagpole is 9 ■ high.

Activity ❻

1. In the hallway or schoolyard, mark off 10 m.
2. Count the steps you take to walk 10 m.
3. Estimate 20-m and 50-m distances by walking.
4. Compare your estimates with a classmate's.

Activity ❼

At a brisk pace, we walk 1 km in about 10 min.

1. In how many hours can we walk 12 km? 21 km? across Canada?
2. Describe two ways to find how long you take to walk 1 km.

Activity ❽

Guess which length is greater. Check by measuring with a partner. Express each difference in centimetres.

1. around your waist or half your height
2. your foot length or around your ankle
3. your arm span or your height
4. your arm length or twice around your neck
5. your leg length or around your waist
6. your hand span or your foot length

4.1 Perimeter

What do running around a track, building a fence around a yard, and sewing trim to the hem of a dress have in common? In each case, we need to know the distance around something, or the **perimeter**.

Activity: Use the Diagram

Julia from grade 7 was helping Esther in the grade 2 class. They fastened building rods together to form a rectangle.

Inquire

1. How did they know they had made a rectangle?
2. How many rods make up the perimeter of the rectangle?
3. Write two different number sentences to show how to calculate the number of rods.
4. Draw 3 more geometric figures that could be built with the same number of building rods.
5. Write a number sentence below each figure to show how to calculate the number of rods.

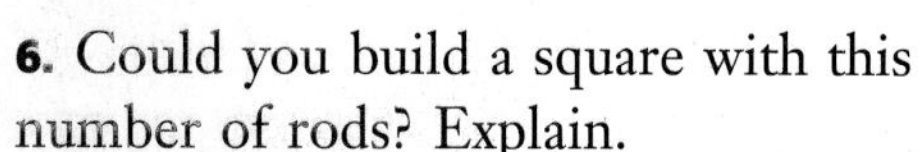

6. Could you build a square with this number of rods? Explain.

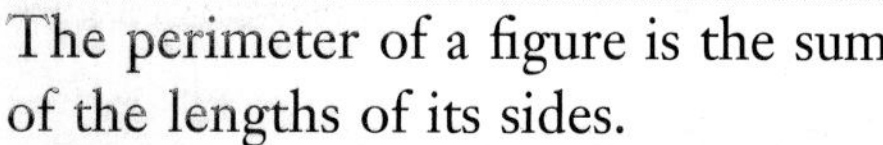

The perimeter of a figure is the sum of the lengths of its sides.

Example

Calculate the perimeter of the courtyard.

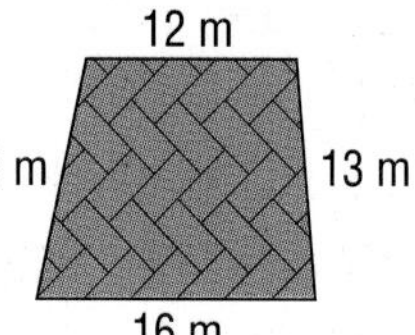

Solution

$P = 12 + 13 + 16 + 14.5$
$= 55.5$

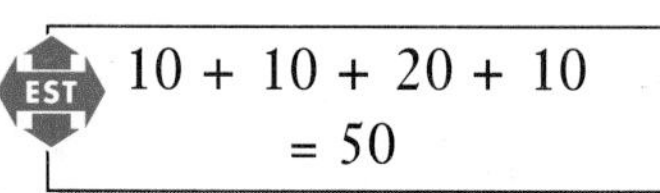

The perimeter of the courtyard is 55.5 m.

Practice

Each figure is made from 10 cm long pieces. Find each perimeter.

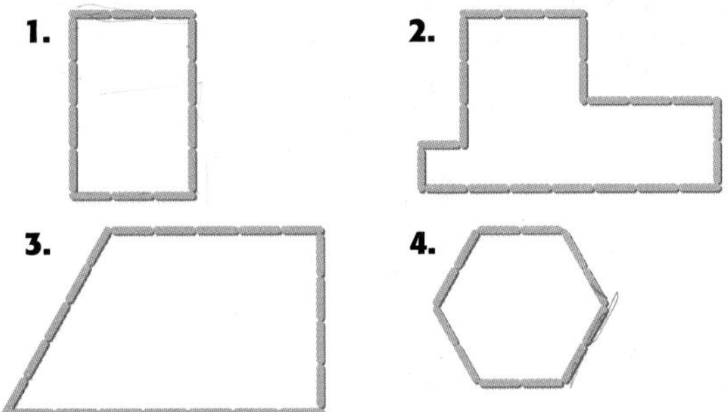

5. Draw 3 figures, each made from 15 equal building rods. If each rod is 10 cm long, state each perimeter.

6. Estimate, then measure each side of the following figure. Calculate its perimeter.

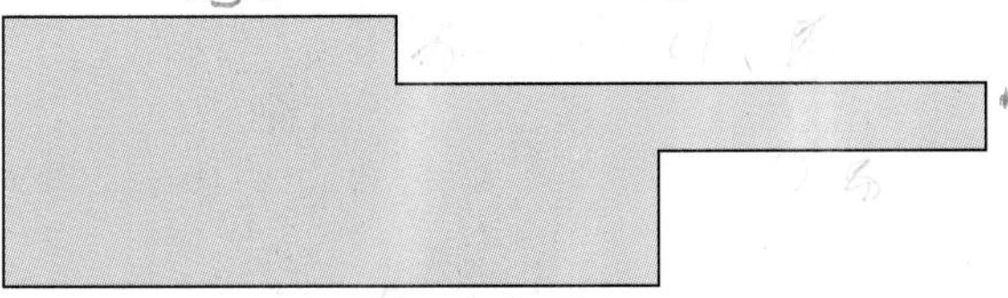

Problems and Applications

Estimate, then calculate the perimeter of each figure.

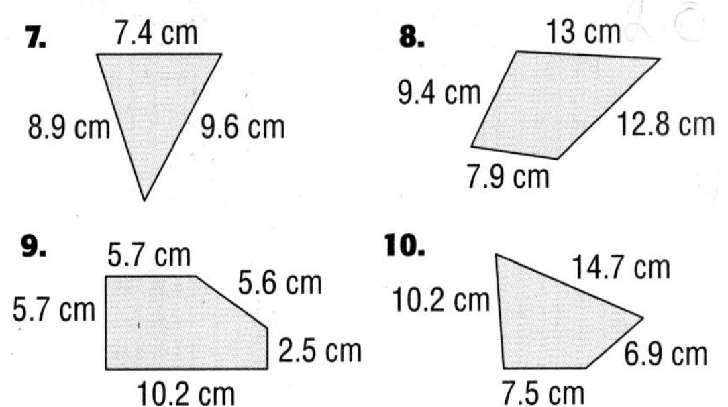

Calculate the missing length. Explain your method.

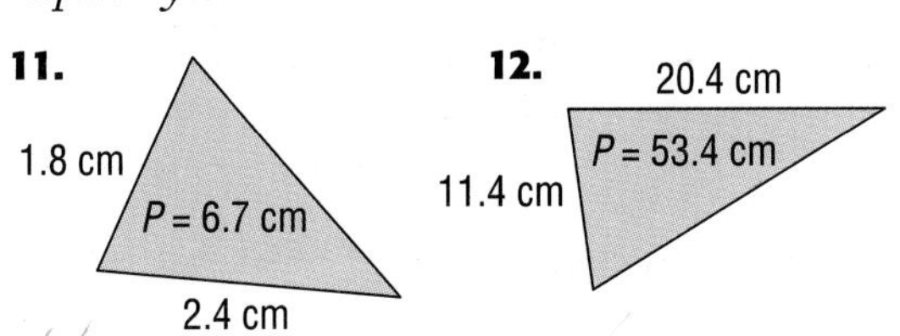

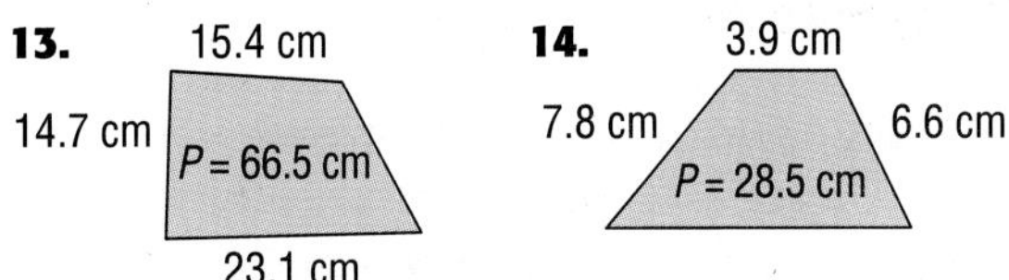

15. Mr. Graham is building a dollhouse. Calculate the perimeter of each room from the plan of the ground floor. The side of each square on the grid represents 5 cm.

Kitchen
Dining Room
Family Room
Hall-way
Living Room

16. A builder charges $660.00 for a fence around 3 sides of a square deck. Each side of the deck is 5.5 m. What is the cost per metre of fence?

17. Take a piece of paper of any shape and cut it into two pieces. Without measuring, decide how the total perimeter of the two new pieces compares with the perimeter of the original piece. Explain your reasoning and compare with a classmate.

PATTERN POWER

a) The side of each square is 2 cm. What is the perimeter of each of the following?

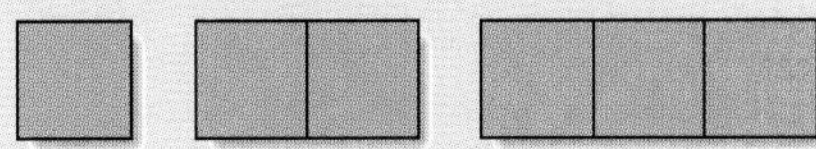

b) What is the perimeter of the rectangle formed from a row of 5 squares? 8 squares? 10 squares?

c) Find the perimeter of the 100th rectangle in this pattern. Explain your method.

4.2 Perimeters of Special Figures

Activity: Determine a Formula

The word "acropolis" means the highest part of an ancient Greek city. The Parthenon was built on the acropolis of Athens. The base of the Parthenon is a rectangle. The length is 72 m and the width is 34 m.

Inquire

1. Sketch the base of the Parthenon and mark the lengths of the sides.
2. Use P for the perimeter, l for the length, and w for the width of the rectangle. In how many ways can you write the formula for the perimeter of the rectangle? Compare with your classmates.
3. Calculate the perimeter of the base of the Parthenon.
4. How would you change the formula to calculate the perimeter of a square? Explain.

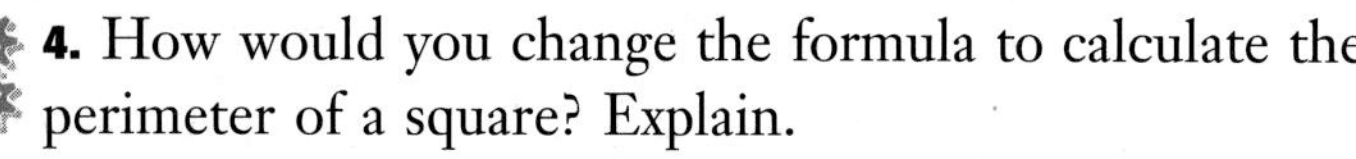

The sides of a regular figure are all equal. There are formulas to calculate the perimeters of regular figures.

Example

Determine the perimeter of each regular figure.

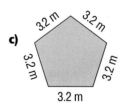

a)

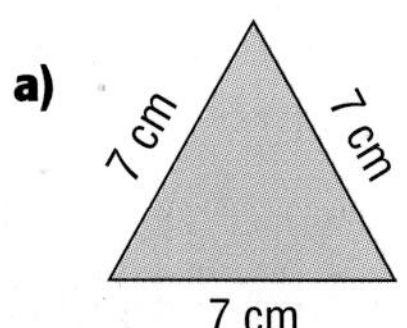

b)

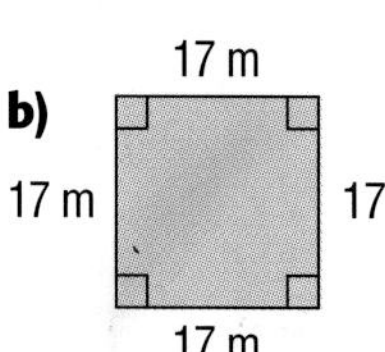

c)

3.2 m
3.2 m
3.2 m
3.2 m
3.2 m

d)

6.7 m
6.7 m
6.7 m
6.7 m
6.7 m
6.7 m
6.7 m
6.7 m

Solution

a) For an equilateral triangle $P = 3 \times s$ $= 3 \times 7$ $= 21$ The perimeter is 21 cm.	**b)** For a square $P = 4 \times s$ $= 4 \times 17$ $= 68$ The perimeter is 68 m.	**c)** For a regular pentagon $P = 5 \times s$ $= 5 \times 3.2$ $= 16$ The perimeter is 16 cm.	**d)** For a regular octagon $P = 8 \times s$ $= 8 \times 6.7$ $= 53.6$ The perimeter is 53.6 m.

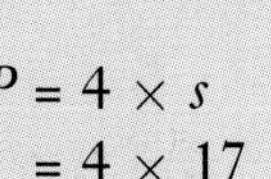

What formula would you use to calculate the perimeter of a regular decagon? How could you use the letters P, n, and s to write a formula for the perimeter of any regular figure?

Practice

Estimate the perimeter of each rectangle. Measure each length and width, then calculate each perimeter.

1. **2.**

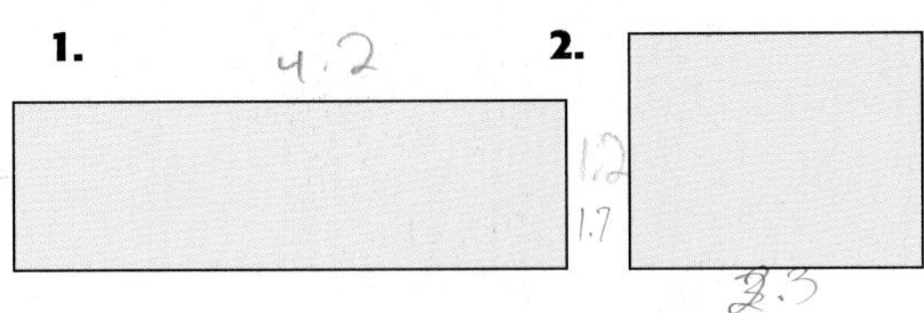

Estimate, then calculate the perimeter of each rectangle.

3. **4.**

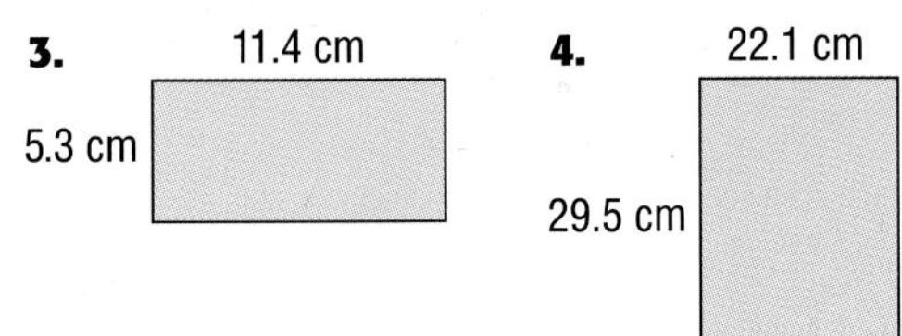

Estimate, then calculate the perimeter of each regular figure.

5. **6.** **7.**

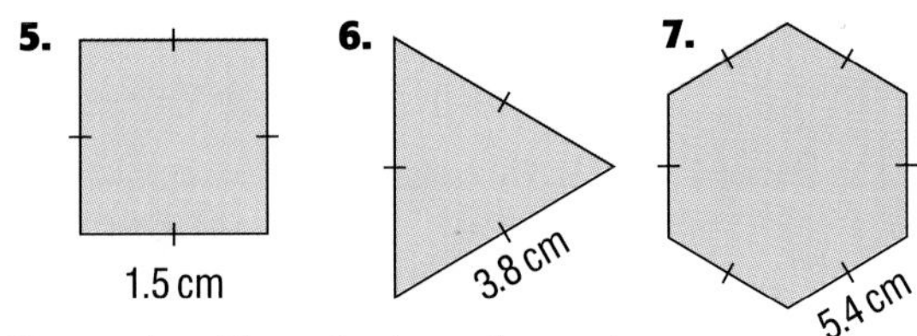

Given the side, calculate the perimeter of each regular figure.

8. triangle, $s = 2.9$ cm

9. octagon, $s = 9.3$ cm

10. hexagon, $s = 8.7$ cm

11. pentagon, $s = 4.8$ cm

12. square, $s = 14.5$ cm

Problems and Applications

Calculate each rectangle's missing dimension. Describe your strategy.

13.

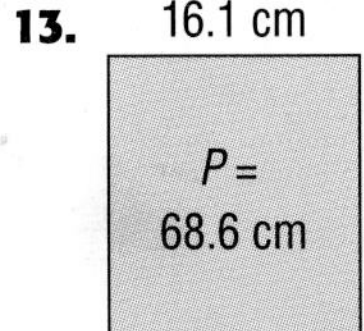

14.

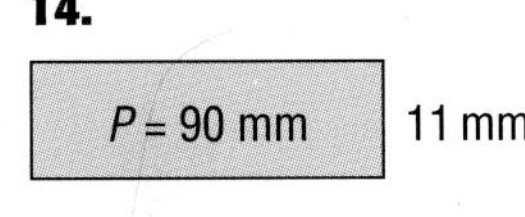

15. The Hammonds' back yard has 4 rectangular sections. Calculate the perimeter of each section.

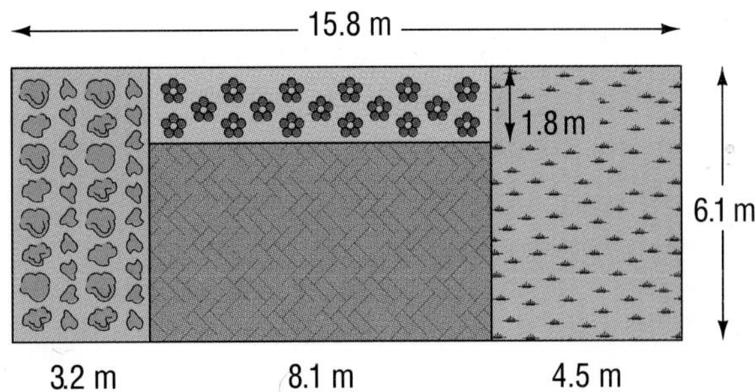

Find the length of each side. Describe your strategy.

16. **17.** **18.**

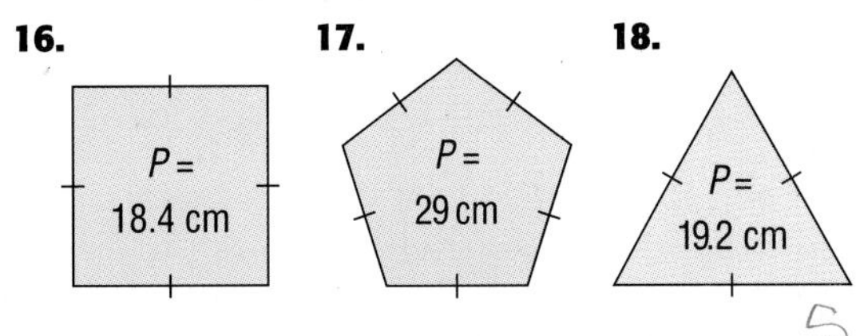

19. The largest office building is the Pentagon in Arlington, Virginia. It is a regular pentagon with each side 281 m. Calculate the perimeter.

20. Draw a regular hexagon, a square, a regular triangle, and four different rectangles, each having a perimeter of 72 cm.

21. Tia and Dee compare the number of times they run around two buildings in the same length of time. Tia runs around a square building with each side 55 m. Dee runs around a rectangular building 65 m by 45 m. Is the comparison fair? Explain.

22. Work with a classmate to measure to the nearest tenth of a centimetre the dimensions of 6 rectangular objects in the classroom. Copy and complete the chart.

Object	Length	Width	Perimeter

4.3 Circumference

Activity: Discover the Relationship

Collect 3 cans of different sizes. On a large piece of grid paper, make a graph by tracing around each can. Wrap masking tape once around each can, without overlapping. Then remove the tape and place it beside the tracing of the same can.

Inquire

1. What dimension of each can equals the length of the tape?
2. What dimension of each can equals the height of the tracing?
3. Copy and complete the chart. For each can, divide the length of tape by the height of the tracing.

Can Number	Height of Tracing	Length of Tape	Length ÷ Height

4. How do your calculated results compare with your classmates'?

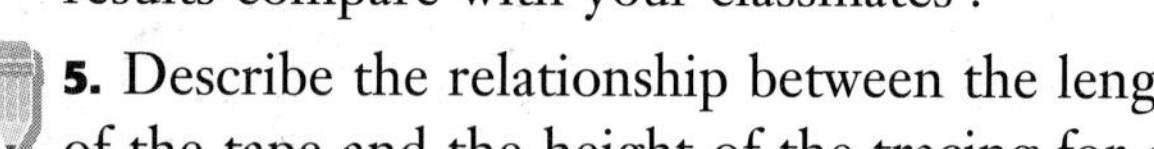

5. Describe the relationship between the length of the tape and the height of the tracing for any can.

The perimeter of a circle is its **circumference**.
The distance across a circle through the centre is its **diameter**.
The circumference divided by the diameter gives a value represented by the Greek letter π. The value of π is approximately 3.14.

We say "pie."

$$\pi = \frac{\text{circumference}}{\text{diameter}} = \frac{C}{d} = 3.14$$

When the diameter is known, we use an approximate value of π to calculate the circumference.

π = 3.141 592 653 589 793.
In this book, we use 3.14.

$$\frac{C}{d} = \pi$$

So, $C = \pi \times d$

Example

Calculate the circumference of a circle with a diameter of 8.5 cm.

Solution

$C = \pi \times d$
$= 3.14 \times 8.5$
$= 26.69$

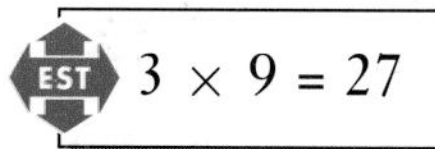

$3 \times 9 = 27$

The circumference is 26.69 cm.

Practice

Measure each diameter. Calculate each circumference to 2 decimal places.

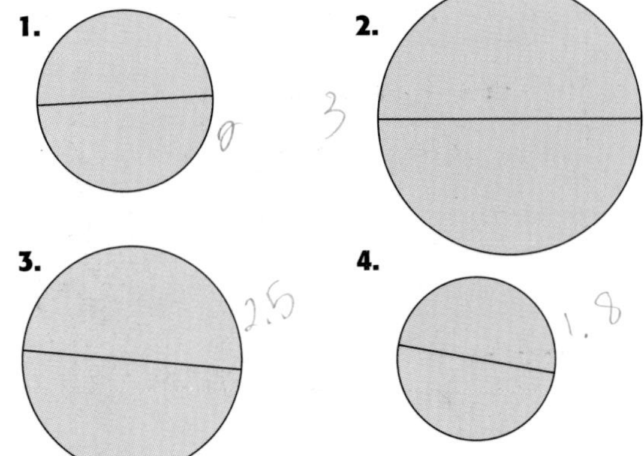

Estimate, then calculate the circumference of each circle.

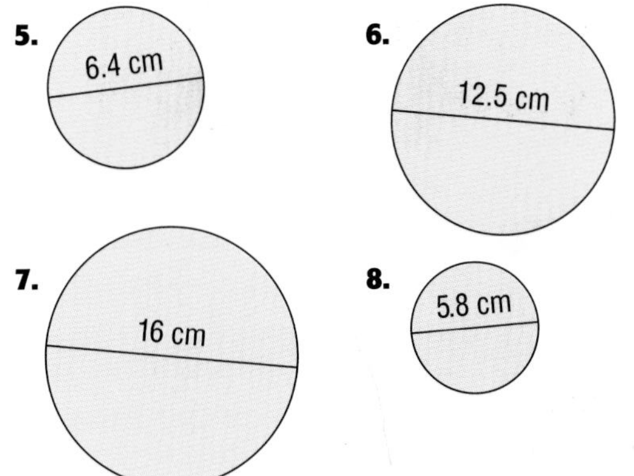

Problems and Applications

9. Use the diagram of the clock to answer each question.

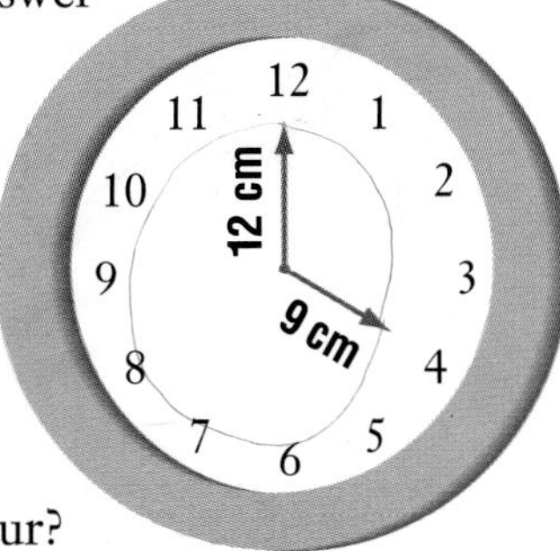

a) To one decimal place, what distance does the tip of the minute hand travel every hour?

b) To one decimal place, what distance does the tip of the hour hand travel every 12 h?

10. Max plans to decorate the lids of some kitchen canisters by gluing a single layer of ribbon around the circumference of each lid. The diameters of the canisters are 11 cm, 13 cm, 14 cm, and 15 cm. To the nearest centimetre, what is the smallest total length of ribbon he can use?

11. The diameter of a circle is twice its **radius**.

$$d = 2 \times r$$

Use each radius to calculate the circumference to 2 decimal places.

a) $r = 5$ cm **b)** $r = 3.5$ cm

c) $r = 9.25$ cm **d)** $r = 1.5$ cm

e) $r = 11.2$ cm **f)** $r = 12.4$ cm

12. The medals at each Olympic Games must be at least 60 mm in diameter. To the nearest millimetre, find the smallest circumference of an Olympic medal.

13. A compact disc has a circumference of 37.7 cm. What is the diameter to the nearest tenth of a centimetre? What is the radius?

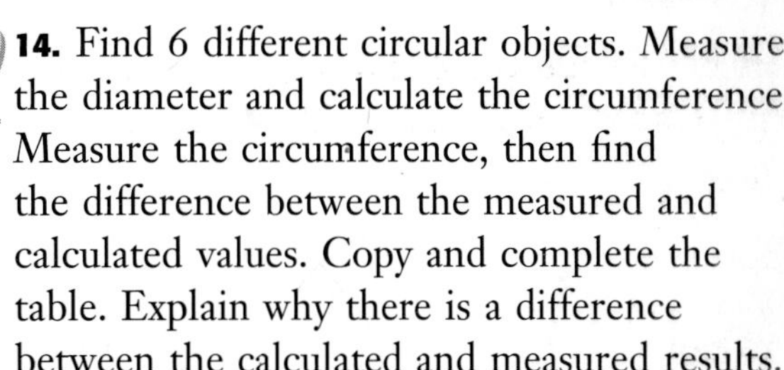

14. Find 6 different circular objects. Measure the diameter and calculate the circumference. Measure the circumference, then find the difference between the measured and calculated values. Copy and complete the table. Explain why there is a difference between the calculated and measured results.

Item	d	π	C calc	C meas	Difference
		3.14			

4.4 Working with Perimeter

Activity: Use the Diagram

The diagram shows the shape of Fort Henry, which is in Kingston, Ontario. The Fort was built during the War of 1812.

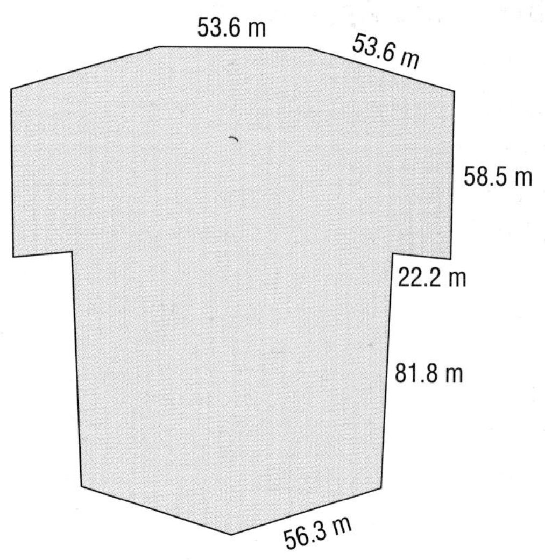

Inquire

1. Copy the diagram and add the missing dimensions. What assumptions have you made?

2. Estimate, then calculate the perimeter.

3. Calculate the perimeter in another way and compare your answers.

4. Compare your methods with a classmate's.

Example

Farrah has a picture to frame. It is a rectangle that measures 62 cm by 43 cm. The width of the frame is 10 cm. What length of frame will Farrah need?

Recall the steps

Understand the Problem

Think of a Plan

Carry Out the Plan

Look Back

Solution

Draw a diagram of the picture and the frame. Adding the lengths of the sides of the picture will not give the correct length of frame. Divide the frame into lengths and add.

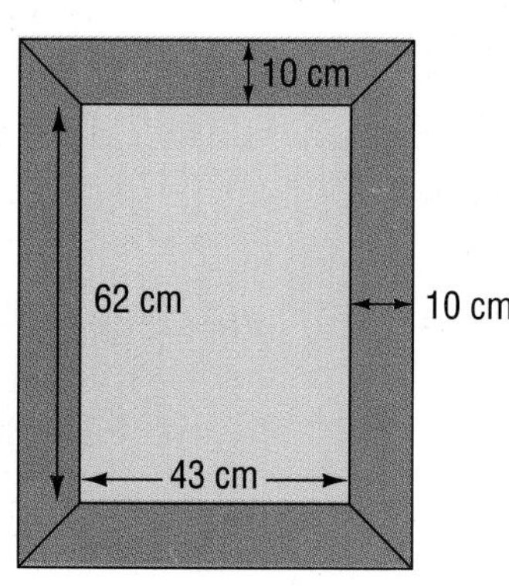

Length of one side $62 + 10 + 10$
$= 82$

Length of two sides 82×2
$= 164$

Length of top $43 + 10 + 10$
$= 63$

Length of top and bottom 2×63
$= 126$

EST $80 + 80 + 60 + 60$
$= 280$

Total length $164 + 126$
$= 290$

Farrah will need 290 cm of frame.

The answer is close to the estimate.

Is there another way to solve the problem?

Problems and Applications

1. The distance between bases on a baseball diamond is 27.4 m. What is the shortest possible distance a player runs after hitting a home run?

2. A furniture company is building coffee tables from glass and wood. Each table is 90 cm by 45 cm. The width of the wood around the top is 7 cm.

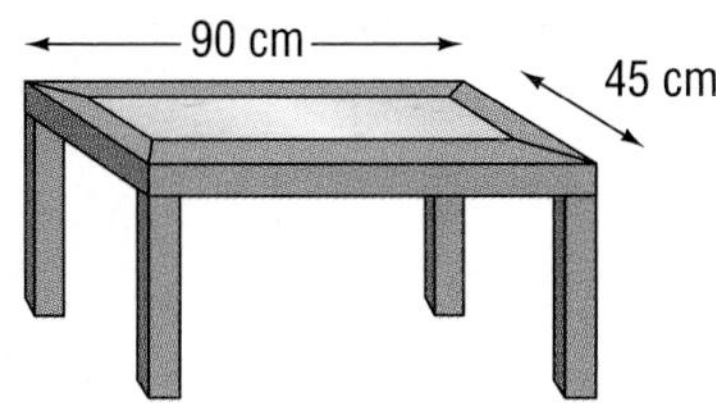

a) What length of wood is needed for the top of each table?

b) If the edges of the glass are protected with a plastic strip, what length of this strip is needed for each table?

3. The Morrisons fence 3 sides of their yard. The back is 14 m and the sides are each 8.75 m. The fence posts are 1.75 m apart.

a) What is the length of the fence?

b) How many fence posts are used?

c) Fence posts cost $13.99 each, and fencing is $4.75/m. Find the total cost of the fence.

d) What assumptions have you made about how the fence is built?

4. Stonehenge is a circular stone monument, built around 2800 BC. It has a diameter of 30 m. To the nearest metre, what is the circumference of Stonehenge?

5. A square field is surrounded by a fence of 3 parallel wires. Each side of the square is 63.2 m. If the wire costs $0.35/m, what is the cost of the wire in the fence?

6. To the nearest millimetre, what is the diameter of a circle made from 36 cm of wire?

7. If each of the following regular polygons is made from 36 cm of wire, what is the length of each side?

a) triangle **b)** square **c)** pentagon
d) hexagon **e)** octagon **f)** decagon

8. The minute hand on a floral clock is 3 m long. The hour hand is 1.5 m long. How much farther does the tip of the minute hand travel than the tip of the hour hand in each of the following lengths of time?

a) 1 h **b)** 1 day

9. There are 12 square gardens of equal size in the conservation area. They all lie inside a rectangle that measures 20 m by 15 m.

a) Sketch the gardens and state the dimensions of each one.

b) Each garden is surrounded by a double-strand wire fence. What length of wire surrounds each garden?

c) The large rectangle is surrounded by a wooden fence. There are two openings in the fence, each 1.2 m wide. Not counting the openings, what is the total length of the fence?

10. Write a perimeter problem about something in your classroom. Have a classmate solve the problem.

LOGIC POWER

Use your knowledge of geography to identify the province that these towns are in. Then check by finding this area on a map.

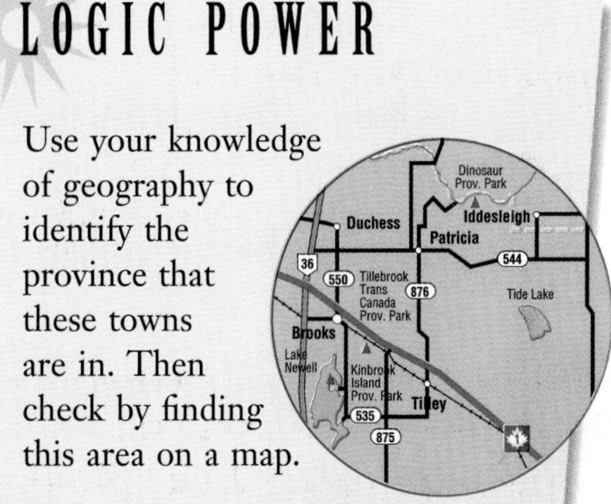

4.5 Find Missing Information

Some problems may not contain all the information you need to solve them. You must research the missing information.

On a school sports day, 200 students sign up for softball. How many teams do they make?

Understand the Problem

1. What information are you given?
2. What are you asked to find?
3. What missing information do you need to solve the problem?

To find the number of teams, you need to know the number of players on a softball team.

Think of a Plan

Find the number of players on a team, then divide 200 by this number.

Carry Out the Plan

There are 9 players on a team.

Paper and Pencil

$$\begin{array}{r} 22 \\ 9\overline{)200} \\ \underline{18} \\ 20 \\ \underline{18} \\ 2 \end{array}$$

EST $\frac{200}{10} = 20$

Calculator C 200 ÷ 9 = 22.222222

There are 22 teams, and 2 players left over.

Look Back

The answer is close to the estimate of 20. Is there another way to solve the problem? How could you use multiplication to check your answer?

Find Missing Information

1. List the given facts.
2. Decide what information is missing.
3. Find the missing information.
4. Solve the problem.
5. Check that your answer is reasonable.

Problems and Applications

Describe the missing information.

1. In an election, Hakim defeated Scully by 38 votes. How many votes did Hakim get?

2. The houses in one block are numbered from 165 to 315. What is the number of the third house on the block?

3. The diameter of Saturn is 52 times the diameter of Pluto. What is the diameter of Pluto?

4. A jogging club wants to run a distance equal to the circumference of the Earth. They estimate it would take about 167 days to run this distance. How fast would they have to run?

5. A chameleon can extend its tongue to equal the length of its body. How long is a chameleon from the tip of its tail to the tip of its extended tongue?

6. A book has 400 pages. How many words are in the book?

Supply the missing information, then solve the problem.

7. The Wright brothers' first flight took place in 1903 in *Flyer 1*. How many years ago was that?

8. The wingspan of the wandering albatross is about twice the arm span of the average man. What is the approximate wingspan of the wandering albatross?

9. A relative promises you some money for your next birthday. The amount will be calculated by taking your age on your next birthday, dividing it by 5, and multiplying the result by $10.00. How much will you get?

10. How old will you be on January 1 in the year 2050?

Locate the missing information, then solve the problem.

11. About 45 000 people could stand on a Canadian football field between the goal posts. How big is the square each person has to stand on?

12. The record length of a strand of seaweed is 60 m. How much longer than an Olympic swimming pool is this?

13. What is the temperature difference between the melting point and boiling point of water?

14. What is the temperature difference between the melting point and boiling point of helium?

Estimate the missing information with a classmate. Use your estimate to solve the problem.

15. By the year 2000, 8 out of 10 Canadian homes are expected to have a home computer. How many homes will have a computer?

16. Ninety ping-pong balls fit into a shoebox. How many ping-pong balls will fit into your classroom?

17. Write a problem that has missing information. Be creative. Make sure that whoever solves the problem has some fun in trying to find the information.

LOGIC POWER

The coins have been placed in the squares so that the two complete rows and two complete columns each hold 7 coins.

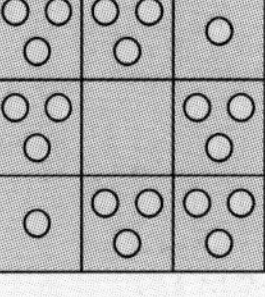

Rearrange the coins so that each complete row and column holds 6 coins.

Estimating and Measuring Area

Activity ❶

Area is the measure of a surface. To wallpaper a room, you need to know the area of the walls.

1. List 5 other situations in which an area is needed.
2. List 5 occupations in which area is used.

Activity ❷

Areas of familiar objects help us to estimate other areas.

A button on a telephone has an area of about 1 cm^2. So does the head of a thumbtack. This square has an area of 1 cm^2.

Say "one square centimetre."

1 cm

1 cm

1. What is the area of the rectangle?

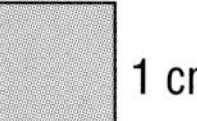

Trace each of the following onto a centimetre grid. Count squares to estimate each area.

2. chalkboard eraser
3. stapler
4. paperback novel
5. bookmark

Find the area of each region. Each square on the grid represents 1 cm^2.

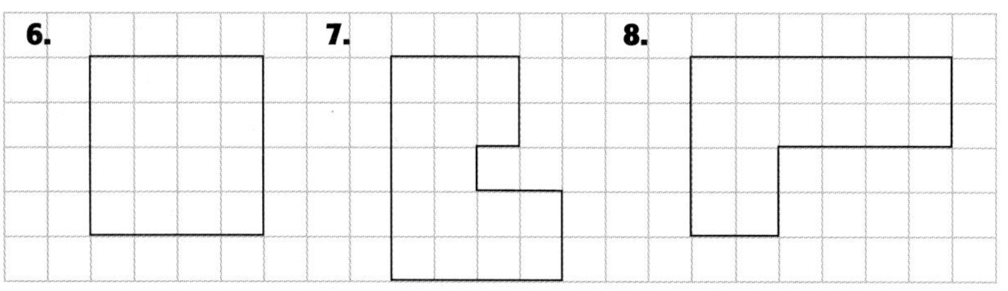

9. Use a geoboard or centimetre grid paper to make 5 different regions, each with an area of 20 cm^2. Repeat for an area of 24 cm^2.

Activity ❸

This shape is made up of 4 whole squares and 4 half squares.

Each square represents 1 cm^2.

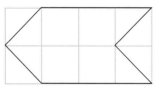

1. Find the area of the shape. Explain your method.

Find the area of each region by counting whole squares and half squares.

2.

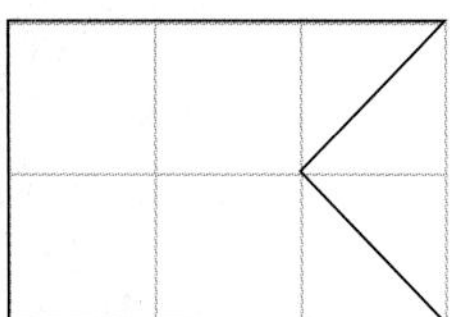

3.

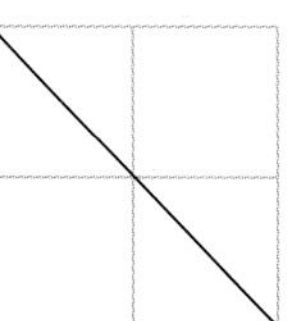

4.

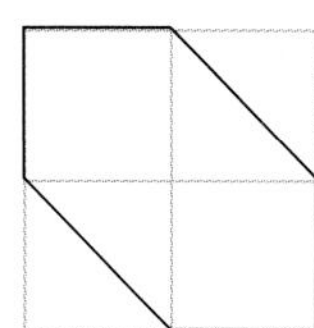

Activity ❹

Areas of irregular shapes can be estimated in two ways.

Method 1

Consider part squares.

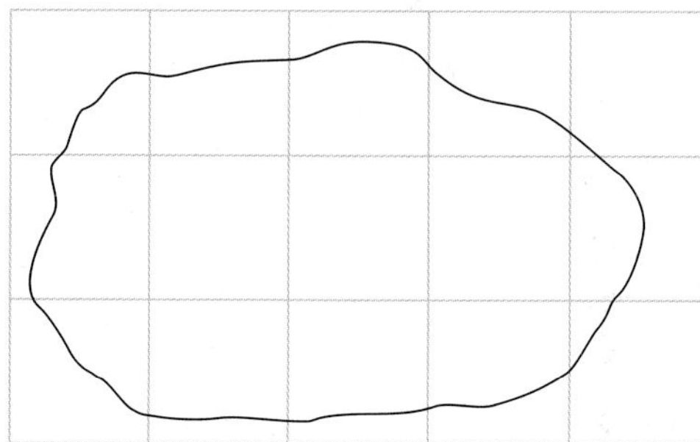

Count squares greater than half as whole squares. Do not count squares less than half. Estimated area is 9 cm^2.

Method 2

Average the number of whole squares inside the shape and the number of squares touched by the shape.

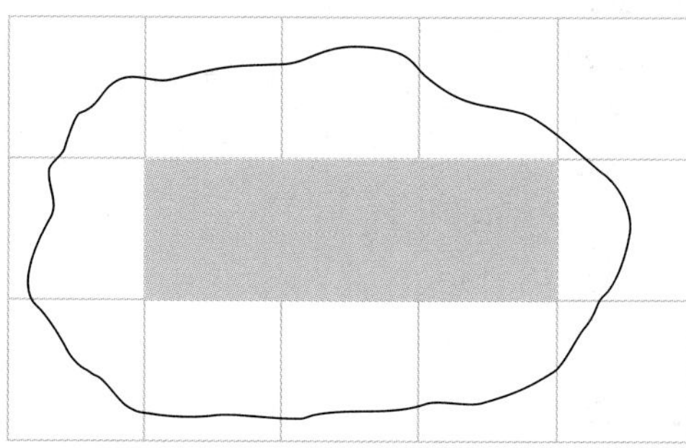

There are 3 whole squares. There are 15 squares touched, including the 3 whole squares.

Average = $(3 + 15) \div 2$
= 9

Estimated area 9 cm^2

Trace each of the objects in questions 1–3 onto a centimetre grid and estimate the area in two ways

1. a shoe **2.** your foot **3.** your hand

Activity ❺

1. A card table is about 1 m by 1 m, so its area is about 1 m^2. How many square centimetres are in 1 m^2? 2.5 m^2?

Complete each statement.

2. 10 m^2 = ■ cm^2

3. 3.5 m^2 = ■ cm^2

4. 20 000 cm^2 = ■ m^2

Construct an area of 1 m^2 from newspaper. Use the square to help you estimate the area of the following.

5. the classroom floor

6. a chalkboard

7. a wall

Activity ❻

1. The hectare (symbol ha) is used to measure areas of land. How many square metres equal 1 ha? 5 ha?

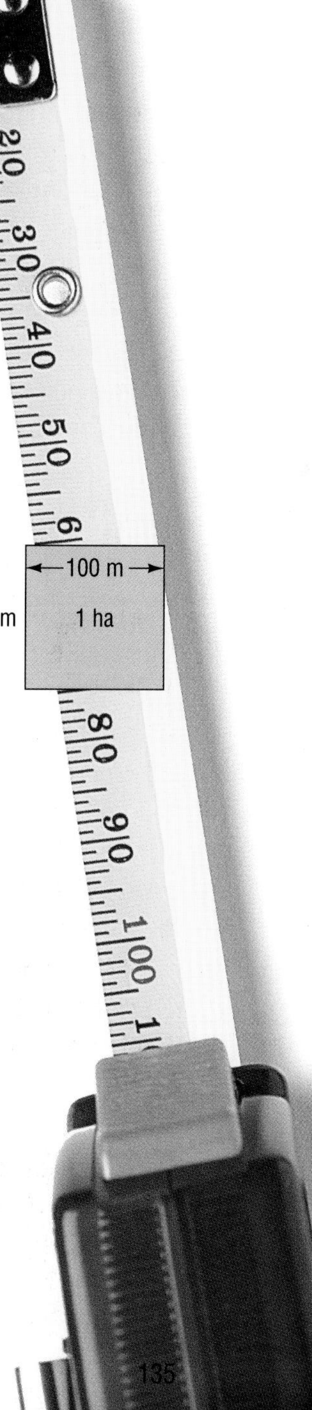

Estimate if the areas in questions 2 and 3 are greater or less than 1 ha.

2. a football field

3. your school grounds

4. Large areas are measured in square kilometres. How many square metres equal 1 km^2? 3 km^2?

Find the area in square kilometres of the following.

5. your county

6. your province

7. Canada

Relating Perimeter and Area

Activity 1

A school has two rectangular skating rinks. One measures 11 m by 9 m, and the other 13 m by 7 m.

After a snowfall, the principal asks two students to shovel the snow from the rinks.

1. Given a choice, which rink would you shovel? Decide as a group and give reasons for your choice.

2. Compare with other groups. How many groups chose rink A? How many chose rink B? How many said there is no difference?

3. If you were asked to shovel a walkway around one of the rinks, which would you choose? Why?

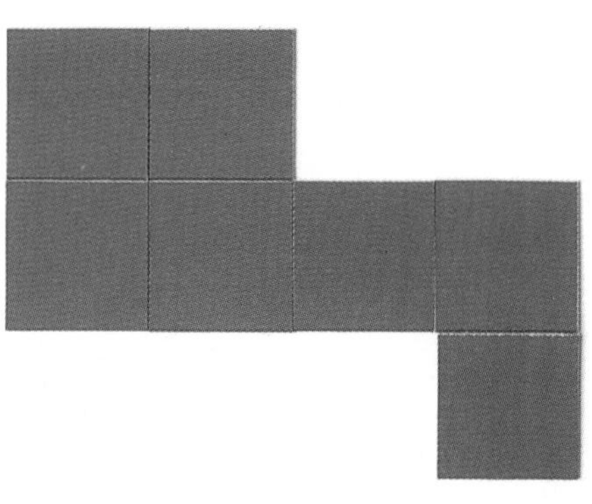

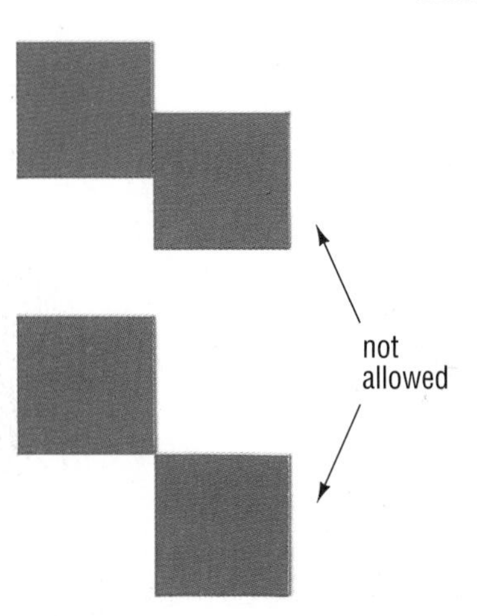

Activity 2

1. Cut out seven identical cardboard squares. Arrange them to form geometric figures. Squares must touch along a whole edge. An example is shown. Make 7 different geometric figures and record each perimeter and area in a table.

Figure	Perimeter	Area
	14	7

2. Why is the area of each figure the same?

3. Why are some of the perimeters different?

4. Make a figure with the greatest possible perimeter. Compare your figure with your classmates'.

5. Make a figure with the smallest possible perimeter. Compare your figure with your classmates'.

Activity ❸

A gardener has 28 m of fence. She wants to enclose a rectangular part of her garden to grow vegetables.

1. Use grid paper to sketch the garden. Draw as many gardens as you can with a perimeter of 28 m. Record your results in a chart.

Rectangle	Length (m)	Width (m)	Perimeter (m)	Area (m^2)
1			28	
2			28	

2. What is the area of the largest rectangular garden that she can enclose with 28 m of fence?

3. What is the area of the largest rectangular garden that she can enclose with 40 m of fence? with 56 m of fence?

Activity ❹

1. Draw a rectangle on grid paper and record its dimensions in a chart.

Rectangle	Length (cm)	Width (cm)	Perimeter (cm)	Area (cm^2)

2. Draw another rectangle whose sides are twice as long as the first. Record the dimensions in the chart.

3. If the sides of a rectangle double, what happens to the perimeter? What happens to the area?

4. Draw another rectangle whose sides are three times as long as the first. Complete the chart. If the sides of a rectangle are multiplied by 3, what happens to the perimeter? What happens to the area?

5. What happens to the perimeter and area if the sides of a rectangle are multiplied by 4?

6. Write a rule for the way the perimeter and area increase when the length and width are multiplied by the same number.

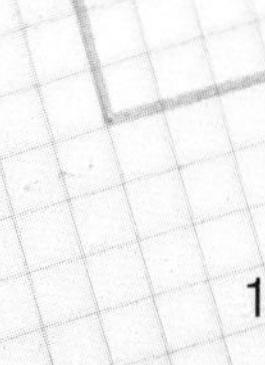

4.6 Area of a Rectangle and Square

Activity: Use the Diagram

In Jane's plan of the Lakeview Student Council Newsletter, each square represents 1 cm^2.

Copy and complete the table to record the size of each section of the newsletter.

Section	Length	Width	Squares Covered
Title			
News and Views			
What's Happening			
Sports			
Lost and Found			

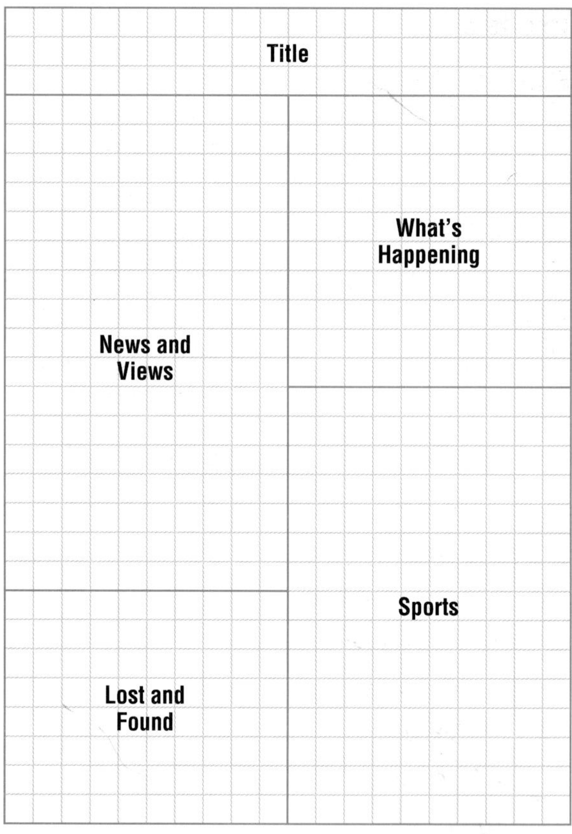

Inquire

1. For any section, what is the relationship between the length, the width, and the number of squares covered?

2. Use the relationship to calculate the area of the entire newsletter.

3. Use the final column of your table to check the area of the newsletter. Describe your method.

4. Use the letters A, l, and w to write a formula for the area of a rectangle.

5. Write a formula for the area of a square.

Example

Last week the sports section included an ad for baseball shirts. The ad was 8 cm by 6.5 cm. What area did the ad cover?

Solution

The ad was an 8 cm by 6.5 cm rectangle.

$$A = l \times w$$
$$= 8 \times 6.5$$
$$= 52$$

EST $10 \times 7 = 70$

The ad covered an area of 52 cm^2.

Practice

Estimate, then calculate the area of each rectangle.

1. 

2. 

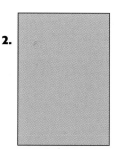

Estimate, then calculate the area of each square.

3. 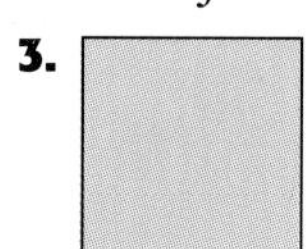

4. 

Estimate, then calculate the area of each rectangle.

5. l = 15 cm, w = 4.6 cm

6. l = 23.2 cm, w = 8.5 cm

7. l = 16.4 km, w = 19.8 km

8. l = 28 m, w = 12.7 m

Calculate the area of each square with the following sides.

9. 14 cm **10.** 9 m **11.** 25 cm

12. 7.5 km **13.** 3.4 cm **14.** 18.1 m

Problems and Applications

15. Estimate, then calculate the area of the address label.

5.9 cm

Judith Black 853 Nowhere Lane Anywhere, Ontario P4A 6W3	1.56 cm

16. Estimate, then calculate the area of the ping-pong table.

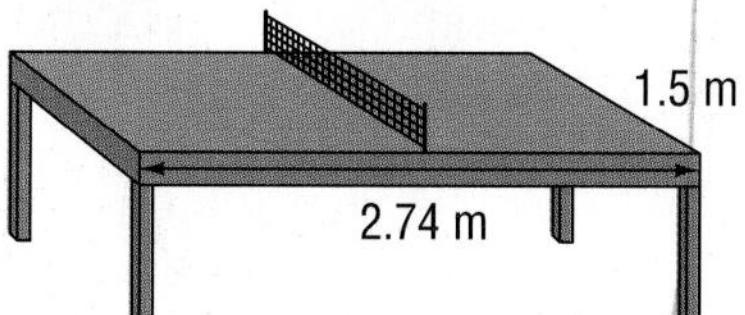

17. Armand built this patio from square paving stones with each side 60 cm. He left 4 areas for plants.

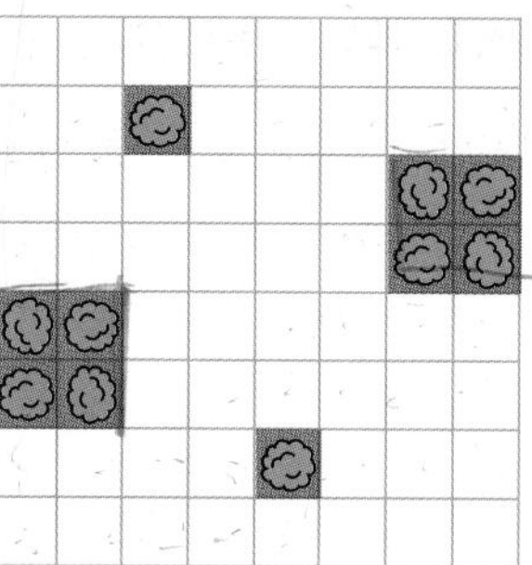

a) What is the total area?

b) What is the paved area?

c) What area is covered by plants?

18. A litre of paint covers 10 m^2. How many litres cover a ceiling 5 m by 3.4 m?

19. A shelf unit has 6 shelves, each 60 cm by 28 cm. What area of shelf paper is needed to cover the tops of all the shelves?

20. The cooking surface of a barbecue is 1536 cm^2. The length is 48 cm.

a) What is the width of the surface?

b) Marko barbecues square hamburger patties with each side 8 cm for a picnic. How many can he cook at the same time?

c) What assumptions have you made?

21. A bulletin board is 2 m by 1.5 m. A teacher wants to cover it with 40 cm by 30 cm sheets of yellow paper. Calculate the smallest number of sheets needed. What assumptions have you made?

22. Jacquie has a mirror 1.2 m by 80 cm. She surrounds it with a border 8 cm wide. What is the total area of the mirror and border?

23. Write an area problem about something in your classroom. Have a classmate solve your problem.

24. As a group, compose an explanation of "area." List as many practical uses of area as you can think of. Compare results with other groups.

4.7 Areas of Figures

The schoolyard at Seven Oaks School wraps around two sides of the building. How can we find the area of the schoolyard?

Activity: Analyze the Solution

We can think of the schoolyard as two separate regions, a square and a rectangle.

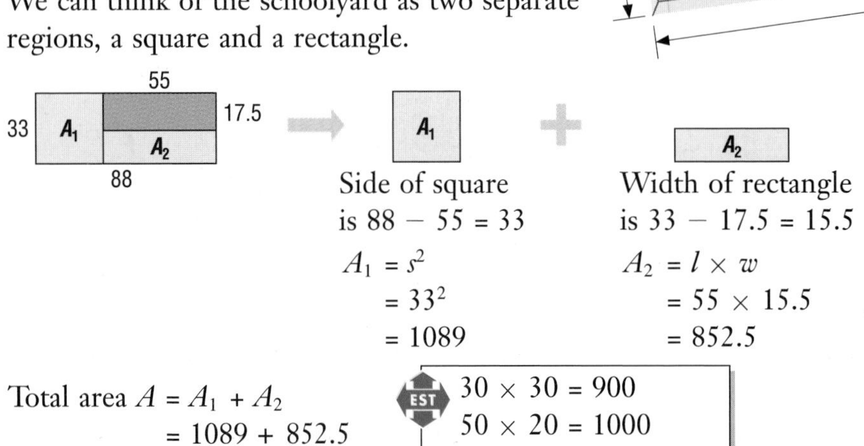

Side of square is 88 − 55 = 33

$A_1 = s^2$
$= 33^2$
$= 1089$

Width of rectangle is 33 − 17.5 = 15.5

$A_2 = l \times w$
$= 55 \times 15.5$
$= 852.5$

Total area $A = A_1 + A_2$
$= 1089 + 852.5$
$= 1941.5$

EST
30 × 30 = 900
50 × 20 = 1000
1000 + 900 = 1900

The area of the schoolyard is 1941.5 m².

Inquire

1. Draw a diagram to show another way of separating the schoolyard into regions.

2. Use the new regions to check the area of the schoolyard.

3. Solve the problem by subtraction instead of addition.

Example

The flag that warns ships of a major gale has a black square on a red background. The flag is 75 cm by 54 cm, with a 24 cm square. What is the area of the red region?

Solution

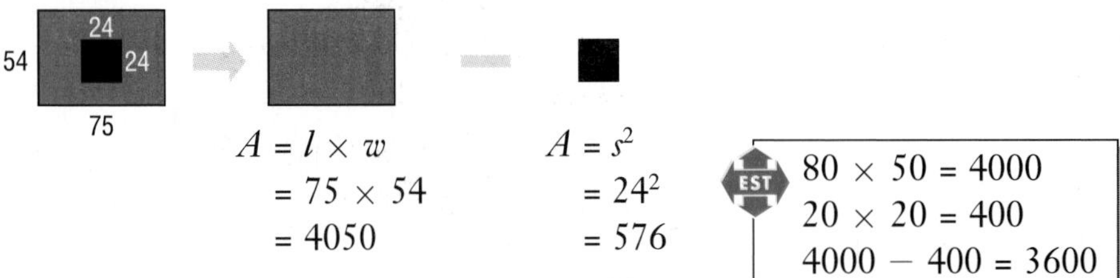

$A = l \times w$
$= 75 \times 54$
$= 4050$

$A = s^2$
$= 24^2$
$= 576$

EST
80 × 50 = 4000
20 × 20 = 400
4000 − 400 = 3600

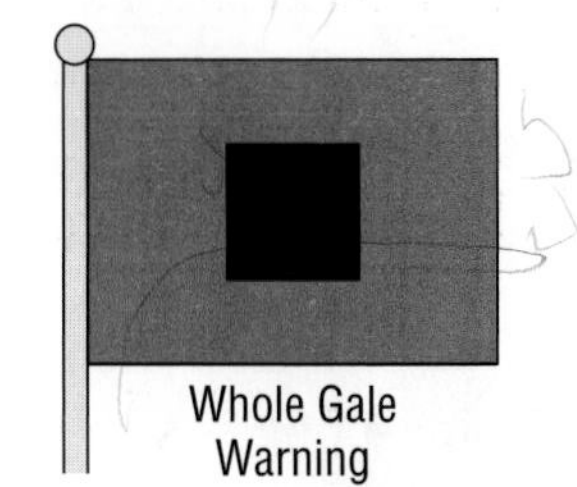

Whole Gale Warning

Area of the region = 4050 − 576
= 3474

The area of the red region is 3474 cm².

Practice

Calculate the area of each figure. Describe your method.

1. **2.**

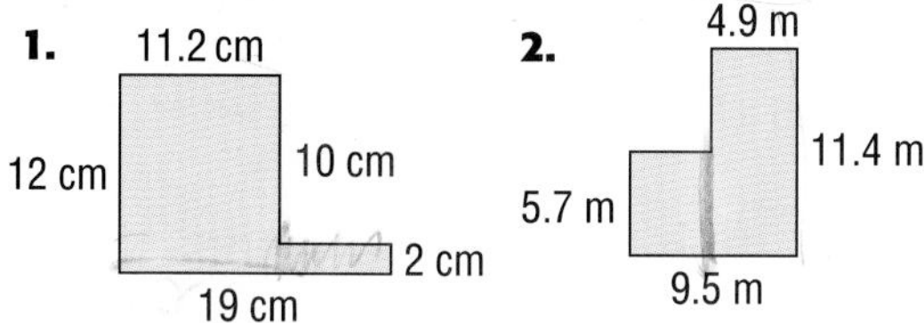

3. **4.**

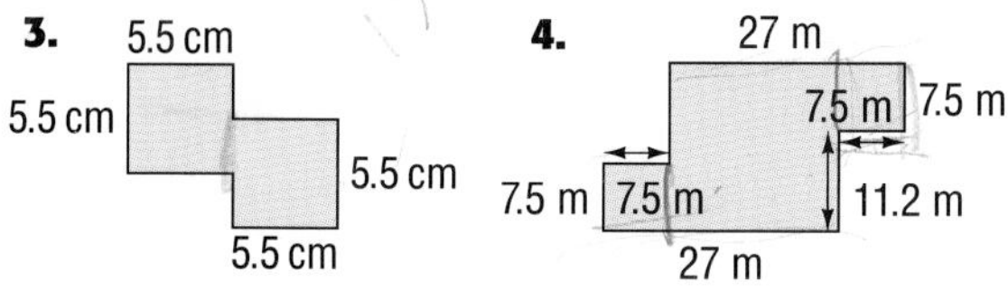

Problems and Applications

5. This plan shows the dimensions, in metres, of the Wilsons' back garden.

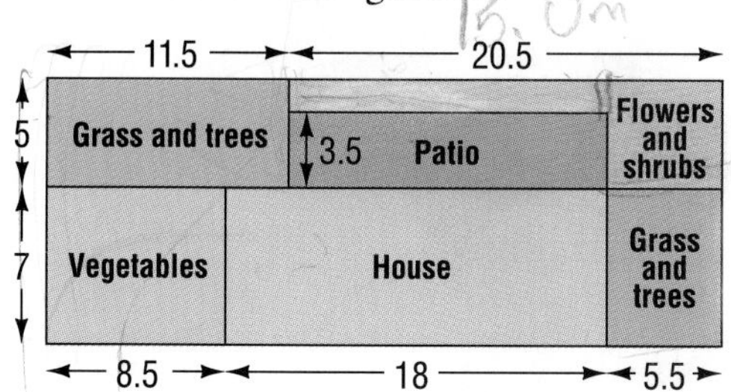

Calculate the area used for each of the following?

a) patio

b) flowers and shrubs

c) vegetables

d) grass and trees

6. The Strauss's living room window has 4 equal square panes of glass and 3 equal rectangular panes. Three panes have been broken in a storm. What total area of glass must be replaced?

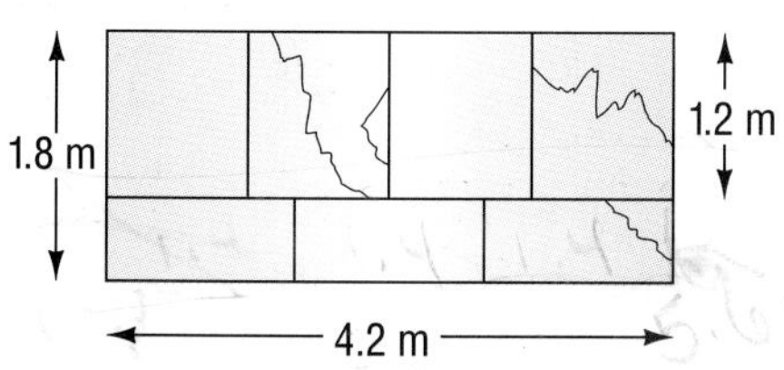

7. The Pattersons want the same carpet for the hallway and dining room. What area of carpet do they need?

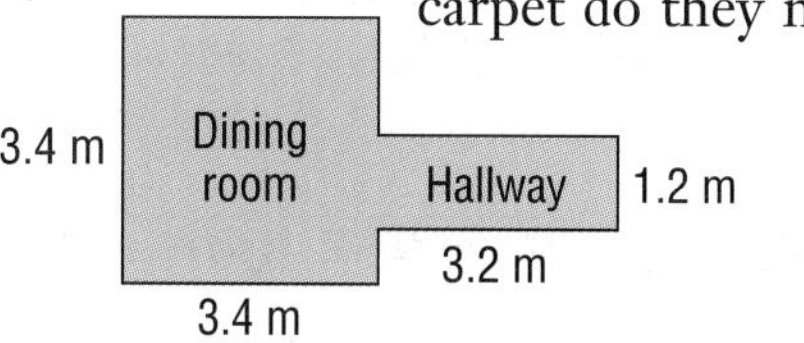

8. The block letters have been drawn on cards that measure 2.5 cm by 3 cm.

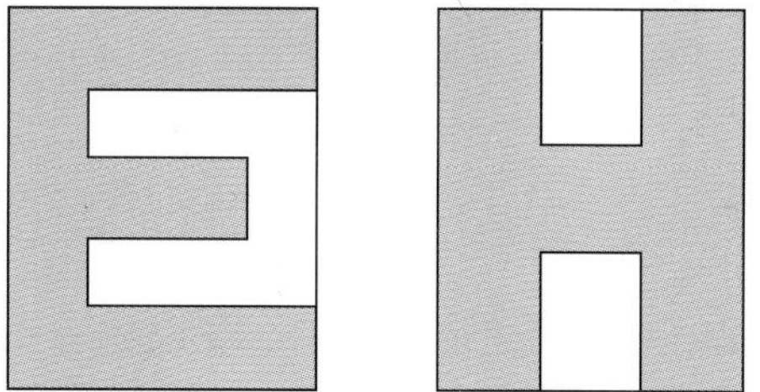

a) Measure each block letter and calculate its area.

b) Using only straight line segments, draw your own initials as they would appear on 2.5 cm by 3 cm cards.

c) Calculate the total area of your initials.

d) Display your results with your classmates'. Sort the initials on the basis of their total area.

NUMBER POWER

1. Liam was born on February 29, 1980. How many birthdays has he had? Explain.

2. How many February 29ths are there between now and December 31, 2020?

3. Was there a February 29th in each of the following years? How do you know?

a) 1957 **b)** 1940 **c)** 1908

4.8 Area of a Parallelogram

One part of the flag of Brazil is a parallelogram. Every parallelogram has a **base** and a **height**. How are they related to the area of the parallelogram?

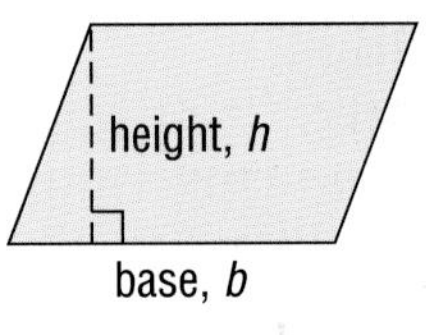

Activity: Discover the Relationship

1. On grid paper, draw 3 parallelograms like the ones shown. Cut them out and number them 1, 2, and 3.

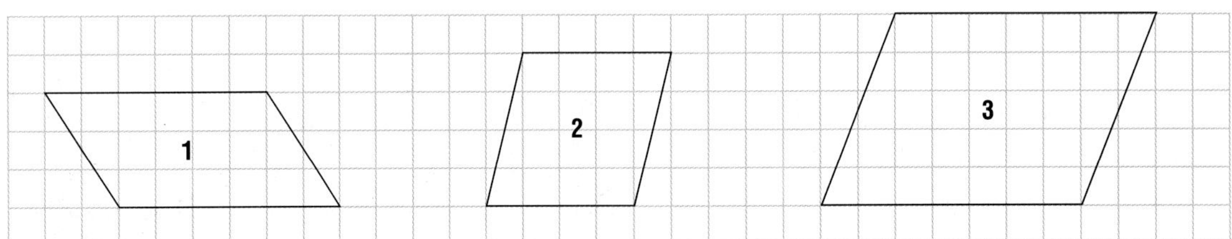

2. Record the base and height of each.

3. Draw a vertical line across parallelogram 1 to divide it into 2 quadrilaterals. Cut along the line and use the two pieces to form a rectangle. Repeat for parallelograms 2 and 3.

Inquire

1. What is the length and width of each rectangle?

2. Compare the length and width of each rectangle to the base and height of the parallelogram you made it from.

3. What is the area of each rectangle?

4. Compare the area of each rectangle to the area of the parallelogram you made it from.

5. Use the letters A, b, and h to write a formula for the area of a parallelogram.

Example

The owner of The Spaghetti House restaurant wants to mark the parking lot for cars. The diagrams show one right-angled parking space and one angled parking space. Which one uses the greater area?

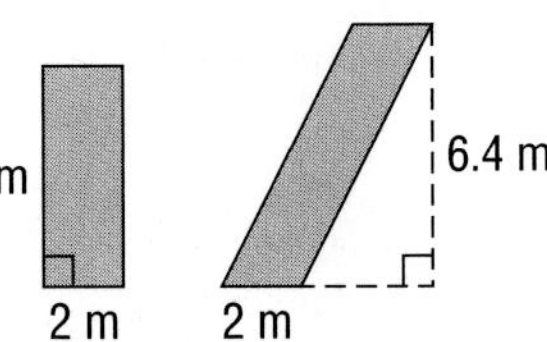

Solution

The right-angled parking space is a rectangle.

$$\begin{aligned} A &= l \times w \\ &= 5.4 \times 2 \\ &= 10.8 \end{aligned}$$

The area is 10.8 m^2.

The angled parking space is a parallelogram.

$$\begin{aligned} A &= b \times h \\ &= 2 \times 6.4 \\ &= 12.8 \end{aligned}$$

The area is 12.8 m^2.

The angled parking space uses the greater area.

Practice

1. Draw a rectangle 8 cm by 5 cm on a centimetre grid. Make a non-vertical cut across 2 opposite sides to make 2 quadrilaterals. Arrange them to make a parallelogram.

a) What is the area of the rectangle?

b) Count squares to find the area of the parallelogram.

c) Find the area of the parallelogram from the formula $A = b \times h$.

2. Measure the base and height of the following parallelogram. Calculate the area.

Estimate, then calculate the area of each parallelogram.

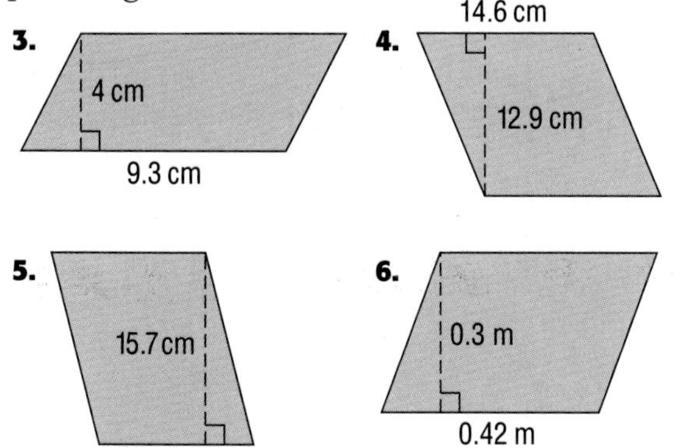

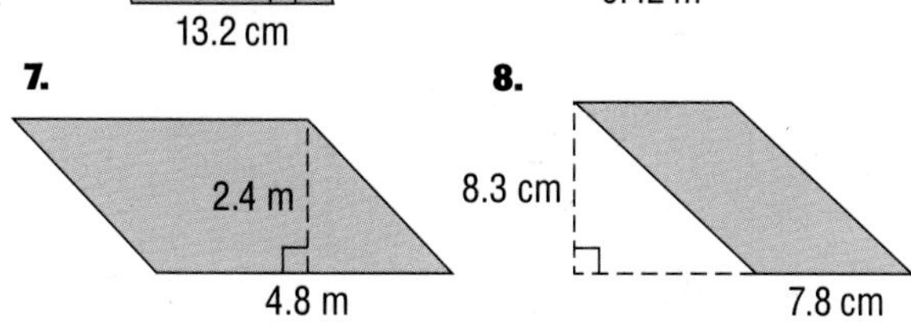

9. Calculate the area of each parallelogram. Explain your results.

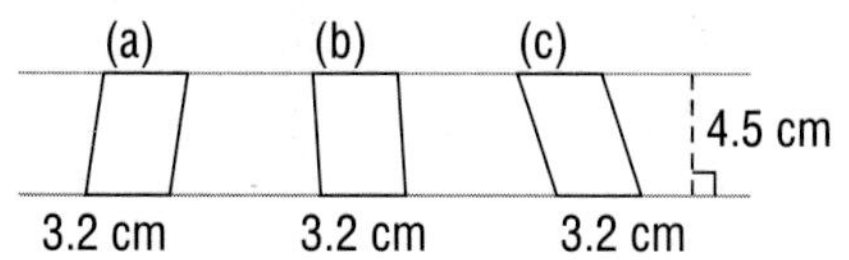

Problems and Applications

10. On centimetre grid paper, draw 2 parallelograms with each of the following areas.

a) 24 cm^2 **b)** 16 cm^2

11. The Chaus put a garden at one end of their rectangular yard and a patio at the other. They put sod in the middle.

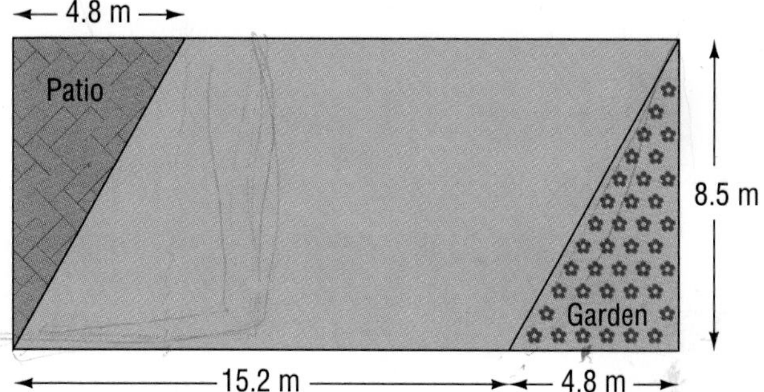

a) Calculate the area of sod.

b) Sod costs \$15.75/m^2. Calculate the total cost of the sod.

c) The patio and the garden are the same size. What is the area of each?

d) Redesign the yard to make the sod a rectangle between the patio and garden. Do not change the areas of the sod, the patio, and the garden. Sketch your design and mark the dimensions of the 3 sections. Compare your sketch with your classmates'.

WORD POWER

CANADA is a one-word name in which the letter A appears 3 times. List other one-word country names that include the letter A 3 times. Compare your list with a classmate's.

4.9 Use a Formula

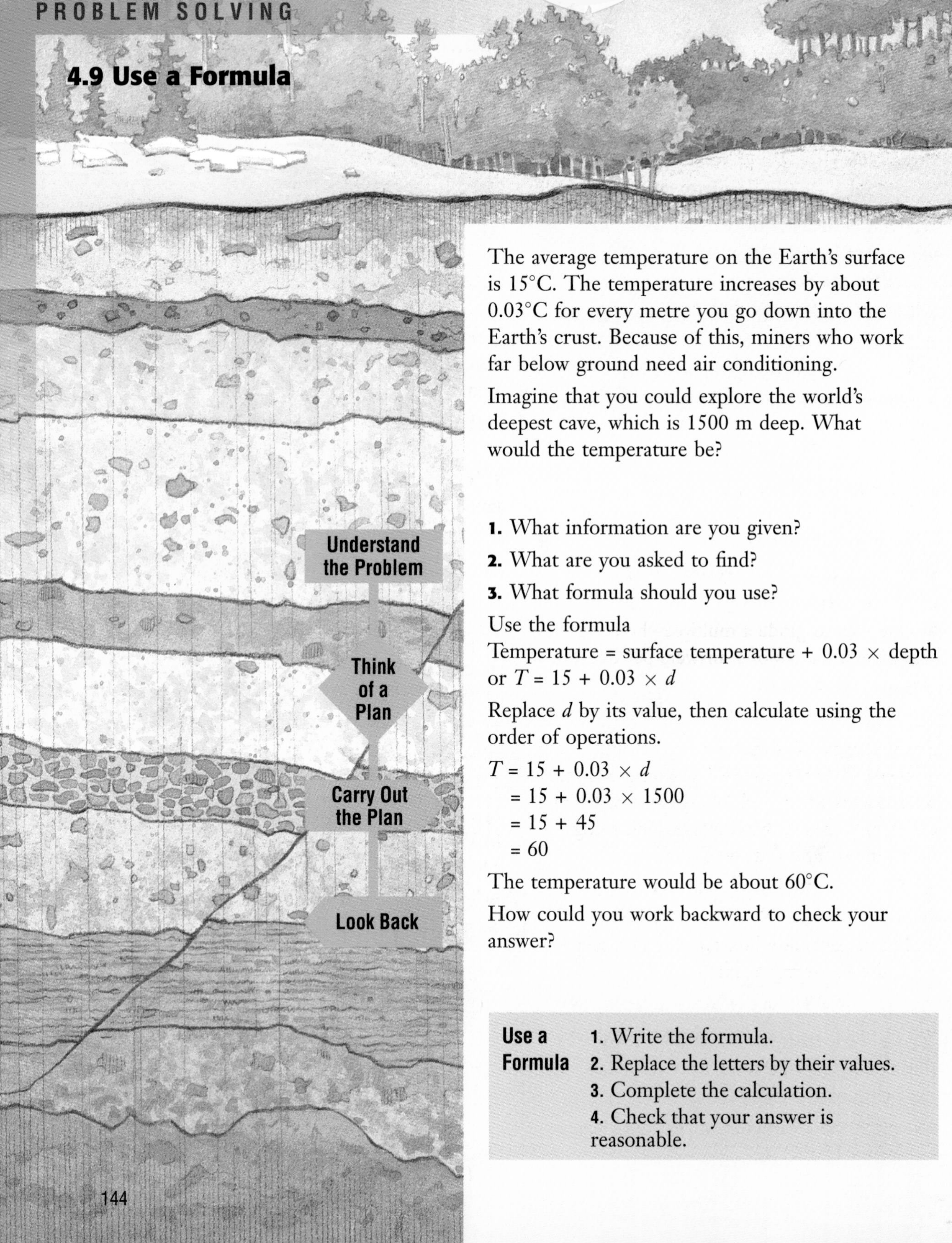

The average temperature on the Earth's surface is 15°C. The temperature increases by about 0.03°C for every metre you go down into the Earth's crust. Because of this, miners who work far below ground need air conditioning.

Imagine that you could explore the world's deepest cave, which is 1500 m deep. What would the temperature be?

1. What information are you given?
2. What are you asked to find?
3. What formula should you use?

Use the formula
Temperature = surface temperature + 0.03 × depth
or $T = 15 + 0.03 \times d$

Replace d by its value, then calculate using the order of operations.

$$\begin{aligned} T &= 15 + 0.03 \times d \\ &= 15 + 0.03 \times 1500 \\ &= 15 + 45 \\ &= 60 \end{aligned}$$

The temperature would be about 60°C.

How could you work backward to check your answer?

Use a Formula

1. Write the formula.
2. Replace the letters by their values.
3. Complete the calculation.
4. Check that your answer is reasonable.

Problems and Applications

1. Mr. Shimja is driving at 80 km/h. The distance he travels is calculated from the following formula.

$$D = 80 \times h$$

D is the distance in kilometres; h is the number of hours of driving.
Calculate the distance he travels in the following numbers of hours.

a) 1 **b)** 3 **c)** 4
d) 5 **e)** 8 **f)** 10

2. One formula for calculating a taxi fare is as follows.

$$F = 2.20 + 1.6 \times k$$

F is the fare in dollars; k is the distance in kilometres. Calculate the fare for each distance in kilometres.

a) 1 **b)** 2 **c)** 4 **d)** 6
e) 12 **f)** 15 **g)** 35 **h)** 30

3. One way to grade a multiple-choice test that gives a choice of 5 answers per question is to use the formula

$$S = R - 0.25 \times W$$

S is the score; R is the number of right answers; W is the number of wrong answers. Six students answer all 100 questions. What are their scores if they have the following numbers of right answers?

a) 20 **b)** 60 **c)** 72
d) 84 **e)** 90 **f)** 100

4. The receipts at a box office are calculated from the following formula.

$$R = 8 \times a + 5 \times s + 3 \times c$$

R equals the receipts in dollars; a is the number of adults; s is the number of students; c is the number of children.

Calculate the receipts from the following numbers of customers.

a) 325 adults, 275 students, 421 children
b) 550 adults, 117 students, 605 children
c) 754 adults, 520 children
d) 216 adults, 825 students

5. Crickets chirp faster or slower depending on the temperature. The formula is

$$T = 5 \times (n + 8) \div 9$$

T is the temperature in degrees Celsius (°C); n is the number of chirps a cricket makes in 1 min.
Find the temperature from the following numbers of chirps per minute.

a) 19 **b)** 23 **c)** 28
d) 37 **e)** 42 **f)** 46

6. The height, in metres, of a highrise building is about 4 times the number of storeys. Write a formula for finding the height from the number of storeys. Calculate the height for the following numbers of storeys.

a) 10 **b)** 15 **c)** 33
d) 50 **e)** 75 **f)** 110

7. Your age in months is the number of complete months since your last birthday, plus 12 times your age in years. Write a formula and use it in parts a) and b).

a) Calculate your age in months.
b) What will your age in months be on December 31, 2010?

8. Write your own problem that requires a formula. Have a classmate solve the problem.

NUMBER POWER

There is 1 number less than 100 that has exactly 7 different factors. What is it?

4.10 Area of a Triangle

At one end of a parking lot, there is a triangle of bare earth. Its **base** is 5 m, and its **height** or **altitude** is 3 m. To work out how much it will cost to sod or pave the earth, we need to know the area of the triangle.

Activity: Find the Relationship

Draw the triangle on centimetre grid paper.

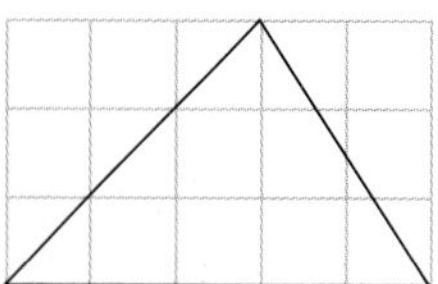

Trace and cut out a second triangle congruent to the first.

Place the two triangles together to form a parallelogram.

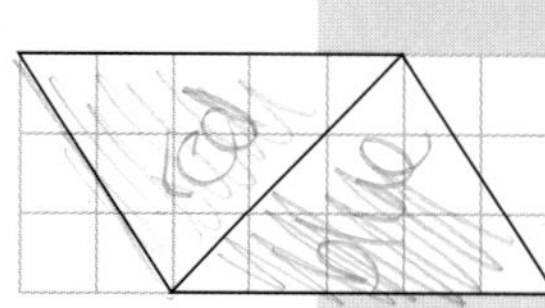

Inquire

1. How does the area of each triangle compare with the area of the parallelogram?

2. How does the base of the triangle compare with the base of the parallelogram?

3. How does the height of the triangle compare with the height of the parallelogram?

4. Use the symbols A, b, and h to write a formula for the area of a triangle.

5. What is the area of the triangle of earth at the end of the parking lot?

Example

Calculate the area of the triangle.

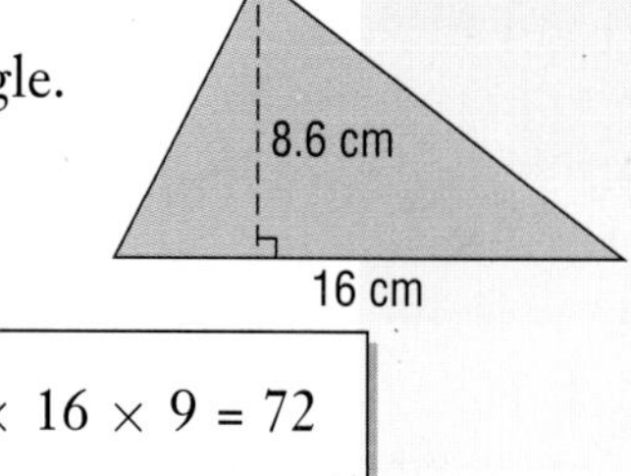

Solution

$$
\begin{aligned}
A &= \tfrac{1}{2} \times b \times h \\
&= \tfrac{1}{2} \times 16 \times 8.6 \\
&= 8 \times 8.6 \\
&= 68.8
\end{aligned}
$$

EST $\frac{1}{2} \times 16 \times 9 = 72$

The area of the triangle is 68.8 cm^2.

Practice

1. Measure the triangle and calculate its area.

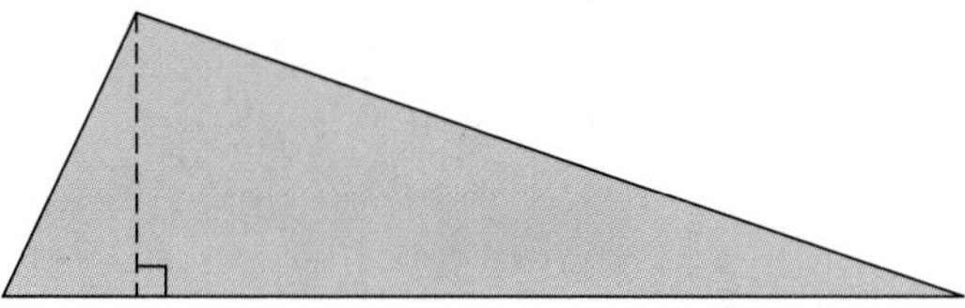

Calculate the area of each shaded region.

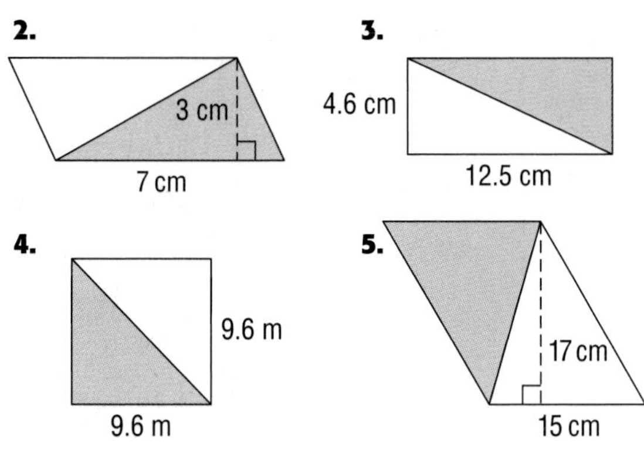

Estimate, then calculate the area of each triangle.

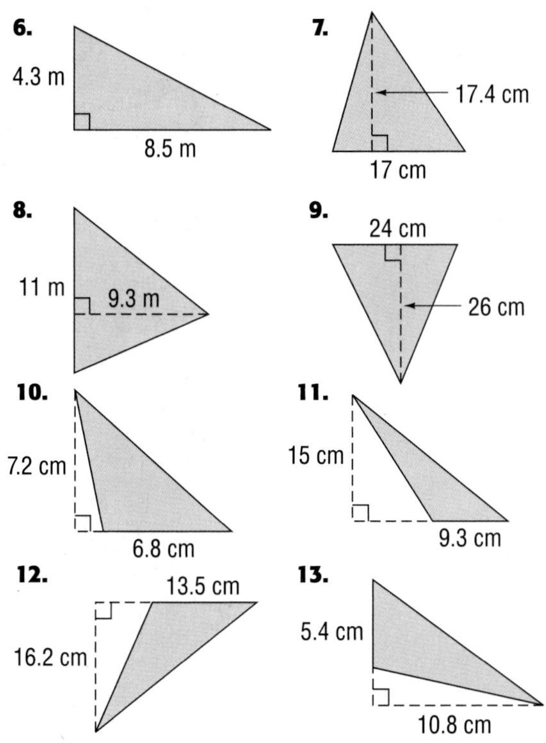

Problems and Applications

Calculate the area of each shaded region.

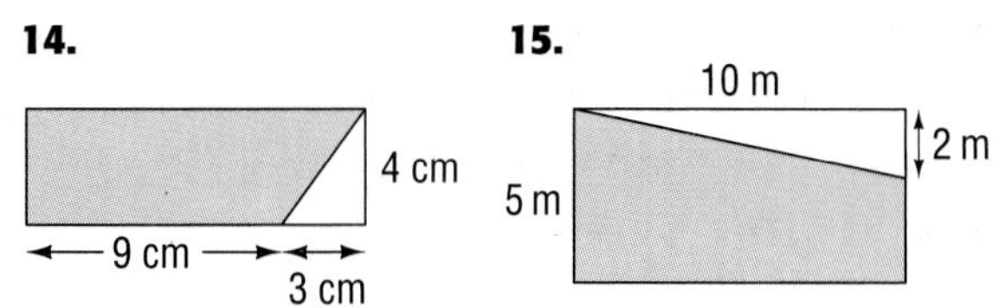

16. The flag is 100 cm by 60 cm.

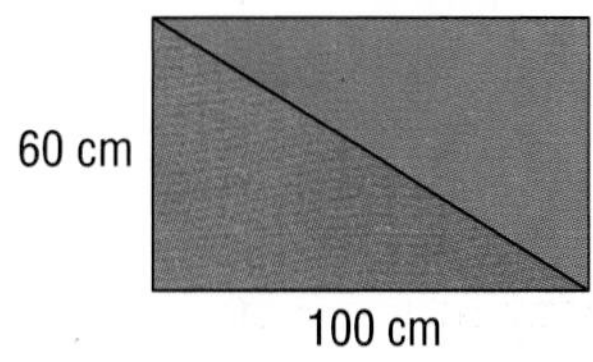

a) Find the area of the flag.

b) Find the area of the red region.

c) Find the area of the blue region.

17. Mr. Jamison dug a flower bed in the corner of his yard. What is the area of the flower bed?

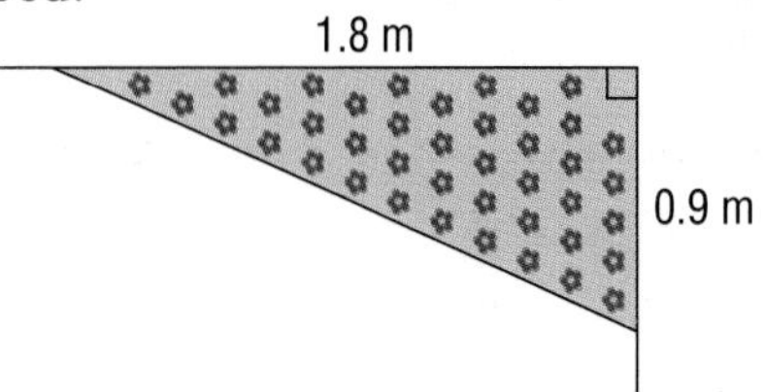

18. The Wongs bought a bedroom mirror. Each square section is 25 cm on each side. The height of each triangular section is 31 cm. What is the area of the mirror?

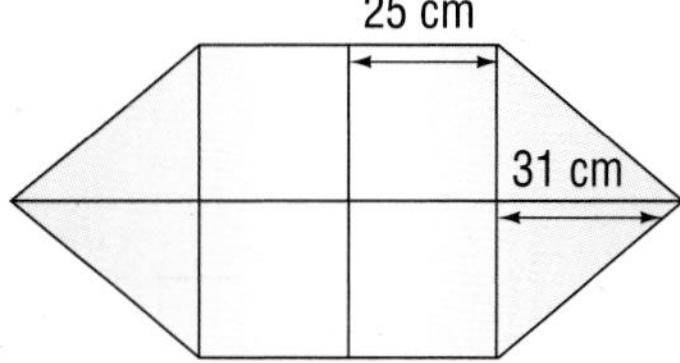

19. Write an area problem that involves two or more triangles. Have a classmate solve the problem.

How Computer Programs Work

A set of instructions we give a computer is called a **program**. By numbering the steps in a program, we tell the computer the order in which to follow the instructions. A computer understands many programming languages. The one we will use here is called BASIC. The chart gives the BASIC symbols for the operations in mathematics.

Operation	Mathematical Symbol	BASIC Symbol
Addition	+	+
Subtraction	−	−
Multiplication	×	*
Division	÷	/
Raising to an exponent	Exponent	↑ or ∧

Activity ❶

The following program tells a computer to add two numbers. Enter the program into the computer by typing each line exactly as shown and pressing ENTER (or RETURN) after each line. The program is "run" when you type RUN and press ENTER.

```
NEW
10 PRINT"ADDING TWO NUMBERS"
20 INPUT"FIRST NUMBER";A         ← Enter the first number.
30 INPUT"SECOND NUMBER";B        ← Enter the second number.
40 PRINT"THE SUM IS"
50 PRINT A;"+";B;"=";A+B         ← The computer prints the sum.
60 END
```

Test the program by adding numbers.

Activity ❷

Modify the program so that the computer performs these operations.

1. subtracts numbers

2. multiplies numbers

3. divides numbers

4. adds three or more numbers

Have a classmate test your programs.

Programming Formulas in BASIC

This program calculates the area of a triangle.

```
NEW
10 PRINT "Area of a Triangle"
20 INPUT "The base is";B
30 INPUT "The height is";H
40 A = .5*B*H
50 PRINT "The area is";A"square units."
60 END
```

Activity ❶

Use the program to calculate the area of each triangle.

1.

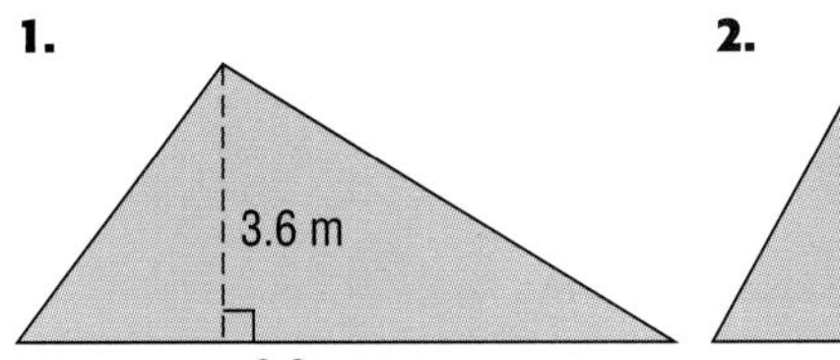

2.

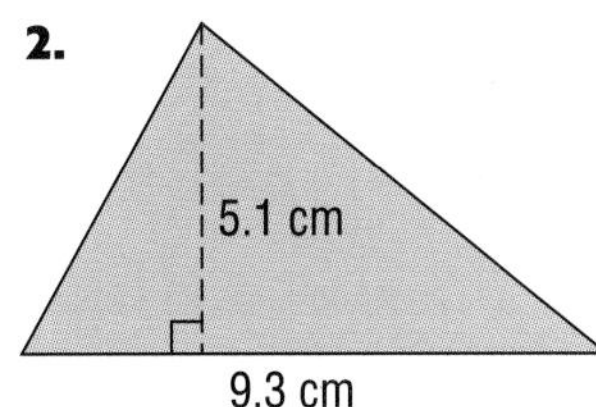

3.

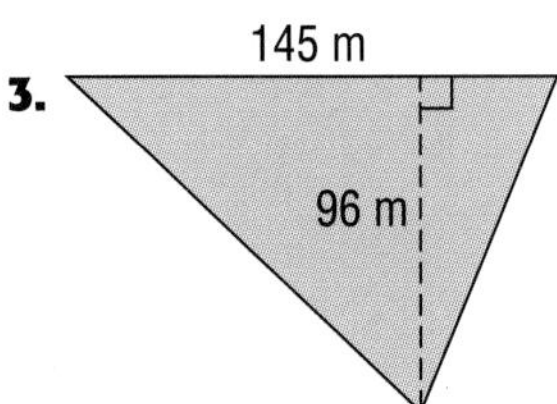

Activity ❷

Modify the program to calculate the following.

1. the area of a rectangle
2. the area of a parallelogram
3. the area of a square
4. the circumference of a circle

Have a classmate test your programs.

Activity ❸

Use your programs to calculate the area for each diagram.

1.

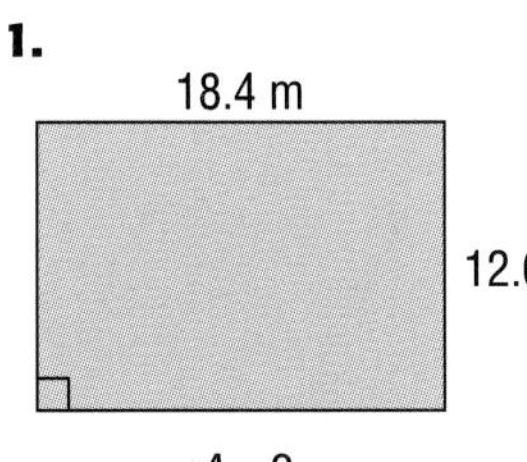

2.

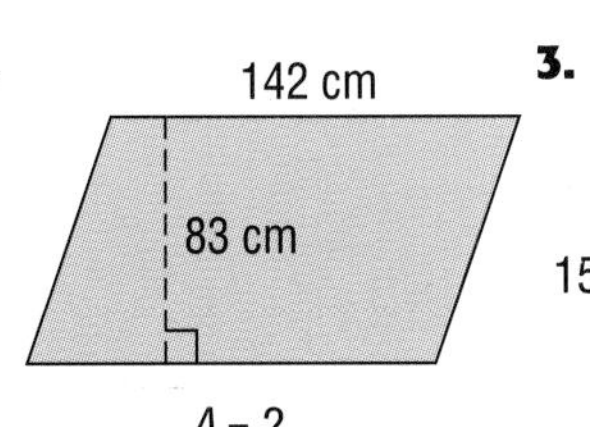

3.

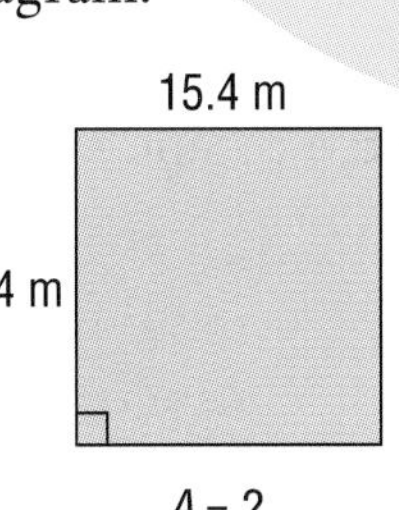

4.11 Working with Area

Activity: Solve the Problem

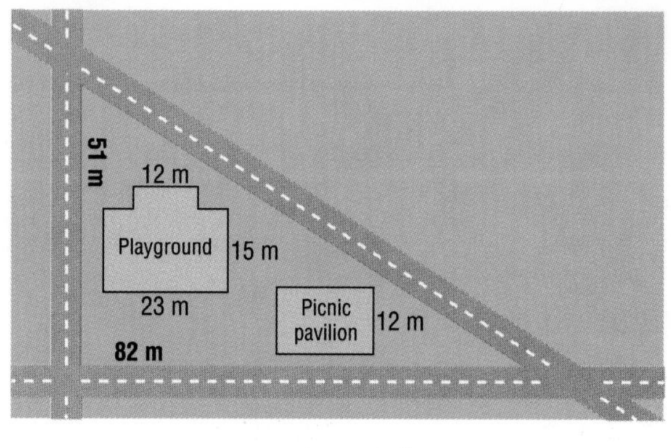

The grass in this triangular park needs to be fertilized. The picnic pavilion and the playground are paved. The rest of the park is grass. What area of the park is grass?

Inquire

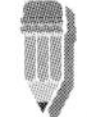

1. What assumptions must you make?

2. Copy the diagram and add the missing information.

3. Calculate the total area of the park, the area of the playground, and the area of the picnic pavilion.

4. Calculate the area of the grass.

5. How could you use addition to check your answer?

Example

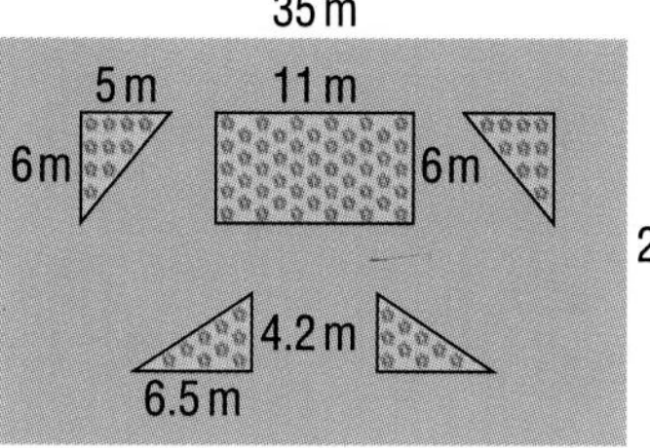

The diagram shows the flower beds on the lawn in front of City Hall.

a) What is the total area of the flower beds?

b) What is the area of the grass?

Solution

Assume that the lawn is a rectangle, one flower bed is a rectangle, and the other flower beds are two pairs of congruent right triangles. Find the area of the flower beds. Subtract it from the total area of the lawn to find the area of the grass.

a) Area of rectangular flower bed 6×11

$= 66$

Area of triangles $2 \times \frac{1}{2} \times 6 \times 5 + 2 \times \frac{1}{2} \times 6.5 \times 4.2$

$= 57.3$

Total area $66 + 57.3$

$= 123.3$

EST $6 \times 5 + 7 \times 4 = 58$

The total area of the flower beds is 123.3 m^2.

b) Total area of lawn 35×22

$= 770$

Area of grass $770 - 123.3$

$= 646.7$

The area of the grass is 646.7 m^2. How could you check your answers?

Recall the steps

Understand the Problem

Think of a Plan

Carry Out the Plan

Look Back

Problems and Applications

The Superstone Patio Company designed these patios. Calculate the area of each. Determine the total cost of each at $23.00/m^2$.

1. **2.**

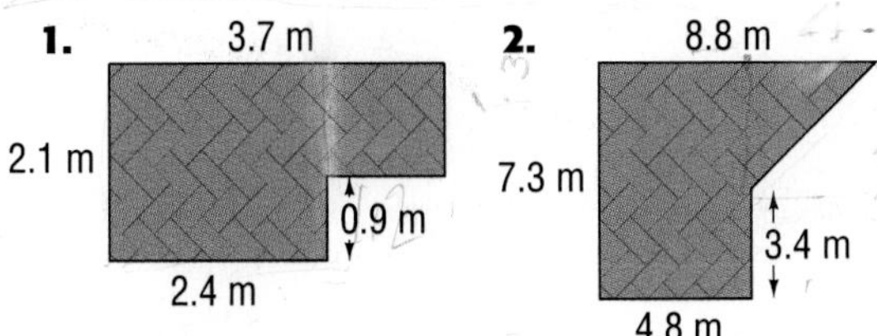

3.

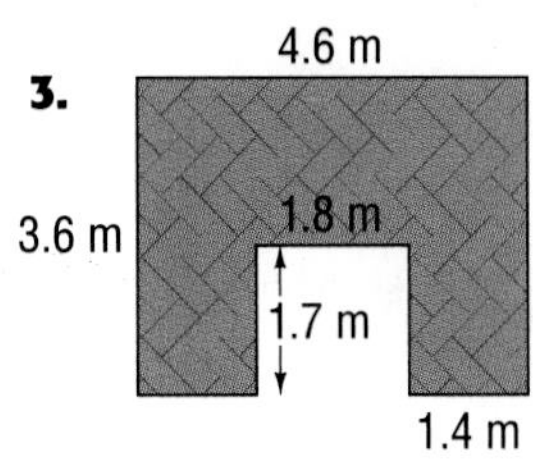

4. The hockey surface at a community centre is 61 m by 30.5 m. Field hockey is played outdoors on a surface 91.5 m by 54.9 m. Which surface has the larger area and by how much?

5. The Taj Mahal in India is a square about 95.4 m on each side. What is the area of the Taj Mahal?

6. A double roll of wallpaper is 10 m long and 51.6 cm wide. What is the maximum area of wall that 1 roll covers?

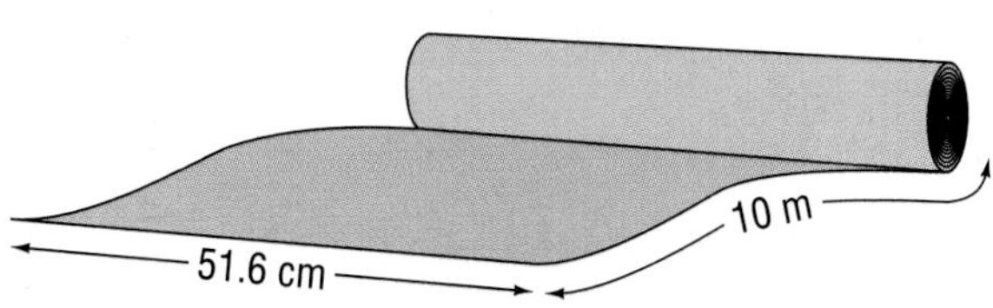

7. The school swimming pool is 50 m long and 21 m wide. The pool is divided lengthwise into six lanes for a swim meet. What is the area of each lane?

8. The Beestons' backyard is in the shape of a parallelogram. There is a sun deck in the yard, as shown in the diagram. Calculate the area of the grass.

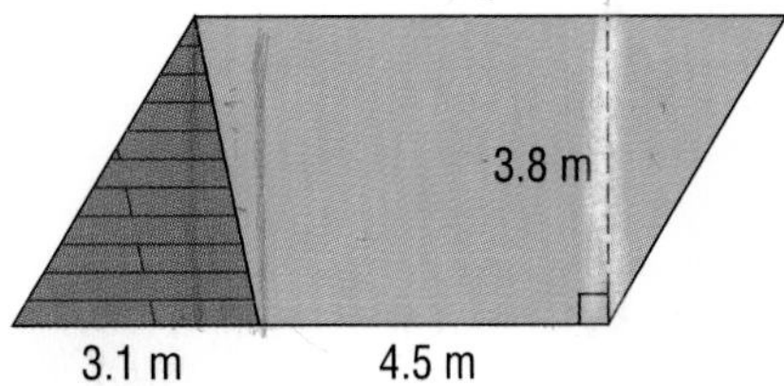

9. A hotel swimming pool measures 20 m by 8 m. The hotel manager wants to put a 2 m wide deck around the pool. Calculate the area of the deck.

10. A brick path between two buildings is a rectangle 30.5 m by 4.1 m. Flowers grow in 4 square holes in the walkway. Each side of the holes is 1.2 m. Calculate the area covered in brick.

11. Design a front lawn for your school. Include areas for flowers and benches. Sketch your design and mark the dimensions. Have a classmate calculate the area of the grass.

LOGIC POWER

Aziza had 142 cans of food to put on shelves at the Food Bank. There were 2 sizes of shelves. The larger one held 24 cans, the smaller one held 14 cans. When Aziza finished, the 142 cans completely filled some shelves. How many shelves of each size did she fill?

Lewis Carroll

Charles Dodgson was an English writer and mathematician. When he wrote math books, he used his real name. But he used the pseudonym Lewis Carroll in the books he wrote for children. His most famous books are *Alice's Adventures in Wonderland* and *Through the Looking Glass*.

The following passage is from one of his nonsense poems, called "Fit the Fifth: The Beaver's Lesson".

The Beaver brought paper, portfolio, pens,
And ink in unfailing supplies:
While strange creepy creatures came out of their dens,
And watched them with wondering eyes.

So engrossed was the Butcher, he heeded them not,
And he wrote with a pen in each hand,
And explained all the while in a popular style
Which the beaver could well understand.

"Taking Three as the subject to reason about—
A convenient number to state—
We add Seven, and Ten, and then multiply out
By One Thousand diminished by Eight.

"The result we proceed to divide, as you see,
By Nine Hundred and Ninety and Two:
Then subtract Seventeen, and the answer must be
Exactly and perfectly true.

"The method employed I would gladly explain,
While I have it so clear in my head,
If I had but the time and you had but the brain—
But much yet remains to be said."

Activity ❶

1. Calculate the answer to the problem in the poem.

2. What is the answer to the problem when you start with 7 instead of 3.

3. Explain the answers and compare with your classmates' explanations.

Activity ❷

Lewis Carroll invented a puzzle called "doublets." In this game, you are given two words. You are asked to get from one word to the other by changing one letter at a time. You must form a new word each time you change a letter.

Here is one way to go from CAT to DOG.

CAT
COT
DOT
DOG

1. Turn a CAR into a BUS.

2. Turn a RUN into a JOG.

3. Turn an EYE into a LID.

4. Turn a BOW into a TIE.

5. Compare your lists of words with a classmate's.

Activity ❸

Lewis Carroll liked to put reflections, or mirror images, in his writing. Tweedledee and Tweedledum in *Through the Looking Glass* are mirror images of each other.

Carroll's poem "Jabberwocky" starts with a stanza that must be read in a mirror.

1. Write your name so that it must be read in a mirror.

2. Where else have you seen writing that must be read in a mirror?

3. What does the mirror image of your right hand look like?

4. In the number 77, are the two digits mirror images of each other? Explain.

5. Write the mirror image of the number 913. Check the result with a mirror.

4.12 Use Logical Reasoning

Brent, Lucas, Abe, and Marris each have a pet. The four pets are a horse, a fish, a parrot, and a dog. Lucas' brother owns the fish. Abe can ride his pet. Marris' pet cannot fly or live under water. Who has each pet?

1. What information are you given?

2. What are you asked to find?

Make a table with rows and columns. Fill in the known facts.

When you enter a "yes," write "no" for the other entries in the same row and column.

Lucas's brother owns the fish, so Lucas does not.

	Brent	Lucas	Abe	Marris
Horse				
Fish		no		
Parrot				
Dog				

Abe can ride his pet, so he has the horse.

	Brent	Lucas	Abe	Marris
Horse	no	no	yes	no
Fish		no	no	
Parrot			no	
Dog			no	

Only the horse and dog cannot fly or live under water. Abe owns the horse, so Marris must have the dog.

	Brent	Lucas	Abe	Marris
Horse	no	no	yes	no
Fish		no	no	no
Parrot			no	no
Dog	no	no	no	yes

Brent must have the fish, because Lucas does not.

	Brent	Lucas	Abe	Marris
Horse	no	no	yes	no
Fish	yes	no	no	no
Parrot	no		no	no
Dog	no	no	no	yes

Lucas must have the parrot.

	Brent	Lucas	Abe	Marris
Horse	no	no	yes	no
Fish	yes	no	no	no
Parrot	no	yes	no	no
Dog	no	no	no	yes

Brent has the fish. Lucas has the parrot. Abe has the horse. Marris has the dog.

Check that the answer agrees with the given information.

Use Logical Reasoning	1. Organize the information. 2. Draw conclusions from the information. 3. Check that your answer is reasonable.

Problems and Applications

1. Pedro, Helena, and Carrie each play a different instrument. The instruments are the trumpet, piano, and guitar. Helena walks to school with the piano and guitar players. Carrie lends the guitar player some money for lunch. Who plays the guitar?

2. Shara, Theresa, and Lance bought a bowl of soup, a salad, and a hot dog for lunch. One of the girls had the soup. Shara put mustard on her lunch. Which item did each person eat?

3. Noreen has 4 new textbooks — French, art, math, and science. The covers are blue, red, green, and black. The art book is not green or red. The math book is black. The French book is not red. What colour is the cover of each book?

4. Nancy, Terry, and Rica own bicycles. One bike is black, one is blue, and one is green. Use the following clues to decide the colour and type of bike that each person owns.

Nancy's bike is not the 10-speed.

The 5-speed bike is blue.

Terry's bike is not green or black.

The 1-speed bike is not black.

5. You are walking down a road when you come to a fork. One way leads to Smithville. Twin brothers are standing at the fork. One always lies, the other always tells the truth. You can ask only one question for information. What question should you ask to be sure of getting to Smithville?

6. Seven coins look the same. But one coin is counterfeit and is lighter than the others. A two-pan balance is available for weighing. What is the smallest number of weighings you need to be sure of finding the counterfeit coin?

7. A nurse, a teacher, and a computer operator live in a row of three houses. When you face the houses, you see that the two-storey house is just to the left of the bungalow. The nurse used to live in the house on the far left. The teacher lives in the split-level. The computer operator lives next door to the teacher. Who lives in which house?

8. Make up a problem that has the answers shown in the chart.

	Adjua	Pierre	Carol	Ravi
Tennis		yes		
Bowling	yes			
Skating				yes
Swimming			yes	

Test your problem to make sure it works, then ask a classmate to solve it.

LOGIC POWER

The triangle is on a 5 by 5 geoboard. There is one pin inside the triangle and no pins on its sides, except at the vertices.

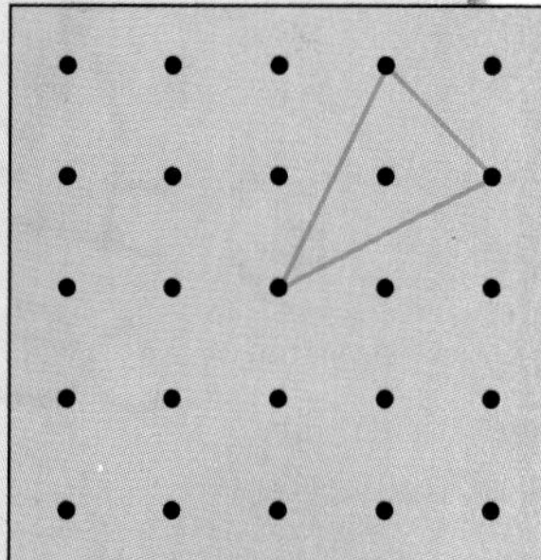

Use this geoboard to make other triangles that have one pin inside and no pins on their sides. How many other triangles of different shapes and sizes can you make?

Review

Measure the dimensions of each figure. Calculate each perimeter.

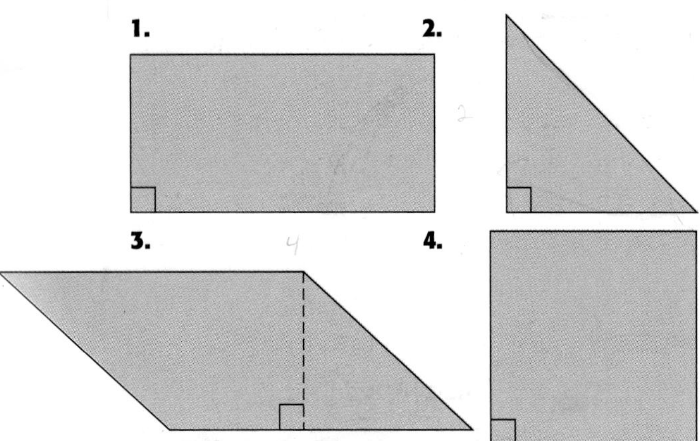

Calculate each perimeter.

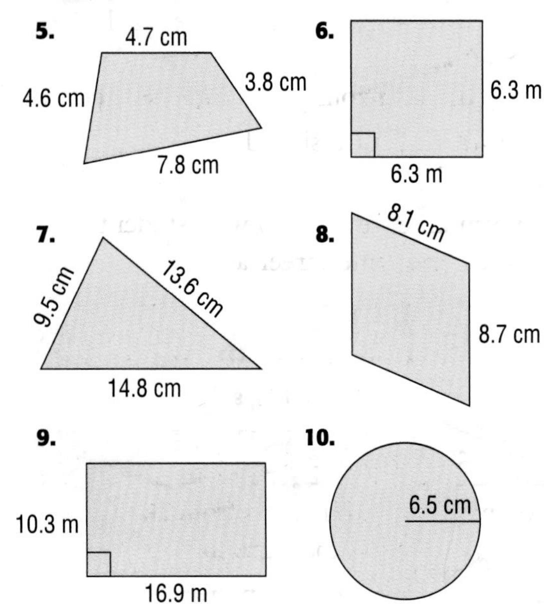

Calculate the perimeter of each figure.

11. rectangle, $l = 16.5$ mm, $w = 9.3$ mm

12. pentagon, $s = 7.2$ cm

13. hexagon, $s = 11.4$ m

14. equilateral triangle, $s = 6.6$ cm

15. square, $s = 14.8$ m

16. octagon, $s = 12.5$ cm

Measure the dimensions of each figure. Calculate each area.

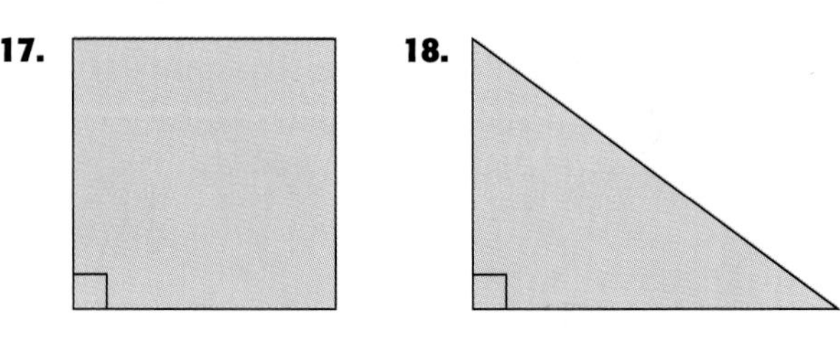

Calculate the area of each figure.

20. square, $s = 5.6$ cm

21. parallelogram, $b = 11.4$ mm, $h = 8.3$ mm

22. rectangle, $l = 14.2$ km, $w = 11$ km

23. triangle, $b = 7$ cm, $h = 4.4$ cm

The following figures were made on a geoboard, with pegs in the same row or column spaced 2 cm apart. What is the area of each figure?

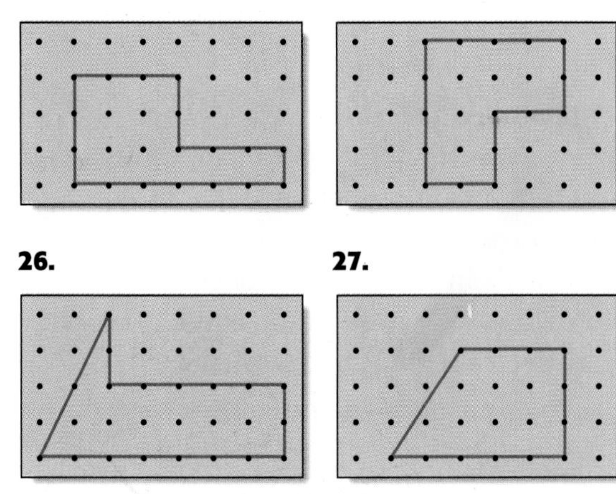

28. A square with side 38 cm is divided into 4 congruent triangles. What is the area of each triangle?

Calculate the area of each figure.

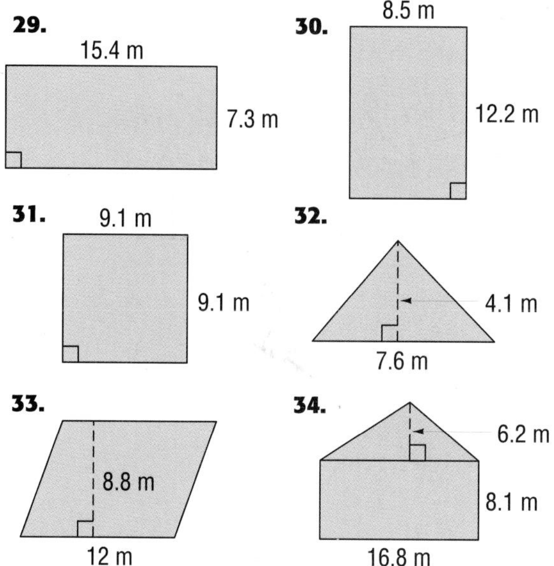

Calculate the area of each patio.

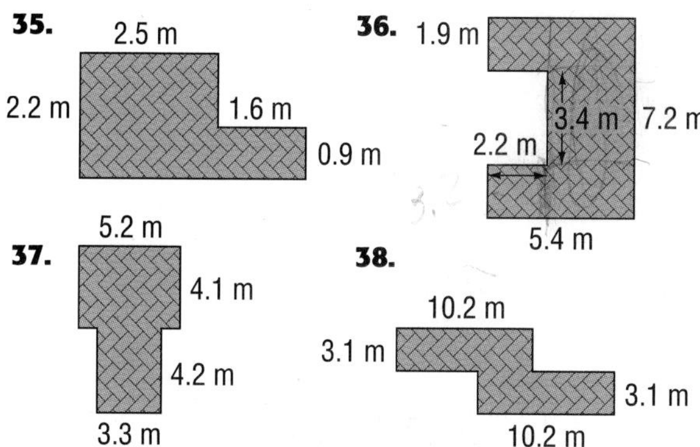

39. A bulletin board is 2.4 m long and 1.2 m high. It is covered in a checkerboard pattern with 288 green and white squares of the same size. Find the side of each square in centimetres.

40. The lawn contains 4 flower beds. Calculate the area of grass to be fertilized.

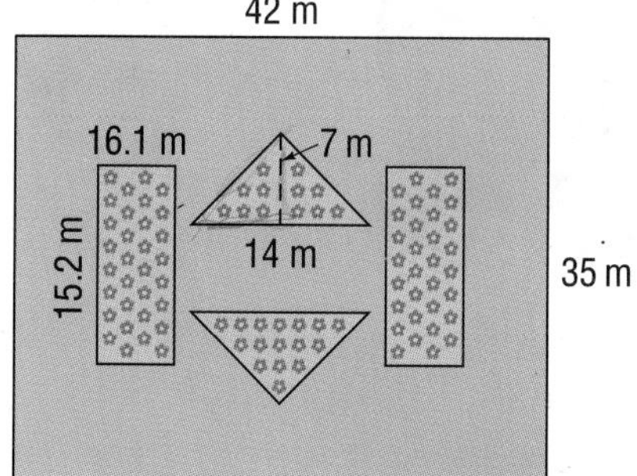

Group Decision Making

Researching Travel Industry Careers

1. Brainstorm with the whole class to decide the careers you would like to investigate. They might include careers like travel agent, airline pilot, bus driver, or mechanic. As a class, choose six careers.

2. Go to home groups.

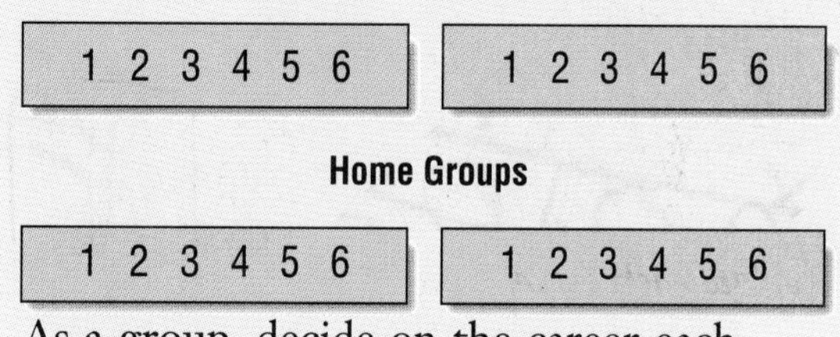

As a group, decide on the career each student will investigate. Decide as a group the questions you want answered.

3. Research your assigned career individually.

4. Form an expert group with students assigned the same career as you.

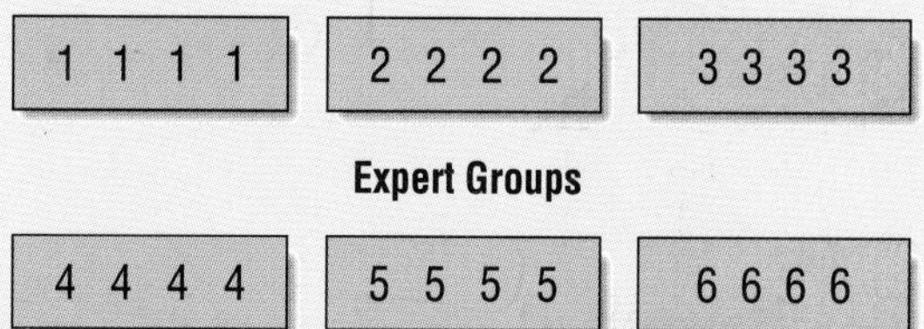

Combine the information from all members of the expert group.

5. In your expert group, prepare a report on the assigned career. Include a description of how the career makes use of math. The report can take any form the group chooses.

6. In your expert group, evaluate the group process and the report. Identify what worked well and what you would do differently next time.

Chapter Check

Calculate the perimeter of each figure.

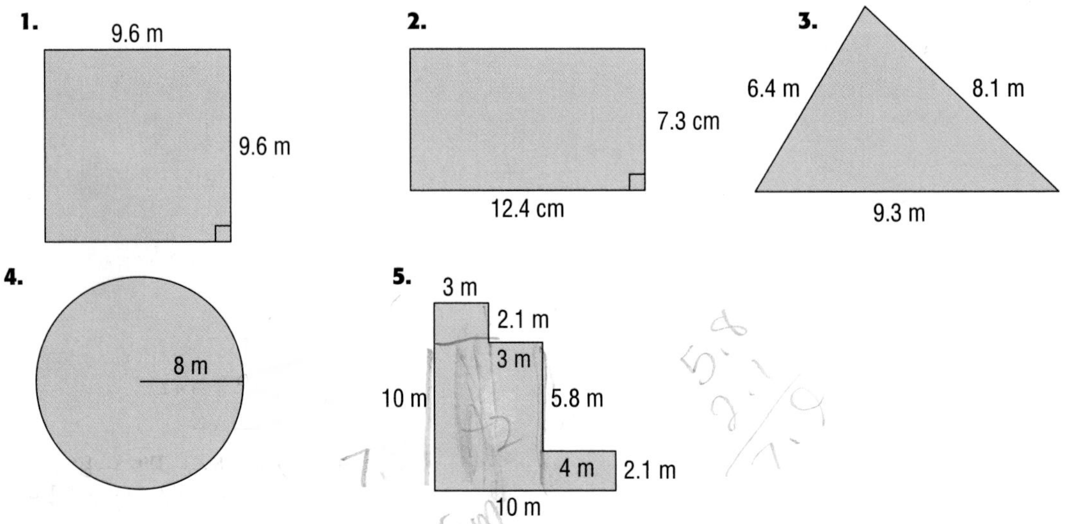

Calculate the area of each figure.

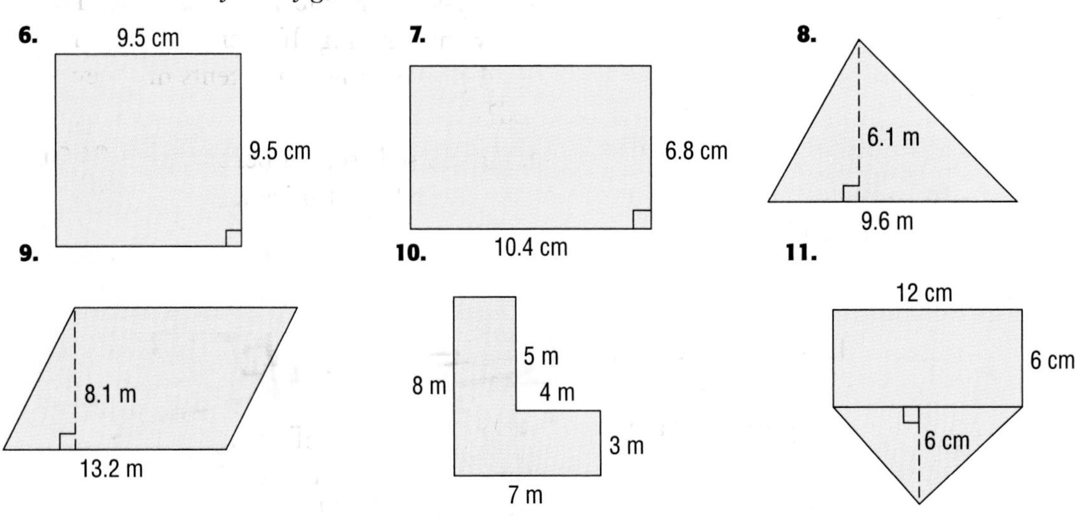

The Reingolds have a square patio in one corner of their yard. A lawn covers the rest of the yard.

12. What is the perimeter of the patio?

13. What is the area of the lawn?

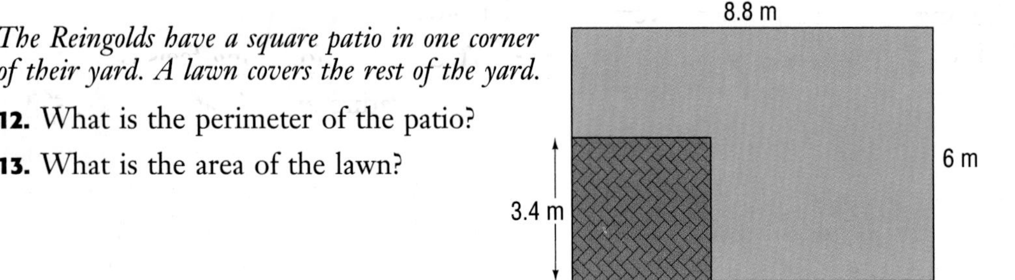

Using the Strategies

In questions 1–12, solve the problem and state the strategy you used.

1. The area of the triangle is 4 cm^2. What is the area of the hexagon?

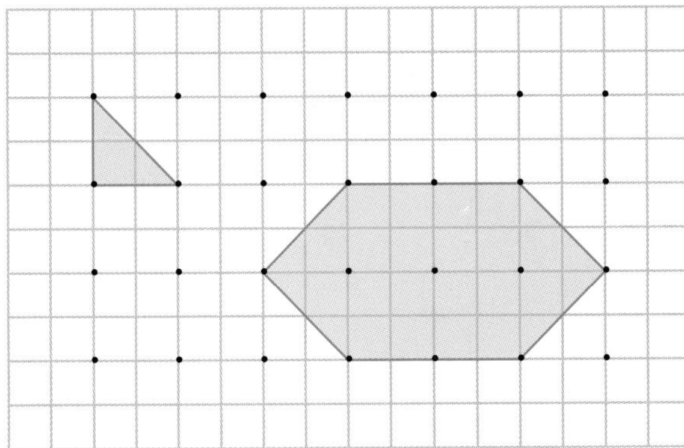

2. In how many different ways can Karl, Andrea, and Heidi line up at the movie theatre to buy tickets?

3. Last Saturday, the Hamilton Red Birds baseball team played two games. The first game started at 13:15 and took 2 h and 48 min to play. The second game took 3 h and 46 min to play. There was a 15 min break between the games. At what time did the second game finish?

4. There are 33 tables in the school cafeteria. There are 6 chairs at each table. If there are 17 empty chairs, how many students are seated in the cafeteria?

5. If you divide a certain number by 3, then add 13, the result is 34. What is the number?

6. A snail is climbing a tree 10 m high. Every day, the snail climbs 3 m. Each night, it slides back 2 m. How many days will the snail take to reach the top of the tree?

7. If the pattern continues, what are the next three numbers?

81, 80, 82, 81, 83, ■, ■, ■

8. Arrows mark the one-way streets. One route from A to K goes from A to D to F to G to K. How many other ways are there?

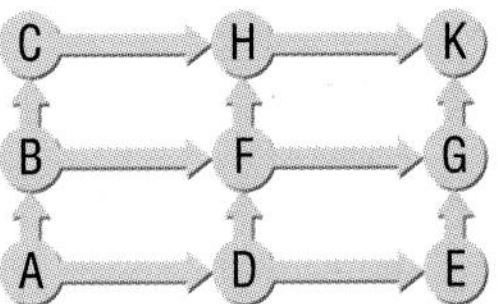

9. The rectangle has a perimeter of 24 m. Sketch 4 other rectangles whose sides are whole numbers of metres and whose perimeters are 24 m.

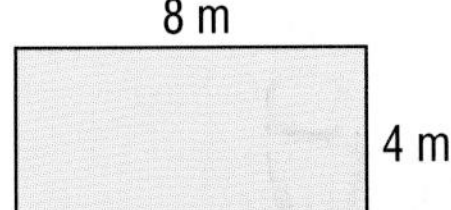

10. The product of two consecutive page numbers in this book is 4160. What are the page numbers?

11. Sixty-seven members of the Wilderness Club went camping. If a tent holds no more than 4 people, how many tents did they need?

12. Harold sells school pens at 3 for $6.50. What is the lowest price he should charge for one pen?

DATA BANK

1. Which of the following distances is longer and by how much?

a) the length of the Nile River

b) the driving distance from Halifax to Vancouver

2. Which of the following feels colder?

a) a temperature of –4°C at a wind speed of 24 km/h

b) a temperature of –1°C at a wind speed of 32 km/h

Chapter 1

Choose a calculation method.

1. You need to calculate a year's earnings from a daily newspaper route.

2. You keep score for a hockey game.

3. Your teacher asks how many hours you studied last month.

Write the total value of the underlined digit in each number.

4. $23\underline{4}5$ **5.** $45.\underline{6}7$ **6.** $\underline{2}3\ 987$

7. $1.0\underline{6}8$ **8.** $46\ \underline{8}23$ **9.** $8.45\underline{6}$

Estimate, then calculate.

10. 456 + 319 + 771 **11.** 2340 − 1123

12. 28.9 + 33.6 + 56.9 **13.** 1.001 − 0.987

14. At the start of the month, Marla had $45.90 in the bank. During the month, she deposited $23.56, $35.00, and $72.00. She wrote one check for $19.05. How much did she have in the bank at the end of the month?

Estimate, then calculate.

15. 23×78 **16.** 294×21

17. 12.6×6.2 **18.** 18.9×1.4

Divide. Use short division.

19. $575 \div 5$ **20.** $388 \div 4$

21. Ravi worked one Saturday for 3.5 h and earned $5.60/h. How much did he earn altogether?

22. Six friends eat at a restaurant. The total bill is $83.70. To share the cost equally, how much should each pay?

Simplify.

23. $21 \div (9 - 7) + 31$

24. $28.8 + 16.2 \times 2 - 9.7$

Chapter 2

List all the factors of each number.

1. 18 **2.** 28 **3.** 33

4. 56 **5.** 44 **6.** 72

Classify as prime or composite.

7. 19 **8.** 14 **9.** 27

10. 41 **11.** 37 **12.** 24

Complete each factor tree.

13.

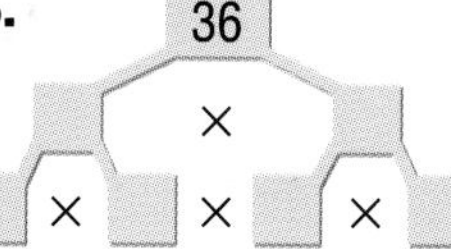

14.

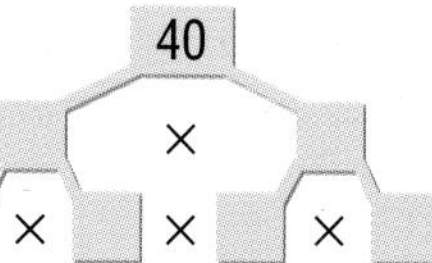

Write as the product of prime factors.

15. 12 **16.** 21 **17.** 100

18. 75 **19.** 44 **20.** 90

Find the greatest common factor.

21. 6, 24 **22.** 12, 18 **23.** 20, 30

24. 12, 32 **25.** 27, 18 **26.** 14, 35

27. 8, 16, 24 **28.** 12, 24, 42 **29.** 10, 15, 20

Find the lowest common multiple.

30. 5, 15 **31.** 6, 4 **32.** 3, 2

33. 4, 3 **34.** 6, 9 **35.** 12, 8

36. 3, 4, 2 **37.** 2, 4, 5 **38.** 2, 5, 3

Write in standard form.

39. 2^3 **40.** 3^4 **41.** 4^2

42. 3^3 **43.** 5^1 **44.** 6^2

Evaluate.

45. $3^3 + 4 - 1$ **46.** $(5 - 3)^4$

47. $12 \div 4 + 5^2$ **48.** $(16 - 2^3) \div 4$

Chapter 3

Use the figure to give the symbols of the following.

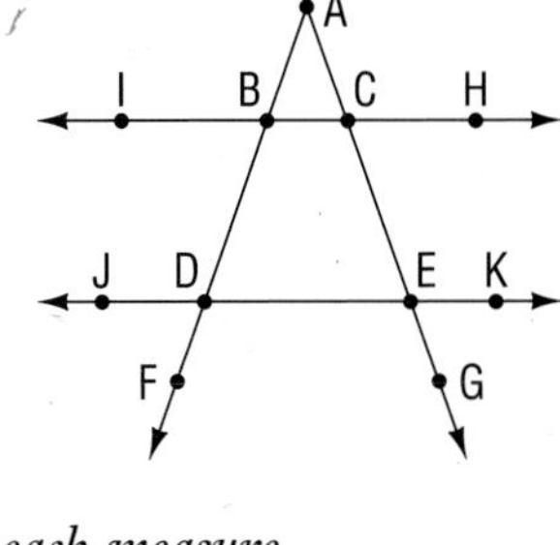

1. 4 points

2. 5 line segments

3. 4 rays

4. 2 lines

5. 6 angles

Draw an angle with each measure. Label and name each angle.

6. 23° **7.** 82° **8.** 90°

9. 113° **10.** 145° **11.** 61°

For each angle, draw the supplementary angle and classify it as acute, right, or obtuse.

12. 45° **13.** 132° **14.** 90°

Determine the measures x, y, and z.

15.

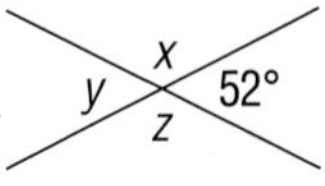

16.

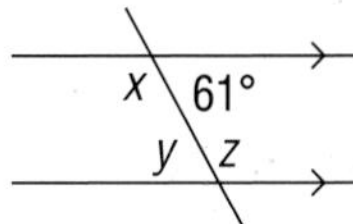

Draw the following triangles.

17. an acute isosceles triangle

18. an equilateral triangle

19. an obtuse scalene triangle

Find the value of x.

20.

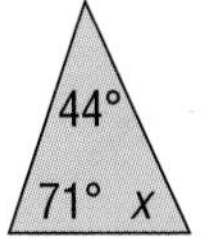

21.

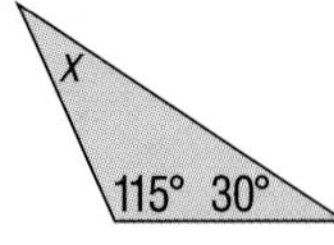

Draw each of the following.

22. a rhombus **23.** a parallelogram

24. The triangles are congruent. State the corresponding parts.

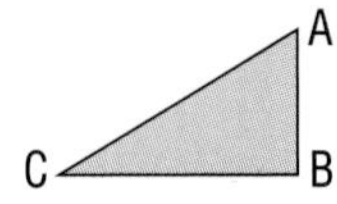

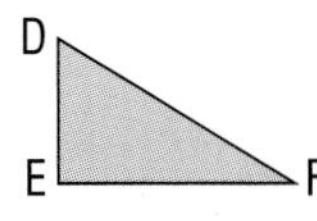

Chapter 4

Calculate the perimeter of each figure.

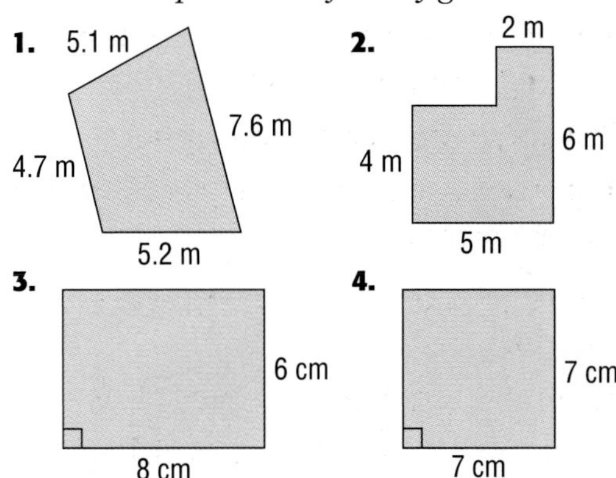

5. Calculate the circumference of a circle with radius 20 cm.

6. A rectangular plot for vegetables is 20 m by 10 m.

a) What length of fence is needed to fence the plot?

b) If fence posts are 2 m apart, how many posts are needed?

Calculate the area of each figure.

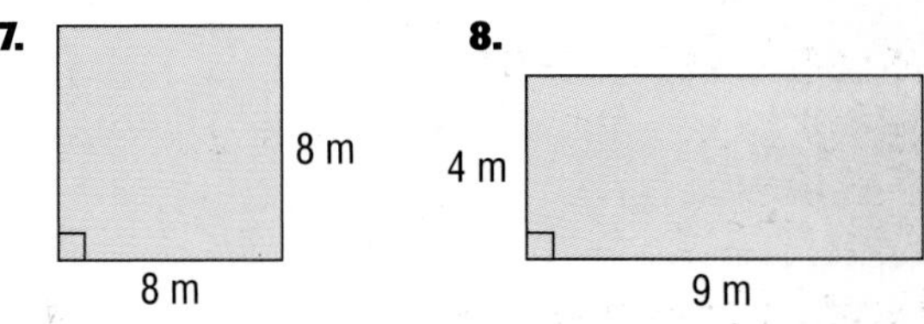

9.

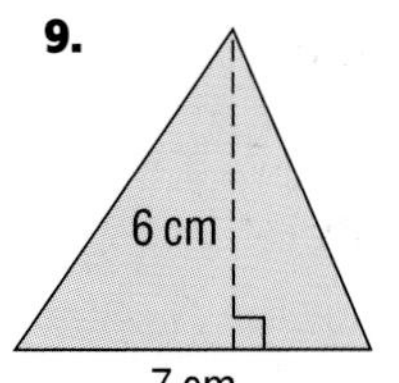

10.

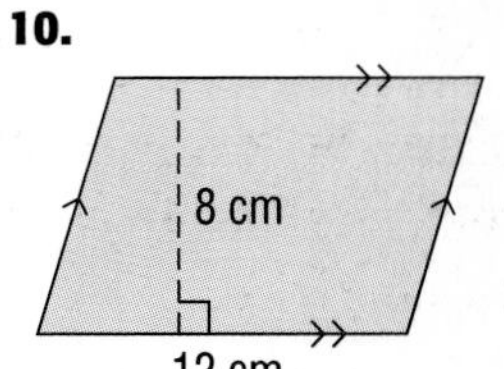

Calculate the area of each figure.

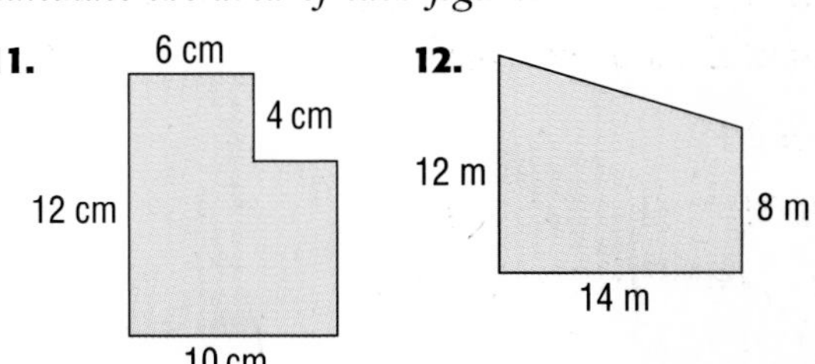

CHAPTER 5

Fractions

The different notes in music tell you how long to hold a note.

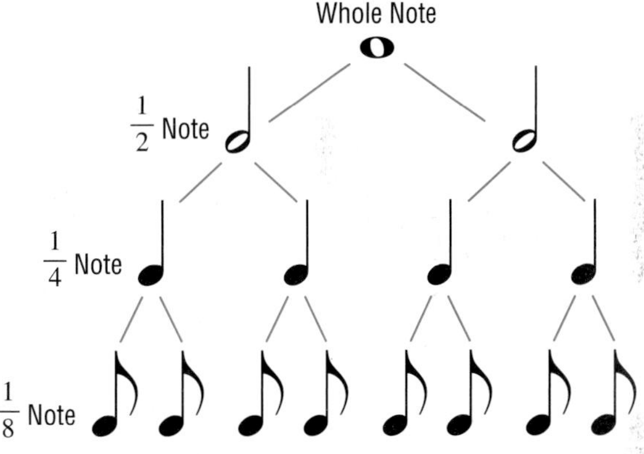

If you hold a whole note for 4 beats, how many beats do you hold a $\frac{1}{2}$ note for? a $\frac{1}{4}$ note? a $\frac{1}{8}$ note?
How many $\frac{1}{8}$ notes equal a whole note? a $\frac{1}{2}$ note?

Fractions

1. Fold paper squares of equal size to show all the ways you can divide a square into halves, quarters, and eighths.

Use a pencil and dot paper, or a geoboard and elastics, to make this square.

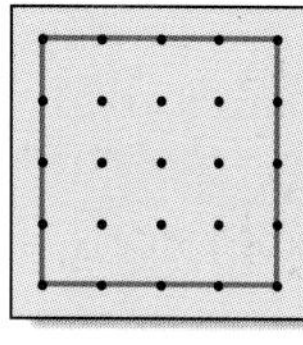

Then make the following pictures. State the fraction shaded in each.

2.

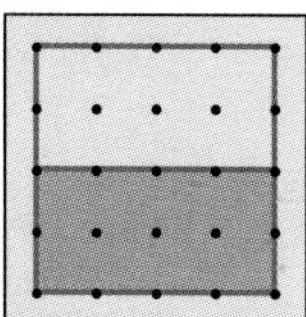

3.

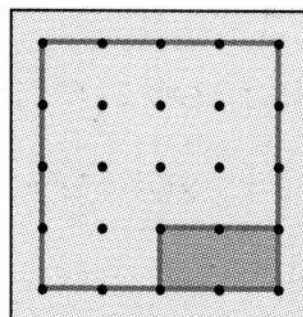

4.

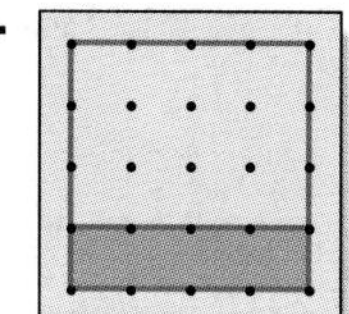

5.

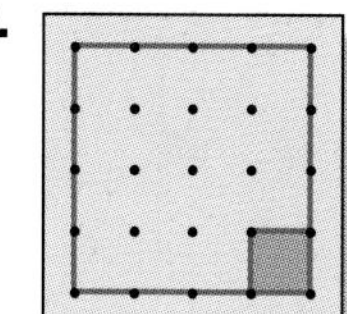

Use a pencil and dot paper, or a geoboard and elastics, to make this square.

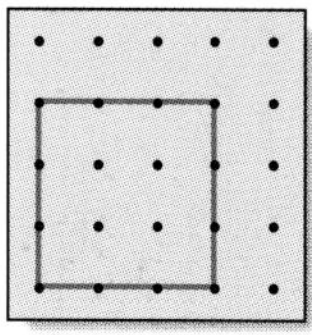

Then make the following pictures. State the fraction shaded in each.

6.

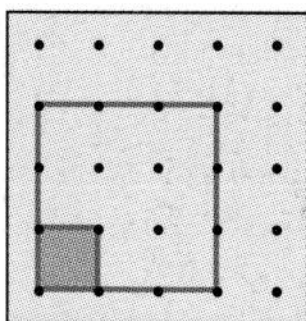

7.

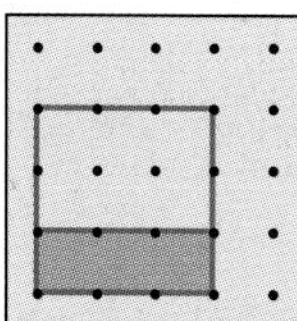

8.

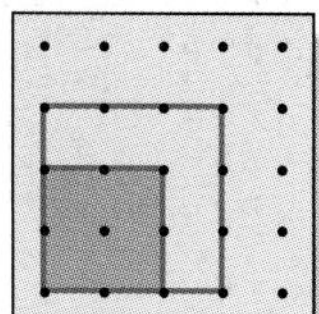

9.

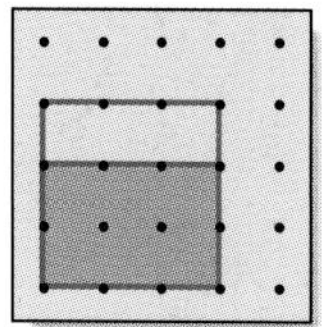

10. What fraction of the people are wearing hats?

11. What fraction of the circle is shaded?

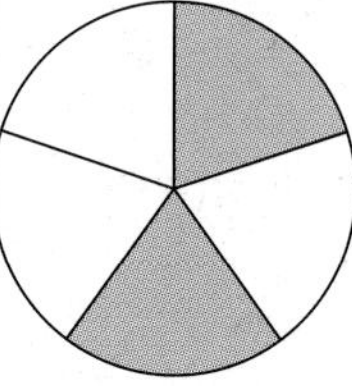

12. What fraction of the books are red?

13. Three students equally share 2 granola bars. What fraction does each student get?

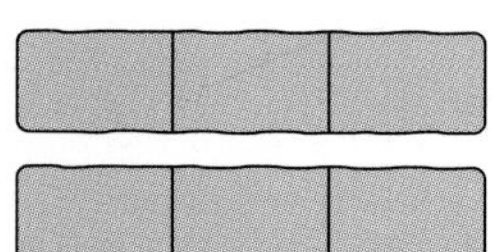

The shaded parts of the figures show fractions. Name each fraction in 2 different ways.

14.

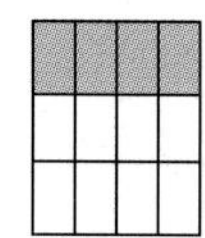

15.

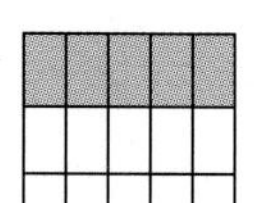

16.

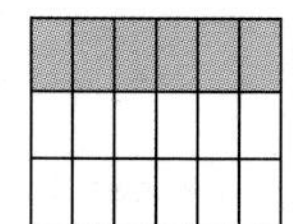

Arrange the fractions from smallest to largest.

17. $\frac{4}{5}$ $\frac{9}{10}$ $\frac{1}{4}$ $\frac{1}{2}$

18. $\frac{2}{3}$ $\frac{5}{6}$ $\frac{3}{4}$ $\frac{3}{8}$

Use the diagrams to find the answers.

19. $4\frac{3}{4} - 2 = \blacksquare$

20. $5\frac{1}{2} - 3 = \blacksquare$

Tangrams

A tangram is a square cut into 7 shapes. There are 2 large triangles, 1 medium-sized triangle, 2 small triangles, 1 square, and 1 parallelogram. The tangram below is on a 4×4 grid.

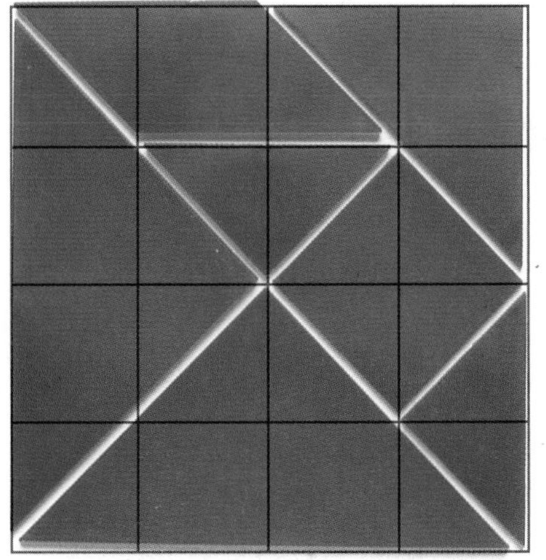

1. What fraction of the grid is covered by each of the following?

a) a large triangle
b) the medium-sized triangle
c) a small triangle
d) the square
e) the parallelogram

2. What fraction of each of the following does a small triangle cover?

a) a large triangle
b) the medium-sized triangle
c) the other small triangle
d) the square
e) the parallelogram

3. What combinations of shapes cover $\frac{1}{2}$ of the grid?

4. Which 3 shapes each cover the same fraction of the grid? Explain how you know.

Mental Math

Add.

1. $\frac{1}{4} + \frac{3}{4}$ **2.** $\frac{3}{5} + \frac{1}{5}$ **3.** $\frac{1}{2} + \frac{1}{2}$ **4.** $\frac{3}{8} + \frac{1}{8}$ **5.** $\frac{3}{10} + \frac{1}{10}$ **6.** $\frac{7}{12} + \frac{1}{12}$

Add.

7. $1\frac{1}{2} + 3\frac{1}{2}$ **8.** $6\frac{1}{4} + 2\frac{1}{4}$ **9.** $4\frac{1}{5} + 3\frac{3}{5}$ **10.** $5\frac{3}{10} + 2\frac{7}{10}$

Subtract.

11. $\frac{7}{8} - \frac{3}{8}$ **12.** $\frac{3}{4} - \frac{1}{4}$ **13.** $\frac{4}{5} - \frac{1}{5}$ **14.** $\frac{9}{10} - \frac{7}{10}$ **15.** $\frac{5}{6} - \frac{1}{6}$ **16.** $\frac{7}{8} - \frac{1}{8}$

Subtract.

17. $1 - \frac{1}{2}$ **18.** $1 - \frac{1}{4}$ **19.** $1 - \frac{2}{5}$ **20.** $3 - \frac{3}{4}$ **21.** $2 - \frac{4}{5}$ **22.** $2 - \frac{1}{2}$

Subtract.

23. $2\frac{1}{2} - 1\frac{1}{2}$ **24.** $4\frac{1}{4} - 1\frac{1}{4}$ **25.** $2\frac{1}{2} - 1\frac{1}{4}$ **26.** $2\frac{3}{4} - 1\frac{1}{4}$

Multiply.

27. $\frac{1}{2}$ of 6 **28.** $\frac{1}{2}$ of 12 **29.** $\frac{1}{2}$ of 10 **30.** $\frac{1}{2}$ of 20

5.1 The Meaning of Fractions

Activity: Examine the Diagrams

A tick-tack-toe game board and playing pieces are shown.

Inquire

1. How many red squares are on the board?

2. What is the total number of squares?

3. What fraction of the squares are red?

4. How many blue playing pieces are there?

5. What is the total number of playing pieces?

6. What fraction of the playing pieces are blue?

A fraction can name parts of a group.

Example 1

Paul collects old coins. He has 7 coins dated 1929. Five of them are dimes.
What fraction of the coins are dimes?

Solution

The numerator represents the number of equal parts being considered. Here, it is the number of dimes.
The denominator represents the total number of equal parts. Here, it is the total number of coins.
So, $\frac{5}{7}$ of the coins are dimes.

A fraction can also name parts of a whole.

Example 2

The line is divided into equal parts.
What fraction of the whole line is the distance from A to E?

A B C D E F

Solution

The line has 5 equal parts.
The distance from A to E is 4 parts.
The distance from A to E is $\frac{4}{5}$ of the whole line.

What fraction of the line is the distance from B to D? from C to F? from B to C? from A to D? from E to B?

Practice

What fraction of each diagram is shaded?

1. 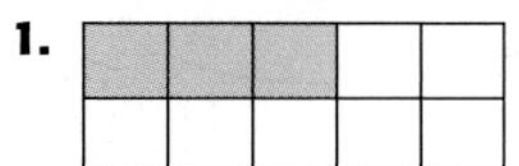

2. 

3. 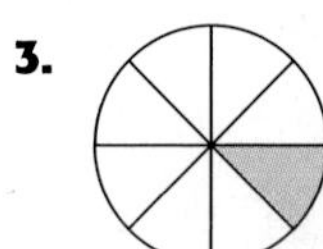

4. 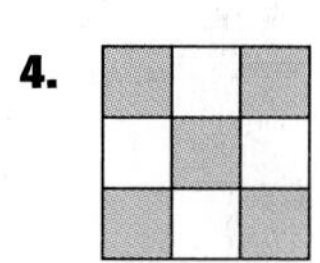

5. 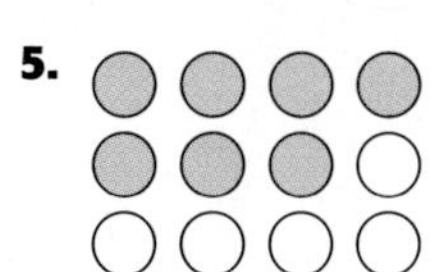

6. 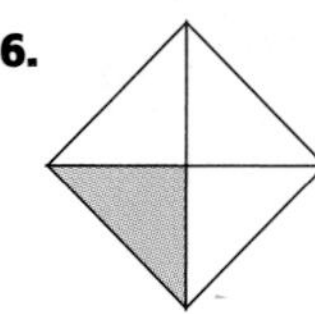

What fraction of each diagram is not shaded?

7. 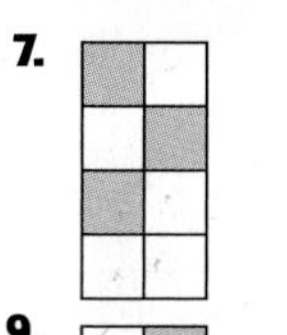

8. 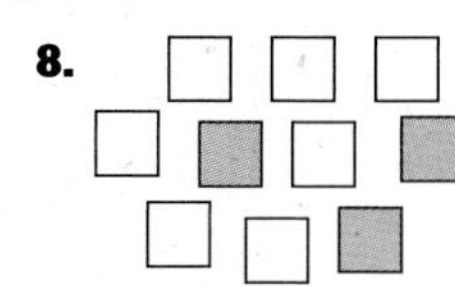

9. 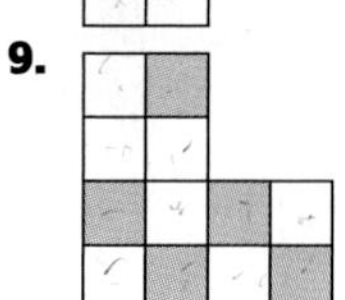

10. 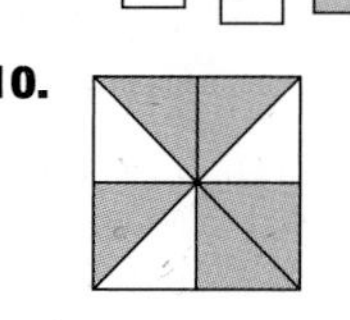

11. 

12. 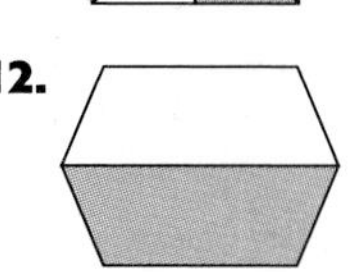

Draw a diagram to show each fraction as part of a whole.

13. $\frac{1}{2}$ **14.** $\frac{2}{3}$ **15.** $\frac{3}{4}$

Draw a diagram to show each fraction as part of a group.

16. $\frac{1}{5}$ **17.** $\frac{9}{10}$ **18.** $\frac{5}{6}$

The line is divided into equal parts.

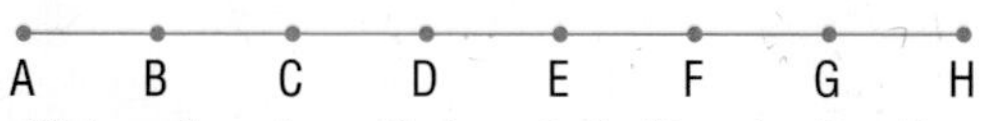

What fraction of the whole line is the distance between these points?

19. A to C **20.** B to F **21.** E to H

22. A to G **23.** D to H **24.** F to G

Problems and Applications

25. Estimate the fraction of each gas tank that is filled.

a) **b)**

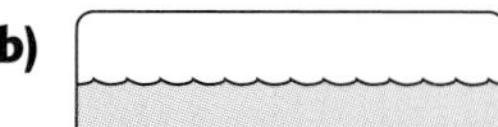

26. There are 50 stamps in the sheet.

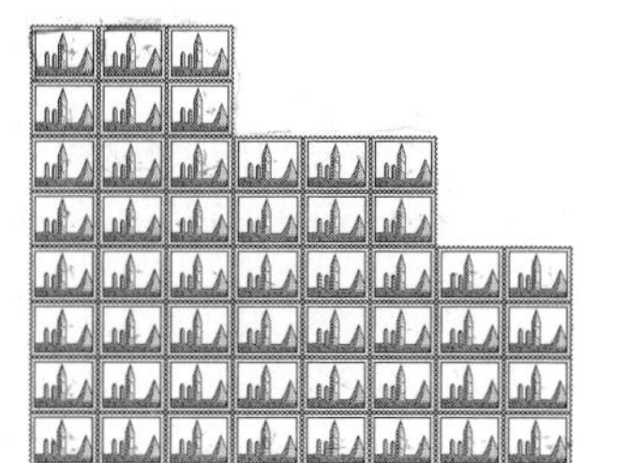

What fraction of the stamps

a) have 1 edge free? **b)** have 2 edges free?

c) have 0 edges free?

d) form the outside border?

27. What fraction of the letters in the word MATHEMATICS are vowels? consonants?

28. Print your name in upper case letters. What fraction of the letters have

a) only straight lines?

b) only curved lines?

c) straight and curved lines?

29. The chart shows the numbers of games won and lost in the American League East at the All-Star Break.

Team	Won	Lost
Baltimore	50	40
Toronto	49	41
Boston	48	42
Milwaukee	48	42
Cleveland	45	45
New York	43	47
Detroit	40	50

What fraction of the teams

a) won more than half of their games?

b) won at least half of their games?

c) lost more than half of their games?

30. What fraction of your class

a) is male? **b)** is female?

c) walks to school? **d)** rides to school?

e) is male and rides to school? **f)** has a first name that starts with a vowel?

g) likes spinach?

5.2 Equivalent Fractions

Activity: Solve the Problem

The Student Council had a group picture taken.

Inquire

1. How many boys are in the picture?
2. How many students are there?
3. What fraction of the students are boys?
4. How many rows of boys are there?
5. How many equal rows of students are there?
6. What fraction of the rows contain boys?

7. Are the two fractions equal? Explain.

Three of the 6 students wore blue shirts.
The fraction of students with blue shirts was $\frac{3}{6}$.
One-half of the students wore blue shirts.
The fraction of students with blue shirts was $\frac{1}{2}$.

$$\frac{3}{6} = \frac{1}{2}$$

The fractions $\frac{3}{6}$ and $\frac{1}{2}$ name the same part of the group. They are called **equivalent fractions** because they have the same value. To write equivalent fractions, multiply or divide the numerator and denominator by the same number.

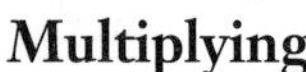

Multiplying

$$\frac{1}{4} = \frac{1 \times 2}{4 \times 2}$$
$$= \frac{2}{8}$$

Dividing

$$\frac{9}{12} = \frac{9 \div 3}{12 \div 3}$$
$$= \frac{3}{4}$$

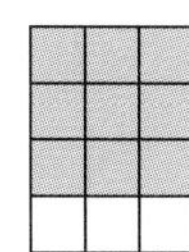

A fraction is in **simplest form** or **lowest terms** when the numerator and denominator have no common factors other than 1.

Example

Express $\frac{6}{8}$ in simplest form.

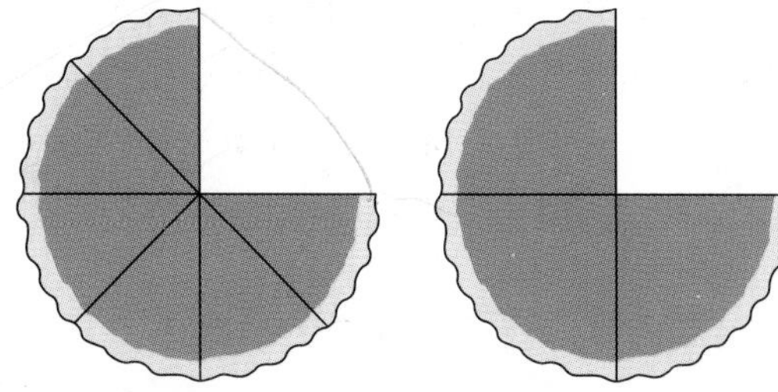

Solution

The factors of 6 are 1, 2, 3, and 6.
The factors of 8 are 1, 2, 4, and 8.
The greatest common factor is 2.

$$\frac{6}{8} = \frac{6 \div 2}{8 \div 2}$$ Divide the numerator and denominator by 2.
$$= \frac{3}{4}$$

So, $\frac{3}{4}$ is the simplest form of $\frac{6}{8}$.

Practice

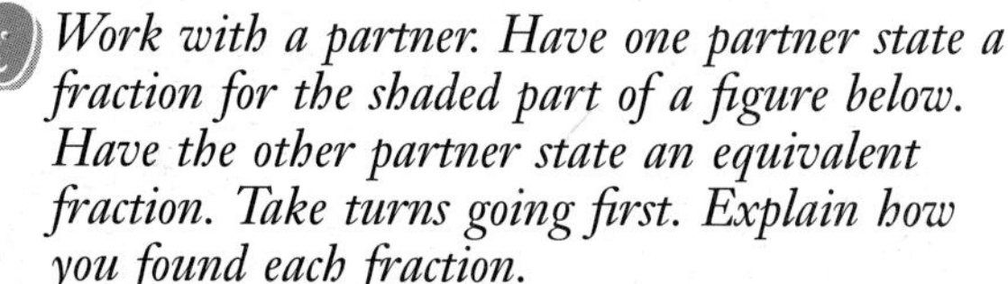

Work with a partner. Have one partner state a fraction for the shaded part of a figure below. Have the other partner state an equivalent fraction. Take turns going first. Explain how you found each fraction.

1.

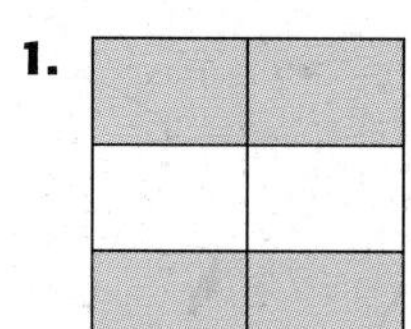

2.

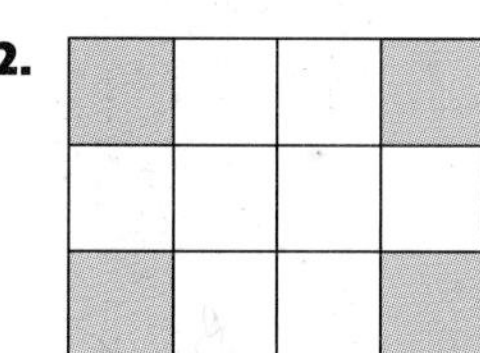

3.

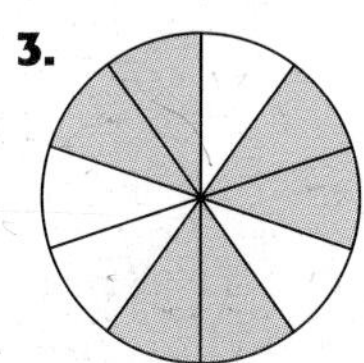

4.

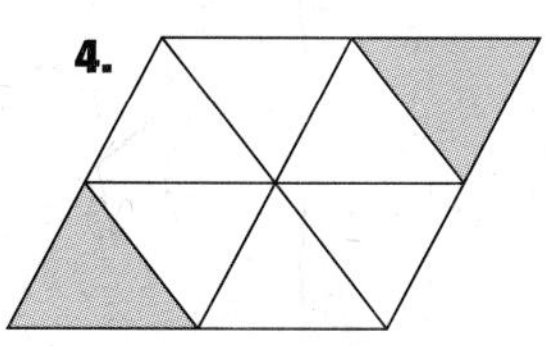

5.

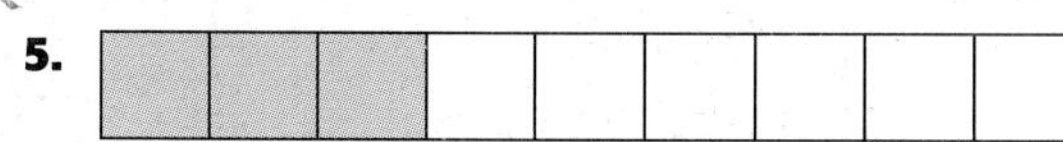

Write a fraction to name the shaded part of each diagram. Then write an equivalent fraction and draw a diagram to represent it.

6.

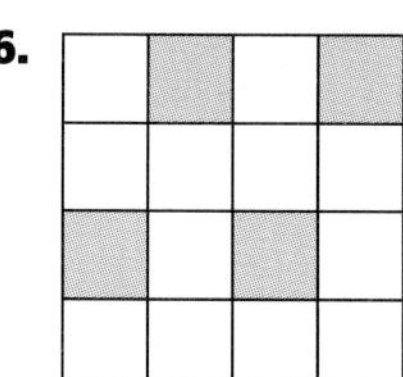

7.

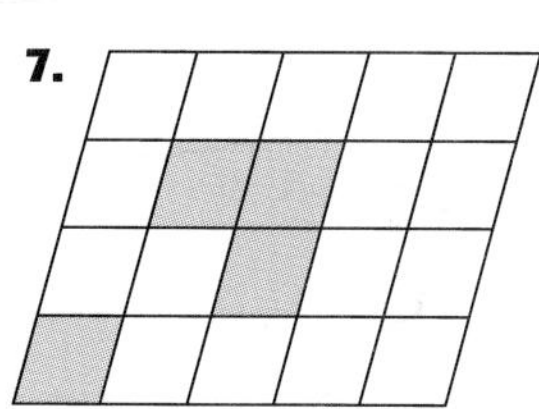

Express the following fractions in lowest terms. Explain how you know that each fraction cannot be written in simpler form.

8. $\frac{7}{21}$ **9.** $\frac{4}{8}$ **10.** $\frac{15}{20}$ **11.** $\frac{9}{12}$

12. $\frac{15}{24}$ **13.** $\frac{9}{15}$ **14.** $\frac{8}{10}$ **15.** $\frac{10}{20}$

Problems and Applications

16. Find pairs of equivalent fractions in the box.

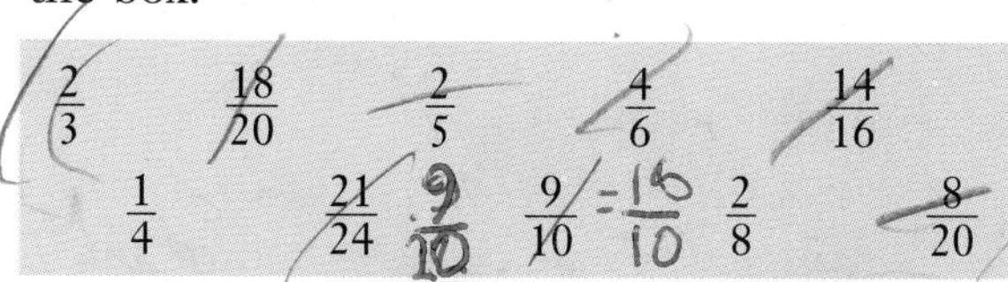

$\frac{2}{3}$ $\frac{18}{20}$ $\frac{2}{5}$ $\frac{4}{6}$ $\frac{14}{16}$

$\frac{1}{4}$ $\frac{21}{24}$ $\frac{9}{10}$ $\frac{2}{8}$ $\frac{8}{20}$

Write the next 3 equivalent fractions. Describe each pattern.

17. $\frac{1}{2}, \frac{2}{4}, \frac{3}{6}, \ldots$ **18.** $\frac{1}{5}, \frac{2}{10}, \frac{3}{15}, \ldots$

19. $\frac{3}{7}, \frac{6}{14}, \frac{9}{21}, \ldots$ **20.** $\frac{3}{3}, \frac{4}{4}, \frac{5}{5}, \ldots$

21. $\frac{3}{4}, \frac{6}{8}, \frac{9}{12}, \ldots$ **22.** $\frac{3}{5}, \frac{6}{10}, \frac{9}{15}, \ldots$

Find the numerator or denominator.

23. $\frac{7}{8} = \frac{■}{16}$ **24.** $\frac{3}{■} = \frac{15}{20}$ **25.** $\frac{5}{6} = \frac{■}{18}$

26. $\frac{3}{■} = \frac{9}{24}$ **27.** $\frac{3}{4} = \frac{■}{16}$ **28.** $\frac{12}{15} = \frac{4}{■}$

29. $\frac{■}{5} = \frac{16}{20}$ **30.** $\frac{1}{4} = \frac{■}{8}$ **31.** $\frac{■}{18} = \frac{3}{9}$

32. Arrange into 3 groups of equivalent fractions.

$\frac{4}{8}$ $\frac{8}{12}$ $\frac{6}{10}$ $\frac{8}{16}$ $\frac{2}{3}$ $\frac{12}{20}$

$\frac{9}{15}$ $\frac{10}{20}$ $\frac{9}{18}$ $\frac{12}{24}$ $\frac{12}{18}$ $\frac{3}{5}$

33. If you take 15 pictures on a 24-exposure roll of film, what fraction of the film have you used? Express your answer in lowest terms.

34. On a hockey team of 24 players, 2 play goal, 8 play defence, and 14 play forward. In lowest terms, what fraction of the team plays

a) goal? **b)** defence? **c)** forward?

35. a) What fraction of Canada's provinces lie to the west of Ontario? Express your answer in simplest form.

b) What fraction of Canada'a provinces lie to the east of Ontario? Express your answer in simplest form.

36. What fraction of each name is made up of vowels? State your answer in lowest terms.

a) Calgary **b)** Saskatoon

c) Gander **d)** Peterborough

e) Rimouski **f)** Dartmouth

g) the capital of your province or territory

5.3 Improper Fractions and Mixed Numbers

Activity: Study the Pictures

Kenji and Mariko ordered 2 medium-sized pizzas. Each pizza had 8 slices. They ate 7 slices.

Inquire

1. How many slices were in two whole pizzas?

2. How many slices were left?

3. What fraction of all the pieces were left?

4. How many whole pizzas were left?

5. What fraction of the partly eaten pizza was left?

6. What is the total of the whole pizza and the partly eaten pizza?

7. Why can $\frac{9}{8}$ be written as $1\frac{1}{8}$?

Kenji and Mariko have two puppies.
They feed them $2\frac{1}{2}$ cans of dog food each day.
We call $2\frac{1}{2}$ a **mixed number**. It is the sum of a whole number and a fraction. We can also write $2\frac{1}{2}$ as $\frac{5}{2}$.
The number $\frac{5}{2}$ is an **improper fraction**. It represents more than one whole. The numerator is bigger than the denominator.

Example 1

Write $\frac{7}{3}$ as a mixed number.

Solution

Divide the numerator by the denominator. The whole number part is the quotient. The fraction is the remainder over the divisor.
So, $\frac{7}{3} = 2\frac{1}{3}$ as a mixed number.

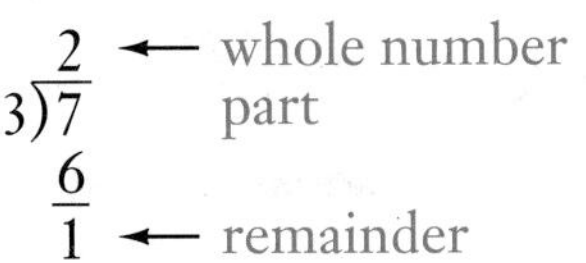

Example 2

Write $2\frac{3}{4}$ as an improper fraction.

Solution

Multiply the whole number by the denominator.
Add the numerator to the product.
Write the sum over the denominator.
So $2\frac{3}{4} = \frac{11}{4}$ as an improper fraction.

denominator
whole number → $2 \times 4 = 8$
$+3$
11 ← numerator

Practice

Express all answers in lowest terms.

1. Describe the difference between an improper fraction and a mixed number.

Write an improper fraction and a mixed number to represent each diagram.

2.

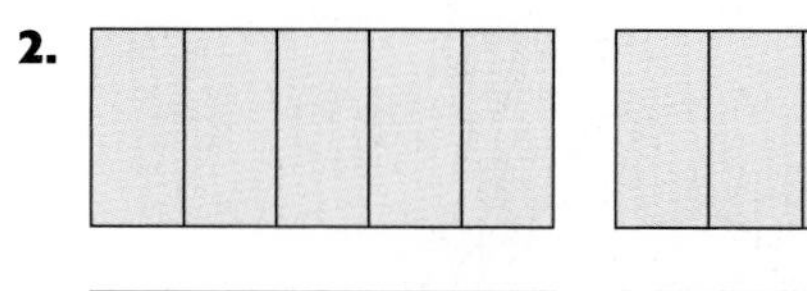

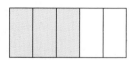

3.

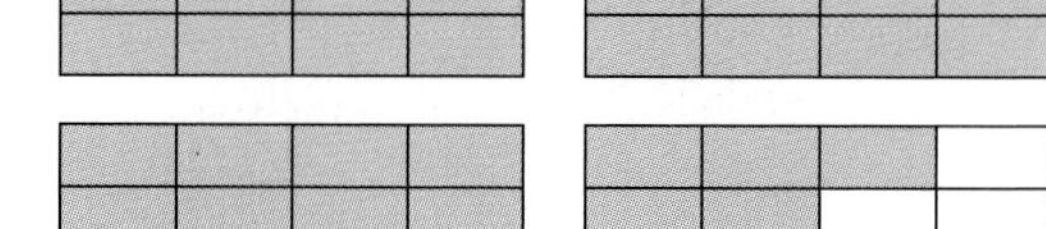

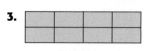

4.

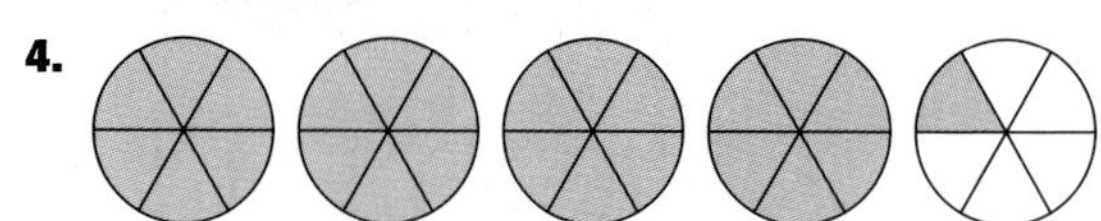

Draw a diagram to represent each mixed number. Write each mixed number as an improper fraction.

5. $1\frac{1}{2}$ **6.** $2\frac{2}{5}$ **7.** $5\frac{1}{3}$

8. $2\frac{1}{4}$ **9.** $3\frac{2}{3}$ **10.** $1\frac{7}{8}$

Write each improper fraction as a mixed number.

11. $\frac{7}{2}$ **12.** $\frac{11}{4}$ **13.** $\frac{19}{5}$ **14.** $\frac{23}{7}$

15. $\frac{63}{8}$ **16.** $\frac{100}{9}$ **17.** $\frac{13}{3}$ **18.** $\frac{15}{6}$

Write each mixed number as an improper fraction.

19. $3\frac{1}{2}$ **20.** $2\frac{2}{3}$ **21.** $3\frac{4}{5}$ **22.** $5\frac{1}{4}$

23. $2\frac{1}{8}$ **24.** $4\frac{3}{8}$ **25.** $8\frac{1}{3}$ **26.** $6\frac{2}{5}$

Problems and Applications

27. Athena ran 3 laps on a 400-m track every day from Monday to Thursday last week. How many kilometres did she run? Express your answer as an improper fraction and a mixed number.

28. Suzette organizes a delivery of flyers every Saturday. She packs them in bags of 10. Last week, she packed 303 flyers. How many bags did she pack? Give your answer as an improper fraction and a mixed number.

29. The Earth turns on its axis once every 24 h. How many turns does it complete in each of the following lengths of time? Express each answer as an improper fraction and a mixed number.

a) 25 h **b)** 26 h **c)** 30 h

d) 36 h **e)** 40 h **f)** 44 h

30. The Bentleys drove for 195 min to reach the lake. Write 195 min as a mixed number of hours.

31. State whether each statement is always true, sometimes true, or never true. Explain.

a) A fraction in which the numerator and denominator are both even can be written in simpler form.

b) A fraction in which the numerator and denominator are both odd can be written in simpler form.

c) A fraction in which the numerator or denominator is a prime number can be written in simpler form.

d) A mixed number is less than one.

e) In the fractional part of a mixed number, the denominator is greater than the numerator by at least 1.

NUMBER POWER

Copy the diagram. Put the numbers from 1 to 9 on the dots so that each line adds to 25.

5.4 Comparing and Ordering Fractions

Activity: Solve the Problem

Each member of the General Assembly of the United Nations has one vote. At least $\frac{2}{3}$ of the nations must vote for an important decision before it is approved. What if $\frac{3}{4}$ of the nations vote in favour?

Inquire

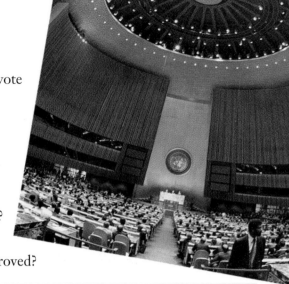

1. List the first 4 equivalent fractions of $\frac{2}{3}$.
2. List the first 4 equivalent fractions of $\frac{3}{4}$.
3. Which of the fractions have the same denominator?
4. How do $\frac{2}{3}$ and $\frac{3}{4}$ compare?
5. If $\frac{3}{4}$ of the nations vote in favour, is a decision approved?

Fractions with the same denominator compare the same way the numerators compare.

$\frac{5}{8} > \frac{3}{8}$ because 5 > 3

To compare fractions when the denominators are different, write equivalent fractions with a common denominator. Then compare the numerators.

Example 1

Compare $\frac{2}{3}$ and $\frac{3}{5}$.

Solution

$\frac{2}{3} = \frac{2 \times 5}{3 \times 5} = \frac{10}{15}$ $\quad \frac{3}{5} = \frac{3 \times 3}{5 \times 3} = \frac{9}{15}$

The lowest common denominator is 15.

Since 10 > 9, $\frac{10}{15} > \frac{9}{15}$.

So, $\frac{2}{3} > \frac{3}{5}$.

Example 2

Compare $2\frac{3}{4}$ and $2\frac{4}{5}$.

Solution

$2\frac{3}{4} \quad 2\frac{4}{5}$

$2\frac{15}{20} \quad 2\frac{16}{20}$

$2\frac{15}{20} < 2\frac{16}{20}$, so $2\frac{3}{4} < 2\frac{4}{5}$

Write the fractions with a common denominator.
The whole numbers are the same. Compare the fractions.

We can also compare fractions by changing them to decimals.

Example 3

Compare $\frac{5}{8}$ and $\frac{4}{7}$.

Solution

C 5 ÷ 8 = 

C 4 ÷ 7 = 0.5714286

0.625 > 0.5714286, so $\frac{5}{8} > \frac{4}{7}$

Practice

Which fraction is larger?

1. $\frac{4}{9}, \frac{5}{9}$
2. $\frac{3}{5}, \frac{2}{5}$
3. $\frac{2}{7}, \frac{3}{7}$
4. $\frac{7}{10}, \frac{5}{10}$
5. $\frac{1}{3}, \frac{2}{3}$
6. $\frac{5}{8}, \frac{7}{8}$

Write each pair of fractions with their lowest common denominator.

7. $\frac{1}{2}, \frac{1}{5}$
8. $\frac{1}{3}, \frac{3}{4}$
9. $\frac{3}{5}, \frac{3}{4}$
10. $\frac{3}{5}, \frac{2}{3}$
11. $\frac{3}{4}, \frac{1}{5}$
12. $\frac{1}{3}, \frac{5}{8}$

Compare the fractions.
Replace each ● with > or <.

13. $\frac{1}{2}$ ● $\frac{3}{8}$
14. $\frac{7}{12}$ ● $\frac{3}{4}$
15. $\frac{2}{5}$ ● $\frac{3}{10}$
16. $\frac{3}{4}$ ● $\frac{7}{8}$
17. $\frac{11}{12}$ ● $\frac{5}{6}$
18. $\frac{2}{3}$ ● $\frac{7}{12}$

Compare the numbers.
Replace each ● with > or <.

19. $2\frac{5}{8}$ ● $2\frac{1}{4}$
20. $3\frac{2}{3}$ ● $3\frac{5}{6}$
21. $2\frac{3}{5}$ ● $2\frac{7}{10}$
22. $5\frac{1}{3}$ ● $5\frac{1}{12}$
23. $2\frac{3}{5}$ ● $2\frac{11}{15}$
24. $1\frac{3}{14}$ ● $1\frac{1}{7}$

Which fraction is larger?

25. $\frac{1}{2}, \frac{2}{3}$
26. $\frac{4}{5}, \frac{3}{4}$
27. $\frac{2}{5}, \frac{1}{3}$
28. $\frac{3}{4}, \frac{5}{6}$
29. $\frac{3}{4}, \frac{2}{3}$
30. $\frac{5}{6}, \frac{7}{9}$

Which fraction is smaller?

31. $\frac{3}{5}, \frac{2}{3}$
32. $\frac{3}{4}, \frac{5}{6}$
33. $\frac{5}{12}, \frac{3}{8}$
34. $\frac{7}{8}, \frac{5}{6}$
35. $\frac{2}{3}, \frac{5}{8}$
36. $\frac{4}{9}, \frac{5}{6}$

Which number is larger?

37. $3\frac{3}{4}, 3\frac{3}{5}$
38. $4\frac{1}{3}, 4\frac{2}{7}$
39. $6\frac{5}{6}, 6\frac{7}{8}$
40. $\frac{4}{3}, \frac{6}{5}$
41. $\frac{6}{5}, \frac{13}{10}$
42. $\frac{10}{4}, \frac{15}{6}$

Problems and Applications

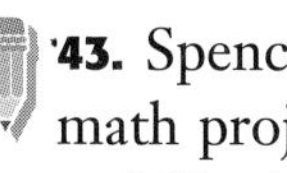

43. Spencer has completed $\frac{7}{10}$ of his math project. Aisha has finished $\frac{3}{4}$ of hers, and Danielle has finished $\frac{4}{5}$ of hers. Who is closest to completing the project? Explain.

44. Which of the 4 quarterbacks is the best passer?

Player	Fraction of Passes Completed
Mike	$\frac{2}{3}$
Nassir	$\frac{7}{12}$
Chris	$\frac{5}{8}$
Kelly	$\frac{3}{4}$

45. Write the names of the Canadian provinces.

a) In simplest form, write the fraction of vowels in each name.

b) Order the fractions from smallest to largest.

46. Do you need to compare $\frac{1}{3}$ and $\frac{2}{7}$ in order to compare $5\frac{1}{3}$ and $4\frac{2}{7}$? Explain.

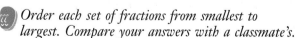

Order each set of fractions from smallest to largest. Compare your answers with a classmate's.

47. $\frac{1}{2}, \frac{1}{3}, \frac{1}{4}$
48. $\frac{5}{9}, \frac{2}{3}, \frac{11}{12}$
49. $\frac{15}{12}, \frac{6}{6}, \frac{3}{4}$
50. $\frac{5}{6}, \frac{3}{4}, \frac{2}{3}$
51. $\frac{11}{6}, \frac{7}{4}, \frac{5}{3}$
52. $\frac{7}{8}, \frac{5}{4}, \frac{3}{2}$

5.5 Estimating Sums and Differences with Fractions

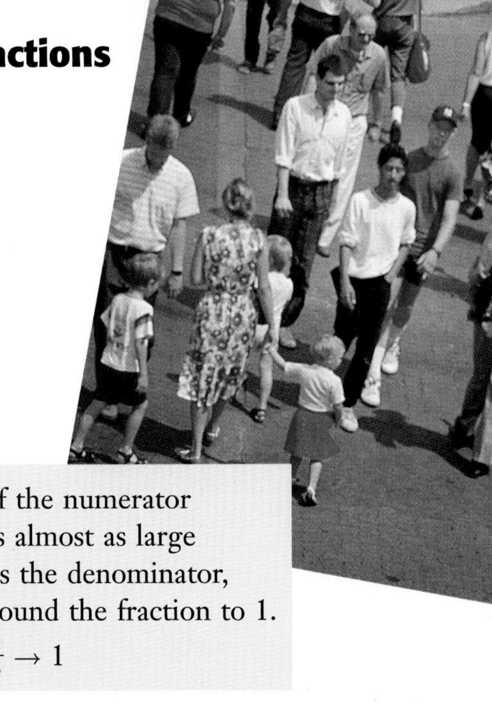

About $\frac{2}{5}$ of Canadians live in Ontario. About $\frac{1}{9}$ live in British Columbia. How can we estimate the fraction of Canadians who live in Ontario and British Columbia?

Activity: Learn About Rounding

Round fractions to estimate sums and differences. When there are no mixed numbers, use the following guidelines.

If the numerator is much smaller than the denominator, round the fraction to 0. $\frac{1}{5} \rightarrow 0$	If the numerator is about half the denominator, round the fraction to $\frac{1}{2}$. $\frac{5}{8} \rightarrow \frac{1}{2}$	If the numerator is almost as large as the denominator, round the fraction to 1. $\frac{5}{6} \rightarrow 1$

Inquire

1. What should you round $\frac{2}{5}$ to? Why?

2. What should you round $\frac{1}{9}$ to? Why?

3. Estimate the fraction of Canadians who live in Ontario and British Columbia.

4. Could you use this rounding method to estimate $\frac{1}{6} + \frac{1}{8}$? Explain.

5. How would you round $\frac{1}{4}$? $\frac{3}{4}$? Explain.

Example 1

Estimate $\frac{4}{5} - \frac{1}{8}$.

Solution

Round $\frac{4}{5}$ to 1. Round $\frac{1}{8}$ to 0.

The difference is about $1 - 0$, or 1.

To estimate sums and differences of mixed numbers, round each mixed number to the nearest whole number.

Example 2

Estimate $3\frac{5}{6} + 2\frac{1}{4}$.

Solution

Round $3\frac{5}{6}$ to 4, since the fraction is greater than $\frac{1}{2}$.

Round $2\frac{1}{4}$ to 2, since the fraction is less than $\frac{1}{2}$.

The sum is about $4 + 2$, or 6.

Example 3

Estimate $5\frac{1}{2} - 3\frac{7}{8}$.

Solution

Round $5\frac{1}{2}$ to 6, since the fraction is $\frac{1}{2}$.

Round $3\frac{7}{8}$ to 4.

The difference is about $6 - 4$, or 2.

Practice

State whether each fraction is closest to 0, $\frac{1}{2}$, or 1.

1. $\frac{1}{5}$ **2.** $\frac{5}{9}$ **3.** $\frac{7}{8}$ **4.** $\frac{5}{6}$

5. $\frac{3}{7}$ **6.** $\frac{2}{3}$ **7.** $\frac{7}{15}$ **8.** $\frac{9}{10}$

9. $\frac{1}{10}$ **10.** $\frac{3}{8}$ **11.** $\frac{1}{8}$ **12.** $\frac{3}{4}$

Choose the better estimate.

13. $\frac{3}{5} + \frac{1}{8}$ about $\frac{1}{2}$ or 1?

14. $\frac{5}{8} + \frac{3}{7}$ about $\frac{1}{2}$ or 1?

15. $\frac{5}{6} - \frac{1}{2}$ about 0 or $\frac{1}{2}$?

16. $\frac{7}{8} - \frac{5}{6}$ about 0 or $\frac{1}{2}$?

17. $\frac{9}{10} + \frac{1}{8}$ about 1 or $1\frac{1}{2}$?

18. $\frac{7}{8} - \frac{1}{10}$ about $\frac{1}{2}$ or 1?

19. $\frac{1}{10} + \frac{1}{8}$ about $\frac{1}{2}$ or 0?

20. $\frac{5}{8} - \frac{3}{10}$ about 0 or $\frac{1}{2}$?

Estimate.

21. $\frac{5}{8} + \frac{4}{7}$ **22.** $\frac{2}{3} + \frac{1}{8}$

23. $\frac{9}{10} - \frac{5}{6}$ **24.** $\frac{3}{8} - \frac{1}{6}$

25. $\frac{3}{4} + \frac{7}{10}$ **26.** $\frac{1}{4} + \frac{5}{8}$

27. $\frac{3}{10} + \frac{5}{6}$ **28.** $\frac{5}{6} - \frac{1}{8}$

29. $\frac{8}{9} + \frac{7}{8}$ **30.** $\frac{8}{9} - \frac{1}{8}$

31. $\frac{5}{6} - \frac{5}{8}$ **32.** $\frac{7}{10} - \frac{1}{3}$

Estimate.

33. $13\frac{3}{8} + 4\frac{5}{6}$ **34.** $9\frac{5}{6} - 6\frac{1}{8}$

35. $15\frac{2}{5} - 9\frac{7}{8}$ **36.** $8\frac{7}{10} + 5\frac{1}{6}$

37. $4\frac{5}{6} - 4\frac{1}{9}$ **38.** $7\frac{2}{3} + 5\frac{2}{7}$

39. $16\frac{1}{10} - 14\frac{9}{10}$ **40.** $8\frac{1}{2} - 6\frac{5}{8}$

41. $5\frac{4}{7} + 2\frac{1}{6}$ **42.** $11\frac{3}{8} + 12\frac{1}{5}$

43. $7\frac{3}{10} - 5\frac{7}{8}$ **44.** $6\frac{5}{6} - 6\frac{1}{5}$

Problems and Applications

45. In 1986, about $\frac{1}{7}$ of the people in Canada were 9 years of age or less. About $\frac{2}{5}$ of the people were 10 to 34 years of age. Estimate the fraction of people who were 34 years of age or less.

46. Emile worked $2\frac{1}{2}$ hours on Thursday, $4\frac{3}{4}$ hours on Friday, and $6\frac{3}{4}$ hours on Saturday. Estimate the total number of hours he worked.

47. Pasquale ate $\frac{3}{8}$ of a pizza, Claudia ate $\frac{1}{2}$, and Linda ate $\frac{3}{4}$. Estimate how much pizza they ate altogether.

48. It is $11\frac{1}{4}$ hours from the time Lydia leaves for work until she gets home. She travels a total of $1\frac{1}{2}$ hours and takes $1\frac{1}{4}$ hours for lunch. Estimate how long she spends at work.

WORD POWER

Place a consonant in the centre ring and the vowels in the second ring to spell 5 three-letter words, reading inward.

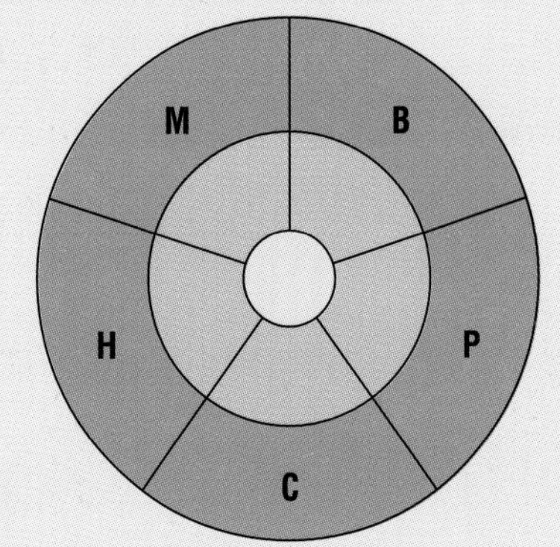

5.6 Adding Fractions

Activity: Use the Diagram

The students at Laurier School set up the gym for an athletic night. What fraction of the whole gym was used for gymnastics competitions plus demonstrations?

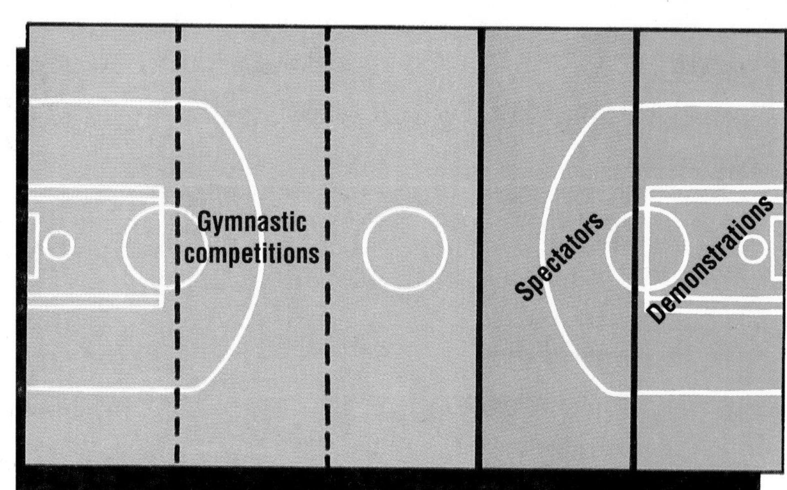

Inquire

1. What fraction was used for demonstrations?

2. What fraction was used for gymnastics competitions?

3. What fraction was used for both together?

To add fractions with the same denominator, add the numerators.

Example 1

Add $\frac{1}{8} + \frac{2}{8}$.

Solution

$$\frac{1}{8} + \frac{2}{8} = \frac{1 + 2}{8}$$
$$= \frac{3}{8}$$

To add fractions with different denominators, write equivalent fractions with the lowest common denominator.

Example 2

The diagram shows how a gym was set up for games. Badminton took up $\frac{1}{2}$ and table tennis $\frac{1}{3}$.

What fraction of the gym was used for games?

Badminton

Table Tennis

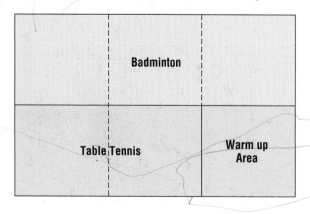

Warm up Area

Solution

The LCD of 2 and 3 is 6.

$$\frac{1}{2} = \frac{1 \times 3}{2 \times 3} = \frac{3}{6}$$

$$\frac{1}{3} = \frac{1 \times 2}{3 \times 2} = \frac{2}{6}$$

EST: $\frac{1}{2} + \frac{1}{2} = 1$

$$\frac{3}{6} + \frac{2}{6} = \frac{5}{6}$$

So, $\frac{5}{6}$ of the gym was used for games.

Practice

Express all answers in lowest terms.

State the sum.

1. $\frac{1}{5} + \frac{3}{5}$ **2.** $\frac{1}{4} + \frac{1}{4}$ **3.** $\frac{7}{8} + \frac{1}{8}$

4. $\frac{1}{3} + \frac{2}{3}$ **5.** $\frac{5}{6} + \frac{5}{6}$ **6.** $\frac{1}{3} + \frac{2}{3} + \frac{2}{3}$

7. $\frac{7}{10} + \frac{1}{10}$ **8.** $\frac{5}{8} + \frac{7}{8}$ **9.** $\frac{1}{5} + \frac{2}{5} + \frac{4}{5}$

Estimate, then add.

10. $\frac{1}{2} + \frac{3}{4}$ **11.** $\frac{9}{10} + \frac{3}{5}$ **12.** $\frac{1}{2} + \frac{5}{7}$

13. $\frac{5}{6} + \frac{2}{3}$ **14.** $\frac{7}{9} + \frac{1}{3}$ **15.** $\frac{1}{4} + \frac{3}{8}$

16. $\frac{3}{4} + \frac{5}{12}$ **17.** $\frac{5}{6} + \frac{1}{12}$ **18.** $\frac{1}{2} + \frac{5}{12}$

Write the LCD for each pair.

19. $\frac{1}{2}, \frac{1}{3}$ **20.** $\frac{1}{4}, \frac{1}{5}$ **21.** $\frac{2}{5}, \frac{3}{4}$

22. $\frac{1}{3}, \frac{2}{5}$ **23.** $\frac{2}{7}, \frac{1}{2}$ **24.** $\frac{1}{3}, \frac{1}{4}$

Estimate, then add.

25. $\frac{1}{2} + \frac{2}{3}$ **26.** $\frac{2}{5} + \frac{1}{4}$ **27.** $\frac{3}{10} + \frac{3}{4}$

28. $\frac{3}{8} + \frac{1}{3}$ **29.** $\frac{2}{9} + \frac{1}{2}$ **30.** $\frac{1}{5} + \frac{1}{2}$

Write the LCD for each pair.

31. $\frac{3}{4}, \frac{3}{10}$ **32.** $\frac{1}{6}, \frac{5}{9}$ **33.** $\frac{1}{8}, \frac{5}{12}$ **34.** $\frac{3}{4}, \frac{5}{6}$

Estimate, then add.

35. $\frac{1}{4} + \frac{5}{6}$ **36.** $\frac{3}{8} + \frac{1}{12}$ **37.** $\frac{2}{5} + \frac{1}{4}$

38. $\frac{5}{6} + \frac{5}{8}$ **39.** $\frac{3}{5} + \frac{2}{3}$ **40.** $\frac{1}{6} + \frac{5}{8}$

Problems and Applications

41. Jacques scored $\frac{1}{2}$ of the total goals for the Red Wings hockey team, and Andres scored $\frac{1}{8}$. What fraction of the goals did these two players score?

42. Olga varnished a table in shop class. She used $\frac{3}{4}$ of a can of varnish for the first coat, $\frac{1}{2}$ of a can for the second coat, and $\frac{1}{3}$ of a can for the third coat. How many cans of varnish did she use?

43. For the average 10–12 year-old, the recommended intake of iron in the diet is at least 8 mg/day. A slice of watermelon contains $\frac{1}{4}$ of this amount, a tomato contains $\frac{1}{10}$, and a serving of apple juice contains $\frac{1}{5}$. What fraction of your daily iron needs do you get from

a) 1 slice of watermelon and 1 serving of apple juice?

b) 1 tomato and 1 serving of apple juice?

c) 1 tomato and 1 slice of watermelon?

d) 1 tomato, 1 slice of watermelon, and 1 serving of apple juice?

44. Write a problem that involves the addition of fractions. Have a classmate solve it.

NUMBER POWER

Unit fractions are fractions that have 1 as the numerator. All fractions can be written as the sum of two or more unit fractions with different denominators. For example:

$$\frac{3}{4} = \frac{2}{4} + \frac{1}{4} = \frac{1}{2} + \frac{1}{4}$$

$$\frac{7}{8} = \frac{4}{8} + \frac{2}{8} + \frac{1}{8} = \frac{1}{2} + \frac{1}{4} + \frac{1}{8}$$

$$\frac{2}{3} = \frac{4}{6} = \frac{3}{6} + \frac{1}{6} = \frac{1}{2} + \frac{1}{6}$$

a) Write each of the following as the sum of unit fractions.

$\frac{9}{16}$ $\frac{2}{5}$ $\frac{1}{3}$ $\frac{7}{10}$

b) Work with a classmate. Choose other fractions and write them as unit fractions.

5.7 Subtracting Fractions

Activity: Study the Diagram

Tara found 7 pieces of cheese in the package in the refrigerator. She packed 1 of the 7 pieces for her lunch.

Inquire

1. What fraction of the whole package did Tara find in the refrigerator?

2. What fraction of the whole package did Tara take?

3. What fraction of the whole package was left?

4. If Tara takes 2 more pieces, what fraction of the whole package will be left?

To subtract fractions with the same denominator, subtract the numerators.

Example 1

Subtract $\frac{3}{5} - \frac{1}{5}$.

Solution

$$\frac{3}{5} - \frac{1}{5} = \frac{3-1}{5}$$
$$= \frac{2}{5}$$

To subtract fractions with different denominators, write equivalent fractions with the lowest common denominator.

Example 2

There was $\frac{2}{3}$ of a 12-slice pizza on the table. Jordan ate 6 slices. What fraction of the whole pizza was left?

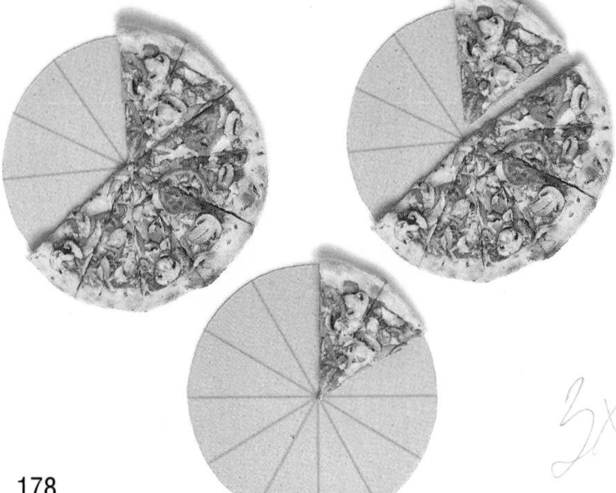

Solution

Jordan ate 6 of the 12 slices, or $\frac{1}{2}$ of the whole pizza.

To find the fraction left, subtract $\frac{2}{3} - \frac{1}{2}$.

The LCD of 3 and 2 is 6.

$$\frac{2}{3} = \frac{2 \times 2}{3 \times 2} = \frac{4}{6}$$

$$\frac{1}{2} = \frac{1 \times 2}{2 \times 2} = \frac{3}{6}$$

$$\frac{4}{6} - \frac{3}{6} = \frac{1}{6}$$

EST $\frac{1}{2} - \frac{1}{2} = 0$

So, $\frac{1}{6}$ of the whole pizza was left.

Practice

Express all answers in lowest terms.

Subtract.

1. $\frac{4}{5} - \frac{3}{5}$ **2.** $\frac{2}{3} - \frac{1}{3}$ **3.** $\frac{3}{4} - \frac{1}{4}$

4. $\frac{5}{6} - \frac{1}{6}$ **5.** $\frac{7}{8} - \frac{5}{8}$ **6.** $\frac{5}{9} - \frac{3}{9}$

Estimate, then subtract.

7. $\frac{3}{4} - \frac{1}{2}$ **8.** $\frac{5}{6} - \frac{1}{3}$ **9.** $\frac{7}{10} - \frac{2}{5}$

10. $\frac{5}{8} - \frac{1}{4}$ **11.** $\frac{9}{10} - \frac{4}{5}$ **12.** $\frac{1}{3} - \frac{1}{6}$

Write the LCD for each pair.

13. $\frac{2}{3}, \frac{1}{2}$ **14.** $\frac{3}{5}, \frac{1}{3}$ **15.** $\frac{1}{4}, \frac{2}{3}$

16. $\frac{3}{4}, \frac{4}{5}$ **17.** $\frac{3}{7}, \frac{1}{3}$ **18.** $\frac{2}{5}, \frac{3}{10}$

Estimate, then subtract.

19. $\frac{1}{2} - \frac{1}{3}$ **20.** $\frac{4}{5} - \frac{1}{3}$ **21.** $\frac{3}{8} - \frac{1}{3}$

22. $\frac{2}{3} - \frac{1}{4}$ **23.** $\frac{2}{3} - \frac{3}{10}$ **24.** $\frac{3}{5} - \frac{1}{2}$

Write the LCD for each pair.

25. $\frac{3}{4}, \frac{3}{10}$ **26.** $\frac{1}{6}, \frac{5}{8}$ **27.** $\frac{7}{12}, \frac{1}{8}$

28. $\frac{5}{6}, \frac{1}{4}$ **29.** $\frac{1}{9}, \frac{1}{6}$ **30.** $\frac{1}{2}, \frac{2}{5}$

Estimate, then subtract.

31. $\frac{3}{7} - \frac{1}{3}$ **32.** $\frac{3}{4} - \frac{1}{6}$ **33.** $\frac{5}{12} - \frac{3}{8}$

34. $\frac{9}{10} - \frac{3}{4}$ **35.** $\frac{8}{9} - \frac{5}{6}$ **36.** $\frac{3}{4} - \frac{3}{10}$

Problems and Applications

37. Suzanne planted $\frac{5}{12}$ of her garden with petunias and $\frac{1}{4}$ of her garden with dahlias. What fraction of her garden did she have left for carnations?

38. Between 1900 and 1986, the fraction of Canadians living in rural areas dropped from $\frac{4}{5}$ to $\frac{1}{4}$. Express the decrease as a fraction.

39. Write your own problem involving the subtraction of fractions. Ask a classmate to solve it.

40. Jamie baked an apple pie and a blueberry pie for the weekend. On Saturday, the family ate $\frac{1}{6}$ of the apple pie and $\frac{5}{8}$ of the blueberry pie. On Sunday, they ate $\frac{1}{2}$ of the apple pie and $\frac{1}{4}$ of the blueberry pie.

a) How much more apple pie was eaten on Sunday than on Saturday?

b) Which pie had more left over at the end of Sunday? Explain.

PATTERN POWER

a) Find the difference between each pair of numbers.

64 and 46 53 and 35 42 and 24

b) What do you notice?

c) Explain the pattern.

d) State 3 other pairs of numbers that fit the same pattern.

e) Repeat, beginning with the following pairs.

74 and 47 63 and 36 52 and 25

5.8 Adding and Subtracting Mixed Numbers

Activity: Analyze the Problem

Melissa studied for $1\frac{1}{2}$ hours on Friday and $3\frac{3}{4}$ hours on Saturday. Melissa's mother wanted to know the total time Melissa studied.

Inquire

1. What is the sum of the whole numbers of hours?
2. What is the sum of the fractions of hours?
3. For how many hours did Melissa study?

4. Write a rule for adding mixed numbers.

Example 1

Add $5\frac{3}{4} + 2\frac{1}{3}$.

Solution

The LCD of 4 and 3 is 12.

$5\frac{3}{4} + 2\frac{1}{3} = 5\frac{9}{12} + 2\frac{4}{12}$ ← Rewrite fractions with the LCD.

$= 7\frac{13}{12}$ ← Add whole numbers and fractions.

$= 8\frac{1}{12}$ ← Write in simplest form.

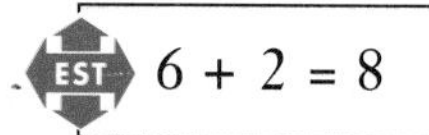

Example 2

Subtract $2\frac{1}{2} - 1\frac{1}{3}$.

Solution

The LCD of 3 and 2 is 6.

$2\frac{1}{2} - 1\frac{1}{3} = 2\frac{3}{6} - 1\frac{2}{6}$ ← Rewrite fractions with the LCD.

$= 1\frac{1}{6}$ ← Subtract whole numbers and fractions.

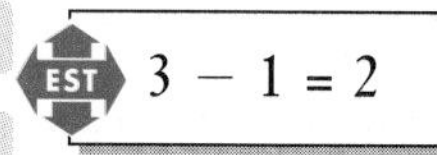

Example 3

Subtract $6 - 4\frac{2}{5}$.

Solution

Rewrite 6 as a mixed number.

$6 - 4\frac{2}{5} = 5\frac{5}{5} - 4\frac{2}{5}$

$= 1\frac{3}{5}$

EST $6 - 4 = 2$

Example 4

Subtract $4\frac{1}{6} - 1\frac{3}{4}$.

Solution

The LCD of 6 and 4 is 12.

EST $4 - 2 = 2$

$4\frac{1}{6} - 1\frac{3}{4} = 4\frac{2}{12} - 1\frac{9}{12}$

$= 3\frac{14}{12} - 1\frac{9}{12}$ ← Because $\frac{2}{12} < \frac{9}{12}$, rewrite the first mixed number.

$= 2\frac{5}{12}$

Practice

Express all answers in lowest terms.

State the sum.

1. $2\frac{1}{4} + 1\frac{1}{4}$ **2.** $3\frac{1}{3} + \frac{2}{3}$ **3.** $4\frac{1}{5} + 2\frac{3}{5}$

4. $2\frac{3}{8} + 1\frac{7}{8}$ **5.** $2\frac{1}{10} + 3\frac{7}{10}$ **6.** $1\frac{5}{6} + \frac{5}{6}$

Estimate, then add.

7. $1\frac{3}{4} + 1\frac{1}{2}$ **8.** $2\frac{5}{6} + 1\frac{2}{3}$ **9.** $2\frac{1}{3} + 1\frac{7}{9}$

10. $1\frac{5}{12} + 1\frac{3}{4}$ **11.** $3\frac{3}{8} + 2\frac{1}{4}$ **12.** $2\frac{5}{6} + 2\frac{1}{12}$

Estimate, then add.

13. $1\frac{1}{2} + 1\frac{2}{3}$ **14.** $2\frac{3}{4} + 3\frac{1}{2}$ **15.** $1\frac{5}{8} + \frac{1}{2}$

16. $2\frac{1}{2} + 1\frac{4}{5}$ **17.** $\frac{7}{8} + 1\frac{3}{4}$ **18.** $1\frac{5}{6} + 2\frac{1}{3}$

Estimate, then subtract.

19. $4\frac{4}{5} - 2\frac{1}{5}$ **20.** $2\frac{3}{4} - 1\frac{1}{4}$ **21.** $2\frac{3}{5} - 1\frac{1}{5}$

22. $3\frac{5}{7} - 1\frac{3}{7}$ **23.** $3\frac{7}{8} - \frac{5}{8}$ **24.** $2\frac{5}{9} - 1\frac{2}{9}$

Estimate, then subtract.

25. $2\frac{1}{3} - 1\frac{1}{6}$ **26.** $3\frac{3}{4} - 2\frac{5}{8}$ **27.** $3\frac{1}{2} - 1\frac{3}{8}$

28. $4\frac{3}{5} - 2\frac{3}{10}$ **29.** $3\frac{1}{6} - 1\frac{1}{12}$ **30.** $5\frac{3}{4} - 3\frac{1}{2}$

Estimate, then subtract.

31. $4 - \frac{2}{5}$ **32.** $5 - \frac{3}{4}$ **33.** $8 - \frac{2}{3}$

34. $3 - \frac{5}{6}$ **35.** $7 - \frac{2}{7}$ **36.** $6 - \frac{3}{10}$

Estimate, then subtract.

37. $2\frac{3}{4} - 1\frac{1}{6}$ **38.** $3\frac{2}{3} - 1\frac{3}{5}$ **39.** $5\frac{5}{6} - 3\frac{1}{2}$

40. $4\frac{3}{4} - 3\frac{2}{5}$ **41.** $4\frac{3}{5} - 2\frac{1}{2}$ **42.** $5\frac{2}{3} - 2\frac{1}{2}$

Estimate, then subtract.

43. $6\frac{1}{4} - 3\frac{1}{2}$ **44.** $4\frac{1}{3} - 2\frac{5}{6}$ **45.** $4\frac{1}{2} - 2\frac{3}{5}$

46. $5\frac{1}{4} - 2\frac{5}{6}$ **47.** $7\frac{3}{7} - 4\frac{1}{2}$ **48.** $8\frac{2}{5} - 3\frac{2}{3}$

Problems and Applications

49. Oren flew to London in $8\frac{1}{4}$ hours and returned in $6\frac{1}{2}$ hours.

a) What was his total flying time?

b) How much shorter was the return trip?

50. The Schmidt family drove from Toronto to Ottawa for Winter Carnival. They drove for $2\frac{2}{3}$ hours in the morning and $2\frac{3}{4}$ hours in the afternoon.

a) For how many hours did they drive?

b) If they stopped for lunch for $\frac{1}{2}$ hour, how long did the trip take?

51. A 1500-m race takes $3\frac{3}{4}$ laps of a track and a 1000-m race takes $2\frac{1}{2}$ laps. How many laps does a 500-m race take?

LOGIC POWER

The 2 triangles intersect at 2 points.

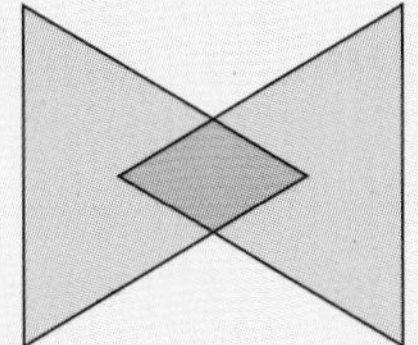

Draw diagrams to show 2 triangles intersecting at 3, 4, 5, and 6 points.

Multiplying Fractions

Activity ❶

1. What is $\frac{1}{2}$ of 6? What is $\frac{1}{3}$ of 12?

2. In mathematics, we write $\frac{1}{2}$ of $6 = 3$ as $\frac{1}{2} \times 6 = 3$
and $\frac{1}{3}$ of $12 = 4$ as $\frac{1}{3} \times 12 = 4$

Use counters to show the following and write each multiplication sentence.

a) $\frac{1}{4}$ of 8 **b)** $\frac{2}{3}$ of 12 **c)** $\frac{1}{5}$ of 15 **d)** $\frac{2}{5}$ of 20 **e)** $\frac{3}{4}$ of 8

Activity ❷

We can shade grid paper to multiply a fraction by a fraction.

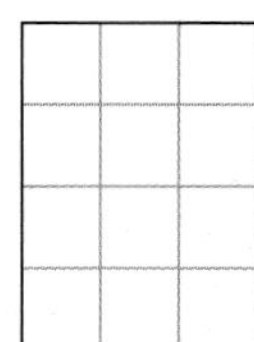

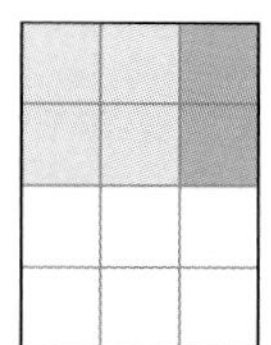

1. Draw a rectangle of 12 squares on grid paper.

2. Shade $\frac{1}{2}$ of the rectangle.

3. Show $\frac{1}{3}$ of the shaded area by shading over the first shading.

4. To describe the fraction with the double shading,
we write $\frac{1}{3}$ of $\frac{1}{2} = \frac{1}{6}$ or $\frac{1}{3} \times \frac{1}{2} = \frac{1}{6}$

Use grid paper to show the following and write each multiplication sentence.

a) $\frac{1}{2}$ of $\frac{2}{3}$ **b)** $\frac{1}{4}$ of $\frac{1}{2}$ **c)** $\frac{3}{4}$ of $\frac{1}{2}$ **d)** $\frac{3}{4}$ of $\frac{1}{3}$

Activity ❸

Shaded circles can help us to multiply a whole number by a mixed number.

1. Use circles to show $1\frac{1}{3}$.

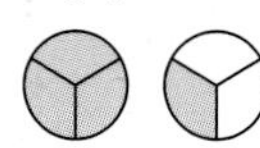

2. Add circles to show $4 \times 1\frac{1}{3}$

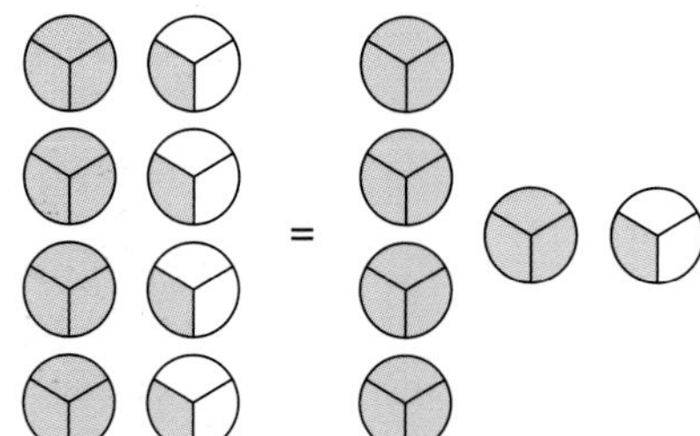

3. We write $4 \times 1\frac{1}{3} = 5\frac{1}{3}$.

Use circles to show the following and write each multiplication sentence.

a) $3 \times 2\frac{1}{2}$ **b)** $2 \times 1\frac{3}{4}$ **c)** $4 \times 2\frac{2}{3}$ **d)** $3 \times 2\frac{1}{4}$

Programming Computer Games In BASIC

Activity ❶

Enter the "Water Dunk Game" into a computer. Play the game with a classmate. The first player picks any letter of the alphabet. The second player has 5 guesses to find the letter and dunk the first player in the water.

```
NEW
 10 PRINT "Pick a letter."
 20 INPUT L$
 30 CLS
 40 PRINT "You have five throws"
 50 PRINT "to hit the right letter."
 60 PRINT "If you hit it, the player"
 70 PRINT "in the chair gets dunked."
 80 PRINT "I will help you."
 90 FOR G = 1 TO 5
100 PRINT "Make a guess."
110 INPUT G$
120 IF G$ = L$ THEN G = 5:GOTO 200
130 IF G$ > L$ THEN PRINT "The letter is before"
140 IF G$ < L$ THEN PRINT "The letter is after"
150 PRINT G$
160 NEXT G
170 PRINT "You missed all 5 throws."
180 PRINT "Now it's your turn in the chair."
190 END
200 PRINT "Splash!!!!"
210 END
```

Activity ❷

1. Modify the program so that the guesser gets only 4 guesses.

2. Add the following lines to the program.

```
PRINT "Do you want to play again?"
INPUT "y or n";Z$
IF Z$ = "y" THEN 10
END
```

What do these lines do to the game? Test your program with a classmate.

5.9 Multiplying Fractions

Activity: Interpret the Diagram

The diagram shows the fraction of the time the average person spends sleeping. It also shows the fraction of sleep time the average person spends dreaming.

Inquire

1. What fraction of the time are people asleep?
2. What fraction of sleep time is spent dreaming?
3. What fraction of the total time does the average person spend dreaming?
4. What is $\frac{1}{4}$ of $\frac{1}{3}$?
5. What fraction of the total time are people asleep but not dreaming?
6. What is $\frac{3}{4}$ of $\frac{1}{3}$?
7. Write a rule for multiplying fractions.

Example 1

Of the land on a farm, $\frac{2}{3}$ is for vegetables. Of the land used for vegetables, $\frac{1}{2}$ is for corn. What fraction of the farmland is for corn?

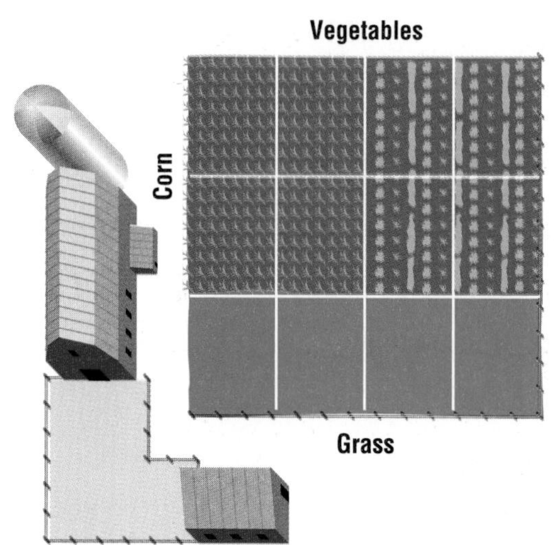

Solution 1

The diagram shows that $\frac{4}{12}$ or $\frac{1}{3}$ of the land is for corn.

Solution 2

We can also find the answer by multiplying fractions.

$$\frac{1}{2} \text{ of } \frac{2}{3} = \frac{1}{2} \times \frac{2}{3}$$
Multiply the numerators.
Multiply the denominators.
$$= \frac{2}{6}$$
$$= \frac{1}{3}$$
Write the answer in simplest form.

Example 2

Multiply.

a) $\frac{3}{5} \times \frac{1}{2}$

b) $\frac{3}{4} \times 5$

Solution

a) $\frac{3}{5} \times \frac{1}{2} = \frac{3 \times 1}{5 \times 2}$
$= \frac{3}{10}$

EST $\frac{1}{2} \times \frac{1}{2} = \frac{1}{4}$

b) $\frac{3}{4} \times 5 = \frac{3}{4} \times \frac{5}{1}$
$= \frac{3 \times 5}{4 \times 1}$
$= \frac{15}{4} = 3\frac{3}{4}$

EST $1 \times 5 = 5$

Practice

Express all answers in lowest terms.

Calculate.

1. $\frac{1}{2}$ of 10 **2.** $\frac{1}{3}$ of 24 **3.** $\frac{1}{4}$ of 12

4. $\frac{1}{5}$ of 15 **5.** $\frac{3}{8}$ of 16 **6.** $\frac{3}{4}$ of 20

7. $\frac{2}{3}$ of 21 **8.** $\frac{3}{4}$ of 30 **9.** $\frac{4}{5}$ of 20

Multiply.

10. $\frac{1}{5} \times \frac{1}{2}$ **11.** $\frac{1}{4} \times \frac{1}{3}$ **12.** $\frac{1}{2} \times \frac{3}{4}$

13. $\frac{1}{3} \times \frac{2}{5}$ **14.** $\frac{3}{5} \times \frac{1}{4}$ **15.** $\frac{5}{8} \times \frac{1}{2}$

16. $\frac{4}{5} \times \frac{2}{3}$ **17.** $\frac{1}{7} \times \frac{2}{3}$ **18.** $\frac{5}{6} \times \frac{1}{2}$

19. $\frac{3}{4} \times \frac{1}{3}$ **20.** $\frac{2}{3} \times \frac{2}{3}$ **21.** $\frac{4}{5} \times \frac{2}{3}$

Estimate, then multiply.

22. $3 \times \frac{5}{12}$ **23.** $\frac{4}{5} \times 3$ **24.** $\frac{3}{4} \times 8$

25. $\frac{7}{8} \times 32$ **26.** $\frac{2}{3} \times 18$ **27.** $10 \times \frac{1}{2}$

Calculate.

28. $\frac{2}{3} \times 4$ **29.** $6 \times \frac{7}{8}$ **30.** $\frac{5}{6} \times 2$

31. $\frac{3}{4} \times 1$ **32.** $3 \times \frac{9}{10}$ **33.** $5 \times \frac{7}{8}$

Problems and Applications

34. A turntable spins a record album through $\frac{5}{9}$ of a turn per second. How many turns is this per minute? Give your answer as a mixed number.

35. Of the students in class 7E, $\frac{5}{6}$ scored 80 or more on a recent math test. There are 30 students in 7E. How many scored 80 or more?

36. A multiple-choice test gives a choice of 4 answers for each question. One way of grading the test is to use the formula

$$S = R - \frac{1}{3} \times W$$

S is the score; R is the number of right answers; W is the number of wrong answers. If 5 students each answer all 50 questions on the test, what scores do they get from the following numbers of right answers?

a) 20 **b)** 50 **c)** 44 **d)** 32 **e)** 35

37. The human body is about $\frac{3}{5}$ water, by mass.

a) What is the mass of an 80-kg adult not including the water?

b) What is your own mass, not including the water in your body?

38. Gersh spent $\frac{3}{5}$ of his vacation in British Columbia. While in that province, he spent $\frac{1}{2}$ of the time in Vancouver.

a) What fraction of his vacation did he spend in Vancouver?

b) If his vacation lasted 20 days, how many days did he spend in Vancouver?

39. How many minutes are there in $\frac{11}{12}$ of a day?

40. In a proper fraction, the numerator is smaller than the denominator. Is the product of two proper fractions ever greater than 1? Explain.

LOGIC POWER

Copy the diagram. Colour 3 squares red, 3 squares green, and 3 squares black so that no two squares with a common boundary have the same colour.

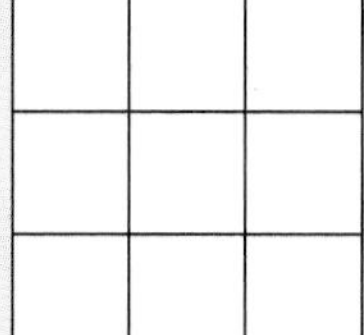

5.10 Reciprocals: Mental Math

Activity: Compare the Solutions

Michelle divided her collection of 44 sea-shells evenly between two kindergarten classes. She knew two ways of working out how many shells each class should get.

Inquire

1. What whole number did she divide by to solve the problem?
2. What fraction did she multiply by to solve the problem?
3. What do you get when you multiply the whole number and fraction you just found?

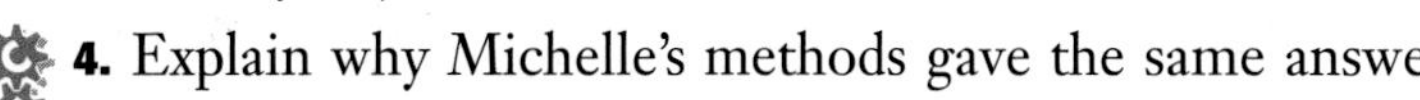

4. Explain why Michelle's methods gave the same answer.
5. How many shells did each class get?

Two numbers whose product is 1 are called **reciprocals**. For example, the numbers 3 and $\frac{1}{3}$ are reciprocals.

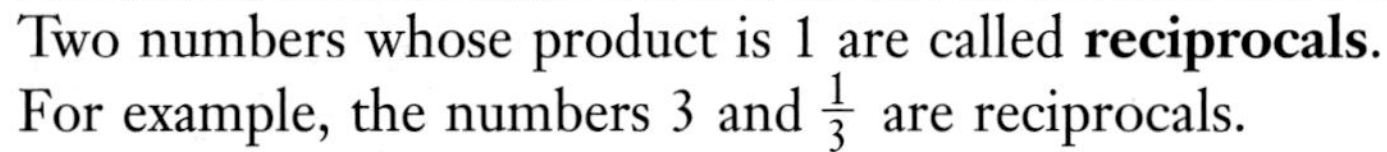

$3 \times \frac{1}{3} = 1$

Dividing by 3 and multiplying by $\frac{1}{3}$ give the same answer.

$12 \div 3 = 4$ and $12 \times \frac{1}{3} = 4$

Example

Find the reciprocals.

a) $\frac{5}{6}$ **b)** 8 **c)** $2\frac{1}{3}$

Solution

a) The reciprocal is $\frac{6}{5}$, since $\frac{5}{6} \times \frac{6}{5} = 1$.

b) The reciprocal is $\frac{1}{8}$, since $8 \times \frac{1}{8} = 1$.

c) Write $2\frac{1}{3}$ as $\frac{7}{3}$. The reciprocal is $\frac{3}{7}$, since $\frac{7}{3} \times \frac{3}{7} = 1$.

Practice

Write a number to make each sentence true.

1. $\frac{2}{9} \times \blacksquare = 1$
2. $\frac{9}{5} \times \blacksquare = 1$
3. $\blacksquare \times \frac{7}{8} = 1$
4. $\blacksquare \times 6 = 1$
5. $\frac{1}{10} \times \blacksquare = 1$
6. $\frac{8}{9} \times \blacksquare = 1$
7. $\blacksquare \times 3\frac{1}{2} = 1$
8. $\blacksquare \times 2\frac{2}{3} = 1$
9. $7 \times \blacksquare = 1$
10. $1 \times \blacksquare = 1$
11. $\blacksquare \times \frac{3}{5} = 1$
12. $\blacksquare \times 1\frac{1}{4} = 1$

Write the reciprocal.

13. $\frac{1}{5}$
14. $\frac{1}{6}$
15. $\frac{2}{3}$
16. $\frac{3}{4}$
17. $\frac{8}{7}$
18. $\frac{9}{8}$
19. 5
20. 6
21. 9
22. $1\frac{1}{3}$
23. $1\frac{5}{6}$
24. $2\frac{3}{4}$
25. 4
26. $\frac{7}{2}$
27. $\frac{4}{5}$
28. $\frac{4}{9}$

Problems and Applications

1. Which number is its own reciprocal? Explain.
2. Which number does not have a reciprocal? Explain.
3. Australia has about $\frac{5}{8}$ as many people as Canada. How many Canadians are there for every Australian?

Dividing Fractions

Activity ❶

1. When we write $3 \div \frac{1}{2}$, we mean:
"How many $\frac{1}{2}$s are in 3?"

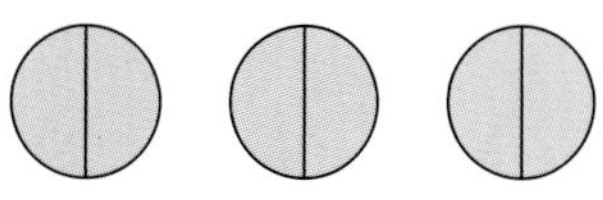

To decide, look at the diagram. Write the division sentence. Use the diagram to write a multiplication sentence that gives the same answer and uses only whole numbers.

2. How many $\frac{1}{3}$s are in 4?

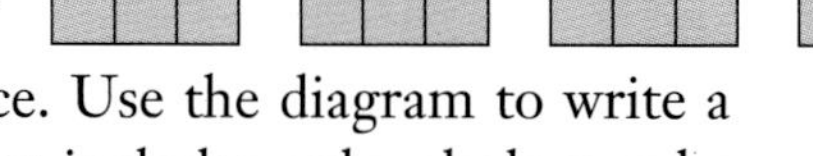

Write the division sentence. Use the diagram to write a multiplication sentence that includes only whole numbers.

3. Draw a diagram to show each of the following. Write each division sentence. In each case, use the diagram to write a multiplication sentence that includes only whole numbers.

a) How many $\frac{1}{2}$s are in 6? **b)** How many $\frac{1}{5}$s are in 2?

c) How many $\frac{1}{4}$s are in 7?

Activity ❷

1. How many $\frac{1}{5}$s are in $\frac{4}{5}$?

Complete the division sentence. $\frac{4}{5} \div \frac{1}{5} = \blacksquare$

Complete the multiplication sentence. $\frac{4}{5} \times \frac{5}{1} = \blacksquare$

2. How many $\frac{1}{8}$s are in $\frac{3}{4}$?

Write the division sentence.

Complete the multiplication sentence. $\frac{3}{4} \times \frac{8}{1} = \blacksquare$

3. Draw a diagram to show each of the following. Write each division sentence. In each case, write a multiplication sentence.

a) How many $\frac{1}{6}$s are in $\frac{5}{6}$? **b)** How many $\frac{1}{10}$s are in $\frac{3}{5}$?

c) How many $\frac{1}{6}$s are in $\frac{2}{3}$?

Activity ❸

1. Copy and complete the table by writing the division sentence and the multiplication sentence for each diagram in Activity 1 and Activity 2. The first line is completed for you.

Division	Multiplication
$3 \div \frac{1}{2} = 6$	$3 \times 2 = 6$

2. Complete the following sentence to give a rule for dividing by fractions. "Dividing by a fraction is the same as...." Compare your rule with your classmates'.

5.11 Dividing Fractions

Activity: Use the Diagram

Rosanna decided to share 3 oranges with her friends. She cut the oranges into $\frac{1}{4}$s.

Inquire

1. How many $\frac{1}{4}$s are in 1 orange?

2. How many $\frac{1}{4}$s are in 3 oranges?

3. How many $\frac{1}{4}$s could Rosanna have cut from 12 oranges?

Example 1

The students at St Matthew's School filled 3 classrooms with activities for an open house. Each activity filled $\frac{1}{2}$ of a classroom. How many activities did the students set up?

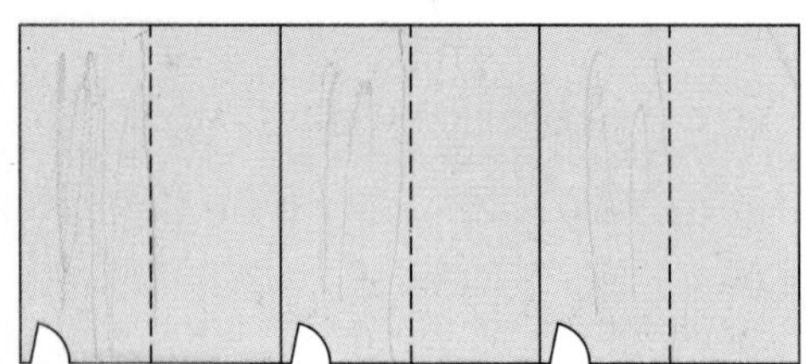

Solution

Dividing by a fraction is the same as multiplying by its reciprocal.

$3 \div \frac{1}{2} = 3 \times \frac{2}{1}$

$= 6$

2 is the reciprocal of $\frac{1}{2}$

The students set up 6 activities.

Example 2

How many $\frac{1}{8}$s are in $\frac{3}{4}$?

Solution

$\frac{3}{4} \div \frac{1}{8} = \frac{3}{4} \times \frac{8}{1}$

$= \frac{24}{4}$

$= 6$

8 is the reciprocal of $\frac{1}{8}$

Example 3

Divide.

a) $\frac{1}{5} \div \frac{2}{3}$ **b)** $\frac{5}{6} \div \frac{3}{4}$ **c)** $\frac{3}{8} \div 2$

Solution

a) $\frac{1}{5} \div \frac{2}{3} = \frac{1}{5} \times \frac{3}{2}$

$= \frac{3}{10}$

b) $\frac{5}{6} \div \frac{3}{4} = \frac{5}{6} \times \frac{4}{3}$

$= \frac{20}{18}$

$= \frac{10}{9}$

$= 1\frac{1}{9}$

c) $\frac{3}{8} \div 2 = \frac{3}{8} \times \frac{1}{2}$

$= \frac{3}{16}$

Practice

Write all answers in simplest form.

Write the reciprocal.

1. $\frac{3}{4}$ **2.** $\frac{1}{2}$ **3.** $\frac{5}{8}$ **4.** $\frac{8}{7}$

5. 3 **6.** $\frac{1}{4}$ **7.** $\frac{9}{5}$ **8.** 7

9. $\frac{2}{5}$ **10.** $\frac{3}{10}$ **11.** 4 **12.** 13

Divide.

13. $\frac{1}{4} \div \frac{1}{2}$ **14.** $\frac{2}{5} \div \frac{1}{3}$ **15.** $\frac{2}{3} \div \frac{3}{4}$

16. $\frac{3}{5} \div \frac{2}{5}$ **17.** $\frac{5}{8} \div \frac{5}{8}$ **18.** $\frac{1}{2} \div \frac{1}{5}$

19. $\frac{5}{6} \div \frac{1}{8}$ **20.** $\frac{1}{8} \div \frac{1}{6}$ **21.** $\frac{5}{4} \div \frac{2}{3}$

22. $\frac{1}{6} \div \frac{3}{2}$ **23.** $\frac{2}{7} \div \frac{1}{7}$ **24.** $\frac{7}{8} \div \frac{1}{3}$

Divide.

25. $\frac{1}{3} \div 2$ **26.** $3 \div \frac{1}{2}$ **27.** $\frac{5}{6} \div 2$

28. $\frac{3}{4} \div 5$ **29.** $4 \div \frac{2}{3}$ **30.** $\frac{1}{6} \div 1$

31. $\frac{2}{5} \div 3$ **32.** $\frac{7}{8} \div 4$ **33.** $6 \div \frac{1}{3}$

Divide.

34. $\frac{7}{8} \div \frac{2}{3}$ **35.** $4 \div \frac{1}{2}$ **36.** $\frac{4}{3} \div 3$

37. $\frac{1}{4} \div \frac{3}{5}$ **38.** $\frac{4}{5} \div \frac{4}{5}$ **39.** $\frac{2}{3} \div \frac{3}{2}$

40. $\frac{2}{8} \div \frac{2}{9}$ **41.** $\frac{4}{9} \div \frac{2}{3}$ **42.** $18 \div \frac{1}{2}$

43. $\frac{1}{2} \div \frac{3}{2}$ **44.** $\frac{3}{2} \div \frac{1}{2}$ **45.** $\frac{5}{6} \div 5$

Problems and Applications

46. Your class is planning a year-end barbecue. Each hamburger takes $\frac{1}{8}$ of a package of ground beef. How many hamburgers can you make from 12 packages?

47. If 2 students equally share $\frac{3}{4}$ of a pizza, how much does each student get?

48. Paul, Lin, and Sue equally shared the weeding of $\frac{3}{4}$ of a park. What fraction of the park did each of them weed?

49. A hurricane has a wind speed of at least 120 km/h. This speed is only $\frac{3}{5}$ of the wind speed from the average human sneeze. What is the wind speed from the average human sneeze?

50. Decide whether each statement is always true, sometimes true, or never true. Explain.

a) Dividing a whole number by an improper fraction gives an answer that is larger than the original whole number.

b) Dividing a fraction by a fraction results in a fraction.

c) Dividing a fraction by a whole number gives a smaller fraction.

d) If you divide a number by a fraction, the smaller the fraction you choose, the larger the answer is.

51. Write a problem that involves the division of fractions. Have a classmate solve it.

LOGIC POWER

Turn the triangle upside down by moving 3 pennies.

5.12 Multiplying and Dividing Mixed Numbers

Activity: Study the Solution

Frank was training for a track meet. Every $2\frac{1}{2}$ laps of the track equalled 1 km. Frank wanted to run 10 km. He needed to know how many laps to run.

Frank changed the number of laps per kilometre to an improper fraction.

$$2\frac{1}{2} = \frac{5}{2}$$

Then he multiplied this fraction by the number of kilometres he wanted to run.

$$\frac{5}{2} \times 10 = \frac{5}{2} \times \frac{10}{1}$$
$$= \frac{50}{2}$$
$$= 25$$

Frank had to run 25 laps.

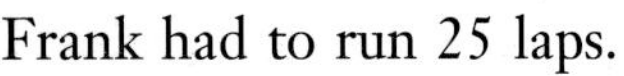

Inquire

1. Why did Frank multiply to get the answer?
2. What answer do you get from this calculator sequence?

C 5 ÷ 2 × 10 = ▭

3. How many laps would Frank run in 5 km?

When multiplying or dividing with mixed numbers, first rewrite them as improper fractions.

Example 1

Sonya ran 15 laps of a track. Every $2\frac{1}{2}$ laps equalled 1 km. How many kilometres did she run?

Solution

Divide.

$$15 \div 2\frac{1}{2} = \frac{15}{1} \div \frac{5}{2}$$
$$= \frac{15}{1} \times \frac{2}{5}$$
$$= \frac{30}{5}$$
$$= 6$$

EST $15 \div 3 = 5$

Sonya ran 6 km.

Example 2

Multiply $2\frac{3}{4} \times 1\frac{1}{2}$.

Solution

$$2\frac{3}{4} \times 1\frac{1}{2} = \frac{11}{4} \times \frac{3}{2}$$
$$= \frac{33}{8}$$
$$= 4\frac{1}{8}$$

EST $3 \times 2 = 6$

Example 3

Divide $2\frac{2}{5} \div 1\frac{1}{2}$.

Solution

$$2\frac{2}{5} \div 1\frac{1}{2} = \frac{12}{5} \div \frac{3}{2}$$
$$= \frac{12}{5} \times \frac{2}{3}$$
$$= \frac{24}{15}$$
$$= \frac{8}{5}$$
$$= 1\frac{3}{5}$$

EST $2 \div 2 = 1$

Practice

Write all answers in simplest form.

Estimate, then multiply.

1. $6 \times 1\frac{1}{2}$ **2.** $3\frac{1}{4} \times 8$ **3.** $2\frac{1}{3} \times 5$

4. $1\frac{3}{4} \times 2$ **5.** $1\frac{1}{5} \times 2\frac{1}{2}$ **6.** $2\frac{1}{3} \times 1\frac{3}{4}$

7. $\frac{2}{3} \times 1\frac{1}{3}$ **8.** $2\frac{1}{2} \times \frac{1}{4}$ **9.** $3\frac{3}{5} \times 2\frac{2}{3}$

Estimate, then divide.

10. $4\frac{1}{2} \div 2$ **11.** $3 \div 1\frac{1}{2}$ **12.** $4 \div 1\frac{1}{4}$

13. $2\frac{2}{3} \div 3$ **14.** $2\frac{1}{2} \div 1\frac{3}{4}$ **15.** $3\frac{2}{5} \div 1\frac{1}{5}$

16. $\frac{2}{3} \div 1\frac{1}{3}$ **17.** $1\frac{1}{2} \div \frac{1}{2}$ **18.** $1\frac{7}{8} \div 1$

Problems and Applications

19. During the summer Paul worked $3\frac{3}{4}$ hours a day at a convenience store. In July, he worked 21 days. How many hours did he work?

20. A department store's regular prices are $1\frac{1}{4}$ times its sale prices. The list gives the regular prices of several items. Calculate the sale prices.

Football jersey	\$66.00
Calculator	\$12.00
Video game	\$80.00
Jeans	\$47.00

21. Antonia writes mystery novels. She takes an average of $2\frac{1}{2}$ hours to write a page.

a) How long did she take to write a 13-page chapter?

b) How many pages can Antonia write in $8\frac{1}{2}$ hours?

22. The sides of a square are $2\frac{1}{2}$ times longer than the sides of another square. How many times greater is the area of the first square than the area of the other?

23. How many hours are there in each of the following numbers of days?

a) $1\frac{1}{2}$ **b)** $3\frac{1}{4}$ **c)** $4\frac{1}{3}$ **d)** $5\frac{1}{6}$

NUMBER POWER

Copy the diagram and put the numbers from 1 to 6 on the dots so that the sum of the numbers on the circumference of each circle is 14.

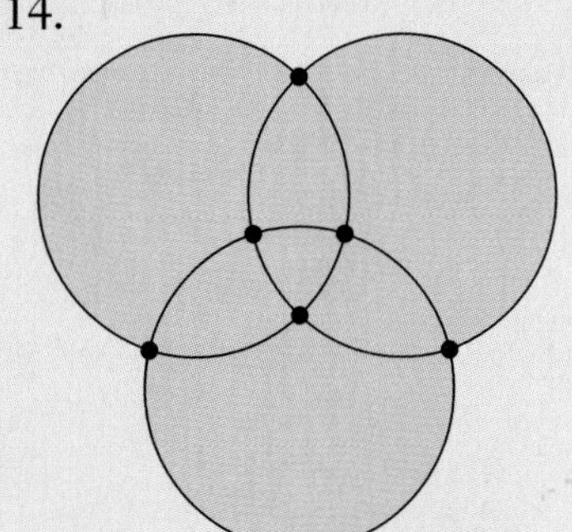

5.13 Decimals and Fractions

We can write fractions as decimals.
The Maritime Provinces are 3 of Canada's 10 provinces.
By the year 2011, 15 of every 100 Canadians will be over age 65.
Of every 1000 Canadians, 243 have French as their first language.

$\frac{3}{10} = 0.3$

$\frac{15}{100} = 0.15$

$\frac{243}{1000} = 0.243$

Activity: Complete the Tables

Copy and complete the first table to change fractions to decimals by writing the equivalent fractions.

Fraction	Equivalent Fraction	Decimal
$\frac{2}{5}$	$\frac{2}{5} \times \frac{2}{2} = \frac{4}{10}$	0.4
$\frac{3}{4}$	$\frac{3}{4} \times \frac{25}{25} = \frac{75}{100}$	0.75
$\frac{1}{2}$		
$\frac{3}{20}$		
$\frac{4}{25}$		

Copy and complete the second table to change fractions to decimals by division.

Fraction	Division	Decimal
$\frac{3}{4}$	$3 \div 4$	0.75
$\frac{2}{5}$		
$\frac{5}{8}$		
$\frac{7}{20}$		
$\frac{1}{6}$		
$\frac{4}{11}$		

Inquire

1. For each table, write the rule you used to change the fractions to decimals.

2. Could you use each of your rules to change any fraction to a decimal? Explain.

3. What is different about the last two decimals in the second table? Could you write them using the rule you found from the first table?

When you divide the numerator by the denominator in a fraction, you may find that the remainder becomes 0 and the division ends. The decimal is called a **terminating decimal.**

$\frac{3}{8} = 8\overline{)3.000} = 0.375$

If the remainder does not become 0 and the decimal repeats, the decimal is called a **repeating decimal**. We use a bar to show the digit or digits that repeat.

$\frac{5}{6} = 6\overline{)5.000} = 0.8333\ldots$
$= 0.8\overline{3}$

Example

Write as decimals.

a) $\frac{3}{5}$ **b)** $1\frac{7}{8}$ **c)** $\frac{5}{11}$

Solution

a) $\frac{3}{5} = \frac{3 \times 2}{5 \times 2}$

$= \frac{6}{10}$

$= 0.6$

b) $\frac{7}{8} = 7 \div 8$

C 7 ÷ 8 = 0.875

$1\frac{7}{8} = 1.875$

c) $\frac{5}{11} = 5 \div 11$

C 5 ÷ 11 = 0.4545454

$\frac{5}{11} = 0.\overline{45}$

Practice

State in decimal form.

1. $\frac{7}{10}$ **2.** $\frac{3}{10}$ **3.** $\frac{33}{100}$ **4.** $\frac{45}{100}$

5. $\frac{131}{1000}$ **6.** $\frac{965}{1000}$ **7.** $\frac{875}{1000}$ **8.** $\frac{1}{100}$

State in decimal form.

9. $1\frac{11}{100}$ **10.** $7\frac{5}{100}$ **11.** $9\frac{6}{10}$

12. $6\frac{91}{1000}$ **13.** $25\frac{150}{1000}$ **14.** $1\frac{1}{100}$

15. $4\frac{39}{100}$ **16.** $9\frac{59}{1000}$ **17.** $23\frac{11}{100}$

Write in decimal form.

18. $\frac{1}{5}$ **19.** $\frac{17}{20}$ **20.** $\frac{5}{8}$ **21.** $\frac{1}{4}$

22. $\frac{3}{8}$ **23.** $\frac{4}{5}$ **24.** $\frac{3}{4}$ **25.** $\frac{8}{25}$

Write in decimal form.

26. $9\frac{1}{4}$ **27.** $3\frac{4}{5}$ **28.** $9\frac{1}{8}$

29. $6\frac{3}{5}$ **30.** $11\frac{7}{20}$ **31.** $12\frac{3}{8}$

32. $4\frac{3}{4}$ **33.** $10\frac{1}{2}$ **34.** $1\frac{2}{5}$

Express in decimal form.

35. $\frac{1}{3}$ **36.** $\frac{5}{6}$ **37.** $\frac{7}{9}$ **38.** $\frac{2}{3}$

39. $\frac{3}{11}$ **40.** $\frac{1}{6}$ **41.** $\frac{1}{12}$ **42.** $\frac{5}{12}$

Write in decimal form. Express each answer to the nearest hundredth.

43. $\frac{1}{8}$ **44.** $3\frac{2}{3}$ **45.** $9\frac{5}{6}$

46. $2\frac{5}{8}$ **47.** $12\frac{7}{11}$ **48.** $8\frac{1}{9}$

49. $2\frac{1}{6}$ **50.** $5\frac{1}{3}$ **51.** $6\frac{3}{11}$

Write as a fraction in simplest form.

52. 0.8 **53.** 0.875 **54.** 2.7 **55.** 4.05

56. 0.2 **57.** 0.6 **58.** 1.75 **59.** 6.5

Problems and Applications

60. Three friends bought 3 blank tapes for \$7.00. Could they share the cost equally? Explain.

61. About $\frac{1}{4}$ of the people in Canada live in Quebec.

a) What fraction of the females in Canada live in Quebec?

b) Express your answer as a decimal.

c) What assumptions have you made?

62. In 1984, swimmer Anne Ottenbrite of Canada won an Olympic Gold medal in the 200-m breaststroke.

a) What fraction of a kilometre did she swim in her winning race?

b) Express your answer as a decimal.

63. About $\frac{1}{11}$ of the Canadian population lives in Alberta.

a) Express this fraction as a decimal.

b) Round your answer to the nearest thousandth.

CALCULATOR POWER

Write $0.0\overline{6}$ as a fraction with 1 as the numerator.

5.14 Order of Operations with Fractions

Activity: Share Your Solution

The finalists in a radio contest were asked to simplify the expression.

$\frac{1}{2}$ of $36 + 8 - 4^2 \div 2$

Inquire

1. Work with a classmate to simplify the expression.

2. One of the finalists got 5 as an answer. What mistake did he make?

3. Another finalist got 3. What mistake did she make?

We simplify expressions involving fractions in the same order as expressions with whole numbers and decimals.

Order of Operations

1. Do operations in **brackets** first. **B**

2. Evaluate **exponents.** **E**

3. Do **divisions** and **multiplications** in the order they appear, from left to right. **D** **M**

4. Do **additions** and **subtractions** in the order they appear, from left to right. **A** **S**

Remember BEDMAS.

Practice

Simplify.

1. $\frac{1}{5} + \frac{1}{2} - \frac{1}{10}$

2. $\frac{2}{3} + \frac{1}{2} \div \frac{1}{8}$

3. $\frac{1}{4} \div \frac{1}{3} + \frac{1}{2}$

4. $\frac{1}{2} - \frac{1}{2} \times \frac{1}{5}$

5. $(\frac{2}{5} + \frac{1}{2}) \div \frac{1}{3}$

6. $\frac{2}{3} \times (\frac{1}{4} - \frac{1}{8})$

Simplify.

7. $\frac{1}{4}$ of $12 + \frac{2}{3}$ of 9

8. $\frac{4}{5} - \frac{1}{2} \times \frac{1}{2}$

9. $\frac{2}{3} - \frac{1}{2} - \frac{1}{3} \times \frac{1}{4}$

10. $(\frac{1}{4} - \frac{1}{8}) \div (\frac{2}{3} + \frac{1}{6})$

11. $\frac{4}{5} + \frac{1}{2} \times \frac{1}{10}$

12. $(\frac{11}{12} - \frac{3}{4}) \div \frac{1}{2}$

Simplify.

13. $\frac{1}{3}$ of $(7 + 8) + 4^2 - 2$

14. $5^2 - \frac{1}{4}$ of $(11 - 7) \div 1$

15. $\frac{1}{5} \times 10 - \frac{1}{4} \times 8 + 11$

16. $4 \div \frac{1}{2} + 3 \div \frac{1}{3} \times 2$

Problems and Applications

17. Two students are absent from a grade 7 class of 26 students. Of those present, $\frac{1}{3}$ want to help with the school play. Of the 28 students in grade 8, $\frac{1}{4}$ want to help. Write an expression to represent the total number of students who want to help. Simplify the expression.

18. Add a set of brackets to each expression so that its value is 8.

a) $\frac{1}{3} \times 12 + 6 + 2$ **b)** $\frac{1}{4} \times 14 - 6 + \frac{2}{3} \times 9$

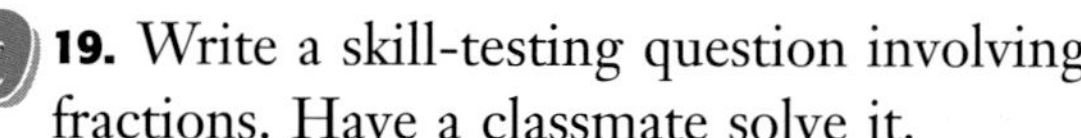

19. Write a skill-testing question involving fractions. Have a classmate solve it.

The Sundial

On a sundial, the gnomon, or pointer, points toward the north star. The angle the gnomon makes with the face of the sundial is the latitude of the sundial's position on the Earth.

Activity ❶

1. Use an atlas or globe to find your latitude.

2. Stand outside on a sunny day and find out where north, south, east, and west are.

3. If it is morning, complete activity 2. If it is afternoon, complete activity 3.

Activity ❷

1. Find a small stick or use a pencil.

2. In the morning, hold your left hand flat with your palm up and your fingers pointing west. Use your thumb to hold the stick at an angle to your palm, as shown in the diagram. Does the stick point, north, south, east, or west?

3. Adjust the angle between your palm and the stick, so that the angle is about equal to your angle of latitude. The position of the shadow tells you the approximate time.

4. Compare with the correct time. How accurate is your sundial?

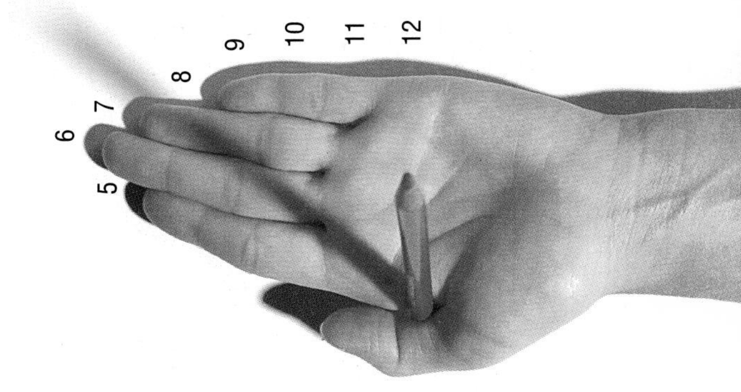

Activity ❸

1. Find a small stick or use a pencil.

2. In the afternoon, hold your right hand flat with your palm up and your fingers pointing east. Use your thumb to hold the stick at an angle to your palm, as shown in the diagram. Does the stick point, north, south, east, or west?

3. Adjust the angle between your palm and the stick, so that the angle is about equal to your angle of latitude. The position of the shadow tells you the approximate time.

4. Compare with the correct time. How accurate is your sundial?

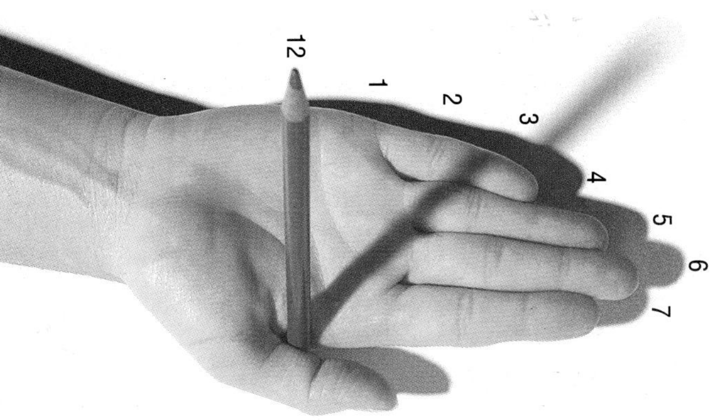

Review

What fraction of each diagram is shaded?

1. 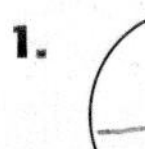 **2.**  **3.** 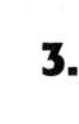 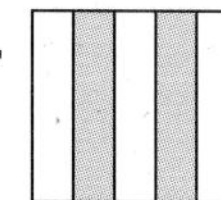

Find the value of ■.

4. $\frac{2}{5} = \frac{■}{15}$ **5.** $\frac{2}{3} = \frac{12}{■}$ **6.** $\frac{■}{10} = \frac{6}{20}$

7. *Find sets of equivalent fractions.*

$\frac{2}{3}$ $\frac{6}{9}$ $\frac{1}{5}$ $\frac{4}{20}$ $\frac{12}{18}$ $\frac{2}{10}$ $\frac{8}{12}$ $\frac{3}{15}$

Express in simplest form.

8. $\frac{3}{24}$ **9.** $\frac{6}{8}$ **10.** $\frac{8}{10}$ **11.** $\frac{4}{12}$

Write as a mixed number in simplest form.

12. $\frac{15}{4}$ **13.** $\frac{9}{2}$ **14.** $\frac{25}{8}$ **15.** $\frac{50}{6}$

State the lowest common multiple.

16. 3 and 5 **17.** 4 and 6 **18.** 8 and 3

Write in order from smallest to largest.

19. $\frac{1}{2}, \frac{1}{3}, \frac{1}{5}, \frac{1}{10}$ **20.** $\frac{2}{3}, \frac{4}{5}, \frac{9}{10}$

State the LCD.

21. $\frac{1}{5}, \frac{1}{3}$ **22.** $\frac{1}{6}, \frac{1}{8}$ **23.** $\frac{1}{2}, \frac{1}{3}, \frac{1}{4}$

Add.

24. $\frac{1}{2} + \frac{1}{3}$ **25.** $\frac{1}{4} + \frac{5}{6}$ **26.** $\frac{3}{4} + \frac{7}{10}$

27. $5\frac{2}{3} + 2\frac{2}{3}$ **28.** $1\frac{1}{2} + 4\frac{9}{10}$ **29.** $2\frac{1}{3} + 5\frac{1}{2}$

Subtract.

30. $\frac{1}{5} - \frac{1}{10}$ **31.** $\frac{3}{5} - \frac{1}{3}$ **32.** $\frac{5}{6} - \frac{1}{4}$

33. $2\frac{1}{2} - \frac{1}{4}$ **34.** $3\frac{1}{3} - \frac{2}{3}$ **35.** $1\frac{9}{10} - \frac{4}{5}$

Multiply.

36. $\frac{1}{4}$ of 2 **37.** $\frac{2}{5}$ of 6 **38.** $5 \times \frac{2}{5}$

39. $\frac{1}{5} \times \frac{3}{5}$ **40.** $\frac{1}{4} \times \frac{1}{3}$ **41.** $\frac{5}{6} \times \frac{2}{3}$

42. $1\frac{1}{4} \times 2\frac{1}{2}$ **43.** $3\frac{1}{4} \times 4\frac{1}{3}$ **44.** $3\frac{1}{2} \times 2\frac{1}{6}$

Write the reciprocal.

45. 4 **46.** $\frac{5}{6}$ **47.** $\frac{1}{10}$

Write a number that makes each sentence true.

48. $\frac{5}{8} \times ■ = 1$ **49.** $\frac{1}{6} \times ■ = 1$

50. $1 = ■ \times \frac{2}{3}$ **51.** $\frac{3}{5} \times \frac{5}{3} = ■$

Divide.

52. $\frac{2}{5} \div \frac{1}{3}$ **53.** $\frac{2}{9} \div \frac{1}{3}$ **54.** $\frac{9}{10} \div \frac{11}{20}$

55. $1\frac{1}{2} \div \frac{1}{4}$ **56.** $2\frac{2}{3} \div \frac{1}{3}$ **57.** $6\frac{1}{3} \div 1\frac{1}{6}$

Evaluate.

58. $\frac{1}{3} + \frac{1}{5} \times \frac{1}{2}$ **59.** $4 - \frac{1}{2}$ of $(3 + 2)$

Write in decimal form.

60. $\frac{9}{10}$ **61.** $\frac{45}{100}$ **62.** $5\frac{675}{1000}$ **63.** $3\frac{15}{100}$

64. $\frac{2}{5}$ **65.** $\frac{5}{8}$ **66.** $3\frac{1}{4}$ **67.** $7\frac{13}{50}$

Write as a fraction in simplest form.

68. 0.7 **69.** 0.16 **70.** 6.4 **71.** 3.25

Express as a repeating decimal.

72. $\frac{2}{3}$ **73.** $\frac{3}{11}$ **74.** $\frac{1}{9}$

75. The Red Sox played 3 games at home. They used $5\frac{1}{4}$ boxes of balls in the first game, $6\frac{1}{2}$ in the second, and $5\frac{3}{4}$ in the third. How many boxes did they use for the 3 games?

76. The \$600.00 earned at the bake sale was shared by 3 groups. The Band got $\frac{1}{2}$. The Chess Club got $\frac{1}{3}$ of what was left. The rest went to the Environment Club. How much did each group get?

77. Telephone companies offer discounts for calls made at certain times. Calculate the cost of long-distance calls with the following discounts.

a) \$15.00 call with $\frac{3}{5}$ off

b) \$8.00 call with $\frac{7}{20}$ off

c) \$12.00 call with $\frac{3}{10}$ off

78. Ernest Charles Manning was Premier of Alberta from 1943 to 1968.

a) In simplest terms, express his years as Premier as a fraction of a century.

b) Express your answer as a decimal.

79. What fraction of a decimetre is a centimetre?

80. Decide whether each situation is possible. Explain.

a) Louis, Lajune, and Rebeccah buy a pizza. Louis and Rebeccah eat $\frac{2}{5}$ each. Lajune eats $\frac{1}{4}$.

b) About $\frac{3}{5}$ of the men in Canada are married. About $\frac{3}{5}$ of the women in Canada are married.

Group Decision Making

Designing a Cross Number Puzzle

Cross number puzzles are like crossword puzzles, except that we complete them with numbers instead of words.

1. Work in your group to make up clues for the shell shown below. Write word problems with whole number answers or numerical expressions with whole number values.

1.	2.		3.	4.	5.	6.
7.			8.		9.	
10.		11.		12.		
		13.	14.			
15.	16.			17.	18.	19.
20.			21.		22.	
23.		24.			25.	

You will need to make up the following clues.

Across	Down
1.	**1.**
3.	**2.**
7.	**3.**
8.	**4.**
9.	**5.**
10.	**6.**
12.	**11.**
13.	**12.**
15.	**14.**
17.	**15.**
20.	**16.**
21.	**18.**
22.	**19.**
23.	**21.**
25.	**24.**

2. Check the clues in your group to make sure that they work.

3. Give your puzzle to other groups to solve.

4. Evaluate the puzzles by deciding how creative the clues are.

Chapter Check

Write an equivalent fraction.

1. $\frac{4}{5}$ **2.** $\frac{2}{3}$ **3.** $\frac{3}{4}$ **4.** $\frac{1}{6}$ **5.** $\frac{7}{10}$

Write each set of fractions from smallest to largest.

6. $\frac{1}{3}, \frac{1}{2}, \frac{1}{4}$ **7.** $\frac{2}{5}, \frac{2}{3}, \frac{7}{15}$ **8.** $2\frac{1}{3}, 2\frac{2}{3}, 2\frac{1}{6}$

Add.

9. $\frac{1}{4} + \frac{1}{4}$ **10.** $\frac{1}{6} + \frac{3}{4}$

11. $1\frac{1}{2} + 1\frac{1}{2}$ **12.** $1\frac{1}{5} + 2\frac{3}{4}$

Subtract.

13. $\frac{2}{3} - \frac{1}{3}$ **14.** $\frac{4}{5} - \frac{1}{10}$

15. $5\frac{1}{2} - 3\frac{1}{4}$ **16.** $10\frac{1}{5} - 9\frac{1}{3}$

Multiply.

17. $\frac{2}{3}$ of 18 **18.** $\frac{4}{5} \times \frac{1}{3}$

19. $\frac{2}{9} \times 27$ **20.** $3\frac{2}{5} \times 5\frac{1}{3}$

Divide.

21. $12 \div \frac{1}{4}$ **22.** $\frac{2}{3} \div \frac{1}{4}$

23. $\frac{8}{9} \div 1\frac{1}{3}$ **24.** $\frac{1}{2} \div 6$

Write as decimals.

25. $\frac{3}{4}$ **26.** $\frac{7}{20}$ **27.** $\frac{3}{8}$ **28.** $\frac{5}{6}$

Simplify.

29. $\frac{1}{2}$ of $(10 - 2) + 3^2$

30. $\frac{1}{2} \times 10 + 5 \div \frac{1}{3} - 4$

Solve.

31. Susan worked $2\frac{1}{2}$ hours on Thursday, $3\frac{3}{4}$ hours on Friday, and $4\frac{3}{4}$ hours on Saturday. How many hours did she work?

32. Frank used $\frac{1}{4}$ of his garden for carrots and $\frac{1}{3}$ for beans.

a) What fraction of the garden did he use?

b) What fraction was left?

33. When Gaetan Boucher won his Olympic gold medals in speedskating, his longer event was $1\frac{1}{2}$ times his shorter event. If his shorter event was the 1000 m, what was his longer event?

PEANUTS reprinted by permission of UFS, Inc.

Using the Strategies

1. In how many different ways can you make change for a quarter?

2. There are four hockey teams in a tournament. Each team will play each of the other teams twice. How many games will be played in the tournament?

3. Draw the bagels. Draw 2 lines across each bagel to make the stated number of pieces.

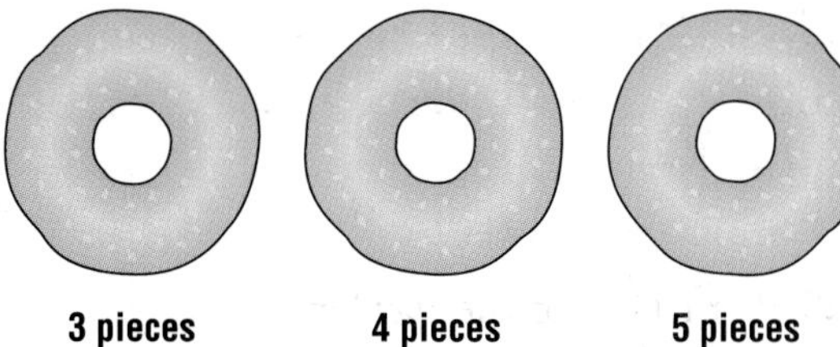

4. Julian bought 3 pens for $1.89 each and 2 notebooks for $5.78 each. If there was no tax, how much change did he get from a twenty-dollar bill?

5. Susan bought 6 antique chairs for $32.00 each. After she refinished them, she sold them to Stephan for $75.00 each.

a) How much profit did she make altogether?

b) If she spent 15 h refinishing the chairs, how much did she make per hour?

6. In a vote for Student Council, Paulo received 36 more votes than Mike. The total number of votes cast for Paulo and Mike was 210. How many votes did they each get?

7. Contestants on a game show won $25.00 worth of prizes for every 5 points they scored. Tamar scored 235 points. How much were her prizes worth?

8. How many page numbers in this book give a remainder of 3 when divided by 50?

9. The lacrosse players were numbered in a circle for passing drill. The 11th player was opposite the 23rd player. How many players were in the circle?

10. Write any fraction.
Double its value.
Add 18.
Halve the result.
Subtract the original fraction.
What number always remains?
Explain.

11. A tripod has $\frac{3}{4}$ as many legs as a horse. A termite has $1\frac{1}{2}$ times as many legs as a horse. How many legs does a termite have?

12. Three times a whole number is 10 more than half the number. What is the number?

13. Facsimile (fax) paper is sold in 30-m rolls. Estimate the number of pages of messages a facsimile machine can print on one of these rolls. What assumptions have you made?

DATA BANK

The Adams family drove from Saint John to Edmonton on the Trans-Canada Highway. They left Saint John on a Saturday morning at 08:00. Their average speed for the trip was 80 km/h.

a) What is the driving distance from Saint John to Edmonton?

b) How many hours did they spend driving from Saint John to Edmonton?

c) Each day they started at 08:00 and drove for 8 h. On what day did they reach Edmonton? What time was it in Edmonton when they arrived?

d) What provincial capitals did they pass through on their trip?

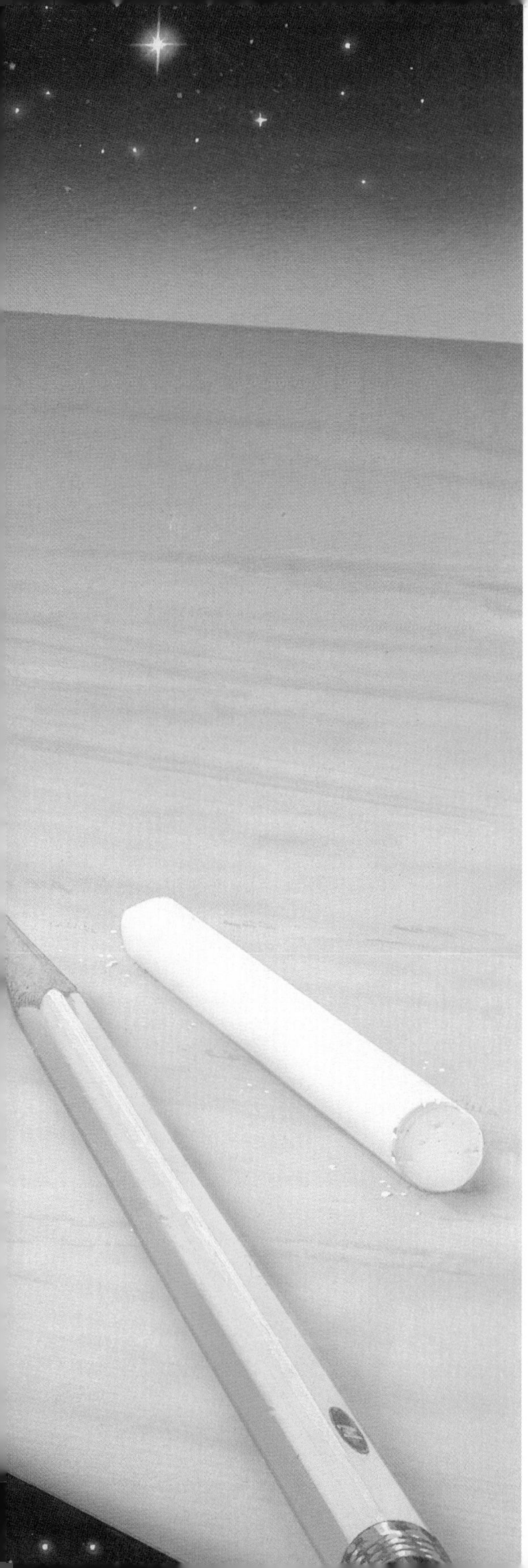

CHAPTER 6

Ratio and Rate

Although we can see lots of stars at night, our universe is mostly empty. Our sun is the closest star to us. The next closest star is Proxima Centauri.

To compare our distances from the two closest stars, put your math book flat on your desk in the position that you would normally read it. Put a chalk mark on the desk at the bottom edge of the book to represent the Earth. Now put a chalk mark on the desk at the top edge of the book to represent the sun.

To represent Proxima Centauri, you would need to put a chalk mark at the top edge of 260 000 math books. The books would be laid so that the top edge of one book touched the bottom edge of the next. How far would the chalk mark be from where you are?

It takes about 8.5 min for light to reach us from the sun. How many years does it take for light to reach us from Proxima Centauri?

Finding Patterns

Activity ❶

Draw the missing diagrams.

1. to is the same as to ?

2. 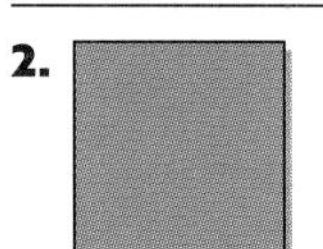 to 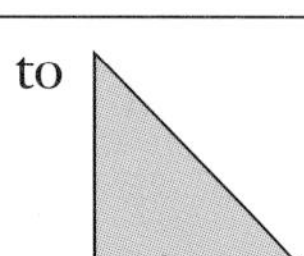 is the same as 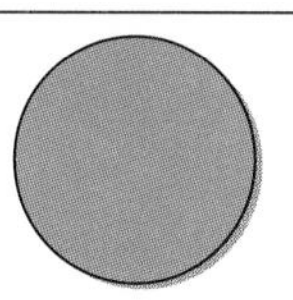 to ?

3. to is the same as to ?

Activity ❷

Find the missing numbers.

1. One horse needs ■ horseshoes.
Three horses need ■ horseshoes.

2. One bicycle needs ■ tires.
Eight bicycles need ■ tires.

3. One baseball team needs ■ players.
Eight baseball teams need ■ players.

Activity ❸

Find the missing numbers.

1. 3 to 12 is the same as 5 to 20 is the same as 8 to ■

2. 14 to 7 is the same as 20 to 10 is the same as 36 to ■

3. 4 to 10 is the same as 8 to 20 is the same as 12 to ■

4. 9 to 6 is the same as 12 to 8 is the same as 15 to ■

Activity ❹

Find the missing numbers.

1. One shirt costs $24.00. Four shirts cost $■.

2. Twelve pens cost $36.00. One pen costs $■. Four pens cost $■

3. Eight calculators cost $132.00. One calculator costs $■.
Four calculators cost $■.

Warm Up

To decode the message, complete each calculation. Find each solution in the code box and replace each number with a letter.

$T = 2 \div \frac{1}{2}$ $R = \frac{3}{4} - \frac{7}{10}$ $B = \frac{3}{8} + \frac{1}{4}$

$W = \frac{2}{5} + \frac{1}{2}$ $V = \frac{2}{3} \div \frac{3}{4}$ $Y = \frac{2}{3} \div \frac{2}{3}$

$W = \frac{1}{10} + \frac{3}{4}$ $A = \frac{2}{3} + \frac{1}{4}$ $O = \frac{1}{6} \div \frac{3}{4}$

$A = \frac{3}{4} + \frac{1}{8}$ $Y = \frac{7}{8} - \frac{1}{6}$ $E = \frac{5}{8} - \frac{1}{4}$

$T = \frac{1}{5} + \frac{1}{2}$ $O = \frac{5}{8} - \frac{1}{3}$ $H = \frac{5}{6} - \frac{5}{8}$

$R = \frac{3}{8} \div 2$ $A = \frac{2}{5} + \frac{1}{3}$ $E = \frac{1}{6} + \frac{1}{4}$

$R = \frac{3}{4} - \frac{1}{5}$ $O = \frac{2}{3} \times \frac{3}{5}$ $M = \frac{3}{8} - \frac{1}{3}$

$A = \frac{3}{4} \times \frac{3}{4}$ $N = \frac{3}{5} - \frac{1}{10}$ $T = \frac{2}{3} \div \frac{4}{5}$

$G = \frac{5}{8} - \frac{1}{6}$ $R = \frac{3}{5} + \frac{1}{3}$ $O = \frac{3}{5} \div \frac{3}{4}$

$E = \frac{1}{3} + \frac{1}{5}$ $N = \frac{1}{5} \div \frac{3}{4}$

Code Box

$\frac{1}{2}$ $\frac{3}{8}$ $\frac{8}{9}$ $\frac{5}{12}$ $\frac{14}{15}$

$\frac{7}{10}$ $\frac{11}{20}$ 1

4 $\frac{7}{24}$

$\frac{5}{6}$ $\frac{5}{24}$ $\frac{1}{20}$ $\frac{2}{5}$ $\frac{17}{20}$

$\frac{9}{16}$ $\frac{9}{10}$ $\frac{11}{15}$ $\frac{17}{24}$

$\frac{7}{8}$

$\frac{5}{8}$ $\frac{4}{5}$ $\frac{2}{9}$ $\frac{1}{24}$ $\frac{8}{15}$ $\frac{3}{16}$ $\frac{11}{12}$ $\frac{4}{15}$ $\frac{11}{24}$

Mental Math

Express in lowest terms.

1. $\frac{4}{8}$ **2.** $\frac{6}{10}$ **3.** $\frac{8}{10}$

4. $\frac{3}{9}$ **5.** $\frac{4}{12}$ **6.** $\frac{5}{15}$

7. $\frac{4}{6}$ **8.** $\frac{10}{15}$ **9.** $\frac{4}{16}$

10. $\frac{12}{16}$ **11.** $\frac{5}{20}$ **12.** $\frac{3}{12}$

13. $\frac{8}{14}$ **14.** $\frac{15}{18}$ **15.** $\frac{16}{20}$

State an equivalent fraction.

16. $\frac{1}{3}$ **17.** $\frac{1}{2}$ **18.** $\frac{2}{3}$

19. $\frac{3}{4}$ **20.** $\frac{3}{5}$ **21.** $\frac{5}{6}$

22. $\frac{1}{6}$ **23.** $\frac{4}{5}$ **24.** $\frac{1}{8}$

25. $\frac{7}{10}$ **26.** $\frac{1}{4}$ **27.** $\frac{2}{5}$

28. $\frac{2}{7}$ **29.** $\frac{5}{8}$ **30.** $\frac{3}{10}$

Express as an improper fraction.

31. $1\frac{1}{2}$ **32.** $2\frac{3}{4}$ **33.** $1\frac{2}{3}$

34. $1\frac{3}{10}$ **35.** $3\frac{1}{4}$ **36.** $2\frac{2}{5}$

37. $3\frac{1}{5}$ **38.** $1\frac{5}{8}$ **39.** $4\frac{3}{8}$

40. $1\frac{4}{5}$ **41.** $2\frac{1}{6}$ **42.** $1\frac{1}{3}$

43. $3\frac{1}{8}$ **44.** $2\frac{7}{10}$ **45.** $1\frac{4}{9}$

Express as a mixed number.

46. $\frac{3}{2}$ **47.** $\frac{8}{5}$ **48.** $\frac{4}{3}$

49. $\frac{6}{5}$ **50.** $\frac{9}{2}$ **51.** $\frac{11}{4}$

52. $\frac{8}{3}$ **53.** $\frac{7}{5}$ **54.** $\frac{7}{6}$

55. $\frac{11}{10}$ **56.** $\frac{7}{4}$ **57.** $\frac{9}{8}$

58. $\frac{11}{5}$ **59.** $\frac{16}{7}$ **60.** $\frac{19}{3}$

6.1 Ratio

Of the 10 Canadian provinces, 4 joined Confederation in 1867, 5 more joined from 1870 to 1905, and 1 joined in 1949.

Activity: Learn About Ratio

A **ratio** is a comparison of two numbers. We say that the ratio of provinces joining Confederation in 1867 to those joining from 1870–1905 is "4 to 5."
In ratio form, we write 4:5.
In fraction form, we write $\frac{4}{5}$.
In words, we write "4 to 5."
The **first term** of the ratio is 4.
The **second term** is 5.

Inquire

1. Write the ratio of provinces joining in 1867 to provinces joining in 1949.
2. Write the ratio of provinces joining in 1949 to provinces joining in 1867.
3. Write the ratio of provinces joining from 1870–1905 to provinces joining in 1949.
4. Write the ratio of provinces joining from 1870–1905 to provinces joining in 1867.

Example

a) Write a ratio to compare the number of triangles to the number of circles.

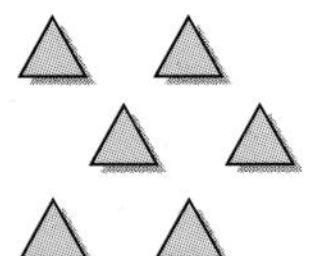

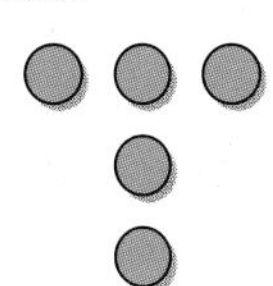

b) Write a ratio to compare the number of red counters to the number of blue counters.

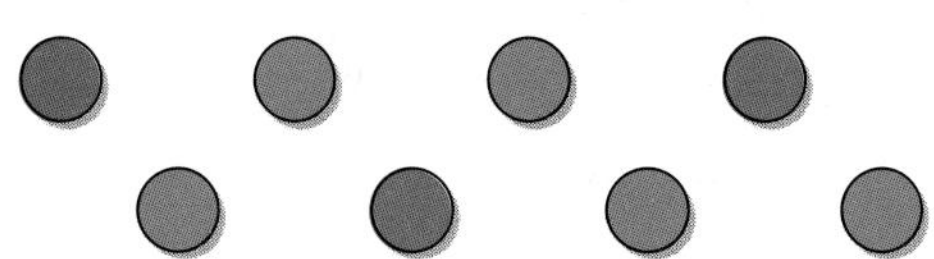

Solution

a) The number of triangles is 6.
The number of circles is 5.
The ratio is 6:5 or $\frac{6}{5}$.

b) The number of red counters is 3.
The number of blue counters is 5.
The ratio is 3:5 or $\frac{3}{5}$.

The order of the terms in a ratio is important.
When you change the order, you change the meaning of the ratio.

If Ron has four dollars and Dana has seven dollars, the ratio of Ron's money to Dana's money is 4:7. What is the ratio of Dana's money to Ron's money?

Practice

1. Work with a classmate. One student uses red and blue counters to represent a ratio with both terms less than 10. The other student writes the ratio of red counters to blue counters. Switch roles and repeat so that each of you makes up and writes 4 ratios.

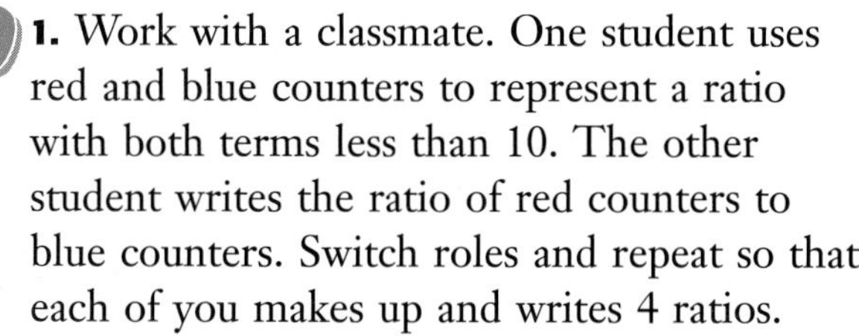

What is the ratio of squares to triangles?

2. **3.**

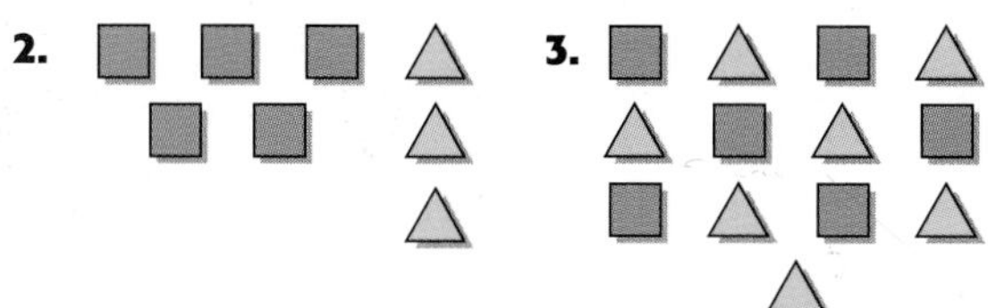

Write each ratio in 2 other ways.

4. 4 to 5 **5.** 1:2 **6.** $\frac{3}{7}$

7. 6:7 **8.** 9 to 4 **9.** $\frac{1}{5}$

10. $\frac{8}{5}$ **11.** 5 to 1 **12.** 3:2

In questions 13–17, use the following diagram and write each ratio in 3 ways.

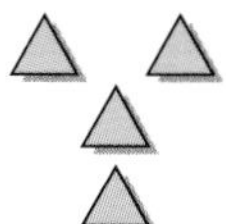
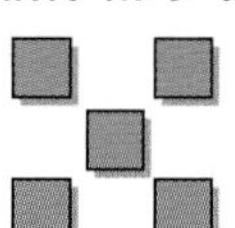
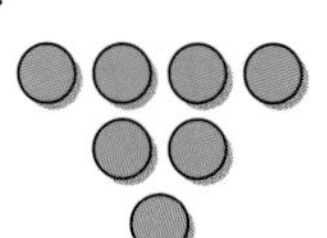

13. triangles to circles

14. circles to squares

15. squares to triangles

16. circles to triangles

17. triangles to squares

Problems and Applications

18. Twelve students tried a swimming test. Seven passed on the first try. What was the ratio of those passing to those failing?

19. There are 23 compact discs, 43 tapes, and 7 music videos in the school library. Find the following ratios.

a) videos to tapes **b)** CDs to videos
c) tapes to CDs **d)** tapes to videos

20. Use the diagram and write the ratios of the lengths.

3 cm 2 cm 4 cm
A B C D

a) AB to CD **b)** BC to AB
c) CD to AC **d)** BC to AD

21. Write the ratio of the number of days in a week to the number of days in a weekend.

22. Write a ratio for the value of a penny to the value of

a) a nickel **b)** a dime
c) a quarter **d)** a dollar

23. Write the ratio of consonants to vowels in each name.

a) Moncton **b)** Victoria
c) Lethbridge **d)** Truro
e) Corner Brook **f)** Niagara Falls

24. Find the following ratios for your class.

a) girls to boys
b) boys to girls
c) teachers to girls
d) students to teachers
e) teachers to students

25. Find the following ratios by totalling the times over 5 school days.

a) hours in school to hours not in school
b) hours in math class to hours in other classes
c) lunch hours to hours in English class
d) hours doing homework to hours in school

NUMBER POWER

Copy the diagram. Place the numbers from 1 to 13 in the circles so that the sum of each line is 21.

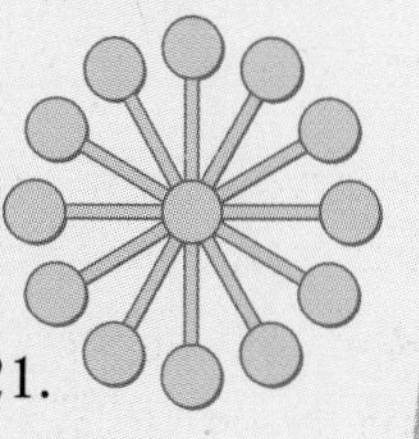

6.2 Equivalent Ratios

Activity: Study the Table

The table shows how cans of concentrate and water are mixed to make orange juice.

Cans of Concentrate	1	2	3	4
Cans of Water	3	6	9	12

Inquire

1. Write 4 ratios of cans of concentrate to cans of water.

2. Are the ratios equal? Explain.

3. Which ratio is in simplest form? Explain.

4. Write a rule for expressing a ratio in simplest form.

The table shows numbers of dollars and quarters that have equal value. The ratios of dollars to quarters are 1:4, 2:8, 3:12, and 4:16, or $\frac{1}{4}$, $\frac{2}{8}$, $\frac{3}{12}$, and $\frac{4}{16}$.

Dollars	1	2	3	4
Quarters	4	8	12	16

These are **equivalent ratios** or **equal ratios**. They make the same comparison.

Example 1

Find ratios equal to

a) 1:2 **b)** 9:12

Solution

a) $1:2 = \frac{1}{2} = \frac{1 \times 4}{2 \times 4} = \frac{4}{8}$

b) $9:12 = \frac{9}{12} = \frac{9 \div 3}{12 \div 3} = \frac{3}{4}$

A ratio is in **simplest form** or **lowest terms** when the greatest common factor of the terms is 1.

Example 2

Express 6:8 in lowest terms.

Solution

The factors of 6 are 1, 2, 3, and 6.
The factors of 8 are 1, 2, 4, and 8.
The greatest common factor is 2.

$6:8 = \frac{6}{8}$

$= \frac{6 \div 2}{8 \div 2}$ Divide the numerator and denominator by 2.

$= \frac{3}{4}$

Practice

Write 2 ratios equal to the ratio of squares to triangles.

1. 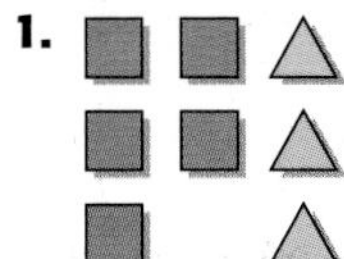

2. 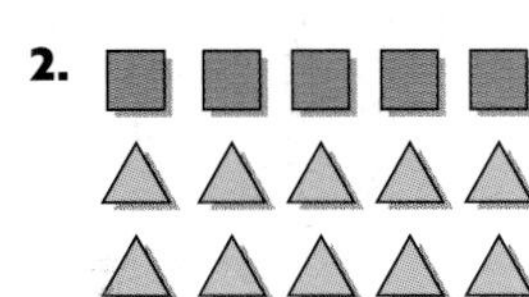

Write 3 equal ratios in the same form.

3. 1:2 **4.** 3 to 2 **5.** $\frac{4}{3}$

6. 1 to 3 **7.** $\frac{5}{2}$ **8.** 2:3

9. $\frac{3}{4}$ **10.** 6:5 **11.** 2 to 1

State whether each ratio is in lowest terms.

12. 4:6 **13.** 5 to 2 **14.** $\frac{2}{6}$

15. 3:5 **16.** $\frac{4}{4}$ **17.** 3 to 9

Write each ratio in lowest terms.

18. 3:12 **19.** 4:10 **20.** 5 to 15

21. $\frac{8}{10}$ **22.** 4 to 12 **23.** 2 to 6

24. $\frac{14}{7}$ **25.** 4 to 4 **26.** 15:10

Write each ratio as a fraction in lowest terms.

27. $\frac{3}{9}$ **28.** 4:8 **29.** $\frac{5}{10}$

30. 12 to 4 **31.** $\frac{4}{12}$ **32.** $\frac{4}{16}$

33. $\frac{22}{12}$ **34.** 24 to 15 **35.** $\frac{25}{15}$

36. 36 to 45 **37.** 17 to 51 **38.** $\frac{20}{28}$

39. 15 wins to 5 losses

40. 16 boys to 12 girls

41. 54 students to 3 teachers

Problems and Applications

42. The ratio of the length to the width of an official Canadian flag is 2:1. Terry has a flag that measures 60 cm by 25 cm. Is it an official flag?

43. Of the 324 tickets for the class concert, 180 were sold to adults and the rest to students. Write the ratio of adults who bought tickets to students who bought tickets. Answer in lowest terms.

44. Ahmed had 12 compact discs and 8 tapes. Bill gave him 4 compact discs.

a) What was Ahmed's original ratio of compact discs to tapes? Answer in lowest terms.

b) What was Ahmed's new ratio of compact discs to tapes? Answer in lowest terms.

45. Express the ratio in lowest terms of vowels to consonants in each name.

a) Chicoutimi **b)** Brandon

c) Ottawa **d)** Summerside

e) Humboldt **f)** your home town

46. The average lynx is 90 cm long and 60 cm tall. Express the length to the height of a lynx as a ratio in lowest terms.

47. State whether each statement is always true, sometimes true, or never true. Explain.

a) A ratio of two odd numbers is in lowest terms.

b) A ratio of two prime numbers is in lowest terms.

c) A ratio of two even numbers is in lowest terms.

48. Marnie has 18 coins in the ratio 1 dollar to 2 quarters. What coins does she spend to give a new ratio of dollars to quarters of 1:3? Give all possible answers and compare with a classmate.

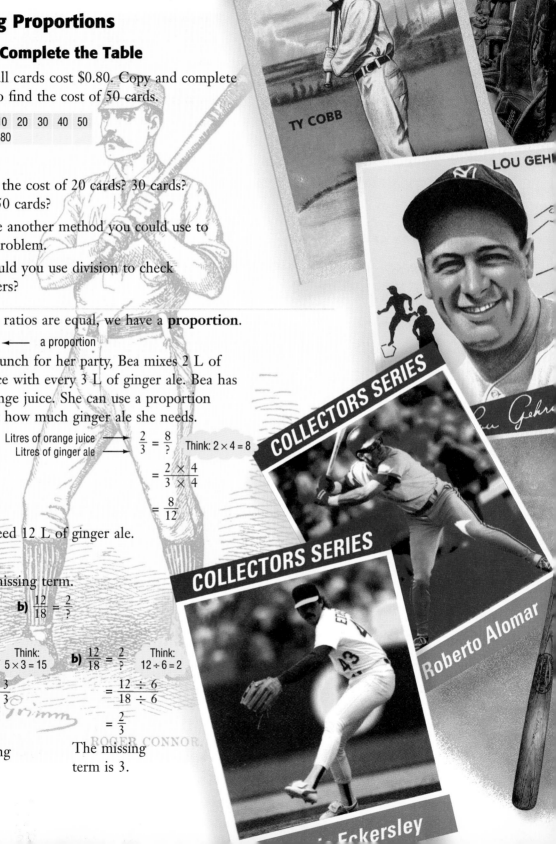

6.3 Solving Proportions

Activity: Complete the Table

Ten baseball cards cost \$0.80. Copy and complete the table to find the cost of 50 cards.

No. of Cards	10	20	30	40	50
Cost (\$)	0.80				

Inquire

1. What is the cost of 20 cards? 30 cards? 40 cards? 50 cards?
2. Describe another method you could use to solve the problem.
3. How could you use division to check your answers?

When two ratios are equal, we have a **proportion**.

$\frac{1}{2} = \frac{3}{6}$ ⟵ a proportion

To make punch for her party, Bea mixes 2 L of orange juice with every 3 L of ginger ale. Bea has 8 L of orange juice. She can use a proportion to find out how much ginger ale she needs.

Litres of orange juice ⟶ / Litres of ginger ale ⟶ $\frac{2}{3} = \frac{8}{?}$ Think: $2 \times 4 = 8$

$$= \frac{2 \times 4}{3 \times 4}$$

$$= \frac{8}{12}$$

Bea will need 12 L of ginger ale.

Example

Find the missing term.

a) $\frac{2}{5} = \frac{?}{15}$ b) $\frac{12}{18} = \frac{2}{?}$

Solution

a) $\frac{2}{5} = \frac{?}{15}$ Think: $5 \times 3 = 15$

$= \frac{2 \times 3}{5 \times 3}$

$= \frac{6}{15}$

The missing term is 6.

b) $\frac{12}{18} = \frac{2}{?}$ Think: $12 \div 6 = 2$

$= \frac{12 \div 6}{18 \div 6}$

$= \frac{2}{3}$

The missing term is 3.

Practice

State whether or not the ratios are equal.

1. $\frac{4}{5}, \frac{8}{10}$ **2.** $\frac{2}{3}, \frac{5}{9}$ **3.** $\frac{4}{4}, \frac{5}{5}$

4. $\frac{12}{10}, \frac{60}{50}$ **5.** $\frac{3}{9}, \frac{4}{12}$ **6.** $\frac{2}{3}, \frac{3}{4}$

7. $\frac{3}{5}, \frac{8}{10}$ **8.** $\frac{3}{5}, \frac{6}{15}$ **9.** $\frac{1}{6}, \frac{4}{24}$

Find the missing term.

10. $\frac{1}{4}, \frac{\blacksquare}{12}$ **11.** $\frac{1}{3}, \frac{\blacksquare}{18}$ **12.** $\frac{\blacksquare}{6}, \frac{12}{24}$

13. $\frac{\blacksquare}{5}, \frac{9}{15}$ **14.** $\frac{6}{15}, \frac{2}{\blacksquare}$ **15.** $\frac{8}{10}, \frac{4}{\blacksquare}$

16. $\frac{5}{\blacksquare}, \frac{25}{10}$ **17.** $\frac{16}{\blacksquare}, \frac{8}{6}$ **18.** $\frac{18}{36}, \frac{\blacksquare}{12}$

19. $\frac{18}{21}, \frac{6}{\blacksquare}$ **20.** $\frac{15}{\blacksquare}, \frac{5}{12}$ **21.** $\frac{\blacksquare}{35}, \frac{28}{5}$

Write the proportion, then solve for the unknown.

22. 1 is to 3 as 4 is to ■

23. 1 is to 2 as 5 is to ■

24. 2 is to 3 as 8 is to ■

25. 3 is to 2 as ■ is to 8

26. 8 is to 12 as ■ is to 6

Write the proportion, then solve for the unknown.

27. 1 h is to $5.00 as 8 h is to $■

28. 50 km is to 1 h as 200 km is to ■ h

29. 6 wins are to 10 games as ■ wins are to 40 games

30. 3 pens are to $1.20 as ■ pens are to $3.60

31. 4 scouts are to 1 tent as 36 scouts are to ■ tents

Problems and Applications

32. Three T-shirts cost $21.00. How much do 9 T-shirts cost?

33. Karen drove 140 km in 2 h.

a) How long will she take to drive 420 km?

b) What assumptions have you made?

34. Twelve muffins cost $7.80. How many muffins can you buy for $2.60?

35. Terry cleans eavestroughs. He earns $17.00 in 2 h. How much should he earn in 12 h?

36. The average newborn baby sleeps $\frac{2}{3}$ of the time. How many hours does the average newborn sleep in a day?

37. How many nickels are worth $3.00?

38. How many metres equal 3 km?

39. A garden flower grows a total of 10 cm in July and August.

a) How much will the flower grow in a year?

b) What assumptions have you made?

c) Are your assumptions reasonable?

40. Write a problem that involves a proportion. Have a classmate solve your problem.

LOGIC POWER

Suppose you have some red paint, some black paint, and some unpainted cubes. You want to paint as many cubes as possible so that no two cubes are exactly the same. You can use only one colour per face. One cube could have 5 red faces and 1 black face. How many different cubes can you paint?

Technology on the Job

Technology can be as complicated as the guidance system on a Space Shuttle or as simple as a pencil. There are many examples of technology in the workplace.

Activity ❶

Describe how you think the following people use technology in their work. You may need to do some research to find out how they do their jobs.

a) Kerri Bourne serves customers at a fast food restaurant.

b) Justine Scarlatti is a police officer.

c) John Rhineman is a treasure hunter. He searches shipwrecks for artifacts, gold, and rare coins.

d) Carl Chancellor is a bank manager.

e) Carol Mak is an air traffic controller.

f) Bill Lee sorts mail for the post office.

Activity ❷

For each job in Activity 1, describe how you think technology will be used in the future.

Activity ❸

Choose any other job that interests you. Describe the technology it requires now and the technology it may use in the future.

Pattern Power from Calculators

Activity ❶

1. When read from left to right, these sums are made from consecutive whole numbers. Determine the pattern and write the next 3 rows. Use your calculator to verify that the additions are correct.

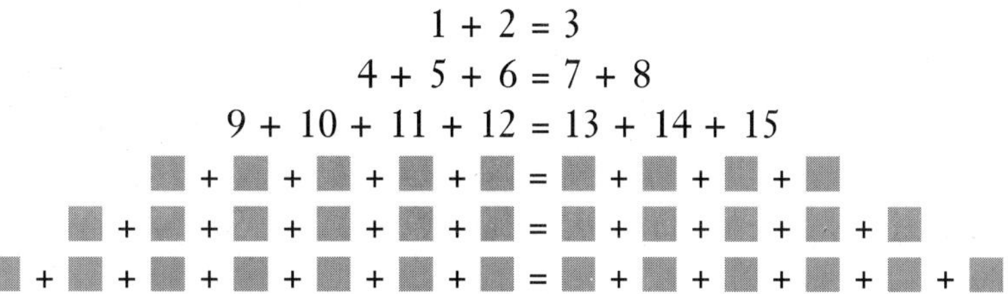

$$1 + 2 = 3$$
$$4 + 5 + 6 = 7 + 8$$
$$9 + 10 + 11 + 12 = 13 + 14 + 15$$
$$\square + \square + \square + \square + \square = \square + \square + \square + \square$$
$$\square + \square + \square + \square + \square + \square = \square + \square + \square + \square + \square$$
$$\square + \square + \square + \square + \square + \square + \square = \square + \square + \square + \square + \square + \square$$

2. Describe the pattern in your own words.

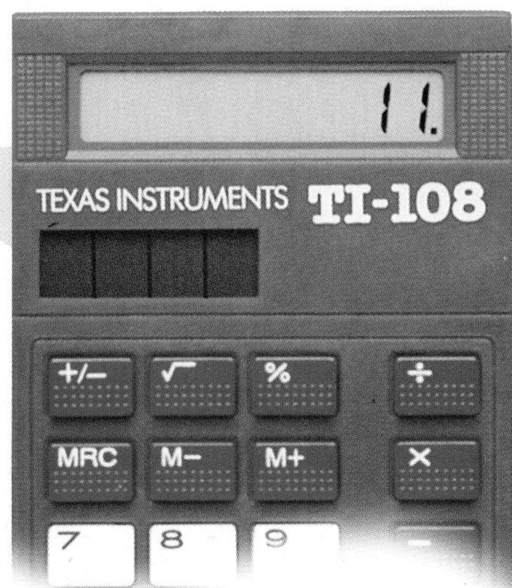

Activity ❷

1. Continue the following pattern. Determine what must be added to the left side to give the smallest possible answer whose digits are all 1s.

$$1 \times 9 + 2 = 11$$
$$12 \times 9 + \square = \square$$
$$123 \times 9 + \square = \square$$
$$1234 \times 9 + \square = \square$$
$$\square \times 9 + \square = \square$$
$$\square \times 9 + \square = \square$$
$$\square \times 9 + \square = \square$$

2. Describe the pattern in your own words.

Activity ❸

1. Determine the pattern for the sum of even numbers and write the next 3 rows.

First	$2 = 2 = 1 \times 2$
First two	$2 + 4 = 6 = 2 \times 3$
First three	$2 + 4 + 6 = 12 = 3 \times 4$
First four	$2 + 4 + 6 + 8 = 20 = \square \times \square$
First five	$\square + \square + \square + \square + \square = \square = \square \times \square$
First six	$\square + \square + \square + \square + \square + \square = \square = \square \times \square$

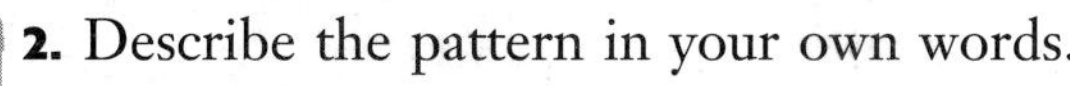

2. Describe the pattern in your own words.

3. What is the sum of the first 29 even numbers?

4. What is the sum of the first 67 even numbers?

6.4 Similar Triangles

A maple leaf appears next to Roberta Bondar's name on the badge she wore on the Space Shuttle *Discovery*. This maple leaf is much smaller than the one on the flag that flies outside your school. The maple leaf on the badge and the one on your school flag have the same shape. Figures that have the same shape are called **similar figures**.

Activity: Discover the Relationship

Draw △ABC on grid paper.

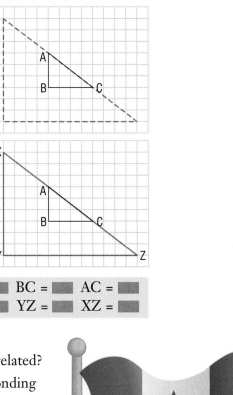

Draw a line parallel to BC, 3 squares below BC.

Draw a line parallel to AB, 4 squares to the left of AB.

Draw a line along AC to form a triangle with the other two lines.

Label the vertices of the larger triangle X, Y, and Z. △ABC is similar to △XYZ. Similar triangles have the same shape.

Measure the angles and sides of both triangles and record the values.

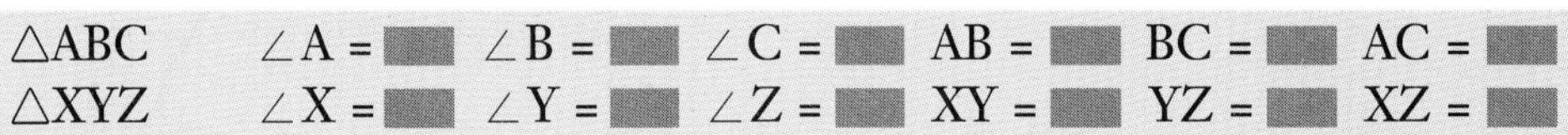

△ABC	∠A = ▇	∠B = ▇	∠C = ▇	AB = ▇	BC = ▇	AC = ▇
△XYZ	∠X = ▇	∠Y = ▇	∠Z = ▇	XY = ▇	YZ = ▇	XZ = ▇

Inquire

1. How are the measures of the corresponding angles related?

2. Write the following ratios of the lengths of corresponding sides in lowest terms.

a) length of AB: length of XY **b)** length of BC: length of YZ

c) length of AC: length of XZ

3. How are the ratios of the corresponding sides related?

4. Write your definition of similar triangles.

Example

△ABC and △DEF are similar.

a) Find the measure of ∠D, ∠E, and ∠F.

b) Find the lengths of EF and DF.

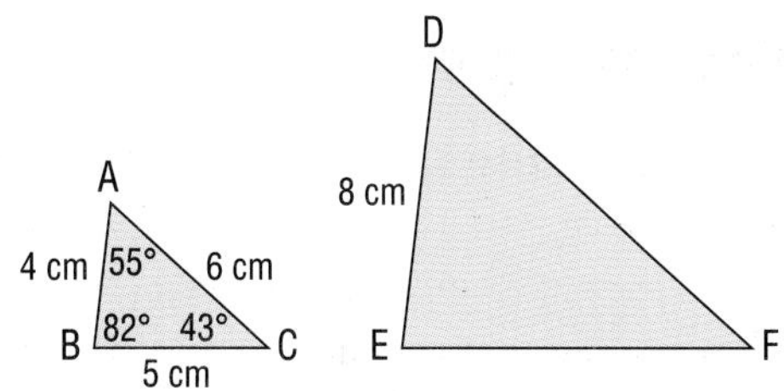

Solution

a) For similar triangles, corresponding angles are equal.

∠D = ∠A = 55°   ∠E = ∠B = 82°   ∠F = ∠C = 43°

b) For similar triangles, the ratios of the corresponding sides are the same.

$\frac{AB}{DE} = \frac{BC}{EF}$ $\frac{AB}{DE} = \frac{AC}{DF}$

So, $\frac{4}{8} = \frac{5}{EF}$ So, $\frac{4}{8} = \frac{6}{DF}$

EF = 10 cm   DF = 12 cm

Think: $\frac{4}{8} = \frac{1}{2}$

Practice

The pairs of triangles are similar. List the pairs of corresponding angles and corresponding sides.

1.

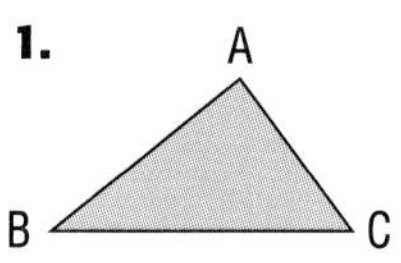

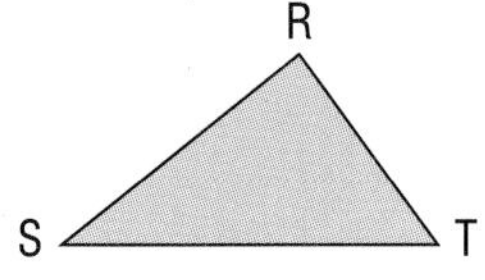

2.

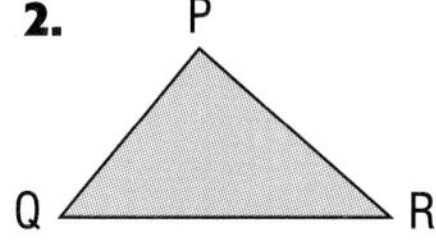

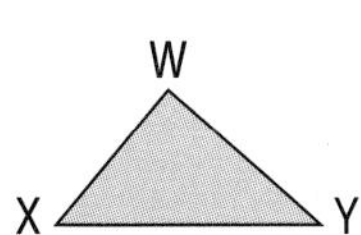

The pairs of triangles are similar. Calculate the missing dimensions.

3.

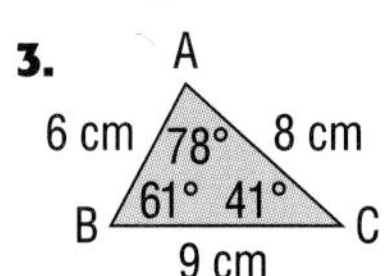

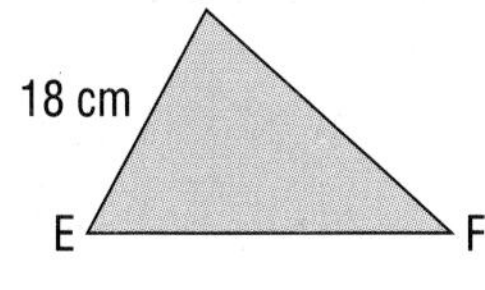

4. **5.**

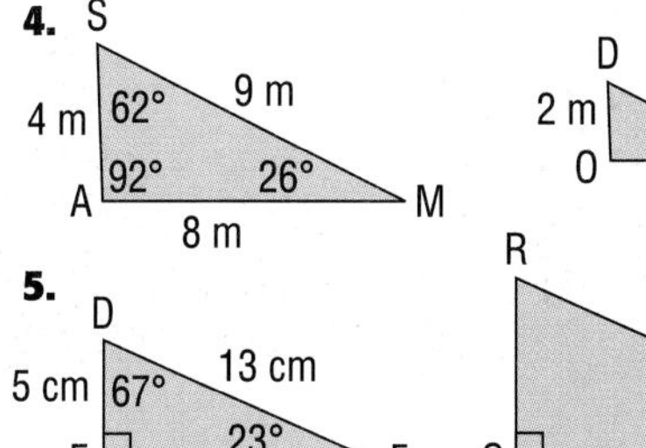

D O G 2 m

R Q P 18 cm

Problems and Applications

6. The flagpole casts a shadow of 12 m when a metre-stick casts a shadow of 2 m. How high is the flagpole?

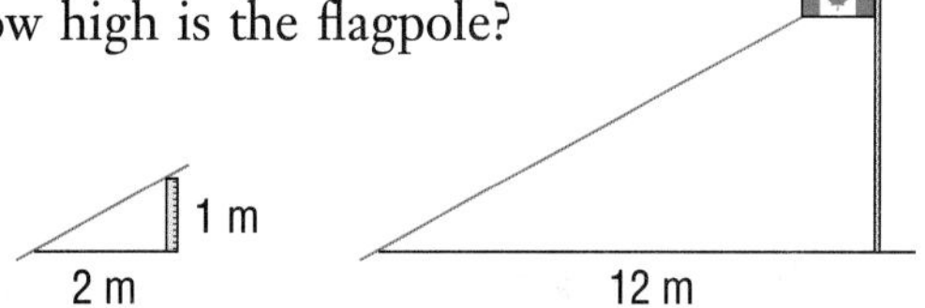

7. Is each statement true or false? Illustrate each answer with a diagram.

a) All rectangles are similar.

b) All squares are similar.

c) All equilateral triangles are similar.

d) All isosceles triangles are similar.

8. If two triangles are congruent are they also similar? Explain.

9. a) Use a protractor and a ruler to draw four similar triangles.

b) Can you draw two triangles whose corresponding angles are equal but which are not similar?

10. Pick a sunny day and work with a classmate. Use a metre-stick and the technique you used in question 6 to calculate the height of your school and objects around your school.

6.5 Scale Drawings

Activity: Study the Drawing

Seven tribes make up the Northwest Pacific cultural unit. They are also known as the Totem Pole Carving People. A totem pole is like a family coat of arms.

A **scale drawing** is used to show something that is too large or too small to draw to its actual size. The totem pole at the right is a scale drawing of a section of a totem pole on the Queen Charlotte Islands, British Columbia.

The totem pole is drawn to a scale of 1 to 30. The scale can be written as a ratio, 1:30. This scale compares the distance on the drawing with the actual distance. One unit of length in the drawing represents 30 units of the same length for the actual totem pole.

Inquire

1. Measure the height of the drawing of this section of totem pole in centimetres.

2. What is the actual height of this section of totem pole in centimetres? in metres?

3. List some other examples of situations in which scale drawings are used.

Example 1

The diagram is a scale drawing of a fin whale.
The scale is 1:200.
What is the actual length of the whale?

10 cm

Solution

The scale is 1:200.
This means that 1 cm in the drawing represents 200 cm on the whale.
Let l represent the actual length of the whale.

1 cm on drawing → numerator of $\frac{1}{200}$; 200 cm actual → denominator; 10 ← length of drawing; l ← actual length of whale

$$\frac{1}{200} = \frac{10}{l}$$

$$\frac{1}{200} = \frac{1 \times 10}{200 \times 10}$$

$$= \frac{10}{2000}$$

The whale is 2000 cm or 20 m long.

Practice

Calculate the actual length of each animal.

1. Giant earthworm from South Africa

Scale 1:100

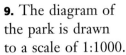

6 cm

2. Brontosaurus—lived 150 000 000 years ago

Scale 1:400

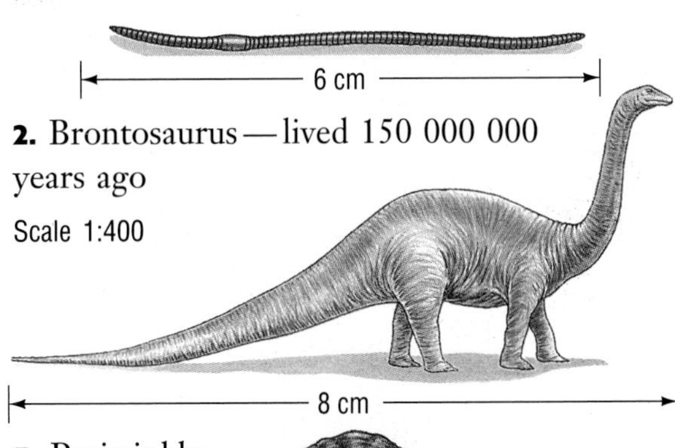

3. Periwinkle

Scale 2:1

4 cm

4. Queen honeybee

Scale 4:1

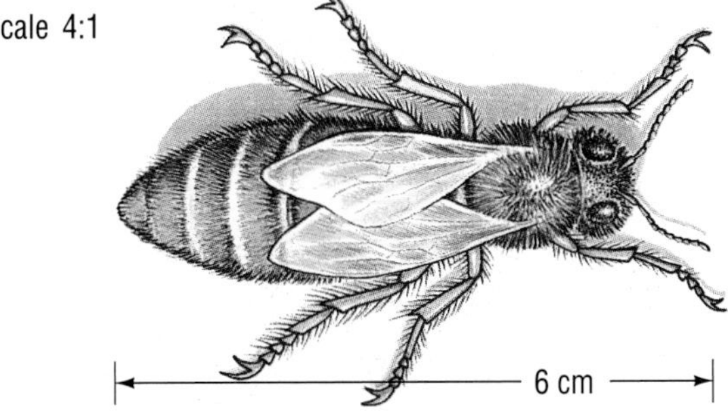

Problems and Applications

5. An insect is 0.5 cm long. What is the length of a diagram of the insect if the scale is 10:1?

6. The width of a sidewalk in a diagram is 8 cm. What is the actual width if the scale is 1:20?

7. The height of a building is 30 m. What is the height of a diagram of the building if the scale is 1:2000?

8. The actual length of a car is 400 cm. The length of the car in a scale drawing is 8 cm. What is the scale?

9. The diagram of the park is drawn to a scale of 1:1000.

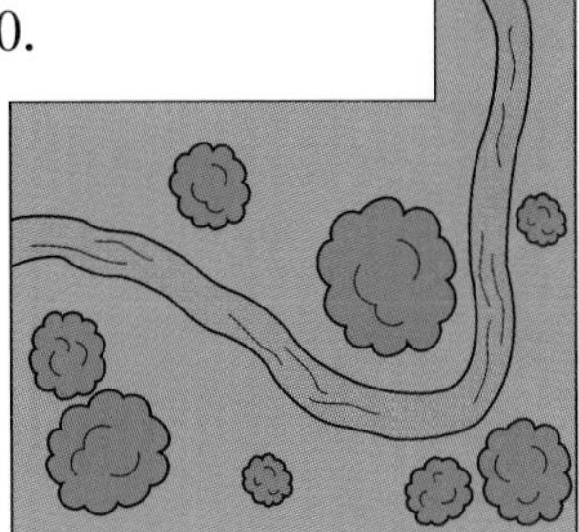

a) Measure the perimeter of the scale drawing.

b) What is the perimeter of the actual park?

10. An area 100 m by 100 m is a hectare. If a scale drawing represents a hectare to a scale of 1:1000, what is the area of the drawing in square centimetres?

11. Decide whether each statement is true or false. Explain.

a) A 1:1 scale drawing of a triangle is a congruent triangle.

b) The length of a 2:1 scale drawing of an insect is 4 times less than the length of a 1:2 scale drawing of the same insect.

12. Estimate the dimensions of the front of your school. Choose a scale to make a scale drawing fit on a page this size.

13. Work with a partner. List occupations that use scale drawings. Why are scale drawings used in these occupations?

NUMBER POWER

A fingernail grows about 0.05 cm a week. Estimate the length of fingernail the average person grows in a lifetime. Compare your estimate and your assumptions with a classmate's.

6.6 Maps and Scales

Activity: Explore the Map

Oak Island is off the South Shore of Nova Scotia. People have been searching for pirate treasure on Oak Island for 200 years. Some say the Money Pit is the hiding place for Captain William Kidd's treasure. Others think Blackbeard buried his treasure in the Pit. The map is drawn to a scale of 1:10 000.

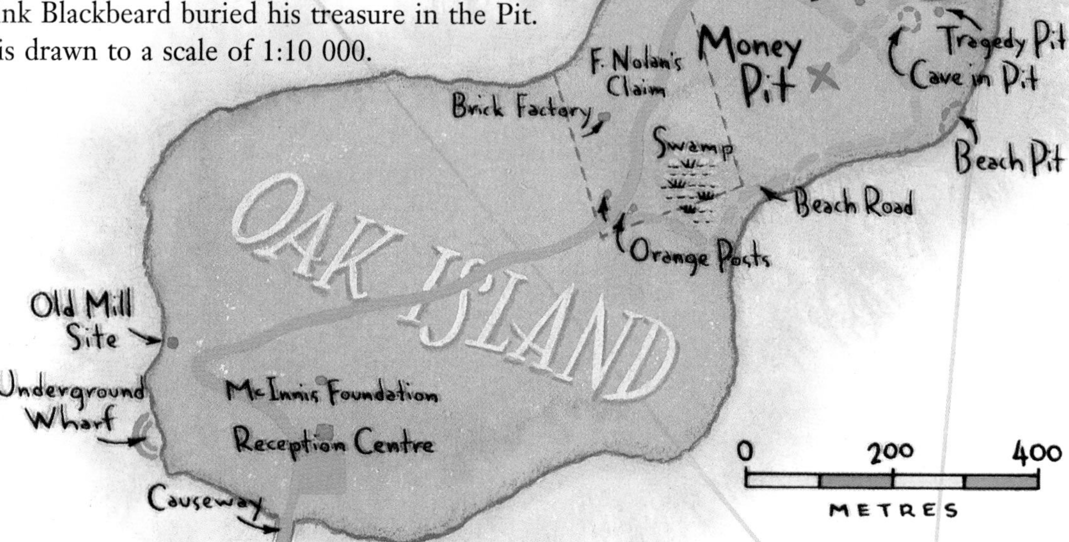

Inquire

1. Measure the distance, in centimetres, from the Underground Wharf to the Money Pit.

2. Calculate the actual distance, in metres, from the Underground Wharf to the Money Pit.

Example

Calculate the distance, in metres, from the Swamp to the Money Pit.

Solution

The scale is 1:10 000.
This means that 1 cm on the map is 10 000 cm on Oak Island, or 1 cm on the map is 100 m on Oak Island.
The distance from the Swamp to the Money Pit on the map is 2.2 cm.

1 cm on map ⟶ , 100 m actual ⟶ $\frac{1}{100} = \frac{2.2}{d}$ ⟵ 2.2 cm on map, ⟵ distance from the Swamp to the Money Pit

$$= \frac{1 \times 2.2}{100 \times 2.2}$$

$$= \frac{2.2}{220}$$

The distance from the Swamp to the Money Pit is 220 m.

Practice

Use the map of Oak Island to find the distance between the following.

1. the Underground Wharf and the Coffer Dams

2. the Swamp and the Beach Pit

3. the Money Pit and the Beach Pit

Problems and Applications

Use the map of Alberta, below, to calculate the following distances by air.

4. Edmonton to Calgary

5. Calgary to Peace River

6. Edmonton to Fort Chipewyan

7. Grande Prairie to Medicine Hat

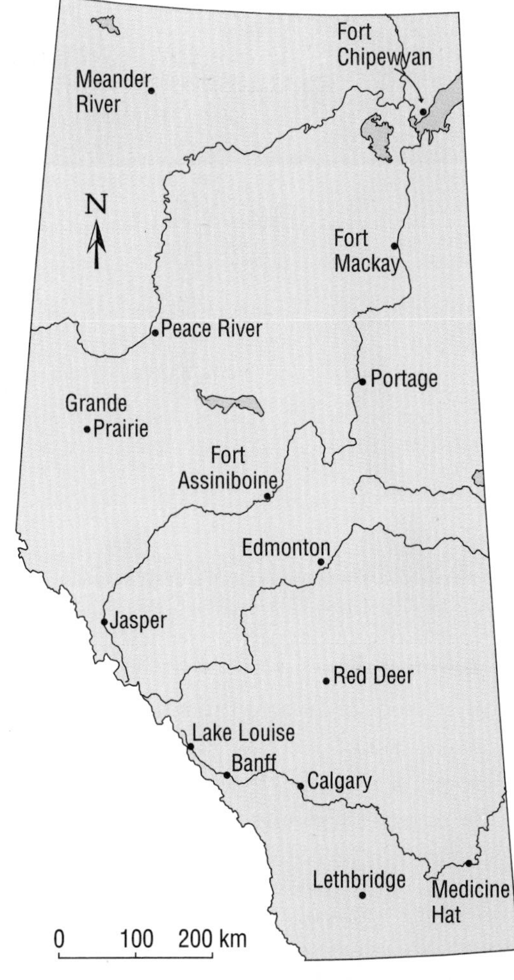

Use the map of Manitoba, below, to calculate the following distances by air.

8. Winnipeg to Thompson

9. Brandon to Lynn Lake

10. Winnipeg to Oxford House

11. Norway House to Ilford

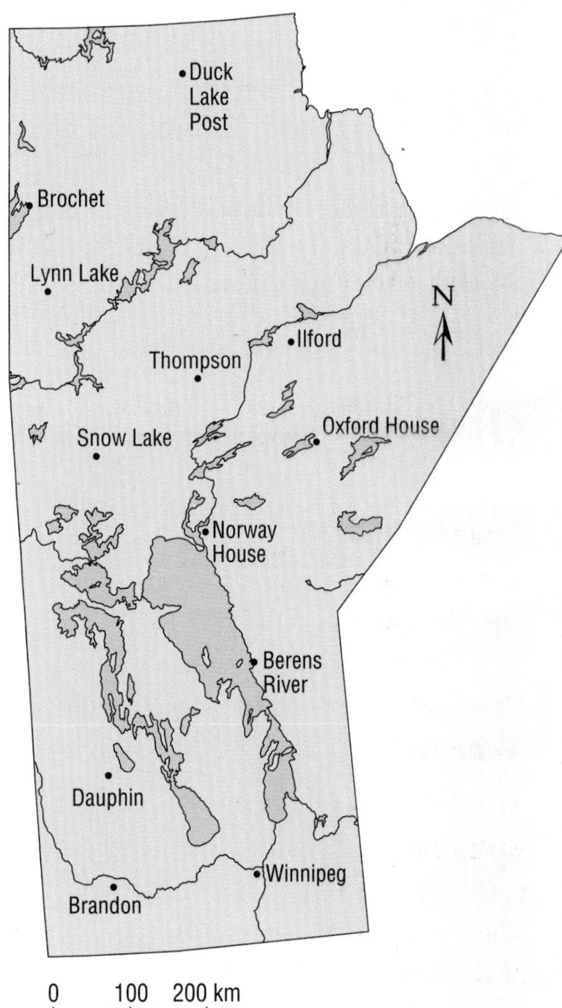

Terry Fox
and the Marathon of Hope

Terry Fox was 21 years old when he started his run across Canada to raise money for cancer research.

The Marathon of Hope began in St. John's, Newfoundland, on April 12, 1980.

Terry had to stop his run on September 1 of that year in Thunder Bay, Ontario, when he became too ill to continue.

Terry's Marathon of Hope raised twenty-five million dollars. The Terry Fox Run continues to raise money for cancer research.

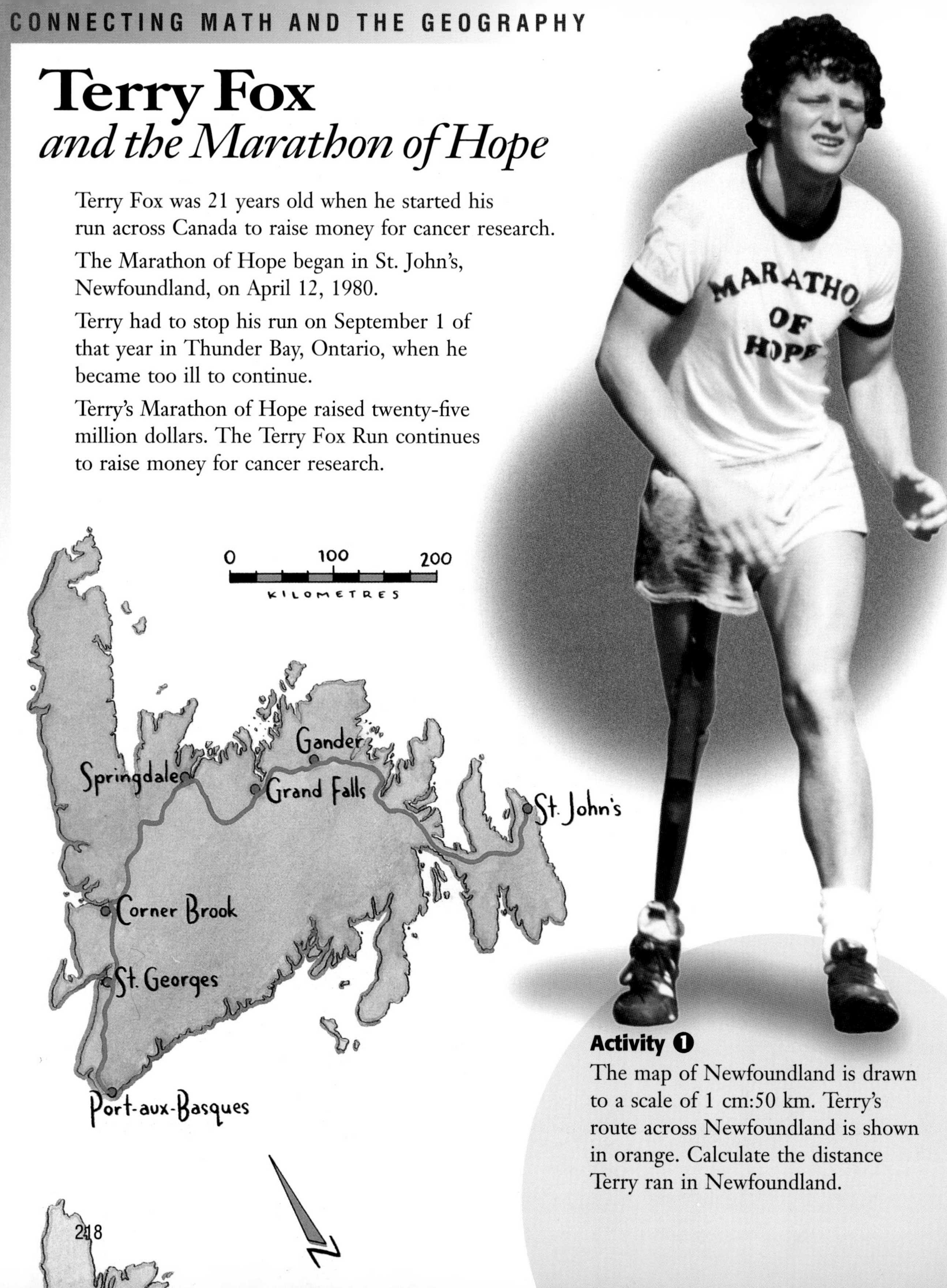

Activity ❶

The map of Newfoundland is drawn to a scale of 1 cm:50 km. Terry's route across Newfoundland is shown in orange. Calculate the distance Terry ran in Newfoundland.

Activity ❷

Terry arrived in North Sydney, Nova Scotia, on May 7. His run to Halifax took him through Port Hawkesbury and Sheet Harbour. From Halifax, he ran to Springhill and on to Amherst. Use a map to calculate how far Terry ran in Nova Scotia.

Activity ❸

On May 24, Terry took the ferry across the Northumberland Strait to Borden, Prince Edward Island. From there, he ran to Charlottetown, before returning to Borden. How far did Terry go in Prince Edward Island?

Activity ❹

Terry took the ferry from Borden to Cape Tormentine, New Brunswick. He ran through Moncton, Saint John, Bristol, and Edmundston. Find how far Terry ran in New Brunswick. Sketch a map of his route.

Activity ❺

Research Terry's route in Quebec and Ontario. Make a poster to show the route. Include some pictures and information about the events Terry attended and the people he met during this part of his run.

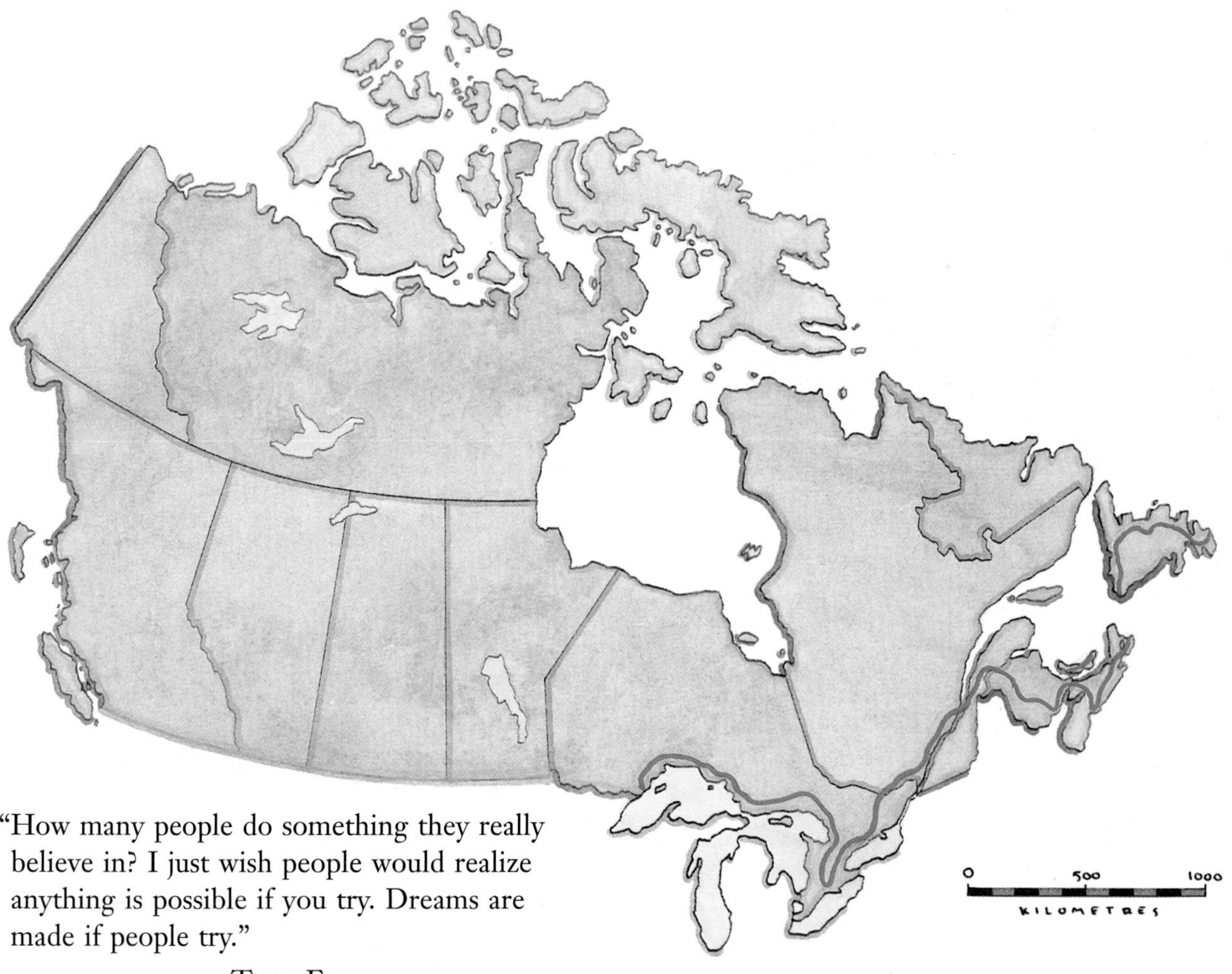

"How many people do something they really believe in? I just wish people would realize anything is possible if you try. Dreams are made if people try."

Terry Fox

Rates

A rate is a special ratio. The two quantities being compared have different units. One rate that you know is speed. If a car travels fifty kilometres in one hour, we say that the speed is fifty kilometres per hour or 50 km/h.

Activity 1

1. Estimate how many words you can say in 1 min. Copy the table and record the estimates for all members of your group.

Name	Estimated Rate (words/min)	Words Spoken in 15 s	Actual Rate (words/min)

2. There are 5 words in the sentence

"I love math and lunch."

One member of your group should say the sentence as many times as possible in 15 s. A group member with a watch that measures seconds should tell the speaker when to start, wait for 15 s, then tell the speaker to stop. Another member should count the number of times the sentence is spoken in 15 s.

3. Record the number of words spoken in 15 s. A speaker who says the sentence 13 times in 15 s has spoken $5 \times 13 = 65$ words in 15 s.

4. Record the actual rate of speaking in words per minute. A person who speaks 65 words in 15 s can speak 4×65 words in one minute, or 260 words/min. This rate is 260 words/min.

5. Complete the table for all other members of the group.

a) Compare each person's estimate with the actual rate in words per minute.

b) Suggest reasons for any large differences between the estimated and actual rates.

Activity 2

1. All members of your group should estimate how many times they blink in 1 h. Copy the table and record the estimates.

Name	Estimated Rate (blinks/h)	Blinks in 1 min	Actual Rate (blinks/h)

2. Count the number of times each person blinks in 1 min. Multiply by 60 to get the number of blinks per hour. Complete the table for each group member.

3. Was anyone's estimated number of blinks per hour close to the actual number of blinks per hour?

4. Suggest reasons for any large differences between the estimated and actual rates.

5. Find out if your rate of blinking changes when you stand in bright light or in a dark corner.

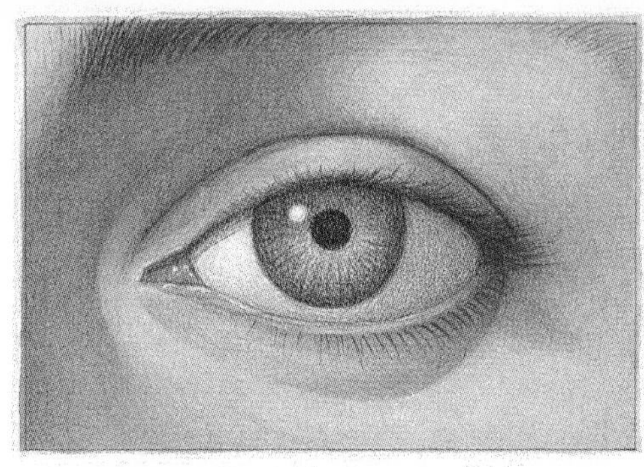

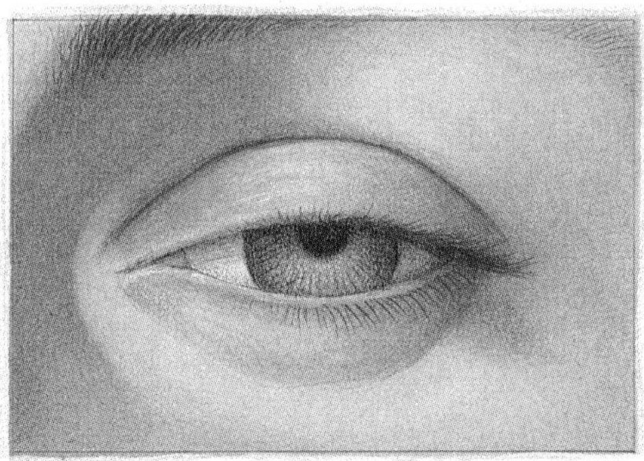

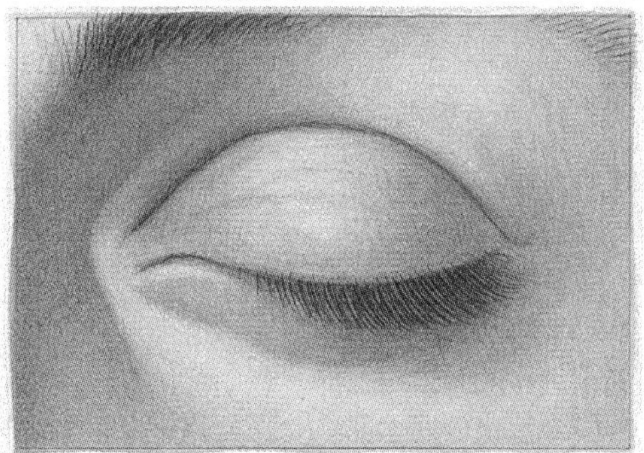

Activity 3

1. All group members should estimate their pulse rates in beats per minute.

2. Determine each group member's pulse rate in beats per minute.

3. Compare the estimated and actual rates.

Activity 4

1. All members of your group should estimate their normal walking rates in kilometres per hour.

2. Decide on a method of calculating a walking rate in kilometres per hour without having the person walk 1 km.

3. Determine each group member's walking rate in kilometres per hour.

4. Compare your method with your classmates'.

6.7 Rates

Activity: Study the Information

The world's slowest mammal is the three-toed sloth of South America. On the ground, it travels an average of 21 m in 10 min. We can write this information as a **rate**, which is a comparison of two quantities with different units.

The rate is $\frac{21\text{ m}}{10\text{ min}}$ or 21 m:10 min.

A rate is usually written as a **unit rate**, in which the second term is 1.

$$\frac{21}{10} = \frac{21 \div 10}{10 \div 10}$$

$$\frac{21}{10} = \frac{2.1}{1}$$

So, the unit rate is $\frac{2.1\text{ m}}{1\text{ min}}$.

A unit rate is usually written in the form 2.1 m/min.

A garden snail can travel 48 m in an hour. We want to know which is slower, the sloth or the snail.

Inquire

1. Write a unit rate for the speed of the snail in metres per hour.
2. Use the units metres and minutes to write a rate for the speed of the snail.
3. Write a unit rate for the speed of the snail in metres per minute.
4. Which is slower, the sloth or the snail?
5. A speed in metres per minute is one example of a unit rate. List other examples of unit rates that you know. Compare your list with your classmates'.

Example

Michael works part-time in the public library. One Saturday, he worked 4 h and earned $32.00. What is Michael's rate of pay?

Solution

$$\text{Rate of pay} = \frac{\text{amount earned}}{\text{time worked}}$$

$$= \frac{\$32.00}{4\text{ h}}$$

$$= \$8.00/\text{h}$$

Practice

Find the value of the unknown.

1. $\frac{10}{2} = \frac{\blacksquare}{1}$ **2.** $\frac{15}{5} = \frac{\blacksquare}{1}$ **3.** $\frac{24}{6} = \frac{\blacksquare}{1}$

4. $\frac{\$8.00}{4} = \frac{\blacksquare}{1}$ **5.** $\frac{28}{14} = \frac{\blacksquare}{1}$ **6.** $\frac{300}{5} = \frac{\blacksquare}{1}$

7. $\frac{\$12.30}{3} = \frac{\blacksquare}{1}$ **8.** $\frac{8.6}{2} = \frac{\blacksquare}{1}$ **9.** $\frac{16}{4} = \frac{\blacksquare}{1}$

Complete the following.

10. 120 km in 2 h = $\blacksquare$ km/h

11. $24 for 3 h = $$\blacksquare$ /h

12. 45 min to paint 5 windows = $\blacksquare$ min/window

13. 24 pens in 3 boxes = $\blacksquare$ pens/box

14. 48 cans in 2 cases = $\blacksquare$ cans/case

15. 120 words in 3 min = $\blacksquare$ words/min

16. $16 for 8 hot dogs = $$\blacksquare$ /hot dog

17. 44 players on 4 teams = $\blacksquare$ players/team.

Write the unit rate for each.

18. 300 km in 5 h

19. 200 m in 40 s

20. 5 lawns in 10 h

21. 40 pencils in 5 boxes

22. 12 suitcases for 4 travellers

23. $440 for 4 rooms

Problems and Applications

24. Henri earns $68.75 for 11 h of work as a packer in a grocery store. What is his hourly rate of pay?

25. Colleen paid $819.00 for 7 nights at a hotel. What was the nightly rate for her room?

26. Franco can type 153 words in 3 min. What is his typing speed in words per minute?

27. While racing around the sun, the Earth travels about 321 000 km in 3 h. What is the Earth's speed in kilometres per hour?

28. Ingvar drove 225 km in 3 h. Justine drove 370 km in 5 h. Who drove faster?

29. The average adult in Canada has about 38.5 h of leisure time per week.

a) Express this rate in hours per day.

b) Do all adults in Canada get this much leisure time every day? Explain.

30. In 1872, railroad engineer Sandford Fleming led a group from Halifax to Victoria to explore a route for the Canadian Pacific Railway. The trip of 8500 km took 103 days.

a) Estimate the rate of travel in kilometres per day.

b) Calculate the rate of travel to the nearest kilometre per day.

31. At the equator, the circumference of the Earth is 40 076 km. If you were standing on the equator, at what speed would you be spinning around the Earth's axis? Give your answer to the nearest kilometre per hour.

LOGIC POWER

A ball was dropped from a height of 60 m. Each time it hit the ground, it bounced up $\frac{1}{2}$ of the height that it dropped. How far had the ball travelled when it hit the ground for the fifth time?

6.8 Unit Pricing

Activity: Make a Comparison

Paul was asked to buy grapefruit for Sunday breakfast. He went to two stores. The price at each store is shown.

FOOD FAIR
Grapefruit
8 for $3.44
ADAM'S
GROCETERIA
Grapefruit
5 for $2.20

Inquire

1. Calculate the cost of 1 grapefruit at Food Fair.

2. Calculate the cost of 1 grapefruit at Adam's Groceteria.

3. Which store offered the better price?

4. Why is it important to know the cost of one item when grocery shopping?

5. What other things should you consider besides price when you buy an item?

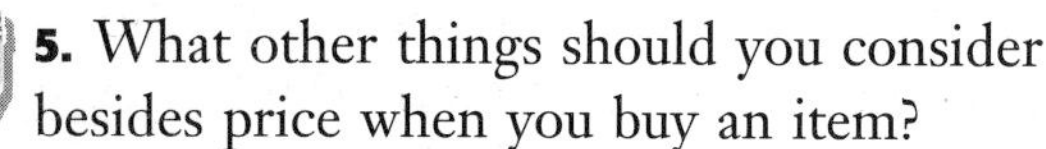

A **unit price** is the cost of one item or unit.

Example

Corn flakes are sold in boxes of 300 g for $2.25 or 550 g for $3.74.

a) Find the unit price for each box.

b) Which size is the better value?

Solution

a) Rewrite the cost of each item in cents. Calculate the cost per gram of each item.

$$\text{Unit price of small size} = \frac{225\ ¢}{300\ \text{g}}$$

$$= 0.75\ ¢/\text{g}$$

C 225 ÷ 300 = 0.75

$$\text{Unit price of large size} = \frac{374\ ¢}{550\ \text{g}}$$

$$= 0.68\ ¢/\text{g}$$

C 374 ÷ 550 = 0.68

The unit price of the small size is 0.75 ¢/g.
The unit price of the large size is 0.68 ¢/g.

b) The large size has the lower unit price.
The large size is the better value.

Practice

Find the unit price for each.

1. \$1.20 for 6 oranges

2. \$3.00 for 5 grapefruit

3. \$10.00 for 5 notebooks

4. \$1.90 for 2 frozen yogurt cones

Find the unit price for each. Round answers to the nearest cent.

5. 3 cookies for \$1.00

6. 3 cartons of milk for \$5.99

7. 4 plums for \$0.99

8. 3 loaves of bread for \$4.49

Which is the better value?

9. a 750-mL bottle of juice for \$2.49 or a 350-mL can for \$0.99

10. a 2-kg box of soap for \$1.99 or a 5-kg box for \$4.49

11. 3 bus tickets for \$3.45 or 10 bus tickets for \$11.00

12. 5 lunch tickets for \$13.00 or 12 lunch tickets for \$30.00

13. a 500-g box of crackers for \$2.29 or a 750-g box of crackers for \$3.50

Problems and Applications

14. The unit price for bananas is \$1.50/kg. What is the cost of 5 kg of bananas?

15. Baseballs cost \$5.95 each. The Eagles use 24 baseballs per home game. What is the cost of baseballs for 42 home games?

16. *The Arts* magazine costs \$17.95 for 12 issues or \$49.95 for 36 issues. How much do you save on each issue if you buy 36 issues instead of 12?

17. Spaghetti costs \$3.29 for a 2-kg package and \$7.95 for a 5-kg package. What is the lowest price you could pay for 10 kg of spaghetti?

18. An order of 6 chicken wings costs \$2.75. A 10-wing order costs \$4.50. What is the lowest price you could pay for 30 wings?

19. In 1990, the Bank of Canada spent about \$50 000 000 to print 834 000 000 new bank notes. What was the unit price of a bank note?

20. An exchange rate is the unit price of the currency of another country.

a) In June 1991, the exchange rate for the US dollar was 1.15. A US dollar cost \$1.15 Canadian. How much did US\$250.00 cost?

b) Look up today's cost of a US dollar in Canadian dollars. How much does US\$250.00 cost?

21. The Student Council wants to sell school crests for \$5.00 each. It costs \$100.00 to set up the cresting machine and \$2.00 for each crest.

a) What is the unit cost of the crests if the school orders 100 crests? 200 crests?

b) Explain why the unit cost changes.

c) Research the meaning of the word "overhead." Write 5 examples of overhead.

22. Many food stores help the shopper decide on the large or small size of a product by showing the unit price.

a) List 5 products priced on the basis of 1 unit.

b) List 5 products that have a unit of 100 g.

c) Describe how a store might decide the size of a unit.

WORD POWER

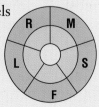

Place a consonant in the centre ring and the 5 vowels in the second ring to spell five 3-letter words reading inward.

R M L S F

Review

Express all answers in simplest form.

1. Write the ratio of apples to oranges.

2. Write the ratio of squares to circles.

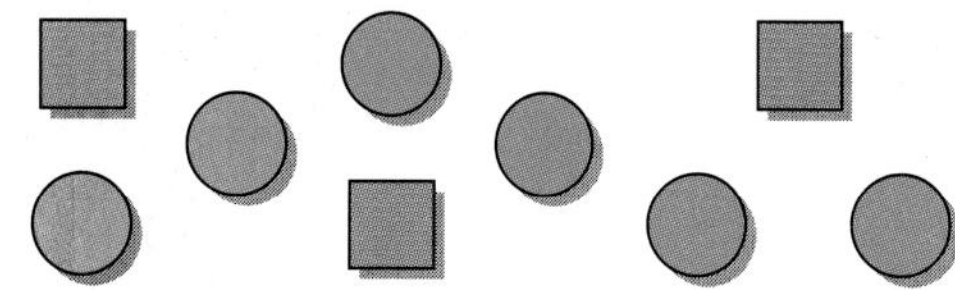

3. Bill has 3 quarters. Eric has 3 dimes. Write the following ratios.

a) $\frac{\text{amount of money Eric has}}{\text{amount of money Bill has}}$

b) $\frac{\text{number of coins Eric has}}{\text{number of coins Bill has}}$

Express in simplest form.

4. 3:9 **5.** 25:10 **6.** $\frac{16}{20}$

7. There were 125 parents and 150 students at the game.
a) Find the ratio of students to parents.
b) Find the ratio of parents to students.

8. Maria is 12 years old and Ardeth is 15 years old.
a) What is the ratio of Ardeth's age to Maria's age?
b) What is the ratio of Maria's age to Ardeth's age?

9. Ari took 24 pictures for the school newspaper. Six of the pictures did not turn out.
a) What is the ratio of pictures that turned out to pictures that did not turn out?
b) What is the ratio of pictures that did not turn out to the total number of pictures taken?

10. An aircraft travels 1800 km in 3 h. What is the rate of travel for the aircraft?

11. Michael's computer printer can print 20 pages in 8 min. Find the rate of printing in seconds per page.

12. Two machines make boxes for hockey cards. One machine makes 200 boxes in 10 min. The other machine makes 300 boxes in 10 min. Find the total number of boxes the two machines make in

a) 1 min **b)** 25 min

Solve for n in the following proportions.

13. $2:3 = n:6$ **14.** $3:5 = n:15$

15. $n:4 = 3:12$ **16.** $n:5 = 6:15$

17. $3:5 = 6:n$ **18.** $1:n = 5:20$

19. $2:n = 4:10$ **20.** $3:n = 9:12$

Solve for n in the following proportions.

21. $\frac{2}{n} = \frac{4}{10}$ **22.** $\frac{3}{9} = \frac{12}{n}$

23. $\frac{n}{3} = \frac{12}{9}$ **24.** $\frac{5}{n} = \frac{15}{9}$

25. $\frac{6}{5} = \frac{18}{n}$ **26.** $\frac{n}{6} = \frac{15}{18}$

27. List the pairs of corresponding sides and corresponding angles in these similar triangles.

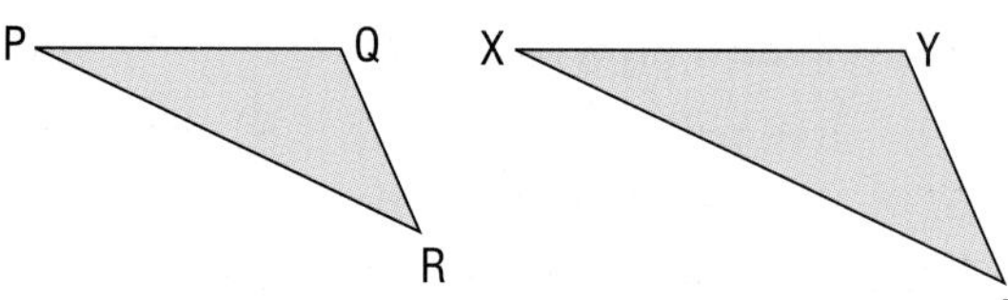

28. The triangles are similar. Calculate the missing dimensions.

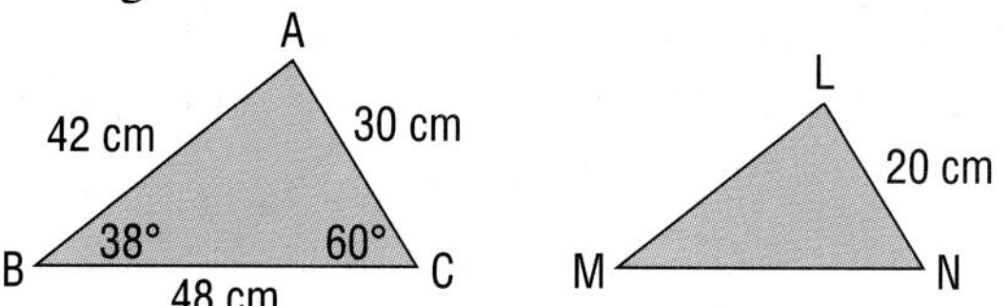

29. A 40 m high building casts a 16-m shadow. A 15 m high tree stands next to the building. How long is the shadow of the tree?

30. Forty students can ride in 1 bus. How many students can ride in 8 buses?

31. A machine makes 8 pens in 1 min. How many pens can the machine make in 5 min?

32. Eighteen players are needed to play a baseball game. How many players are needed to play 6 baseball games at the same time?

33. The ratio of red cherries to black cherries in a bowl is 2:3. There are 50 cherries in the bowl. How many red cherries are in the bowl?

34. A survey found that there were 7 television sets to every 5 households. How many television sets would there be in 1000 households?

Find the unit price for each.

35. 3 apples for $1.50

36. 10 cookies for $1.20

37. 4 balloons for $2.00

38. 5 pencils for $1.00

Solve.

39. Matt earns $9.75/h. Caroline earns $235.20 for 24 h of work. Who has the higher rate of pay?

40. Two places are 4 cm apart on a map. The scale of the map is 1:1000. How far apart are the places on the Earth?

41. Canada's wheat production is the sixth largest in the world. In 1989, Canada produced about 24 000 000 t of wheat. That year, India produced about 54 000 000 t. State the ratio of wheat produced in Canada to wheat produced in India.

42. What is the ratio of the months of the year that begin with the letter "J" to those that do not?

Group Decision Making

Designing a Classroom Of the Future

The purpose of this activity is to make a scale drawing of a grade 7 classroom of the future.

1. Meet with your group to decide how many years into the future you will design the classroom for.

2. Brainstorm as a group the kinds of things that would be in your classroom of the future. Make sure there are good reasons for your choices.

3. Decide on the size and location of everything in the room. Select the size of paper you need for the scale drawing. Choose a scale.

4. Make your scale drawing.

5. Present your drawing to the class. Give reasons for the items in the classroom and where they are located.

6. Meet as a group to discuss your classroom of the future. If you could change anything in the drawing, what would you do differently and what would you keep the same?

Chapter Check

Write the ratio.

1. circles to squares

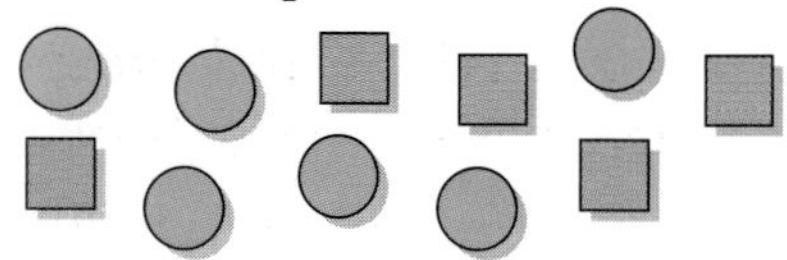

2. red squares to blue squares

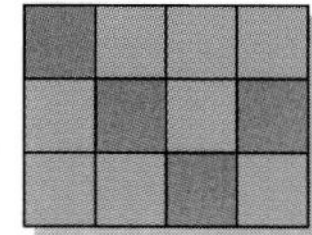

3. Write three ratios equivalent to 6:2.

4. In lowest terms, write the ratio of the number of pins used in 10-pin bowling to the number of pins used in 5-pin bowling.

Solve for n in questions 5 and 6.

5. $2:3 = n:9$

6. $\frac{n}{3} = \frac{8}{12}$

7. Two pencils cost $1.50. Solve a proportion to find the cost of 7 pencils.

8. List the pairs of corresponding sides and corresponding angles in these similar triangles.

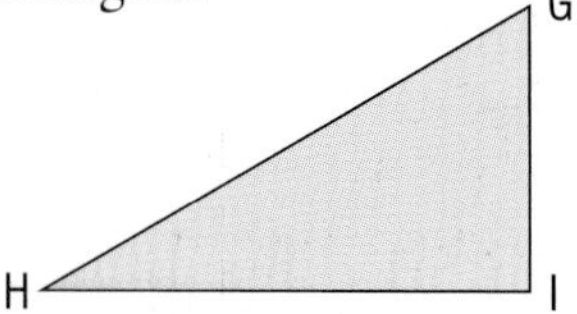

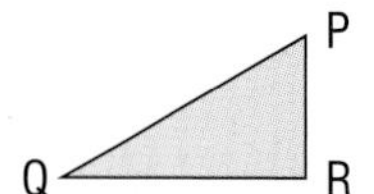

9. The triangles are similar. Find the missing dimensions.

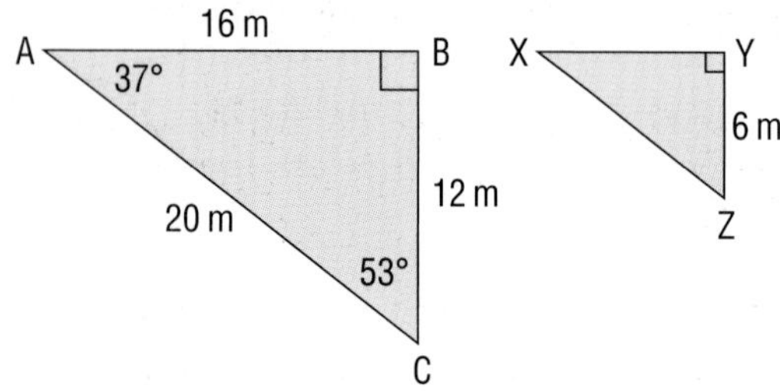

10. Habib earns $22.50 for 3 h work after school. What is his hourly rate of pay?

11. The Bears won 3 out of every 5 games they played in the season. The season had 80 games. How many games did the Bears win?

12. Find the unit price for each.

a) 3 tickets for $12.00

b) $8.00 for 4 notebooks

13. The length of a plant in a drawing is 8 cm. The scale is 1:4. What is the length of the real plant?

14. On a map, 1 cm represents 12 km on Earth. What is the actual distance between two places that are 6 cm apart on the map?

"This fellow here hiccups 14 times per minute and he shrugs his shoulders 22 times per minute."

Reprinted by permission: Tribune Media Services

Using the Strategies

1. Sandra's grandmother on Sandra's father's side had 2 children. Each of these children had 2 children. Sandra's grandmother on Sandra's mother's side had 3 children. Each of these children had 2 children. How many cousins does Sandra have?

2. What is the distance from
a) Elmswood to Pierce?
b) Pierce to Thorton?
c) Thorton to Elmswood?

3. The concert starts at 20:00. You want to arrive half an hour before it starts. You will take 20 min to get there on the bus from your friend's house. You are going to have pizza at your friend's house before you catch the bus. You will take 5 min to walk to your friend's house, 15 min to get the pizza, and 20 min to eat. At what time should you leave home to go to your friend's house?

4. Carl bought 4 shirts at $28.80 each and 3 pairs of socks at $9.75 a pair. How much did he spend?

5. Sharon and Gino start from the same place and drive in opposite directions. Sharon drives at 45 km/h. Gino drives at 55 km/h.
a) How far apart are they after 2 h?
b) How far apart are they after 4.5 h?
c) If they drove in the same direction from the start, how far apart would they be after 2.5 h?

6. How many rectangles of different sizes can you make if the sides can only be 10 cm, 15 cm, or 20 cm. Remember that a square is also a rectangle.

7. Tara, Marcia, Paul, and Emil are guides at the Parliament Buildings. Two guides must be on duty at all times. How many different teams of 2 guides are possible?

8. On Monday, February 1, the rock group *Laserbeam* released a new recording. Sales averaged 5000 a day, 7 days a week. At this rate, on which day and date will the millionth recording be sold. What assumptions have you made?

9. A golf tournament gave $270 000 in prizes. The winner received $\frac{1}{2}$. The runner-up got $\frac{1}{4}$. The remainder was divided equally between the third-, fourth-, and fifth-place finishers. How much did the fifth-place finisher receive?

10. The 3 coins start out as shown.

Turning over 2 coins next to each other is 1 move. Describe how you can get 3 heads in a row in 2 moves.

11. Anar wants to put new carpet in an L-shaped room. The larger part of the room measures 6 m by 3 m. The smaller part measures 4 m by 2 m. If carpet costs Anar $27.50/m^2, how much will it cost her to carpet the room?

DATA BANK

1. How many times larger is the province of Manitoba than the province of Nova Scotia?

2. Which Canadian Prime Minister was in office for the longest period of time in total?

There are many different languages in the

anguage, Language, Language, Language, Lang

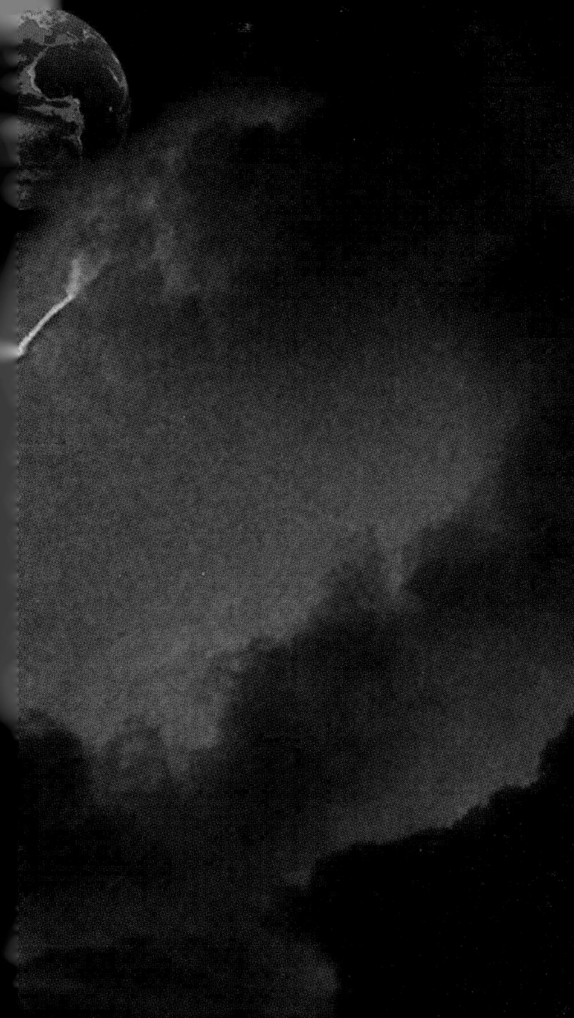

CHAPTER 7

Percent

About 5000 languages and dialects are spoken in the world. A dialect is a variation of a language.

The map shows a few of the world's languages. The coloured rectangle represents the fraction of people who speak each language.

Is the Chinese-language or English-language area larger on the map? Are there more people who speak Chinese or more people who speak English? Explain.

List at least 4 languages included in the group of "other languages." Compare your list with a classmate's.

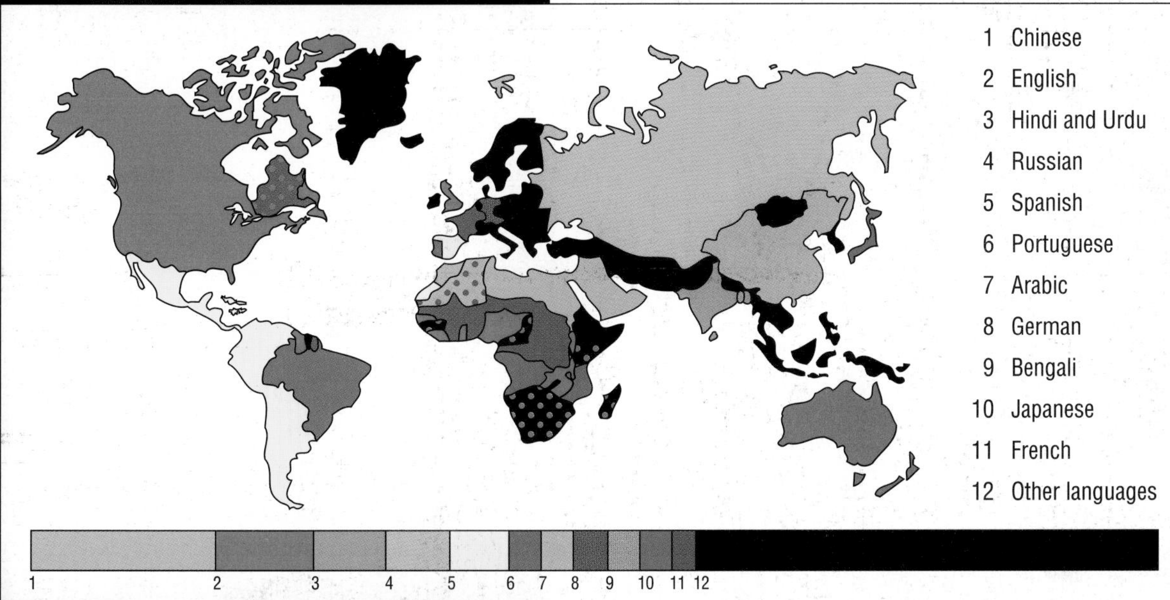

Parts of 100

There are 100 squares on the 10 by 10 grid.

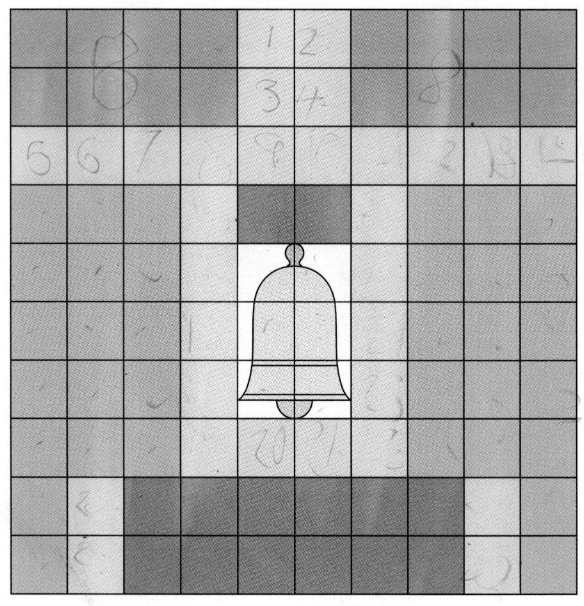

Activity ❶

Write fractions with a denominator of 100, then simplify.

a) the fraction of the grid shaded blue
b) the fraction of the grid shaded yellow
c) the fraction of the grid shaded red
d) the fraction of the grid shaded green
e) the fraction of the grid covered by the bell

Activity ❷

1. Make your own diagrams to show the following fractions.

a) $\frac{1}{2}$ **b)** $\frac{1}{3}$ **c)** $\frac{1}{4}$ **d)** $\frac{1}{10}$ **e)** $\frac{1}{100}$

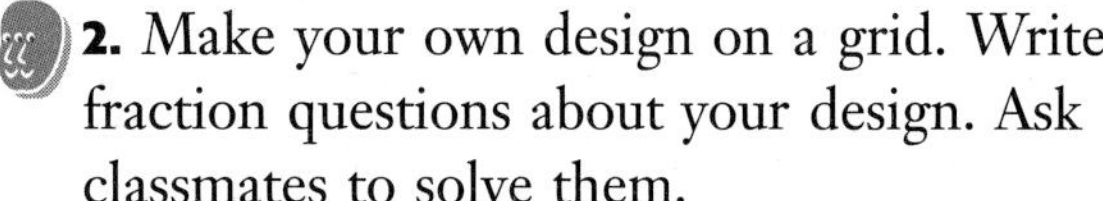

2. Make your own design on a grid. Write fraction questions about your design. Ask classmates to solve them.

Advertising

Advertisements use percents to show discounts.

Activity ❶

1. What does the word "discount" mean?

2. List things other than price that affect where you shop. Compare your list with your classmates'.

Activity ❷

1. Design an advertisement to sell an item of your choice at a discount.

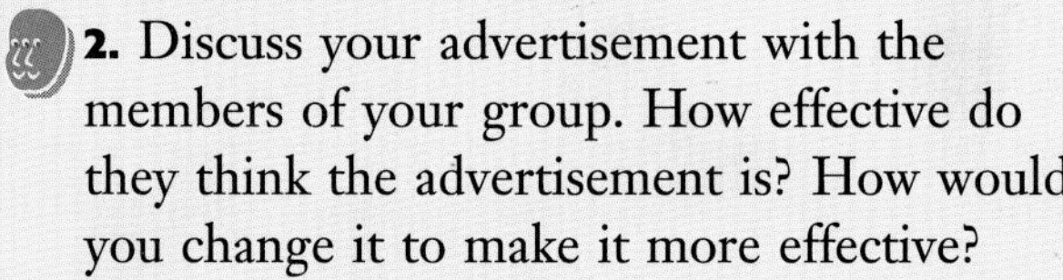

2. Discuss your advertisement with the members of your group. How effective do they think the advertisement is? How would you change it to make it more effective?

Decimals and Fractions

Express as a decimal.

1. $\frac{1}{2}$ **2.** $\frac{1}{4}$ **3.** $\frac{3}{4}$

4. $\frac{1}{5}$ **5.** $\frac{2}{5}$ **6.** $\frac{3}{5}$

7. $\frac{3}{10}$ **8.** $\frac{3}{100}$ **9.** $\frac{3}{1000}$

Express as a fraction in simplest form.

10. 0.2 **11.** 0.4 **12.** 0.6

13. 0.8 **14.** 0.15 **15.** 0.35

16. 0.45 **17.** 0.55 **18.** 0.65

Express in simplest form.

19. $\frac{3}{9}$ **20.** $\frac{2}{8}$ **21.** $\frac{3}{12}$

22. $\frac{4}{12}$ **23.** $\frac{8}{12}$ **24.** $\frac{10}{12}$

25. $\frac{10}{30}$ **26.** $\frac{5}{25}$ **27.** $\frac{7}{28}$

Express as an improper fraction.

28. $2\frac{1}{4}$ **29.** $3\frac{1}{2}$ **30.** $2\frac{1}{5}$

31. $7\frac{1}{3}$ **32.** $1\frac{1}{8}$ **33.** $2\frac{2}{3}$

34. $3\frac{1}{4}$ **35.** $2\frac{5}{8}$ **36.** $1\frac{2}{3}$

Express as a mixed number in simplest form.

37. $\frac{13}{4}$ **38.** $\frac{9}{2}$ **39.** $\frac{5}{4}$

40. $\frac{19}{5}$ **41.** $\frac{24}{7}$ **42.** $\frac{32}{5}$

43. $\frac{9}{4}$ **44.** $\frac{17}{4}$ **45.** $\frac{13}{4}$

Find the missing numerator.

46. $\frac{1}{2} = \frac{■}{100}$ **47.** $\frac{3}{4} = \frac{■}{100}$

48. $\frac{2}{5} = \frac{■}{100}$ **49.** $\frac{7}{10} = \frac{■}{100}$

50. $\frac{3}{15} = \frac{■}{100}$ **51.** $\frac{9}{20} = \frac{■}{100}$

Mental Math

Add.

1. 36 + 10 **2.** 810 + 100 **3.** 45 + 5

4. 325 + 5 **5.** 75 + 25 **6.** 30 + 50

7. 18 + 2 **8.** 18 + 12

Subtract.

9. 85 − 5 **10.** 96 − 6 **11.** 425 − 100

12. 615 − 15 **13.** 66 − 6 **14.** 66 − 16

15. 54 − 14 **16.** 54 − 24

Multiply.

17. 6 × 12 **18.** 12 × 12

19. 25 × 10 **20.** 75 × 1000

21. 36 × 100 **22.** 540 × 100

23. 5 × 70 **24.** 6 × 200

Divide.

25. 42 ÷ 7 **26.** 4200 ÷ 7

27. 36 ÷ 6 **28.** 360 ÷ 6

29. 240 ÷ 10 **30.** 1500 ÷ 100

31. 75 000 ÷ 100 **32.** 1000 ÷ 50

State the remainder.

33. 12 ÷ 5 **34.** 15 ÷ 4 **35.** 36 ÷ 9

36. 40 ÷ 9 **37.** 85 ÷ 10 **38.** 75 ÷ 9

39. 40 ÷ 7 **40.** 40 ÷ 5

Simplify.

41. $\frac{1}{5} + \frac{2}{5}$ **42.** $1 - \frac{2}{5}$ **43.** $\frac{2}{3} \times \frac{1}{5}$

44. $\frac{4}{7} - \frac{1}{7}$ **45.** $\frac{1}{3} \div \frac{1}{2}$ **46.** $\frac{3}{4} - \frac{1}{2}$

47. $\frac{1}{2}$ of 24 **48.** $\frac{1}{3}$ of 24 **49.** $\frac{5}{8} + \frac{3}{8}$

50. $\frac{5}{8} - \frac{1}{4}$ **51.** $\frac{2}{3} \times \frac{1}{2}$ **52.** $\frac{3}{4} \div \frac{1}{4}$

53. a) How many dimes are in $5.00?
b) How many nickels are in $2.00?
c) How many quarters are in $10.00?

Percents

An amusement park might charge $10.00 per person to get in. The term "per person" means "for each person."

The word "percent" means "for each 100" or "out of 100."

You can think of the percent symbol, %, as being made up of a 1 and two 0s.

If you get $\frac{87}{100}$ on a math test, you can write your score as 87% and say you got "eighty-seven percent."

Activity 1

There are 100 small triangles in the design.

What percent of the triangles have each of the following colours?

1. red **2.** orange **3.** white

4. blue **5.** green

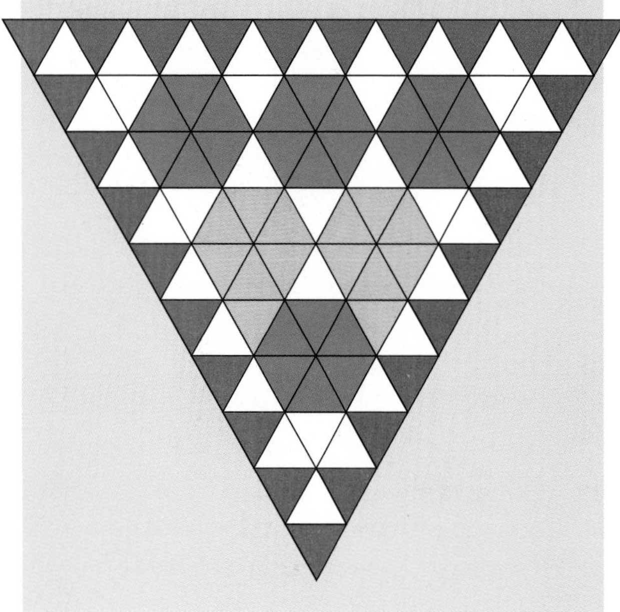

Activity 2

Use a grid of 16 squares on a geoboard or squared paper.

The following figures represent 50% or $\frac{1}{2}$ of the squares.

These are polygons.

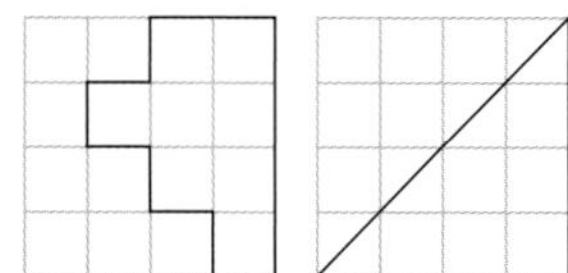

These are not polygons.

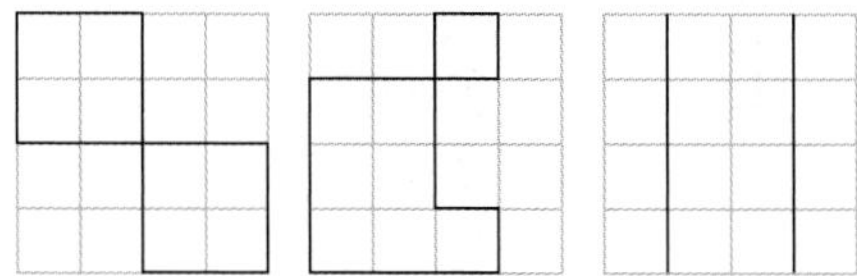

Remember that these polygons are all the same.

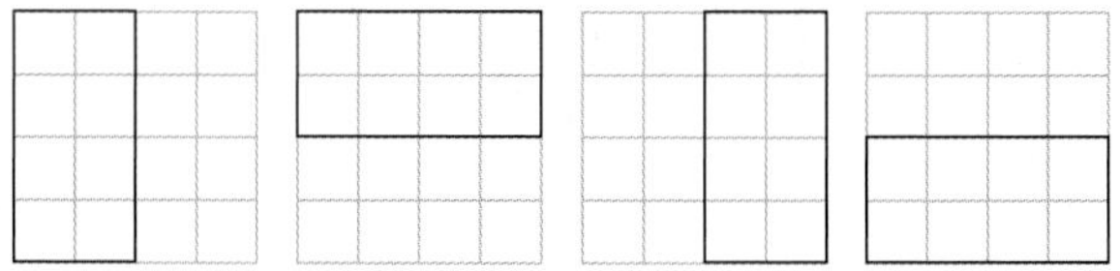

1. Make as many different polygons as you can that represent 50% or $\frac{1}{2}$ of the squares.

2. Compare your number of polygons with a classmate's.

Activity ❸

If the length of your hand span is 15 cm, it is $\frac{15}{100}$ or 15% of a metre.

Use a ruler and string to determine the following lengths. Express each length as a percent of a metre.

1. your hand span
2. your arm span
3. the length of your foot
4. the length of your arm
5. the length of your hand
6. the distance around your head

Activity ❹

Express each of the following as a percent of a metre.

1. the distance of your chair seat from the floor
2. the distance from the door knob to the floor
3. the width of this textbook
4. the length of your pencil
5. the height of your desk
6. the height of the teacher's desk

Activity ❺

Use the diagrams or make each solid from 100 cubes.

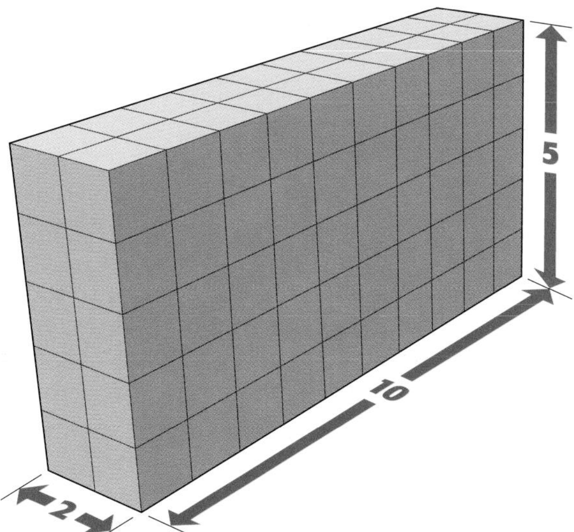

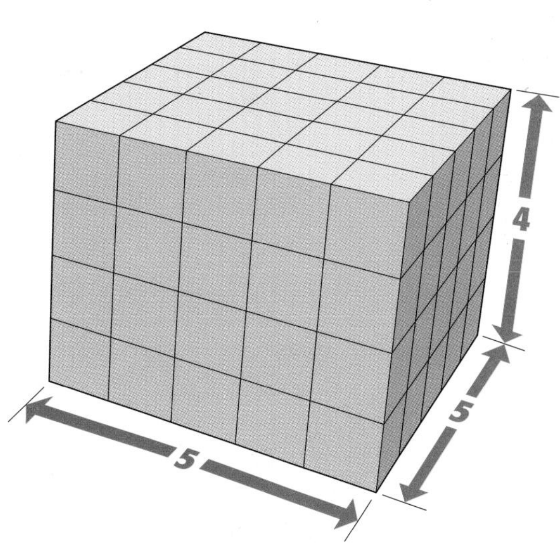

Suppose we painted the outsides of the solids red. For each solid, state the percent of the 100 cubes with the following numbers of red faces.

1. 3 **2.** 2 **3.** 1 **4.** 0

7.1 Percent

The average Canadian eats for 6 h of every 100 h. The fraction of the time spent eating is $\frac{6}{100}$.

Percent means "out of 100." So, the percent of the time spent eating is 6%.

Activity: Make a Design

Draw a rectangle that contains 100 squares. To make a design, colour each square red or black, or leave it white.

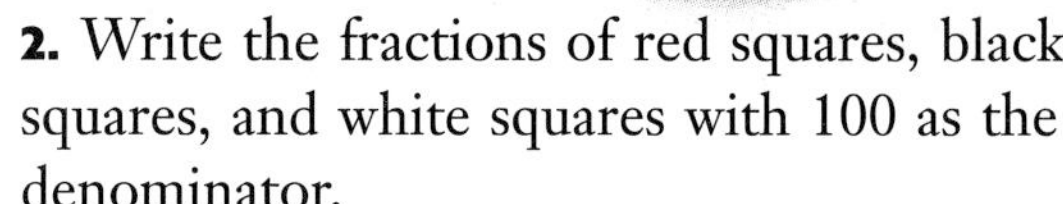

Inquire

1. Write the numbers of red squares, black squares, and white squares.

2. Write the fractions of red squares, black squares, and white squares with 100 as the denominator.

3. What percent of the squares are

a) red? **b)** black? **c)** white?

4. Repeat steps 1–3 for a classmate's design.

Example 1

It will take 100 tiles to cover a kitchen floor.

a) What percent of the floor is covered with 1 tile? 30 tiles? 45 tiles? 100 tiles?

b) Express each answer as a decimal.

Solution

a)

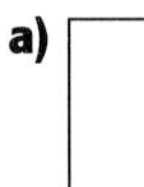

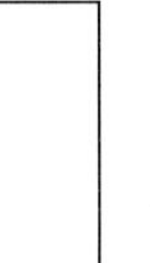

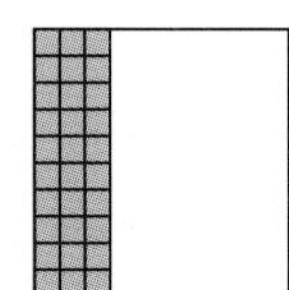

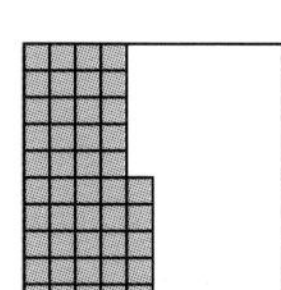

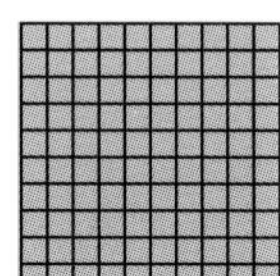

$\frac{1}{100} = 1\%$ $\frac{30}{100} = 30\%$ $\frac{45}{100} = 45\%$ $\frac{100}{100} = 100\%$

b) $\frac{1}{100} = 0.01$ $\frac{30}{100} = 0.3$ $\frac{45}{100} = 0.45$ $\frac{100}{100} = 1$

Example 2

In this design, what percent of the squares are green?

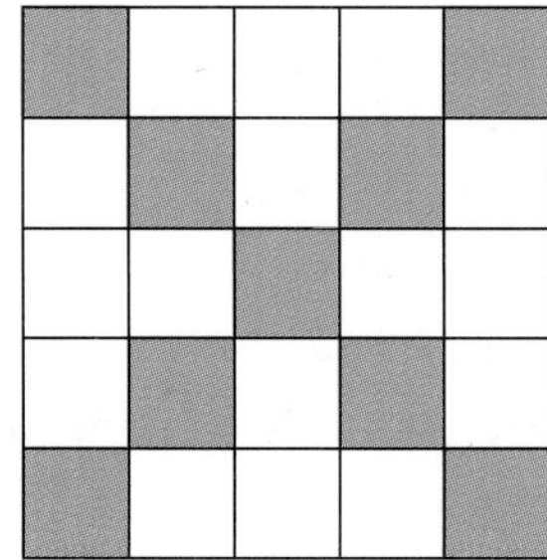

Solution

The fraction of green squares is $\frac{9}{25}$. Write the fraction with 100 as the denominator.

$$\frac{9}{25} = \frac{9 \times 4}{25 \times 4}$$

Think: 100 = 25 × 4

$$= \frac{36}{100}$$

$$= 36\%$$

So, 36% of the squares are green.

Practice

In questions 1–4, express the shaded part of each figure as a percent.

1. 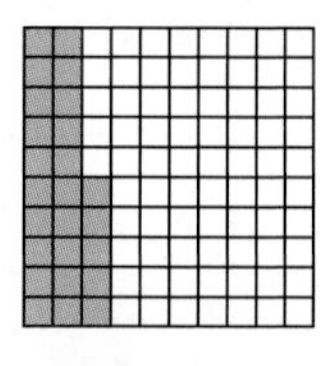

2. 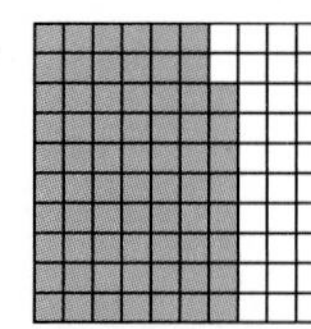

3. 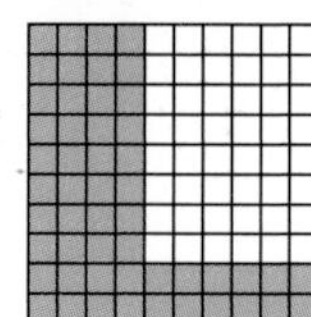

4. 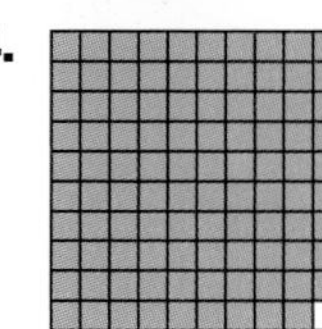

What percent of each figure in questions 5–8 is shaded?

5. 

6. 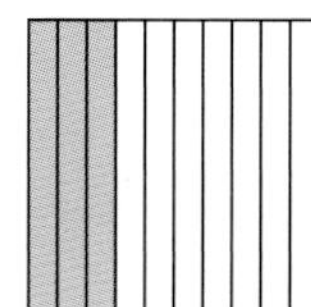

7. 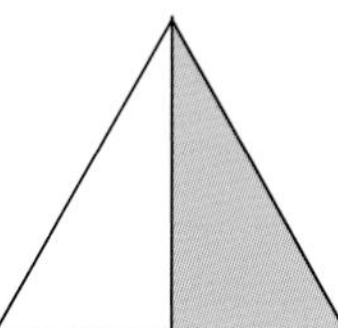

8. 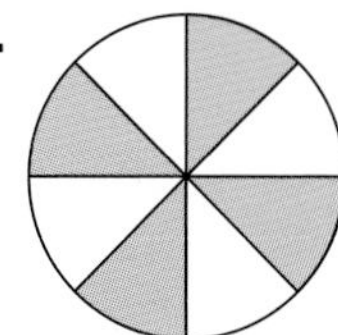

What percent of each figure in questions 9–10 is not shaded?

9. 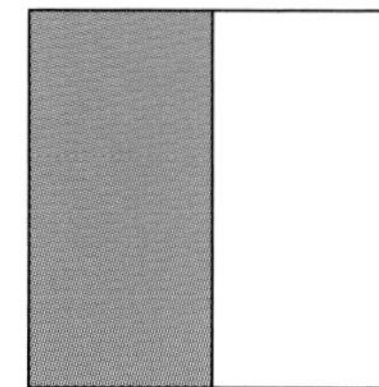

10. 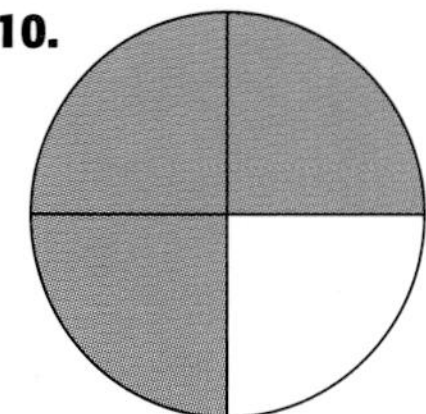

Complete the following.

11. $\frac{1}{10} = \frac{■}{100} = ■\%$ **12.** $\frac{7}{50} = \frac{■}{100} = ■\%$

13. $\frac{4}{5} = \frac{■}{100} = ■\%$ **14.** $\frac{4}{50} = \frac{■}{100} = ■\%$

Write as a percent.

15. $\frac{21}{100}$ **16.** $\frac{9}{100}$ **17.** $\frac{35}{100}$

18. $\frac{7}{50}$ **19.** $\frac{21}{50}$ **20.** $\frac{9}{10}$

21. $\frac{1}{4}$ **22.** $\frac{2}{5}$ **23.** $\frac{1}{25}$

Problems and Applications

24. Sales tax is expressed as a percent. How many cents on a dollar would you pay at each rate of tax?

a) 8% **b)** 10% **c)** 12%

d) 4% **e)** 7% **f)** 5%

25. A sweater is one-half natural fibre. What percent is natural fibre?

26. On a typical day, Monique spends 25% of her time at school, 33% sleeping, and 8% eating. What percent of her day does she spend on other things?

In questions 27–32, choose the better test score.

27. 8 out of 10 or 12 out of 20

28. 3 out of 5 or 50%

29. 7 out of 10 or 65%

30. 15 out of 20 or 35 out of 50

31. 21 out of 25 or 85 out of 100

32. 11 out of 20 or 20 out of 40

33. From 1975 to 1984, the Edmonton Eskimos won 6 out of 10 Grey Cup finals. What percent did they win?

34. Find a list of today's top 10 songs.

a) What percent do you like?

b) What percent were recorded by groups?

c) What percent were recorded by solo artists?

35. We can write $\frac{3}{4}$ as 75% and $\frac{4}{5}$ as 80%. Is it easier to compare $\frac{3}{4}$ with $\frac{4}{5}$ or to compare 75% with 80%? Explain.

36. Make a list of things that are often expressed as percents. Share your list with your classmates.

7.2 Fractions and Decimals as Percents

Activity: Solve the Problem

Asia has $\frac{3}{5}$ of the world's population.

We want to know what percent of the world's population this is.

Inquire

1. Write the fraction with a denominator of 100.

2. Use short division to write $\frac{3}{5}$ as a decimal.

3. Write the decimal as a fraction with a denominator of 100.

4. Compare the fractions you found in 1 and 3.

5. Write the fraction as a percent.

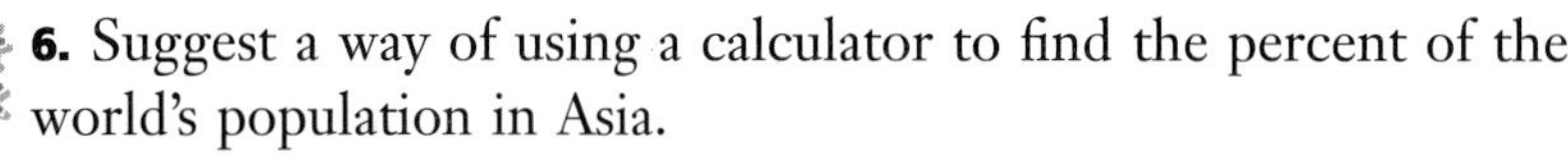

6. Suggest a way of using a calculator to find the percent of the world's population in Asia.

Example 1

A young child grows 20 temporary teeth, called milk teeth. Between the ages of 6 and 10, permanent teeth push out the milk teeth. What percent of the milk teeth are gone when 9 teeth have been pushed out?

Solution

The fraction of milk teeth gone is $\frac{9}{20}$.
Express this fraction with a denominator of 100.

$$\begin{aligned}\frac{9}{20} &= \frac{9 \times 5}{20 \times 5} \\ &= \frac{45}{100} \\ &= 45\%\end{aligned}$$

So, 45% of the milk teeth are gone.

Example 2

Write 0.325 as a percent.

Solution

Express the decimal as a fraction with a denominator of 100.

$$\begin{aligned}0.325 &= \frac{0.325}{1} \\ &= \frac{0.325 \times 100}{1 \times 100} \\ &= \frac{32.5}{100} \\ &= 32.5\%\end{aligned}$$

Example 3

Use a calculator to express $\frac{42}{70}$ as a percent.

Solution

C 42 ÷ 70 % 60.

$\frac{42}{70} = 60\%$

If your calculator does not have a % key, what could you press instead?

Practice

Express as percents.

1. $\frac{17}{100}$ **2.** $\frac{27}{100}$ **3.** $\frac{7}{100}$ **4.** $\frac{29}{100}$

5. $\frac{99}{100}$ **6.** $\frac{63}{100}$ **7.** $\frac{33}{100}$ **8.** $\frac{1}{100}$

Complete the following.

9. $\frac{1}{2} = \frac{\blacksquare}{100}$ **10.** $\frac{31}{50} = \frac{\blacksquare}{100}$

11. $\frac{7}{10} = \frac{\blacksquare}{100}$ **12.** $\frac{25}{25} = \frac{\blacksquare}{100}$

Complete the following.

13. $0.65 = \frac{\blacksquare}{100}$ **14.** $0.7 = \frac{\blacksquare}{100}$

15. $0.01 = \frac{\blacksquare}{100}$ **16.** $0.99 = \frac{\blacksquare}{100}$

Write each fraction as a percent.

17. $\frac{7}{10}$ **18.** $\frac{9}{20}$ **19.** $\frac{3}{50}$

20. $\frac{15}{45}$ **21.** $\frac{120}{1000}$ **22.** $\frac{500}{10\ 000}$

Complete the following.

23. $0.3 = \frac{\blacksquare}{100} = \blacksquare\%$

24. $0.9 = \frac{\blacksquare}{100} = \blacksquare\%$

25. $0.33 = \frac{\blacksquare}{100} = \blacksquare\%$

Write each decimal as a percent.

26. 0.4 **27.** 0.8 **28.** 0.75

29. 0.01 **30.** 0.055 **31.** 0.635

Replace ● with <, >, or = to make each statement true.

32. 0.25 ● 30% **33.** $\frac{1}{3}$ ● 30%

34. $\frac{3}{5}$ ● 75% **35.** 0.35 ● 40%

36. $\frac{27}{50}$ ● 55% **37.** $\frac{7}{10}$ ● 80%

Problems and Applications

38. About 12 000 people voted in an election. About 16 000 people could have voted. What percent of the people voted?

39. The table shows the numbers of students in the grades 6, 7, and 8 classes

Grade	Number of Students
6	12 girls 14 boys
7	20 girls 12 boys
8	16 girls 26 boys

a) What percent of the students are in grade 6?
b) What percent of the students are in grade 8?
c) What percent of all the students are girls?
d) What percent of grade 7 students are boys?

40. About $\frac{4}{5}$ of the people in Canada live within 160 km of the border with the U.S. What percent of Canadians live at least 160 km from the border?

41. We expect a millipede to have 1000 legs because its name means "a thousand feet." The largest number of legs ever found on a millipede is 750. What percent is this of the expected number?

42. a) In 1991, the average Canadian family spent about 0.45 of its income on various kinds of tax. Express this decimal as a percent.
b) Research and describe the meaning of "Tax Freedom Day"?

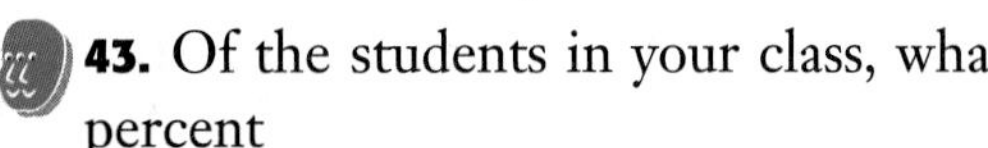

43. Of the students in your class, what percent
a) are girls?
b) are boys?
c) walk to school?
d) take a bus to school?

7.3 Percents as Fractions and Decimals

Activity: Study the Graph

The Recreation Department keeps a record of where children are injured on playgrounds. The results, shown on the circle graph, are given to playground supervisors each year.

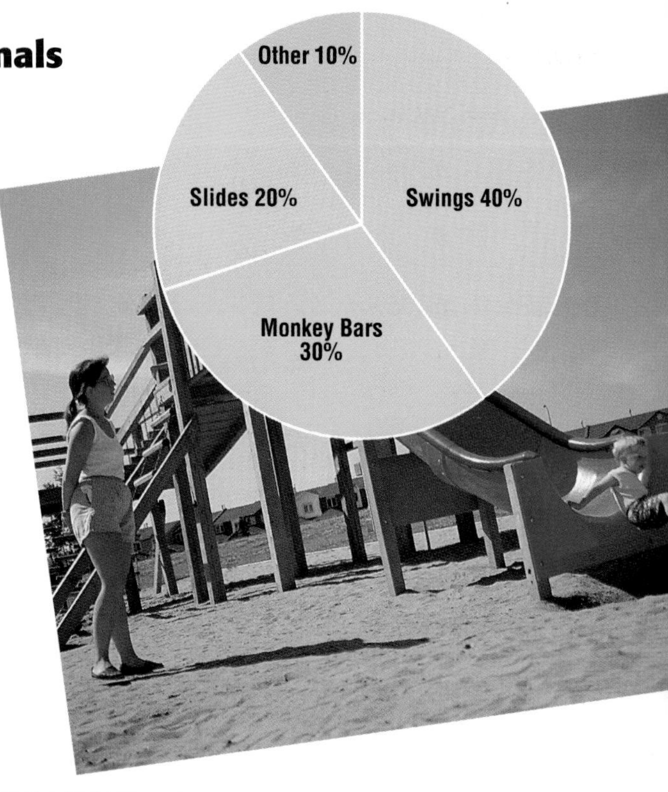

Inquire

1. What percent of injuries happen on swings?

2. Write this percent as a fraction with a denominator of 100. Write the fraction in lowest terms.

3. What percent of injuries happen on slides?

4. Write this percent as a fraction with a denominator of 100. Change the fraction to a decimal.

5. Suggest why playground supervisors should know where children are injured.

Example

The circle graph shows where people get their pets. Express each percent as a fraction and as a decimal.

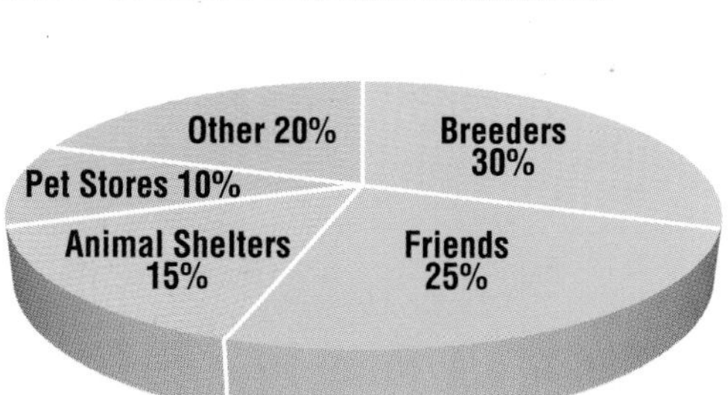

Solution

To write a percent as a fraction, first write a fraction with a denominator of 100. Reduce to lowest terms if possible.

To write a percent as a decimal, first write a fraction with a denominator of 100. Divide the numerator by the denominator.

Percent	Fraction	Decimal
Breeders 30%	$30\% = \frac{30}{100} = \frac{3}{10}$	$30\% = \frac{30}{100} = 0.3$
Friends 25%	$25\% = \frac{25}{100} = \frac{1}{4}$	$25\% = \frac{25}{100} = 0.25$
Animal Shelters 15%	$15\% = \frac{15}{100} = \frac{3}{20}$	$15\% = \frac{15}{100} = 0.15$
Pet Stores 10%	$10\% = \frac{10}{100} = \frac{1}{10}$	$10\% = \frac{10}{100} = 0.1$
Other 20%	$20\% = \frac{20}{100} = \frac{1}{5}$	$20\% = \frac{20}{100} = 0.2$

Practice

Express each percent as a decimal.

1. 21% **2.** 25% **3.** 18% **4.** 5%
5. 9% **6.** 7% **7.** 100% **8.** 50%

Express each percent as a fraction in lowest terms.

9. 25% **10.** 50% **11.** 75% **12.** 10%
13. 20% **14.** 30% **15.** 40% **16.** 90%
17. 60% **18.** 80% **19.** 70% **20.** 1%

Express each percent as a decimal.

21. 27% **22.** 15% **23.** 37% **24.** 52%
25. 95% **26.** 99% **27.** 62% **28.** 19%

Express each percent as a fraction in lowest terms.

29. 15% **30.** 35% **31.** 18% **32.** 5%
33. 65% **34.** 55% **35.** 68% **36.** 44%
37. 8% **38.** 14% **39.** 2% **40.** 4%

41. Copy and complete the chart.

Percent	Fraction	Decimal
75%		
80%		
	$\frac{2}{5}$	
		0.2
30%		
	$\frac{3}{4}$	
56%		
	$\frac{1}{20}$	
		0.08
6%		

Replace each ● with <, >, or = to make each statement true.

42. $21\% \bullet \frac{11}{25}$ **43.** $31\% \bullet 0.31$

44. $5\% \bullet 0.5$ **45.** $16\% \bullet \frac{2}{25}$

46. $35\% \bullet \frac{7}{10}$ **47.** $70\% \bullet 0.7$

48. $\frac{29}{50} \bullet 59\%$ **49.** $0.06 \bullet 6\%$

Problems and Applications

50. The circle graph shows the most popular breakfast foods ordered in a restaurant.

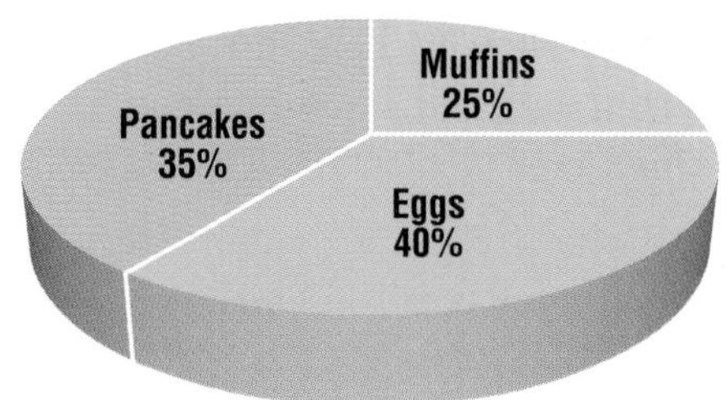

a) Express each percent as a decimal.
b) Express each percent as a fraction in lowest terms.
c) What fraction of the people had eggs or pancakes?
d) What fraction of the people did not have eggs?

51. Ask members of your class where they and their friends got their pets. Express your results as percents. Compare your results with the results of the survey on the previous page.

WORD POWER

You can change the word PIT into 4 other real words by changing the vowel. Write another 3-letter word beginning with the letter P so that changing the vowel gives 4 other real words.

7.4 Finding a Percent of a Number

Activity: Use the Information

Baseball players are elected to the Baseball Hall of Fame in Cooperstown, New York, by the Baseball Writers Association. To be elected, a player must be selected by at least 75% of the writers who vote.

In 1991, pitcher Ferguson Jenkins from Chatham, Ontario, received 334 votes from 443 writers.

Inquire

1. Write 75% as a decimal.

2. What operation does the word "of" mean?

3. Calculate 75% of 443.

4. Was Ferguson Jenkins elected to the Baseball Hall of Fame? Explain?

Example 1

The Lees' restaurant bill was $45.00. They left 15% of the bill as a tip. How much did they leave?

Solution

To find a percent of a number, write the percent as a decimal or a fraction and then multiply by the number.

$$15\% = \frac{15}{100}$$
$$= 0.15$$

$$15\% \text{ of } \$45.00 = 0.15 \times \$45.00$$
$$= \$6.75$$

Example 2

On average, teenagers in Canada watch television 11% of the time. For how many hours does the average teenager watch television in a year?

Solution

Assume there are 365 days in a year. The number of hours in a year is $365 \times 24 = 8760$

$$11\% = \frac{11}{100}$$
$$= 0.11$$

$$11\% \text{ of } 8760 = 0.11 \times 8760$$
$$= 963.6$$

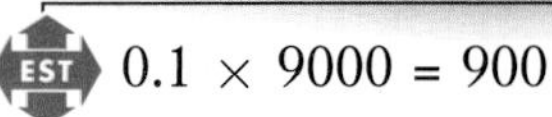

$0.1 \times 9000 = 900$

C 8760 × 11 % 

When you use the % key, enter the percent last.

The average teenager watches television for 963.6 h in a year.

Practice

Express as a fraction.

1. 50% **2.** 25% **3.** 75%

4. 10% **5.** 1% **6.** 100%

Evaluate.

7. 50% of 20 **8.** 50% of 80

9. 10% of 1000 **10.** 25% of 8

11. 25% of 200 **12.** 50% of 200

13. 25% of 40 **14.** 10% of 70

Estimate.

15. 50% of 195 **16.** 25% of 35

17. 50% of 49 **18.** 50% of 595

19. 25% of 19 **20.** 25% of 99

Express as a decimal.

21. 15% **22.** 50% **23.** 5%

24. 18% **25.** 37% **26.** 80%

27. 9% **28.** 24% **29.** 12%

Calculate.

30. 50% of 36 **31.** 10% of 42

32. 25% of 88 **33.** 75% of 12

34. 25% of 144 **35.** 50% of 252

36. 12% of 35 **37.** 15% of 76

Replace each ● with <, >, or = to make each statement true.

38. 10% of 80 ● 5% of 50

39. 6% of 25 ● 5% of 30

40. 12% of 356 ● 15% of 300

Problems and Applications

In questions 41–46, calculate to the nearest cent.

41. 10% of \$75.00 **42.** 25% of \$99.00

43. 30% of \$99.00 **44.** 20% of \$995.00

45. 8% of \$32.50 **46.** 15% of \$64.95

47. The Ascot hotel has 180 rooms. From Monday to Thursday, the hotel is 80% full. From Friday to Sunday, the hotel is 45% full. How many rooms does the hotel rent each week?

48. The Toronto Blue Jays play in the Skydome, which has 50 516 seats. If the Skydome is 75% full, how many spectators are there?

49. About 900 people use the mini golf course on an average day. On a holiday, the number increases by about 25%. How many people use the mini golf course on a holiday?

50. The Glenwood Park Restaurant adds a 15% tip to all bills. Grant's bill is \$54.85. How much is the tip?

51. In its first year, an infant averages 40% of each day awake, 25% of each day sleeping and dreaming, and 35% of each day sleeping without dreaming. How many hours does the infant spend on each activity during its first year?

52. In 1986, 21% of the people in Canada were under 15 years of age. Another 49% were aged 15 to 44, and 30% were 45 or older.

a) Predict the number of people in each age group in a town of 5000 people.

b) Can you use these percents to predict the number of people in each age group in your school? Explain.

53. The table gives the results of a health survey.

Health Condition	Excellent	Very Good	Good	Fair	Poor
Percent	25%	36%	27%	9%	3%

Look up the population of Canada and work out how many people in Canada belong to each category. Compare your results with your classmates'.

7.5 Estimating with Percent: Mental Math

Activity: Use the Information

In 1985–1986, with the Edmonton Oilers, Wayne Gretzky broke the record for most points in one season. He scored 52 goals and had 163 assists for a total of 215 points.

Inquire

1. What fraction of his points came from goals?

2. Round the numerator and denominator to give a simple fraction.

3. Estimate the percent of his points that came from goals by changing the simple fraction to a percent.

Use your rounding skills to estimate percents.

Example 1

In 1981–1982, Wayne first broke the record for points in one season. He scored 92 goals and had 120 assists for 212 points. Estimate the percent of his points that came from goals.

Solution 1

$\frac{92}{212}$ is about $\frac{90}{200}$.

$\frac{90}{200} = \frac{45}{100}$

$= 45\%$

About 45% of his points came from goals.

Solution 2

$\frac{92}{212}$ is about $\frac{100}{200}$.

$\frac{100}{200} = \frac{1}{2}$

$= 50\%$

About 50% of his points came from goals.

Example 2

Estimate 35% of \$152.00.

Solution

35% is about $33\frac{1}{3}\%$ or $\frac{1}{3}$.
\$152.00 is about \$150.00.
$\frac{1}{3}$ of \$150.00 is \$50.00.

Example 3

Estimate 22% of \$312.00.

Solution

22% is about 20% or 0.2.
\$312.00 is about \$300.00.
$0.2 \times \$300.00$ is \$60.00.

Practice

Estimate the percent of each area that is shaded.

1\.

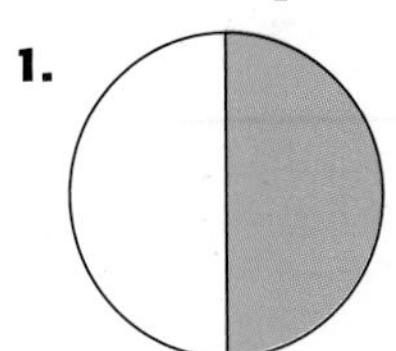

2\.

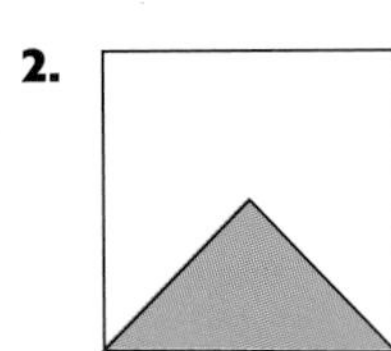

3\.

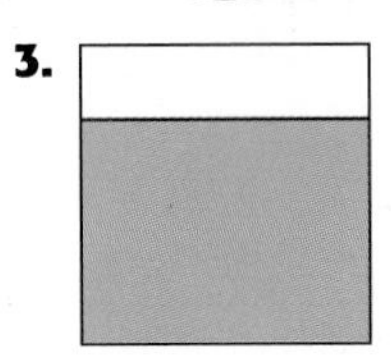

4\.

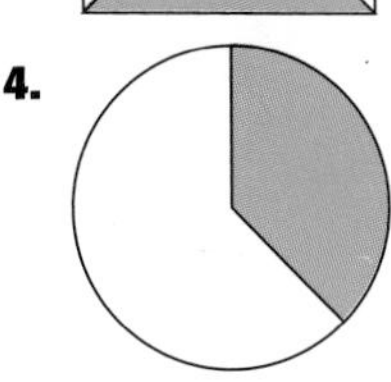

5\.

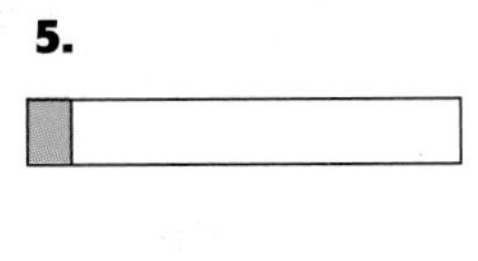

6\.

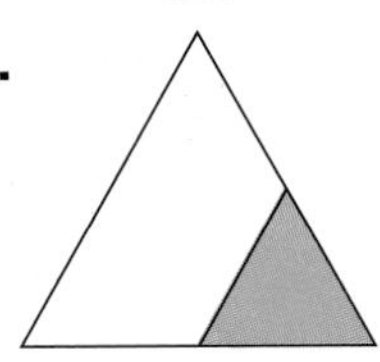

Estimate the percent of each number mentally.

7. 50% of 600 **8.** 25% of 80

9. 10% of 60 **10.** 20% of 50

11. 30% of 70 **12.** 40% of 500

Estimate the percent of each amount mentally.

13. 12% of \$50.00 **14.** 21% of \$700.00

15. 34% of \$89.00 **16.** 8% of \$123.00

17. 42% of \$560.00 **18.** 18% of \$452.00

Problems and Applications

In questions 19–24, estimate the percent for each test score.

19. 33 out of 50 **20.** 21 out of 25

21. 8 out of 12 **22.** 22 out of 33

23. 43 out of 80 **24.** 42 out of 52

25. The 2 highest cities in Canada are Calgary and Edmonton. Calgary is 1045 m above sea level. Edmonton is 666 m above sea level. Estimate the percent that Edmonton's height is of Calgary's height.

26. The table gives the approximate area of each of the Great Lakes.

Lake	Area (km²)
Erie	26 000
Huron	60 000
Michigan	58 000
Ontario	19 000
Superior	82 000
Total	245 000

Estimate the percent of the total area that each lake covers.

27. Canada became a country in 1867. Estimate the percent that your age is of Canada's age.

Estimate the 15% restaurant tip for the following bills. Compare your estimates with your classmates'.

28. \$60.00 **29.** \$21.00 **30.** \$33.00

31. \$45.78 **32.** \$18.50 **33.** \$7.75

34. \$9.44 **35.** \$135.80 **36.** \$89.25

37. Write a problem that involves estimating a percent. Ask a classmate to solve your problem.

PATTERN POWER

In the figure, the coloured circles in a row are determined by the coloured circles in the row above.

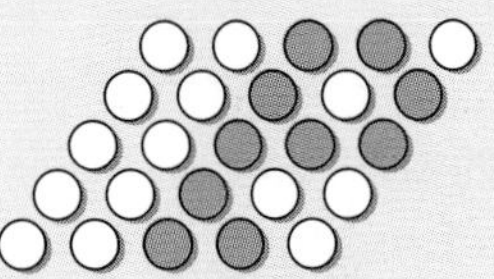

a) What is the rule?

b) Make your own puzzle. Use more than two colours if you like.

c) Ask a classmate to find your rule or rules.

7.6 Finding the Percent

Activity: Study the Information

Navin and Bea collected the following numbers of coins while on a trip to 6 countries in Europe.

United Kingdom 26	France 59	Finland 20
Germany 34	Austria 17	Sweden 44

Inquire

1. What was the total number of coins they collected?
2. How many of the coins were from Sweden?
3. What fraction of the coins were from Sweden?
4. What percent of the coins were from Sweden?

We can find a percent using fractions.

Example 1

Of the 200 coins, 34 were from Germany. What percent of the coins were from Germany?

Solution

$$\frac{34}{200} = \frac{17}{100}$$

$$= 17\%$$

So, 17% of the coins were from Germany.

We can also find a percent using decimals.

Example 2

Of the 200 coins, 26 were from the United Kingdom, and 44 were from Sweden. What percent of the coins were from the United Kingdom or Sweden?

Solution

$$\frac{26 + 44}{200} = \frac{70}{200}$$

$$= 0.35$$

$$= 35\%$$

So, 35% of the coins were from the United Kingdom or Sweden.

Example 3

Navin and Bea sold 16 of their 26 coins from the United Kingdom. What percent did they sell? Answer to the nearest tenth.

Solution

Fraction sold $\frac{16}{26}$

EST $\frac{16}{26}$ is about $\frac{3}{5}$ or 60%

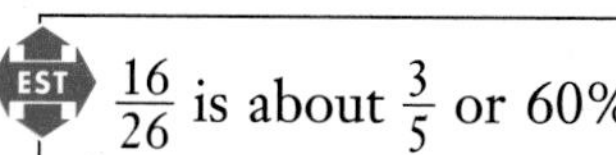

They sold 61.5% of their coins from the United Kingdom.

Practice

Express each decimal as a percent.

1. 0.35 **2.** 0.63 **3.** 0.27

4. 0.4 **5.** 0.1 **6.** 0.9

7. 0.07 **8.** 0.01 **9.** 0.05

10. 0.345 **11.** 0.025 **12.** 0.105

Express each fraction as a percent.

13. $\frac{1}{2}$ **14.** $\frac{2}{5}$ **15.** $\frac{3}{5}$

16. $\frac{3}{10}$ **17.** $\frac{7}{10}$ **18.** $\frac{11}{100}$

19. $\frac{5}{100}$ **20.** $\frac{5}{10}$ **21.** $\frac{5}{500}$

22. $\frac{1}{4}$ **23.** $\frac{2}{4}$ **24.** $\frac{3}{4}$

What percent of the first number is the second number?

25. 100, 45 **26.** 10, 5 **27.** 4, 1

28. 10, 2 **29.** 5, 5 **30.** 50, 4

Express each fraction as a percent to the nearest tenth.

31. $\frac{1}{3}$ **32.** $\frac{2}{3}$ **33.** $\frac{1}{6}$

34. $\frac{5}{6}$ **35.** $\frac{1}{30}$ **36.** $\frac{7}{30}$

37. $\frac{27}{40}$ **38.** $\frac{29}{40}$ **39.** $\frac{1}{40}$

What percent of the first number is the second number? Express each answer to the nearest tenth.

40. 40, 35 **41.** 35, 25 **42.** 68, 42

43. 81, 19 **44.** 27, 14 **45.** 55, 18

Problems and Applications

46. In the 1990–1991 season, the Calgary Flames won 46 of the 80 games they played. What percent of the games did they win?

47. Marilyn got 34 out of 50 questions correct on a test. Nadia wrote a different test and got 21 out of 28 questions correct. Who had the better score?

48. From 1948 to 1992, the United States won 9 out of 12 Olympic finals in men's basketball. What percent of the finals did the United States win?

49. In 1991, Nelson Santovenia of the Montreal Expos got 24 hits in 96 times at bat. What percent of the times at bat did he hit?

50. Ms. Chan gave her students a math test. The table shows the results.

Name	Number Correct	Number Attempted
Henry	35	45
Margot	25	30
Joshua	28	40
Paola	35	40
Nanette	25	35
Ali	46	50

To determine each student's score, she expressed the number of correct answers as a percent of the number of questions attempted.

a) Calculate each percent. Round to the nearest tenth, if necessary.
b) Who had the highest percent score?
c) Who had the lowest percent score?

51. The carat, which equals 200 mg, is the unit of mass for precious stones, such as diamonds. A 1-carat diamond has $\frac{1}{2}$ or 50% of the mass of a 2-carat diamond.
Express the mass of a 2-carat diamond as a percent of each of the following diamonds.
a) 5-carat **b)** 10-carat **c)** 25-carat

NUMBER POWER

Copy the diagram. Put the numbers from 1 to 9 on the dots so that the numbers on each line add to 23.

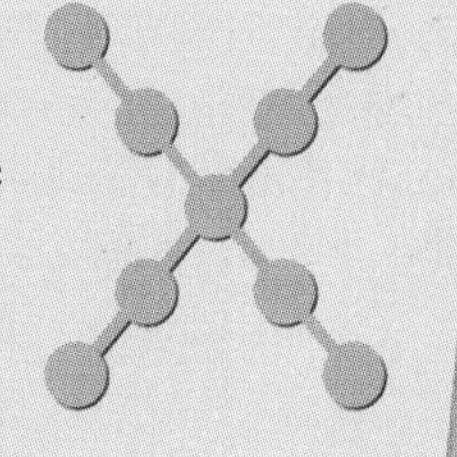

The Arts

Use your research skills in the following activities.

Activity ❶

1. How does word processing allow a playwrite to make changes to a play without retyping all of it?

2. Describe how computers can be used to
a) cast a play **b)** produce a play **c)** sell tickets

3. How can computers be used to control the sound and lights for a play?

4. How can writers use computer technology to generate poetry?

5. Suggest some future uses of technology in writing.

Activity ❷

Movies were originally made with celluloid film. The film had to be developed, like photographic film. Editing was done by cutting the film and joining it with glue. Today, videotape can be used instead.

1. How does the use of videotape reduce the time and expense of putting together the scenes of a movie?

2. The cost of the 8-mm film for a 3-min home movie was $6.00. What was the cost of the 8-mm film for a 2-h home movie? Compare with the cost of a videotape long enough for a 2-h home movie.

3. What other advantages does videotape have over celluloid film?

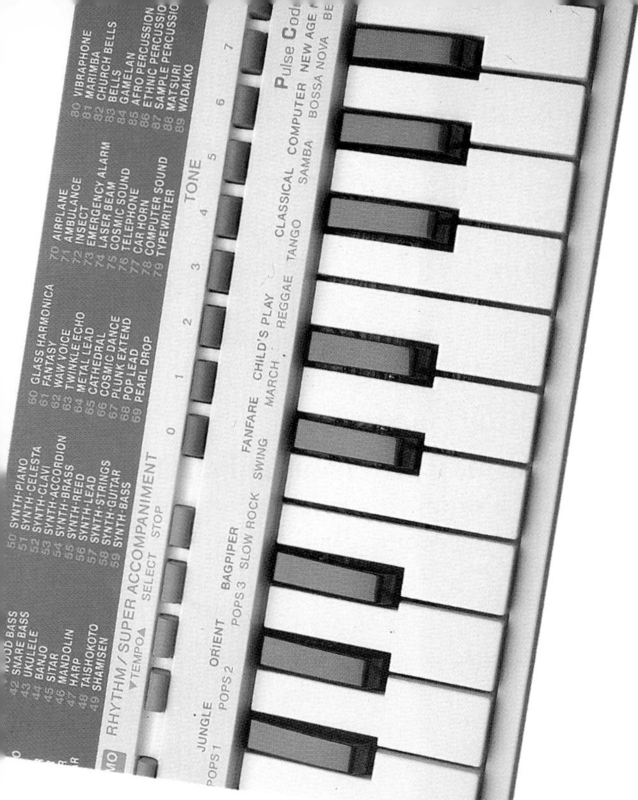

More Pattern Power from Calculators

Activity ❶

1. Determine the pattern in the sum of the odd numbers.

$$1 = 1 = 1^2$$
$$1 + 3 = 4 = 2^2$$
$$1 + 3 + 5 = 9 = ■$$
$$1 + 3 + 5 + 7 = 16 = ■$$
$$1 + 3 + 5 + 7 + 9 = 25 = ■$$
$$1 + 3 + 5 + 7 + 9 + 11 = 36 = ■$$

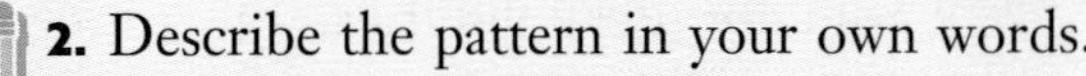

2. Describe the pattern in your own words.

3. What is the sum of the first 32 odd numbers?

4. What is the sum of the first 67 odd numbers?

5. Explain how the following diagram shows that the sum of the first four odd numbers is 16.

1	*	*	*	*
3	*	*	*	*
5	*	*	*	*
7	*	*	*	*

6. Draw a diagram to show the following sum.

$$1 + 3 + 5 + 7 + 9 + 11 + 13 + 15 + 17$$

Activity ❷

1. Determine the pattern in the sum of the following odd numbers.

$$1 = 1 = 1^3$$
$$3 + 5 = 8 = 2^3$$
$$7 + 9 + 11 = ■ = ■$$
$$13 + 15 + 17 + 19 = ■ = ■$$
$$21 + 23 + 25 + 27 + 29 = ■ = ■$$
$$31 + 33 + 35 + 37 + 39 + 41 = ■ = ■$$
$$43 + 45 + 47 + 49 + 51 + 53 + 55 = ■ = ■$$

2. Describe the pattern in your own words.

Activity ❸

From the development of new instruments to the use of modern amplifiers, technology has played an important part in music. Today, computer technology is used to compose music and to print musical arrangements. Computerized synthesizers are used to make new sounds.

1. What do the following numbers mean in recorded music?

a) 78 **b)** 45 **c)** $33\frac{1}{3}$

2. In what years were the following technologies developed for recording music?

a) wax cylinders **b)** vinyl recordings

c) cassette tapes **d)** compact discs

3. What are the advantages of using computers to write music?

4. What are the advantages and disadvantages of using computers to play music?

5. Describe the future of technology in music.

7.7 Percents Greater Than 100%

Activity: Study the Data

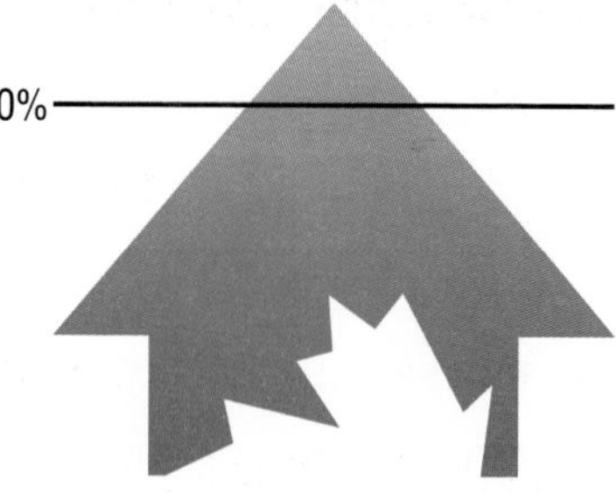

The Canadian Consumer Price Index shows the cost of living as a percent of the cost in 1986. The 1990 Index was about 120, so the cost of living in 1990 was 120% of the cost in 1986.

Inquire

1. What is 100% of $1000.00?

2. What is 20% of $1000.00?

3. For each $1000.00 a family needed to live in 1986, how much did it need in 1990?

4. Look up the latest Consumer Price Index. Work out how much a family needs for each $1000.00 it needed in 1986.

As with percents less than 100%, percents greater than 100% can be written as fractions or decimals.

$$140\% = \frac{140}{100}$$

$$= \frac{7}{5} \text{ or } 1.4$$

Think: $\frac{140}{100} = \frac{140 \div 20}{100 \div 20}$

Practice

State each percent as a decimal.

1. 35% **2.** 100% **3.** 300%

4. 175% **5.** 1000% **6.** 2500%

Express as a percent.

7. 0.125 **8.** 1.25 **9.** 3

10. 4.5 **11.** 0.35 **12.** 0.05

Express as a percent.

13. $\frac{150}{100}$ **14.** $\frac{18}{10}$ **15.** $\frac{200}{100}$

16. $\frac{11}{10}$ **17.** $\frac{3}{2}$ **18.** $1\frac{1}{4}$

19. $1\frac{1}{5}$ **20.** $3\frac{1}{2}$ **21.** $5\frac{3}{10}$

Find.

22. 150% of $60.00 **23.** 300% of $2500.00

24. 110% of $20.00 **25.** 250% of $18.00

26. 180% of $250.00 **27.** 225% of $160.00

28. 200% of $300.00 **29.** 130% of $35.00

Problems and Applications

30. A poster costs $8.00. The price is increased to 125% of the old price. What is the new price?

31. The price of a baseball card increased from $20.00 to $25.00. What percent of the old price was the new price?

32. The name "centipede" means "100 feet," so we expect a centipede to have 100 legs. The actual number of legs on a centipede can be as high as 354. What percent is this number of the expected number?

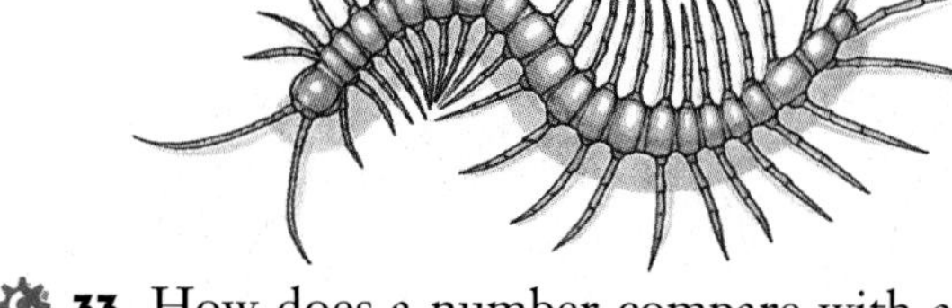

33. How does a number compare with a percent of the number, if the percent is
a) <100%? **b)** 100%? **c)** >100%?

7.8 Simple Interest

When you deposit money in a bank, the bank pays you for the right to use your money. This payment is called **interest**. When you borrow money, you have to pay to use it. This payment is also called interest.

Activity: Solve the Problem

Terry deposited $200.00 in the bank for one year. The bank paid 6% interest per year. Terry wanted to know how much money she would have in her account at the end of one year.

Inquire

1. How much did Terry deposit?

2. What was the interest rate?

3. What is 6% of $200.00?

4. How much did Terry have in her account at the end of one year?

Problems and Applications

Calculate the amount of interest on each deposit for one year.

1. $800.00 at 9% **2.** $1000.00 at 11%

3. $500.00 at 12% **4.** $600.00 at 10%

5. $2000.00 at 7% **6.** $500.00 at 5%

For each deposit, calculate the total amount in the account after one year.

7. $200.00 at 7% **8.** $550.00 at 6%

9. $1000.00 at 9% **10.** $1500.00 at 8%

11. $2300.00 at 11% **12.** $769.00 at 5%

When you borrow money, interest is added to give the total amount you owe. Complete the table.

	Amount Borrowed	Interest Rate	Interest Owed	Total Owed
13.	$725.00	12%		
14.	$325.00	9%		
15.	$1250.00	10%		
16.	$3750.00	11%		
17.	$4625.00	7%		
18.	$5780.00	6%		

19. Armand borrowed $300.00 for one year at 11% interest. Calculate the total amount Armand owed at the end of the year.

20. Jenny's grandfather bought her a $500.00 savings bond. The interest paid on the bond for one year was 9%. Calculate the amount of interest for one year.

21. The interest on savings bonds one year was 9.5%. Calculate the amount of interest earned on a $500.00 bond that year.

22. State whether each statement is always true, sometimes true, or never true. Explain.
a) A deposit at a higher interest rate earns more interest than a deposit at a lower interest rate.
b) The best type of deposit to make is the one with the highest interest rate.

23. Research today's interest rates for deposits and for borrowing money. Compare your findings with your classmates'.

7.9 Discount and Sale Price

Activity: Study the Picture

A **discount** is the difference between a regular price and a sale price. A discount may be expressed as a percent or as a dollar amount. We want to work out the sale price of the AM/FM portable stereo.

Inquire

1. What is the regular price of the stereo?
2. What is the percent discount?
3. Write the discount as a dollar amount.
4. Calculate the sale price of the stereo.

5. Describe another way to work out the sale price.

Example

The regular price of a pair of sneakers is \$79.95. What is the sale price after a discount of 15%?

Solution

Calculate the discount.

15% of $\$79.95 = 0.15 \times 79.95$
$= 11.9925$

The discount is \$11.99.

C 79.95 × 15 % M+
11.9925 is in the memory

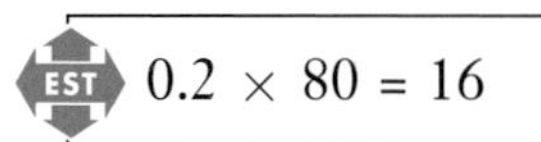

Calculate the sale price.

regular price − discount = sale price

$\$79.95 - \$11.99 = \$67.96$

C 79.95 − MRC =

EST 80 − 12 = 68

The sale price is \$67.96.

Problems and Applications

Estimate each discount.

1. 10% off a shirt at \$40.00
2. 10% off a jacket at \$49.95
3. 50% off a roll of film at \$5.99
4. 25% off a calculator at \$99.99

Find the sale price of each item in questions 5–9.

5. a \$79.95 sweater at 15% off
6. a \$65.00 pair of jeans at 25% off
7. a \$1295.00 furniture set at 50% off
8. a \$19.99 T-shirt at 20% off
9. a \$22 500.00 truck at 3% off

10. Check newspapers and flyers to find 6 items selling at a discount. Find the discount in each case.

7.10 Goods and Services Tax (GST)

Activity: Study the Picture

The Goods and Services Tax is applied by the Federal Government. The Tax is expressed as a percent. We want to know the cost of the bike, including GST.

Inquire

1. What is the rate of the GST?

2. How much is the GST on the bike?

Example

The selling price of a ball is $24.00.
Find the cost of the ball with GST added.

Solution

If the GST rate is 7%
GST = 0.07 × $24.00
= $1.68
Selling Price = $24.00
Cost = $24.00 + $1.68
= $25.68

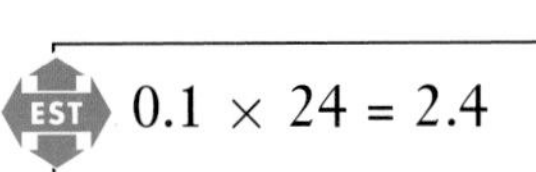

Problems and Applications

Estimate the amount of GST.

	Item	Price
1.	sweater	$89.50
2.	shoes	$212.50
3.	ball glove	$99.99
4.	computer	$1295.00
5.	new car	$24 000.00
6.	armchair	$349.50
7.	shirt	$65.00
8.	book	$8.50
9.	school supplies	$37.81
10.	compact disc	$21.50

Calculate the cost including GST.

	Item	Price
11.	coat	$179.50
12.	skis	$225.00
13.	chair	$99.50
14.	stereo	$595.00
15.	show ticket	$11.50
16.	jacket	$125.00
17.	television	$799.95
18.	writing paper	$2.99

19. If the GST increases by 1%, what will be the increase in the total cost of the items in questions 11–18?

20. An item with a regular price of $200.00 is on sale at 25% off. How much GST do you save?

21. List items that are exempt from the GST. Compare your list with a classmate's.

7.11 Provincial Sales Tax (PST)

Activity: Study the Example

The rate of Provincial Sales Tax (PST) is determined by each province. In some provinces, the PST is calculated on just the selling price of an item. In other provinces, the PST is calculated on the sum of the selling price and the GST. Consider both methods for a pair of skis with a selling price of $400.00. Assume that the GST is 7% and the PST is 8%.

1—PST calculated on the selling price:

Selling price = $400.00
GST = 0.07 × $400.00 = $28.00
PST = 0.08 × $400.00 = <u>$32.00</u>
Total cost = $460.00

2—PST calculated on the selling price plus GST:

Selling price = $400.00
GST = 0.07 × $400.00 = <u>$28.00</u>
Total = $428.00
PST = 0.08 × $428.00 = <u>$34.24</u>
Total cost = $462.24

Inquire

1. What is the rate of PST in your province?

2. Which method is used to calculate the PST in your province?

3. Make a chart to show the rate of PST for each province in Canada.

Problems and Applications

For each item, estimate the total of the GST and PST in your province.

	Item	Price
1.	sweat shirt	$40.00
2.	camera	$250.00
3.	new car	$35 000.00
4.	television	$469.00
5.	ring	$995.00
6.	book	$22.50
7.	plant	$8.77

Calculate the total cost of each item, including GST and PST, in your province.

	Item	Price
8.	birdfeeder	$30.00
9.	personal stereo	$200.00
10.	blouse	$55.00
11.	camcorder	$1094.00
12.	new car	$23 790.00
13.	jeans	$34.95
14.	compact disc	$11.50

15. List items that are exempt from PST in your province. Compare your list with a classmate's.

7.12 Commission

Activity: Look for a Pattern

Tara is a sales clerk. She is paid a percent of what she sells. This type of payment is called a **commission**. The chart shows Tara's earnings one Thursday night.

Sale	Amount	Commission
1	$100.00	$3.00
2	$500.00	$15.00
3	$800.00	$24.00
4	$200.00	$6.00
5	$300.00	▬

Inquire

1. What is Tara's percent commission?

2. What is Tara's commission on the $300 sale?

3. What are Tara's total earnings?

Some salespeople earn a salary plus a commission.

Example

Tor sells clothes. He earns $250.00 a week, plus a commission of 2% of his sales. How much does he earn if he sells $12 000.00 worth of clothes in a week?

Solution

Salary = $250.00

Commission = 0.02 × $12 000.00 = $240.00

Total = $490.00

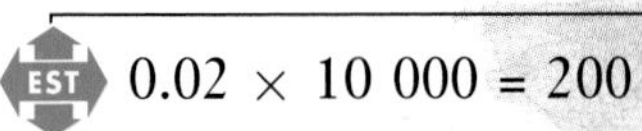

Tor earns $490.00.

Practice

Estimate.

1. 11% of $900.00 **2.** 9% of $1150.00

3. 15% of $680.00 **4.** 7% of $1250.00

5. 11% of $545.00 **6.** 9% of $899.00

Problems and Applications

7. Mark sold souvenirs at a baseball park. Here are his sales for 6 days.

Monday	$275.00	Thursday	$454.00
Tuesday	$318.00	Friday	$537.00
Wednesday	$380.00	Saturday	$672.00

Mark earned 15% commission on his sales.

a) How much did he earn each day?

b) What were his total earnings for 6 days?

8. The Chans sold their home for $160 000.00. They paid 5% in real estate commission. Calculate the amount of commission.

9. Pat works in a shoe store. She makes $300.00 per week, plus 2% of her sales. Last week her sales were $2235.00. How much did she earn?

10. You have been offered a job in a sporting goods store. You have to choose how you will be paid. One option is $300.00 a week, plus 5% of your sales. The other option is 15% of your sales. The store owner says an average sales person sells $2500.00 worth of goods a week.

a) Which method of payment do you choose? Give reasons for your answer.

b) Use a table to determine the sales that give the same weekly pay by both methods.

The Shrinking World of The Grizzly

Grizzly bears get their name from the flecked hair on their flanks, back, and shoulders. (The word "grizzly" means greyish.) Grizzlies are larger than black bears and smaller than polar bears. Grizzlies have masses between 70 kg and 530 kg. In the fall, grizzlies dig dens. They hibernate from 4 to 6 months through the winter. As the human population has expanded, the grizzly population has declined. The table shows the population of grizzly bears in North America.

Province/State/Territory	Population
Alaska	32 000–43 000
Northwest Territories	4000–5000
Yukon Territory	6000–7000
British Columbia	10 000
Alberta	780
Montana	500–700
Wyoming	200
Idaho	20–30
Washington	10–20

Black Bear

Polar Bear

Grizzly Bear

Activity ❶

1. Estimate the total grizzly population in North America.

2. Estimate the total grizzly population in Canada.

3. What percent of the total grizzly population is in Canada?

4. What percent of the Canadian grizzly population is in British Columbia?

5. In the 1850s, the grizzly population in the United States (excluding Alaska) was 100 000. What percent of this number is left in these states?

The map shows where grizzly bears once lived in North America and where they live now.

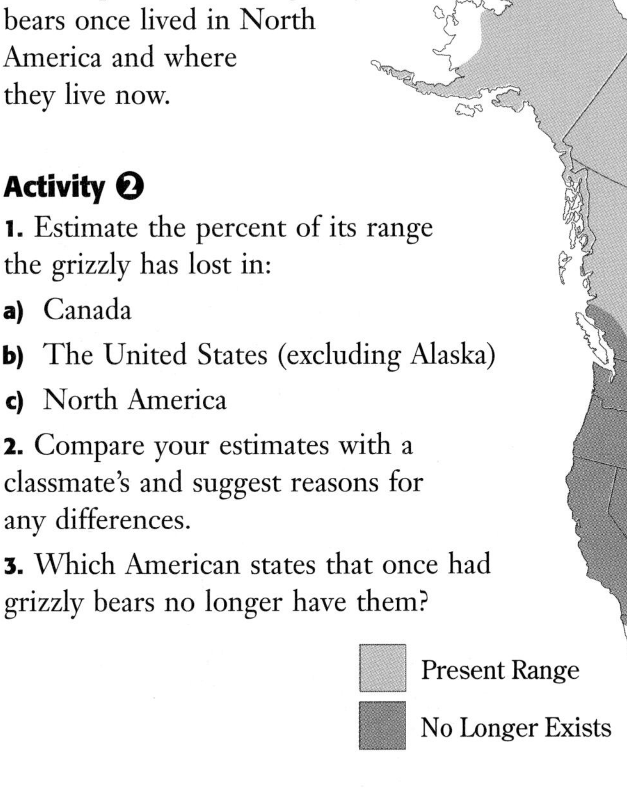

Activity ❷

1. Estimate the percent of its range the grizzly has lost in:

a) Canada

b) The United States (excluding Alaska)

c) North America

2. Compare your estimates with a classmate's and suggest reasons for any differences.

3. Which American states that once had grizzly bears no longer have them?

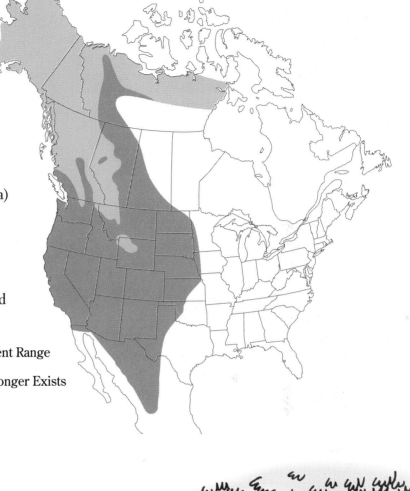

Activity ❸

1. Discuss how animals have been described in children's stories and other fiction. List examples that show animals to be "good," like the horse in *The Black Stallion*. List other examples that show them to be "bad," like the wolf in *Little Red Riding Hood*. Do you agree with the descriptions of the animals?

2. List some examples of "good" and "bad" animals in movies and TV shows. Do you agree with the descriptions?

3. How do you think a grizzly bear lives and behaves? Look up information about the grizzly to check if your ideas are correct.

Review

1.

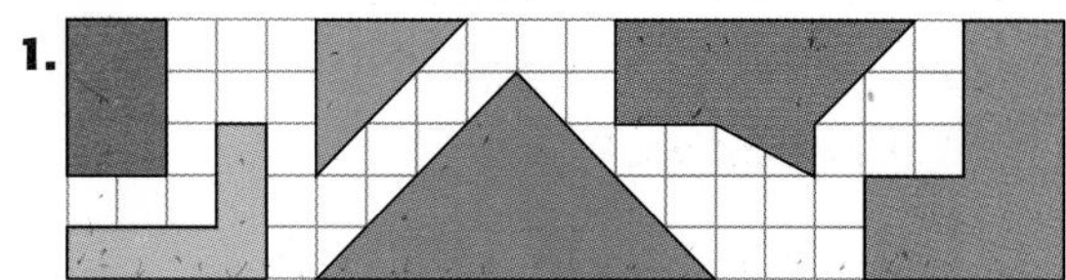

a) What percent of the grid is covered by each coloured region?
b) What percent of the grid is coloured?
c) What percent of the grid is white?

2. Copy and complete the table.

Fraction	$\frac{\blacksquare}{100}$	Percent
$\frac{7}{10}$		
$\frac{2}{5}$		
$\frac{9}{25}$		
$\frac{20}{1000}$		
$\frac{3}{4}$		

Write each decimal as a percent.

3. 0.75 **4.** 0.6 **5.** 0.02
6. 0.125 **7.** 0.99 **8.** 0.375
9. 0.075 **10.** 1.2 **11.** 2.45

Express each percent as a fraction in lowest terms.

12. 50% **13.** 75% **14.** 80%
15. 25% **16.** 90% **17.** 7%
18. 99% **19.** 15% **20.** 38%

Express each percent as a decimal.

21. 25% **22.** 50% **23.** 75%
24. 5% **25.** 1% **26.** 7.5%
27. 17.6% **28.** 125% **29.** 200%

Replace ■ with <, =, or > to make each statement true.

30. 0.2 ■ 15% **31.** 1.25 ■ 125%
32. 60% ■ $\frac{2}{3}$ **33.** $\frac{1}{4}$ ■ 25%
34. 0.5 ■ 5% **35.** 0.35 ■ 70%
36. 0.125 ■ $\frac{1}{8}$ **37.** $\frac{1}{8}$ ■ 12.5%

Calculate.

38. 25% of 100 **39.** 30% of 200
40. 75% of 12 **41.** 35% of 1000
42. 5% of 300 **43.** 125% of 60

Express the first number as a percent of the second number.

44. 30, 60 **45.** 75, 100
46. 80, 120 **47.** 125, 100
48. 65, 260 **49.** 312, 416

Estimate, then calculate 8% of each amount.

50. $65.00 **51.** $125.00
52. $9.95 **53.** $16.50
54. $175.80 **55.** $499.95

Estimate, then calculate 9% of each amount.

56. $2005.00 **57.** $65.75
58. $18 750.00 **59.** $429.50
60. $5.05 **61.** $5256.75

For each deposit, find the total amount in the account after one year.

62. $400.00 at 7% **63.** $850.00 at 8%
64. $1260.00 at 9% **65.** $730.00 at 11%

Find the sale price of each item.

66. a $185.00 tent at 25% off
67. a $45.00 shirt at 10% off
68. a $380.00 television at 15% off
69. $89.99 roller skates at 20% off

Calculate the GST payable on each selling price.

70.

71.

Calculate the PST payable on each selling price in your province.

72. 

73. 

Calculate the commission earned on each amount.

74. $500.00 at 8%

75. $7500.00 at 3%

76. $525.00 at 1%

77. $850.00 at 15%

78. $6500.00 at 2%

79. $7586.00 at 12%

80. Gomez rented an apartment for 12 months at $650.00 per month. He paid a real estate broker a commission of 10% of the year's rent for finding the apartment. How much commission did Gomez pay?

81. The average wind speed in Dawson, Yukon Territories, is 3.7 km/h. The average wind speed in St. John's, Newfoundland, is 24.3 km/h. Express the wind speed in Dawson as a percent of the wind speed in St. John's. Round your answer to the nearest percent.

82. St. John's, Newfoundland, is foggy 34% of the days in the year. How many days a year are foggy?

83. Mr. Mathias bought a house for $25 000.00. He sold it years later for $140 000.00. Express the selling price as a percent of the purchase price.

84. Petra saved 15% of the money she made from babysitting. In two weeks, she babysat 4 times and earned $8.00, $9.50, $7.50, and $12.00. How much did she save?

85. At one store, sneakers have a regular price of $69.95 with a 10% discount. Another store sells the same sneakers for a regular price of $74.95 with a 15% discount. Where would you buy the sneakers and why?

Group Decision Making

Researching Community Service Careers

1. As a class, brainstorm possible careers to investigate. They might include such careers as police officer, firefighter, social worker, community planner, or elected official. As a class, select 6 careers.

2. Go to home groups.

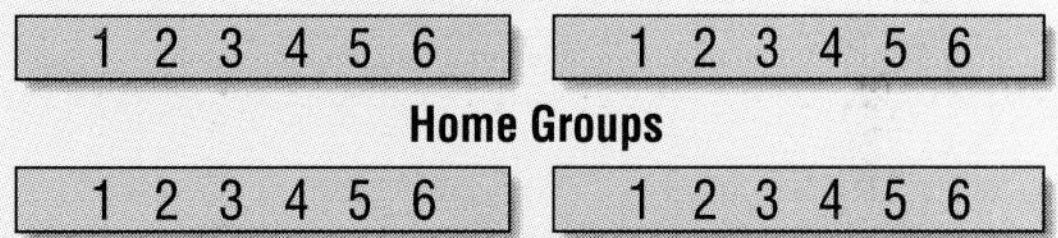

As a group, decide which career each member will research.

3. Form an expert group with students who are researching the same career as you.

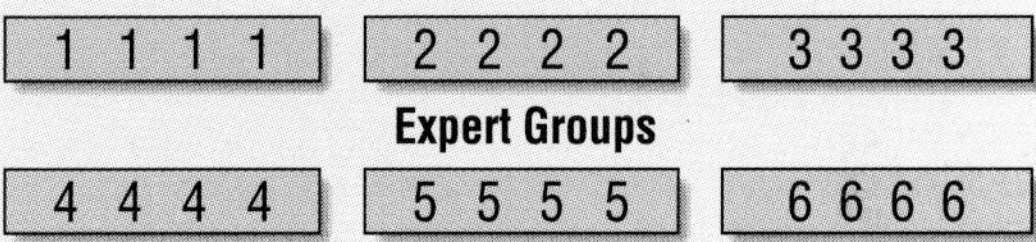

As an expert group, choose the questions you want to answer and research the career.

4. Return to your home group and share your findings from your expert group. Ask for questions and comments from your home group.

5. Return to your expert group and give the feedback from your home group. Decide on the format your expert group will use for its report. Prepare a report on the career. Include a description of how the career makes use of math.

6. In your expert group, evaluate the process and your report. Identify what went well and what you would do differently another time.

Chapter Check

Express as a percent.

1. $\frac{53}{100}$ **2.** 0.3 **3.** 4 out of 5

4. $\frac{3}{4}$ **5.** 0.05 **6.** $\frac{5}{20}$

7. Express 65%

a) as a decimal

b) as a fraction in simplest form

Calculate.

8. 12% of 65 **9.** 125% of 60

10. 65% of 80 **11.** 83% of 2000

12. What percent of 20 is 12?

13. In 1988, 6 of every 10 students who graduated as veterinarians in Canada were women. Express the number of female graduates as a percent of the number of male graduates.

14. Rosa put $125.00 in the bank at 8% interest for one year.

a) Calculate the interest she earned.

b) Calculate her total amount in the bank after one year.

15. A pair of gloves sells for $19.95. Calculate the following for your province.

a) the GST

b) the PST

16. A pair of shoes is on sale at 20% off the regular price of $85.00. What is the sale price?

17. At the end of 1990, 20 nuclear reactors were operating in Canada. Of these, 18 were in Ontario, 1 was in Quebec, and 1 was in New Brunswick. Calculate the percent of the reactors that were in these locations.

a) Ontario **b)** Quebec

c) New Brunswick **d)** the rest of the country

18. Carl earned 3% commission on a house he sold for $120 000.00. How much was his commission?

THE WIZARD OF ID **Brant parker and Johnny hart**

By permission of Johnny Hart and Creators Syndicate Inc.

Using the Strategies

1. The parking meter contained 43 coins in quarters and dollars. The value of the coins was $29.50. How many of each type of coin were there?

2. The diagrams show the floor plans of 2 houses.

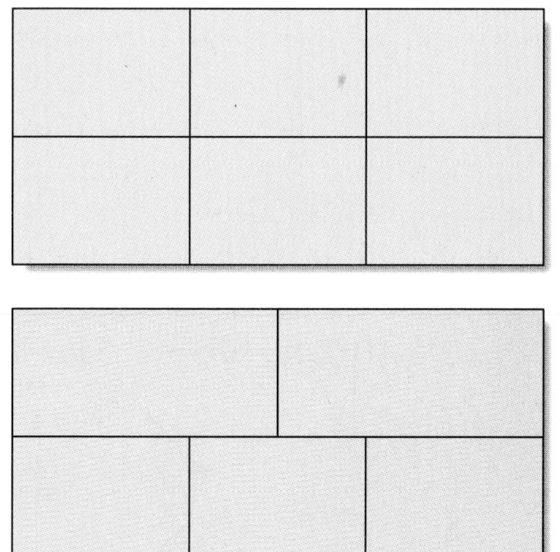

Copy each floor plan. Without lifting your pencil, try to draw one line that crosses each wall of each room once and only once.

3. The kindergarten class has a box of building cubes. When 2, 3, 4, 5, or 6 students share the cubes, there is always 1 cube left over. When 7 students share the cubes, there are no cubes left over. What is the smallest possible number of cubes in the box?

4. Joe bought three cartons of milk that cost $2.69 each. What was his change from a $10.00 bill?

5. Ramon, Mary, Inga, and Paul go to the movies in a car. Two sit in the front and two in the back. Only Ramon and Mary can drive. In how many possible ways can they sit in the car?

6. The product of two consecutive whole numbers is 1482. What are the numbers?

7. Adam and Beth started running at the same end of the track. They ran at the same speed but in opposite directions.

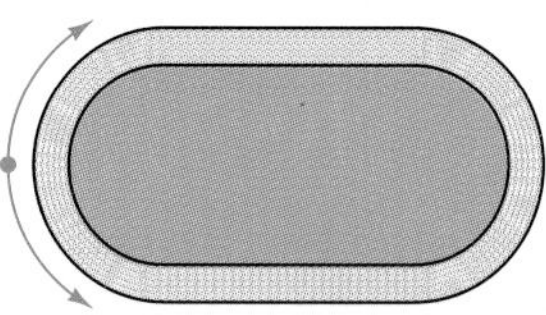

They both ran 4 times around the track. How many times did they pass each other before they met at the end of 4 laps?

8. Shirley left for school at 08:35 and returned home at 16:16. How long was Shirley away from home?

9. The High Flyer roller coaster has 15 cars. Each car holds 3 people. Each ride is 3 min long. It takes 1 min between rides to unload and load the riders.

a) How many people can ride in 1 h?

b) What assumptions did you make?

10. Determine the pattern. Copy and complete the table.

9	14	?	9	?	10
4	6	9	?	5	?
5	8	7	6	?	?
20	48	?	?	45	21

DATA BANK

1. How much deeper than Lake Erie is Lake Huron?

2. The Lee family drove from Winnipeg to Regina and back. When they started, the odometer on their car read 12 452 km. While in Regina, they drove 355 km. What was the approximate number of kilometres on the odometer when they got back to Winnipeg?

CHAPTER 8

Three-Dimensional Geometry

The diagrams show 2 different polyominoids.
Each is made up of 4 cubes joined face to face.

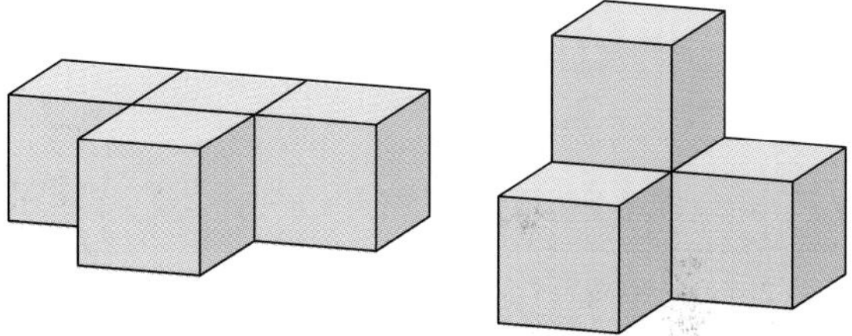

How many other different polyominoids can you make with 4 cubes?

Models in Three Dimensions

Activity ❶

1. a) Cut 2 identical triangles from Bristol board to use as the bases of a prism. Make a small hole in each corner, as shown.

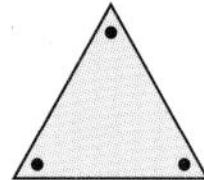
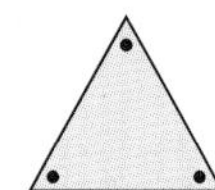

b) Take 3 equal lengths of plastic straw. Thread lengths of yarn or string through each straw, then through the corners of your triangles. Knot each piece of yarn or string at each end.

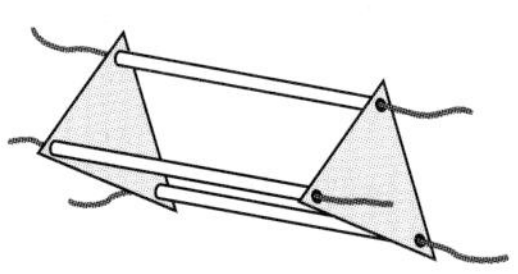
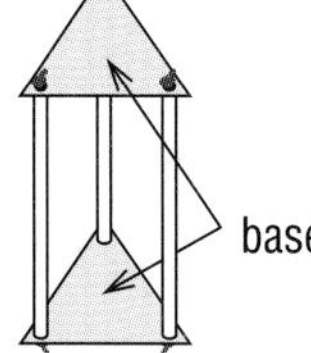

c) Label your model "TRIANGULAR PRISM."

2. Make models with each of the following shapes as the 2 bases.

a)
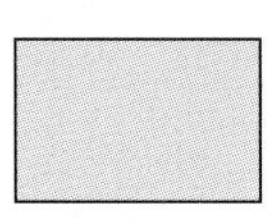
b)

c)
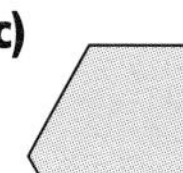

3. Label the models from step 2 as follows.

a) RECTANGULAR PRISM
b) PENTAGONAL PRISM
c) HEXAGONAL PRISM

4. a) Describe the ways in which all 4 of your models are the same.
b) State the part of each model that determines its name.

5. Use Bristol board, plastic straws, and yarn or string to make and label an OCTAGONAL PRISM.

Activity ❷

1. a) Cut a triangle from Bristol board to use as the base of a pyramid. Make a small hole in each corner.

b) Take 3 equal lengths of plastic straw. Thread lengths of yarn or string through each straw, then through the corners of your triangle. Knot each piece of yarn or string at each corner.

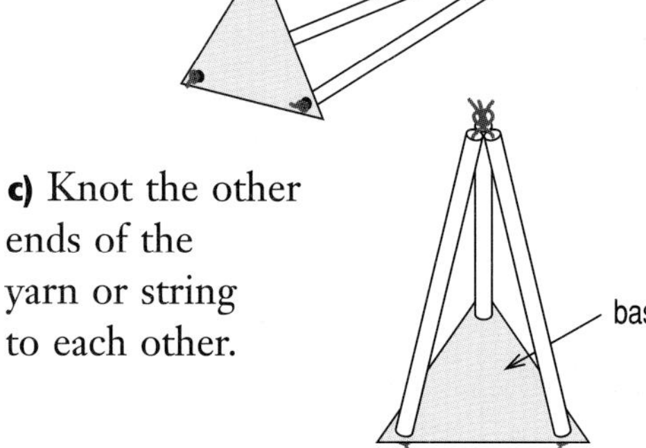

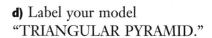

c) Knot the other ends of the yarn or string to each other.

d) Label your model "TRIANGULAR PYRAMID."

2. Make models with each of the following shapes as the base.

a)
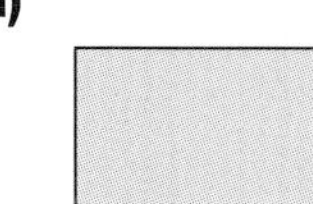
b)
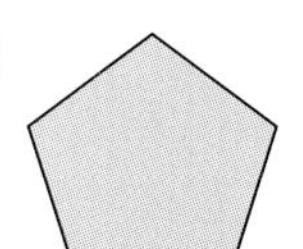
c)
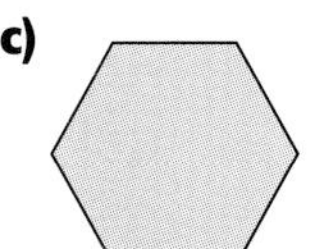

3. Label the models from step 2 as follows.

a) RECTANGULAR PYRAMID
b) PENTAGONAL PYRAMID
c) HEXAGONAL PYRAMID

4. a) Describe the ways in which all 4 of your models are the same.
b) State the part of each model that determines its name.

5. Use Bristol board, plastic straws, and yarn or string to make and label a SQUARE PYRAMID.

Polygons and Lines of Symmetry

1. Use the following description to sketch and name each polygon. Compare your answers with a classmate's.

a) 4 sides, 4 right angles, adjacent sides not equal
b) 6 equal sides, 6 equal angles
c) 3 sides, 1 right angle
d) 4 sides, opposite sides parallel, no right angles, adjacent sides not equal
e) 5 sides
f) 3 equal sides

2. Sketch each sign. Name the polygon in each sign.

a) stop sign
b) school zone sign
c) yield sign
d) no parking sign

3. Use the diagram below to name

a) 2 pairs of perpendicular lines
b) 2 pairs of parallel lines
c) 2 pairs of congruent line segments
d) a right angle
e) a parallelogram
f) a triangle

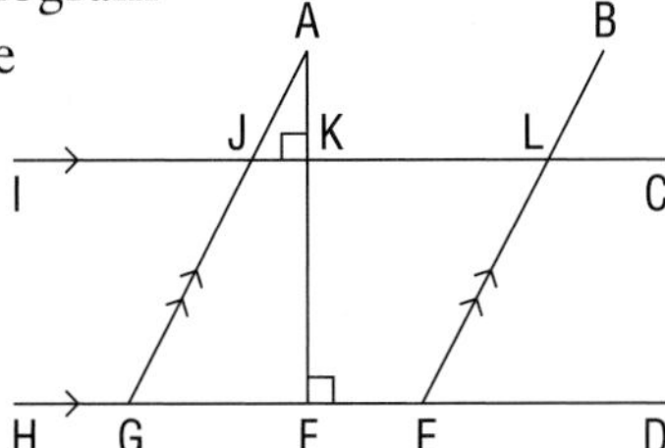

4. Copy each figure and draw all the lines of symmetry.

a)
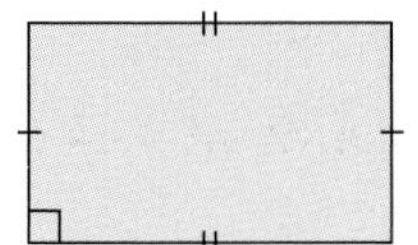

b)
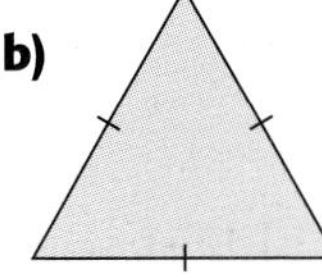

c)
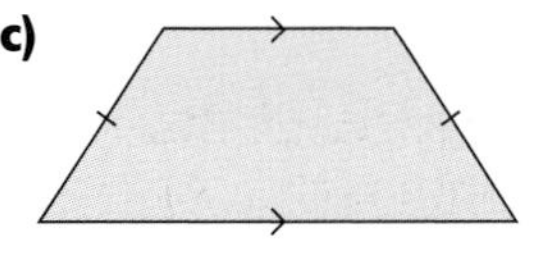

d)
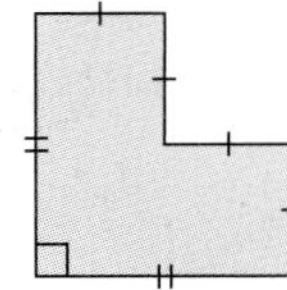

Mental Math

Calculate.

1. $2 \times 3 \times 4$
2. $6 \times 7 \times 1$
3. $5 \times 6 \times 2$
4. $8 \times 0 \times 9$
5. $3 \times 1 \times 8$
6. $5 \times 10 \times 5$

Calculate.

7. $4 \times 6 + 5$
8. $8 \times 7 - 6$
9. $9 \times 3 - 4$
10. $5 \times 10 + 8$
11. $11 \times 2 + 8$
12. $9 \times 6 - 5$
13. $7 \times 7 + 6$
14. $4 \times 3 - 9$

Simplify.

15. $(5 \times 4) + (9 \times 2)$
16. $(4 \times 2) + (4 \times 5)$
17. $(5 \times 5) + (2 \times 3)$
18. $(7 \times 3) + (5 \times 2)$
19. $(10 \times 10) + (10 \times 2)$
20. $(7 \times 0) + (7 \times 4)$

Evaluate.

21. 6^2
22. 10^3
23. 9^2
24. 3^3
25. 2^4
26. 7^2
27. 10^5
28. 1^3
29. 11^2

Multiply.

30. 1.5×10
31. 6.4×100
32. 2.25×100
33. 0.8×1000
34. 5.36×10
35. 7×100
36. 14.1×10
37. 0.05×1000

Use each of the following prices to state the cost of 1 item.

38. 6 for $36.00
39. 5 for $3.50
40. 3 for $1.20
41. 8 for $4.00
42. 10 for $6.40
43. 2 for $8.60
44. 4 for $10.00
45. 9 for $2.70

8.1 Three-Dimensional Figures

We live in a three-dimensional world. Many common objects are made in the shapes of three-dimensional geometric figures.

Activity: Examine the Pictures

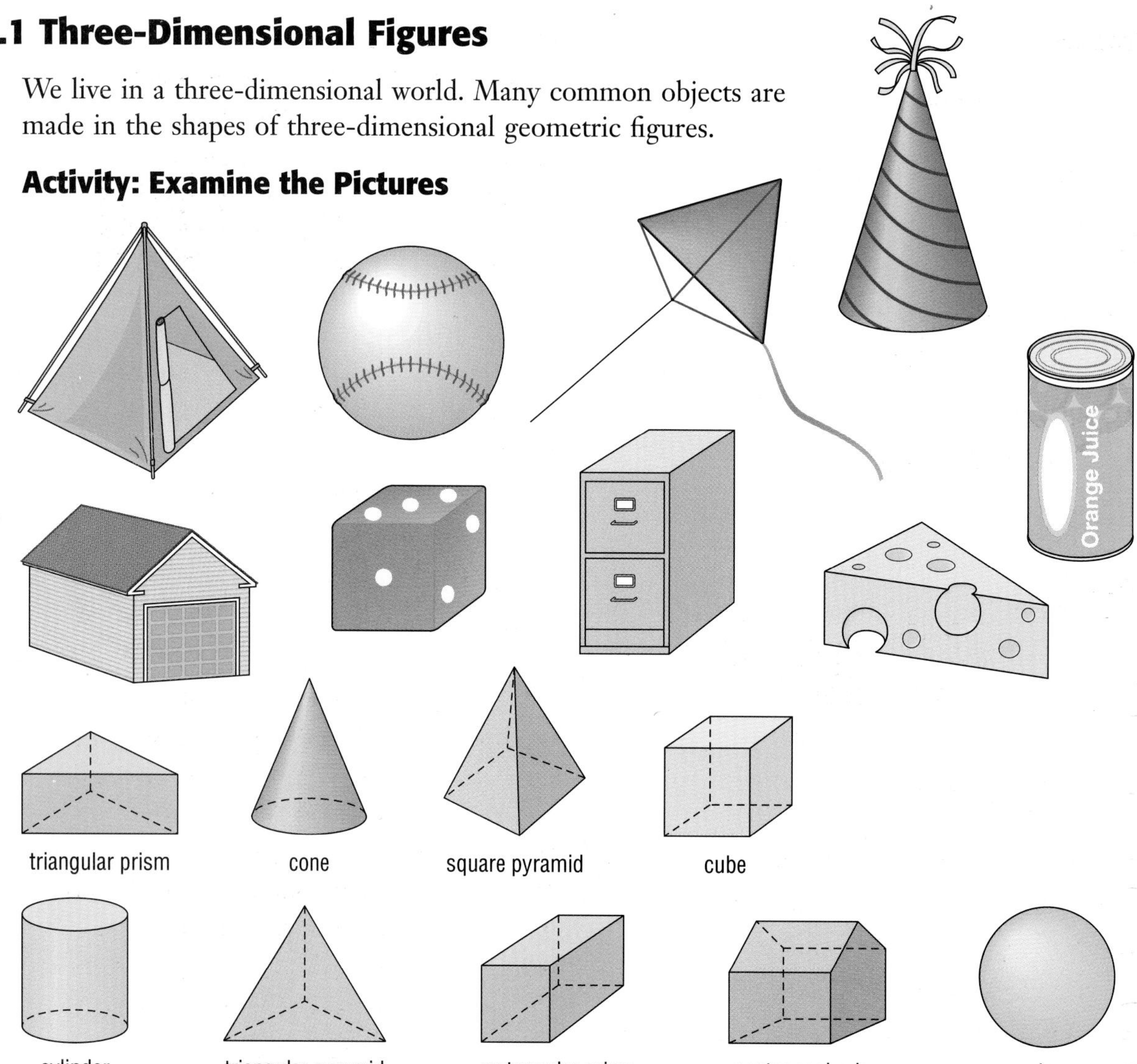

Inquire

1. Examine the above pictures of the 9 geometric figures and the 9 real-life objects. Match each object with its corresponding three-dimensional figure.

2. Name 6 objects around your classroom that are examples of 6 of the above three-dimensional figures.

3. Use cut-out shapes to construct a group set of three-dimensional figures from Bristol board.
Describe the differences and similarities you can identify by studying the shapes.

Practice

Trace the base of each figure and name the shape that is formed.

1. cylinder
2. triangular prism
3. cube
4. square pyramid
5. cone
6. rectangular prism

Name each prism from the shape of its base.

7. pentagon
8. hexagon
9. octagon
10. triangle

Problems and Applications

Pairs of faces of three-dimensional figures meet at ***edges.***

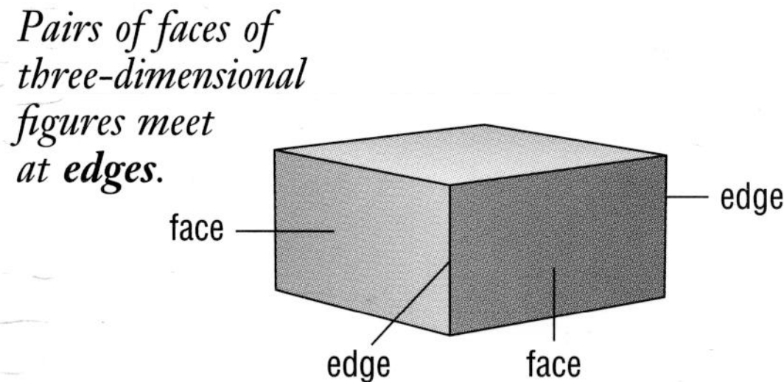

Use your models to determine the number of edges of each figure in questions 11-18.

11. triangular pyramid
12. rectangular prism
13. cylinder
14. pentagonal prism
15. square pyramid
16. cube
17. triangular prism
18. cone

19. Name a three-dimensional figure that has no edges.

20. Sketch the paths traced by the edges of a cylinder and a cone when they are rolled on a flat surface.

State the number of triangular surfaces on each of the following.

21. triangular pyramid

22. square pyramid

23. pentagonal pyramid

24. hexagonal pyramid

25. octagonal pyramid

26. Use your answers to questions 21–25 to state what determines the number of triangular faces on a pyramid.

The edges of 3 or more flat faces on a three-dimensional figure meet at a ***vertex.***

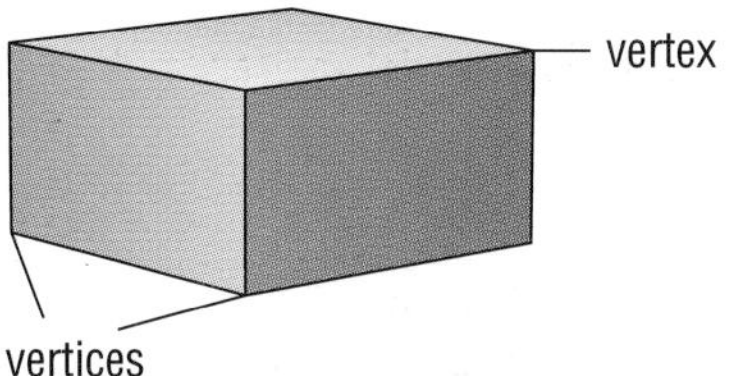

Use your models to determine the number of vertices each figure in questions 27-31 has.

27. cube

28. triangular prism

29. square pyramid

30. pentagonal prism

31. triangular pyramid

32. Name 2 three-dimensional figures on the previous page whose surfaces are all the same shape. Work with a partner to construct another figure whose faces are all the same shape. Name the figure.

33. With a partner, compose a paragraph that describes how a cube and a rectangular prism are the same and how they are different.

34. a) Work with your group to find three-dimensional figures that fit each clue below.

I have more than 5 faces.
I have only 2 faces.
I have 12 edges.
I have 2 pentagonal faces.
I have 5 vertices.
I have 2 circular faces.
I have only triangular faces.
I have 6 vertices.

b) Is there more than one answer for any of the clues? Explain.

35. Write a clue like those in question 34. Have a classmate find the three-dimensional figure.

8.2 Identifying and Classifying Polyhedra

Activity: Use the Definitions

We use a type of **prism** to separate light into its different colours. A prism has 2 parallel, congruent bases joined by the same number of parallelograms as there are sides on each base.

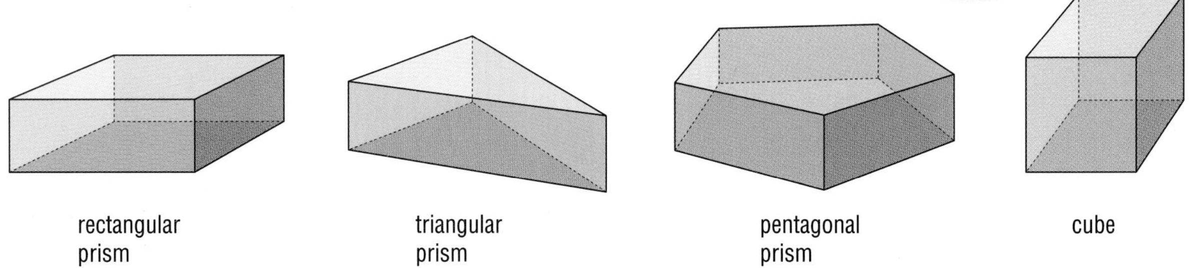

rectangular prism

triangular prism

pentagonal prism

cube

A prism is an example of a **polyhedron**, which is a three-dimensional figure with flat faces. Polyhedra have faces, edges, and vertices.

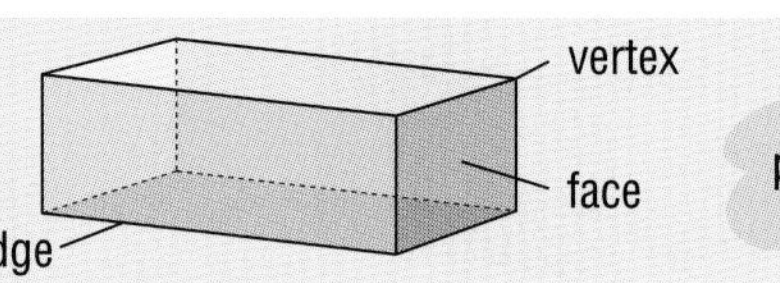

The plural of polyhedron is polyhedra or polyhedrons.

Inquire

1. With a partner, compose definitions of face, edge, and vertex. Compare your definitions with your classmates'.

2. Name the shape of the base for each prism named above.

3. How many parallelograms form the faces of each prism, excluding the bases?

4. What gives each prism its name?

5. Suggest an alternative name for the cube.

Activity: Use the Definitions

A **pyramid** is a polyhedron that has one base and the same number of triangular faces as there are sides on the base.

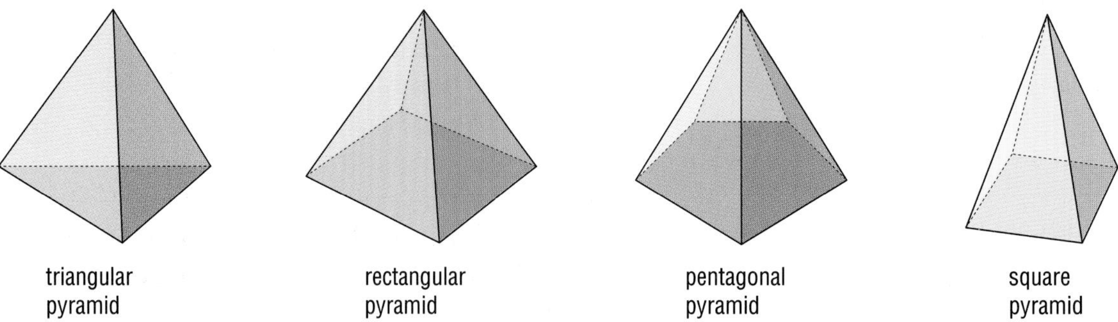

triangular pyramid

rectangular pyramid

pentagonal pyramid

square pyramid

Inquire

1. Name the shape of the base for each pyramid shown.

2. Count the number of triangular faces for each pyramid.

3. Describe a hexagonal pyramid.

4. Look up the meaning of "tetrahedron" in your dictionary. With your classmates, describe how the meaning can be applied to your understanding of pyramids.

Practice

1. Use the diagram to name the following.

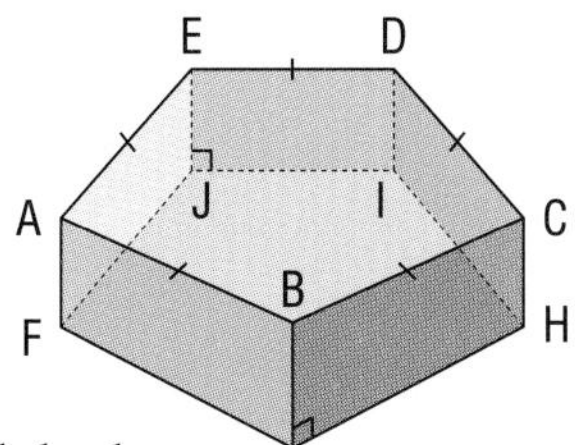

a) the type of polyhedron
b) 3 pairs of parallel edges
c) 3 pairs of equal edges
d) 3 pairs of perpendicular edges
e) 2 pairs of congruent faces

2. Use the diagram to name the following.

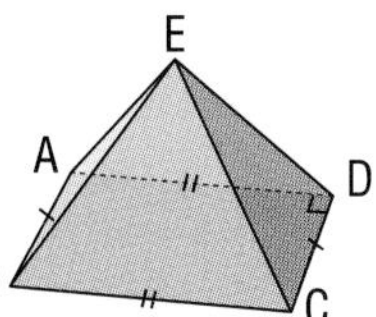

a) the type of polyhedron
b) 2 pairs of parallel edges
c) 2 pairs of equal edges
d) 2 pairs of perpendicular edges
e) 2 pairs of congruent faces

Problems and Applications

3. Models of polyhedra can be constructed with drinking straws as edges, joined by wire or plasticine.

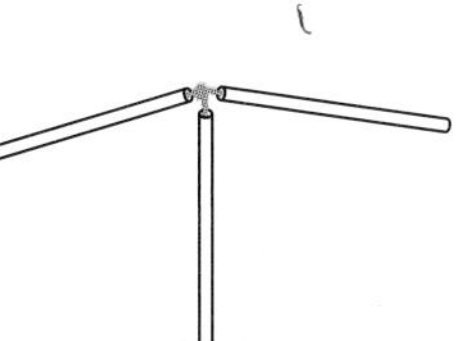

Construct and name a polyhedron with these numbers of equal lengths of straw.

a) 12 **b)** 15 **c)** 6 **d)** 8

4. Sheila constructed a polyhedron from the following materials. Sketch a polyhedron she could have made.

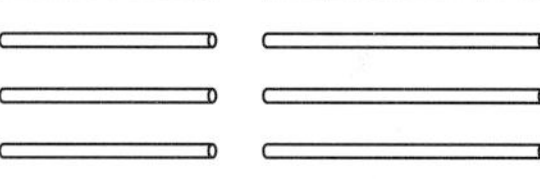

5. The sides of the bases of the hexagonal prism are equal, and the vertical edges are equal.

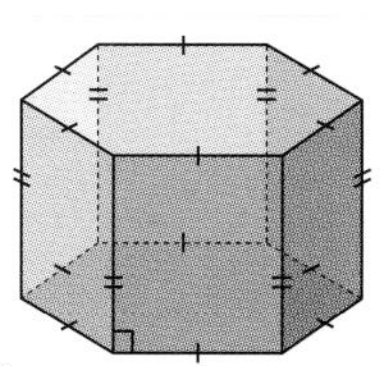

To construct this polyhedron,

a) how many equal pieces of drinking straw would you use for the bases?
b) how many equal pieces would you use for the vertical edges?
c) what shape would you make the vertical faces of the prism?

6. Use models to help you name each polyhedron and state the number of right angles it contains.

a)

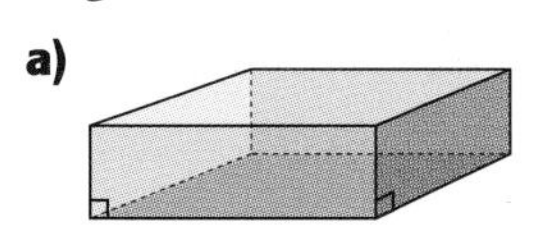

b)

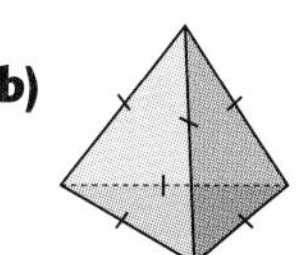

c)

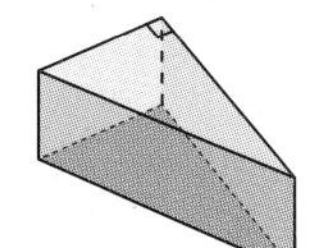

d)

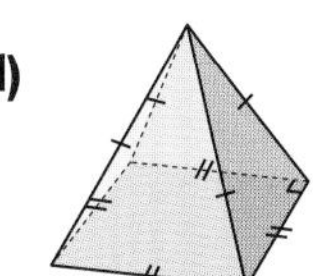

7. Look through several magazines for examples of polyhedra. Share your examples with a classmate. Describe the types of polyhedra you found.

8.3 Solids, Shells, and Skeletons

Activity: Read the Statements

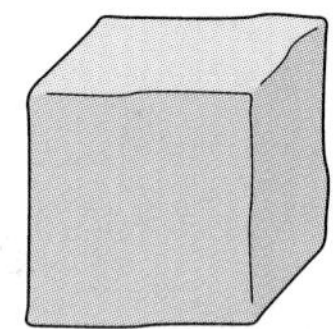

Peter formed a solid cube from plasticine.

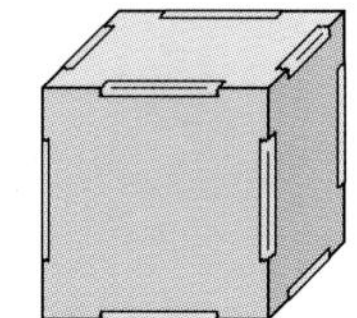

Maria made the shell of a cube from Bristol board.

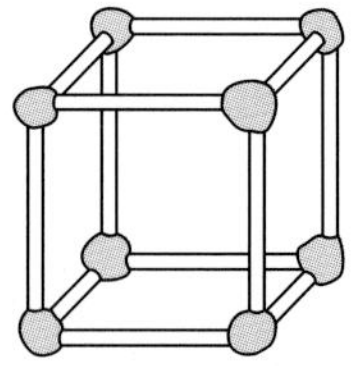

Sandro constructed the skeleton of a cube from sticks and plasticine.

Inquire

1. Work with a classmate to decide why Peter's cube is called a solid, Maria's cube is called a shell, and Sandro's cube is called a skeleton.

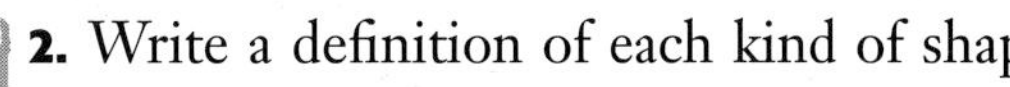

2. Write a definition of each kind of shape.

3. Name another object that is

a) a solid. **b)** a shell. **c)** a skeleton.

Practice

Identify each object as a solid, a shell, or a skeleton.

1.

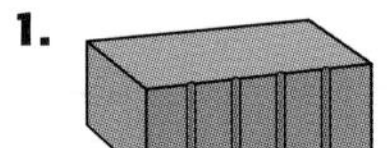

2.

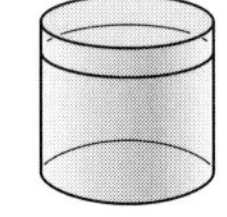

3.

4.

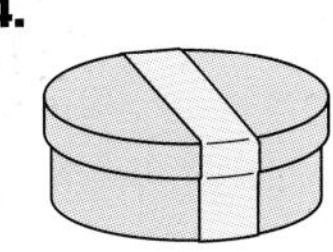

Problems and Applications

5. How many of each of these shapes are needed to form the shell of each polyhedron?

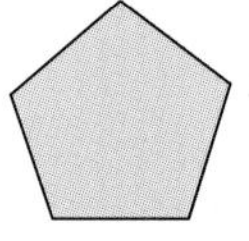

pentagon

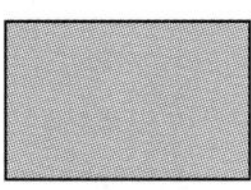

rectangle

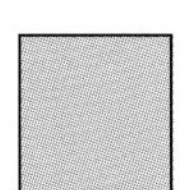

square

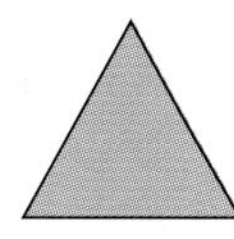

triangle

a) triangular prism **b)** cube
c) pentagonal pyramid **d)** rectangular prism
e) square pyramid **f)** pentagonal prism

6. Classify each object as a solid, a shell, or a skeleton. Explain how you know.

a) a book **b)** an apple
c) a bird cage **d)** a volleyball

7. With a partner, make and name the polyhedron whose skeleton is made from the following sticks.

a) six, 10 cm long
b) eight, 15 cm long; four, 8 cm long
c) ten, 12 cm long; five, 6 cm long
d) four, 10 cm long; four, 18 cm long
e) eight, 5 cm long; four, 12 cm long
f) six, 7 cm long; three, 10 cm long

8. Work with a group to make a chart. Name one object that can be described by each of the following. Compare with other groups.

a) a skeleton of a rectangular prism
b) a shell of a sphere
c) a solid cylinder
d) a shell of a cube
e) a skeleton of a triangular prism

8.4 Planes of Symmetry

Activity: Study the Statements

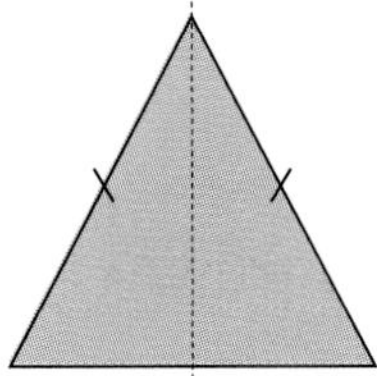

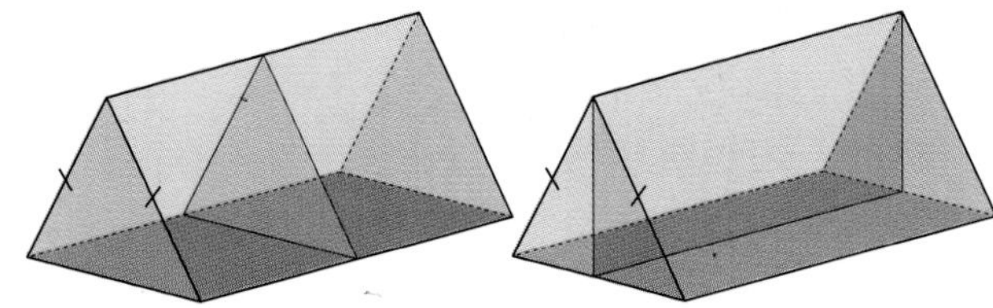

A line of symmetry divides the isosceles triangle into 2 congruent parts.

A plane of symmetry divides the isosceles triangular prism into 2 congruent parts.

Inquire

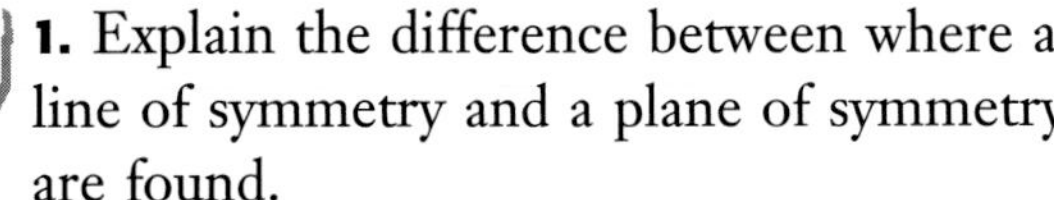

1. Explain the difference between where a line of symmetry and a plane of symmetry are found.

2. Explain why the isosceles triangular prism has 2 different planes of symmetry.

3. Sketch a scalene triangular prism and an equilateral triangular prism. How many planes of symmetry does each have? Compare your answers with a partner's.

Practice

Sketch each figure and show its planes of symmetry.

1. square pyramid

2. rectangular prism

3. hexagonal prism

4. cylinder

Problems and Applications

Sketch each object and show its planes of symmetry.

5.

6.

7.

8.

9.

10.

State whether each shaded region shows a way to cut the food into two congruent pieces. Explain.

11.

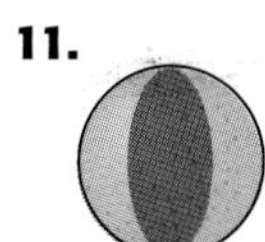

12.

13.

One-half of each model has been removed at the indicated plane of symmetry. Build the complete model with centimetre cubes and sketch the results on grid or dot paper.

14.

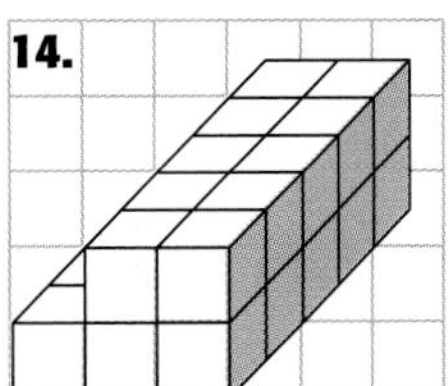

15.

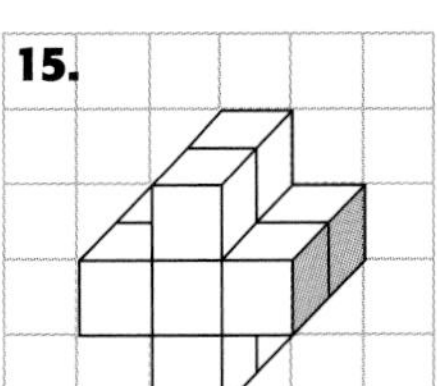

16. In a group, make several cubes of the same size from plasticine. Cut each one once to show the different planes of symmetry. Make a chart to show your results.

Designing with LOGO

This program draws a square whose sides are 70 units long.

```
TO SQUARE
REPEAT 4[FD 70 RT 90]
END
```

To save this program, hold down the Ctrl key and the C key. The computer will answer with **SQUARE DEFINED**. Now that the **SQUARE** program is stored, the **REPEAT** command can be used to make a design.

```
REPEAT 4[RT 90 SQUARE]
```

The above program instructs the computer to draw 4 squares, each rotated 90° from the previous starting direction of the turtle.

```
REPEAT 8[LT 45 SQUARE]
```

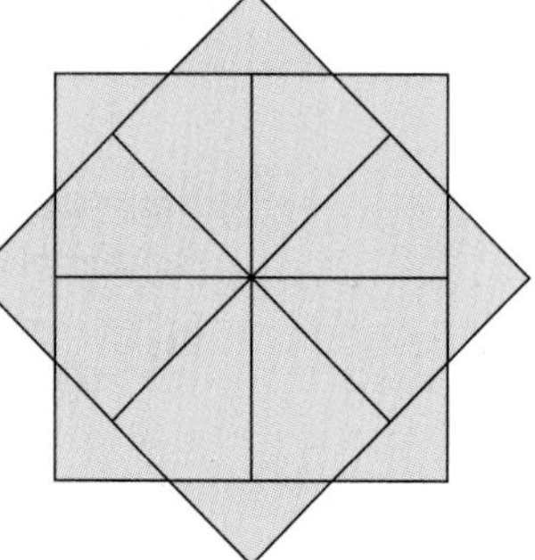

The above program draws 8 squares, each rotated 45° from the previous starting direction of the turtle.

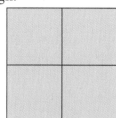

The following program draws a rhombus with sides 50 units long.

```
TO RHOMBUS
RT 30 FD 50
RT 60 FD 50
RT 120 FD 50
RT 60 FD 50
RT 90
END
```

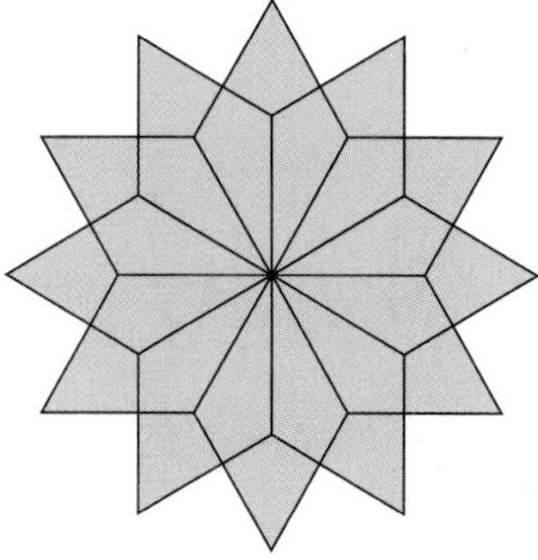

The following program draws the rhombus 12 times, each rotated 30° from the previous starting direction of the turtle.

```
REPEAT 12[RT 30 RHOMBUS]
```

Activity ❶

1. Write a program to draw the equilateral triangle.

2. Write a program to draw the triangle 6 times, each rotated 60° from the previous starting direction of the turtle. Draw the design.

3. Write a program to draw the triangle 12 times, each rotated 30° from the previous starting direction of the turtle. Draw the design.

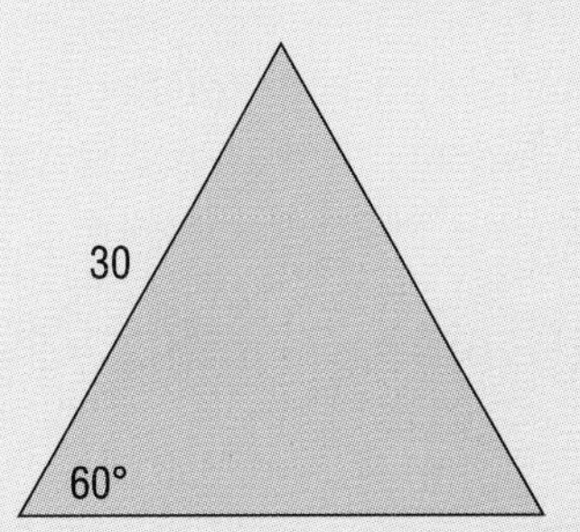

Activity ❷

1. Write a program to draw the figure. Draw the figure.

2. Write a program to draw the figure 8 times, each rotated 45° from the previous starting direction of the turtle. Draw the figure.

Activity ❸

Write a program to draw the design. Draw the design.

Activity ❹

Write a program to make a design of your own. Draw the design.

8.5 Nets of Polyhedra

When Praya bought a sweater for her father, the sales clerk gave her a flattened box to use for gift-wrapping it.

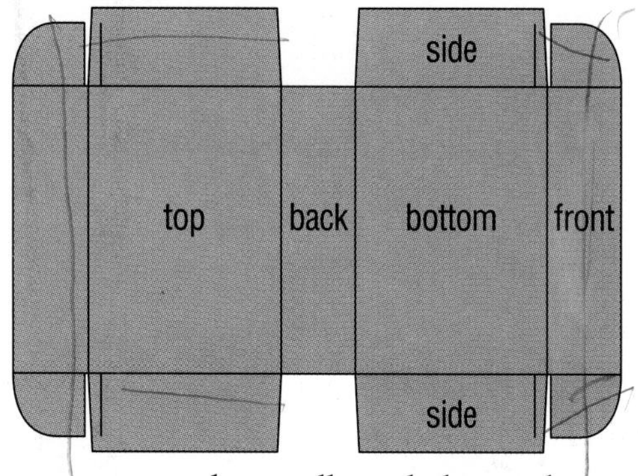

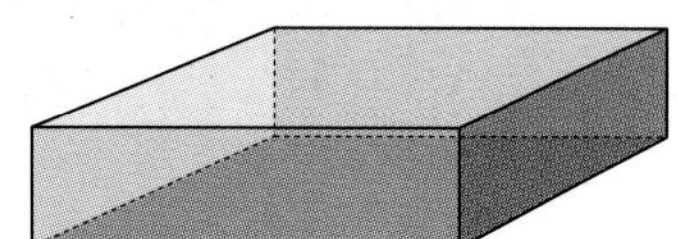

The pattern on the cardboard shows the parts of the box and extra flaps. This kind of pattern, which folds to form a polyhedron, is called a **net**.

When the cardboard is folded, it forms a rectangular prism.

Activity: Do an Experiment

Carefully take apart an empty cereal box by undoing the flaps. Lay it flat on your desk. Label the front, bottom, sides, top, and back of the box.

Inquire

1. Compare your net with the one shown above. Describe the similarities and differences.

2. Can any polyhedron be formed from its two-dimensional net? Explain.

3. What determines the positions of the faces in a net?

4. Take a different box. Sketch the predicted shape of its net. Open up the box and compare the actual net with your prediction.

Practice

Name the polyhedron formed from each net. List the edges that are joined when the net is assembled.

1.

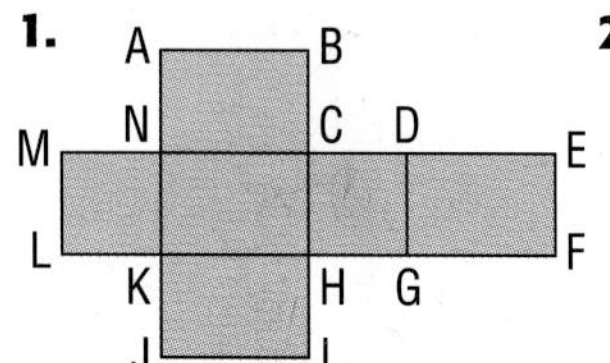

2.

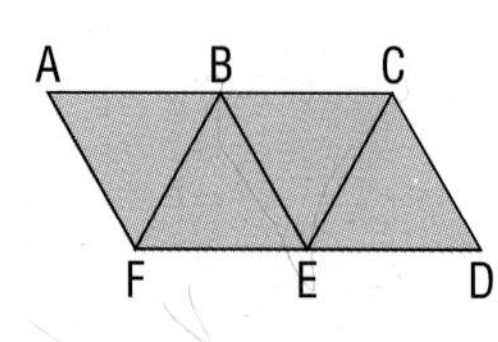

3.

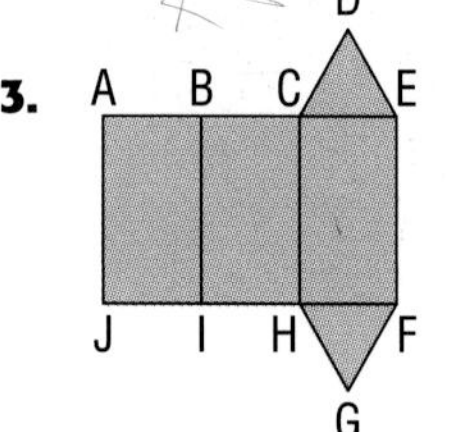

4.

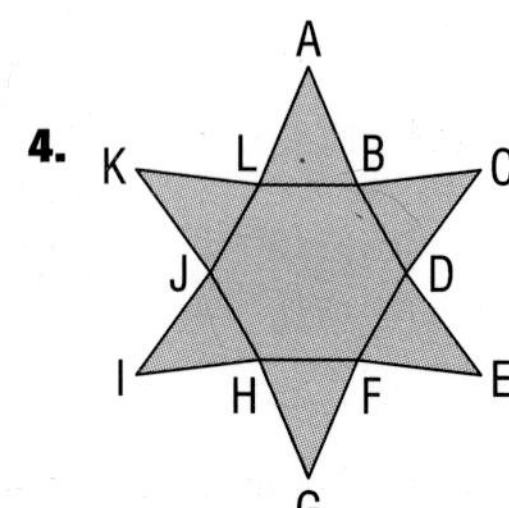

5. A square pyramid has a square base and 4 triangular faces.

  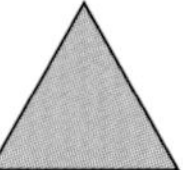 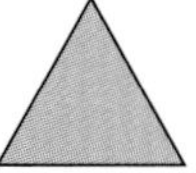 

Draw the net of a square pyramid.

6. A pentagonal prism has 2 pentagonal bases and 5 rectangular faces.

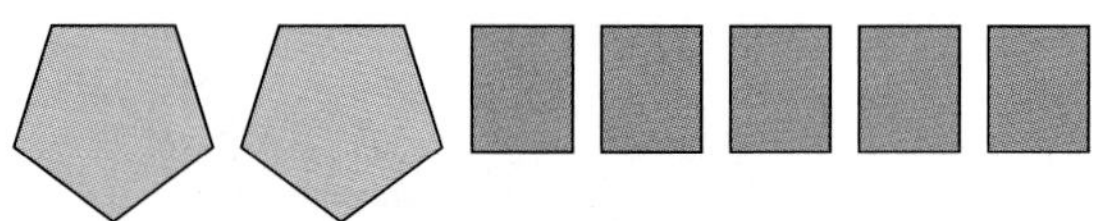

Draw the net of a pentagonal prism.

Draw 2 possible nets for each of the following polyhedra. Count the number of edges that must be folded to form the model from each net. Count the number of edges that need to be sealed. Are the two numbers the same for each model?

7.

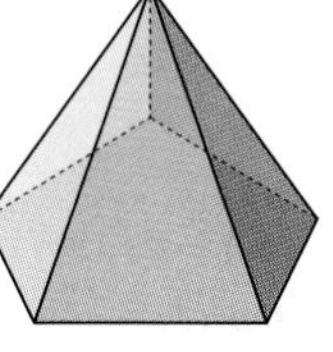

8.

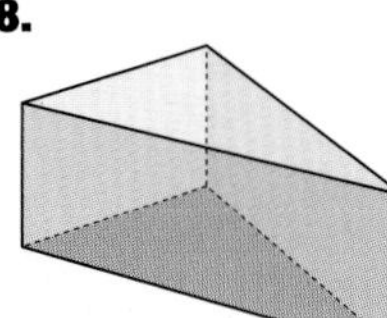

9.

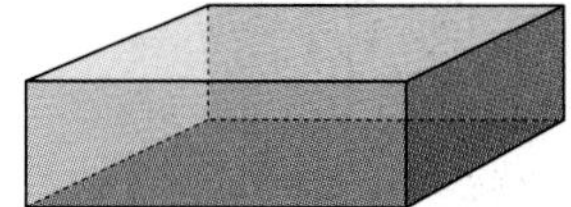

Problems and Applications

10. The plastic cube in the playground has identical holes in two opposite sides.

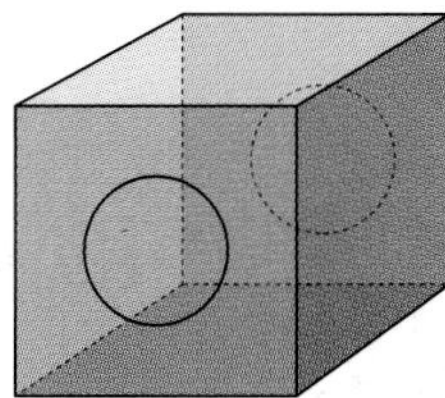

Draw a net of the cube. Show the positions of the holes.

11. With a partner, draw on 2-cm grid paper as many ways as you can find for connecting 6 identical squares. They must be joined along complete edges.

YES NO

Compare your results with those of other pairs. Cut out your arrangements. Predict, then determine which ones fold to form a cube. Record your results in a chart.

12. Work in a group. Collect several boxes in the shape of rectangular prisms. Seal all the edges. Investigate the smallest number of cuts you must make to open a rectangular prism to show its net. Use sketches to help describe your findings.

13. Design a polyhedral package for a product of your choice. Draw a net that will allow the package to be made. Explain why you chose your package design and how you chose the net. Compare your designs with your classmates'.

PATTERN POWER

1. Copy the chart. Use pictures or models to help you complete the chart with the number of vertices, V, number of faces, F, and number of edges, E.

Polyhedron	V	F	E	V + F	V + F − E
cube					
triangular prism					
square pyramid					
pentagonal prism					
triangular pyramid					

2. Describe the pattern in the chart.

3. Use 2 additional polyhedra. Is the pattern true for them?

8.6 Surface Area

Activity: Measure the Container

To work out the cost of making a package, a manufacturer needs to know the amount of material needed. It is useful to know the sum of the areas of the faces of the package. The sum of the areas of the faces of a three-dimensional figure is called the **surface area** of the figure. Consider the surface area of a cereal box.

Inquire

1. How many faces does the box have?

2. List any pairs of faces with the same area.

3. Measure the height, length, and width of the box.

4. Calculate the area of each face.

5. Calculate the surface area of the box.

6. Have you accounted for all the cardboard in the box? If not, describe how to improve the method.

One way to calculate the surface area of a figure is to use a net of the figure.

Example

The pyramid of Khufu was built around 2500 B.C. Calculate its surface area.

Solution

Draw a net of the pyramid. The surface area includes the area of the base, which is 230 m by 230 m. The sides are 4 identical triangles, each 186 m high and with a base of 230 m. Calculate the areas of the base and the 4 sides, then add.

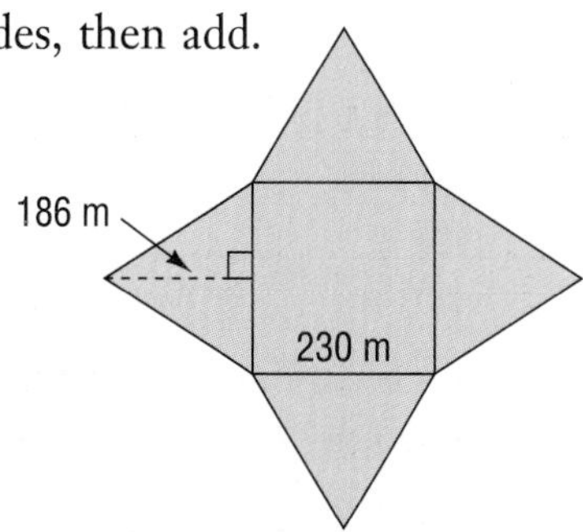

Area of base	$230 \times 230 = 52\ 900$
Area of side	$\frac{1}{2} \times 230 \times 186 = 21\ 390$
Area of 4 sides	$4 \times 21\ 390 = 85\ 560$

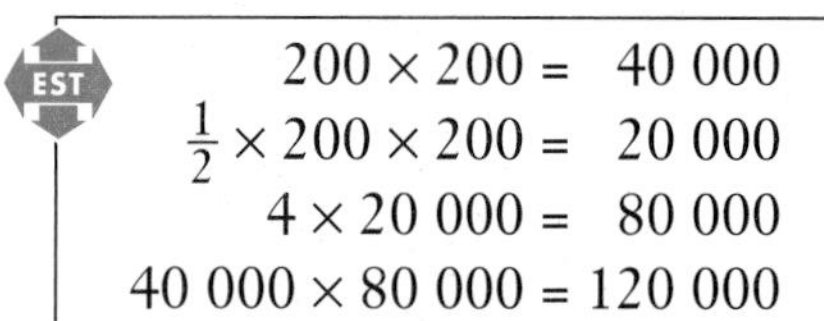

EST

$200 \times 200 = 40\ 000$

$\frac{1}{2} \times 200 \times 200 = 20\ 000$

$4 \times 20\ 000 = 80\ 000$

$40\ 000 \times 80\ 000 = 120\ 000$

Surface area $\quad 52\ 900 + 85\ 560 = 138\ 460$

The surface area is 138 460 m^2.

How could you use subtraction to check your answer?

Practice

Calculate the surface area of each rectangular prism.

1.

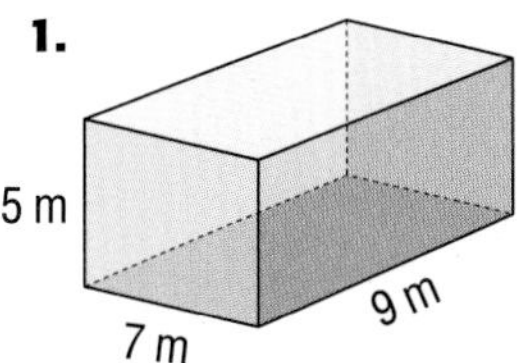

2.

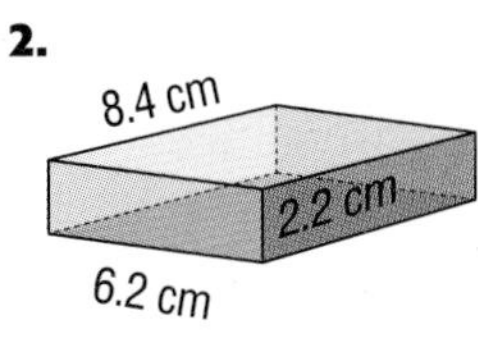

Calculate the surface area of each pyramid.

3.

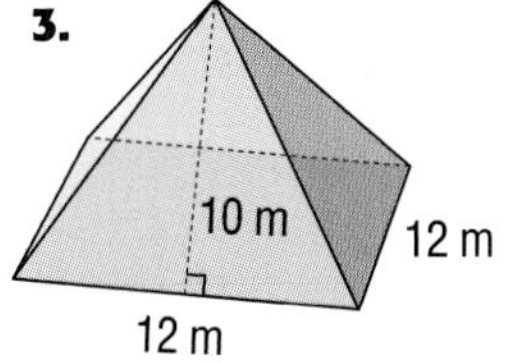

4.

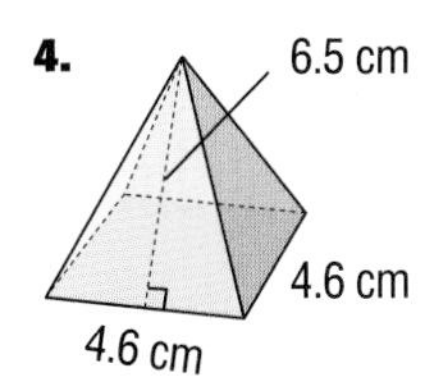

Calculate the surface area of each triangular prism.

5. **6.**

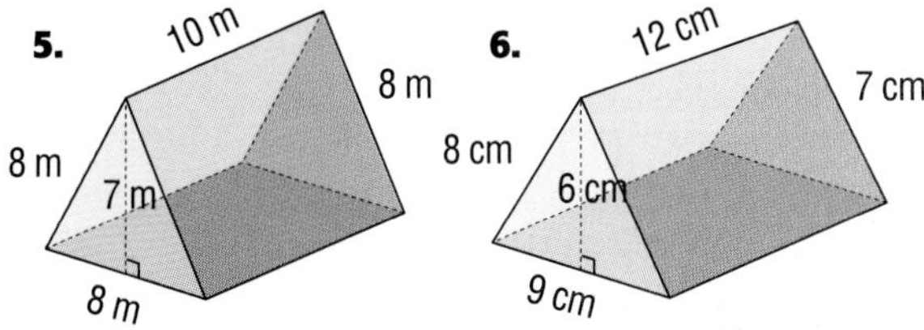

Problems and Applications

7. a) Calculate the surface area of the rectangular prism.

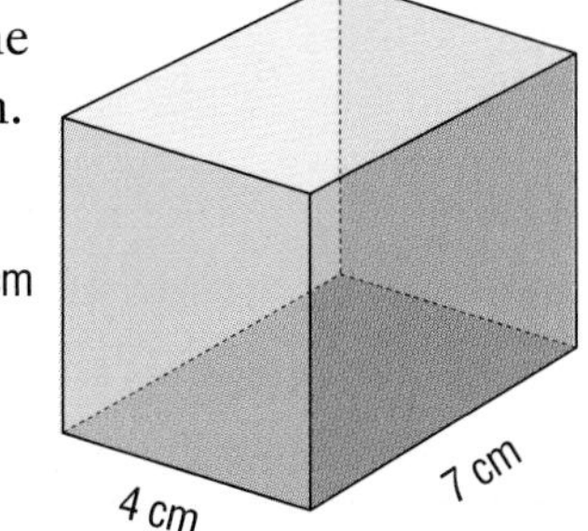

b) Double each dimension, then calculate the surface area of the new prism.

c) What happens to the surface area of a rectangular prism when the dimensions are doubled?

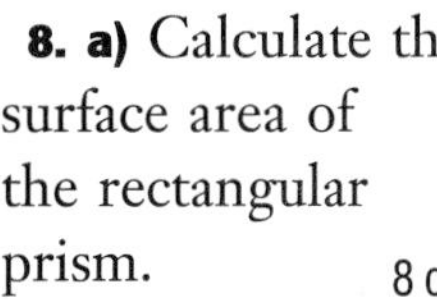

8. a) Calculate the surface area of the rectangular prism.

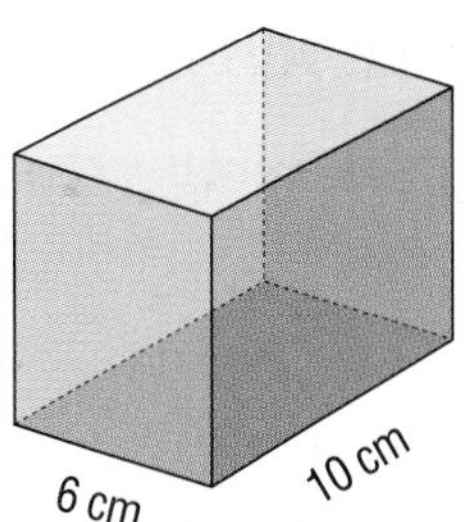

b) Halve each dimension, then calculate the surface area of the new prism.

c) What happens to the surface area of a rectangular prism when the dimensions are halved?

9. a) From your answers to questions 7 and 8, state what happens to the surface area of a polyhedron when each of the dimensions is multiplied by the same number.

b) Test your conclusion on a polyhedron of your choice.

10. The skeleton of a cube is made from 60 cm of wire. Cardboard faces are added to form a cubic shell. What is the surface area of the shell?

11. a) What is the surface area of a solid cube with 10-cm sides?

b) The solid cube is cut into 2 equal pieces along a plane of symmetry parallel to a face of the cube. What is the total surface area of the 2 new pieces?

c) What happens to the total surface area when any solid polyhedron is cut into smaller pieces? Explain.

NUMBER POWER

There are 4 numbers less than 100 that each have exactly 3 different factors, including themselves and 1. What are the numbers?

8.7 Regular Polyhedra: The Platonic Solids

Recall that a regular polygon has all sides equal.
Here are a few examples.

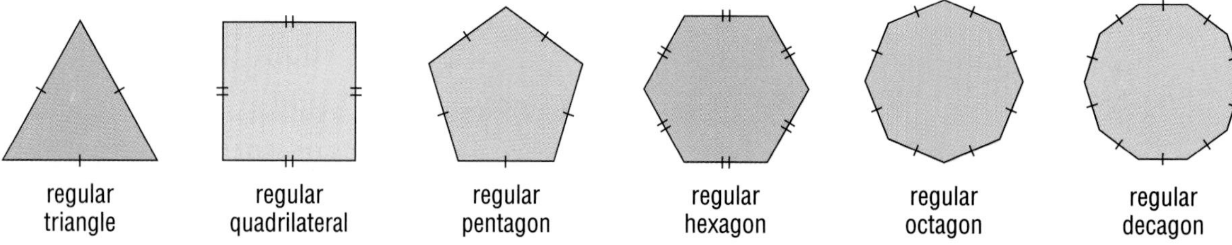

Activity: Learn About Regular Polyhedra

In a **regular polyhedron**, all the faces are congruent regular polygons.
There are only 5 regular polyhedra.

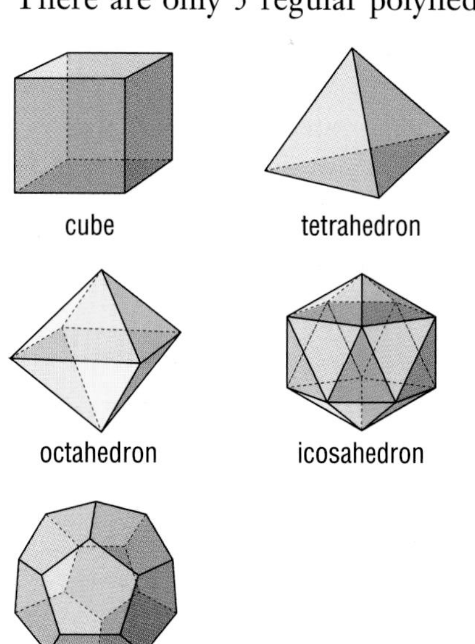

The regular polyhedra are called the **Platonic solids**. They are named after the Greek scholar Plato who discovered that there are only 5 of them. Plato set up the world's first academy. It was a school where he brought together experts in all branches of learning to teach and do research. The school was in an olive grove near Athens. The land had once been owned by a man named Akademus, a Greek hero in the Trojan War.

Inquire

1. How many faces does a tetrahedron have?

2. How many faces does an octahedron have?

3. What do the prefixes "tetra-" and "octa-" mean?

4. What determines the name of a regular polyhedron?

5. Use your answer to question 4 to give another name for a cube.

6. Write a description of each regular polyhedron.

7. Why do you think Plato's school was called an "academy"?

Practice

Use the nets in the following questions to build a set of Platonic solids from heavy cardboard. In each case, flaps for gluing are shown.

1. The cube is made from 6 squares.

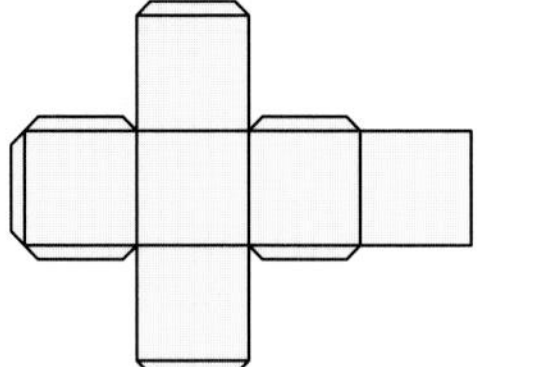

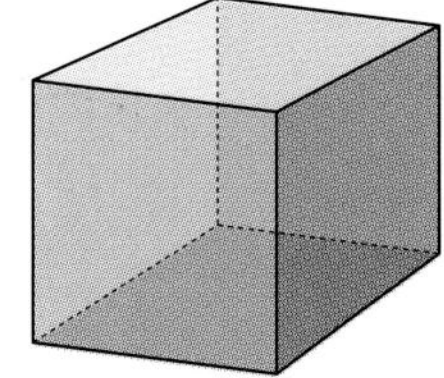

How many squares meet at each vertex?

2. The tetrahedron is made from 4 equilateral triangles.

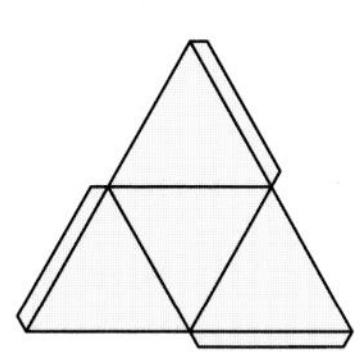

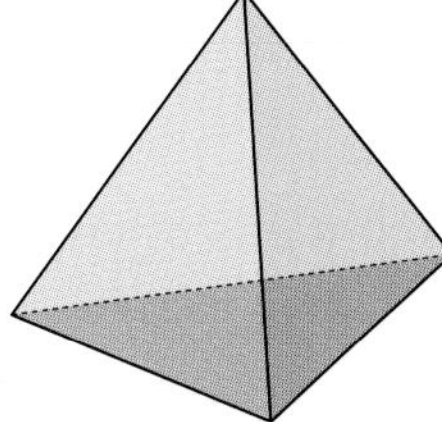

How many triangles meet at each vertex?

3. An octahedron is made from 8 equilateral triangles.

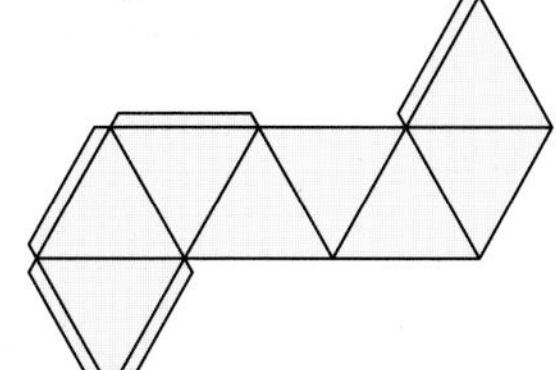

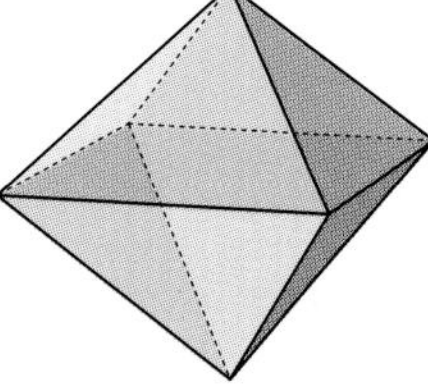

How many triangles meet at each vertex?

4. An icosahedron is made from 20 equilateral triangles.

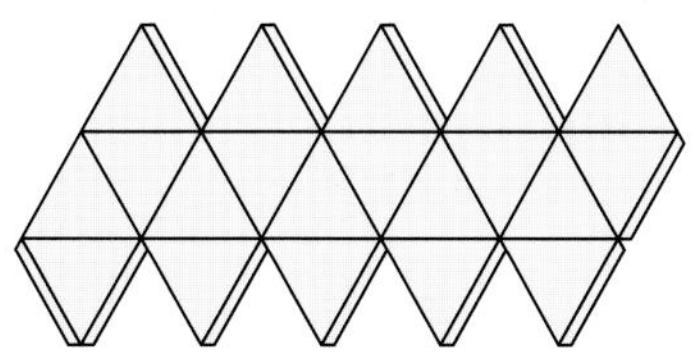

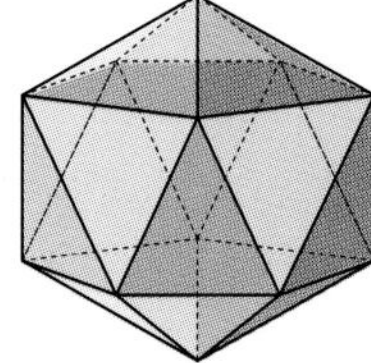

How many triangles meet at each vertex?

5. A dodecahedron is made from 12 regular pentagons.

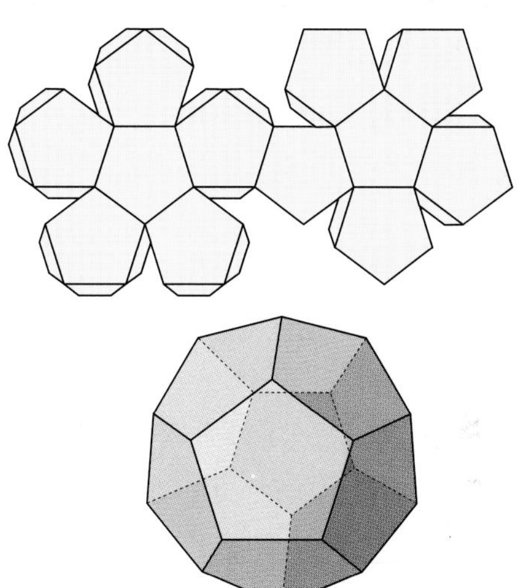

How many pentagons meet at each vertex?

Problems and Applications

6. What are the meanings of the prefixes "dodeca-" and "icosa-"? Explain.

7. If the faces of a tetrahedron and an octahedron are congruent, how do the surface areas of the 2 polyhedra compare?

8. If the faces of an octahedron and an icosahedron are congruent, how do the surface areas of the 2 polyhedra compare?

9. With a classmate, decorate a set of Platonic solids and make a mobile.

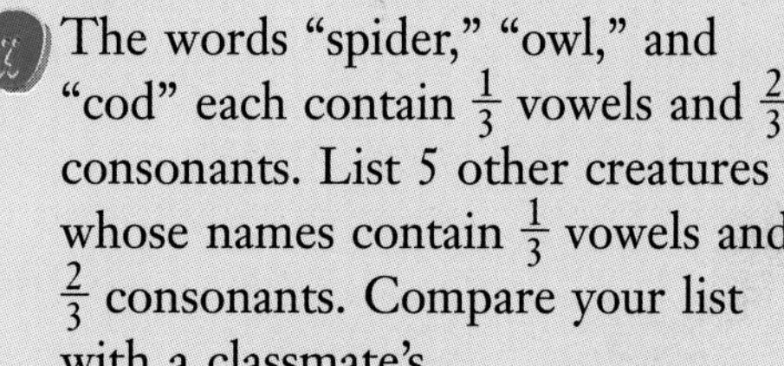

WORD POWER

The words "spider," "owl," and "cod" each contain $\frac{1}{3}$ vowels and $\frac{2}{3}$ consonants. List 5 other creatures whose names contain $\frac{1}{3}$ vowels and $\frac{2}{3}$ consonants. Compare your list with a classmate's.

8.8 Perspectives of Objects

We can view three-dimensional objects from several different directions or **perspectives**. The image we see depends on the point of view.

Activity: Study the Pictures

An advertising brochure showed a new model of a jeep from 3 perspectives.

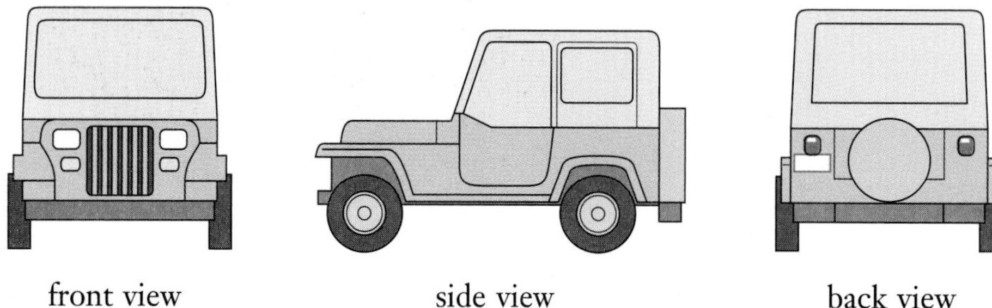

front view side view back view

Inquire

1. Sketch the jeep as it might look from the top.

2. Sketch a bus as you might see it from different perspectives if you were in a car.

3. Sketch a cube as you would see it from different perspectives. Include some views that are not perpendicular to faces of the cube.

4. Look at several polyhedra from different perspectives. Compare your observations with your classmates'. Can one polyhedron look the same as a different polyhedron if you change your point of view? If so, sketch examples.

Practice

The objects are viewed from above. Name each object.

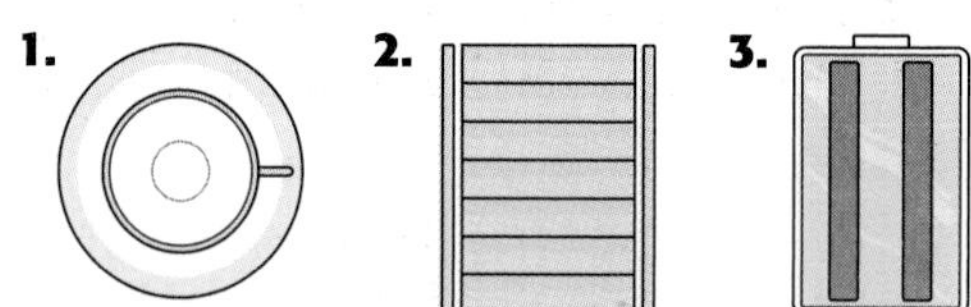

4. Sketch the house as it would look from each view.

a) front

b) side

c) top

Draw the front view, top view, and two side views of the following objects. The front of each object is shaded.

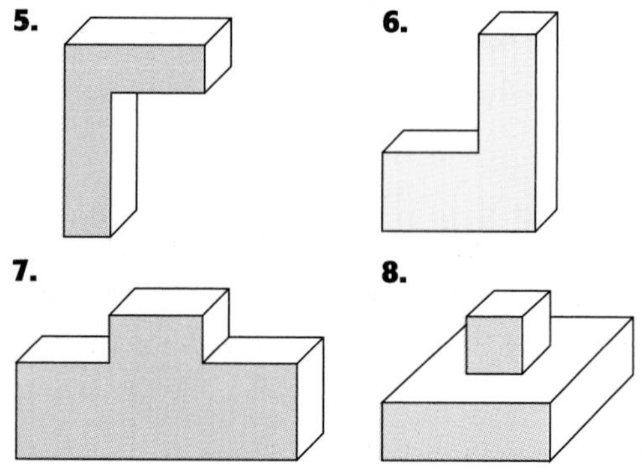

Problems and Applications

Draw a front view, side view, and top view of each object.

9.

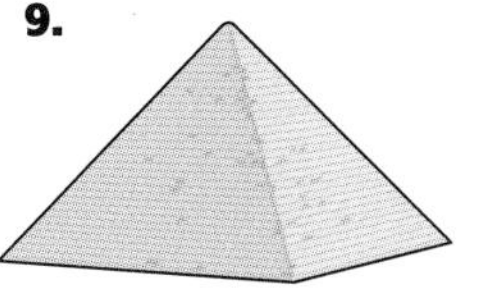

10.

11.

12.

13.

14.

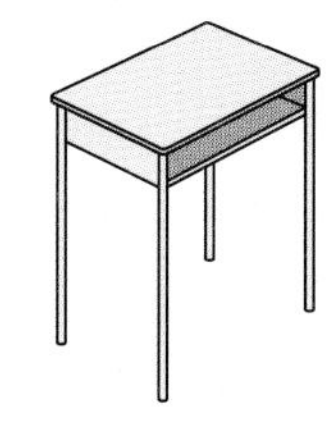

15. Sketch the top view of your classroom, as if it did not have a ceiling or roof.

16. The diagrams show the net of a cube and a view of the cube from one perspective.

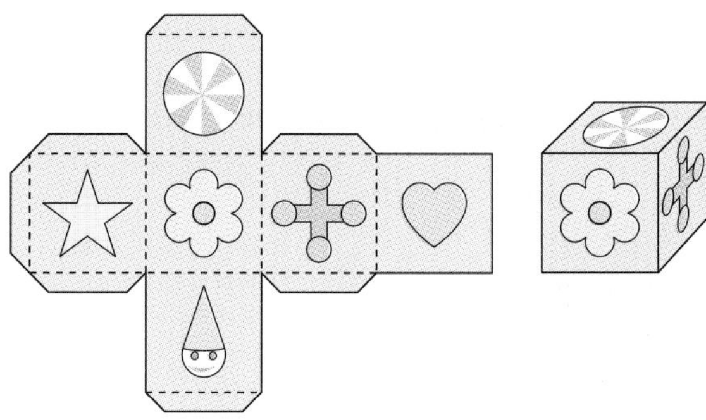

Copy the net, including the pictures, and construct the cube. Place the cube as shown, with the flower at the front. Draw the cube viewed from

a) above **b)** below **c)** the left
d) the right **e)** the back

The diagrams show the front view, side view, and top view of the same object. Make a sketch that shows the overall shape of the object. Compare your sketches with your classmates'.

17.

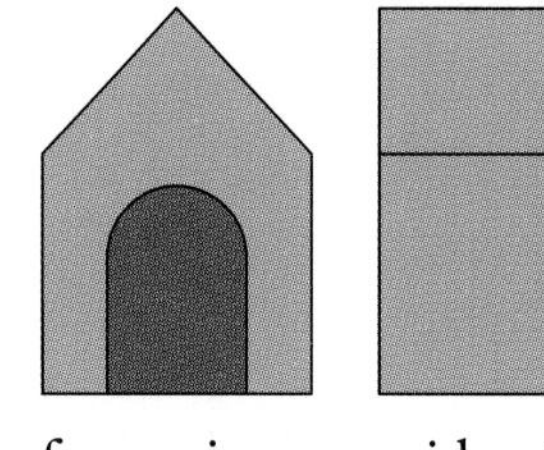

front view

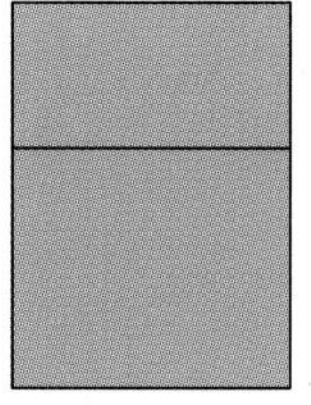

side view

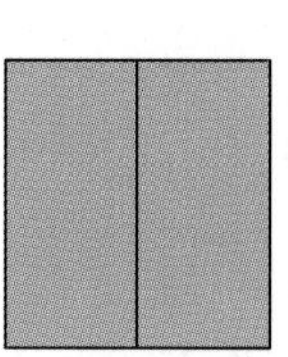

top view

18.

front view

side view

top view

19. Work with a partner. Sketch the front view, back view, and top view of your school. Compare your sketches with your classmates'.

LOGIC POWER

Nina, Mary, Dan, and Pierre are seated at a square table. One likes swimming, another bowling, another tennis, and another skating. The bowler is across from Dan. The skater is on Nina's left. Mary and Pierre are next to each other. A girl is on the tennis player's left. Act out the scene to find out which sport each person likes.

Estimating and Measuring Volume

Length is the distance between 2 points.
Length has 1 dimension.
Length is measured in linear units.
The length of the line is 3 cm.

3 cm

Area is the measure of a surface.
Area has 2 dimensions.
Area is measured in square units.
The area of the rectangle is 6 cm^2.

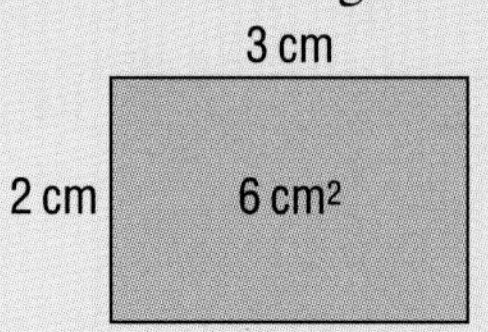

Volume is the amount of space filled by an object. Volume has 3 dimensions. Volume is measured in cubic units. The volume of the rectangular prism is 9 cm^3.

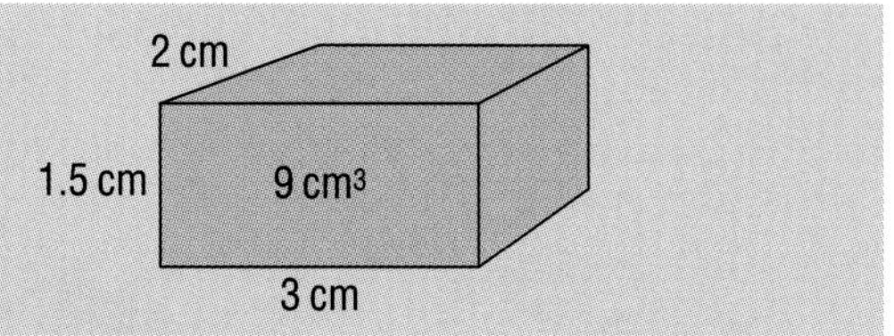

Activity ❶

A centicube has a volume of 1 cm^3. Choose the best estimate for the volume of each of the following. Explain your choice to a classmate.

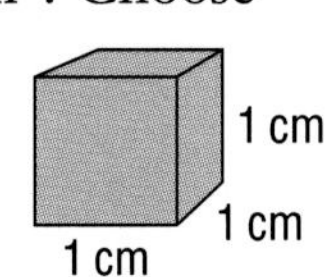

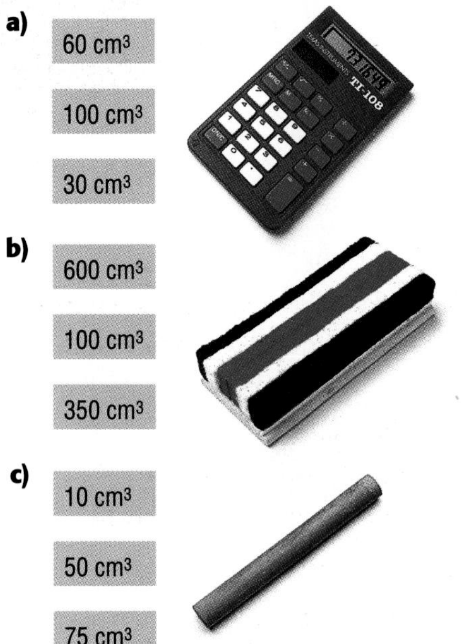

Activity ❷

1. Construct a cube from a net of cardboard, with each face 10 cm by 10 cm.

2. How many centicubes would you need to fill the cube you constructed?

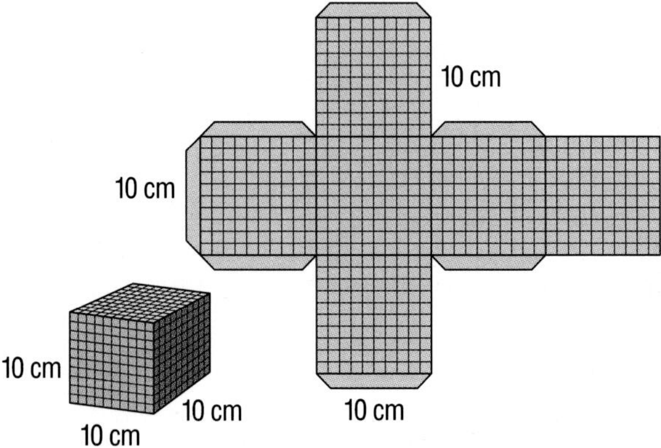

3. Use your cube to estimate the volume of

a) your desk
b) a bookshelf
c) a waste basket
d) a filing cabinet
e) a box of tissues

4. Describe how you obtained each estimate.

5. Compare your estimates with your classmates'.

Activity ❸

Construct each object from centicubes.
Determine the volume of each object.

a)

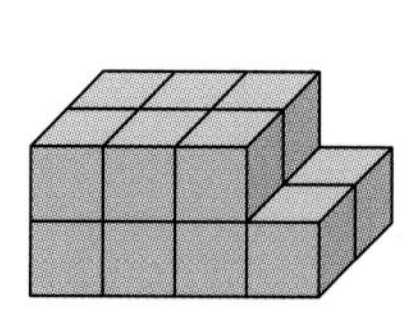

b)

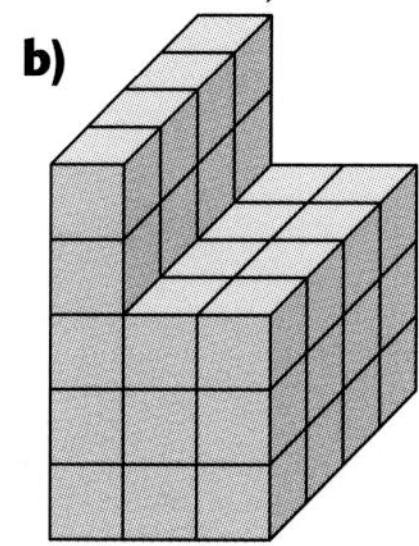

c)

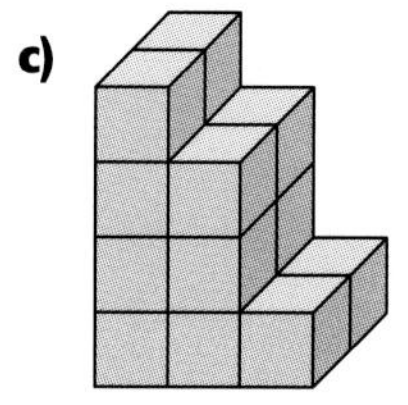

d)

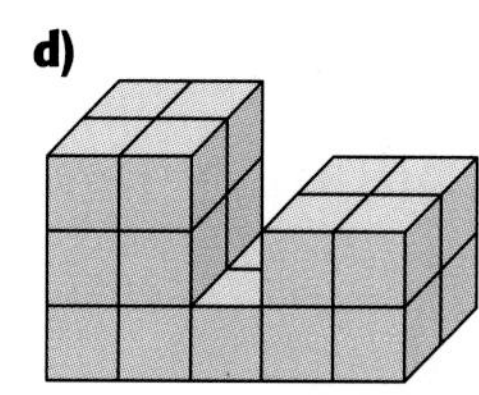

Activity ❹

When you cannot measure the dimensions of an object, you can measure its volume by finding the volume of water it displaces.

1. Fill an overflow can with water. Place an irregular object, such as a small stone, in the can. Catch the water the stone displaces and pour it into a graduated cylinder. Measure the volume of displaced water to find the volume of the object. For example, if the stone displaces 8 mL of water, the volume of the stone is 8 cm^3.

2. Estimate, then determine the volumes of several objects by displacement.

Activity ❺

1. Fasten metre-sticks together with rubber bands or tape to form a 1-m^3 skeleton.

2. How many centicubes would be needed to fill the skeleton?

3. Estimate the volume of each of the following in cubic metres.

a) a teacher's desk **b)** your classroom
c) a refrigerator **d)** the gymnasium
e) a school bus

4. Describe how you obtained each estimate.

5. Compare your estimates with your classmates'.

Activity ❻

1. If you tried to build a cube with a volume of 1 m^3 from centicubes, how many would you need?

2. Express in cubic centimetres.

a) 2 m^3 **b)** 3.25 m^3 **c)** 1.4 m^3
d) 0.7 m^3 **e)** 4.38 m^3 **f)** 0.06 m^3

3. Express in cubic metres.

a) 15 000 000 cm^3 **b)** 6000 cm^3
c) 4 500 000 cm^3 **d)** 75 000 cm^3
e) 2800 cm^3 **f)** 930 000 cm^3

8.9 Volumes of Prisms

Ms. Petrie bought a bag of centicubes for the classroom. Each cube measures 1 cm on every edge. The volume of each cube is 1 cm^3.

Activity: Study the Picture

Ms. Petrie asked Juanita to store as many cubes as possible in a clear plastic box. The picture shows the result.

Inquire

1. How many cubes covered the base of the box?

2. How many layers of cubes were there?

3. How many cubes were in each layer?

4. How many cubes did Juanita use to fill the box?

5. What is the volume of the box?

6. Use the words "length," "width," and "height" in a sentence that explains how the volume of a rectangular prism can be calculated. Rewrite your sentence using symbols.

Example

Calculate the volume of the triangular prism.

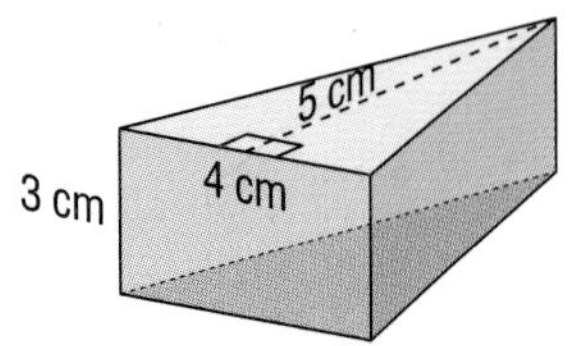

Solution

The volume of a prism is the area of the base multiplied by the height.

Area of base $\frac{1}{2} \times 4 \times 5 = 10$

Volume $10 \times 3 = 30$

The volume is 30 cm^2.

Practice

Each solid is made from centicubes. Determine the dimensions of each figure and calculate its volume.

1. **2.**

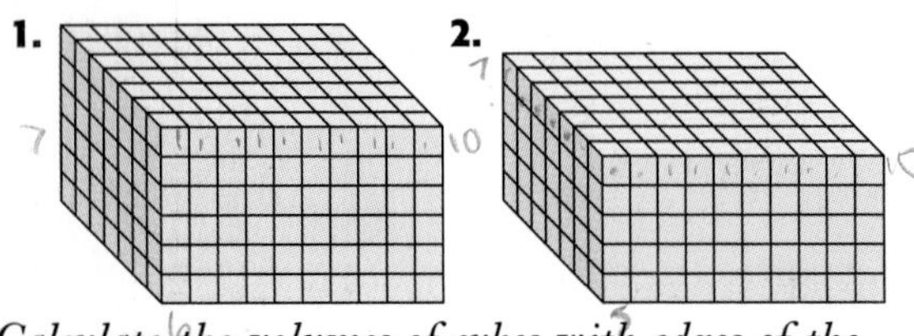

Calculate the volumes of cubes with edges of the following lengths.

3. 2 cm **4.** 5 cm **5.** 8 cm **6.** 12 cm

7. a) Draw the net and construct the triangular prism.

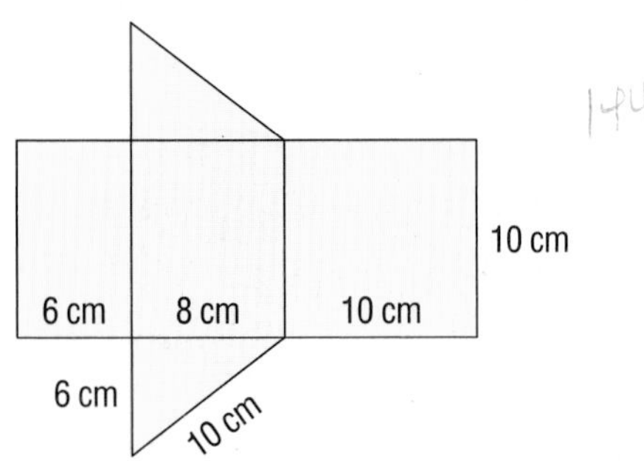

b) Calculate the volume of the prism.

Problems and Applications

Some of Anton's building blocks are triangular prisms. Calculate the volume of each. The base of each is shaded.

8. **9.**

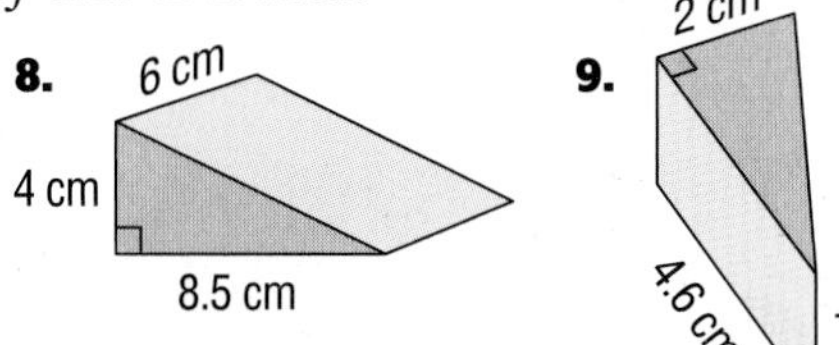

10. **11.**

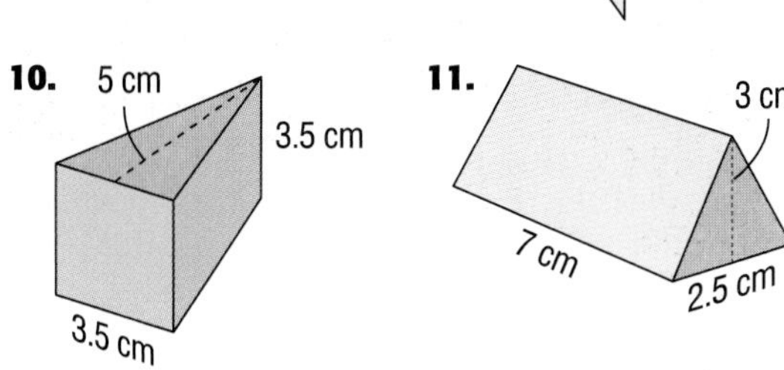

Calculate the largest volume that each gift box can hold.

12. **13.**

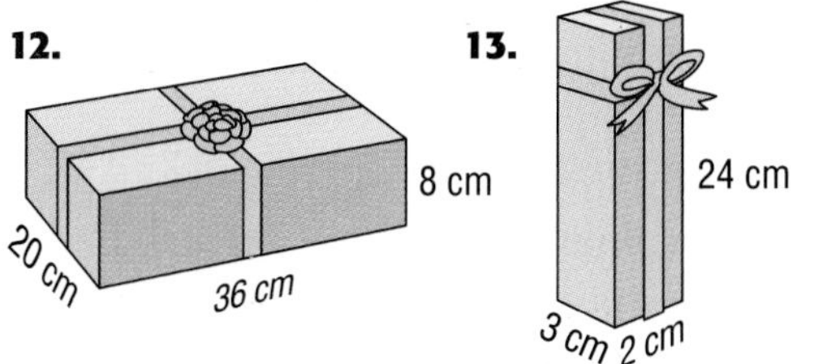

14. **15.**

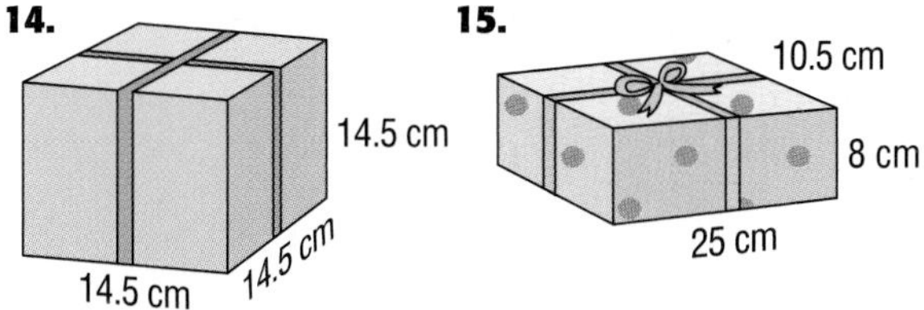

16. A display of toys in a store is 3 boxes long, 4 boxes wide, and 3 boxes high. Each box is 12 cm long, 8.5 cm wide, and 10 cm high.

a) What is the volume of each box?
b) What is the total volume of the display?

17. Construct and sketch 2 different rectangular prisms, each with a volume of 1000 cm^3. Label each sketch with the dimensions of the prism.

18. Each piece in a set of triangular prisms is the same size. A second and third prism are built from the pieces.

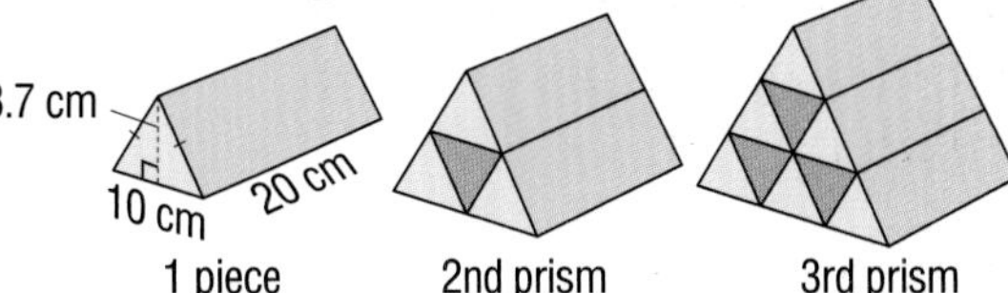

a) What is the volume of one piece?
b) What are the dimensions of the second and third prisms? What is the volume of each?
c) Sketch the fourth prism. State its dimensions and calculate its volume.
d) Describe the pattern in the 4 prisms.

19. Work with a partner. Measure the following objects to the nearest centimetre. Calculate the volume of each. Record your answers in a chart.

a) this book
b) a tissue box
c) a bookshelf
d) your desk

LOGIC POWER

A food company needs a box for its new product, Nut-n-Honey Pieces. The company orders a box that will hold 50 cm^3 of the product.

a) If the box maker uses whole number dimensions, what are all the possible sets of dimensions for the box?
b) Which box would you choose? Give reasons for your decision.
c) What additional information might affect your decision?

Estimating and Measuring Mass

The **mass** of an object is a measure of the quantity of matter it is made up of. Mass is measured in milligrams, grams, kilograms, and tonnes.

1000 mg = 1 g
1000 g = 1 kg
1000 kg = 1 t

Activity ❶

A straight pin has a mass of 100 mg.

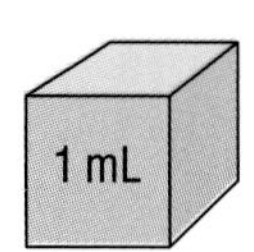

One millilitre of water has a mass of 1 g.

A roll of breath mints has a mass of 20 g.

A hamburger patty has a mass of 100 g.

Estimate the mass of each of the following.
Explain your reasoning. Compare your estimates with your classmates'.

a) granola bar **b)** paper clip **c)** pencil **d)** container of yogurt **e)** paperback book

Activity ❷

1. Use a scale to find your mass in kilograms.
2. Find your mass while holding a chair.
3. Subtract your mass to find the mass of the chair.
4. Use the same method to calculate the mass of

a) a stack of 6 books **b)** a school bag
c) a tape recorder **d)** a package of foolscap paper
e) something of your choice

Activity ❸

A 747 jumbo jet has a maximum take-off mass of about 350 t. Research the masses of these large objects.

a) African elephant **b)** tour bus
c) oil tanker **d)** Saturn V rocket
e) blue whale **f)** the *Silver Dart*

Activity ❹

Express each mass in the given unit.

a) 1500 mg = ■ g **b)** 3750 g = ■ kg
c) 4.6 g = ■ mg **d)** 2.8 t = ■ kg
e) 12 900 kg = ■ t **f)** 0.95 kg = ■ g

Estimating and Measuring Capacity

1000 mL = 1 L

The **capacity** of a container is the greatest volume it will hold. Capacity is measured in litres and millilitres. If the volume of the inside of a container is 1 cm^3, the container can hold up to 1 mL.

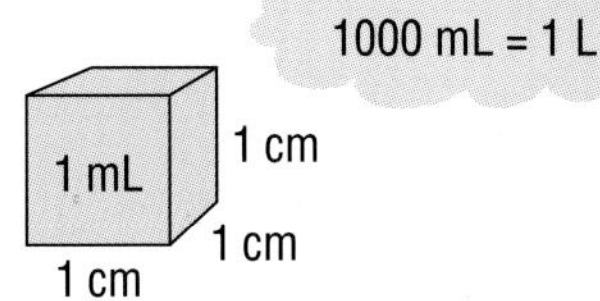

Activity ❶

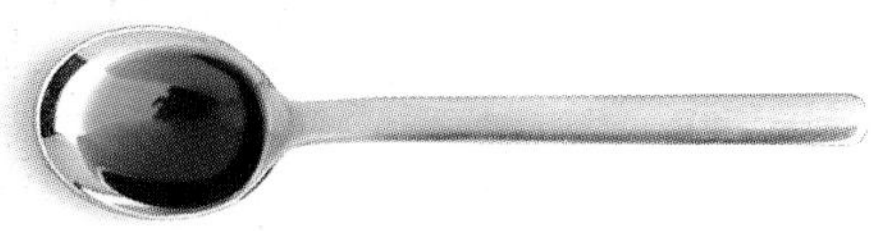

A teaspoon holds about 5 mL.

A measuring cup holds 250 mL.

Choose the best estimate for each capacity.

a)

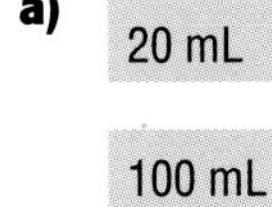

20 mL

100 mL

2 mL

b)

35 mL

135 mL

350 mL

c)

300 mL

100 mL

500 mL

Activity ❷

1. Use an empty 2-L milk or juice carton.

a) Measure the length and width of the base.
b) Mark the side in 1-cm units up to 10 cm.
c) Cut the carton just above the 10-cm mark.

When filled to the 10-cm mark, your container holds 1000 mL or 1 L.

2. Locate an example of each container, below. Sketch it, label its dimensions, and use your litre measure to estimate its capacity.

a) fish tank **b)** bucket **c)** pop bottle
d) paint can **e)** container for liquid detergent

Activity ❸

1. Do some research to find each capacity.

a) your bath tub
b) an Olympic swimming pool
c) your refrigerator
d) your home hot water tank

2. Describe how you found your results.

Activity ❹

1. Express each capacity in the given unit.

a) 500 mL = ■ L **b)** 4 L = ■ mL
c) 12.5 L = ■ mL **d)** 80 mL = ■ L
e) 9635 mL = ■ L **f)** 1.208 L = ■ mL

2. If 1 cm^3 = 1 mL and 1000 mL = 1 L, how many litres equal 1 m^3?

8.10 Volume, Capacity, and Mass

Activity: Look for Examples

The capacity of a container is the greatest volume it will hold. Capacity is measured in millilitres and litres. Large capacities may be expressed in kilolitres.

1000 mL = 1 L
1000 L = 1 kL

Inquire

1. Work with a group to list as many types of containers as possible that measure in units of capacity.

2. List products that are sold in units of capacity.

3. Compare your lists with those of your classmates.

4. Do the products that are sold in units of capacity have anything in common?

Activity: Study the Information

The mass of an object is a measure of the quantity of matter it is made up of. Mass is measured in milligrams, grams, kilograms, and tonnes.

1000 mg = 1 g
1000 g = 1 kg
1000 kg = 1 t

There is a special relationship between the volume and mass of water. Consider the situation in which the following containers are filled with water. Note that the diagrams are not drawn to scale.

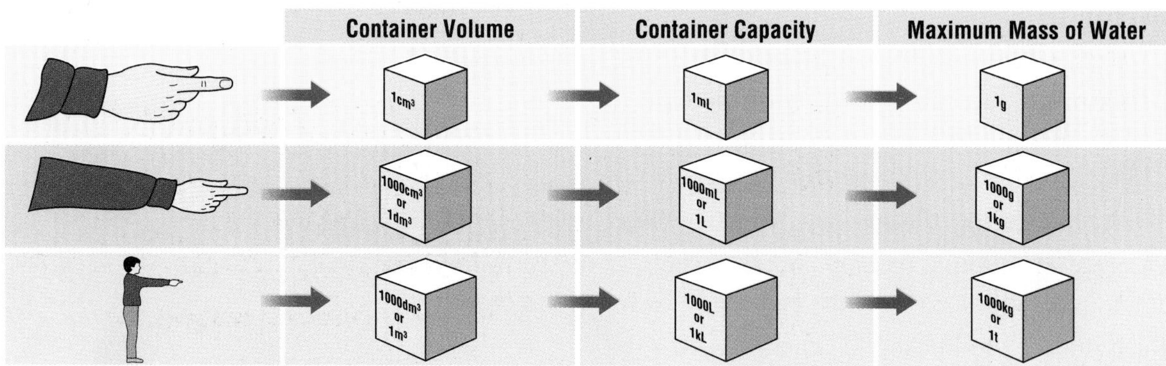

Inquire

1. Divide a large piece of chart paper into 4 sections, headed "milligram," "gram," "kilogram," and "tonne." In each section, sketch as many different objects as you can that are measured in the given unit of mass. Display your chart with those of other groups.

2. What is the capacity of a container whose volume is 250 cm^3?

3. What mass of water could the 250-cm^3 container hold?

4. In your own words, distinguish the meanings of the terms "volume" and "capacity."

Practice

Express in litres.

1. 250 mL **2.** 50 mL **3.** 2400 mL
4. 5000 mL **5.** 3 kL **6.** 4.5 kL

Express in millilitres.

7. 3 L **8.** 8.5 L **9.** 0.9 L
10. 35 L **11.** 12.65 L **12.** 2.08 L

Express in grams.

13. 4 kg **14.** 125 mg **15.** 2500 mg
16. 0.3 kg **17.** 1.75 kg **18.** 1360 mg

Express in kilograms.

19. 8000 g **20.** 5 t **21.** 250 g
22. 0.15 t **23.** 75 g **24.** 50 000 mg

Problems and Applications

What units of measurement are used for each of the following products?

25.

26.

27.

28.

29.

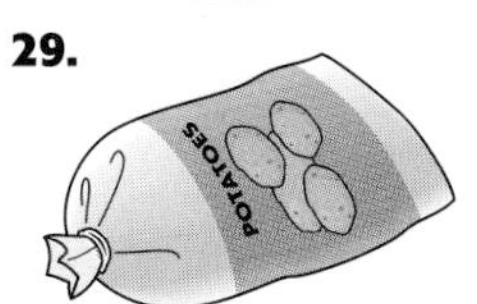

30.

31. A medium-sized apple has a mass of 60 g. About how many apples make up 1 kg?

32. A case of pop contains twenty-four 280-mL cans. How many 750-mL bottles contain about as much pop as 1 case?

33. A can of frozen orange juice and a can of frozen lemonade each hold 355 mL of concentrate. The juice concentrate is mixed with 3 cans of water. The lemonade concentrate is mixed with 4 cans of water.

a) What quantity of orange juice comes from 1 can of concentrate?
b) What quantity of lemonade comes from 1 can of concentrate?

34. Colin had a mass of 3.8 kg when he was born. His mass is now 15 times his mass at birth.

a) What is Colin's present mass?
b) What is the difference between Colin's mass and your mass?

35. Calculate the volume of water with each mass.

a) 150 g **b)** 5.2 g
c) 2.4 kg **d)** 1 mg

36. The Rashids' swimming pool is 7.5 m long and 6 m wide. It is filled to a depth of 1.6 m.

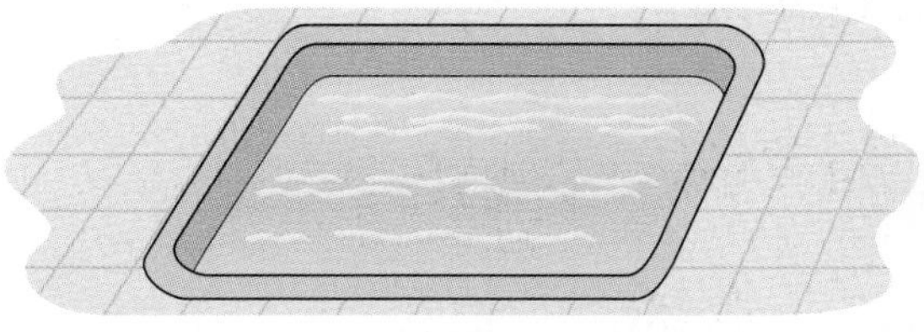

a) What is the volume of water in the swimming pool?
b) If the pool is 80% full, what is the capacity of the pool?
c) What mass of water is in the pool?

37. A cube has a volume of 125 cm^3 but a capacity of 0 mL. How is this possible?

38. Work with a partner. Use your research skills to find information about mass, capacity, or volume in *The Guinness Book of Records* or another source. Use the information to design a poster.

Geometry in Nature

Geometric shapes are common in nature. For example, the shapes of snowflakes show many variations, determined mainly by the temperature. The following pictures show a variety of geometric shapes found in nature.

Activity ❶

1. Name any geometric shapes you recognize in the pictures.

2. Research and list some other natural geometric shapes.

3. Compare your list with your classmates'.

Activity ❷

Design a poster that includes various natural geometric shapes.

Review

Name each three-dimensional figure.

1. **2.** **3.** **4.**

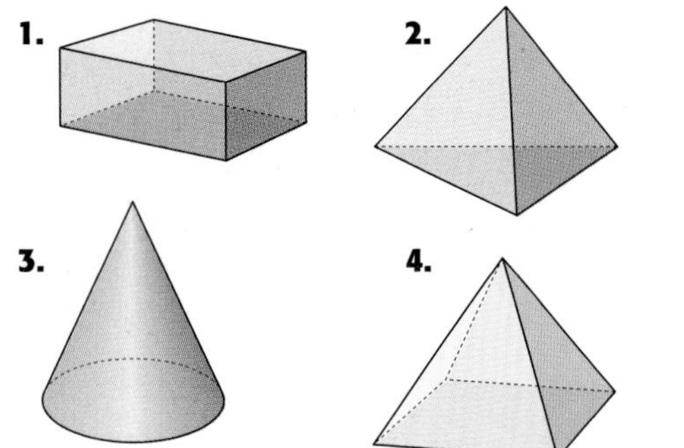

5. Name the parts indicated on the diagram.

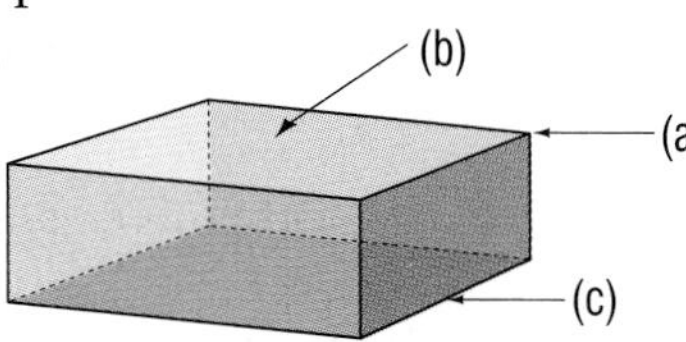

Name a three-dimensional figure that has the following parts.

6. 4 faces
7. 9 edges
8. no vertices
9. 6 congruent faces
10. 5 vertices
11. 6 edges

State the number of faces, edges, and vertices for each of the following.

12. cube

13. pentagonal prism

14. triangular prism

15. hexagonal pyramid

From the diagram, name the following.

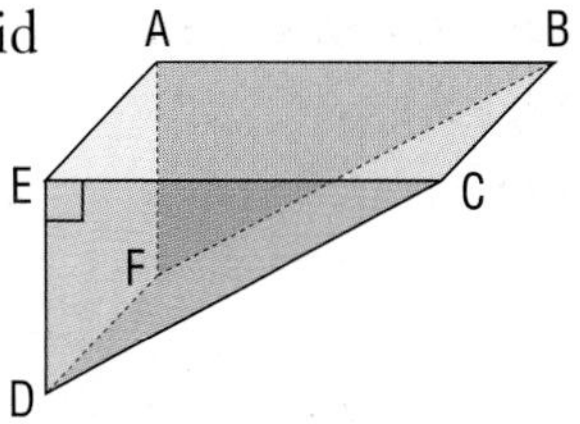

16. 2 pairs of parallel edges

17. 1 pair of congruent faces

18. 2 pairs of perpendicular edges

19. the edges that are equal in length

20. the type of polyhedron

State the number of right angles on each of the following polyhedra.

21. rectangular prism

22. square pyramid

23. triangular pyramid

24. cube

Identify each object as a solid, shell, or skeleton.

25.

26.

27.

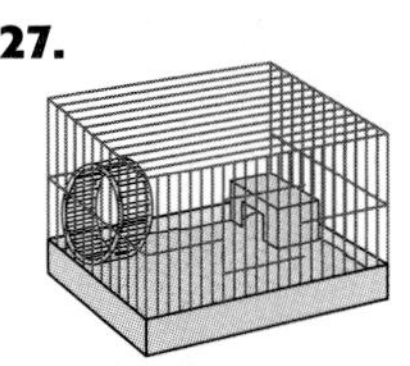

28.

Sketch each object and show 2 planes of symmetry.

29.

30.

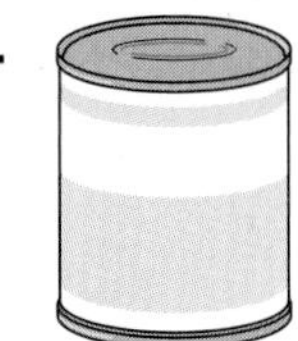

One-half of each model has been removed along a plane of symmetry shaded gray. Sketch the complete model on grid or dot paper.

31.

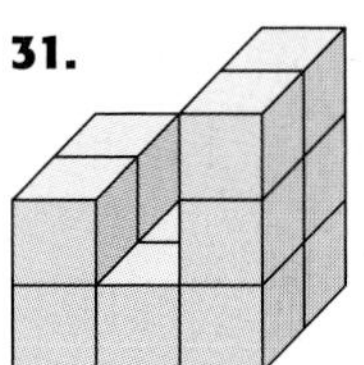

32.

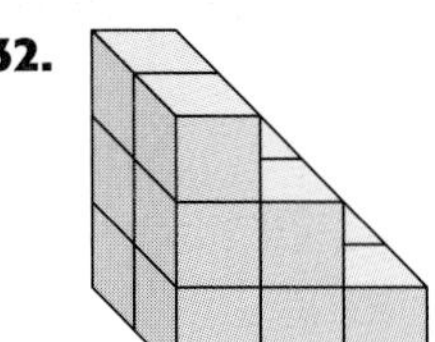

Name each figure whose net is shown. List the edges that will be joined when the figure is assembled.

33. **34.**

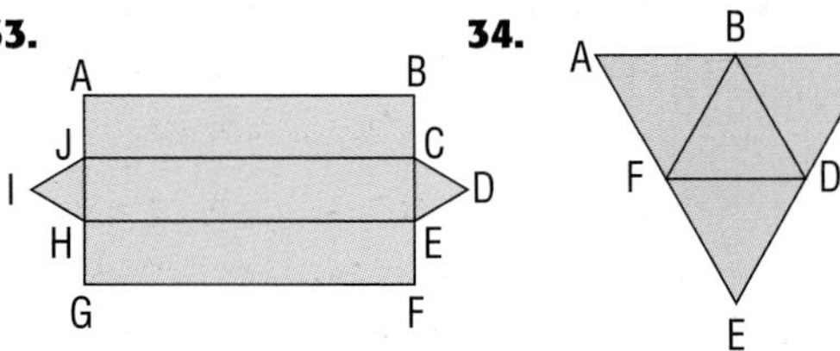

Calculate the surface area.

35.

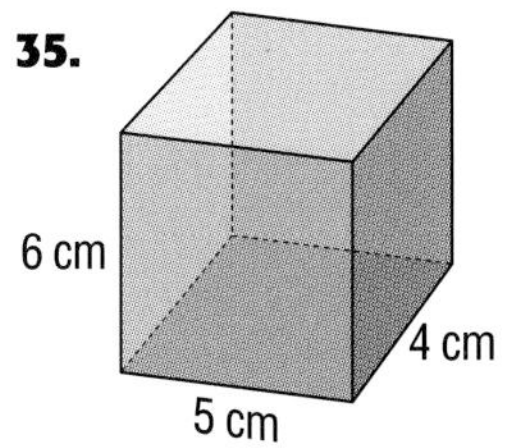

36.

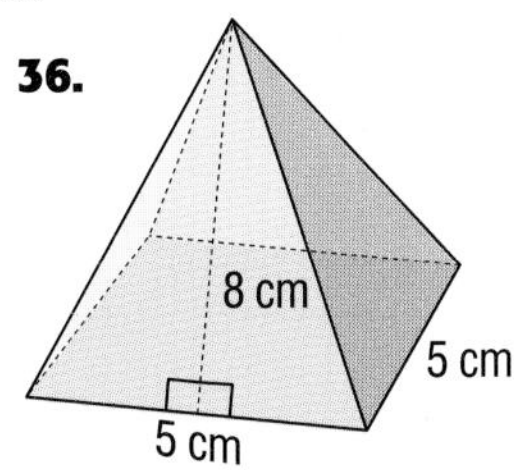

Calculate the volume.

37. **38.**

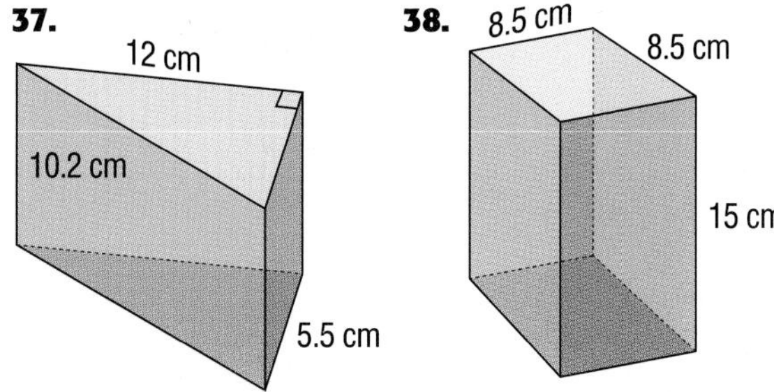

39. Cheryl used this pattern to make a box for her sewing equipment. Find the volume of the box.

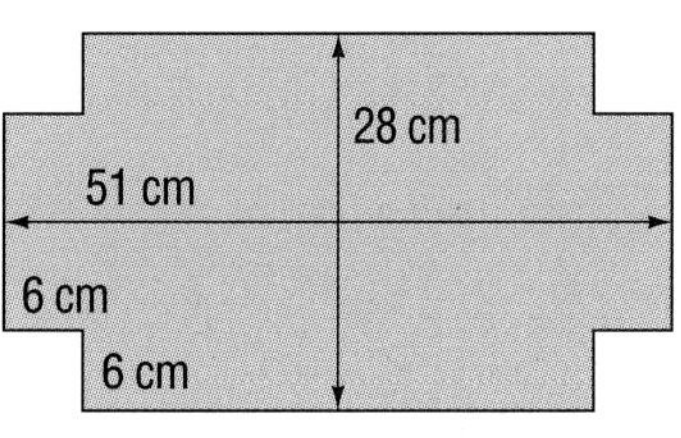

At a craft show, an artist displayed flower vases made in the shape of triangular prisms. Calculate the volume and capacity of each vase. What assumptions have you made?

40. **41.**

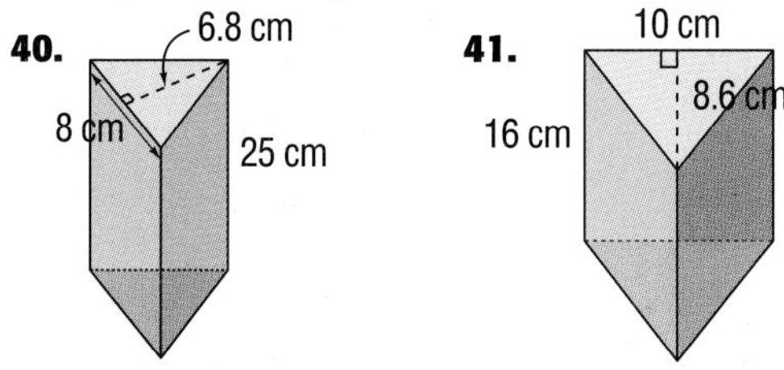

42. The Renauds bought 24 cans of orange juice. Each can held 355 mL. About how many 750-mL bottles of orange juice would hold the same amount as the 24 cans?

43. A container with a mass of 50 g and a capacity of 100 mL is filled with water. What is the total mass of the container and water?

Group Decision Making
Volunteering in the Community

Volunteers are a very important part of the community. You will now choose a voluntary activity for your group.

1. As a class, brainstorm the parts of your community in which volunteers are important. Possibilities include senior citizens' homes, hospitals, parks, animal shelters, and nursery schools.

2. As a class, choose 5 or 6 parts of the community that need volunteers. Assign one part to each group.

3. In your group, brainstorm a voluntary activity that would take the group three or four hours to carry out. For example, if your group wants to volunteer in a senior citizens' home, you might visit senior citizens there, do odd jobs at the home, or give a party. List as many activities as you can think of.

4. As a group, choose the best 4 or 5 ideas on your list. Select 2 members of the group to contact and visit possible locations to discuss your plans with the person in charge.

5. After the 2 members report back to the group, decide on your activity, plan it, and carry it out.

6. After you complete the activity, prepare a group report and present it to the class. Describe what you did and what you learned about the benefits of voluntary work. Describe how you used math in planning and carrying out your activity. Include in your report your opinions of how effective your group work was and how you could improve it.

Chapter Check

Name each polyhedron.

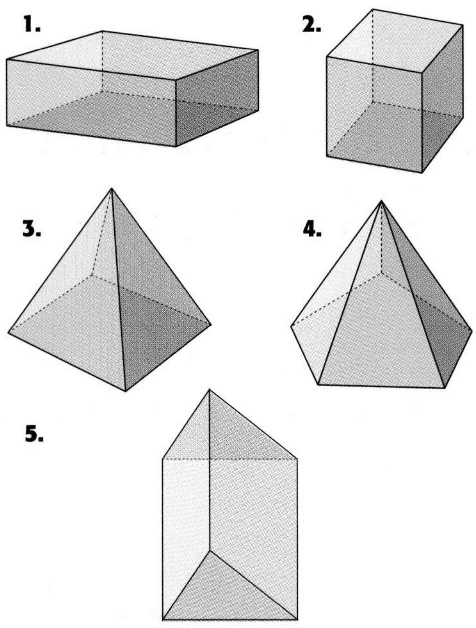

List the number of faces, edges, and vertices for each of the following.

6. triangular pyramid

7. cube

8. hexagonal prism

In questions 9–13, use the diagram of the rectangular prism.

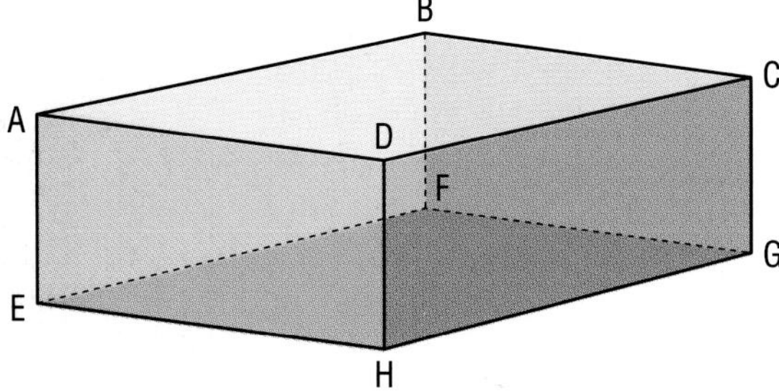

9. Name 2 pairs of congruent faces.

10. Name 2 pairs of equal edges.

11. Name 2 pairs of parallel edges.

12. Name 2 pairs of perpendicular edges.

13. State the number of right angles.

Sketch and name the polyhedron made from each net.

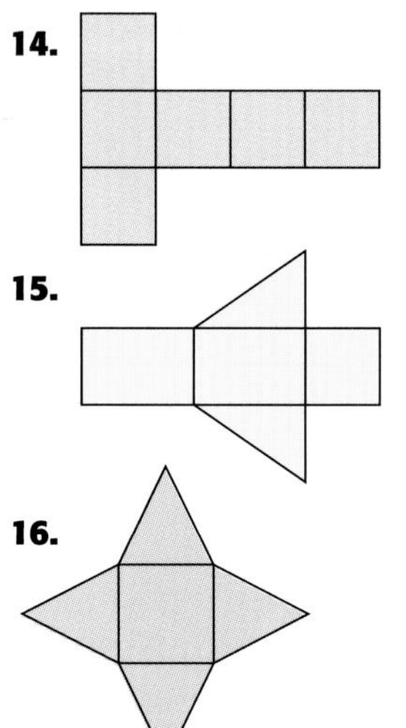

Draw the net for each polyhedron.

17. rectangular prism

18. triangular prism

Use the top view to name each polyhedron.

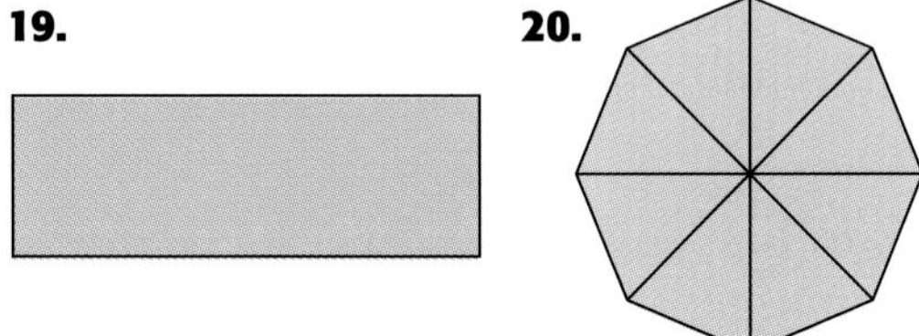

Calculate the volume and surface area.

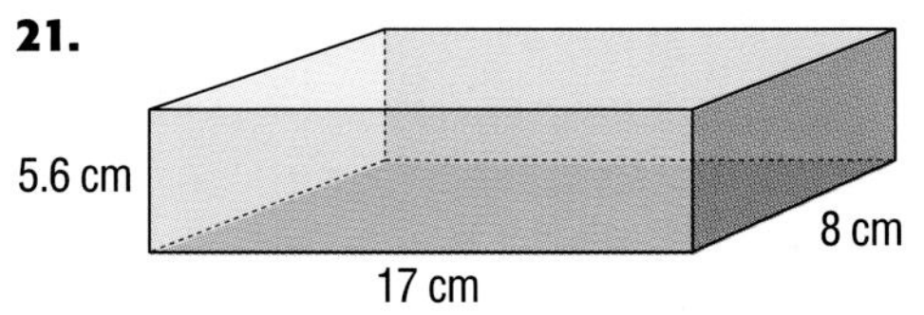

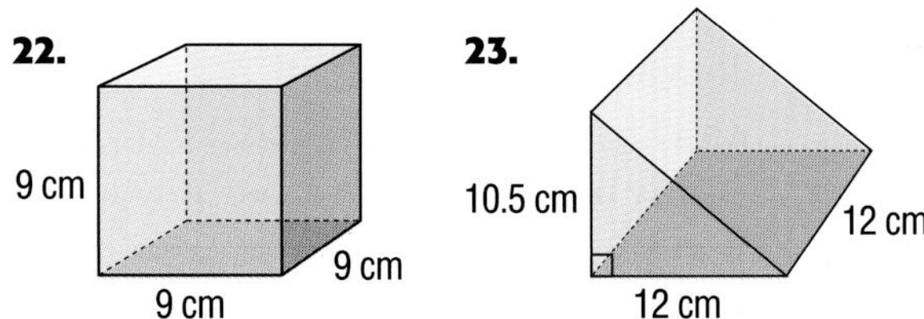

24. What mass of water fills a beaker with a capacity of 400 mL?

Using the Strategies

1. The sides of each cube are 1 cm long.

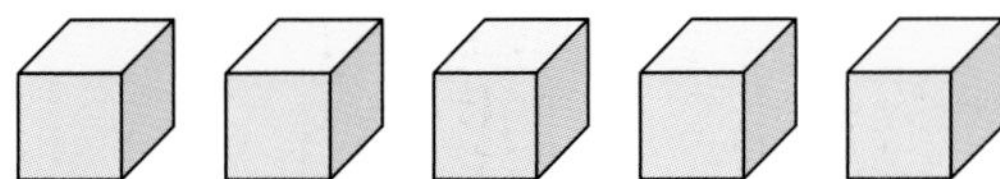

a) What is the total surface area of the 5 cubes?

b) The cubes have been arranged to make a solid. The total surface area of the solid is 22 cm^2.

Arrange the cubes to make 3 other solids, each with a surface area of 22 cm^2.

c) Arrange the cubes to make a solid with a surface area of 20 cm^2.

2. Use the digits 3, 4, 5, and 6 to find the largest product.

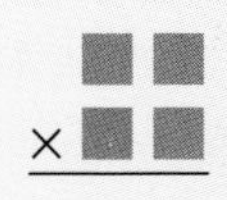

3. Jim put a new battery in his watch on March 12. The battery lasted 318 days. On what date did Jim's watch stop?

4. The teachers of the three grade 7 classes each sent a student to the office to pick up Fitness Participation Certificates. The first student took $\frac{1}{3}$ of the certificates. The second student took $\frac{1}{3}$ of the remaining certificates, and the last student took $\frac{1}{3}$ of the remaining certificates. There were 32 certificates left in the office. How many were there to begin with?

5. The net is folded along the edges to make a cube. What letter is on the face opposite the letter E?

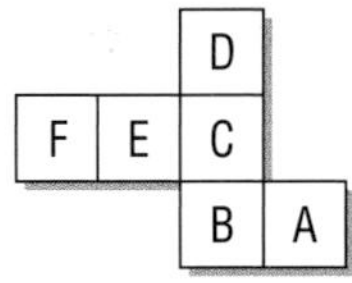

6. Jacob paved his driveway with paving stones that were 40 cm by 20 cm. His driveway was 10 m by 4 m. How many stones did he need? What assumptions have you made?

7. Place the numbers 1 to 12 in the 2 left columns so that the sums of the first 6 rows are equal, the sums of the 2 columns on the left are equal, and the sum of the two columns on the left equals the sum of the right column.

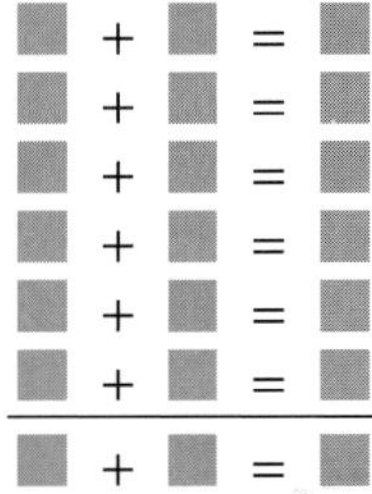

8. Aniela has three photographs on her dresser. In how many different ways can she arrange them in a row?

9. Five students paid a total of $175.00 for 5 concert tickets when they ordered the tickets by phone. This price included a $2.50 service charge on each ticket. What was the cost of each ticket without the service charge?

DATA BANK

1. How many times longer than a black right whale is a fin whale? Express your answer as a mixed number in lowest terms.

2. It takes 7 h to fly from Toronto to London, England. If you left Toronto at 20:15 on a Monday, at what time on what day would you arrive in London?

Chapter 5

Write an equivalent fraction.

1. $\frac{1}{3}$ **2.** $\frac{2}{5}$ **3.** $\frac{4}{3}$ **4.** $\frac{3}{10}$

Order from smallest to largest.

5. $\frac{3}{4}, \frac{4}{5}, \frac{7}{10}$ **6.** $1\frac{1}{2}, 1\frac{3}{5}, 1\frac{3}{4}$

Estimate, then add.

7. $\frac{1}{2} + \frac{2}{3}$ **8.** $\frac{3}{4} + \frac{3}{8}$ **9.** $\frac{3}{8} + \frac{5}{6}$

10. $1\frac{2}{5} + \frac{1}{4}$ **11.** $2\frac{5}{6} + 3\frac{1}{2}$ **12.** $5\frac{1}{4} + 2\frac{2}{3}$

Estimate, then subtract.

13. $\frac{3}{4} - \frac{1}{3}$ **14.** $\frac{5}{6} - \frac{1}{2}$ **15.** $\frac{7}{8} - \frac{2}{3}$

16. $2\frac{1}{2} - 1\frac{1}{4}$ **17.** $5\frac{1}{6} - 2\frac{2}{3}$ **18.** $4\frac{5}{6} - 1\frac{3}{4}$

Estimate, then multiply.

19. $\frac{1}{2} \times \frac{3}{4}$ **20.** $\frac{2}{3} \times \frac{3}{5}$ **21.** $\frac{5}{6} \times \frac{1}{4}$

22. $2\frac{1}{2} \times \frac{1}{3}$ **23.** $3\frac{1}{3} \times 3$ **24.** $2\frac{3}{4} \times 1\frac{1}{2}$

Estimate, then divide.

25. $\frac{2}{3} \div \frac{1}{2}$ **26.** $\frac{3}{4} \div \frac{3}{8}$ **27.** $\frac{3}{5} \div \frac{2}{5}$

28. $5 \div \frac{1}{2}$ **29.** $\frac{3}{4} \div 2$ **30.** $1\frac{1}{2} \div 2\frac{1}{2}$

Change to a decimal.

31. $\frac{5}{4}$ **32.** $\frac{7}{8}$ **33.** $\frac{5}{6}$

34. Of Canadian families with their children living at home, about $\frac{2}{5}$ have 1 child, $\frac{2}{5}$ have 2 children, and $\frac{1}{5}$ have 3 or more children. What fraction of these families have 2 or more children?

35. The Earth turns on its axis once every 24 h. In simplest form, what fraction of a turn does it make in each of the following times.

a) 1 h **b)** 2 h **c)** 3 h **d)** 10 h **e)** 18 h

Chapter 6

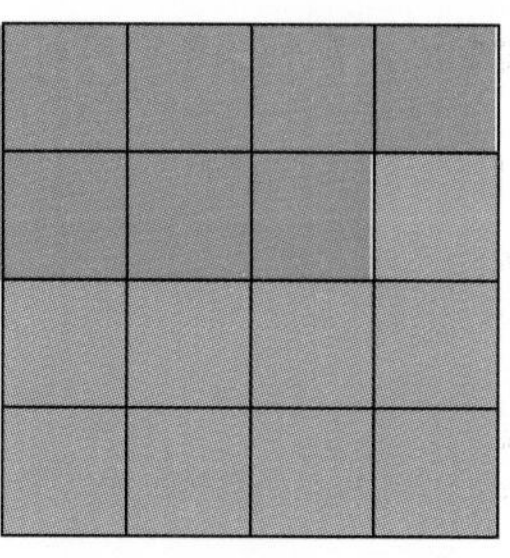

1. Write the ratio of red squares to green squares.

The power rating of a light bulb is measured in watts, symbol W. Write the ratio of a 60-W rating to each of the following ratings. Express each answer in lowest terms.

2. 40 W **3.** 100 W **4.** 150 W

Write 3 ratios equivalent to each of the following.

5. 1:2 **6.** 2 to 3 **7.** $\frac{8}{3}$

Find the missing term.

8. $\frac{1}{4} = \frac{■}{12}$ **9.** $\frac{■}{5} = \frac{6}{10}$

10. $\frac{18}{24} = \frac{3}{■}$ **11.** $\frac{2}{■} = \frac{8}{20}$

12. Five tickets cost $35.00. What would 8 tickets cost?

13. Bob earned $55.80 in 9 h. What was his hourly rate of pay?

14. Choose the better value — 5 kg of birdseed for $6.50 or 8 kg for $10.80.

15. The actual length of a sparrow is 8 cm. What is the length of a sparrow in a drawing if the scale is 5:1?

16. The width of a door in a drawing is 2 cm. What is the actual width of the door if the scale is 1:40?

17. The triangles are similar. Find the missing dimensions.

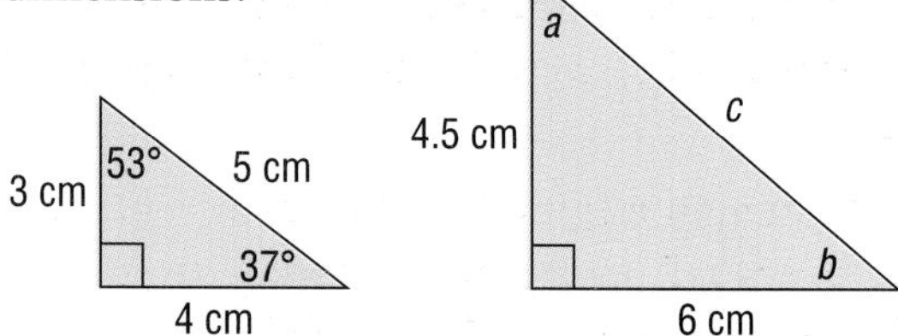

Chapter 7

What percent of each diagram is shaded?

1.  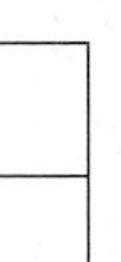

2. 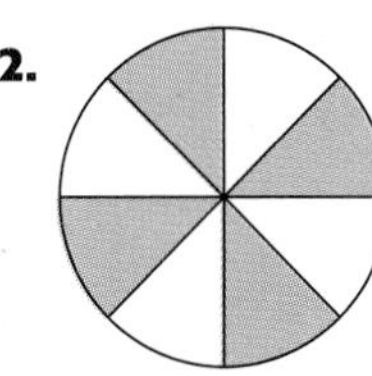

Express as a percent.

3. $\frac{3}{4}$ **4.** $\frac{2}{5}$ **5.** $\frac{4}{25}$

6. 0.34 **7.** 0.56 **8.** 0.425

Express as a decimal.

9. 21% **10.** 46% **11.** 8%

Express as a fraction in lowest terms.

12. 24% **13.** 15% **14.** 68%

Calculate.

15. 25% of 80 **16.** 35% of 800

17. the percent that 17 is of 20

18. the percent that 45 is of 60

19. 150% of $200.00

20. Susan deposited $300.00 in the bank for 1 year. She received 7% interest. How much did she have in her account at the end of the year?

21. A sweater that regularly costs $90.00 is on sale at 20% off. What is the sale price?

22. A radio costs $68.00. What is the cost in your province including

a) GST? **b)** GST and PST?

23. Diego works in a clothing store. He is paid $200.00 a week, plus a commission of 2% of his sales. One week, his sales were $7500.00. What were his total earnings that week?

24. At the 1988 Summer Olympics, Canada won 3 gold, 2 silver, and 5 bronze medals. What percent were gold medals?

Chapter 8

How many faces, edges, and vertices does each of the following have?

1. triangular prism **2.** cylinder

3. rectangular prism

Name an object that is an example of each of the following.

4. a solid **5.** a shell

6. a skeleton

Calculate the surface area of each prism.

7.

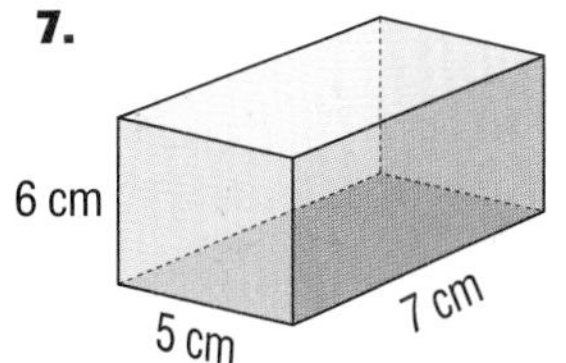

8.

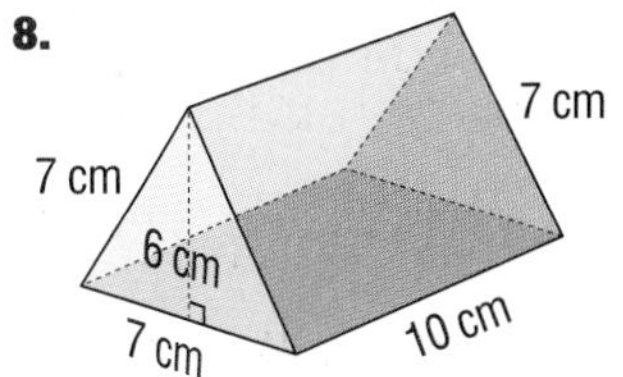

9. Name an object that has 1 plane of symmetry.

10. Draw the front view, side view, and top view of the computer.

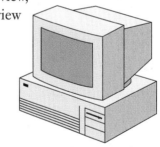

11. Calculate the volume of the prism.

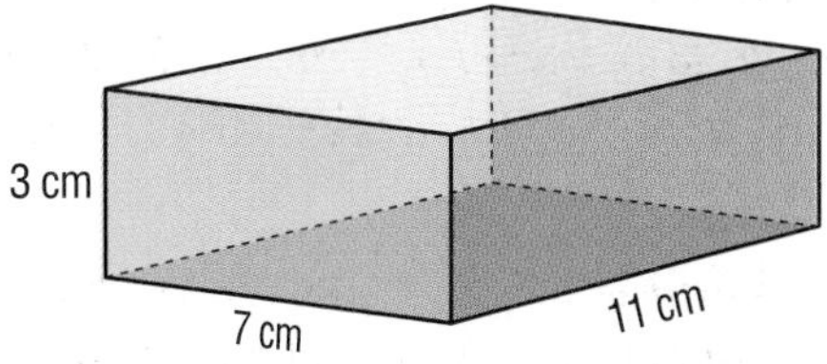

12. A bucket holds 10 kg of water. What is the capacity of the bucket?

13. A can of frozen grapefruit juice, holding 355 mL of concentrate, is mixed with 3 cans of water. What volume of juice is obtained?

CHAPTER 9

Statistics

Did you know that about 40% of the households in Canada have at least 1 pet?

Make a list of your relatives and friends. Do not list more than 1 person from any household. Write *pet* or *no pet* beside each name. What percent of the people on your list have pets?

Combine your list with those of 3 of your classmates. What percent of the people on the combined list have pets?

If the percent is much greater or much less than 40%, give reasons for the difference.

Testing Computer Games

A software company is developing 4 computer games — *Tennis*, *Baseball*, *The Maze*, and *Skiing*. The company wants to have the games tested by students, so it gives one copy of each game to a school for 4 weeks. Four classes have been chosen to test the games. Each class must test one game a week.

Activity ❶

Copy the chart. To organize the testing, fill in the names of the games so that each class will test a different game each week for four weeks. This way of testing products is called a "Latin Square."

	Class 1	Class 2	Class 3	Class 4
First Week				
Second Week				
Third Week				
Fourth Week				

Activity ❷

Complete the chart from Activity 1 in as many other ways as you can. Make sure that all the ways are different from each other.

In how many ways can you complete the chart? Compare your answers with your classmates' to make sure that you find all the possibilities.

Math Skills for Statistics

Express as a decimal.

1. 50% **2.** 25% **3.** 30%

4. 45% **5.** 13% **6.** 7%

7. 2% **8.** 77% **9.** 61%

Calculate.

10. 50% of 200 **11.** 25% of 500

12. 10% of 800 **13.** 15% of 120

14. 20% of 70 **15.** 5% of 160

16. 2% of 88 **17.** 75% of 30

Express as a percent.

18. $\frac{33}{50}$ **19.** $\frac{29}{50}$ **20.** $\frac{12}{25}$

21. $\frac{7}{25}$ **22.** $\frac{13}{20}$ **23.** $\frac{9}{10}$

24. $\frac{3}{5}$ **25.** $\frac{56}{200}$ **26.** $\frac{60}{150}$

Express as a fraction in lowest terms.

27. 25% **28.** 14% **29.** 75%

30. 20% **31.** 50% **32.** 10%

33. 60% **34.** 65% **35.** 8%

Arrange the numbers from smallest to largest.

36. 23, 35, 28, 31, 45, 26, 32, 27, 34

37. 181, 184, 179, 180, 177, 182, 186, 189, 173

38. 34, 35, 36, 34, 37, 32, 35, 34, 38, 31, 30, 36

Add the following numbers and divide the result by 5.

39. 30, 40, 35, 40, 25

40. 73, 62, 41, 54, 50

41. 122, 121, 124, 123, 120

42. 87, 98, 55, 56, 49

Mental Math

Add.

1. $\frac{3}{8} + \frac{1}{8}$ **2.** $\frac{2}{5} + \frac{1}{5}$

3. $\frac{3}{10} + \frac{7}{10}$ **4.** $\frac{1}{4} + \frac{1}{2}$

Subtract.

5. $\frac{7}{8} - \frac{3}{8}$ **6.** $\frac{4}{5} - \frac{1}{5}$

7. $\frac{9}{10} - \frac{1}{10}$ **8.** $\frac{3}{4} - \frac{1}{2}$

Multiply.

9. $\frac{1}{4} \times \frac{1}{2}$ **10.** $\frac{2}{3} \times \frac{1}{4}$

11. $\frac{1}{5} \times 10$ **12.** $6 \times \frac{2}{3}$

Divide.

13. $\frac{1}{4} \div \frac{1}{2}$ **14.** $\frac{1}{3} \div \frac{2}{3}$

15. $6 \div \frac{1}{2}$ **16.** $\frac{1}{2} \div 2$

Calculate.

17. 50% of 60 **18.** 50% of 80

19. 50% of 200 **20.** 50% of 1000

Calculate.

21. 25% of 100 **22.** 25% of 40

23. 25% of 200 **24.** 25% of 1000

Calculate.

25. 10% of 100 **26.** 10% of 200

27. 10% of 500 **28.** 10% of 1000

Calculate.

29. $\frac{1}{2}$ of 200 **30.** $\frac{1}{3}$ of 66

31. $\frac{1}{4}$ of 80 **32.** $\frac{1}{5}$ of 20

9.1 Collecting Data

Activity: Learn About Sampling

To taste the soup of the day, a chef does not taste all the soup. The chef just takes a spoonful or a **sample**.

Suppose you were asked to find out the favourite colour of bicycles among the students in your town. Instead of asking all the students, you could ask just some of them. The students that you ask are a sample of all the students. When you ask people their opinion about something, you are taking a **survey**.

Sandra conducted the bicycle survey in her school. She used a survey sheet to collect the data. Sandra used tally marks to record the number of students who gave each colour as their favourite.

SURVEY SHEET		
Colour	**Tally**	**Frequency**
Blue	~~IIII~~ III	
Green	~~IIII~~ ~~IIII~~ ~~IIII~~ II	
White	~~IIII~~ ~~IIII~~ I	
Red	~~IIII~~ ~~IIII~~ ~~IIII~~ ~~IIII~~	
Black	~~IIII~~ IIII	

After she finished her survey, Sandra counted the tally marks and wrote the number in the frequency column. The **frequency** for a colour is the number of students who chose that colour.

SURVEY SHEET		
Colour	**Tally**	**Frequency**
Blue	~~IIII~~ III	8
Green	~~IIII~~ ~~IIII~~ ~~IIII~~ II	17
White	~~IIII~~ ~~IIII~~ I	11
Red	~~IIII~~ ~~IIII~~ ~~IIII~~ ~~IIII~~	20
Black	~~IIII~~ IIII	9

Then Sandra organized the data.

Unorganized Data	
Blue	8
Green	17
White	11
Red	20
Black	9

Organized Data	
Red	20
Green	17
White	11
Black	9
Blue	8

Inquire

1. Which colour was the most popular?

2. Which colour was the least popular?

3. How many students did Sandra survey?

A personal survey, like the one Sandra used, is just one of the ways to collect information. You could also

- conduct a phone survey
- ask an expert
- use a data bank
- conduct a mail survey
- survery people at an event
- use books, magazines, and newspapers

Problems and Applications

1. Roger conducted a survey about people's favourite TV shows.

MOST POPULAR SHOWS		
Type of Program	**Tally**	**Frequency**
Drama	卌 卌 卌	
Suspense	卌 |||	
Feature Film	卌 卌 卌 卌		
Sitcom	卌 卌 卌 卌 |||	
Adventure	卌 卌 |||	

a) Complete the frequency column on Roger's survey sheet.
b) How many people chose drama?
c) List the kinds of programs in order from most popular to least popular.
d) Which was the most popular kind of program?
e) Which was the least popular?
f) How many people were surveyed? What assumption have you made?

2. The Recreation Department asked Monika to survey the team sports students prefer to play.

FAVOURITE SPORTS		
Sport	**Tally**	**Frequency**
Volleyball	卌 卌 卌 |||	
Baseball	卌 卌 卌 卌 卌 ||	
Basketball	卌 卌 |||	
Soccer	卌 卌 ||	
Hockey	卌 卌 卌 ||	
Tennis	卌 卌		

a) Complete the frequency column.
b) List the sports in order from most popular to least popular.
c) Which sport was least popular?
d) How many students were surveyed?

3. Jessica conducted a survey about favourite seasons. The list gives the student choices. W means winter; S means spring; J means summer; F means fall.

W	S	W	J	F	J	W	J	S	J
W	J	F	S	S	W	J	W	S	J
F	W	S	F	J	W	S	J	J	W

a) Draw and complete a survey sheet for the data.
b) Order the seasons from most popular to least popular.
c) How many students preferred summer?
d) How many students were surveyed?

4. Carlos surveyed the most popular way of listening to music. In the list, A means AM radio; F means FM radio; T means tapes; R means records; C means compact discs.

F	F	A	T	T	C	T	T	A	A	T	C	T
T	F	A	A	T	C	F	T	A	T	T	A	A
C	A	C	T	T	A	A	T	T	T	A	T	T
A	F	F	T	C	C	A	A	T	A	F	C	T
A	T	T	F	F	T	T						

a) Draw and complete a survey sheet for the data.
b) Order the ways of listening from most popular to least popular.
c) By how many votes did the most popular choice beat the second most popular?
d) How many people were surveyed?

5. Work with a classmate. Record the method you would use to gather data on the following. Give reasons for your answers.

a) the most popular fast-food restaurant for students in your school
b) the names and lengths of the 5 longest rivers in Canada
c) the person who will be the next mayor of your town
d) the most popular months for tourists to visit Italy
e) the going rate of pay for baby-sitting
f) the most popular magazines in your town
g) the weather in July in Melbourne, Australia
h) the most popular ride at an amusement park
i) the most common illnesses among babies

Collecting Data

In the following activities, work in groups to collect data from the students in your class and in your school.

Activity ❶

1. In your group, list 6 items that you would like to survey. Your list might include such items as

- colour of eyes
- favourite singer
- favourite school subject
- favourite food
- least favourite food

Do not include items that could be embarrassing to other students.

2. Write your list on a large sheet of paper or on the chalkboard, so that all students can read each list.

3. As a class, use the group lists to write another list of the 10 or 12 most popular items. There should be enough items for each group to have 2 items to survey.

4. As a class, decide on a method of choosing which group has first pick of the items on the list, which group has second pick, and so on.

5. As a group, select the two items you will survey. Decide on the questions you will ask.

6. As a group, make a survey sheet and collect the data from the other students in your class.

7. As a group, organize the data.

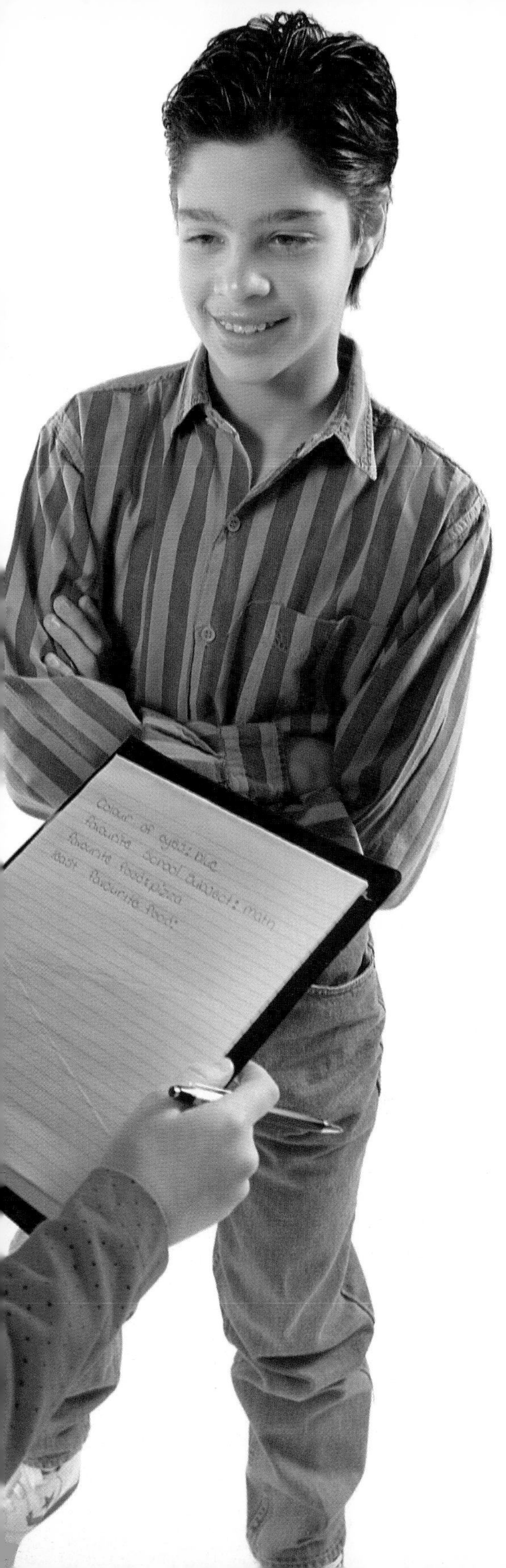

Activity ❷

1. To collect data from students in other classes in the school, your group should select 5 students from each of the other classes. Different groups should work together to make sure that they do not all choose the same students in another class. It is important that every student in each of the other classes be asked at least one question.

2. In your group, assign each group member at least one class to survey.

3. Have each group member survey the assigned class by collecting the data from the 5 students selected in that class.

4. As a group, combine the data from the other classes and organize the data.

Activity ❸

1. In your group, compare the results of your school survey with the results of the survey in your class.

2. Give reasons for the similarities and differences.

Activity ❹

1. In your group, prepare a report for the rest of the class.

2. Post the results of your surveys in the school, so that students from other classes can see them.

3. As a group, evaluate your work. If you had to survey your class and school again, what would you do in the same way and what would you do differently?

9.2 Using a Sample to Make Predictions

Activity: Think About the Process

There were about 400 000 people living in Bent Creek. Mark wanted a new swimming pool to be built. He decided to find out how many people agreed with him.

Instead of asking each person, Mark decided to ask a sample of people. He planned to use their answers to predict how many people in Bent Creek wanted a new pool.

Mark first had to decide on the number of people to ask. This number is called the **sample size**. Mark decided to ask 100 people.

When choosing the people to ask, Mark had to be sure that his sample was not distorted or **biased**.

Inquire

1. What is wrong with asking a very large sample of people, such as a sample of 100 000?

2. What is wrong with asking a very small sample, such as a sample of 3 people?

3. Would asking 100 people on the beach give a biased sample? Explain.

Suppose Mark's sample was not biased, and he found that 60 people out of 100 said they were in favour of a new pool.

This means that $\frac{60}{100}$ or 60% of the sample wanted the pool.

Mark applied the percent from the sample to the whole population of Bent Creek.

$$60\% \text{ of } 400\ 000 = 0.6 \times 400\ 000$$
$$= 240\ 000$$

From his sample, Mark predicted that, if he had asked everyone in Bent Creek, 240 000 would have wanted a new pool.

Problems and Applications

1. There were 500 students at Paul's school. Paul was asked to find out how many could swim. Paul surveyed 50 students. He found that 35 students in his sample could swim. How many of the 500 students would Paul predict could swim?

2. Clara was asked to find out how many students at her school could ski. There were 600 students in her school. Clara surveyed 80 of them and found that 20 could ski. Using the data, decide how many students Clara predicted could ski.

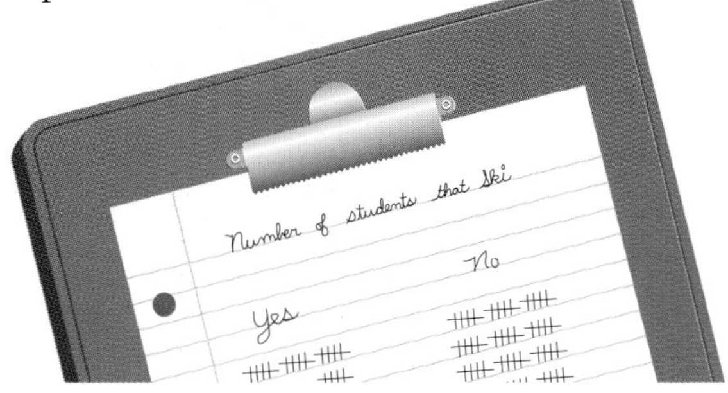

3. The town council of Hammerstein wanted to know if the public was in favour of building a new theatre. There were about 60 000 people in Hammerstein. Charles sampled 100 of them.

New Theatre Survey

Opinion	Number	Percent
Yes	45	
No	33	
Undecided	22	

a) Copy the table and complete the percent column.
b) Use the percents from the sample to predict how many people in the town wanted a new theatre, how many did not want a new theatre, and how many were undecided.

4. Rakia was asked by Giant Video to find out which section of the store people buy the most videos from. There are about 20 000 people in Rakia's town who buy videos. She surveyed 400 customers at the video store.

Videos Bought the Most

Type of Video	Number	Percent
Classics	40	
New Releases	154	
Exercise	34	
Feature Films	98	
Children's	74	

a) Copy the table and complete the percent column.
b) Use the percents to predict the number of people who buy each kind of video.
c) Why would a video store owner want to know this information?
d) Might there be any bias in Rakia's sample? Explain.

5. Work with a classmate.
a) Decide on a strategy to estimate how many Canadians are left handed. Use your strategy to make an estimate.
b) Could you use the same strategy to decide how many Canadians wear eyeglasses or contact lenses? Explain.

LOGIC POWER

Ted and Mary Bevan have 5 daughters. Each daughter has a brother. How many people are in the Bevan family?

9.3 Reading and Drawing Pictographs

Activity: Study the Graphs

A **pictograph** or **picture graph** uses pictures or symbols to compare similar things. The pictographs show the best-selling children's hardcover books and paperbacks in North America.

Best-selling Hardcover Books	
The Littlest Angel	.7
The Cat in the Hat	.7
The Tale of Peter Rabbit	
Pat the Bunny	.9
Each represents 1 000 000 books.	

Best-selling Paperbacks	
Charlotte's Web	.6
The Outsiders	.9
The Tales of a Fourth Grade Nothing	.6
Are You There God? It's me, Margaret.	.3
Each represents 1 000 000 books.	

Inquire

1. About how many copies has the most popular hardcover book sold?

2. About how may copies has *Pat the Bunny* sold?

3. What is the best-selling paperback?

4. About how many copies has *Charlotte's Web* sold?

5. How might a book store manager use this information?

Example

The table gives weekly sweat shirt sales at Meadowvale School. Display the data on a pictograph.

Week	Sales
1	$600.00
2	$710.00
3	$380.00
4	$420.00
5	$160.00
6	$90.00

Solution

Choose a symbol to represent the data. Let one represent $100.00.

Round the data to convenient numbers. In this case, round to the nearest $50.00.

Week	Sales (rounded)
1	$600
2	$700
3	$400
4	$400
5	$150
6	$100

Draw a pictograph and give it a title.

Sweat Shirt Sales
Week 1
Week 2
Week 3
Week 4
Week 5
Week 6
Each represents $100.

Why did we round the data before drawing the pictograph?

Problems and Applications

1. The pictograph shows the top choices for dinner for grade 7 and 8 students at Greenwood School.

Dinner Choices
Chicken
Pizza
Spaghetti
Hamburger
Steak
Each represents 5 students.

a) How many chose each meal?
b) How many students were surveyed?
c) How many more chose pizza than hamburger?

2. The pictograph shows where and when people like to use personal stereos.

Personal Stereos: Where and When
Walking
At Home
Studying
Playing Sports
At Work
Other
Each represents 10 users.

a) Where are personal stereos used most?
b) How many people like to use a personal stereo while walking?
c) How many like to use a personal stereo while playing sports?
d) How many more like to use a personal stereo while studying than at work?
e) Can you tell how many users were surveyed? Explain.

3. The table gives the results of a survey about where people go on vacation.

Vacation Spot	Frequency
Beach	50
Visit Family/Friends	70
Camping	40
Car Trip/Sightseeing	25
Historic Sites	15

Display these data on a pictograph.

4. The table shows the numbers of letters in the longest words in various languages.

Language	Letters in Longest Word
English	29
French	25
German	80
Japanese	12
Mohawk	50
Swedish	130

Represent the data on a pictograph.

5. The largest litters recorded for various kinds of pets are shown.

Pet	Largest Litter
Dog	23
Ferret	15
Guinea Pig	12
Mouse	34
Rabbit	24

Draw a pictograph to represent the data.

6. Describe some advantages and disadvantages of using pictographs to represent data.

7. Write a question based on the pictograph from question 3, 4, or 5. Have a classmate solve the question.

8. Draw a pictograph about a feature of Canada. Here are some ideas.
- the populations of the provinces
- the number of daily newspapers in each province

Write 3 questions based on your graph. Have a classmate solve them.

9.4 Reading Bar Graphs and Broken-Line Graphs

Bar graphs are used to compare similar things.

Activity: Study the Graph

Stacey Bain is a camp counsellor at a summer music camp for grades 7 and 8 students. The campers are divided into two teams, the Eagles and the Hawks.

One camp activity involves recording wildlife sightings. The bar graph shows the numbers of animals the teams spotted near the camp.

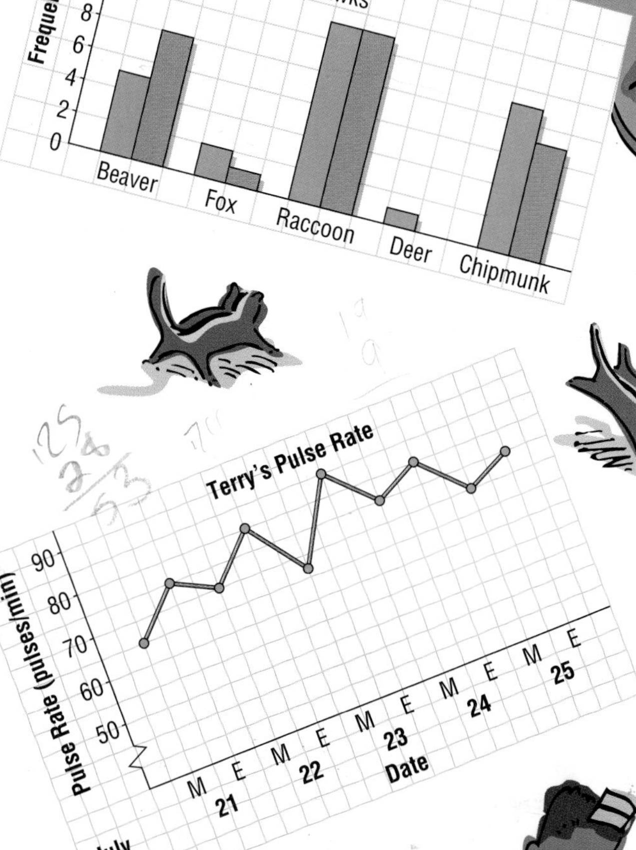

Inquire

1. What do the bars stand for?
2. What determines the height of each bar?
3. Which team spotted more chipmunks?
4. How many raccoons did each team spot?
5. Which team spotted more animals?

Broken-line graphs are used to show how something changes with time. They are called broken-line graphs because they include several line segments.

Activity: Study the Graph

The camp nurse checked Terry's pulse rate every morning and evening while he was sick. The graph shows his pulse rate over one week.

Inquire

1. Why does the vertical axis not need to start at 0?
2. What was Terry's pulse rate on the morning of July 21?
3. What was Terry's pulse rate on the evening of July 25?
4. What was Terry's highest pulse rate that week?
5. What was Terry's lowest pulse rate?
6. A normal pulse rate is between 72 pulses/min and 80 pulses/min. At what times was Terry's pulse rate out of the normal range?
7. Could Terry's pulse rate have been out of the normal range at any other times in the week? Explain.

Problems and Applications

1. The bar graph shows the approximate masses of several animals when they are full-grown.

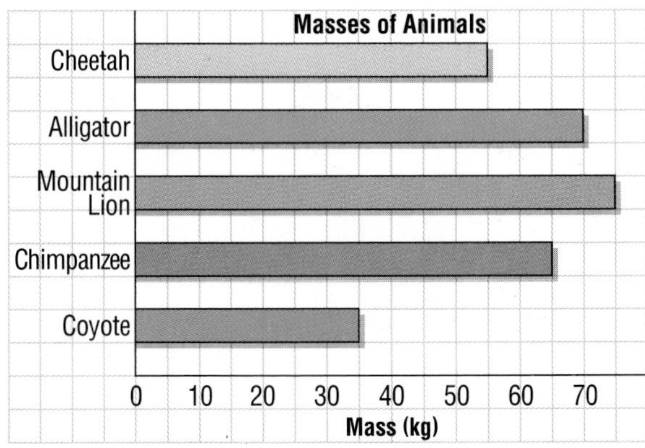

a) Name the heaviest animal.
b) Name the lightest animal.
c) What is the mass of an alligator?
d) What is the mass of a cheetah?
e) What is the difference in mass between a chimpanzee and a coyote?

2. The double bar graph shows the instruments played at music camp.

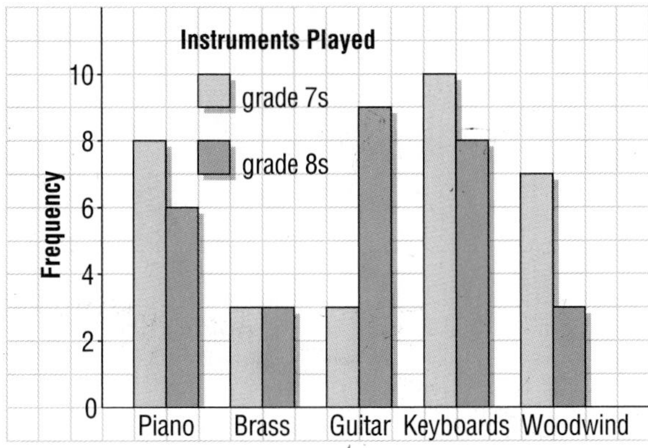

a) Which instrument was most popular with the grade 8s?
b) How many grade 7s played guitar?
c) Which instrument was most popular at the camp?
d) How many grade 8s were at the camp?

3. The broken-line graph shows Carla's pulse rate during 10 min on a rowing machine.

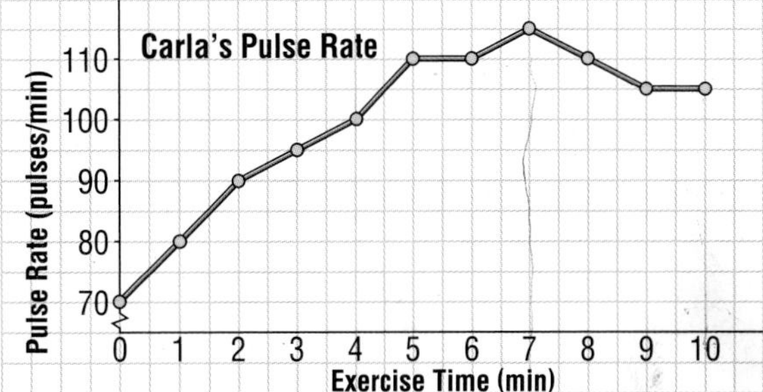

a) State her pulse rate at the start.
b) State her pulse rate at the end of 10 min.
c) State her highest pulse rate.
d) After how many minutes did her pulse rate reach its highest value?

4. The double broken-line graph gives the daily high and low temperatures in Hamilton, Ontario, during one week.

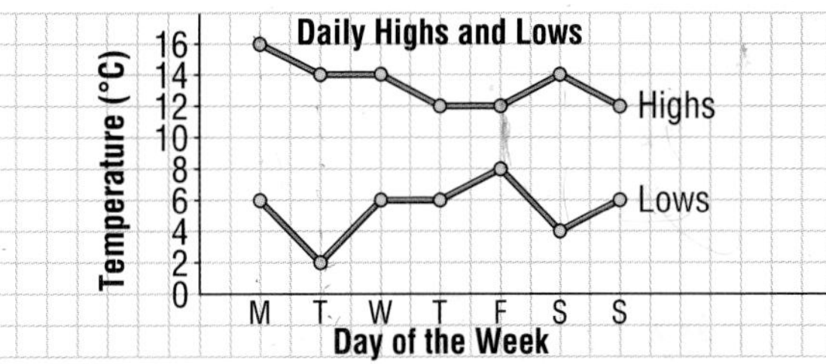

a) Which day had the highest temperature?
b) Which day had the lowest temperature?
c) Which day had the greatest difference in temperatures?
d) Which day had the smallest difference in temperatures?

WORD POWER

A change in one letter changes the word "five" into the real words "dive," "give," "fire," and "fine." How many real words can you make from the word "fate" in the same way?

9.5 Drawing Bar Graphs

Activity: Study the Example

Seven of the planets that orbit our sun have moons.
The table gives the numbers of moons discovered by 1992.

Planet	Number of Moons
Earth	1
Mars	2
Jupiter	16
Saturn	18
Uranus	15
Neptune	8
Pluto	1

To display this information on a bar graph, follow the steps.

1. Decide on the width of each bar.
Draw and label the horizontal axis.

2. Draw and label the vertical axis.

3. Plot the number of moons.
Choose a scale so that all the data can be shown.

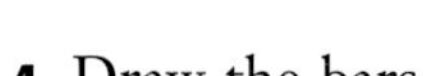

4. Draw the bars.

5. Give the graph a title.

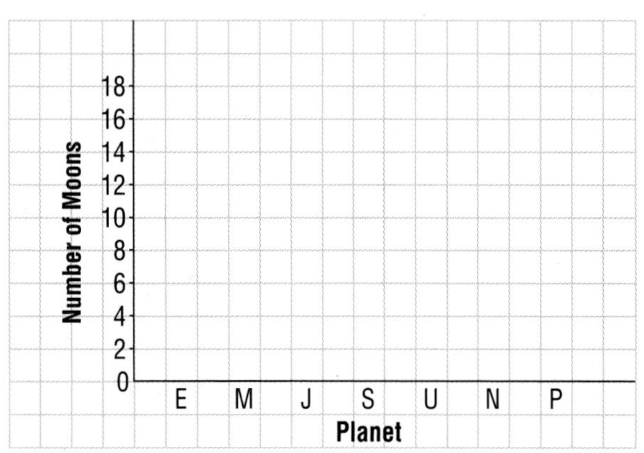

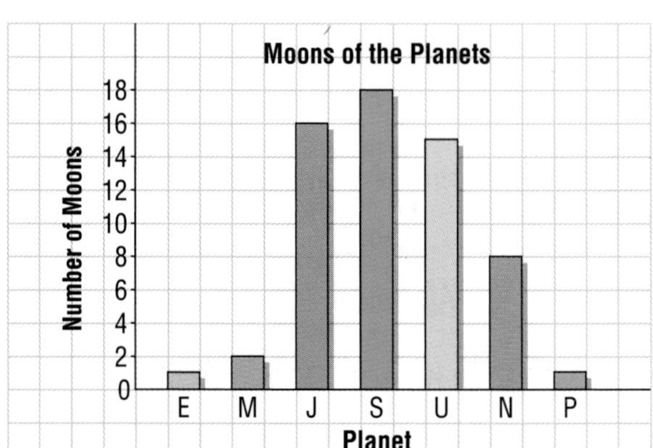

Inquire

1. What are the advantages of displaying the data on a bar graph instead of leaving them in a table?

2. The data could be displayed on a pictograph. Is it better to use a bar graph or a pictograph in this case? Explain.

3. Explain why we would not display the data on a broken-line graph.

4. Find examples of bar graphs in newspapers and magazines.
Give reasons why you think the data are displayed on bar graphs.

Problems and Applications

1. The table gives the distance walked per day by people in several jobs.

Job	Distance Per Day (km)
Nurse	8
Secretary	4
Salesperson	6
Dentist	1
Security Guard	7
Reporter	3

a) Display this information on a bar graph.

b) How would you determine how far you walk on a typical school day?

2. The table gives the numbers of tourists some countries have in a year.

Country	Tourists Per Year (millions)
Italy	26
Canada	15
France	37
Spain	33
Austria	16
U.S.A.	28
U.K.	16

Display this information on a bar graph.

3. The table shows the number of chemists of different nationalities who won Nobel Prizes from 1969 to 1991.

Nationality	Number of Winners
American	20
British	5
Canadian	3
German	4
Swiss	2
Other	6

a) Draw a bar graph to display the information.

b) American chemists won 5 times more prizes than chemists of which nationality?

c) What percent of the winners were Canadian?

4. The Fresh Fruit and Vegetable Association conducted a survey to find students' most popular snack fruits. The table gives the results.

Fruit	Number of Votes
Seedless Grapes	27
Bananas	32
Oranges	23
Strawberries	10
Apples	45

a) Display this information on a bar graph.

b) If 100 students were surveyed, why is the total number of votes greater than 100?

c) Survey the students in your class. Draw a bar graph of the results. Compare your classmates' choices with those of the 100 students in the survey.

5. Survey the students in your class to find out the types of pets they have. Display the data on a bar graph. Write 3 questions you could ask based on the data in your graph. Have a classmate answer the questions.

6. Many young people do voluntary work. Survey your class to find out what types of voluntary work they would like to do. Draw a double bar graph showing the types of work and the numbers of boys and girls who would choose each type.

NUMBER POWER

Copy the diagram. Place the numbers from 1 to 9 on the dots so that the numbers on each side of the triangle add to 20. The 4 has been placed for you.

9.6 Drawing Broken-Line Graphs

Activity: Study the Example

To promote safety on the water, the City of Burlington has posted the following information next to the boat-launch ramp.

MONTH	WATER TEMP.	SURVIVAL TIME
JANUARY	0°C	10 min
FEBRUARY	0°C	10 min
MARCH	1°C	12 min
APRIL	2°C	18 min
MAY	5°C	30 min
JUNE	10°C	1 h 20 min
JULY	18°C	5 h
AUGUST	21°C	6 h
SEPTEMBER	19°C	5 h
OCTOBER	12°C	2 h
NOVEMBER	7°C	45 min
DECEMBER	3°C	20 min

To draw a graph of the water temperature in different months of the year, follow the steps.

1. Draw and label the horizontal axis.

2. Draw and label the vertical axis. Choose a scale that allows all the temperatures to be shown

3. Plot the temperatures.

4. Join the points with straight lines.

5. Give the graph a title.

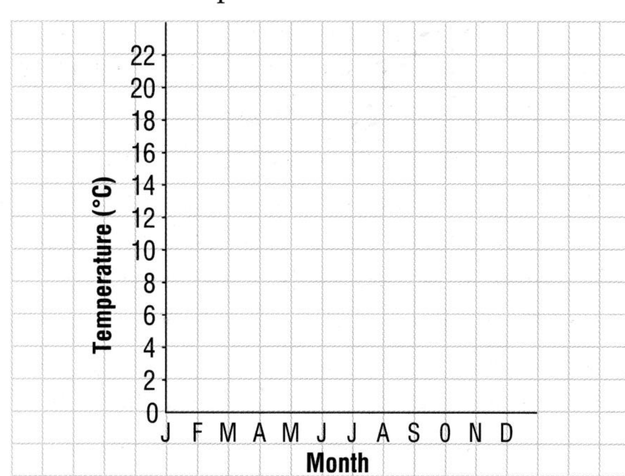

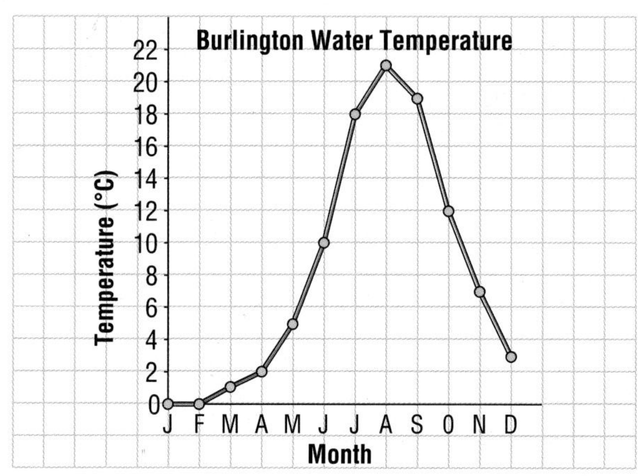

Inquire

1. Why is the broken-line graph more effective than the table?

2. Use the data to draw a broken-line graph of survival times in different months of the year.

3. Explain why a pictograph would not be the best way to represent survival times.

4. Find examples of broken-line graphs in newspapers and magazines. Explain why the data are displayed on broken-line graphs.

Problems and Applications

1. Brendan helped the Student Council to sell school baseball caps. The table gives the amount of time he spent each day selling caps.

Day	Time (min)
Monday	25
Tuesday	30
Wednesday	45
Thursday	20
Friday	50
Saturday	60

a) Display this information on a broken-line graph.
b) On how many days did he work more than half an hour?
c) How much longer did he work on Friday than on Monday?
d) How many minutes did he work during the week?

2. The table gives the approximate number of minutes of daylight per day for different months of the year in Southern Canada.

Month	Daylight (min)
January	550
February	600
March	675
April	750
May	850
June	900
July	900
August	875
September	800
October	700
November	625
December	550

a) Display this information on a broken-line graph.
b) Which months have the same amounts of daylight?
c) Which months have the least daylight?
d) Can the table be true for all parts of Canada? Explain.

3. The table gives the population of Canada, rounded to the nearest half million, since 1867.

Year	Population (millions)
1867	3.5
1871	3.5
1881	4.5
1891	5.0
1901	5.5
1911	7.0
1921	9.0
1931	10.5
1941	11.5
1951	14.0
1961	18.0
1971	21.5
1981	24.5
1991	27.0

a) Display this information on a broken-line graph.
b) In which 10-year period did the population increase the most? Do you know why?
c) Use your graph to predict when the population of Canada should reach thirty million. What assumptions have you made?

4. Suppose you plotted a broken-line graph to show your height each year up to age 12. Could you use the graph to predict what your height will be at age 30? Explain.

5. a) Research the winning times for the men's 50-km walk at the Olympic Games. Plot this information on a broken-line graph.
b) Use your graph to predict the year when the winning time could be 3 h. What assumption have you made?
c) How long would it take you to walk 50 km? Describe how you found out.

6. a) Research the winning distances for the women's javelin throw in the Olympic Games. Plot this information on a broken-line graph.
b) Use your graph to predict the year when the winning distance could be 90 m. What assumption have you made?

9.7 Reading Circle Graphs

Activity: Study the Graph

A circle graph shows how something is divided into parts.

Tourists spend about $4 000 000 000.00 in Canada each year. The circle graph shows how the tourist dollars are divided.

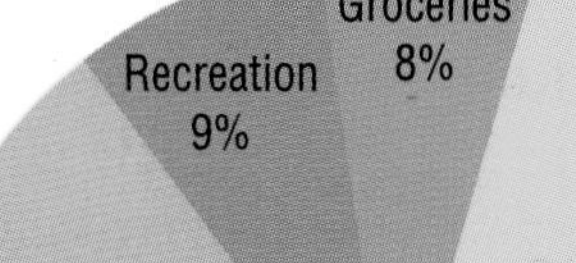

Inquire

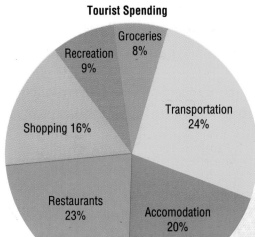

1. From the graph, how many times more money do tourists spend on transportation than on groceries?

2. What fraction of the amount spent on accomodation is the amount spent on groceries?

3. How much do tourists spend on accomodation each year?

4. How much do tourists spend on recreation each year?

5. What percent of the total is spent on food?

6. Which 2 categories together account for about half the spending?

7. What is the difference between the amount spent on groceries and the amount spent on recreation?

Problems and Applications

1. The circle graph shows the results of a survey that asked people which meal they were most likely to buy at a fast-food restaurant.

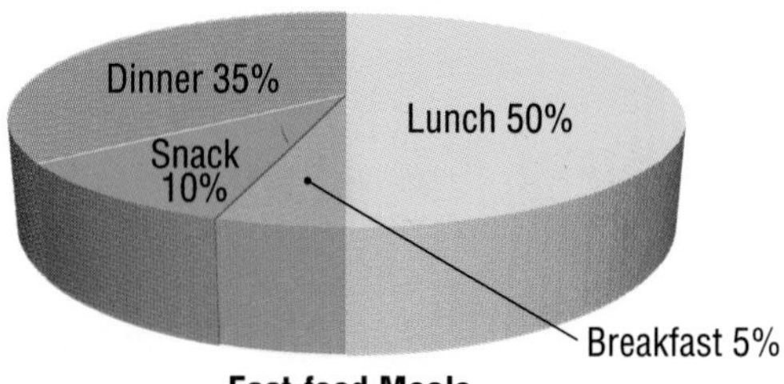

Fast-food Meals

Two thousand people were surveyed.

a) How many said dinner?
b) How many said lunch?
c) How many said a snack?
d) How many said breakfast?

2. The circle graph shows where people eat the food they buy at a restaurant.

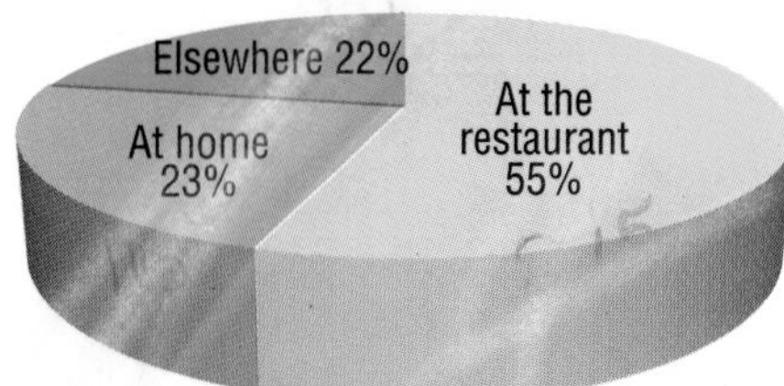

Eating Locations

Five hundred people were surveyed. How many people chose each category?

3. The circle graph shows the areas of the world's oceans.

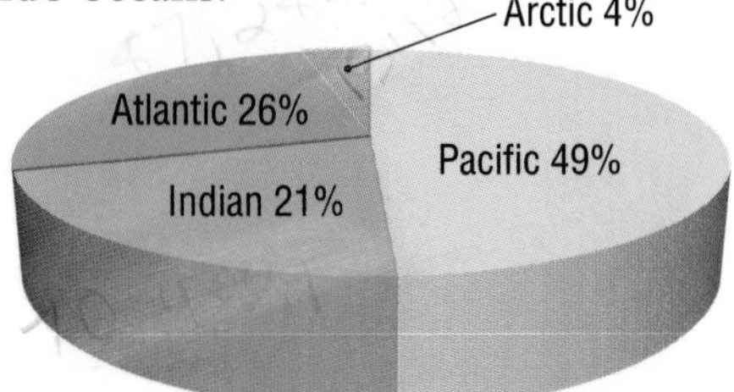

Areas of Oceans

The total area of the oceans is 335 710 000 km^2. What is the area of each ocean?

4. The circle graph shows how one hour of a radio station's time is divided.

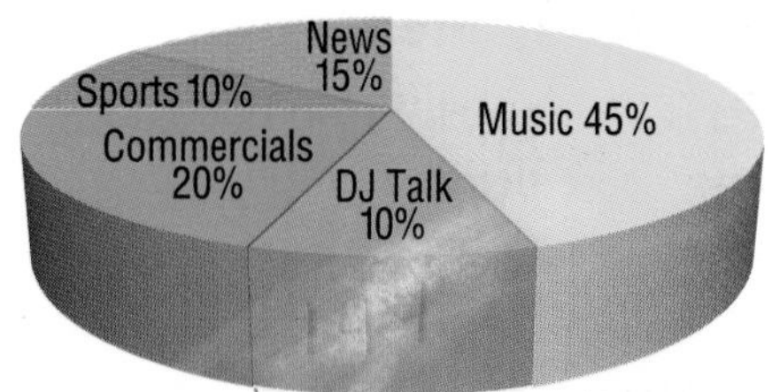

Radio Station's Time

If the station broadcasts for 24 h a day, how many minutes per day are spent on each category?

5. The circle graph shows the destinations of Canadians on trips outside Canada in one year.

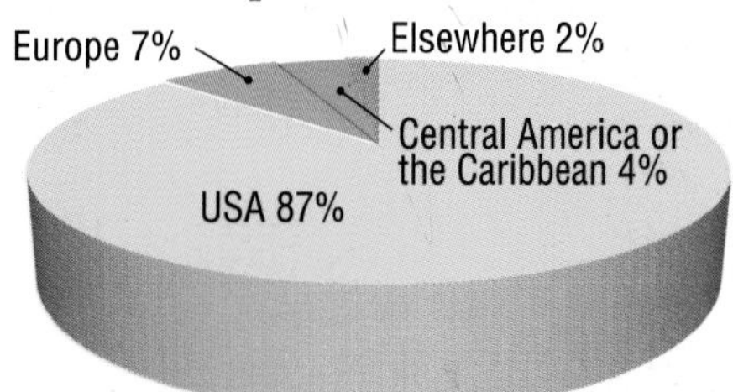

Canadian Trip Destinations

Canadians made 39 000 000 trips outside the country that year. Calculate the number of trips to each destination.

$1^2 = 1$
$11^2 = 121$
$111^2 = ■$
$1111^2 = ■$
$11111^2 = ■$

a) Use your calculator to complete the third and fourth rows in the pattern.
b) Predict the missing number on the fifth row.
c) Describe the pattern in words.

9.8 Drawing Circle Graphs

Activity: Study the Example

It cost a TV network $1 000 000.00 to produce a 1-h special. The costs were divided as follows.

Cast salaries	$600 000.00
Staff salaries	$100 000.00
Writers	$50 000.00
Sets, music, costumes, etc.	$150 000.00
Props, lighting, sound	$100 000.00
Total	$1 000 000.00

To show these costs on a circle graph, follow these steps.

1. Write each cost as a percent of the total cost.

Cast salaries $\frac{600\ 000.00}{1\ 000\ 000.00} \times 100\% = 60\%$

Staff salaries $\frac{100\ 000.00}{1\ 000\ 000.00} \times 100\% = 10\%$

Writers $\frac{50\ 000.00}{1\ 000\ 000.00} \times 100\% = 5\%$

Sets, etc. $\frac{150\ 000.00}{1\ 000\ 000.00} \times 100\% = 15\%$

Props, etc. $\frac{100\ 000.00}{1\ 000\ 000.00} \times 100\% = 10\%$

Total 100%

2. Find the size of each angle for the circle graph. The angle at the centre of a circle is 360°.

Cast Salaries	60% of $360° = 0.60 \times 360° = 216°$
Staff Salaries	10% of $360° = 0.10 \times 360° = 36°$
Writers	5% of $360° = 0.05 \times 360° = 18°$
Sets, etc.	15% of $360° = 0.15 \times 360° = 54°$
Props, etc.	10% of $360° = 0.10 \times 360° = 36°$
Total	360°

3. Draw a circle.

4. Draw the angles with a protractor.

5. Label each sector with a percent.

6. Give the graph a title.

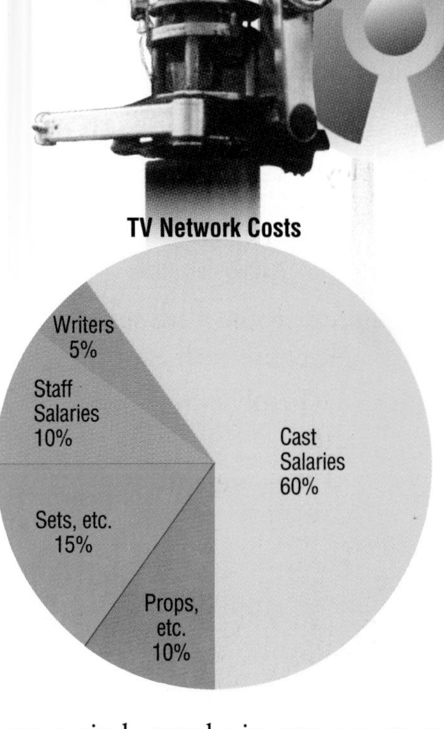

Inquire

1. What does it tell you if the sum of the angles is not 360°? What should you do in that case?

2. Find some circle graphs in newspapers and magazines. Why are the graphs effective?

Problems and Applications

In questions 1–7, display the information on a circle graph.

1. The surface area of the Earth is 71% water and 29% land.

2. Our sun is made up of 90% hydrogen, 8% helium, and 2% other elements.

3. The time in Mike's day is divided as follows.

School	25%
Studying	10%
Sleeping	40%
Meals	10%
Recreation	15%

4. The table shows how we use water in our homes.

Personal Hygiene	30%
Drinking and Eating	3%
Toilet	32%
Dishwashing	10%
Laundry	9%
Garden	3%
Waste	13%

5. The table shows the industries Canadians were employed by in 1990.

Manufacturing	16%
Sales and Distribution	18%
Construction	6%
Utilities	8%
Finance	6%
Services	34%
Government	7%
Other Industries	5%

6. A survey found the ages of people who owned personal stereos. The table gives the results.

Age	Frequency
1 – 9	38
10 – 19	46
20 – 29	34
30 – 39	28
40 – 49	14
50 +	40

7. A fully developed set of human teeth includes the following.

Incisors	8
Canines	4
Bicuspids	8
Molars	12

8. The table shows where every $100 of advertising money is spent.

TV	$19
Magazines	$5
Radio	$7
Newspapers	$30
Mail	$15
Other	$24

a) Display this information on a circle graph.
b) Where would the advertising money in the "other" category be spent?

9. Could you use a circle graph to represent each of the following? Explain.

a) your height at different ages
b) the way you spend your money
c) the percents of crocodiles that are mammals, reptiles, and insects

10. Work with a classmate. Draw a circle graph to show how your time at school is divided.

11. Conduct a survey in your class to find how many schools each of your classmates has attended. Draw a circle graph that shows the percent who have attended one school, the percent who have attended two schools, and so on.

12. Work with a classmate.

a) Choose a topic that you would like to gather information about. Have your topic approved by your teacher.
b) Gather the data and display the results on a circle graph.
c) Write 3 questions based on the graph. Have a classmate solve them.

Computer Databases

A database organizes and stores information so that it is easier to find what you want.

Activity ❶

You have already used many databases. The telephone book is one example.

1. List some databases that you know.

2. Describe the purpose of each database on your list.

Activity ❷

Computer databases let you store, organize, and manage information quickly and easily. To use a computer database, you need to know how the information is stored.

Mark Cliff collects sports cards. He is setting up a database to organize his collection. His first step is to make a **record** of the information he wants for each card. A record is a set of information. Each piece of information is called a **field**.

Here is one of Mark's records. The first column shows the field names he chose. The second column shows the fields.

SPORT	Baseball	These are called character fields. The information does not change for a particular card.
CARD	Topps	
LASTNAME	Bell	
FIRSTNAME	George	
YEAR	1984	
TEAM	Blue Jays	
CARDNUMBER	278	
ROOKIE	No	
COST	1.00	This is a numeric field. The information will change.
VALUE	1.25	

1. List the field names your school principal might choose for a computer database to store information about students. State which field names are for character fields and which ones are for numeric fields.

2. List other examples of the types of information that might usefully be stored on a computer database.

3. Choose a computer database of your own. List the field names you would include in the record.

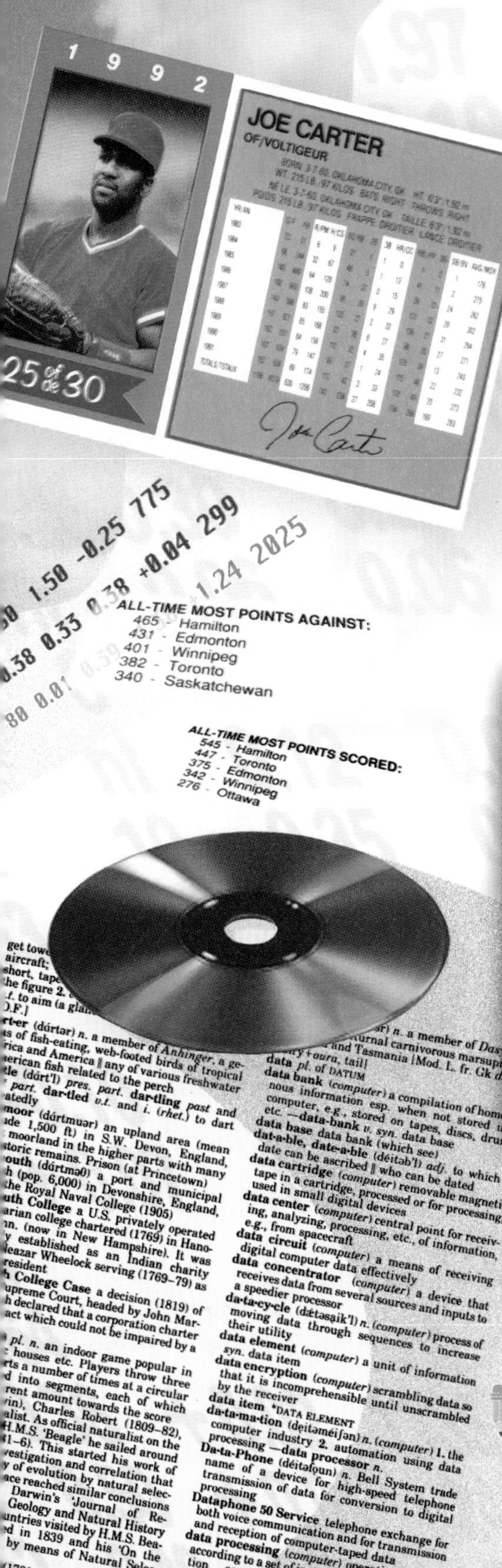

Activity ❸

Once Mark completes his records, he can use the database in many ways.

For example, he can:

- list all his baseball cards
- list all his Topps baseball cards
- list all his Topps rookie baseball cards
- calculate the total he paid for his cards
- calculate the total value of his cards

Suppose Mark instructs his computer to list all the 1986 baseball cards with a value of $0.15 or more. He also requests the first and last names, the card maker, and what the card cost him.

Mark sees the following *Browse* screen.

Records Organize Fields Go to Exit

Card	Lastname	Firstname	Cost	Value
Donruss	Bell	George	1.00	.30
Donruss	Canseco	Jose	15.00	50.00
Donruss	Davis	Glen	2.00	3.75
Donruss	Mattingly	Don	3.00	5.00
Fleer	Bell	George	1.00	.30
Fleer	Clemens	Roger	1.50	3.00
Fleer	Henke	Tom	2.00	.25
Topps	Gooden	Dwight	1.00	1.75
Topps	Jackson	Bo	3.50	9.00
Topps	Ryan	Nolan	1.00	.60
Topps	Stieb	Dave	0	.15

1. What is the total value of these cards?

2. What was the total amount Mark paid for these cards?

3. If he sold his cards, would Mark make a profit or a loss?
How much would he make or lose?

4. If your school principal had student records on a database, what types of information would your principal be most likely to pull up on a *Browse* screen?

9.9 The Mean or Average

Activity: Analyze the Data

The table shows the total numbers of points scored in 4 Grey Cup finals.

Year	Points
1988	43
1989	83
1990	61
1991	57

You want to know the average number of points scored.

Inquire

1. Do you require an exact or approximate answer?
2. Write your definition of average. Compare your definition with your classmates'.
3. What method of calculation will you choose?
4. What was the average number of points scored?

Example

In their first 4 seasons, the Toronto Blue Jays won 54, 59, 53, and 67 games. Determine their average number of wins in their first 4 seasons.

Solution

To find the average of a set of numbers, add the numbers then divide by the number of numbers you added.

$$\frac{54 + 59 + 53 + 67}{4} = \frac{233}{4}$$

$$= 58.25$$

The Toronto Blue Jays averaged 58.25 wins in their first 4 seasons.

The average is also called the **mean**.
The **range** of a set of numbers is the "spread" between the highest number and the lowest number. For the set of Blue Jays' wins, the range is 67 − 53 or 14.

Practice

Find the range of each set of temperatures.

1. 9°C, 5°C, 8°C, 3°C, 6°C, 1°C

2. 18°C, 16°C, 17°C

3. 29°C, 22°C, 24°C, 24°C, 28°C

Find the range of each set of golf scores.

4. 67, 66, 69, 71, 72

5. 88, 78, 92, 91, 69, 76

6. 99, 101, 105, 110, 96, 115

Find the mean and range of each set of test marks.

7. 20, 21, 24, 27

8. 60, 56, 59, 59, 61

9. 83, 81, 74, 75, 86, 87

Find the average of each set of test marks to the nearest tenth.

10. 22, 33, 38, 29

11. 54, 57, 53, 66, 69

12. 82, 81, 74, 75, 61, 66

Problems and Applications

List the following.

13. 3 different numbers with a mean of 50

14. 5 different numbers with a mean of 100

15. 4 different numbers with a mean of 66

16. 6 different numbers with a mean of 82

17. 5 different numbers with a mean of 75 and a range of 8

18. On his first history test, Paul got 75. On his second test, he got 83. He got 98 on the third test.

a) Find his average after the first 2 tests.
b) Find his average after the third test.

19. Carson went to 5 stores and priced socks for the basketball team. The prices he found were \$9.45, \$9.95, \$8.75, \$9.70, and \$9.50 per pair. What was the average price?

20. Donna is in a bowling league. The table shows her scores for 3 weeks.

Week	1st Game	2nd Game	3rd Game
1	176	188	194
2	183	180	213
3	191	175	192

Find her average

a) at the end of the first week,
b) at the end of the second week, and
c) at the end of the third week.

21. During the first 6 weeks of school, Franco averaged \$31.50 a week for lunches. How much did he spend for lunches during the 6 weeks?

22. Nabila bowled 203 and 198 in her first 2 games. What will she have to bowl in the third game to have an average of 205?

23. The inflation rate is the percent by which the cost of living increases each year. Some Canadian inflation rates are shown in the table

Year	Inflation Rate %
1983	5.7
1984	4.4
1985	3.9
1986	4.2
1987	4.4
1988	4.0
1989	5.0
1990	4.8

What was the average inflation rate in Canada from 1983 to 1990?

24. The mean of 2 numbers is 10. Can you identify the numbers? Explain.

25. a) Take your pulse to find how many times your heart beats in a minute.
b) Find the mean and range of the heart rates in your class.

26. Work with a classmate. List 5 situations in which an average is used. Describe how the average is used in each situation.

9.10 The Median and the Mode

The middle number in a set of numbers arranged in order is called the **median**.
The number that occurs most often in a set of numbers is called the **mode**.
For the numbers 14, 15, 16, 18, and 18, the median is 16, and the mode is 18.

Activity: Analyze the Data

Karen helps train golden retrievers and Labrador retrievers as guide dogs. The dogs live in foster homes for their first year. Then they are old enough to be trained.

There are 9 golden retrievers to be trained. Their masses are

39 kg, 41 kg, 43 kg, 42 kg, 39 kg,
40 kg, 38 kg, 41 kg, 39 kg

Inquire

1. Arrange the masses in order from smallest to largest.

2. What is the median mass?

3. What mass is the mode?

4. Why is it important to know the masses and heights of guide dogs?

Suppose one of the 39-kg dogs was bought as a guide dog. The masses of the remaining dogs would be as follows.

38 kg, 39 kg, 39 kg, 40 kg, 41 kg, 41 kg, 42 kg, 43 kg

There are now two middle masses, 40 kg and 41 kg. The new median is the average of these two masses.

$$\frac{40 + 41}{2} = \frac{81}{2}$$
$$= 40.5$$

The new median mass is 40.5 kg.

The masses 39 kg and 41 kg now occur most often. There are two modes, 39 kg and 41 kg.

Practice

Find the mode or modes of the test scores.

1. 8, 9, 8, 7, 7, 8, 9, 6

2. 56, 55, 57, 59, 56, 60

3. 12, 13, 14, 12, 13, 15, 16, 17

Find the median.

4. 34, 36, 33, 32, 37

5. 81, 88, 89, 98, 87, 86, 82

6. 45, 46, 43, 42

7. 18, 22, 17, 19, 21, 23

8. 56, 57, 59, 47, 48, 50, 40

9. 9, 8, 7, 8, 6, 9, 5, 6

Problems and Applications

List the following.

10. 5 different numbers with a median of 67

11. 7 different numbers with a median of 75

12. 4 different numbers with a median of 28

13. 6 different numbers with a median of 61

14. The heights of the 6 players on a basketball team are as follows.

175 cm   182 cm   189 cm
193 cm   169 cm   184 cm

a) Find the median height.
b) Find the mean height.
c) If a player who is 203 cm tall joins the team, what are the new median height and mean height?

15. The table shows the times for a 50-m dash.

Runner	Time (s)
Jennifer	6.9
Ingrid	6.7
Shima	7.4
Chantal	6.5
Karen	6.5

a) Calculate the median time.
b) Calculate the mean time.
c) State the mode.
d) How many runners were faster than the median time?
e) How many runners were faster than the mean time?
f) How many runners had times that were faster than the mode?

16. The following marks were received by 11 students on a swimming test.

80, 73, 71, 70, 24, 68, 72, 74, 75, 50, 80

a) Calculate the mean, median, and mode of these marks.
b) How many marks are greater than the median?
c) How many marks are less than the median?
d) How many marks are greater than the mean?
e) How many marks are less than the mean?
f) How many marks are greater than the mode?
g) How many marks are less than the mode?
h) Compare how effective the mean, median, and mode are at showing the centre of the data. Explain your reasoning.

17. To the nearest hour, estimate the amount of time you spend watching TV in a week.

a) Determine the mean and median values of the estimates in your group.
b) Compare your results with those of other groups.

NUMBER POWER

The lowest and highest of a set of 7 whole numbers are 6 and 16. The mode is 15. The median is 10. The mean is 11. Find the numbers.

9.11 Stem-and-Leaf Plots

A stem-and-leaf plot is a very efficient way to organize data in increasing order.

Activity: Analyze the Data

Two police officers surveyed the speeds of cars passing Oakdale School. Francine Geneva used a radar gun to determine the speed of each car in kilometres per hour. She recorded the following speeds.

48, 37, 54, 38, 44
46, 29, 42, 41, 52
51, 40, 38, 50, 39
43, 54, 38, 48

As she called out each speed to her partner, Wayne Carson, he recorded it as a stem and a leaf.

For each piece of data, the first digit was the stem and the second the leaf.

The stems for the car speeds were 2, 3, 4, and 5. The diagrams show how Wayne recorded the speeds.

2	
3	
4	
5	

"48"

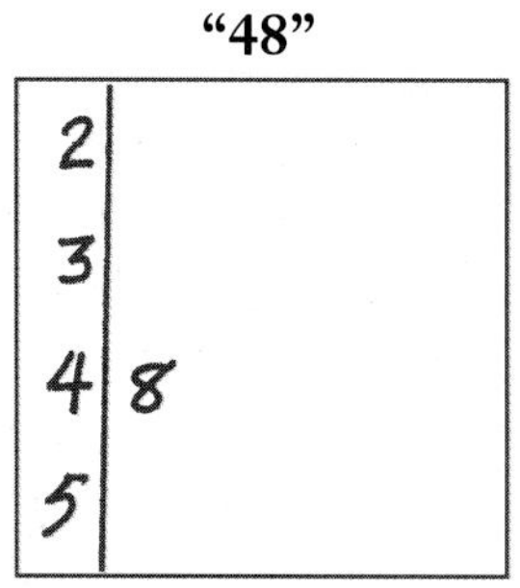

2	
3	
4	8
5	

"37, 54, 38"

2	
3	78
4	8
5	4

"44, 46, 29"

2	9
3	78
4	846
5	4

"42, 41, 52"

2	9
3	78
4	84621
5	42

"51, 40, 38"

2	9
3	788
4	846210
5	421

"50, 39, 43"

2	9
3	7889
4	8462103
5	4210

"54, 38, 48"

2	9
3	78898
4	84621038
5	42104

To find the median speed, Wayne arranged the leaves in order from smallest to largest. The result was this stem-and-leaf plot.

Car Speeds (km/h)	
2	9
3	7 8 8 8 9
4	0 1 2 3 4 6 8 8
5	0 1 2 4 4

Inquire

1. What was the range of speeds?
2. How many speeds were recorded in the plot?
3. What was the median speed? How do you know?
4. What speed was the mode?

Practice

Find the median, mode, and range.

1.

Nursery Plant Heights (cm)	
2	5 6 8 9 9 2
3	6 1 1 2 0 1 7
4	0 1 2 3 7
5	3 1 0

2.

Hotel Room Rates ($)	
7	7 9 4 6
8	1 8 4 6 2 9 0
9	4 2 2 9 4 2 3 5 7
10	1 0 1 3

3.

Masses of Horses (kg)	
22	0 1 0 2
23	2 0 8 3 5 7
24	4 6 1 7 9 5
25	2 5 6 7
26	3 0

Problems and Applications

4. The list shows the ages of Canada's Prime Ministers at the start of their terms.

52, 51, 70, 47, 70, 74, 54, 57, 46,
47, 60, 66, 61, 65, 48, 39, 55, 45

a) Construct a stem-and-leaf plot for the ages.
b) Find the median, mode, and range.
c) Name the youngest Prime Minister.

5. Major League baseball teams play 162 games a season. The list shows the number of games won by the Montreal Expos in their first 22 seasons.

52, 73, 71, 70, 79, 79, 75,
55, 75, 76, 95, 90, 86, 82,
78, 84, 78, 91, 81, 81, 85, 70

a) Construct a stem-and-leaf plot for the games won.
b) Find the median, mode, and range.
c) In how many seasons did they win more than half of their games?
d) Research the number of wins per season for the Toronto Blue Jays since 1977. (Do not include the shortened 1981 season.) Use a stem-and-leaf plot to determine the median, mode, and range. Compare the values with those for the Montreal Expos.

6. Describe the advantages and disadvantages of using a stem-and-leaf plot to organize data. Compare your opinions with your classmates'.

Misleading Graphs

Graphs display information clearly and attractively. Be careful when you read graphs. Some graphs are misleading.

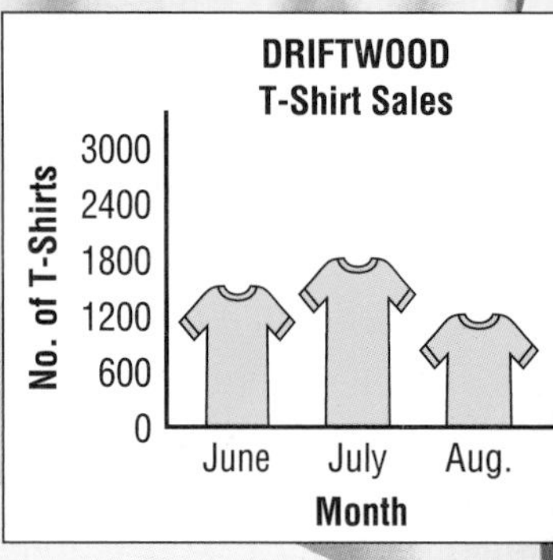

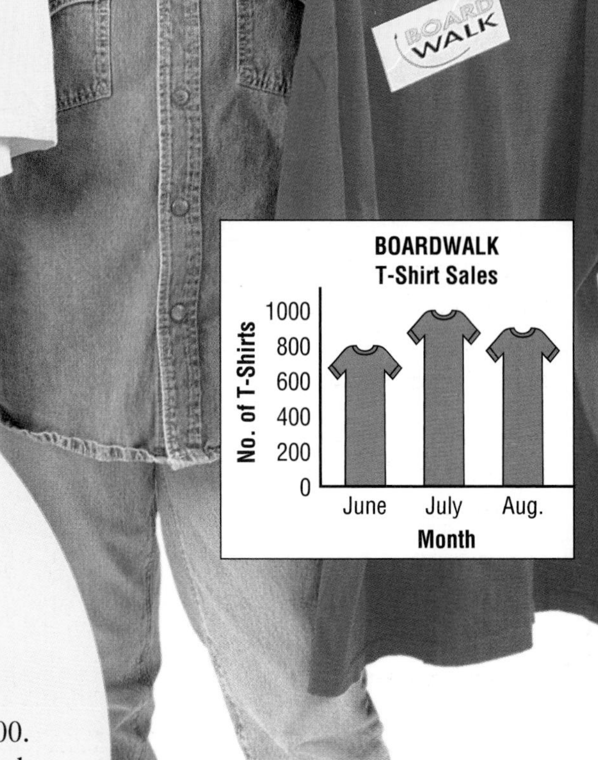

Activity ❶

The two graphs show the number of T-shirts sold by two stores, the Boardwalk and the Driftwood, in three months.

When you first look, you may think that the Boardwalk sold more T-shirts.

But look at the vertical axes. On the Boardwalk graph, the vertical axis is marked off in units of 200. On the Driftwood graph, the vertical axis is marked off in units of 600.

1. How many T-shirts did each store sell in June?

2. How many T-shirts did each store sell altogether in three months?

When you compare graphs, make sure you look at the scales on the axes.

Activity ❷

The graphs both display the number of bicycle sales for Milanetti Cycle for the same six months.

1. How are the graphs different?
2. What impression does each graph give?

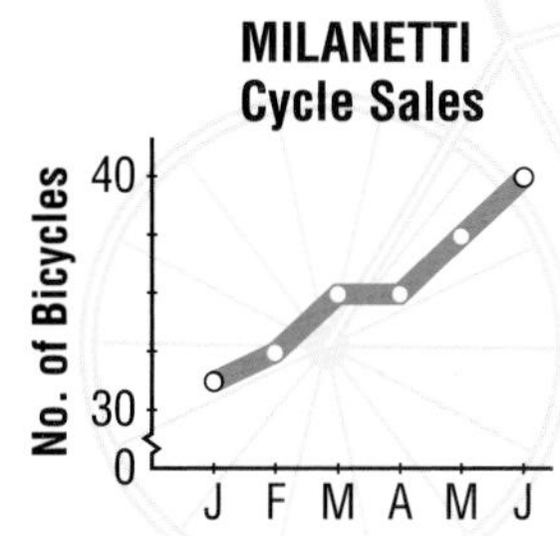

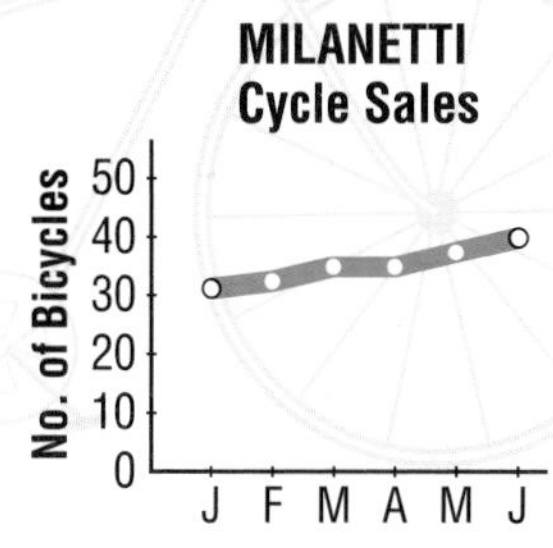

Activity ❸

Two classes at St. Paul's School compete to see who can sell the most boxes of oranges.

Class 7 sells 100 boxes.
Class 8 sells 200 boxes.

Carl, who is in Class 8, uses this pictograph to display the results. He claims it is fair. He makes the lines twice as long for Class 8, because it sells twice as many boxes of oranges.

Debbie, who is in Class 7, argues that Carl's graph is misleading.

Why? What makes it look as though Class 8 sells more than twice as many oranges as Class 7?

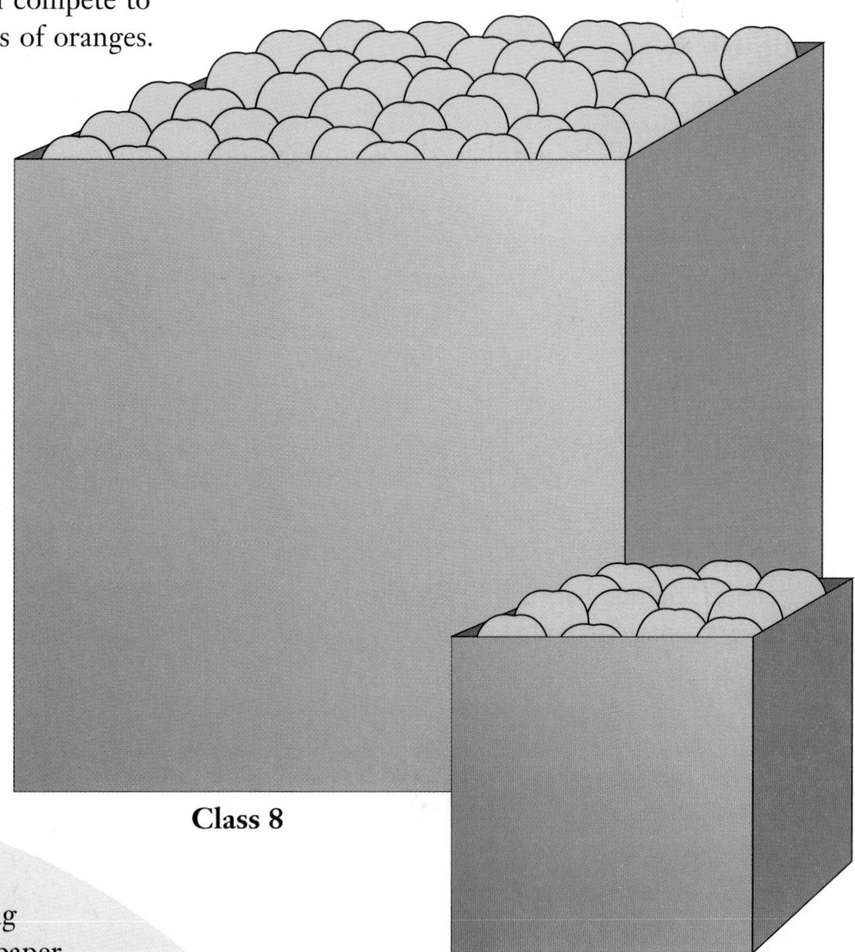

Activity ❹

Find an example of a misleading graph in a magazine or a newspaper. If you cannot find one, draw one.

Explain why the graph is misleading.
Describe how to make the graph more realistic.

9.12 Possible Outcomes

Activity: Conduct an Experiment

Work with a classmate. Roll a die and toss a coin at the same time. Record your results in a table, like the one shown.

Outcome	Die	Coin
1	6	H
2	4	T

Each result you get is known as an **outcome**. Repeat the experiment 25 times and record the outcomes.

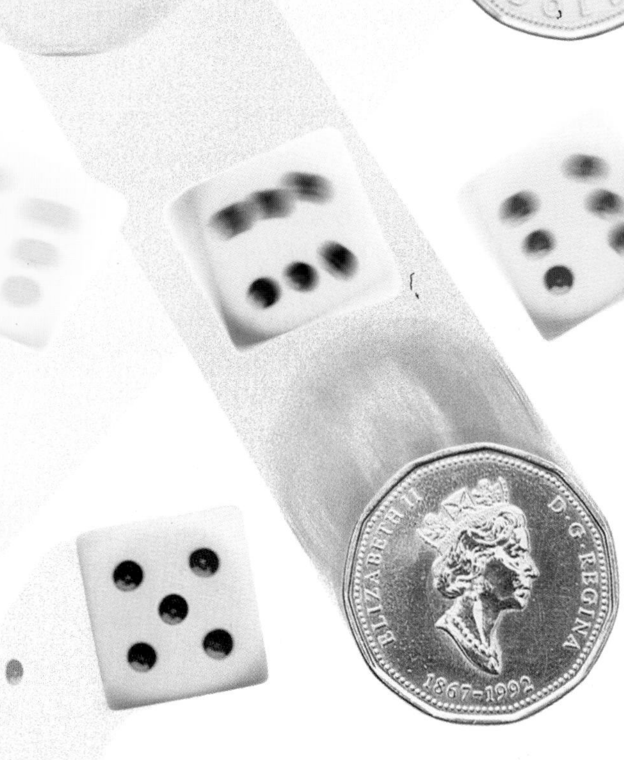

Inquire

1. What are all the possible outcomes when you roll a die?

2. What are all the possible outcomes when you toss a coin?

3. One possible outcome of the experiment is a head and a 5. What are all the other possible outcomes?

When you toss a coin, the chance of getting a head or a tail is the same. We say that the outcomes are **equally likely**.

When you roll a die, the chance of getting each of the numbers 1 to 6 is the same. Again, the outcomes are equally likely.

Example

If you spin the spinner, there are three possible outcomes — red, yellow, or blue. Are the outcomes equally likely? If not, which outcome is most likely?

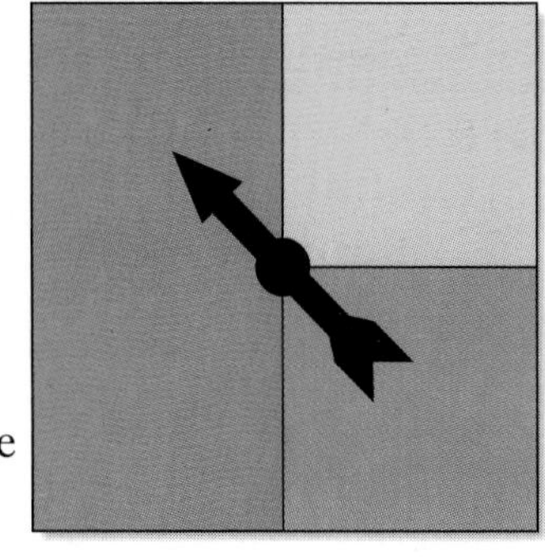

Solution

The outcomes are not equally likely, because the 3 coloured sections are not equal in area.

The red section is larger than the others. The chance of the outcome being red is greater than the chance of the outcome being yellow or blue. Red is the most likely outcome.

Problems and Applications

For each experiment, state the possible outcomes. Decide if the possible outcomes are equally likely or not. If the possible outcomes are not equally likely, state the most likely outcome.

1. Spin the spinner.

2. Flip a baseball card.

3. Drop a thumbtack on the floor.

4. Spin the spinner.

5. Roll a cube with faces lettered A, B, C, D, E, and F.

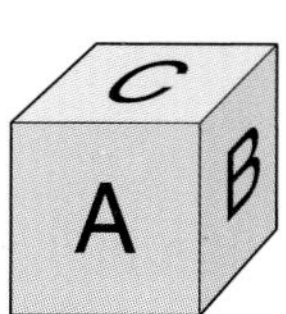

6. Drop a plastic cup on the floor.

7. Shoot a foul shot.

8. Spin the spinner.

9. Toss a nickel and a penny at the same time.

10. Roll a red die and a blue die at the same time.

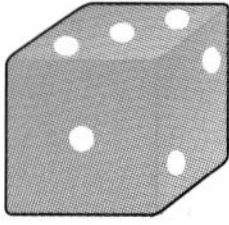

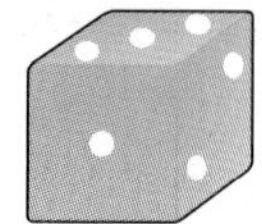

11. Design 2 experiments. One should have equally likely outcomes. The other should not. Ask a classmate to identify which is which.

CALCULATOR POWER

Use a calculator to complete the calculations.

$1^2 + 2^2 + 2^2 = 3^2$
$2^2 + 3^2 + 6^2 = \blacksquare$
$3^2 + 4^2 + 12^2 = \blacksquare$
$4^2 + 5^2 + 20^2 = \blacksquare$

a) How are the numbers on the left determined?
b) How can you predict the number that will be squared on the right?
c) Write the next 3 rows and check your answer with a calculator.

9.13 Probability

Activity: Conduct An Experiment

Work with a classmate. Place 6 markers in a bag —3 red, 2 blue, and 1 white. Draw a marker from the bag, record the colour, and return the marker to the bag. Carry out the experiment 30 times.

Inquire

1. Predict the number of times you expect each colour to be drawn in 30 trials.

2. Compare your prediction with the actual results.

3. Compare your results with those of your classmates.

4. What results would you expect if you did the experiment 6000 times?

Example 1

What is the chance of spinning a 4?

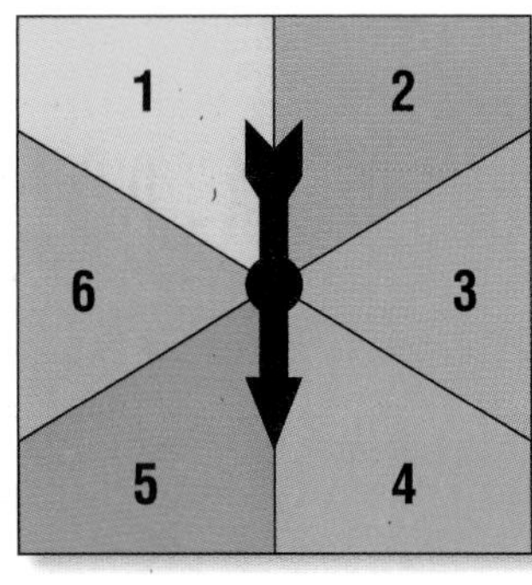

Solution

The 6 possible outcomes are 1, 2, 3, 4, 5, and 6. Each outcome is equally likely. Spinning a 4 is a **favourable outcome**. The chance of spinning a 4 is "one out of six" or 1 out of 6 or $\frac{1}{6}$.

We normally use the word **probability** instead of chance. We write the probability of spinning a 4 as $P(4)$.

So, $P(4) = \frac{1}{6}$.

Example 2

What is the probability of spinning a 5 or a 6?

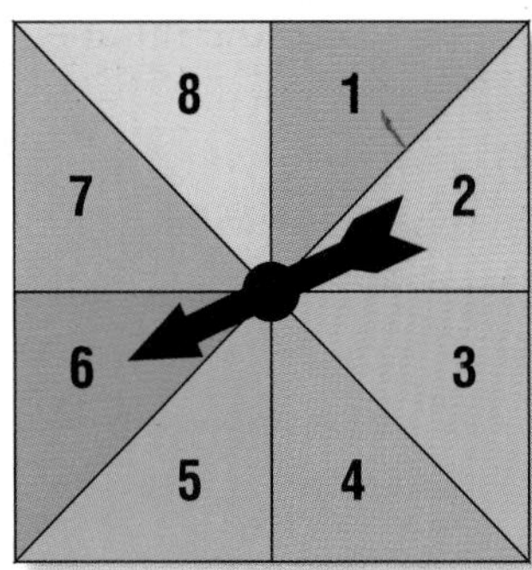

Solution

The 8 possible outcomes are 1, 2, 3, 4, 5, 6, 7 and 8. All are equally likely. The 2 favourable outcomes are 5 and 6.

$P(5 \text{ or } 6) = \frac{2}{8}$ or $\frac{1}{4}$

The probability of spinning a 5 or a 6 is $\frac{1}{4}$.

Example 3

What is the probability of spinning a 7?

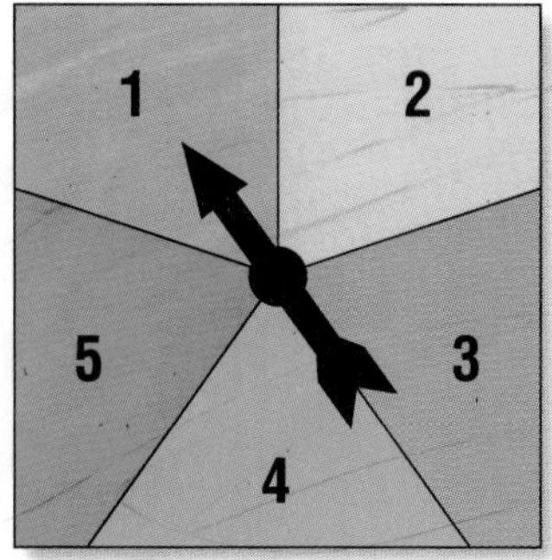

Solution

The 5 possible outcomes are 1, 2, 3, 4, and 5. The favourable outcome, 7, is not possible.

$P(7) = \frac{0}{5} = 0$

Problems and Applications

In questions 1–8, find the probability of each event.

1. Spin the spinner.
a) P(red) **b)** P(blue)
c) P(yellow) **d)** P(white)

2. Toss the coin.
a) P(head) **b)** P(tail)

3. Roll the die.
a) $P(2)$ **b)** $P(5)$
c) $P(3$ or $4)$ **d)** P(even number)

4. Choose one marble without looking.
a) P(red) **b)** P(blue)
c) P(green) **d)** P(yellow)

5. Choose one card without looking.

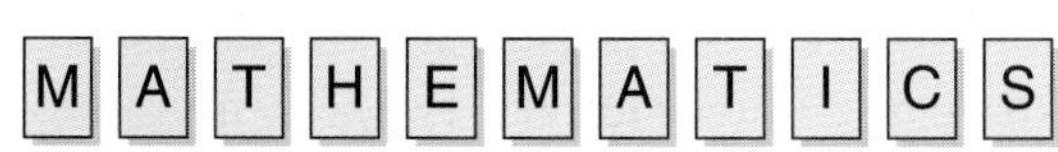

a) P(M)
b) P(A)
c) P(vowel)
d) P(W)

6. The outcomes on this spinner are not equally likely. Spin the spinner.
a) P(red) **b)** P(blue)
c) P(yellow) **d)** P(purple)

7. The outcomes on this spinner are not equally likely. Spin the spinner.
a) P(red) **b)** P(blue)
c) P(green) **d)** P(yellow)

8. Choose one card without looking.

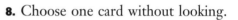

a) $P(3)$
b) $P(15)$
c) P(multiple of 3)
d) P(even number)
e) P(prime number)
f) P(number less than 13)

9. a) Draw a spinner that would give these probabilities.

$P(\text{yellow}) = \frac{1}{3}$ $P(\text{blue}) = \frac{1}{2}$

$P(\text{white}) = \frac{1}{6}$ $P(\text{red}) = 0$

b) Predict the outcomes if you spun the spinner 3000 times.

10. Design an event that has a probability of $\frac{1}{5}$.

11. Can you draw a spinner that gives 4 possible outcomes with the following probabilities? Explain.

$\frac{1}{4}$ $\frac{1}{5}$ $\frac{3}{10}$ $\frac{2}{5}$

THE GAME SHOW

Gerry was the contestant on a television game show called *It's Your Move*. Gerry answered all the questions correctly. He then had the chance to win the big prize, a new car.

The host led Gerry to three doors on the stage. The doors were numbered 1, 2, and 3. The host explained that there was a new car behind one of the doors and nothing behind the other two. The host said that she knew which door hid the car.

The host asked Gerry to pick a door. Gerry chose door number 2. The host then walked over to the doors and opened door number 3. There was nothing behind door number 3. Then the host asked Gerry if he would like to change his mind about door number 2 and take door number 1.

Gerry thought for a minute and said, "I will take door number 1."

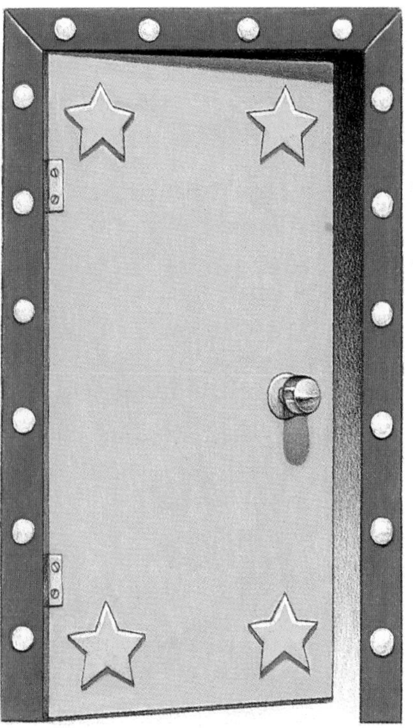

Activity 1

1. Did Gerry make the choice that gave him the best chance to win the car? Explain why you think Gerry should or should not have changed his mind.

2. Compare your decision with your classmates'.

Activity 2

1. Test whether Gerry was right to change his mind. Work in groups and set up the game. You could use cups for the doors and a piece of chalk for the car. Choose a host, a contestant, and a recorder. Play the game and have the the recorder write the result in a table, like the one shown.

Gerry should have changed his mind.	Gerry should not have changed his mind.

2. Take turns at being the host, the contestant, and the recorder. Play the game a total of 20 times. Record all the results. Use the results to decide whether Gerry was right.

The Dinosaur Museum

A display was being set up in a new wing of the Dinosaur Museum. Five dinosaurs were to be displayed in 6 rooms. Only 1 dinosaur would fit into any room at one time.

The diagram shows where the staff set up the dinosaurs. Unfortunately, the *Brontosaurus* and the *Tyrannosaurus* were in the wrong rooms.

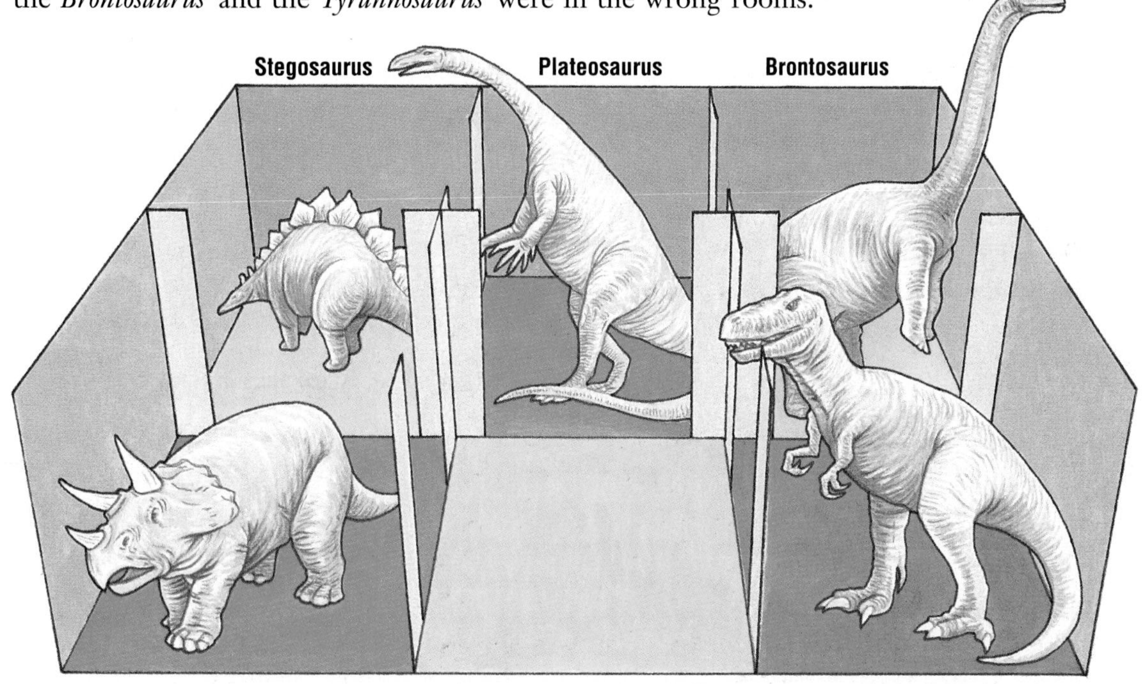

The staff must now switch the *Brontosaurus* and the *Tyrannosaurus* by moving 1 dinosaur at a time into a vacant room. The doors are shown on the diagram.

There are many ways to switch the *Brontosaurus* and the *Tyrannosaurus*. The problem is to make the switch in as few moves as possible. It is not important which rooms the other 3 dinosaurs end up in. However, the empty room shown in the diagram must be empty after all the moves.

Activity

1. Copy the floor plan of the Museum and label pieces of paper to represent the dinosaurs. Determine the smallest number of moves needed to switch the *Brontosaurus* and the *Tyrannosaurus*. Moving a single dinosaur is 1 move.

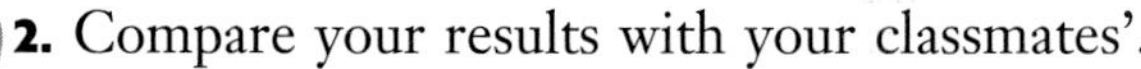

2. Compare your results with your classmates'.

Review

1. Monica surveyed some students at her school to determine their favourite method of travel for short trips. In the following list of results, c means car, b means bus, and t means train.

c c c b t b c t b c b c c
t b t b c c c t b t b t t
c b c t b c c t t b c c b
c b t c c b b c t t b c c

a) Complete a survey sheet for the data.
b) How many chose the train?
c) How many chose the bus?
d) How many chose the car?
e) How many students did Monica survey?

2. There are 600 students in Masao's school. Masao surveyed 50 of them and found that 32 would buy school baseball caps. Predict how many students in the school would buy school baseball caps.

3. The bar graph shows the results of a survey to determine the favourite hockey team among students at Riverside School.

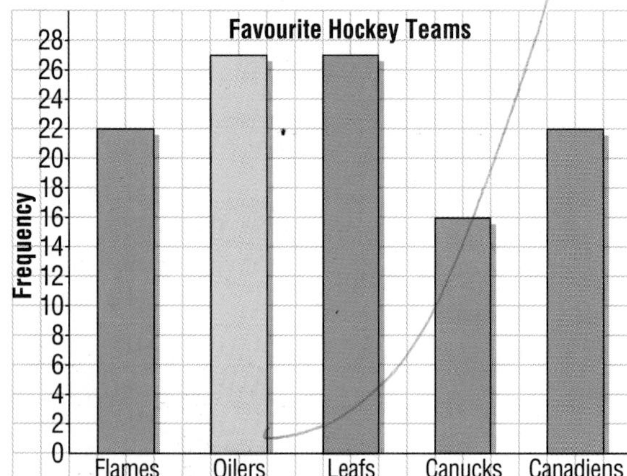

a) Which team was the most popular?
b) Which team got the fewest votes?
c) How many students voted for the Canadiens?
d) How many students were surveyed?

4. The table gives the results of a survey about favourite school subjects.

Subject	Tally	Frequency
History	卌 卌 ||||	
Science	卌 卌 ||	
Math	卌 卌 卌 卌	
Physical Education	卌 卌 卌 卌 ||	
Art	卌 卌 |||	

a) Complete the frequency column.
b) How many students were surveyed?
c) Display the data on a bar graph.
d) Display the data on a pictograph.

5. The broken-line graph shows the mean daily temperature in Victoria, British Columbia, for each month of the year.

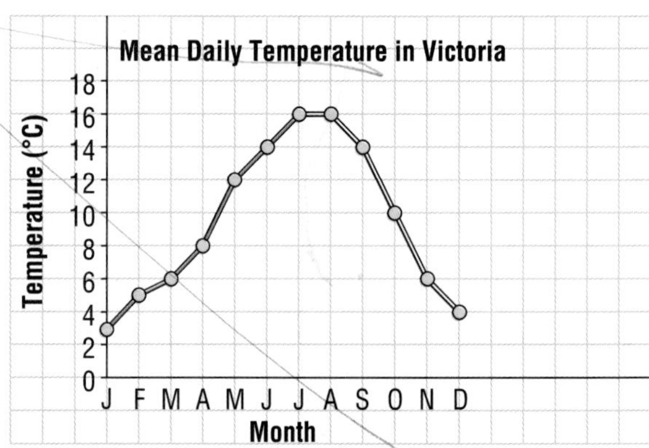

a) State the 2 warmest months.
b) State the coldest month.
c) State the range of the data.

6. The table shows Canadian wheat exports for various years.

Subject	Wheat Exports (million tonnes)
1984	21.8
1985	17.5
1986	17.7
1987	20.8
1988	23.5
1989	12.4
1990	17.4

a) Display this information on a broken-line graph.
b) What were the total wheat exports in these 7 years?

7. The table shows the percents of the gases in dry air at sea level.

Gas	Percent
Nitrogen	78%
Oxygen	20%
Argon	1%
Other gases	1%

Display these data on a circle graph.

8. Calculate the mean, median, mode, and range of each set of data.

a) 22, 18, 18, 19, 20, 21, 19, 24, 19

b) 76, 81, 77, 80, 78, 79, 79, 78

9. a) Construct a stem-and-leaf plot for the following test scores.

70, 80, 81, 82, 67, 68, 90, 91
93, 82, 84, 85, 70, 71, 72, 75
75, 86, 68, 73, 90, 92, 83, 85
93, 76, 76, 69, 77, 78, 79

b) Find the median and range for the scores.

Find the probability of the following events.

10. Choose one marble without looking.

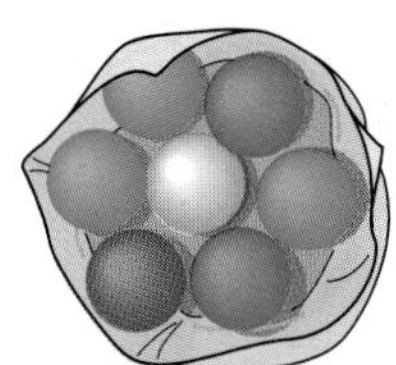

a) P(red) **b)** P(blue)
c) P(green) **d)** P(white)

11. Spin the spinner.

a) P(blue)
b) P(red)
c) P(white)

Group Decision Making
Researching Health Careers

1. As a class, brainstorm the careers you might investigate. They might include such careers as doctor, nurse, medical technician, dentist, dental assistant, dental hygienist, or physiotherapist. As a class, choose 6 careers.

2. Go to home groups and arrange yourselves in pairs. Decide as a group which career each pair will investigate.

1 2 3 4 5 6	1 2 3 4 5 6
PAIRS WITHIN HOME GROUPS	
1 2 3 4 5 6	1 2 3 4 5 6

3. In your pair, list the questions you want to answer about your career. Include a question about how the career makes use of math. Research the answers.

4. Exchange questions with a pair that researched a different career. Research the other pair's set of questions. Assess your findings to make sure you have answered the questions.

5. Pool your information with the pair that gave you questions. Work as a group of 4 to prepare a report on both careers you investigated.

6. In your group of 4, evaluate the group process and your report. Identify what went well and what you would do differently next time.

Chapter Check

1. There are about 10 000 people in Dunhaven. Sarah found that 31 of the 50 people she surveyed were in favour of a new mall. Predict how many people in Dunhaven were in favour of the mall.

2. The bar graph shows how some students get to school.

a) How many take the bus?
b) How many walk?
c) How many ride a bicycle?
d) How many were surveyed?

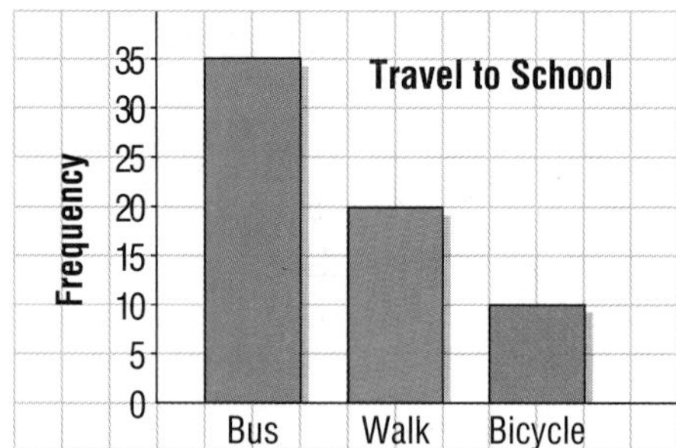

3. The pictograph shows the percent of Canadian households that owned various appliances in 1990.

a) What percent of households had cable TV?
b) What percent had air conditioners?
c) Did more households have dishwashers or CD players?
d) How many times more households had radios than had dishwashers?

Percent with Appliances

Air Conditioner ● ● ◖
Cable TV ● ● ● ● ● ● ●
CD Player ● ◖
Dishwasher ● ● ● ●
Radio ● ● ● ● ● ● ● ● ● ●

Each ● represents 10%.

4. The table gives the temperature at noon in Sydney, Nova Scotia, for 1 week. Display this information on a broken-line graph.

Day	Temperature (°C)
Monday	19
Tuesday	14
Wednesday	9
Thursday	11
Friday	7
Saturday	13
Sunday	16

5. The circle graph shows how a school is divided by grade. If there are 600 students, how many are in each grade?

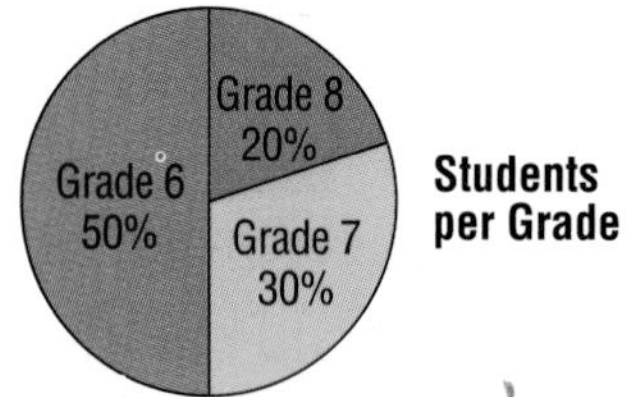

6. Calculate the mean, median, mode, and range of the following data.

23, 26, 25, 33, 24, 27, 24

7. Construct a stem-and-leaf plot for the following test scores.

14, 21, 22, 30, 25, 26, 28, 20
30, 15, 19, 23, 24, 29, 31

8. Choose one marble without looking. Find the following probabilities.

a) $P(\text{red})$ **b)** $P(\text{blue})$

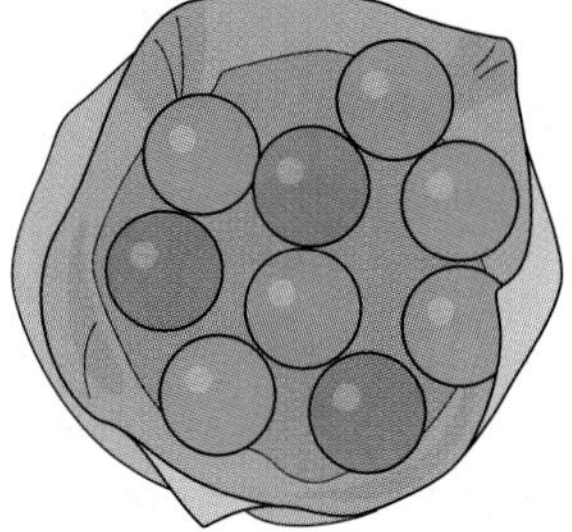

Using the Strategies

1. While investigating a crime, a detective learned that a cruise ship left port on the morning of February 20, 1992, and returned on the afternoon of March 3, 1992. How many nights did the passengers spend on the ship?

2. Before school started, Erin bought 4 shirts at $28.80 each and 3 pairs of socks at $4.65 a pair. What was the total cost before tax?

3. The area of the square is one-half the area of the rectangle.

Use the same number of whole toothpicks to make 2 four-sided figures so that one figure has an area one-quarter the area of the other.

4. Find the patterns and complete the tables.

a)

9	19
12	25
14	29
8	?
17	?
?	41

b)

16	7
20	9
32	15
12	?
44	?
?	11

5. Paula, Kirsten, Erica, and Zanana played a video game. Erica scored more points than Kirsten. Zanana scored less than Kirsten. Zanana scored more points than Paula.

a) Who scored the most points?

b) Who was second?

c) Who was third?

6. Mahmud's eyeglasses cost $310.00 The lenses cost him $45.00 more than the frames. What was the cost of the frames?

7. How many rectangles are in the figure? (Remember a square is also a rectangle.)

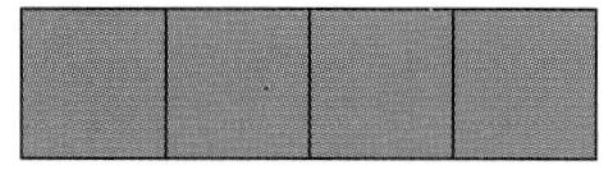

8. If you use 4 straight cuts, what is the largest number of pieces you can get from a round pizza?

9. The diagram shows the four parking lots at a fairground. Assume that when cars come to an intersection, half go one way and half the other way. If 2000 cars enter the parking area, how many end up in each lot?

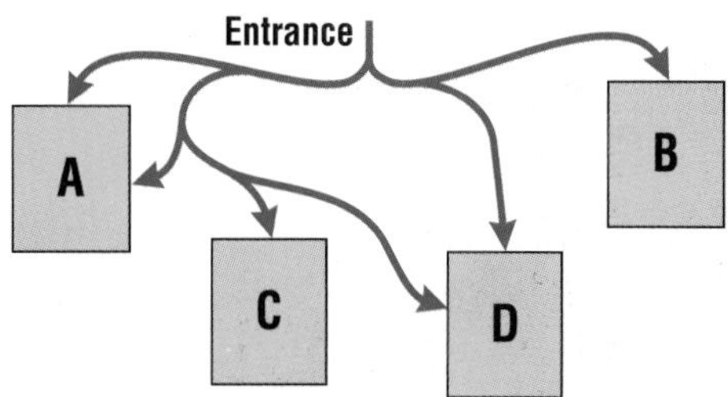

10. Susan packed 3 pairs of jeans and 3 shirts for a camping trip. How many different combinations of jeans and shirts can she wear?

11. Lester B. Pearson was born on April 23, 1897. He served as Prime Minister of Canada from April 22, 1963, until April 20, 1968. How old was he when his term as Prime Minister ended?

DATA BANK

1. If a plane flies at 800 km/h and you leave Regina at 08:00, about what time will you arrive in Toronto?

2. Use the DATA BANK to create a problem. Have a classmate solve the problem.

28
27
26
25
24
23
22
21
20
19
18
17
16
15
14
13
12
11
10
THORNHILL

CHAPTER 10

Integers

The St. Lawrence Seaway-Great Lakes Waterway System links the Great Lakes and the St. Lawrence River to the Atlantic Ocean.

The diagram shows the elevations or heights above sea level of parts of the route from Thunder Bay to Montreal. Use the diagram to answer the following questions.

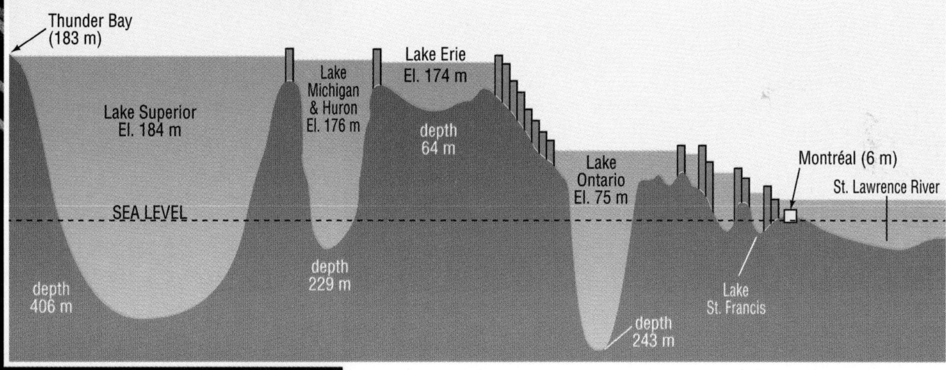

1. How far below sea level are the bottoms of Lakes Superior, Huron, and Ontario?

2. What do the red markings on the diagram mean?

3. How far must ships be raised or lowered between Lakes Erie and Ontario?

4. How far must ships be raised or lowered between Thunder Bay and Montreal?

A Number Jigsaw

Fit the 5 pieces below into the spaces in the puzzle so that the numbers add to 15 in every direction.

A Lock

Solve this problem with a classmate.

Sandra has designed a clever lock for the safe. The lock has 16 buttons, numbered from 1 to 16. The numbers in each row and column and along each diagonal add to 34. So do the numbers in the 4 corners.

All the numbers are hidden until you press ENTER.

When you press ENTER, the numbers 12, 7, 3, 10, 15, 5, and 4 appear on the buttons as shown.

To open the lock, you have up to 2 min to find and press button number 2. If you press any other button, the alarm will go off.

Find button number 2 in less than 2 min.

Warm Up

Find the number of cubes in each figure. In questions 2 and 3, the hole goes right through each figure.

1.

2.

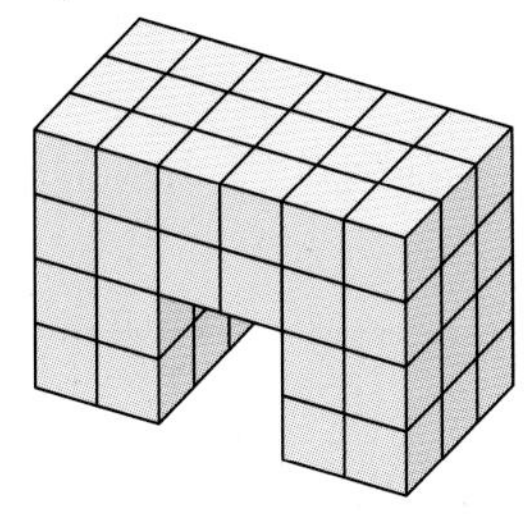

3.

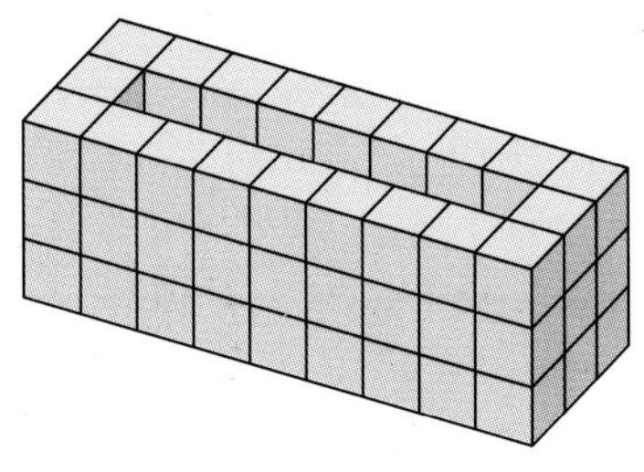

4.

Graph on a whole number line.

5. 5, 6, 7, 8, … **6.** 6, 5, 4, 3, … **7.** $x > 7$ **8.** $x < 5$ **9.** $x \geq 9$ **10.** $x \leq 4$

Mental Math

Add.

1. 303 + 123 **2.** 456 + 111
3. 666 + 222 **4.** 131 + 313
5. 4002 + 3001 **6.** 5010 + 2121
7. 33 + 21 + 14 **8.** 22 + 34 + 11
9. 70 + 80 + 90 **10.** 200 + 300 + 400
11. 55 + 55 + 55 **12.** 500 + 600 + 700

Subtract.

13. 404 − 201 **14.** 888 − 333
15. 765 − 123 **16.** 465 − 354
17. 3456 − 1212 **18.** 4007 − 1006
19. 60 − 30 − 20 **20.** 88 − 22 − 44
21. 25 − 7 − 9 **22.** 828 − 727

Multiply.

23. 333 × 2 **24.** 222 × 3
25. 404 × 2 **26.** 1001 × 6
27. 30 × 70 **28.** 200 × 20
29. 5000 × 3 **30.** 3123 × 3
31. 90 × 60 × 10 **32.** 300 × 200
33. 6000 × 4000 **34.** 20 × 40 × 60

Divide.

35. 444 ÷ 2 **36.** 6393 ÷ 3
37. 50 000 ÷ 5 **38.** 2700 ÷ 9
39. 6400 ÷ 8 **40.** 484 000 ÷ 4
41. 56 000 ÷ 80 **42.** 2100 ÷ 70
43. 4800 ÷ 600 **44.** 100 000 ÷ 100
45. 6018 ÷ 6 **46.** 200 000 ÷ 20 000

Calculate.

47. 60 − 40 + 30 **48.** 77 − 66 + 11
49. 40 × 2 − 60 **50.** 900 + 600 − 200
51. 80 ÷ 2 − 1 **52.** 33 + 44 − 55
53. 20 × 30 × 20 **54.** 100 ÷ 2 ÷ 5
55. 444 ÷ 444 + 1 **56.** 606 − 101 − 303
57. 909 − 101 + 4 **58.** 333 − 111 + 333

10.1 Integers

Activity: Learn About Integers

The Celsius temperature scale sets the freezing point of water at 0°C and the boiling point of water at +100°C.

Temperatures greater than 0°C are represented by **positive numbers**. For example, the hottest place on Earth is Dallol, Ethiopia, where the average temperature is +34°C. We read +34 as "positive thirty-four."

Temperatures below 0°C are represented by **negative numbers**. For example, the coldest place on Earth is Plateau Station in Antarctica, where the average temperature is −57°C. We read −57 as "negative fifty-seven."

Numbers like 0, +100, +34, and −57 are called **integers**. Positive whole numbers, negative whole numbers, and zero are integers. Integers are sometimes called signed numbers or directed numbers.

Integers have many uses, aside from recording temperatures. One use is to state the distance of a place on Earth above or below sea level. This distance is called **elevation**. Sea level has an elevation of 0 m.

Inquire

1. Use an atlas to find the following elevations.

a) Canada's highest mountain **b)** your town
c) Death Valley in California **d)** the Dead Sea

2. Use an almanac or other source to find the highest and lowest temperatures ever recorded in Canada. Round each value to the nearest integer, if necessary.

3. We can represent an amount of rainfall by a positive integer, but not by a negative integer. Why not?

Integers can be shown on a number line.

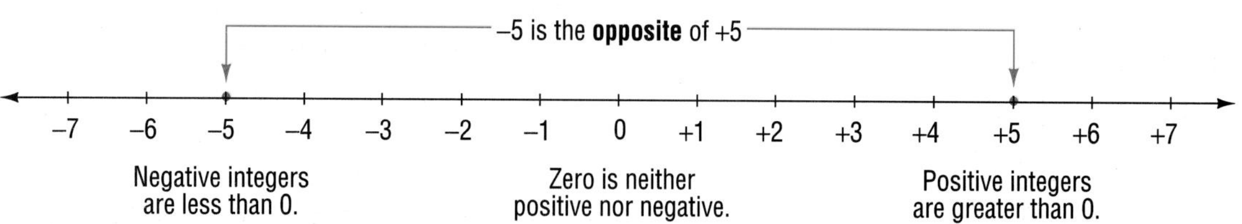
–5 is the **opposite** of +5
–7 –6 –5 –4 –3 –2 –1 0 +1 +2 +3 +4 +5 +6 +7
Negative integers are less than 0.
Zero is neither positive nor negative.
Positive integers are greater than 0.

Practice

1. Read each integer.

a) +5 **b)** −4 **c)** +11 **d)** −7
e) −15 **f)** +8 **g)** +25 **h)** −21

Represent with an integer.

2. five seconds after liftoff

3. twelve seconds before liftoff

4. seven degrees Celsius below zero

5. nine degrees Celsius above zero

6. a gain in mass of 2 kg

7. eighty-two metres below sea level

8. a gain of twelve points

9. a loss of seven points

Write each integer in words.

10. −5 **11.** +8 **12.** −3 **13.** +9

14. −1 **15.** +11 **16.** +15 **17.** −25

State the opposite of each integer.

18. +3 **19.** −7 **20.** +9 **21.** −1

22. −21 **23.** +32 **24.** −45 **25.** +56

Problems and Applications

26. Copy and complete the table.

Temperatures (°C)		
Start	**Change**	**Final**
+12	down 5	
+7	down 8	
−2	down 3	
−4	up 6	
−3	up 2	
0	down 7	

Write the next 3 integers.

27. +2, +1, 0, ■, ■, ■

28. −7, −6, −5, ■, ■, ■

29. +7, +4, +1, ■, ■, ■

30. −10, −11, −12, ■, ■, ■

Use an integer to represent each statement and its opposite.

31. six degrees Celsius above zero

32. thirty metres below sea level

33. seven seconds after liftoff

34. a loss of thirteen points

35. twelve steps down

36. earnings of eleven dollars

37. At noon, the temperature was +2°C. From noon to 17:00, the temperature went down 3°C, up 1°C, down 4°C, up 2°C, and down 3°C. What was the temperature at 17:00?

38. Bill starts the game Reach for the Top with 0 points. If he gains 6 points, loses 8 points, loses 3 points, and gains 2 points, what is his final score?

39. Golfers keep score with integers. If par is 72 and you take 70 strokes to play one round, your score is 2 below par or −2. If par is 72, express the scores of these golfers as integers.

a) Marie 77 **b)** Harold 71 **c)** Tamar 68
d) Doc 69 **e)** J.R. 92 **f)** Sally 85

40. a) What is the opposite of the opposite of −5? Explain.

b) Does 0 have an opposite? Explain.

41. With a classmate, research the Kelvin temperature scale. Explain why it does not use negative integers.

LOGIC POWER

Shelly, Lucia, and Buzz guessed the temperature on a cold morning. Lucia's guess was 3°C too high. Buzz guessed −4°C. Shelly's guess was 2°C lower than Buzz's. Lucia's guess was 1°C lower than Shelly's. What was the temperature?

10.2 Comparing and Ordering Integers

Activity: Represent the Data

The arctic fox lives in places where the winter temperature is –40°C.

Tennis players like the temperature around +22°C.

The desert rattlesnake sunbathes when the temperature is +40°C.

Antarctic penguins are comfortable at –2°C.

The kangaroo lives where the average temperature is +29°C.

Numbers such as these can be ordered and compared by putting them on a number line.

Inquire

1. Draw a horizontal number line with positive numbers on the right and negative numbers on the left.

2. Mark the temperatures on the number line.

3. Do integers increase or decrease from right to left on the number line?

4. Do integers increase or decrease from left to right on the number line?

Example

Compare –4 and +5.

Solution 1

Put the integers on a number line.

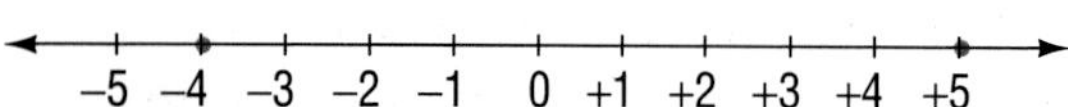

The integer on the left is smaller.
We say "–4 **is less than** +5."
We write –4 < +5.

Solution 2

Put the integers on a number line.

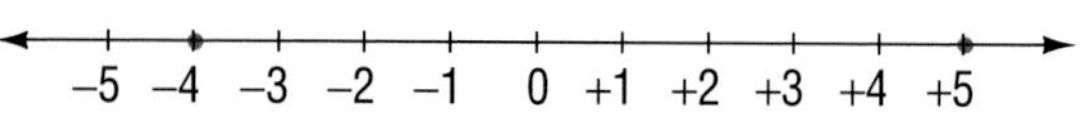

The integer on the right is larger.
We say "+5 is greater than –4."
We write +5 > –4.

Practice

Replace ● with > or < to make each statement true.

1. +5°C ● +2°C **2.** +3°C ● +7°C
3. −3°C ● +4°C **4.** +8°C ● −1°C
5. −3°C ● −5°C **6.** −4°C ● −9°C

Which integer is farther to the right on a number line?

7. +7 or +9 **8.** +6 or −2 **9.** −3 or −5
10. −1 or +6 **11.** +2 or 0 **12.** 0 or −3

Which integer is greater in each pair?

13. +4, +8 **14.** −1, +2 **15.** −3, −5
16. +9, −1 **17.** +1, −4 **18.** −7, −2

Which integer is smaller in each pair?

19. +3, +5 **20.** 0, −2 **21.** −3, +4
22. −2, −5 **23.** −6, −4 **24.** +5, −1

Which integers are greater than +2?

25. +5 **26.** +1 **27.** +8
28. −3 **29.** −1 **30.** 0

Which integers are less than +3?

31. +1 **32.** +7 **33.** −2
34. −6 **35.** 0 **36.** +5

Which integers are greater than −3?

37. +4 **38.** 0 **39.** −5
40. −1 **41.** −7 **42.** +1

Which integers are less than −2?

43. +4 **44.** −8 **45.** −1
46. 0 **47.** −3 **48.** +1

Replace ● with > or < to make each statement true.

49. +4 ● −3 **50.** −4 ● +1
51. −2 ● −6 **52.** −7 ● −5
53. 0 ● −2 **54.** 0 ● +7

Write in order from smallest to largest.

55. +6, −3, +7, −1, 0
56. −2, −4, +1, −6, +3
57. −1, −6, −3, −9, −2

Write in order from largest to smallest.

58. +6, −4, +8, −1, +5
59. −2, +1, −7, −3, 0
60. −1, −9, −5, −8, −10

Problems and Applications

61. Arrange the following average temperatures from warmest to coldest.

Planet/Moon	Average Temperature (°C)
Earth	+20
Venus	+470
Saturn	−180
Moon	−30
Mercury	+120
Jupiter	−150
Mars	0

62. If 2 integers have different signs which one is greater?

63. If 2 different integers have the same sign which one is greater?

64. Describe how comparing integers is different from comparing whole numbers.

65. Paul said, "−25°C is colder than −15°C, so −25 is greater than −15." Is Paul's statement true? Explain.

66. The data show Ottawa's mean daily temperature in degrees Celsius for each month of the year. Use the data to write 2 questions. Have a classmate solve them.

Jan −11 Feb −10 Mar −3 Apr +6
May +13 Jun +18 Jul +21 Aug +19
Sep +14 Oct +8 Nov +1 Dec −8

Investigating Integers

Before building a real bridge an engineer would first build a **model** of the bridge. Then the engineer could see how well the real bridge would work. We also use models in mathematics.

We can use static electricity as a model for integers. Static electricity has positive and negative charges. Integers include positive and negative whole numbers. In our model, we use red disks to represent positive charges and blue disks to represent negative charges.

One red disk represents a charge of +1.
One blue disk represents a charge of −1.

A positive and a negative charge cancel each other to produce a charge of zero. In our model, a red disk (+1) and a blue disk (−1) together represent a charge of zero. = zero charge

Different numbers of positive and negative charges result in different charges on a metal plate. We can use our disks to represent the charge on a plate. The charge represented in the diagram is +2.

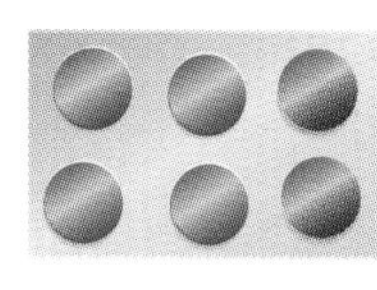

Activity ❶

State the charge represented by each group of disks.

1.

2. 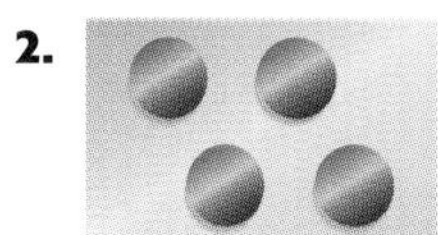

3. 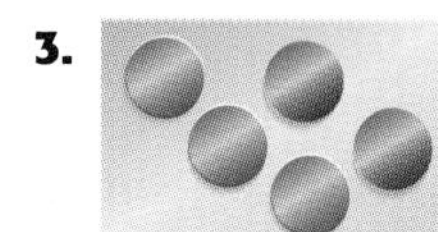

4. 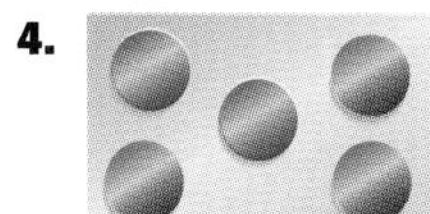

5. 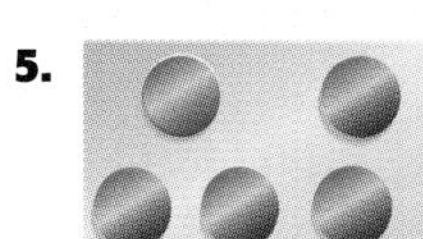

6. 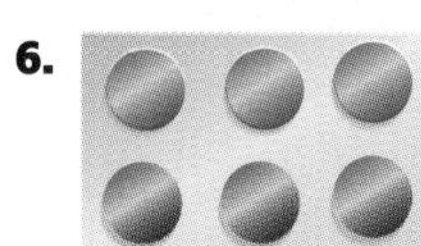

7. 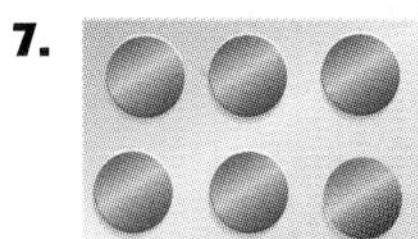

8. 

9. 

Activity ❷

There are many ways to show the same charge. The disks show 3 ways to make a charge of −2.

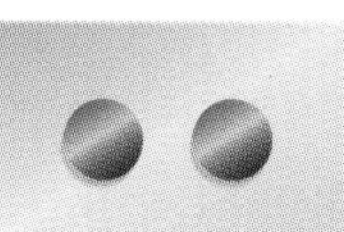

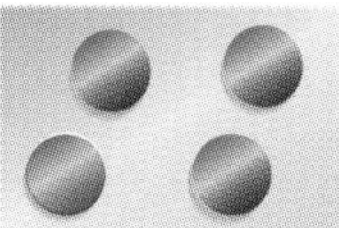

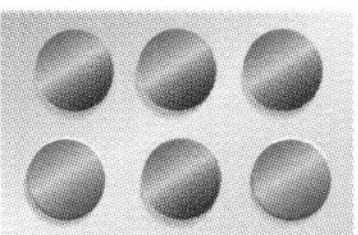

Use disks to show 3 different ways of making each of the following charges.

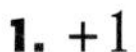

1. +1 **2.** −1 **3.** +3 **4.** −4

Activity ❸

To show what happens when integers are added, we add charges to the plate.

Charge is +3.	Add 2 negatives.	Make zero charges. Remove paired disks.	Final charge is +1.
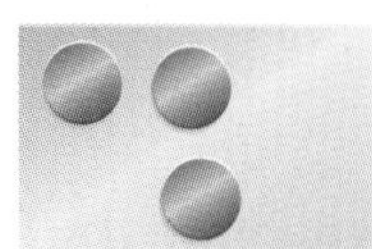	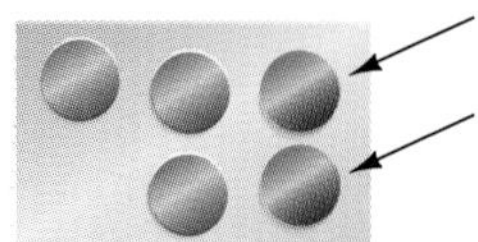	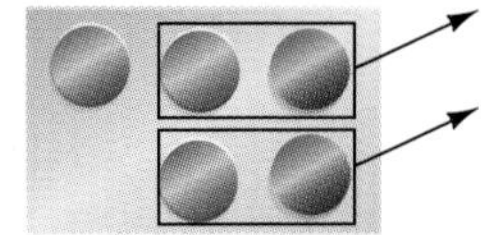	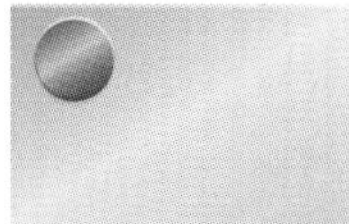

The addition is $(+3) + (-2) = +1$

Use the disks to answer the following.

1. $(-4) + (-2) =$ ■ **2.** $(+4) + (-2) =$ ■ **3.** $(-3) + (+4) =$ ■
4. $(-5) + (+6) =$ ■ **5.** $(-3) + (+2) =$ ■ **6.** $(+4) + (-5) =$ ■

Activity ❹

To show what happens when integers are subtracted, we remove charges from the plate.

Charge is +3.	Remove 2 negatives.	Charge is +5. 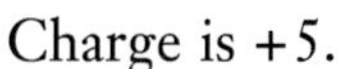
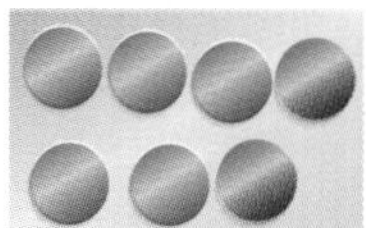		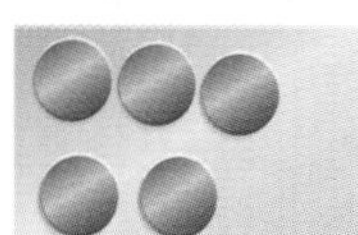

The subtraction is $(+3) - (-2) = +5$

Suppose you want to remove 4 negative charges, but there are only 2 negative charges on the plate. Add 2 pairs of positive and negative charges. By doing this, you do not change the charge on the plate.

Charge is +2.	Charge is +2. 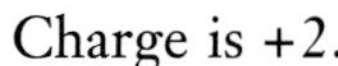	Remove 4 negatives.	Charge is +6. 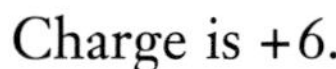
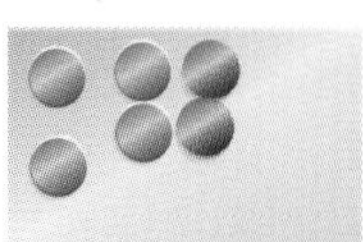	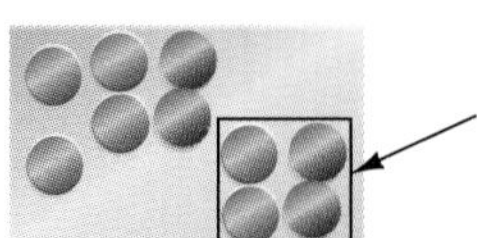	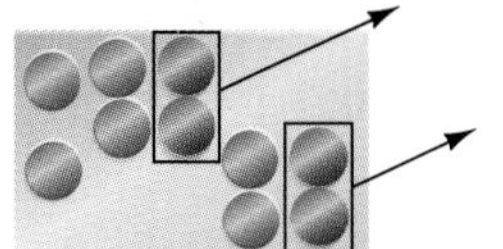	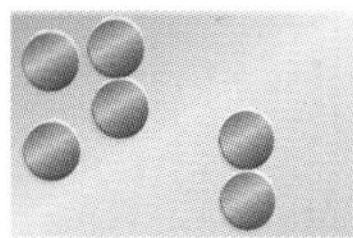

The subtraction is $(+2) - (-4) = +6$

Use the disks to answer the following.

1. $(+5) - (+2) =$ ■ **2.** $(+4) - (-2) =$ ■ **3.** $(-2) - (-4) =$ ■

4. $(-5) + (+6) =$ ■ **5.** $(-3) + (+2) =$ ■ **6.** $(+4) + (-5) =$ ■

10.3 Adding Integers

Activity: Use the Integer Disks

We can think of red and blue disks as **integer disks**.
A red disk represents the integer +1.
A blue disk represents the integer −1.

The integer is +4 or (+4).	The integer (−3) is added.	Pairs of red and blue disks are removed.	The final integer is +1 or (+1).
	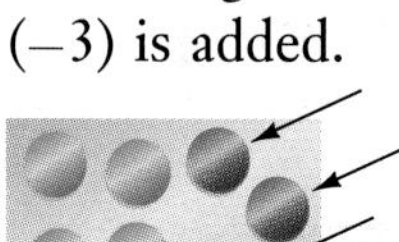	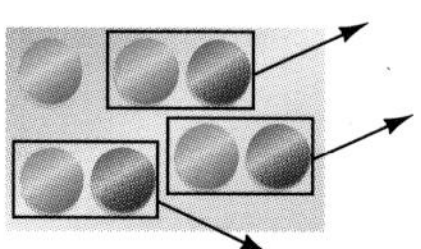	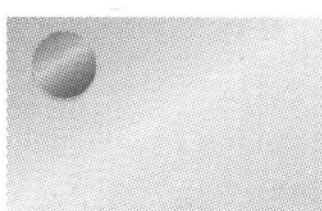

Say "positive 4 plus negative 3 equals positive 1."
Write (+4) + (−3) = +1.

Inquire

1. Use a set of positive disks and negative disks to answer the following. Write the addition statement for each.

a) (+3) + (+2) **b)** (−4) + (−2) **c)** (+3) + (−3)
d) (+5) + (+3) **e)** (−5) + (+1) **f)** (−3) + (+5)
g) (−1) + (−4) **h)** (+2) + (−6) **i)** (−6) + (+2)

2. Write a rule for the sum of two positive integers.

3. Write a rule for the sum of two negative integers.

4. Write a rule for the sum of a positive and a negative integer.

To show addition on a number line, start at 0.
Go to the left for negative integers.
Go to the right for positive integers.

(+3) + (−2)

(+3) + (−2) = +1

(−5) + (+2)

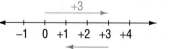

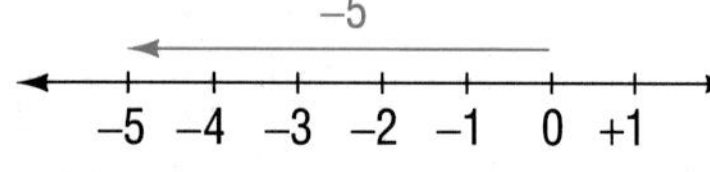

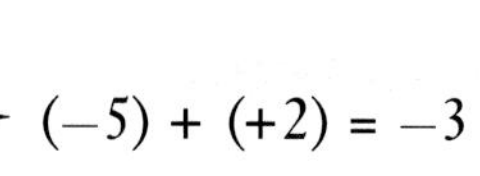

(−5) + (+2) = −3

(+2) + (−2)

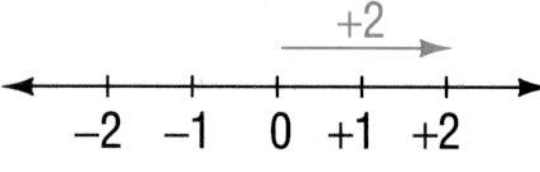

(+2) + (−2) = 0

Practice

Write the addition statement.

1. Add 2 negatives.

2. Add 4 positives.

3. Add 5 negatives.

4. Add 1 positive.

Write the addition statement.

5.

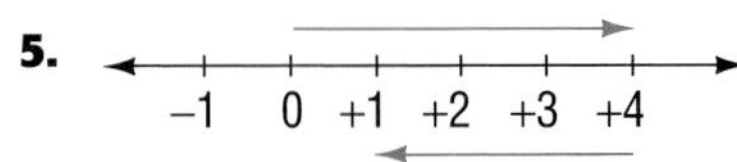

−1 0 +1 +2 +3 +4

6.

−3 −2 −1 0 +1 +2

7.

−6 −5 −4 −3 −2 −1 0 +1

8.

−2 −1 0 +1 +2 +3 +4

Model each addition with integer disks. Write the addition statement.

9. (+5) + (+2) **10.** (+4) + (−3)

11. (+2) + (−4) **12.** (−3) + (−1)

13. (−3) + (+3) **14.** (−5) + (+6)

Add.

15. (+4) + (+3) **16.** (+2) + (+7)

17. (−6) + (−1) **18.** (−5) + (−4)

19. (+4) + (−2) **20.** (−3) + (+5)

21. (−6) + (+1) **22.** (+6) + (−9)

Problems and Applications

Find the missing integer.

23. (+4) + (■) = +9 **24.** (−5) + (■) = −8

25. (+6) + (■) = −1 **26.** (■) + (−2) = −5

27. (■) + (+6) = +1 **28.** (■) + (−7) = −7

29. A spacecraft countdown is at −8 s. In how many seconds will the spacecraft be 15 s into its flight?

30. A chinook is a warm wind that can suddenly affect parts of Alberta and Saskatchewan in winter. If it is −11°C in Calgary at 13:00, and a chinook raises the temperature by 18°C in the next hour, what is the temperature at 14:00?

31. The Melvilles sell records at a flea market every Saturday. On 4 Saturdays in June, they had a profit of $30, lost $20, lost $40, and had a profit of $60. How much was their profit or loss in June?

Use the integer disks to model these additions.

32. (+2) + (+5) + (−4) **33.** (−3) + (+7) + (+1)

34. (−6) + (−1) + (−3) **35.** (+8) + (−3) + (+2)

36. What is the sum of any non-zero integer and its opposite? Explain.

37. Make each calculation. Replace each answer with the letter in the box. Decode the message to find out what barbers know.

(−4) + (−3) = ■
(+8) + (−4) = ■
(−2) + (+6) = ■
(+5) + (−11) = ■
(+8) + (−6) = ■
(−6) + (−8) = ■
(+8) + (+4) = ■

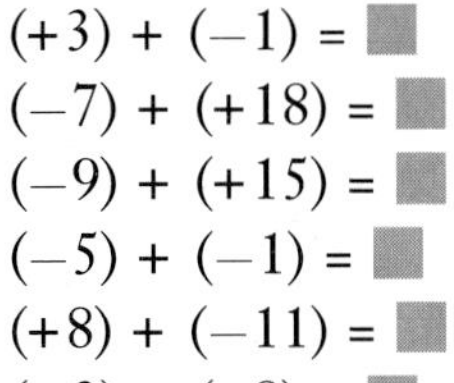

(+3) + (−1) = ■
(−7) + (+18) = ■
(−9) + (+15) = ■
(−5) + (−1) = ■
(+8) + (−11) = ■

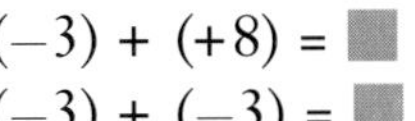

(−3) + (+8) = ■
(−3) + (−3) = ■
(−3) + (+15) = ■

A −7	B −4	C −3
D +1	E −14	F +13
G −5	H +2	I −1
J −10	K +8	L +4
M −8	N −2	O +11
P +3	Q +7	R +6
S +12	T −6	U +5
V −9	W +9	X −11
Y −12	Z −13	

CODE

38. Make up your own coded message that requires the addition of integers. Have a classmate decode it.

10.4 Subtracting Integers

Activity: Use the Integer Disks

We can use integer disks to show the subtraction of integers.
The following sequence shows the subtraction (+2) − (−3).

The integer is (+2).

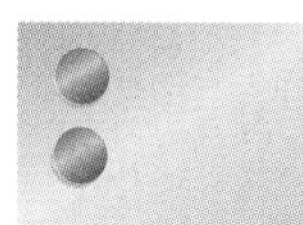

Three pairs of disks are added. The integer is still (+2).

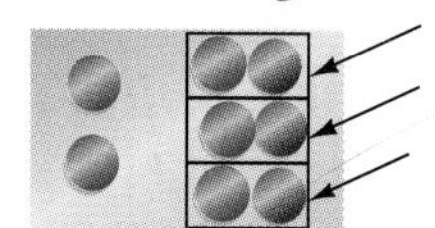

Three negative disks (−3) are removed.

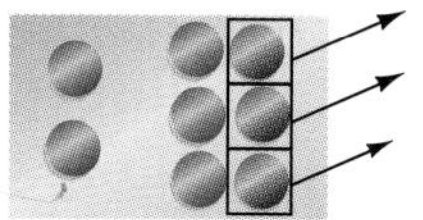

The final integer is (+5) or +5.

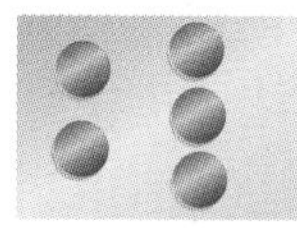

Say "positive 2 subtract negative 3 equals positive 5."
Write (+2) − (−3) = +5

Inquire

1. Use a set of positive disks and negative disks to answer the following. Write the subtraction statement for each.

a) (−4) − (−1) **b)** (+2) − (+5) **c)** (−2) − (−3)
d) (−3) − (+2) **e)** (−1) − (+4) **f)** (+4) − (−4)

2. Use the disks to compare the result of the subtraction (+7) − (+3) with the result of the addition (+7) + (−3).

3. Work with a partner and calculate the following pairs. Write a number sentence in each case.

a) (−2) − (+5)
(−2) + (−5)

b) (+4) − (−2)
(+4) + (+2)

c) (+5) − (+3)
(+5) + (−3)

d) (−3) − (−1)
(−3) + (+1)

e) (−3) − (+2)
(−3) + (−2)

f) (+3) − (+4)
(+3) + (−4)

4. Study the pairs of number sentences from question 3. Look for a pattern. Write a rule for using addition to subtract integers.

Example

Use addition to subtract the following.

a) (+2) − (−6) **b)** (+4) − (+7) **c)** (−2) − (−5)

Solution

To subtract an integer, add its opposite.
First, rewrite each subtraction sentence as an addition sentence.

a) (+2) − (−6)
= (+2) + (+6)
= +8

b) (+4) − (+7)
= (+4) + (−7)
= −3

c) (−2) − (−5)
= (−2) + (+5)
= +3

Practice

Write the subtraction statement.

1. Subtract 2 positives.

2. Subtract 1 negative.

3. Subtract 2 positives.

4. Subtract 1 negative.

5. Subtract 2 negatives.

Write the opposite of each integer.

6. +4 **7.** −3 **8.** +5 **9.** −7

10. +2 **11.** −3 **12.** +11 **13.** −23

Write the addition sentence and simplify.

14. (+7) − (+4) **15.** (−6) − (+1)

16. (−5) − (−8) **17.** (+9) − (−6)

18. (+4) − (+7) **19.** (+1) − (−8)

Subtract.

20. (+7) − (+3) **21.** (−9) − (−5)

22. (+4) − (+7) **23.** (−2) − (−4)

24. (−1) − (−4) **25.** (+3) − (+6)

Subtract.

26. (+4) − (−2) **27.** (−6) − (+7)

28. (+8) − (+9) **29.** (−4) − (+3)

30. (−3) − (+7) **31.** (+2) − (−4)

Problems and Applications

Find the missing integer.

32. (+8) − (■) = +2 **33.** (+4) − (■) = −3

34. (−7) − (■) = −3 **35.** (■) − (−2) = +6

36. (■) − (+1) = −5 **37.** (■) − (−3) = −7

38. The temperature on the side of a space shuttle that faces the sun is +250°C. The temperature on the shaded side is −130°C. What is the difference in these temperatures?

39. Copy and complete the temperature chart, which shows high and low temperatures on a winter day.

City	High (°C)	Low (°C)	Change (°C) (High − Low)
Calgary	−5	−11	
Regina	−3	−15	
Winnipeg	+1	−6	
Moncton	−2	−3	
Halifax	+5	−4	
St.John's	−4	−6	

Which city had the greatest temperature change? smallest temperature change?

40. a) Determine the difference between any non-zero integer and its opposite.
b) How many results are there? Explain.
c) How do the results compare with the integer and its opposite? Explain.

41. a) Use an almanac or other source to find the highest and lowest temperatures ever recorded where you live. Calculate the difference.
b) Find the highest and lowest temperatures ever recorded on Earth. Calculate the difference.

LOGIC POWER

These identical cubes are stacked in a corner. How many cubes are you unable to see?

Codes and Cyphers

People have been sending and receiving secret messages for many years. The message shown here was thrown into a crowd of people in 1730 by the pirate Le Vasseur, while he was being led to the gallows. It is supposed to give directions to Le Vasseur's treasure, now worth billions of dollars. No one has found the treasure.

Activity ❶

The following message is coded using a Caesar cypher. This cypher is named after Julius Caesar, who used this method to send messages.

ZDWFK DQWRQB KH FDQW EH WUXVWHG

In a Caesar cypher, all the letters are shifted the same number of places to the right in the alphabet. In the message above, the letters are shifted 3 places to the right, so that D means A, E means B, F means C, and so on.

1. Decode the message.

2. Encode a message by shifting the letters of the alphabet a different number of places to the right. Ask a classmate to decode it.

3. Use a computer to list all the Caesar alphabets. They start as follows.

A B C D E F G H I J K L M N O P Q R S T U V W X Y Z
B C D E F G H I J K L M N O P Q R S T U V W X Y Z A
C D E F G H I J K L M N O P Q R S T U V W X Y Z A B
D E F G H I J K L M N O P Q R S T U V W X Y Z A B C

Activity ❷

The ADFGX cypher was first used during World War I. The ADFGX cypher uses a grid like the one at the right.

	A	D	F	G	X
A	A	B	C	D	E
D	F	G	H	I	K
F	L	M	N	O	P
G	Q	R	S	T	U
X	V	W	X	Y	Z

1. Decode this message.

GG DF AX DD AX FD GF AA GD AX FD DG GF GF DG FF DD

2. In the ADFGX cypher, there are two letters with the same code. Which ones do you think they are? Why?

3. Use the ADFGX cypher to encode a message for a classmate to decode.

Activity ❸

In a message written with a null cypher, all the real letters of the message are there. They are just hidden by letters that are not part of the message.

1. Decode the following message by reading only the second letter in each group.

XHOP WETC ALIX QPTS ZMIO TEYL

2. The letter you read need not be the second letter in each group. Decode the following message.

SWMT RTEP QAEH UPTR RTOD NQNP AFTP WPRI
RAAB TPIL QVNP WOAH FPTE LJNW CTOW YPOC
TMNQ

3. Use a null cypher to encode a message for a classmate to decode.

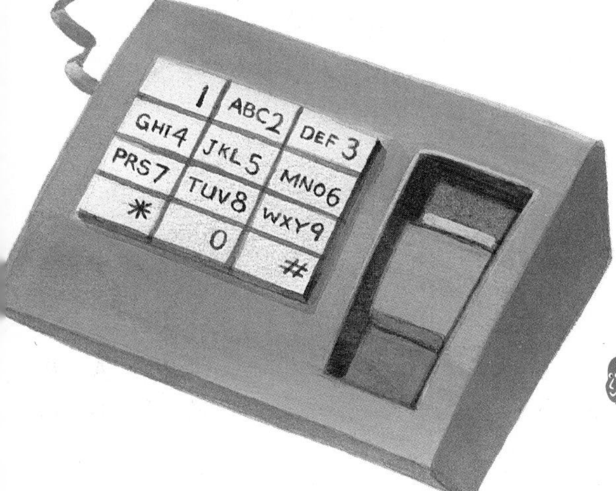

Activity ❹

The following message has been encoded using the number pad on a telephone. The letter A is 21, B is 22, C is 23, D is 31, and so on.

1. Write the other letters in the alphabet as numbers and decode the message.

42 32 21 72 72 43 83 32 31 53 21 73 81
62 43 41 42 81 23 21 53 53 61 32 81 63
31 21 93

2. Use the telephone cypher to encode a message for a classmate to decode.

10.5 Multiplying Integers

Activity: Use the Integer Disks

$2 \times 3 = 3 + 3$

2 groups of 3

Multiplication can be shown as repeated addition.

You can use integer disks to show multiplication. Think of multiplying by +2 as adding 2 groups of the same number of disks.

$(+2) \times (+3)$	The integer is 0.	Add 2 groups of disks, each representing +3.	The final integer is (+6) or +6. So, $(+2) \times (+3) = +6$.

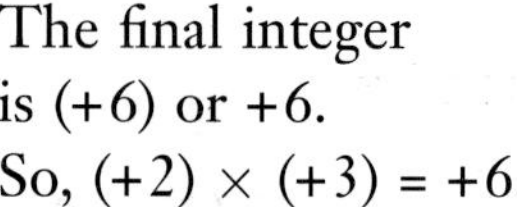

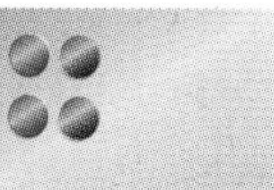

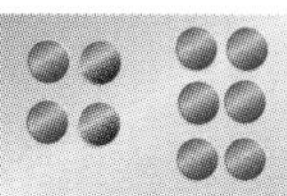

$(+2) \times (-3)$	The integer is 0.	Add 2 groups of disks, each representing −3.	The final integer is (−6) or −6. So, $(+2) \times (-3) = -6$.

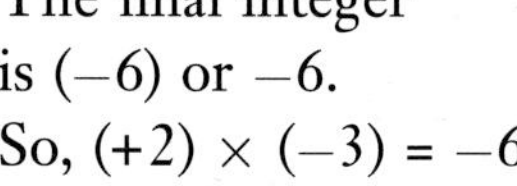

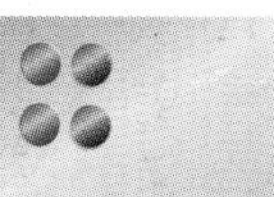

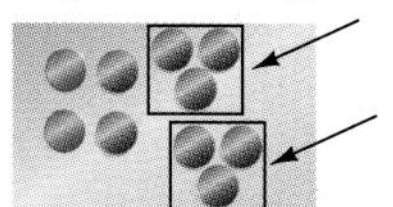

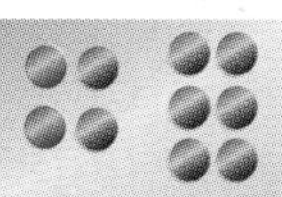

Think of multiplying by −2 as removing 2 groups of the same number of disks.

$(-2) \times (+3)$	The integer is 0.	Remove 2 groups of disks, each representing +3.	The final integer is (−6) or −6. So, $(-2) \times (+3) = -6$.

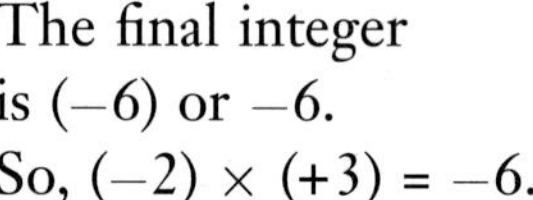

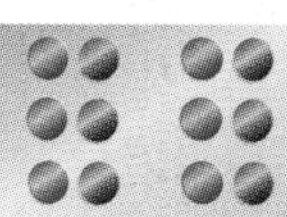

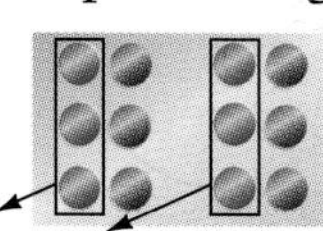

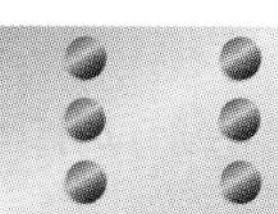

$(-2) \times (-3)$	The integer is 0.	Remove 2 groups of disks, each representing −3.	The final integer is (+6) or +6. So, $(-2) \times (-3) = +6$.

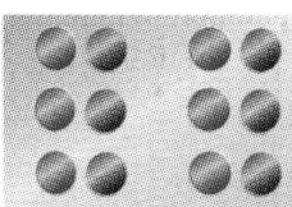

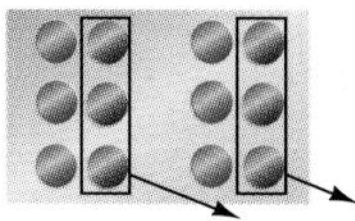

Inquire

1. Use the disks to show these multiplications. Write the multiplication statement for each.

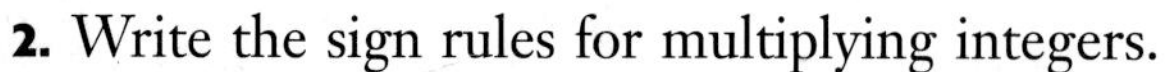

a) $(+2) \times (+4)$	**b)** $(+2) \times (-4)$	**c)** $(-2) \times (+4)$	**d)** $(-2) \times (-4)$
e) $(+3) \times (+4)$	**f)** $(-3) \times (-4)$	**g)** $(-3) \times (+4)$	**h)** $(+3) \times (-4)$
i) $(+3) \times (-2)$	**j)** $(-3) \times (+2)$	**k)** $(-3) \times (-2)$	**l)** $(+3) \times (+2)$

2. Write the sign rules for multiplying integers.

Example

Multiply.

a) $(+3) \times (+5)$
b) $(-3) \times (-5)$
c) $(-3) \times (+5)$

Solution

The product of 2 positive integers or 2 negative integers is a positive integer.
The product of a positive and a negative integer is a negative integer.

a) $(+3) \times (+5) = +15$ **b)** $(-3) \times (-5) = +15$ **c)** $(-3) \times (+5) = -15$

Practice

State whether each answer is positive or negative.

1. $(+4) \times (+5) = ■20$ **2.** $(-2) \times (+3) = ■6$
3. $(+4) \times (-4) = ■16$ **4.** $(-1) \times (-8) = ■8$
5. $(+6) \times (-2) = ■12$ **6.** $(-3) \times (+1) = ■3$

Multiply.

7. $(+6) \times (+3)$ **8.** $(-4) \times (-5)$
9. $(-2) \times (+6)$ **10.** $(+4) \times (-8)$
11. $(-3) \times (-3)$ **12.** $(-8) \times (+8)$

Multiply.

13. $(+11) \times (+11)$ **14.** $(+20) \times (-20)$
15. $(-30) \times (-20)$ **16.** $(+15) \times (-10)$
17. $(-40) \times (+5)$ **18.** $(+22) \times (+4)$

Problems and Applications

Find the missing integer.

19. $(+3) \times (■) = +15$ **20.** $(■) \times (-2) = -12$
21. $(-6) \times (■) = -30$ **22.** $(+2) \times (■) = +10$

Identify each pair of integers, given their sum and product.

23. sum -1, product -20
24. sum $+4$, product $+4$
25. sum $+3$, product -10
26. sum -8, product $+12$

27. If the outside temperature reaches the freezing point at midnight and drops 2°C/h through the night, what is the temperature at 06:00?

28. Make each calculation. Replace each answer by a letter from the code box. Decode the message to find out what the judge said when the skunk entered.

$(+4) \times (-3) = ■$
$(+6) \times (+3) = ■$
$(-6) \times (+2) = ■$
$(+6) \times (-5) = ■$
$(-4) \times (+4) = ■$
$(-8) \times (-2) = ■$
$(+9) \times (-4) = ■$
$(-10) \times (+2) = ■$
$(-3) \times (-12) = ■$
$(+6) \times (-4) = ■$
$(-4) \times (+8) = ■$
$(+3) \times (-4) = ■$
$(-5) \times (+6) = ■$
$(+8) \times (-2) = ■$
$(-4) \times (+5) = ■$

A +24	B +12	C −32
D +18	E −24	F −14
G +30	H +36	I +16
J −21	K +31	L +14
M +21	N −36	O −12
P +23	Q −18	R −16
S +15	T −20	U −30
V +21	W +28	X +20
Y −15	Z −28	

CODE

29. Use multiplication of integers to make a coded message. Ask a classmate to decode it.

NUMBER POWER

Copy the diagram. Place the numbers from 1 to 9 on the dots so that each line adds to 24.

10.6 Dividing Integers

Activity: Discover the Relationship

You have discovered the sign rules for multiplying integers.

$(+3) \times (+4) = +12$ $\quad$ $(-3) \times (-4) = +12$
$(-3) \times (+4) = -12$ $\quad$ $(+3) \times (-4) = -12$

You also know that each multiplication fact has two related division facts.

Multiplication fact	**Division facts**
$4 \times 5 = 20$	$20 \div 5 = 4$ and $20 \div 4 = 5$

You will now use these ideas to discover the sign rules for dividing integers.

Inquire

1. Write the two division facts for each multiplication.

a) $(+4) \times (+3) = +12$ $\quad$ **b)** $(+2) \times (+7) = +14$
c) $(-4) \times (-2) = +8$ $\quad$ **d)** $(-5) \times (-3) = +15$
e) $(+2) \times (-3) = -6$ $\quad$ **f)** $(+5) \times (-2) = -10$
g) $(-4) \times (+3) = -12$ $\quad$ **h)** $(-6) \times (+4) = -24$
i) $(+6) \times (+3) = +18$ $\quad$ **j)** $(-8) \times (+5) = -40$

2. What is the sign of the quotient when

a) a positive integer is divided by a positive integer?
b) a positive integer is divided by a negative integer?
c) a negative integer is divided by a positive integer?
d) a negative integer is divided by a negative integer?

3. How many related division facts are there for $(+3) \times 0$? Explain.

4. What is the quotient when 0 is divided by any integer?

Example

Divide.

a) $(+10) \div (+5)$ $\quad$ **b)** $(-10) \div (-5)$
c) $(+10) \div (-5)$ $\quad$ **d)** $(-10) \div (+5)$

Solution

The quotient of 2 positive integers or 2 negative integers is a positive integer. The quotient of a positive integer and a negative integer is a negative integer.

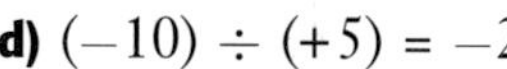

a) $(+10) \div (+5) = +2$ $\quad$ **b)** $(-10) \div (-5) = +2$
c) $(+10) \div (-5) = -2$ $\quad$ **d)** $(-10) \div (+5) = -2$

Practice

State whether each answer is positive or negative.

1. $(+15) \div (+5) = \blacksquare 3$
2. $(-12) \div (+3) = \blacksquare 4$
3. $(-9) \div (-3) = \blacksquare 3$
4. $(-8) \div (+2) = \blacksquare 4$
5. $(+9) \div (+1) = \blacksquare 9$
6. $(+4) \div (-4) = \blacksquare 1$
7. $(-16) \div (-8) = \blacksquare 2$
8. $(+20) \div (-2) = \blacksquare 10$

Divide.

9. $(-8) \div (-2)$
10. $(-12) \div (+6)$
11. $(-9) \div (+9)$
12. $(+6) \div (-1)$
13. $(+24) \div (+8)$
14. $(-21) \div (-3)$

Divide.

15. $\frac{(-14)}{(-7)}$
16. $\frac{(+24)}{(-12)}$
17. $\frac{(+40)}{(-8)}$
18. $\frac{(-27)}{(+3)}$
19. $\frac{0}{(-2)}$
20. $\frac{(+36)}{(+9)}$

Divide.

21. $(+188) \div (-4)$
22. $(-126) \div (-6)$
23. $(-300) \div (-10)$
24. $(+175) \div (+5)$
25. $(+121) \div (-11)$
26. $(-108) \div (+9)$

Problems and Applications

Find the missing integer.

27. $(+8) \div (\blacksquare) = +4$
28. $(-6) \div (\blacksquare) = -1$
29. $(\blacksquare) \div (+4) = -7$
30. $(+20) \div (\blacksquare) = +5$
31. $(\blacksquare) \div (-3) = +9$
32. $(-8) \div (\blacksquare) = +8$
33. $(-6) \div (\blacksquare) = -2$
34. $(\blacksquare) \div (-9) = -2$

35. If the temperature drops steadily from 0°C at midnight to −12°C at 0:400, what is the temperature at 02:00?

36. If the lowest temperatures on 4 winter nights are +2°C, −4°C, −5°C, and −1°C, what is the average low for the 4 nights?

37. What is the quotient when any non-zero integer is divided by its opposite?

38. Make each calculation. Replace each answer by a letter from the code box. Decode the message to find out what quadruplets are.

$(-32) \div (+2) = \blacksquare$
$(-20) \div (-4) = \blacksquare$
$(-21) \div (+7) = \blacksquare$
$(+16) \div (+2) = \blacksquare$
$(-22) \div (+2) = \blacksquare$
$(+8) \div (+1) = \blacksquare$
$(+30) \div (-2) = \blacksquare$
$(-20) \div (-2) = \blacksquare$
$(-6) \div (-6) = \blacksquare$
$(+24) \div (-2) = \blacksquare$
$(-10) \div (-2) = \blacksquare$
$(+12) \div (-4) = \blacksquare$
$(-18) \div (-9) = \blacksquare$
$(+10) \div (-5) = \blacksquare$
$(-15) \div (-3) = \blacksquare$
$(+9) \div (-3) = \blacksquare$
$(+24) \div (-3) = \blacksquare$

A −1	B −7	C −11
D −8	E +3	F −16
G −12	H −6	I +10
J −10	K +14	L −2
M −14	N +1	O +5
P −9	Q +7	R +8
S +12	T +2	U −3
V +9	W +15	X +6
Y −15	Z −13	

CODE

39. Make up a coded message using integer division. Have a classmate decode the message.

PATTERN POWER

a) Complete the calculations.

$1^2 - 0^2 = 1$
$2^2 - 1^2 = \blacksquare$
$3^2 - 2^2 = \blacksquare$
$4^2 - 3^2 = \blacksquare$
$5^2 - 4^2 = \blacksquare$

b) Describe the pattern in words.

c) Use the pattern to find $93^2 - 92^2$ without using a calculator.

Integers on a Calculator

Activity ❶

To enter positive integers on a calculator, you do not need to enter the [+] sign.
On a calculator, if there is no sign the number is positive.

The [+/–] key on a calculator is used to enter negative numbers.

1. Write the display you get from each of the following sequences.

a) [C] 5 [+/–]

b) [C] [+/–] 5

c) [C] 3 4 [+/–]

d) [C] 3 [+/–] 4

e) [C] [+/–] 3 4

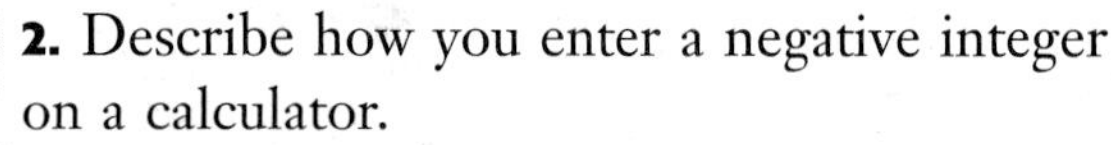

2. Describe how you enter a negative integer on a calculator.

3. If you enter –3 on a calculator when you intend to enter +3, how can you correct your mistake? Compare your suggestion with your classmates'.

Activity ❷

To add (+8) + (–3)

press	[C]	8	[+]	3	[+/–]	[=]
display	0	8	8	3	-3	5

To add (–7) + (+4)

press	[C]	7	[+/–]	[+]	4	[=]
display	0	7	-7	-7	4	-3

Estimate, then add.

1. (+37) + (–44)

2. (–56) + (–95)

3. (+43) + (–35)

4. (–89) + (+27)

5. (–16) + (–48)

6. (–79) + (–59)

7. (+39) + (–74)

8. (–35) + (+88)

9. (+67) + (–23)

10. (–42) + (+69)

Activity ❸

To subtract (–2) – (+5)

press	C	2	+/–	–	5	=
display	0	2	-2	-2	5	-7

To subtract (–6) – (–8)

press	C	6	+/–	–	8	+/–	=
display	0	6	-6	-6	8	-8	2

Estimate, then subtract.

1. (+47) – (+23) **2.** (–84) – (+52)
3. (–58) – (–89) **4.** (–39) – (–18)
5. (–11) – (+34) **6.** (+32) – (–12)
7. (–34) – (–21) **8.** (+83) – (–62)
9. (+34) – (+39) **10.** (–23) – (+37)

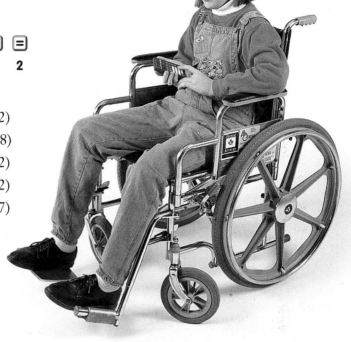

Activity ❹

To multiply (–3) × (+5)

press	C	3	+/–	×	5	=
display	0	3	-3	-3	5	-15

To multiply (–4) × (–6)

press	C	4	+/–	×	6	+/–	=
display	0	4	-4	-4	6	-6	24

Estimate, then multiply.

1. (+15) × (–16) **2.** (–12) × (+18)
3. (–23) × (–7) **4.** (–28) × (–77)
5. (+21) × (–91) **6.** (+12) × (+16)
7. (–24) × (+44) **8.** (–54) × (+67)
9. (+16) × (–17) **10.** (–32) × (–46)

Activity ❺

To divide (–8) ÷ (+4)

press	C	8	+/–	÷	4	=
display	0	8	-8	-8	4	-2

To divide (–6) ÷ (–2)

press	C	6	+/–	÷	2	+/–	=
display	0	6	-6	-6	2	-2	3

Estimate, then divide.

1. (–144) ÷ (+16) **2.** (+224) ÷ (–8)
3. (–32) ÷ (–16) **4.** (+126) ÷ (–16)
5. (–231) ÷ (–11) **6.** (+182) ÷ (–13)
7. (–126) ÷ (–6) **8.** (–736) ÷ (+32)
9. (–322) ÷ (–23) **10.** (–448) ÷ (+14)

Review

Write as an integer.

1. eleven degrees Celsius below zero
2. seventy-four metres above sea level
3. five seconds before air time
4. twenty dollars spent
5. thirty-three dollars earned

Write the opposite of each integer.

6. -5 **7.** $+6$ **8.** $+7$ **9.** -8

Write the next 3 integers.

10. $+5, +3, +1, \blacksquare, \blacksquare, \blacksquare$
11. $-10, -8, -6, \blacksquare, \blacksquare, \blacksquare$
12. $+7, +3, -1, \blacksquare, \blacksquare, \blacksquare$
13. $-1, -6, -11, \blacksquare, \blacksquare, \blacksquare$

Which integers are less than −3?

14. $+5$ **15.** -4 **16.** -1
17. 0 **18.** -7 **19.** -2

Which integers are greater than −5?

20. -7 **21.** -1 **22.** $+2$
23. -8 **24.** -4 **25.** 0

Replace the ● by > or < to make each statement true.

26. $+4 \bullet +2$ **27.** $-3 \bullet +1$ **28.** $-5 \bullet -6$
29. $+2 \bullet -1$ **30.** $-8 \bullet -7$ **31.** $-4 \bullet 0$

Write the integers from smallest to largest.

32. $-3, +4, -5, -1, +1, -6$
33. $-9, -2, -11, -4, -13, -16$
34. $+3, 0, -1, -6, -7, +11, +15$

Add.

35. $(+5) + (+6)$ **36.** $(-3) + (+6)$
37. $(-7) + (-2)$ **38.** $(-8) + (+5)$
39. $(+2) + (-4)$ **40.** $(+3) + (-1)$
41. $(+9) + (-9)$ **42.** $(-4) + (-4)$

Find the missing integer.

43. $(+6) + (\blacksquare) = +8$ **44.** $(-4) + (\blacksquare) = -6$
45. $(-7) + (\blacksquare) = -2$ **46.** $(\blacksquare) + (-2) = +7$
47. $(\blacksquare) + (+3) = +2$ **48.** $(\blacksquare) + (+5) = -4$

Simplify.

49. $(+7) + (+1) + (+2)$
50. $(-3) + (-4) + (+5)$
51. $(-6) + (-2) + (+7)$
52. $(+6) + (-5) + (-2)$

Subtract.

53. $(+7) - (+2)$ **54.** $(+4) - (-3)$
55. $(-6) - (-2)$ **56.** $(-3) - (+5)$
57. $(+1) - (+8)$ **58.** $(-1) - (-8)$
59. $(-3) - (-3)$ **60.** $0 - (-6)$

Find the missing integer.

61. $(+7) - (\blacksquare) = +1$ **62.** $(+2) - (\blacksquare) = +5$
63. $(-5) - (\blacksquare) = -6$ **64.** $(\blacksquare) - (-3) = +2$
65. $(\blacksquare) - (-2) = +8$ **66.** $(\blacksquare) - (+6) = -4$

Multiply.

67. $(+4) \times (+3)$ **68.** $(-3) \times (+2)$
69. $(-1) \times (-7)$ **70.** $(+7) \times (-6)$
71. $(-8) \times (-9)$ **72.** $(+2) \times (+4)$
73. $(-5) \times (-5)$ **74.** $(-4) \times 0$

Find the missing integer.

75. $(+7) \times (\blacksquare) = +42$ **76.** $(-4) \times (\blacksquare) = -12$
77. $(\blacksquare) \times (+2) = -8$ **78.** $(\blacksquare) \times (-3) = +9$
79. $(-9) \times (\blacksquare) = +27$ **80.** $(\blacksquare) \times (-1) = -12$

Divide.

81. $(+20) \div (+4)$ **82.** $(-18) \div (-2)$
83. $(-15) \div (+5)$ **84.** $(+14) \div (-2)$
85. $(+10) \div (+5)$ **86.** $(-16) \div (-8)$
87. $(-21) \div (+3)$ **88.** $(+35) \div (-7)$

Find the missing integer.

89. $(-32) \div (\blacksquare) = -8$

90. $(+72) \div (\blacksquare) = -9$

91. $(\blacksquare) \div (-3) = +4$

92. $(\blacksquare) \div (+2) = -7$

93. $(+14) \div (\blacksquare) = -14$

94. a) State the smallest positive integer.
b) State the greatest negative integer.

95. Hockey players can be rated with integers. Paul was on the ice when his team scored 15 goals and the other teams scored 20 goals. His rating is found from

goals for − goals against
$(+15) - (+20) = -5$

a) Rate the hockey players.

Name	Goals For	Goals Against
Fragnito	+38	+42
Chan	+59	+41
George	+26	+24
Petty	+34	+55
Lloyd	+45	+51

b) Use the ratings to order the players from best to worst.

96. The ground temperature at an airport was 10°C. The temperature dropped 5°C for every 1000 m above the ground. What was the temperature outside an airplane that took off from this airport and climbed to 5000 m?

97. One winter, the lowest temperatures in some cities across Canada were as follows.

City	Lowest Temperature (°C)
St. John's	−24
Halifax	−22
Montreal	−24
Toronto	−20
Winnipeg	−35
Edmonton	−36
Vancouver	−14

Find the average of these temperatures.

Group Decision Making

Planning a Vacation

In this activity, your group will plan a Canadian vacation for a family travelling by car. The vacation should be 2 to 3 weeks long. The emphasis should be on sightseeing. The trip could include one or more provinces, or only part of a province. One possible tour would be around the Maritime Provinces, including visits to the provincial capitals.

1. Decide where to spend the vacation and where you would leave from. Get maps and travel brochures for the trip.

2. Brainstorm a possible list of places to visit and things to do. Then, still in your group, make selections from the list. Decide how many people would take the trip and whether they would camp or stay in hotels.

3. Plan the trip day by day. Take into account the distance to travel, speed limits, rest stops, overnight stays, sightseeing, and visits to other tourist attractions.

4. Estimate the cost of meals, gasoline, lodgings, and other expenses. Allow for the cost of any souvenirs you might buy and the cost of any tickets, to a zoo or a whale watch, for example.

5. Prepare a report for the class. Include a map of the trip, and a description of how long it would take and what you would do.

6. Evaluate your work. If you had to plan another trip, what would you do in the same way and what would you do differently?

Chapter Check

Write each of the following as an integer.

1. eight degrees Celsius above zero

2. seven floors up

3. nine seconds before liftoff

4. a loss of three kilograms

Write the opposite of each integer.

5. +5 **6.** −6 **7.** −2

Replace each ● with > or < to make each statement true.

8. −7 ● −3 **9.** −7 ● +4

10. −6 ● −1 **11.** −8 ● −9

12. +3 ● +1 **13.** −2 ● −5

Add.

14. (+6) + (+2) **15.** (−7) + (+3)

16. (−4) + (−5) **17.** (+3) − (−6)

Subtract.

18. (+8) − (+3) **19.** (−2) − (+5)

20. (−7) − (−6) **21.** (+3) − (−6)

Multiply.

22. (+6) × (+2) **23.** (−3) × (−4)

24. (−4) × (+3) **25.** (+4) × (−5)

Divide.

26. (+8) ÷ (+2) **27.** (−6) ÷ (−3)

28. (+12) ÷ (−4) **29.** (−10) ÷ (+5)

30. At 08:00, the temperature was −13°C. The temperature then dropped 2°C/h until 12:00. What was the temperature at 12:00?

31. Toshiko works at a flea market. On Wednesday, she made a profit of $40, on Thursday a loss of $15, on Friday a loss of $60, and on Saturday a profit of $15. What was her profit or loss over 4 days?

32. In January, the mean daily temperature in Saint John, New Brunswick, is −7°C. In July, the mean is +17°C. What is the difference in these mean temperatures?

33. The table gives Frank's change in mass for 5 weeks while he was training for a sports meet.

Week 1	Week 2	Week 3	Week 4	Week 5
−2 kg	−1 kg	+1 kg	+1 kg	−2 kg

What was his total gain or loss in mass over the 5 weeks?

PEANUTS reprinted by permission of UFS, Inc.

Using the Strategies

1. The building block is decorated with the last six letters of the alphabet.

U is opposite V
W is opposite X
Y is opposite Z

Draw a net of the cube.

2. Can a year have 53 Mondays? Explain.

3. Find 6 different digits that give this sum.

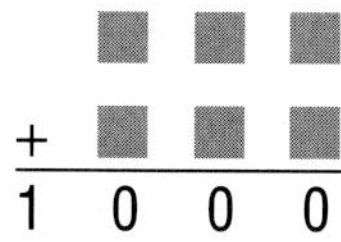

4. On average, Canadians of age 15 or more spend 0.75 h/day on sports and hobbies, and 3.15 h/week on leisure-time reading. Express the daily reading time as a fraction of the daily time spent on sports and hobbies. Write your answer in lowest terms.

5. Terry ate one-quarter of an apple pie for lunch and one-half of what was left for dinner. How much of the pie was left after dinner?

6. One piece of string has been passed through the holes in a piece of cardboard. Copy the diagram and show how the string could look on the back of the cardboard.

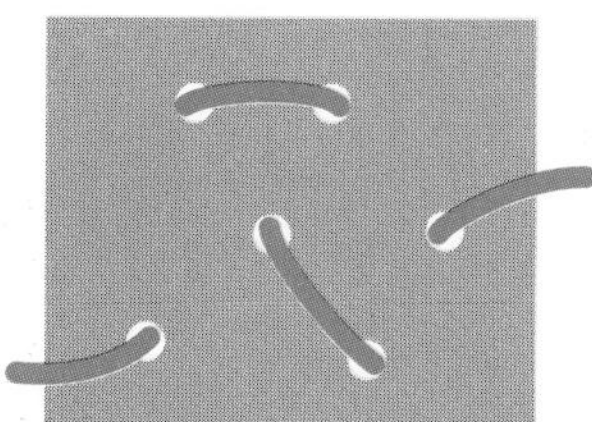

7. Each letter represents a different digit. What are the digits?

$$\begin{array}{r} DE \\ \times\ DE \\ \hline CDE \end{array}$$

8. Susan has to be in Winnipeg at 11:15. It takes her 1 h and 15 min to drive there. She needs 45 min to dress and eat breakfast. Before that, she needs 20 min to do her exercises. Walking her dog after breakfast takes 15 min. For what time should she set her alarm?

9. Which of the following containers holds the most?

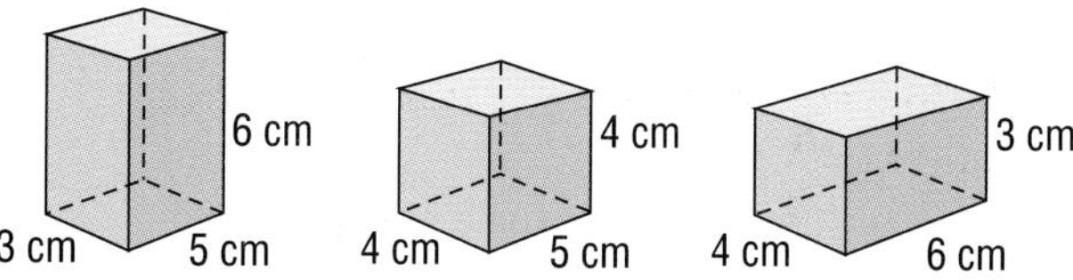

10. Take 4 shots at the target and hit 4 numbers that total 100.

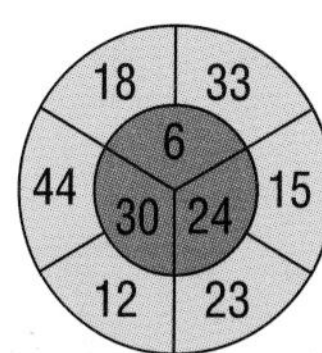

11. The English language contains about 800 000 words.

a) Estimate how many of the words a person with a college education uses.

b) If you take the smallest odd number as a percent, it tells you what percent of the 800 000 words the average college-educated person uses. Calculate the number of words. How close was your estimate?

DATA BANK

1. How much farther from the sun is Pluto than the Earth?

2. How much higher is the highest mountain in Asia than the highest mountain in North America?

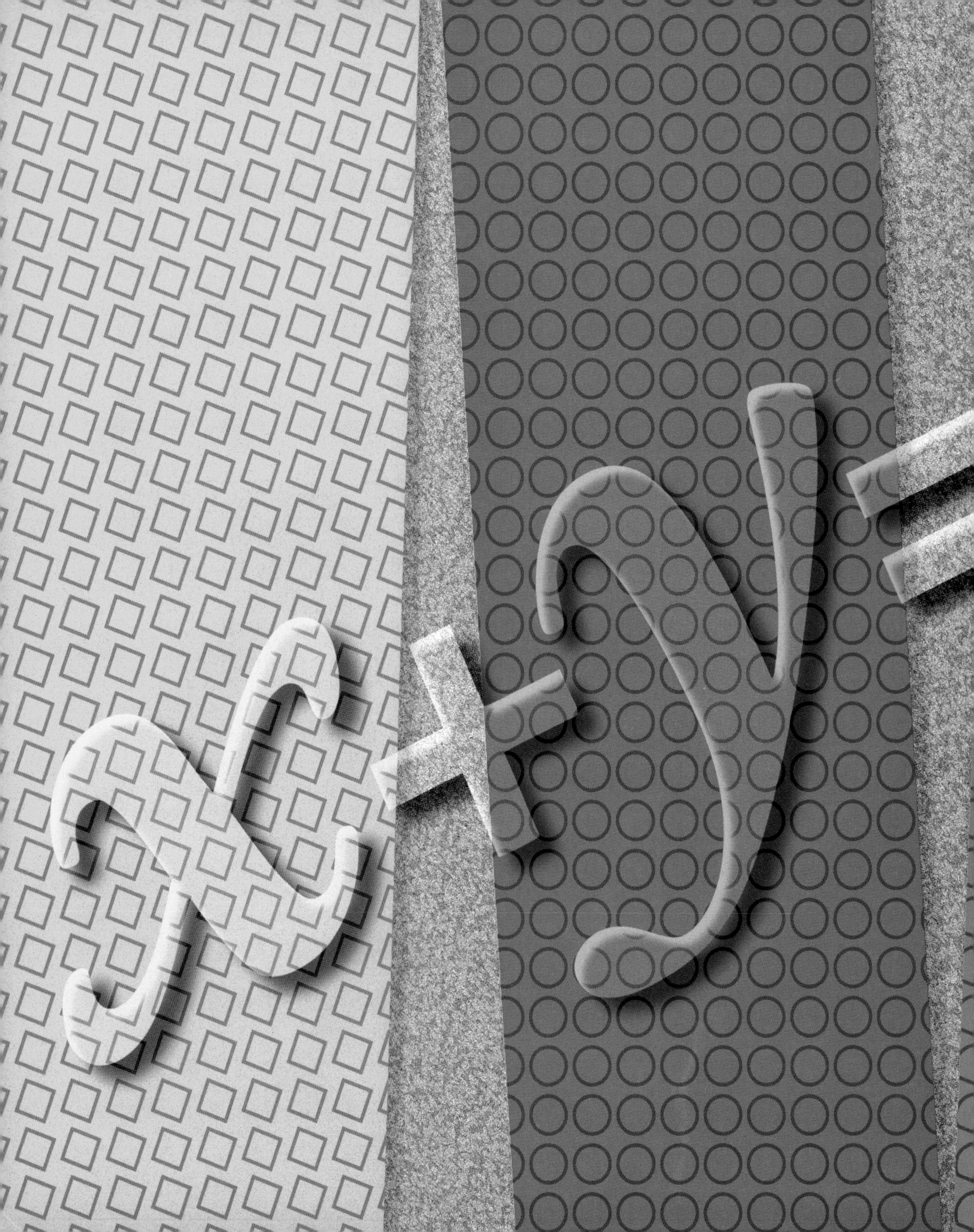

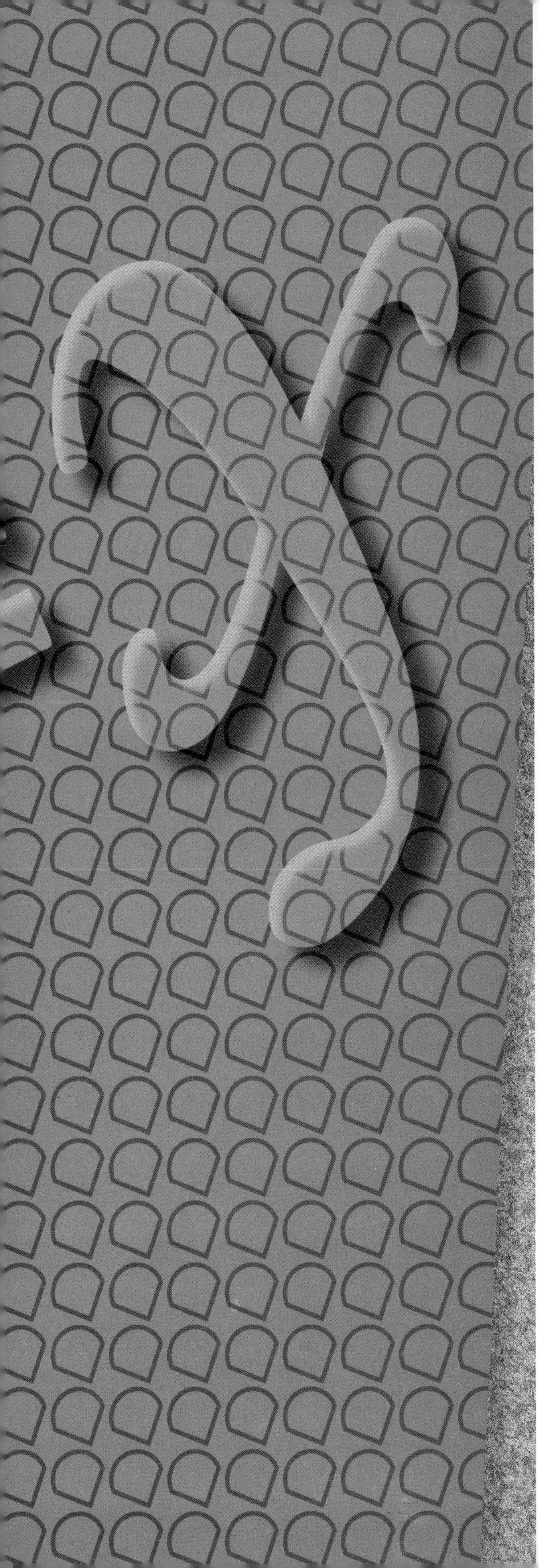

CHAPTER 11

Algebra

There are about 5000 languages and dialects in the world. However, many people understand at least some of the international signs and symbols shown here. State the meaning of all the ones you know.

Compare the ones you know with the ones that your classmates know.

Number Tiles

You will need a set of tiles numbered 0 to 9 for these activities. Small cardboard squares with the numbers printed on them will be fine.

Look for clues to decide where to place your tiles in the following activities. For example, if you see 7 ÷ ■, the ■ will be 7 or 1 because all operations have whole number answers.

Activity ❶

Use each of the 10 tiles once to make these equations correct.

1. 7 ÷ ■ + 6 ÷ ■ = 3

2. ■ × 2 − ■ = 4

3. 4 × ■ + 1 − ■ = 0

4. 5 ÷ ■ − ■ = 1

5. 5 ÷ ■ − 4 ÷ ■ = 4

Activity ❷

Use each of the 10 tiles once to make these equations correct.

1. 9 ÷ ■ − ■ = 2

2. ■ × ■ − 7 = 8

3. 7 × ■ + ■ = 9

4. 4 ÷ ■ + ■ = 7

5. ■ − 3 × ■ = 2

Activity ❸

Use each of the 10 tiles once to make these equations correct.

1. 4 ÷ ■ + ■ = 8

2. ■ × 2 − ■ = 1

3. 3 + ■ ÷ ■ = 5

4. 3 ÷ ■ + 4 − ■ = 4

5. ■ × 1 + ■ = 7

Warm Up

1. There were 2 candidates in the election for class president. The winner received 22 votes. The loser received 1 less than half as many votes as the winner. How many students voted?

2. The teacher gave 18 sheets of construction paper to Nate and Maria. Nate needed 4 sheets more than Maria. How many sheets did each receive?

3. Calculate the perimeter of each figure.

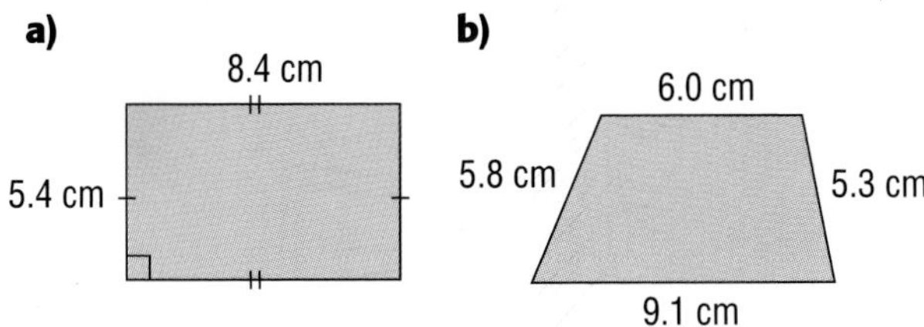

4. Find the area of each figure.

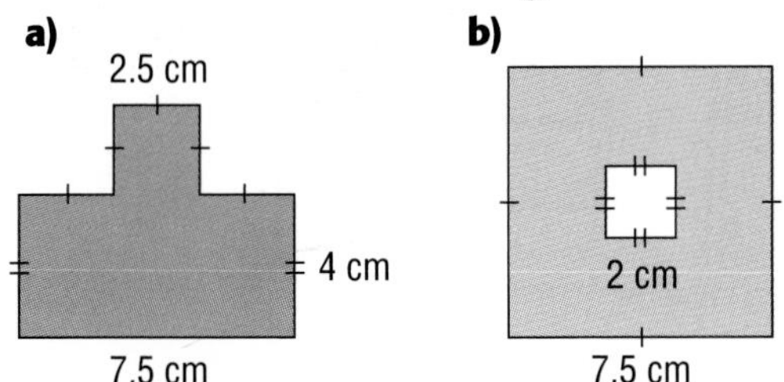

5. Find the volume of each figure.

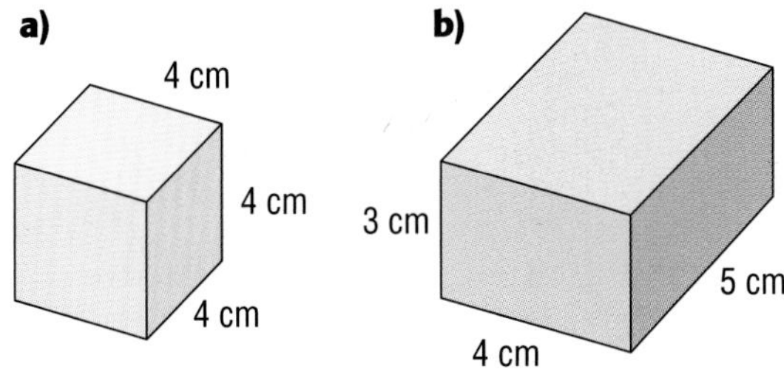

6. The distance formula is $d = st$, where d = distance, s = speed, and t = time. If Jack ran at an average speed of 8.5 m/s for 13 s, how far did he run?

7. The formula to find the nth odd number, starting with 1, is $2n - 1$. What is the 1000th odd number?

Mental Math

Calculate.

1. $12 + 6$ **2.** $18 + 2$ **3.** $7 + 23$

4. $14 + 26$ **5.** $38 - 8$ **6.** $44 - 14$

7. $56 - 16$ **8.** $88 - 28$ **9.** 20×7

10. 25×4 **11.** 30×8 **12.** 50×6

13. $320 \div 8$ **14.** $450 \div 9$ **15.** $600 \div 3$

Calculate.

16. $\frac{1}{5} + \frac{3}{5}$ **17.** $\frac{1}{2} + \frac{1}{4}$ **18.** $\frac{3}{7} - \frac{1}{7}$

19. $\frac{5}{6} - \frac{1}{2}$ **20.** $\frac{1}{2} \times \frac{1}{3}$ **21.** $\frac{2}{5} \times \frac{2}{3}$

22. $\frac{1}{3} \times 12$ **23.** $\frac{1}{4} \times 20$ **24.** $5 \div \frac{1}{2}$

Calculate.

25. $1.5 + 0.5$ **26.** $3.6 + 0.4$

27. $6.8 - 1.8$ **28.** $7.4 - 3.4$

29. 4.5×100 **30.** 7.25×1000

31. 0.25×100 **32.** 1.05×100

33. $550 \div 10$ **34.** $2500 \div 100$

35. $525 \div 100$ **36.** $625 \div 1000$

Calculate.

37. $4.8 + 1.2$ **38.** $6.5 + 1.5$

39. $25.5 - 0.5$ **40.** $35.5 - 5.5$

41. 45×0.1 **42.** 550×0.01

43. 15×0.01 **44.** 150×0.01

45. $15 \div 0.1$ **46.** $25.5 \div 0.1$

47. $65 \div 0.01$ **48.** $750 \div 0.01$

Calculate.

49. $n + 5, n = 3$ **50.** $n - 7, n = 2$

51. $3 \times n, n = 6$ **52.** $n \div 2, n = 18$

53. $20 \div n, n = 5$ **54.** $n^2, n = 6$

11.1 Variables in Expressions

Activity: Study the Table

Bill sells tickets for the county fair. The price of each ticket is $8.75. He made up this table, so that he could quickly determine how much to charge for the different numbers of tickets he might sell.

Tickets #	Cost $
1	8.75
2	17.50
3	26.25
4	35.00
5	43.75

Inquire

1. How did Bill calculate $26.25 as the price for 3 tickets?

2. How did he calculate $43.75 as the price for 5 tickets?

3. What would be the price for 8 tickets?

4. Write a formula for the price of n tickets.

Bill also sells $7.00 tickets for the grandstand show. He used the following formula to find the price of any number of tickets, where n represents the number of tickets sold:

$$\text{Price of Tickets} = 7 \times n$$

Bill wrote $7 \times n$ to show that 7 is multiplied by the number represented by n. We usually write $7 \times n$ as $7n$.

In the **expression** $7n$, the letter n is a **variable.**

Replacing a variable by a number is called **substitution.**

Remember to use the order of operations when you evaluate expressions.

Find the value of each expression by substituting 3 for n.

a) $n + 5$ **b)** $5n$ **c)** $3n - 4$

Solution

a) $n + 5 = 3 + 5$
$= 8$

b) $5n = 5(3)$
$= 15$

c) $3n - 4 = 3(3) - 4$
$= 9 - 4$
$= 5$

Practice

Evaluate the following.

1. $n + 5, n = 4$ **2.** $3n, n = 2$

3. $n - 2, n = 5$ **4.** $7 + n, n = 0$

5. $4n, n = 0$ **6.** $2n + 1, n = 3$

7. $3n - 2, n = 1$ **8.** $3 + 2n, n = 5$

9. $10 - 3n, n = 2$ **10.** $4n - 6, n = 3$

Substitute 3 for m in each expression and then simplify.

11. $4m$ **12.** $m + 5$ **13.** $m - 1$

14. $7 - m$ **15.** $12 - m$ **16.** $m + m$

Substitute 4 for x in each expression and then simplify each expression.

17. $x + 5$ **18.** $5x$ **19.** $2x + 3$

20. $10 - x$ **21.** $10 - 2x$ **22.** $3x + 5$

Substitute $y = 2$ and then simplify each of the following.

23. $5 - y$ **24.** $y - 2$ **25.** $2y$

26. $2y - 3$ **27.** $7 - 2y$ **28.** $6 - 3y$

Evaluate the following expressions for $m = 2$ and $n = 3$.

29. $m + n$ **30.** $2m + n$ **31.** $m + 4n$

32. $n - m$ **33.** $3m - n$ **34.** $3(m + n)$

Evaluate these expressions for $x = 2.4$ and $y = 4.2$.

35. $x + y$ **36.** $2x + y$ **37.** $x + 3y$

38. $4x + 5y$ **39.** $5x - 2y$ **40.** $3(y - x)$

Problems and Applications

41. An expression for the perimeter of a rectangle is $2(l + w)$. Find the perimeter for $l = 2$ m and $w = 1.3$ m.

42. The cost of team pennants at the stadium souvenir stand is represented by the expression $12.50n$, where n is the number of pennants. What is the cost of the following?

a) 4 pennants **b)** 7 pennants

43. The cost of hamburgers and drinks is represented by the following expression. The variable, m, is the number of hamburgers and the variable, n, is the number of drinks.

$$4.50m + 1.50n$$

a) What is the cost of a hamburger? a drink?

b) What is the cost of 1 hamburger and 1 drink?

c) How many hamburgers and drinks can you buy for $13.50?

44. Write a problem that uses the expression $3n + 10$. Ask others to solve it.

45. Work with a classmate to find values for x and y that give the expression $2x - 3y$ a value of 1.

46. Create your own expressions and challenge your classmates to find values for the variables to produce a certain number.

WORD POWER

The word TIP gives the real word PIT when it is written backwards. Find 4 other 3-letter words that give real words when they are written backwards.

11.2 Words and Symbols

Activity: Complete the Table

Francoise sells picture frames for the cost of the materials, plus \$7.00 for assembly.

Copy and complete the table.

Cost of Materials (\$)	10	11	18	24	35	46
Selling Price (\$)						

Inquire

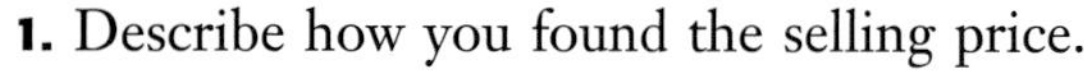

1. Describe how you found the selling price.
2. Write an expression for the selling price if the cost of materials is m dollars.

3. If the cost of materials doubles, does the selling price double? Explain.

Example 1

Golf balls are sold in packages of 3.
One package costs \$7.00. The table shows the prices of different numbers of packages.

Number of Packages	1	2	3	4	5	6
Number of Golf Balls	3	6	9	12	15	18
Price (\$)	7	14	21	28	35	42

a) Write an expression for the number of golf balls in a number of packages.
b) Write an expression for the price of a number of packages.

Solution

Let n represent the number of packages of golf balls.

a) The number of golf balls is the number of balls in a package multiplied by the number of packages. An expression for the number of golf balls in n packages is $3n$.

b) The price is given by the price of each package multiplied by the number of packages. An expression for the price of n packages is $7n$.

Example 2

Write an expression for each phrase.
a) three times a number n
b) a number d increased by three
c) twice a number y decreased by five
d) the square of a number x

Solution

The expressions are as follows:
a) $3n$
b) $d + 3$
c) $2y - 5$
d) x^2

Practice

Choose an expression from the cloud to match the words for each of the following statements.

1. a number increased by 5

2. a number decreased by 6

3. a number multiplied by 4

4. a number divided by 2

5. 8 subtracted from a number

6. the sum of 5 and a number

7. a number subtracted from 9

8. 5 divided by a number

$5x \quad 6 - x \quad \frac{x}{2} \quad n - 8 \quad 8 - n$

$5 + y \quad x + 5 \quad \frac{x}{5} \quad x - 6 \quad 9x$

$9 - m \quad 4n \quad 2x \quad \frac{5}{x} \quad \frac{2}{x}$

The variable x represents a number. Write the words that can be represented by each of these expressions.

9. $x + 6$ **10.** $x - 5$ **11.** $4x$

12. $2x$ **13.** $9 + x$ **14.** $7 - x$

15. $\frac{x}{3}$ **16.** $\frac{7}{x}$ **17.** $\frac{x}{2} - 3$

Write each of the following using symbols.

18. m divided by 4

19. n increased by 2

20. 10 decreased by n

21. 12 divided by x

Write each statement using symbols.

22. half of a number

23. five times a number

24. six less than a number

25. twenty-five divided by a number

Problems and Applications

26. Write expressions for each of the following.

a) Sondra's height increased by five centimetres

b) the width decreased by six metres

c) the length multiplied by ten

d) the time divided by three

e) six times the number of pens

f) In 1992, the number of Canadians who had flown in space increased by 2.

g) The mass of a Siberian tiger is ten times the mass of a Canadian beaver.

h) In the 1992 World Series, the Toronto Blue Jays won two more games than the Atlanta Braves.

27. P.J. earns \$5.00/h cutting lawns in the neighbourhood. The table shows the number of hours she worked.

Time (h)	1	2	3	4	5	6	7	8
Pay (\$)								

a) How can each earned amount be calculated?

b) Copy and complete the table.

c) Write an expression for the amount earned.

LOGIC POWER

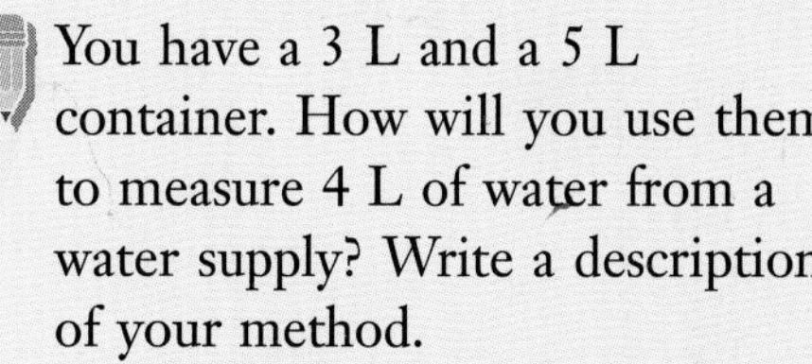

You have a 3 L and a 5 L container. How will you use them to measure 4 L of water from a water supply? Write a description of your method.

11.3 Solving Equations

Activity: Interpret the Data

It costs \$8.00, plus \$3.00/h, to rent a motor scooter.

Inquire

1. How much does it cost to rent a scooter for 1 h?

2. How much does it cost to rent one for 7 h?

3. Write an expression that represents the cost of renting a scooter for n hours.

Example 1

Masa wants to rent a faster motor scooter. It costs \$10.00, plus \$4.25/h. He has \$27.00. How many hours can he afford?

Solution

Use the guess and check strategy.

Guess		Check
Number of Hours (h)	Total Cost ($)	Is the result 27?
1	4.25(1) + 10 = 14.25	No, too small
2	4.25(2) + 10 = 18.50	No, too small
3	4.25(3) + 10 = 22.75	No, too small
4	4.25(4) + 10 = 27.00	Yes, it checks

Masa can afford to rent the scooter for 4 h.

In Example 1, the number sentence for the total cost can be written using a variable. If n represents the number of hours, then the sentence is $4n + 10 = 27$. Sentences such as $4n + 10 = 27$ are either true or false, depending on the value we assign to n. These sentences are called **equations**.

Example 2

Solve $n + 5 = 9$.

Solution

Find the value of n that makes $n + 5 = 9$ a true statement.

Since $4 + 5 = 9$, then $n = 4$.
$n = 4$ is the solution.

Think: What number gives 9 when it is added to 5?

Practice

Does the number in brackets make each sentence a true statement?

1. $n + 7 = 10$ (3) **2.** $x - 5 = 0$ (5)

3. $3b = 18$ (15) **4.** $5u = 20$ (4)

5. $\frac{x}{5} = 2$ (15) **6.** $2w = 6$ (3)

7. $2z + 1 = 7$ (3) **8.** $3e - 2 = 10$ (4)

Solve each equation.

9. $x + 3 = 7$ **10.** $f + 3 = 4$

11. $m + 2 = 9$ **12.** $n + 1 = 6$

13. $y + 4 = 8$ **14.** $z + 8 = 12$

Solve each equation.

15. $x - 5 = 7$ **16.** $a - 3 = 7$

17. $z - 1 = 6$ **18.** $4 - n = 0$

Solve the following equations.

19. $3n = 6$ **20.** $2s = 10$ **21.** $6x = 24$

22. $5y = 20$ **23.** $10t = 30$ **24.** $7n = 35$

Solve each equation.

25. $\frac{x}{4} = 3$ **26.** $\frac{y}{2} = 4$ **27.** $\frac{c}{7} = 3$

28. $\frac{r}{2} = 8$ **29.** $\frac{m}{4} = 1$ **30.** $\frac{n}{3} = 6$

Solve the following equations.

31. $5 + x = 12$ **32.** $y + 7 = 13$

33. $\frac{m}{7} = 11$ **34.** $\frac{n}{5} = 15$

35. $8a = 32$ **36.** $12q = 60$

Solve these equations.

37. $2n + 7 = 15$ **38.** $3x - 4 = 14$

39. $4p + 2 = 22$ **40.** $2t - 9 = 11$

41. $3m + 5 = 26$ **42.** $6b + 8 = 56$

Find the correct value for each variable.

43. $x + 1.5 = 2.8$ **44.** $y - 3.2 = 1.2$

45. $z + 3.7 = 4.8$ **46.** $x + 4.2 = 6.5$

47. $2x = 4.6$ **48.** $3y = 6.3$

49. $5x = 7.25$ **50.** $10x = 65$

Problems and Applications

Write an equation in the form shown by replacing the ▲ and ■ with numbers. The solution for x is shown in brackets.

51. $x +$ ▲ $=$ ■ (5)

52. ▲ $+ x =$ ■ (3)

53. ▲$x =$ ■ (6)

54. $\frac{x}{▲} =$ ■ (4)

55. $x -$ ▲ $=$ ■ (11)

56. A copy shop charges 9¢/page for the first 225 copies and 3¢/page for additional copies. How many pages can you copy for $24.00?

57. Why are number sentences like $4n + 10 = 30$ called equations?

Work with a classmate and write an equation for the next 2 problems. Then, solve the equation.

58. The cost for a bus to cross the bridge is $5.00 for the bus and driver plus $1.25 for each passenger. Including the driver, how many can cross the bridge for $15.00?

59. A ride in a taxi costs $3.00 plus $1.25 for each kilometre driven. How far can you go if you have $28.00?

LOGIC POWER

What relation is a man to his mother's only brother's only nephew?

See-Saw Math

Activity

Copy the diagrams and use the clues to find out what is on the last see-saw in each case.

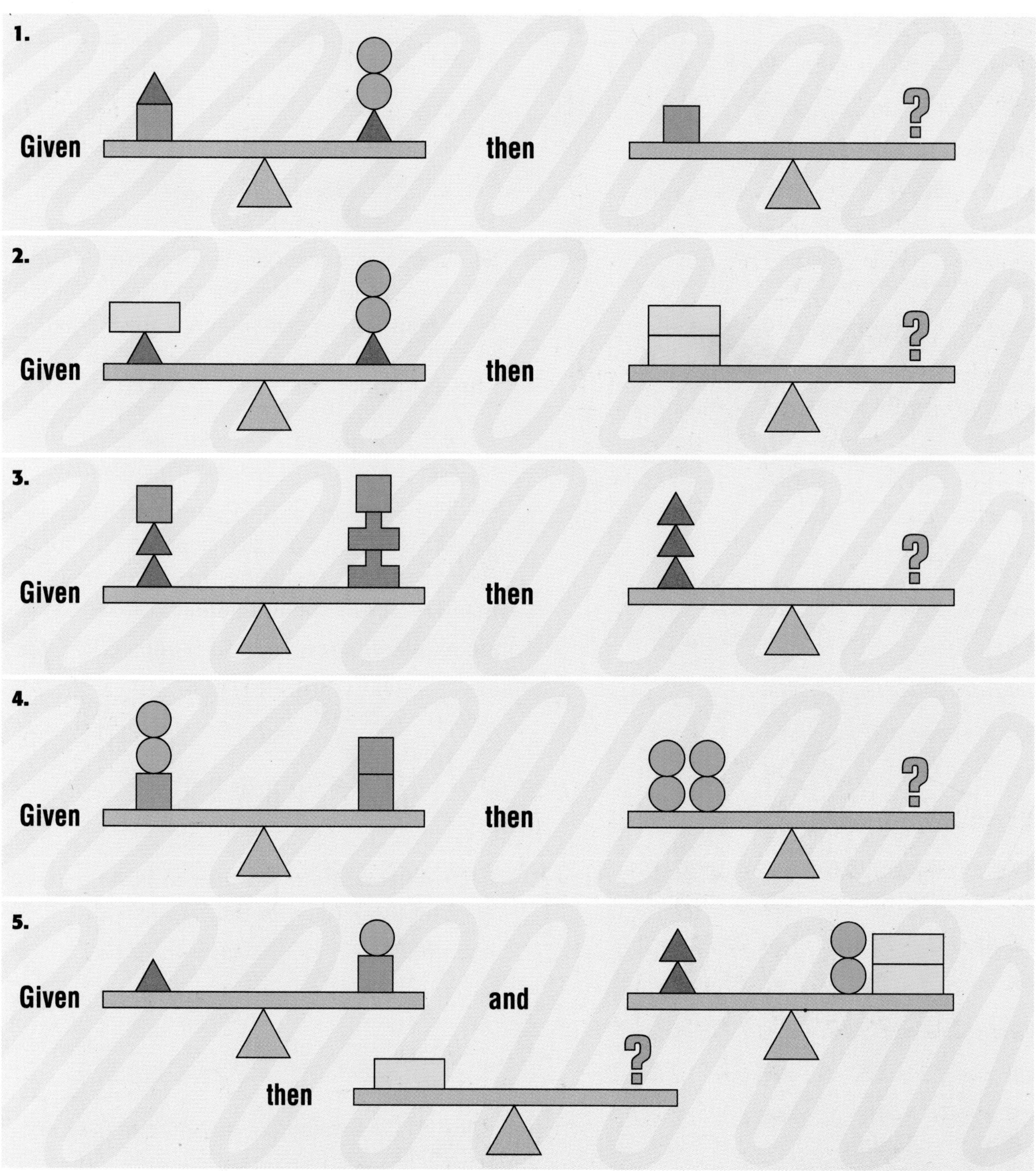

11.4 Solving Equations by Subtraction

Activity: Use Algebra Tiles

An equation is like a balance scale. We can use algebra tiles to represent equations. A *red* tile means *add 1*. A *green* rectangle represents the *variable x*.

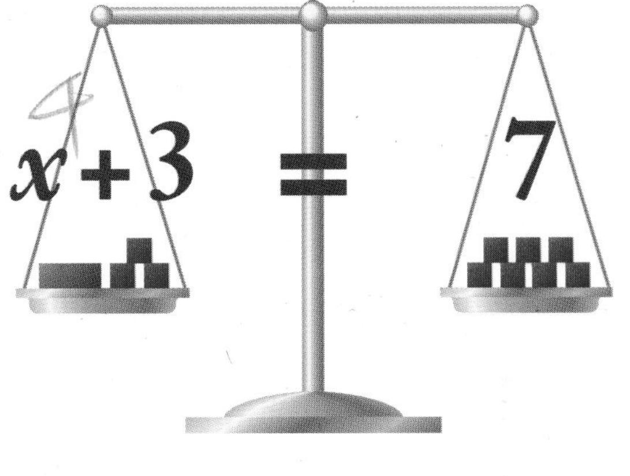

The diagram on the right represents the equation $x + 3 = 7$. Find the value of x.

Inquire

1. If you remove 3 red tiles from each side of the scale in the diagram, what is the new equation? What is the value of x?

2. What must you subtract from both sides of $x + 5 = 8$ to solve it?

3. What must you subtract from both sides of the following equations to solve them?

a) $x + 1 = 7$ **b)** $x + 2 = 10$ **c)** $x + 5 = 6$

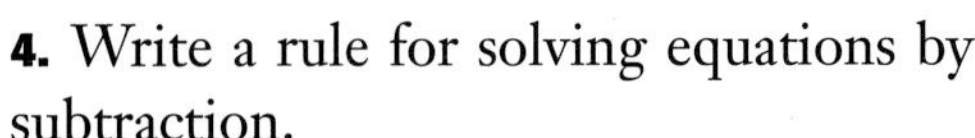

4. Write a rule for solving equations by subtraction.

Example

Solve $x + 6 = 14$.

Solution

Subtract 6 from both sides.

$$x + 6 = 14$$
$$x + 6 - 6 = 14 - 6$$
$$x = 8$$

Check:
$8 + 6 = 14$

The solution is 8.

Practice

What number would you subtract from both sides of these equations to solve them?

1. $x + 6 = 13$ **2.** $c + 1 = 8$ **3.** $y + 2 = 7$

4. $m + 5 = 5$ **5.** $x + 3 = 9$ **6.** $z + 7 = 10$

Solve these equations.

7. $p + 11 = 19$ **8.** $y + 2 = 3$

9. $r + 8 = 12$ **10.** $p + 5 = 11$

Solve the following equations.

11. $m + 12 = 22$ **12.** $n + 15 = 35$

13. $x + 7 = 17$ **14.** $y + 11 = 33$

15. $y + 13 = 33$ **16.** $p + 17 = 37$

Solve.

17. $x + 3 = 5.8$ **18.** $y + 5 = 7.8$

19. $n + 2 = 4.4$ **20.** $p + 9 = 18.2$

21. $r + 6 = 12.7$ **22.** $t + 8 = 13.6$

11.5 Solving Equations By Addition

Activity: Use Algebra Tiles

Recall that a red tile means add 1 and a green rectangle represents the variable x. A *white* tile means *subtract 1*. A red and white tile together make 0.

The diagram represents the equation $x - 2 = 5$. Find the value of x.

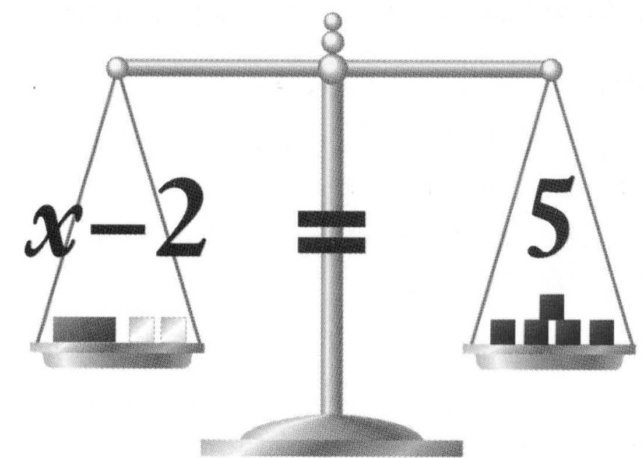

Inquire

1. If you add 2 red tiles to each side of the scale in the diagram, what is the new equation?

2. What is the value of x?

3. What must you add to both sides of $x - 1 = 4$ to solve the equation?

4. What must you add to both sides of these equations to solve them?

a) $x - 3 = 7$ **b)** $x - 4 = 9$ **c)** $x - 5 = 6$

5. Write a rule for solving equations by addition.

Example

Solve $x - 5 = 12$.

Solution

Add 5 to both sides of the equation.

$$x - 5 = 12$$
$$x - 5 + 5 = 12 + 5$$
$$x = 17$$

Check: $17 - 5 = 12$

The solution is 17.

Practice

What number would you add to both sides to solve each equation?

1. $x - 3 = 11$ **2.** $d - 1 = 5$ **3.** $n - 7 = 8$

4. $m - 4 = 8$ **5.** $y - 10 = 3$ **6.** $z - 10 = 1$

7. $x - 15 = 3$ **8.** $y - 19 = 1$ **9.** $t - 24 = 2$

Solve these equations.

10. $m - 5 = 4$ **11.** $n - 3 = 2$ **12.** $p - 7 = 3$

13. $r - 7 = 9$ **14.** $s - 5 = 3$ **15.** $t - 8 = 5$

Solve each of the following equations.

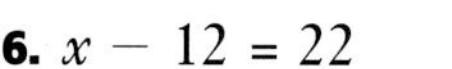

16. $x - 12 = 22$ **17.** $y - 10 = 18$

18. $m - 15 = 25$ **19.** $n - 11 = 33$

20. $x - 21 = 31$ **21.** $y - 9 = 24$

Solve these equations.

22. $m - 6 = 8.3$ **23.** $r - 7 = 9.8$

24. $m - 15 = 25$ **25.** $s - 4 = 4.5$

26. $p - 9 = 0.9$ **27.** $t - 5 = 7.8$

11.6 Solving Equations By Division

Activity: Use Algebra Tiles

Remember that a red tile means add 1 and a green rectangle represents the variable x.

The diagram represents the equation $2x = 8$. Find the value of x.

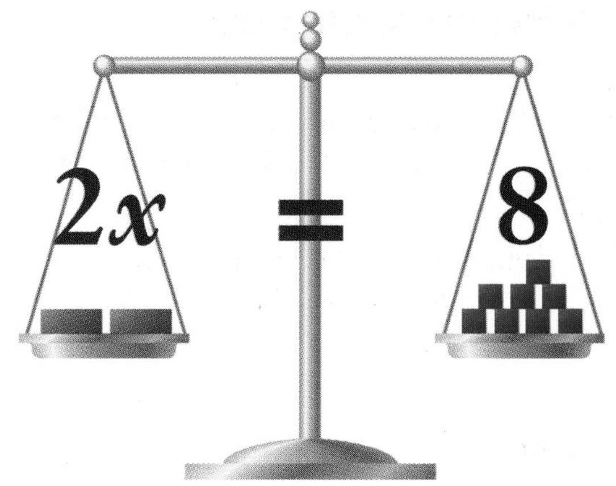

Inquire

1. How many equal parts are there on the left-hand side of the equation?

2. Divide the right-hand side of the equation into the same number of equal parts. What is the value of each part? What is the value of x?

3. To solve the following equations, what must you divide both sides by?

a) $3x = 6$ **b)** $4x = 12$ **c)** $5x = 20$

4. Write a rule for solving equations by division.

Example

Solve $4x = 8$.

Solution

Divide both sides of the equation by 4.

$$4x = 8$$
$$\frac{4x}{4} = \frac{8}{4}$$
$$x = 2$$

Check:
4(2) = 8

The solution is 2.

Practice

By what number would you divide both sides to solve each equation?

1. $6x = 12$ **2.** $2x = 8$ **3.** $2y = 10$

4. $5m = 5$ **5.** $3x = 9$ **6.** $7z = 14$

7. $11r = 22$ **8.** $6n = 18$ **9.** $10p = 40$

Solve each of these equations.

10. $3x = 15$ **11.** $2y = 12$ **12.** $8x = 16$

13. $5p = 15$ **14.** $6m = 24$ **15.** $3s = 12$

Solve each of the following equations.

16. $12m = 24$ **17.** $5a = 25$ **18.** $7x = 21$

19. $11y = 33$ **20.** $9q = 27$ **21.** $3p = 3$

Solve these equations.

22. $3x = 2.1$ **23.** $5y = 1.5$ **24.** $2n = 4.4$

25. $9p = 1.8$ **26.** $6r = 2.4$ **27.** $8t = 1.6$

11.7 Solving Equations By Multiplication

Activity: Interpret the Diagram

The balance shows the equation $\frac{x}{2} = 3$.
Find the value of x.

Inquire

1. By what number should you multiply the left-hand side of the equation to give x?

2. Multiply the right-hand side of the equation by the same number. What is the value of x?

3. To solve the following equations, what number must you multiply both sides by?
a) $\frac{x}{3} = 8$ **b)** $\frac{x}{2} = 5$ **c)** $\frac{x}{4} = 1$

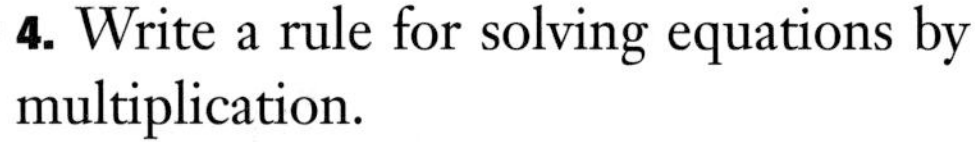

4. Write a rule for solving equations by multiplication.

Example

Solve $\frac{x}{3} = 4$.

Solution

Multiply both sides by 3.

$$\frac{x}{3} = 4$$
$$3 \times \frac{x}{3} = 3 \times 4$$
$$x = 12$$

Check: $\frac{12}{3} = 4$

The solution is 12.

Practice

By what number would you multiply both sides to solve each equation?

1. $\frac{x}{3} = 5$ **2.** $\frac{x}{2} = 4$ **3.** $\frac{y}{7} = 4$

Solve each of the following equations.

4. $\frac{m}{5} = 1$ **5.** $\frac{t}{4} = 2$ **6.** $\frac{c}{6} = 5$

7. $\frac{x}{2} = 0$ **8.** $\frac{m}{7} = 8$ **9.** $\frac{r}{9} = 3$

10. $\frac{n}{3} = 6$ **11.** $\frac{b}{2} = 7$ **12.** $\frac{c}{8} = 8$

13. $\frac{x}{6} = 2$ **14.** $\frac{y}{4} = 5$ **15.** $\frac{w}{3} = 3$

Solve these equations.

16. $\frac{x}{3} = 1.2$ **17.** $\frac{y}{2} = 3.5$ **18.** $\frac{z}{6} = 0.2$

19. $\frac{t}{4} = 2.4$ **20.** $\frac{a}{7} = 0.9$ **21.** $\frac{b}{5} = 1.9$

WORD POWER

Which consonant appears most often in the names of the 10 Canadian provinces?

11.8 Solving Equations in Two Steps

Activity: Use Algebra Tiles

The balance at the right shows the equation $2x + 1 = 9$. Solve the equation.

Inquire

1. Subtract 1 from both sides of the equation. What is the new equation?
2. Divide both sides of the new equation by 2. What is the value of x?

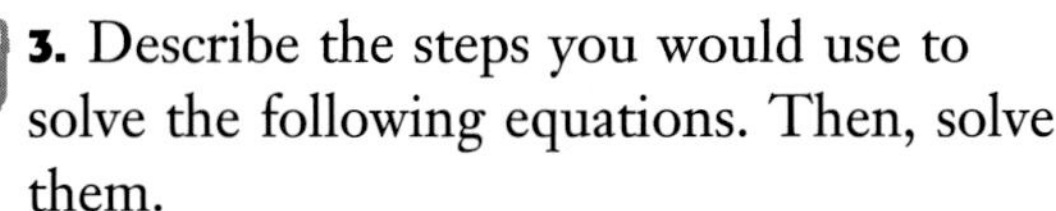

3. Describe the steps you would use to solve the following equations. Then, solve them.

a) $2x + 2 = 8$ **b)** $3x + 1 = 13$

Example

Solve $3x - 2 = 13$.

Solution

First, add 2 to both sides.

$$3x - 2 = 13$$
$$3x - 2 + 2 = 13 + 2$$
$$3x = 15$$

Then, divide both sides by 3.

$$\frac{3x}{3} = \frac{15}{3}$$
$$x = 5$$

The solution is 5.

Check: $3(5) - 2 = 13$

Practice

Solve each equation.

1. $2x + 1 = 7$ **2.** $3n + 1 = 13$
3. $4t + 5 = 21$ **4.** $2y + 7 = 11$
5. $3p + 4 = 22$ **6.** $4m + 7 = 27$
7. $2t + 5 = 8 + 15$ **8.** $7e + 2 = 21 - 5$

Solve the following equations.

9. $2x - 1 = 9$ **10.** $5x - 2 = 13$
11. $2x - 5 = 11$ **12.** $4x - 7 = 17$
13. $5x - 6 = 24$ **14.** $3x - 11 = 10$
15. $2x - 4 = 11 + 1$ **16.** $6x - 5 = 23 - 4$

Solve each equation.

17. $3x + 1.2 = 4.2$ **18.** $2x - 2.3 = 3.7$
19. $4x - 1.1 = 7.7$ **20.** $5x + 3.1 = 9.6$

NUMBER POWER

Copy the diagram. Place the numbers from 1 to 9 in the circles, so that each side of the triangle adds to 23. The 4 has been placed for you.

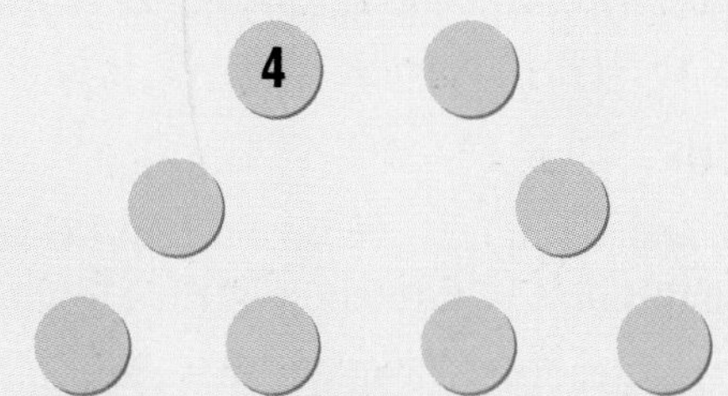

11.9 Writing and Reading Equations

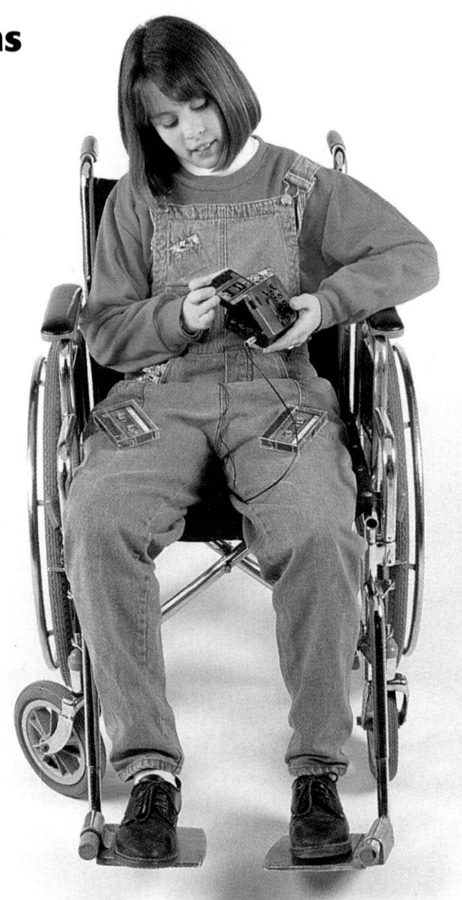

Activity: Use an Equation

Alicia bought a package of cassette tapes for her personal stereo. She gave the sales clerk a \$10.00 bill and received \$3.50 change. Use an equation to find the cost of the tapes.

Inquire

1. What was the sum of the cost of the cassettes and the amount of change?

2. Write the preceding equation in words.

3. Let the cost of the cassettes be n. Write the equation in symbols.

4. Solve the equation.

Example 1

Write an equation for each sentence.

a) Five more than a number, x, is twelve.
b) Five times a number, y, is fifteen.
c) Four less than a number, m, is six.
d) A number, n, divided by two is five.

Solution

The equations are as follows.

a) $x + 5 = 12$
b) $5y = 15$
c) $m - 4 = 6$
d) $\frac{n}{2} = 5$

Example 2

Write a word problem that can be solved with the equation $x + 5 = 15$. Then, solve it to check if your problem works.

Solution

Gunter and Gretchen are brother and sister. Gretchen is 5 years older than Gunter. Gretchen is 15. How old is Gunter?

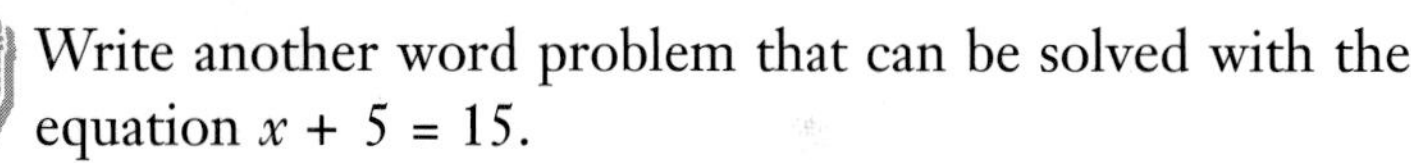

Write another word problem that can be solved with the equation $x + 5 = 15$.

Practice

Choose the correct equation from the cloud.

1. Three subtracted from a number is seven.

2. A number multiplied by three is eighteen.

3. A number increased by seven is thirteen.

4. Four added to a number is nine.

5. Twelve reduced by a number is four.

6. A number divided by three is twelve.

$3x = 18$ $12 - s = 4$

$y - 3 = 7$ $\frac{x}{3} = 12$

$r + 7 = 13$ $n + 4 = 9$ $x - 5 = 12$

Write an equation for each sentence.

7. 4 added to a number is 16.

8. 7 subtracted from a number is 5.

9. A number multiplied by 2 is 18.

10. A number divided by 3 is 6.

11. One half of a number is 5.

12. One quarter of a number is 2.

Write an equation for each statement.

13. A number divided by 3 is 12.

14. A number increased by 7 is 11.

15. A number multiplied by 6 is 6.

16. A number decreased by 4 is 8.

17. 14 divided by a number is 2.

18. A number increased by 3 is 5.

Write each of the following in words.

19. $n + 15 = 25$ **20.** $t - 4 = 11$

21. $5x = 30$ **22.** $\frac{w}{3} = 6$

23. $r + 21 = 33$ **24.** $m - 9 = 20$

25. $4t = 32$ **26.** $\frac{x}{5} = 7$

Problems and Applications

Write and solve an equation for each statement.

27. Earl's age increased by 5 is 17.

28. Saleena's age decreased by 5 is 18.

29. Twice Bob's age is 24.

30. Half of Anne's age is 12.

31. Julio's age divided by 3 is 5.

32. Shirley's age in 3 years will be 14.

Write and solve an equation for each of the following.

33. The length is 3 more than the width. The length is 15.

34. Maria's age is twice Jane's age. Maria is 24.

35. Brett has sold half as many papers as Tom. Brett sold 250 papers.

36. Elaine's book has 3 fewer pages than Margarite's book. Elaine's book has 200 pages.

Read the statements in questions 37 and 38, then write and solve the equation.

37. Fossils of prehistoric creatures, found in southern Alberta, indicate that they lived three times as long ago as people have lived. One of the oldest prehistoric creatures lived 15 000 000 years ago. How long ago did one of the oldest humans live?

38. Canada's Atlantic coastline is 10 600 km longer than its Pacific coastline. The Pacific coastline is 18 700 km long. How long is the Atlantic coastline?

39. Write a short problem that can be expressed by the equation $x - 7 = 8$. Challenge a classmate to solve your problem.

11.10 Using Equations to Solve Problems

Activity: Solve the Problem

Sharon bought a Luc Robitaille rookie card and an Adam Oates rookie card.

The total cost of both cards was $32.50.

If the Adam Oates card cost $25.00, how much did the Luc Robitaille rookie card cost?

Inquire

1. What is the total cost of the 2 cards?

2. Write the equation in words.

3. Write the equation in symbols.

4. Solve the equation to find the cost of the Luc Robitaille rookie card.

Writing and solving equations is a common problem solving strategy.

Recall the steps

Understand the Problem

Think of a Plan

Carry Out the Plan

Look Back

Example 1

Sharon works in a sports card shop.

Card binders cost $6.00 each. One week, she sold $180.00 worth of binders. How many did she sell?

Solution

Let n represent the number of binders sold. Write and solve an equation.

$$6n = 180$$
$$\frac{6n}{6} = \frac{180}{6}$$
$$n = 30$$

Check: $6(30) = 180$

Sharon sold 30 binders.

Example 2

Rick and Chuck also work at the card shop. Rick worked 5 h less than Chuck. The sum of their hours is 27. How many hours each did Rick and Chuck work?

Solution

Let Chuck's hours be x. Then, Rick's hours are $x - 5$. The equation is:

$$x + (x - 5) = 27$$
$$2x - 5 = 27$$
$$2x - 5 + 5 = 27 + 5$$
$$2x = 32$$
$$x = 16$$

Chuck worked 16 h.

$$x - 5 = 16 - 5$$
$$= 11$$

Rick worked 11 h.

Check:
$x + (x - 5) = 27$
$16 + (16 - 5) = 27$

Problems and Applications

1. Find the following numbers.
a) When it is increased by 5, the result is 11.
b) When it is divided by 3, the quotient is 5.
c) The product of 4 and itself is 12.
d) The difference between itself and 8 is 2.
e) When it is subtracted from 18, the result is 8.

2. The formula for the area of a rectangle is $A = l \times w$.

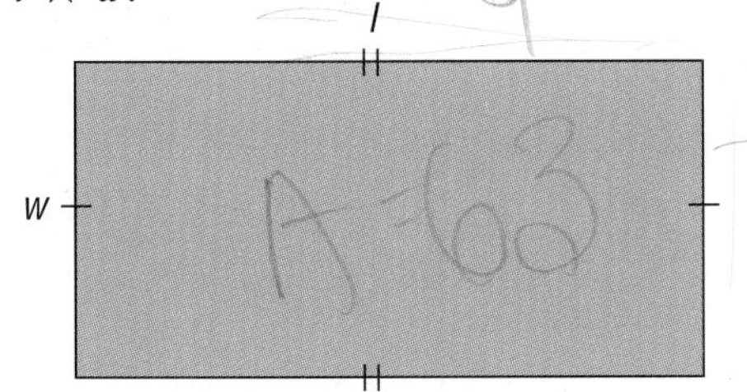

a) The area of the rectangle is 63 cm^2. If its width is 7 cm, what is its length?
b) If the area of the rectangle is increased to 72 cm^2, but its length remains the same, what is its new width?

3. A Cal Ripken baseball card sells for \$18.50. This is \$11.75 more than a Joe Carter card. What is the cost of a Joe Carter card?

4. Soula bought 2 new skirts for school. One cost \$10.00 more than the other. If the cost of both skirts was \$70.00, what was the cost of each skirt?

5. The sum of 2 numbers is 24. One number is 3 times as great as the other. What are the 2 numbers?

6. The difference between 2 numbers is 36. The larger number is 4 times as great as the smaller. What are the 2 numbers?

7. In hockey standings, a team is given 2 points for a win and 1 point for a tie. The Cougars had 27 points with 3 ties. How many wins did they have?

8. Melanie and Paolo both worked the same number of hours. Five times the number of hours Melanie worked increased by nine is equal to three times the number of hours Paolo worked plus seventeen. How many hours did Melanie and Paolo work?

9. The sum of 3 numbers is 15. The second number is double the first. The third number is 5 less than the first. What are the 3 numbers?

10. Create your own problem that can be solved with an equation. Have a classmate solve it. Check your classmate's answer.

11.11 Inequalities

Activity: Use the Data

The table shows the amount of energy, in kilojoules, used by a 50-kg person in each activity for 15 min.

Activity	Energy Used (kJ)	Activity	Energy Used (kJ)
Basketball	320	Hiking	370
Dancing	190	Running	640
Field Hockey	570	Soccer	410

Inquire

1. The activities are listed alphabetically. In what other ways could you list them?

2. Which activity uses the most energy?

3. Which activity uses the least energy?

This number line shows the names and heights of a team of high school volleyball players.

Heather	Marion	Orval	Rose	Mitch	Chan
165 cm	172 cm	176 cm	180 cm	185 cm	190 cm

Orval is taller than Heather because 176 is greater than 165. We write $176 > 165$.

Marion is shorter than Chan because 172 is less than 190. We write $172 < 190$.

These expressions are called **inequalities.**

Let x represent the heights greater than or equal to 180 cm. The inequality $x \geq 180$ may be true or false, depending on the value we assign to x.

The values that make the inequality $x \geq 180$ true for the volleyball players are 180 (Rose), 185 (Mitch), and 190 (Chan).

≥ means greater than or equal to

Example 1

Solve $x + 3 > 5$, where x is a whole number. Graph the solution.

Solution

When x is a whole number greater than 2, $x + 3 > 5$ is true. We write the solution as $x > 2$ or $x = 3, 4, 5, \ldots$ The red arrow shows that the solution continues without end.

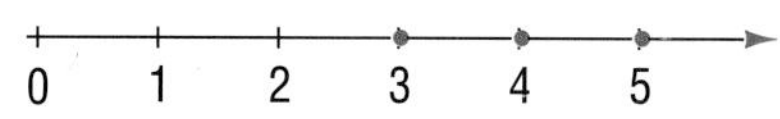

Example 2

Solve $x + 2 \leq 6$ for whole number values.

Solution

For $x = 0$: $0 + 2 \leq 6$

For $x = 1$: $1 + 2 \leq 6$

For $x = 2$: $2 + 2 \leq 6$

For $x = 3$: $3 + 2 \leq 6$

For $x = 4$: $4 + 2 = 6$

When $x = 5$, the inequality is no longer true because $5 + 2 > 6$.
The solution is 0, 1, 2, 3, 4.

$\leq$ means less than or equal to

Practice

Which of the following statements are true?

1. $2 + 3 > 5$ **2.** $2 + 5 = 11 - 4$

3. $3 + 8 \geq 11$ **4.** $9 - 5 \leq 4$

5. $3 + 5 < 2 + 5$ **6.** $7 > 4 + 5$

Write an inequality using x for each of the following graphs.

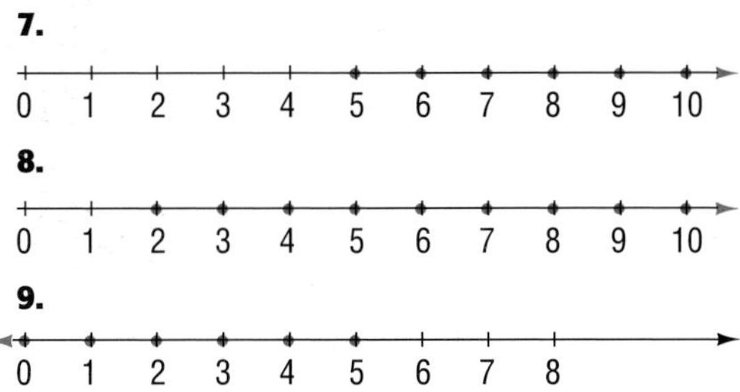

The variables are whole numbers from 0 to 10. Write each solution.

10. $x < 5$ **11.** $y > 4$ **12.** $x \leq 3$

13. $x \geq 2$ **14.** $m > 8$ **15.** $n < 7$

16. $x \geq 6$ **17.** $b \leq 6$ **18.** $s + 2 < 8$

19. $t + 3 > 5$ **20.** $p - 1 > 0$ **21.** $3q < 9$

The variables are whole numbers. Solve each inequality and graph its solution on a number line.

22. $n > 6$ **23.** $x < 9$ **24.** $y + 3 > 5$

25. $p - 2 < 3$ **26.** $4t > 12$ **27.** $x = 7$

Problems and Applications

28. The tallest trees in the world are shown in this table.

Type of Tree	Location	Height (m)
Douglas Fir	British Columbia	138
Redwood	California	123
Mountain Ash	Tasmania	108

a) Draw a number line to arrange their heights in ascending order.
b) Write an inequality that describes your number line.

29. Write 4 different inequalities that could describe the amount of energy used in the 6 different activities shown in the table on page 386.

30. a) If x is a whole number, solve the inequality $x \neq 5$.
b) Graph the solution on a number line.

PATTERN POWER

Diagram 1

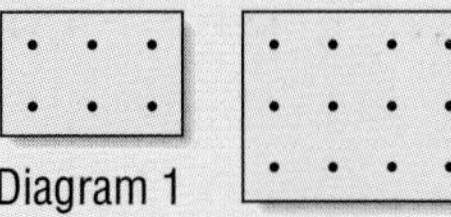

Diagram 2

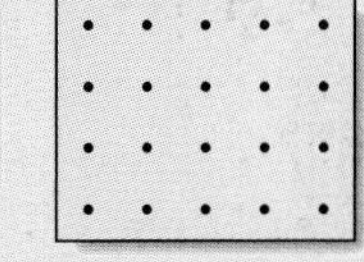

Diagram 3

How many dots will there be in these diagrams?

a) 5th diagram **b)** 10th diagram

11.12 Tables of Values

Activity: Look for a Pattern

Copy and complete these tables.

a)

x	y
1	2
2	3
3	4
4	5
5	
6	

b)

x	y
2	0
3	1
4	2
5	3
6	
7	

c)

x	y
0	0
1	2
2	4
3	6
4	
5	

d)

x	y
1	1
2	4
3	9
4	16
5	
6	

Inquire

1. What is the pattern in each table?

2. For each table, write an equation that relates x and y.

3. Calculate the missing values of y in each table.

4. Make up your own table and have a classmate discover the equation you used.

Example 1

a) Construct a table to show 5 values for the expression $3 + 5x$. Use the values $x = 1, 2, 3, 4$, and 5.

b) Describe the pattern.

Solution

The expression values for $3 + 5x$ are as follows.

a) For $x = 1$: $3 + 5(1) = 8$
For $x = 2$: $3 + 5(2) = 13$
For $x = 3$: $3 + 5(3) = 18$
For $x = 4$: $3 + 5(4) = 23$
For $x = 5$: $3 + 5(5) = 28$

x	y
1	8
2	13
3	18
4	23
5	28

b) For every unit increase in x, the value of $3 + 5x$ increases by 5.

Example 2

All clothing is being sold at 25% off in a sports store. Copy and complete the table to show the sale prices.

Item	Regular Price ($)	Sale Price ($)
Sneakers	60.00	
Sweat shirt	49.00	
Shorts	29.95	
T-shirt	19.99	

Solution

If all items are 25% off, the sale price is 75% of the regular price. Multiply each regular price by 0.75.

Item	Regular Price ($)	Sale Price ($)
Sneakers	60.00	45.00
Sweat shirt	49.00	36.75
Shorts	29.95	22.46
T-shirt	19.99	14.99

Practice

Complete each table and describe the pattern.

1.

x	$x-5$
1	
2	
3	
4	
5	

2.

x	$2x+1$
1	
2	
3	
4	
5	

3.

x	$3x-2$
1	
2	
3	
4	
5	

4.

x	$5x+1$
1	
2	
3	
4	
5	

Problems and Applications

5. Theatre tickets cost \$45.00 each. Copy and complete this table and write an equation.

Number of Tickets (n)	Cost (\$)
1	
2	
3	
4	

6. The weather person on a cruise ship determines the exact time interval between seeing lightning and hearing a thunderclap. If t, in seconds, is the time interval recorded, then the expression $\frac{t}{3}$ will give the distance in kilometres between the observer and the storm.

Copy and complete the table in your notebook.

Time Between Lightning and Thunder (s)	Distance From the Storm (km)
1.5	
3	
4.5	
6	
9	

7. School shirts cost \$200.00 for the design of the crest plus \$20.00 per shirt. To determine the cost of an order of shirts, the following formula is used, where n is the number of shirts. Complete the table.

$$20n + 200$$

Number of Shirts (n)	Cost (\$)
10	
20	
50	
100	
200	
500	

8.

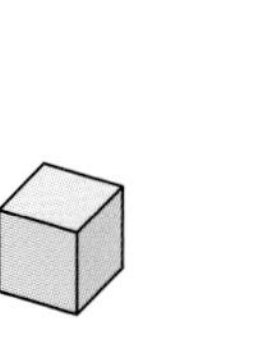

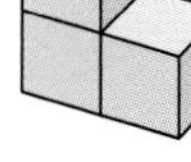

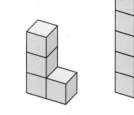

Diagram 1 Diagram 2 Diagram 3

a) Set up a table of values to include the number of cubes in the first 5 diagrams.
b) Predict how many cubes will be in the 8th diagram.
c) Predict how many cubes will be in the 10th diagram.

LOGIC POWER

Gear 2 rotates clockwise. Which way do the other gears rotate?

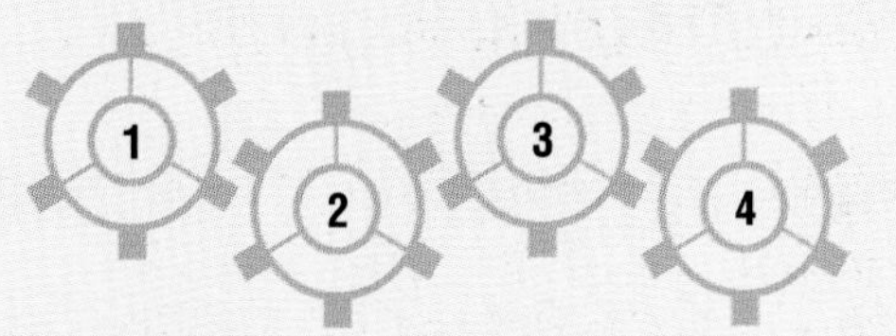

Computer Spreadsheets

Spreadsheets organize information into rows and columns, so that we can work with the information more easily.

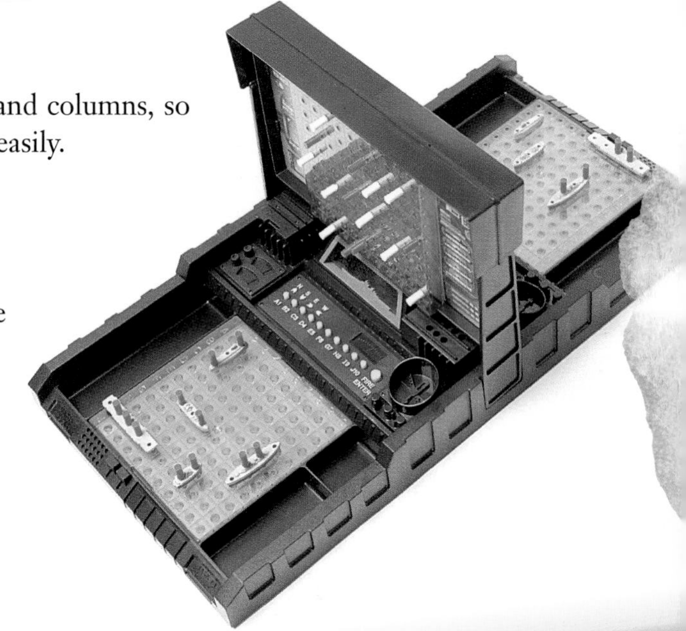

Activity ❶

Manual spreadsheets have been used for centuries. For example, some baseball fans use manual spreadsheets to record the events at a game. The game Battleship is also a manual spreadsheet.

1. List examples of manual spreadsheets that you know.

2. Find examples of manual spreadsheets in the newspaper. Cut them out and make a spreadsheet poster.

Activity ❷

To set up a computer or electronic spreadsheet, we need a way of locating a particular entry. The **cursor** is a highlighted rectangle on the screen. The position of the cursor is called a **cell.** Each cell is given a name according to the column and row it is in. In the diagram, the cursor is in cell A2 because it is in column A and row 2.

Set up the game, Battleship, using a spreadsheet for each player. Use seven columns labelled A, B, C, D, E, F, G, and seven rows labelled 1, 2, 3, 4, 5, 6, and 7. Play the game with a classmate.

Activity ❸

As with manual spreadsheets, you can enter letters, words, numbers, and numerical expressions in a computer spreadsheet. The advantage of computer spreadsheets is that you can also enter formulas and instruct the computer to do calculations for you.

The spreadsheet below has been set up by Jennifer Lee to keep track of her money. The spreadsheet shows the titles for the rows and columns, the entries for 3 weeks, and the formulas that Jennifer wants to use.

	A	B	C	D	E
1		Week 1	Week 2	Week 3	Totals
2	INCOME				@SUM(B3..D3)
3	Allowance	$10.00	$10.00	$10.00	@SUM(B4..D4)
4	Work	$14.00	$13.00	$16.00	@SUM(B5..D5)
5	Total Income	+B3+B4	+C3+C4	+D3+D4	
6	EXPENSES				@SUM(B7..D7)
7	Food	$5.00	$4.50	$3.25	@SUM(B8..D8)
8	Other	$8.00	$11.00	$9.50	@SUM(B9..D9)
9	Total Expenses	+B7+B8	+C7+C8	+D7+D8	@SUM(B10..D10)
10	SAVINGS	+B5-B9	+C5-C9	+D5-D9	

1. What are the entries in B1, C1, and D1?

2. What do the entries in A2, A3, A4, and A5 mean?

3. What do the entries in A6, A7, A8, and A9 mean?

4. What does the entry in B3 tell you?

5. What does the entry in B4 tell you?

6. What does the formula in B5 tell the computer to do?

7. What does the entry in B7 tell you?

8. What does the entry in B8 tell you?

9. What does the formula in B9 tell the computer to do?

10. What does the formula in B10 tell the computer to do?

11. a) What does the formula in E4 tell the computer to do?

b) When the computer makes this calculation, what will the answer tell Jennifer?

12. When the computer makes the calculation for E10, what will this answer mean to Jennifer?

13. Complete Jennifer's spreadsheet by making the calculations.

11.13 Ordered Pairs

Activity: Study the Map

An easy way to locate places on a map is to place a numbered grid on the map.

A numbered grid has been placed on this map of Ottawa.

To find the Parliament Buildings on the map, move horizontally from 0 to 8, then vertically from 0 to 6. Their location can be written as (8, 6).

The order of the numbers is important—the horizontal value is written first, then the vertical. We call (8, 6) an **ordered pair.**

The 2 numbers in an ordered pair are the **coordinates** of a point.

Inquire

1. What is located at each of these points?

a) (1, 5) **b)** (10, 2) **c)** (14, 10)

2. State the coordinates of these locations.

a) Mint **b)** Supreme Court **c)** Bank of Canada **d)** Mall
e) Library **f)** By Ward Market **g)** Postal Museum **h)** Arts Centre

3. Why is it important to know the order of the coordinates in an ordered pair?

Some equations such as $x + 3 = 5$ have only one variable. Here, the value of the variable, x, is 2.

Other equations, like $x + y = 4$, have two variables and many solutions

Example

Find all the whole number solutions for the equation $x + y = 4$.

Solution

The solutions are all those whole number values that add to 4.

x	0	1	2	4	3
y	4	3	2	0	1

The solutions can be written as ordered pairs in the form (x, y).
They are (0, 4), (1, 3), (2, 2), (4, 0), and (3, 1).

Practice

Write the letter of the point named by each ordered pair.

1. (3, 3) **2.** (0, 4) **3.** (5, 5)

4. (2, 8) **5.** (1, 1) **6.** (5, 0)

7. (8, 8) **8.** (9, 6) **9.** (3, 5)

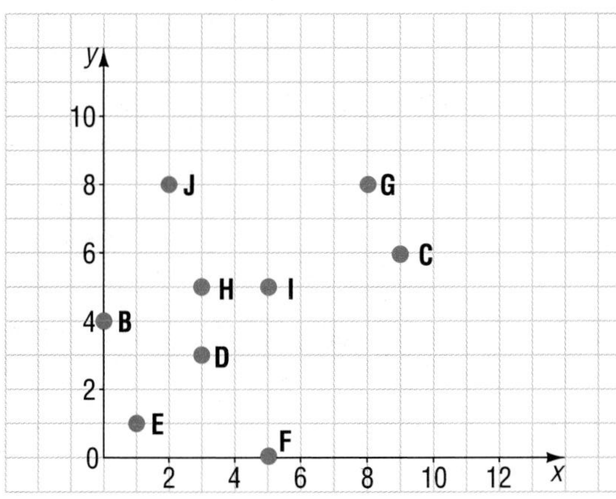

10. Write the coordinates for each letter on the graph.

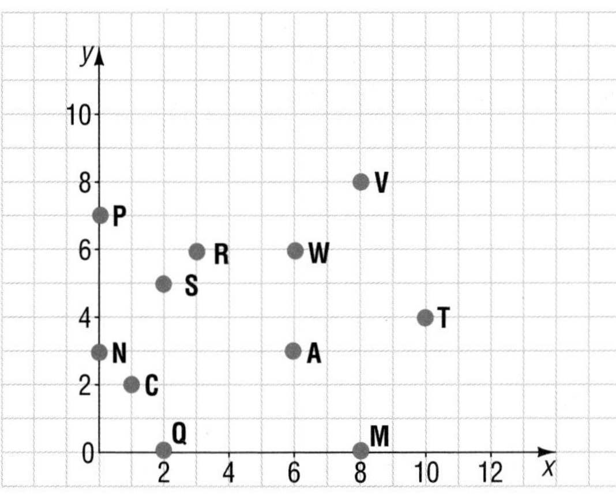

Problems and Applications

11. Graph each set of ordered pairs on a grid. Join the points in order to form a polygon. Identify each polygon.

a) (0, 0), (0, 5), (5, 5), (5, 0)

b) (1, 2), (4, 3), (3, 7)

12. a) Plot the points A(1, 7), B(1, 2), C(6, 2), and D(6, 7).

b) Join the points in order.

c) Name the polygon formed.

d) Calculate the perimeter and area of the polygon.

13. a) Plot the points A(0, 2), B(0, 8), C(8, 8), and D(8, 2).

b) Join the points in order.

c) Name the polygon formed.

d) Calculate the perimeter and area of the polygon.

14. a) Plot the points A(1, 1), B(2, 5), C(7, 5), D(8, 1).

b) Join the points in order to form a polygon.

c) Calculate the area of the polygon.

15. Plot the sets of points. What pattern, if any, is formed by each set?

a) (1, 2), (2, 4), (3, 6), (4, 8)

b) (8, 0), (6, 2), (4, 4), (2, 6)

c) (2, 0), (2, 1), (2, 3), (2, 4)

d) (0, 5), (1, 5), (2, 5), (3, 5)

For each equation, find 4 ordered pairs that are solutions of the equation. Graph each set of points and identify each pattern.

16. $x + y = 5$ **17.** $x + y = 10$

18. $x - y = 2$ **19.** $y = x$

20. a) On a grid, draw a design that uses connected straight lines. Record the coordinates of the points where the line segments meet.

b) Give the coordinates to a classmate in the order they should be joined. Have your classmate draw the design.

c) Check the design against your own. Do they match or do you have to give your classmate more information?

11.14 The Coordinate Plane

Activity: Study the Graph

The grid at the right is called a **coordinate plane.**

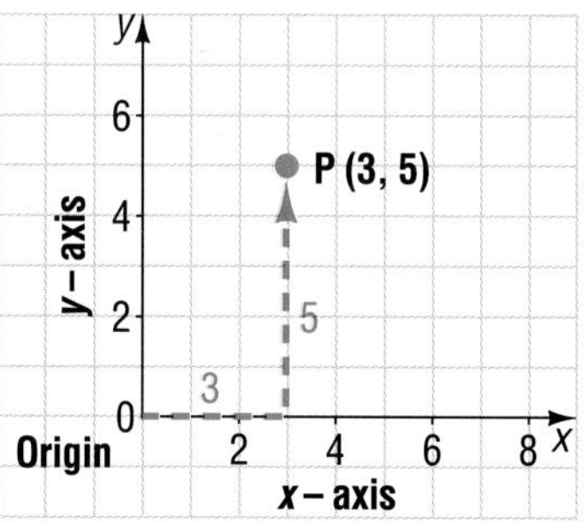

In a coordinate plane, the horizontal number line is called the ***x*-axis**; the vertical number line is called the ***y*-axis.**

The two number lines meet at a point called the **origin.** Its coordinates are (0, 0).

To locate point P(3, 5) on the plane, start at the origin, and move 3 units to the right and 5 units up.

The graph shows 14 points plotted on the coordinate plane.

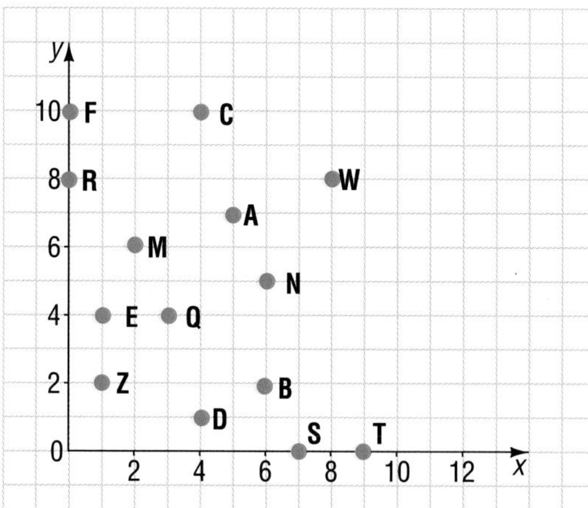

Inquire

1. Identify the letter at each of the following coordinates.

a) (3, 4) **b)** (6, 2) **c)** (2, 6)
d) (8, 8) **e)** (9, 0) **f)** (0, 8)

2. State the coordinates of each of the following points.

a) A **b)** Z **c)** N **d)** C
e) D **f)** E **g)** S **h)** F

Example

a) Plot the points (0, 0), (1, 1), (2, 2), (3, 3), (4, 4), and (5, 5).
b) How are the points related?

Solution

a)

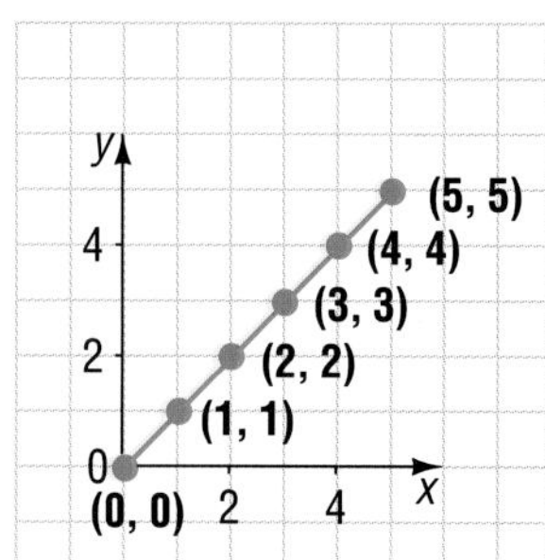

b) The points lie on a straight line.

Practice

Copy and complete these tables. Write the solutions as ordered pairs.

1. $x + y = 3$

x	y
0	
1	
2	
3	

2. $x + y = 8$

x	y
0	
1	
2	
3	

3. $x - y = 0$

x	y
	0
	1
	2
	3

4. $y - x = 2$

x	y
	2
	3
	4
	5

5. $y = x + 5$

x	y
0	
	6
2	
	8

6. $y = x - 4$

x	y
4	
	1
6	
	3

Find 4 ordered pairs that are solutions for each of these equations.

7. $x + y = 8$

8. $x + y = 12$

9. $x + y = 15$

10. $x - y = 5$

11. $x - y = 10$

12. $y = x + 3$

Write an equation that relates x and y.

13.

x	y
0	6
1	5
2	4
3	3
4	2

14.

x	y
1	0
2	1
3	2
4	3
5	4

Problems and Applications

15. Write an equation that relates the terms in each list of ordered pairs.

a) (3, 4), (5, 6), (7, 8), (9, 10)

b) (1, 1), (2, 3), (3, 5), (4, 7)

c) (1, 1), (2, 4), (3, 9), (4, 16)

16. The squash club charges you a fee of $10.00 per month plus $4.00 per game.

a) What is the fixed cost and the variable cost per month?

b) If you play one game a week, what are your fees for that month?

c) Write a general equation to describe your squash club costs.

d) Write 2 ordered pairs that satisfy the equation.

17. Renate's father says that while she helps him renovate their house, he will pay her $5.00/h on top of her $10.00 weekly allowance.

a) Write an appropriate equation for her weekly income.

b) How many hours will it take Renate to earn $45.00?

c) What is the least amount of time she must work to earn $32.00?

d) Write 2 ordered pairs that will satisfy the equation.

CALCULATOR POWER

a) Use your calculator to find the next 3 rows in this pattern.

$1 \times 2 \times 3 \times 4 + 1 = 25$ or 5^2

$2 \times 3 \times 4 \times 5 + 1 = 121$ or 11^2

b) Describe the pattern in words.

11.15 Graphing Ordered Pairs

The coordinate plane can be extended with integers.

As before, points are plotted by moving horizontally then vertically. However, this time the horizontal move can be left or right, and the vertical move can be up or down.

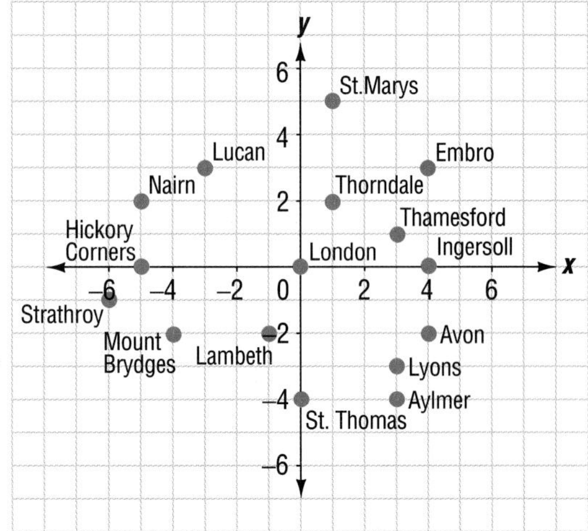

Activity: Study the Graph

The approximate locations of communities around London, Ontario, are shown on the grid to the right.

London is at the origin, (0, 0).

To locate Lucan, you move horizontally to −3 and vertically to +3. Lucan has coordinates (−3, +3), which we usually write as (−3, 3).

Inquire

1. What are the coordinates of each of the following?

a) Thorndale **b)** Mount Brydges **c)** Strathroy
d) Nairn **e)** Ingersoll **f)** St. Thomas

2. Which communities are located at the following coordinates?

a) (−1, −2) **b)** (−5, 0) **c)** (3, −3)

Example

Plot the points A(4, −1), B(4, 2), C(−2, 2) and D(−2, −1) on a grid.
Join the points in order. Identify the figure and calculate its area.

Solution

For each point, begin plotting from the origin and make the moves indicated in units.

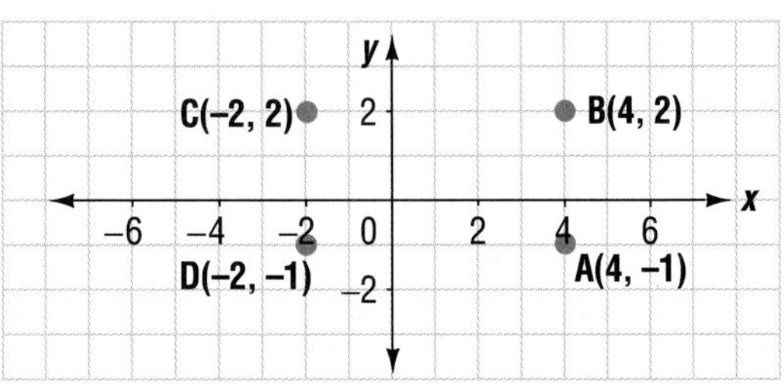

A(4, −1): 4 to the right and 1 down
B(4, 2): 4 to the right and 2 up
C(−2, 2): 2 to the left and 2 up
D(−2, −1): 2 to the left and 1 down

Join the points in order. The figure ABCD is a rectangle. Its area is:

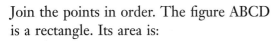

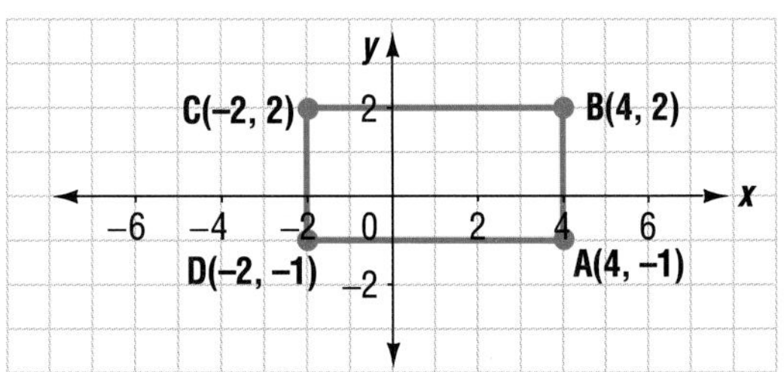

$A = l \times w$

$= 6 \times 3$ or 18 square units.

Practice

1. Name the coordinates of each point on the grid.

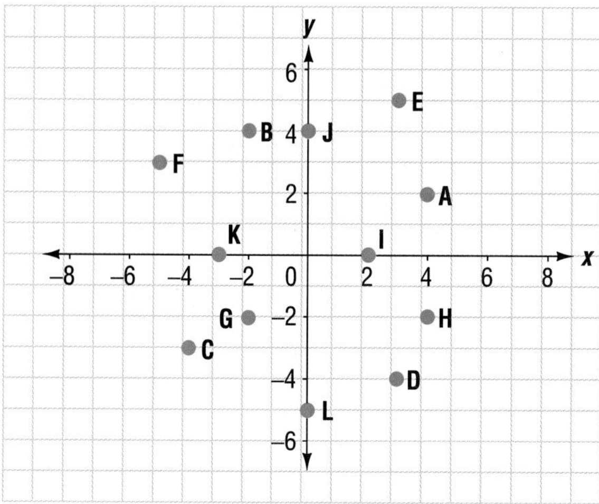

2. Name the points with the following coordinates on the grid below.

a) (–3, 3) **b)** (4, 1) **c)** (–4, –2)
d) (3, –3) **e)** (0, 3) **f)** (0, –3)
g) (–1, 1) **h)** (–5, 0) **i)** (0, 5)

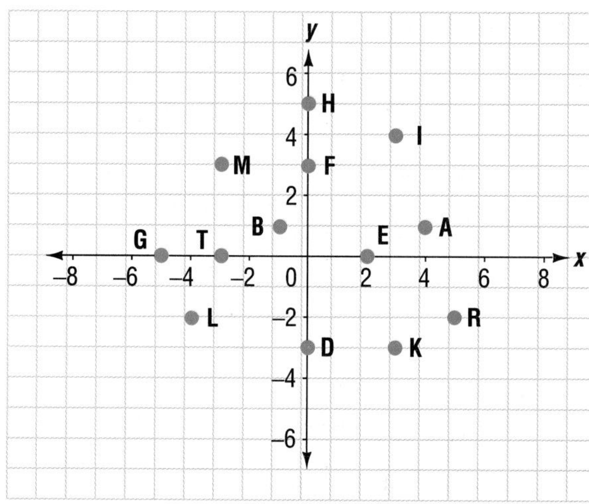

Problems and Applications

3. Plot the points P(–2, 1), Q(0, 4), R(6, 4), and S(4, 1) on a grid. Join the points in order to form a figure. Identify the figure and calculate its area.

4. Plot the points A(–4, 3), B(–4, –3), C(4, –3), D(4, –1), E(2, –1), and F(2, 3) on a grid. Join the points in order to form a figure and calculate the area of the figure.

5. a) List four points that have the same x-coordinate as (3, 4).
b) Plot the points on a grid, join them, and describe your results.

The x-axis and the y-axis divide the grid into 4 quadrants. They are named as shown in the diagram.

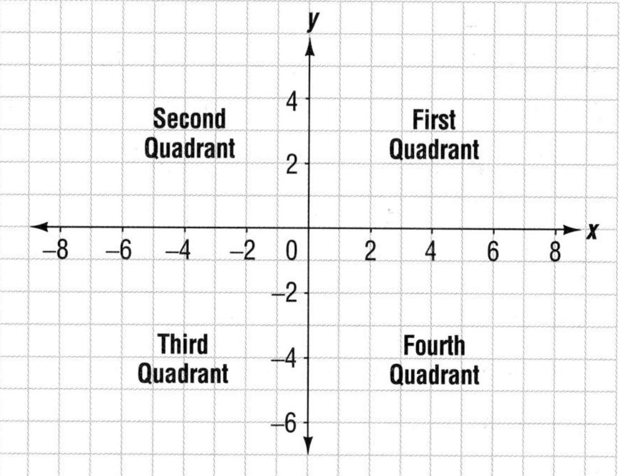

In which quadrants are the following points located?

6. K(4, 5) **7.** M(–2, –4)
8. T(–4, 1) **9.** R(3, –5)
10. N(1, –2) **11.** Q(–1, –1)
12. W(5, 5) **13.** S(–3, 4)

14. a) What is different about the coordinates of the points in each quadrant?
b) Use the ordered pair (x, y) and the appropriate sign to write an ordered pair for each of the 4 quadrants.

Braille

Braille is a way of writing and printing for blind people. It was invented by Louis Braille (1809–1852), who taught blind people in France. Louis Braille was himself blind.

The braille alphabet uses six dots. A raised dot, or combination of dots, represents a letter.

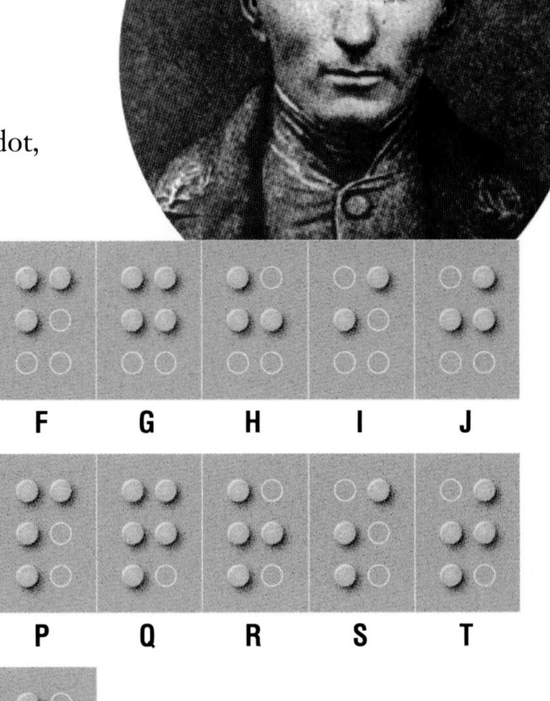

A B C D E F G H I J

K L M N O P Q R S T

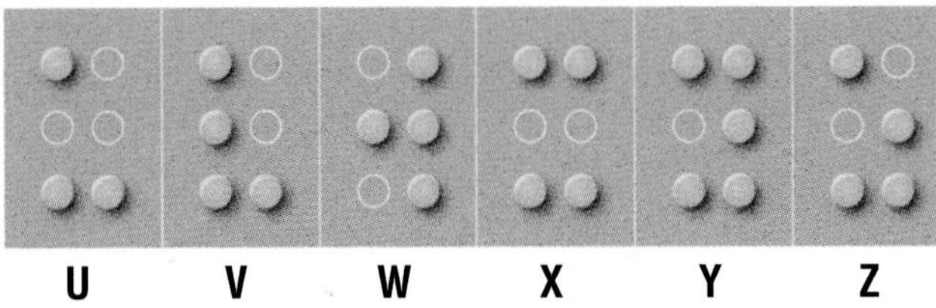

Activity ❶

1. What does this braille message say?

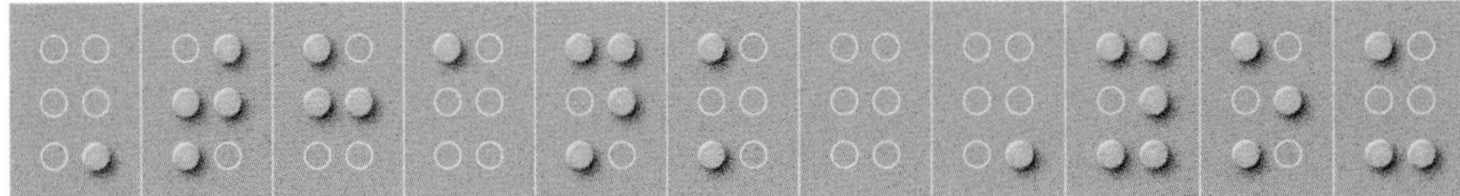

2. What is the purpose of the dot in this position?

3. Braille a message and have a classmate read it.

Activity ❷

Numbers can also be written in braille.

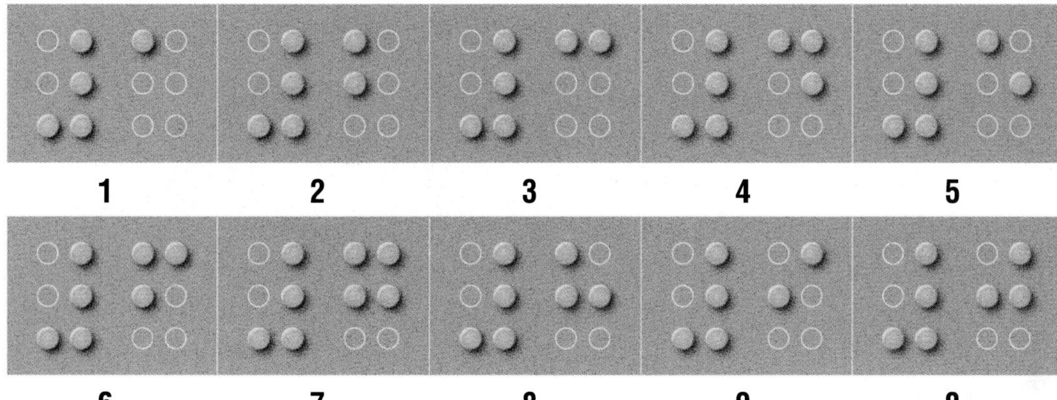

1. How are braille numbers different from braille letters?

2. Compare the second part of each braille number to letters in the braille alphabet. What do you notice?

3. Braille your telephone number and your address.

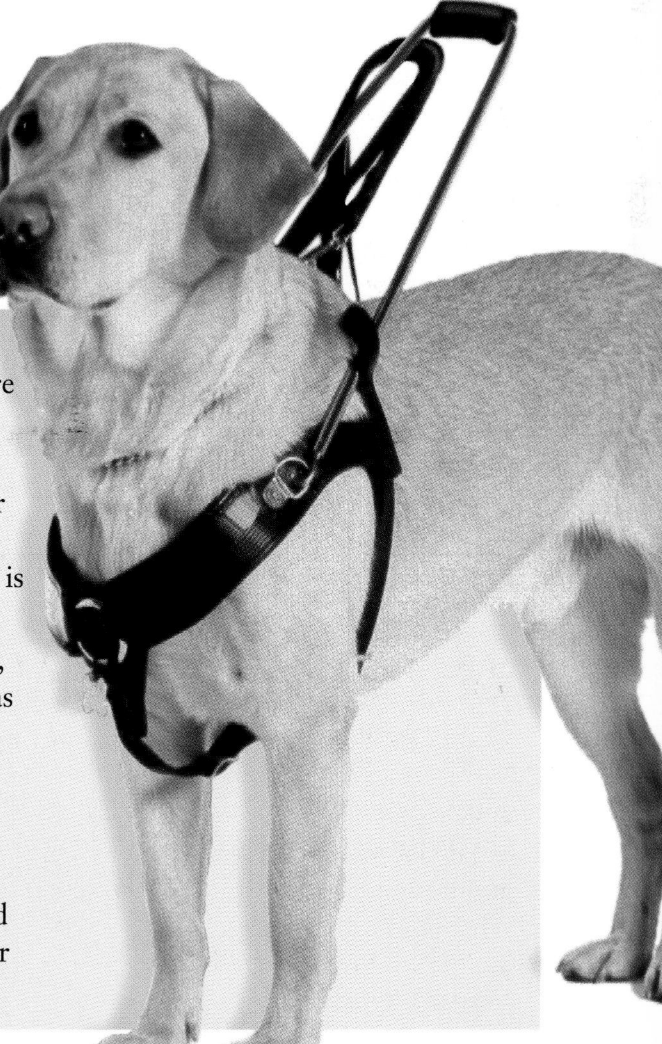

Activity ❸

Many blind people have guide dogs. These dogs are trained specifically to safely guide a blind person from place to place.

A guide dog responds to commands from its owner such as *left*, *right*, *forward*, Therefore, it is very important not to distract or touch the dog when it is wearing its harness.

Because the guide dog is so important to its owner, the dog is allowed access to all public places such as restaurants, theatres, and public transportation.

1. Investigate how guide dogs are trained.

2. How many commands does a guide dog learn?

3. How long does the training take?

4. Is there a specific breed of dog that is best suited to being a guide? If there is, what are the particular characteristics of that type of dog?

Review

Substitute 5 for x in each of the following expressions.

1. $3x$ **2.** $x + 3$ **3.** $x - 5$

4. $7 - x$ **5.** $2x + 2$ **6.** $3x - 1$

Evaluate the following expressions for $x = 2$ and $y = 3$.

7. $x + y$ **8.** $y - x$ **9.** $2x - y$

10. $2x + 3y$ **11.** $3x - 2y$ **12.** $\frac{x}{2} + y$

Write an expression for each phrase.

13. 3 more than y **14.** 4 less than x

15. n divided by 4 **16.** s minus 3

Find these numbers.

17. 5 added to it gives 12.

18. 8 subtracted from it gives 3.

19. 3 multiplied by it gives 27.

20. 3 divided into it gives 7.

Solve the following equations.

21. $x + 5 = 8$ **22.** $y - 2 = 5$

23. $m + 3 = 6$ **24.** $n - 3 = 3$

25. $2a = 10$ **26.** $10u = 60$

27. $\frac{x}{3} = 6$ **28.** $\frac{p}{4} = 5$

29. $2x + 1 = 7$ **30.** $2y - 1 = 9$

31. $3m + 2 = 14$ **32.** $2n - 5 = 15$

Solve the following for x.

33. $x + 2.5 = 3.8$ **34.** $x - 1.6 = 2.4$

35. $x - 3.6 = 0$ **36.** $5x = 3.5$

37. Edwin's shirt cost $4 less than Peter's shirt. The sum of the costs of the shirts is $28. What did each shirt cost?

38. Five more than twice Al's shoe size is 29. What is Al's shoe size?

Write each solution for x using whole numbers from 0 to 10.

39. $x < 6$ **40.** $x > 4$

41. $x \geq 7$ **42.** $x \leq 5$

43. $x + 2 > 6$ **44.** $x + 3 \leq 4$

45. $2x < 8$ **46.** $2x - 1 \geq 5$

Write the whole number solution for each inequality and draw its graph on a number line.

47. $x < 7$ **48.** $x > 4$ **49.** $2x > 6$

50. $3x \leq 12$ **51.** $x + 1 < 3$ **52.** $x + 4 \leq 8$

53. Copy and complete these tables.

a)

x	$2x + 3$
1	
2	
3	
4	
5	

b)

x	$3x - 2$
1	
2	
3	
4	
5	

54. A banquet costs $200 to rent the hall plus $8 per person for the caterer to provide food. The formula for the cost is shown as follows, where n is the number of people.

Banquet Cost = $8n + 200$

a) Copy and complete this table of values.

People (n)	100	200	500	1000	2000
Cost ($)					

b) Write 2 other ordered pairs that satisfy this equation.

55. a) Plot the points D(0, 0), E(4, 4), F(7, 4), and G(11, 0).
b) Identify the figure DEFG.
c) Find the area of DEFG.

56. a) Plot the points A(−2, 2), B(4, 2), C(4, −3), and D(−2, −3).
b) Identify the figure ABCD.
c) Find the area of ABCD.

57. Write the coordinates of each of the points shown in the following graph.

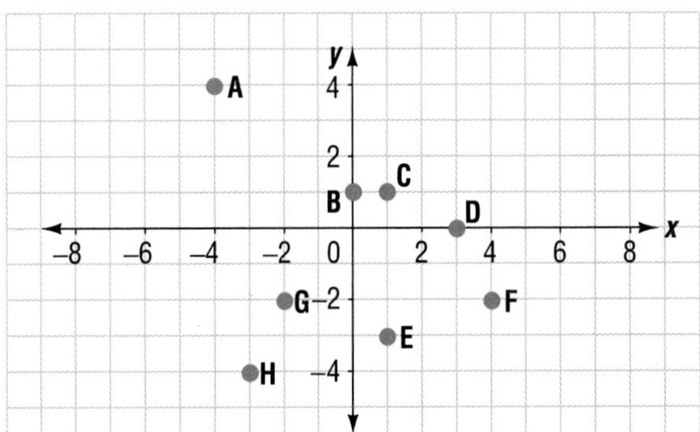

Find 4 ordered pairs that are solutions to each of the following equations and graph each set of points.

58. $x + y = 8$

59. $x - y = 2$

60. $y = x - 3$

61. $y = x + 2$

Copy and complete these tables. Write the solutions as ordered pairs.

62. $x + y = 9$

x	y
1	
2	
3	
4	
5	
6	

63. $x - y = 3$

x	y
	0
	2
	4
	6
	8
	10

64. $y = 2x + 1$

x	y
1	
2	
3	
4	
5	
6	

65. $y = 3x - 2$

x	y
0	
1	
	7
	13
4	
6	

Group Decision Making
Researching Business Careers

1. As a class, brainstorm some business careers that you would like to know more about. They could include the following: stock-broker, computer programmer, computer systems analyst, draftsperson, architect, engineer, retail seller, or accountant.

2. Choose a career to research on your own. Make a list of questions about the career. Include a question about how math is used in the career.

3. In your home group, decide on some other questions that could be addressed by each individual on his or her topic.

1 2 3 4 5 6	1 2 3 4 5 6

Home Groups

1 2 3 4 5 6	1 2 3 4 5 6

4. Carry out your individual research and prepare a report. Include a description of how mathematics is used in the career you chose.

5. Evaluate the process you used and your report. Identify what went well and what you would do differently with your next research topic.

6. Have other students in your class evaluate your report.

7. Finally, as a class, evaluate the entire process.

Chapter Check

Write each statement using symbols.

1. One number is five more than another.

2. Franklin worked three hours more than Cam.

3. Jason saved \$60 more than Heidi.

Write an equation and solve.

4. Murray has \$3.00 more than Petra. Together they have \$21.00. How much money does each person have?

Solve the following equations,

5. $x + 7 = 12$ **6.** $5y = 35$

7. $p - 3 = 12$ **8.** $2c - 5 = 17$

9. $7b = 49$ **10.** $\frac{a}{5} = 11$

Graph the whole number solution for each of the following on a number line.

11. $x < 4$ **12.** $x \geq 5$ **13.** $x \leq 3$

Write the whole number solution for each inequality.

14. $x - 3 > 2$ **15.** $4x \leq 12$ **16.** $x + 1 > 4$

17. Complete these tables of values.

a)

x	$x + 7$
2	
3	
4	
5	
6	

b)

x	$2x - 3$
2	
3	
4	
5	
6	

18. Find 5 points for each of the following equations and draw a graph.

a) $x + y = 9$ **b)** $y = x + 1$

19. Name the coordinates of the points shown on the graph.

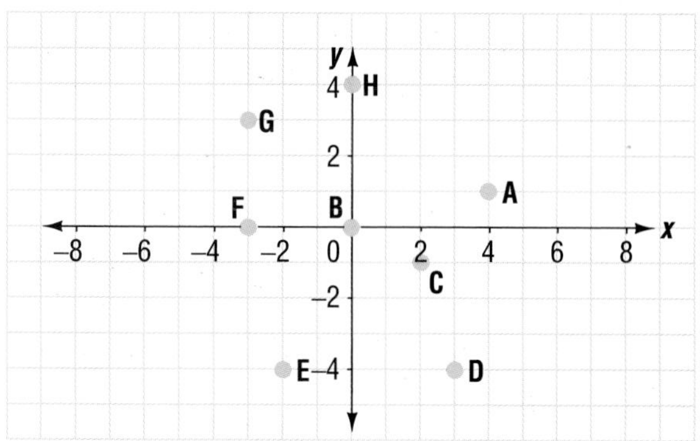

Reprinted by permission: Tribune Media Services

Using the Strategies

1. A full glass of orange juice has a mass of 430 g. A half glass of orange juice has a mass of 260 g. What is the mass of the glass?

2. Sherri noticed that the numbers on her digital clock had a horizontal line of symmetry when the time was 11:31.

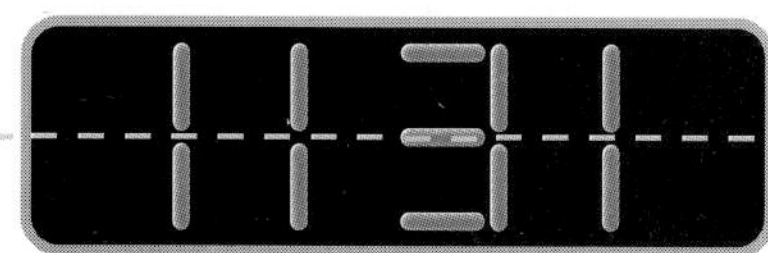

a) At what other times do the numbers on a digital clock have a horizontal line of symmetry?
b) Are there any times when a digital clock's numbers have a vertical line of symmetry?

3. Franco bought a book for $13.95. The cashier made an error and gave him $12.45 change from a $20.00 bill. How much change should Franco receive?

4. Complete each pattern and write a sentence to describe the pattern.
a) 3, 5, 8, 12, ■, ■, ■, 38
b) 1, 7, 13, ■, ■, 31
c) 91, 79, 69, 61, ■, ■, 49

5. The numbers in the squares are found by adding the numbers in the circles that lead into the squares. Find the numbers in the circles.

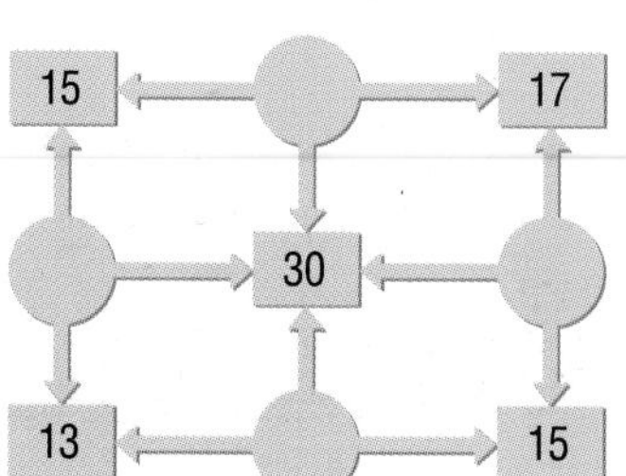

6. The occupations of Adams, Gorski, Stapoulos, and Devereaux are a doctor, a fire fighter, an automobile mechanic, and a journalist, but not necessarily in that order. Use the following clues to match each person with their profession.
a) Devereaux visited the doctor last week.
b) The mechanic fixed Gorski's car.
c) The fire fighter and Devereaux are friends and they both play golf with the automobile mechanic.
d) Adams and Gorski did not attend university.

7. Carl's dog eats half a can of food each day. Carl bought 12 cans of dog food for $18.48. How much does it cost to feed his dog every day?

8. Natasha's car holds 55 L of gasoline. The gas gauge reads as follows:

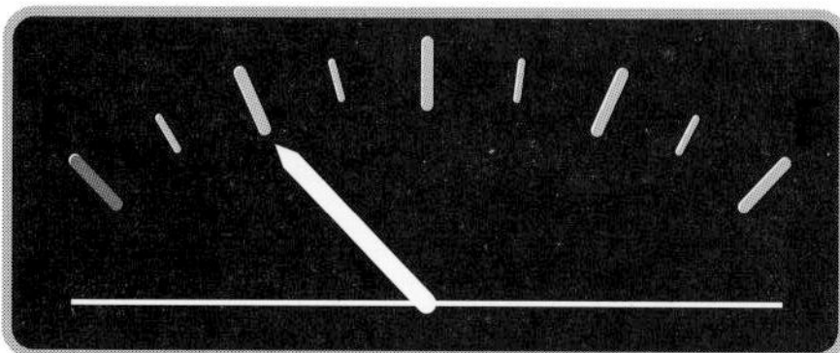

About how many litres of gasoline will it take to fill Natasha's gasoline tank?

DATA BANK

1. If you and your classmates stood with your arms stretched wide and your fingers just touching, how many people would reach from one end of a blue whale to the other?

2. a) What is the longest river in Canada?
b) How many times longer is the longest river in the world?

CHAPTER 12

Transformations

Take a strip of paper and attach the ends to form a loop.
How many sides and edges does it have?
How many colours would you need to colour each side a different colour?
If you cut the strip around the centre, what would you have?

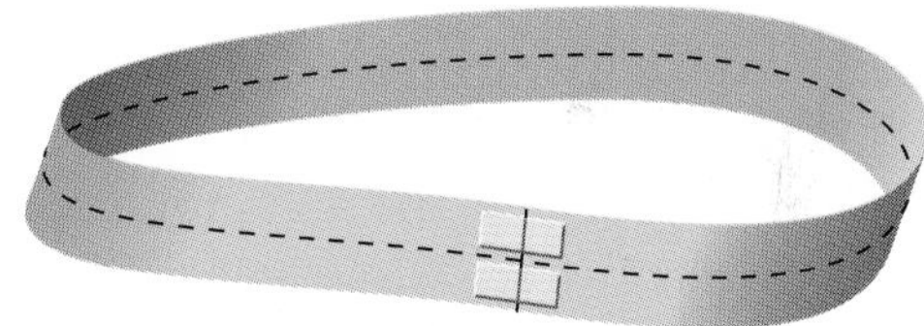

Take another strip of paper and make a half twist in one end before attaching the ends. You have made a **Möbius strip**.
Try colouring one side of your strip.
How many colours do you need to colour the whole strip?
If you cut your strip around the centre, what would you have?

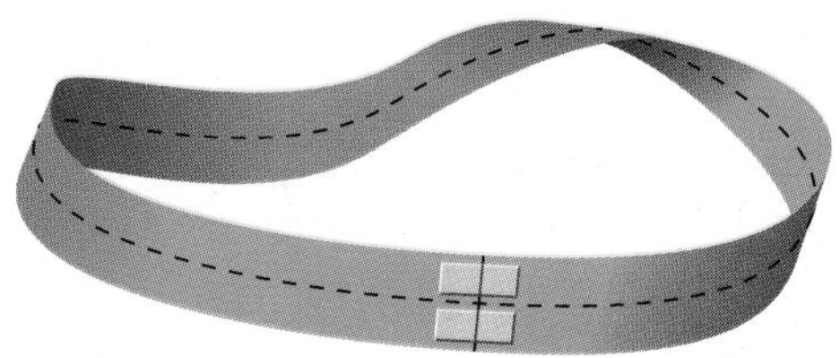

Dominoes

A domino has two sets of dots on it.
The number of dots can be 6, 5, 4, 3, 2, 1, or 0 (blank).
A full set of dominoes contains all the possible number pairs from double blank (double zero) to double six.
The set of dominoes you have seen is called a double six set because double six is the highest double.

Activity ❶

1. How many dominoes are there in a complete double six set?
One way to find out is to list them in some sort of order.
You might start with

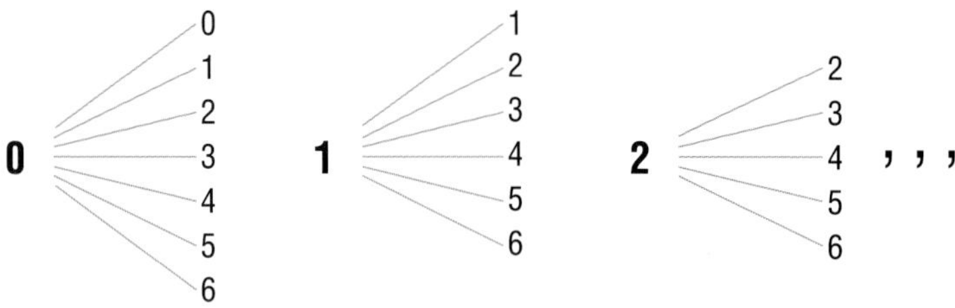

2. How many dots are on a double six set?

3. Suppose you remove all the dominoes that have sixes on them. You have a double five set. How many dominoes are in a double five set? How many dots are on a double five set?

4. How are the number of dominoes in a set and the number of dots on a set related?

Activity ❷

1. Suppose you begin with a double six set of dominoes and start a chain. The rule for the chain is that touching numbers on adjacent dominoes must be the same.

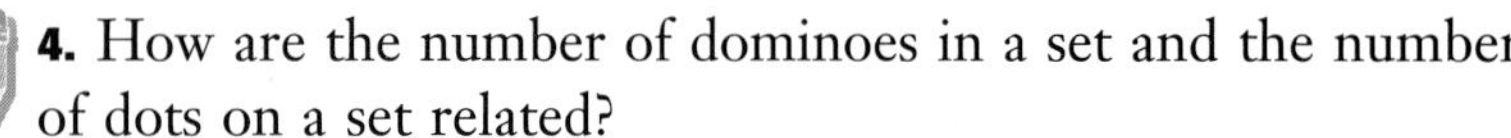

Suppose the starting end of the chain has 5 dots. If all the dominoes are used, how many dots will the other end have?

2. Suppose you start a chain with a 6 and make sure that touching numbers are the same. What is the shortest chain you can make that uses all the dominoes with 6s on them?

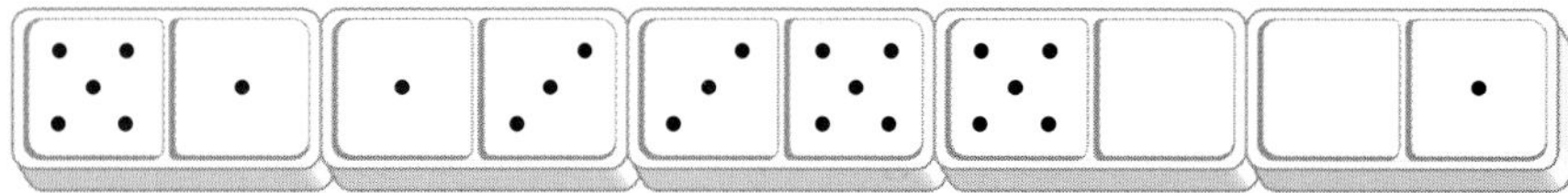

Polyominoes

A polyomino is a shape made up of squares joined along whole edges.

These are polyominoes.

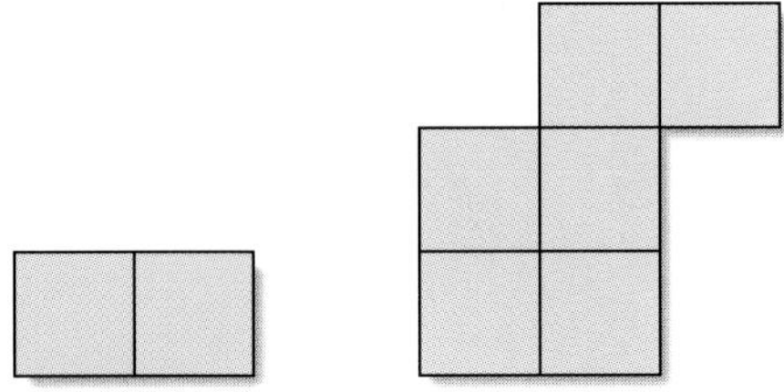

These are not polyominoes.

Name	Number of Squares	Diagram
Monomino	1	
Domino	2	
Triomino	3	
Tetromino	4	
Pentomino	5	

Activity ❶

1. The diagram shows one of the five different tetrominoes.

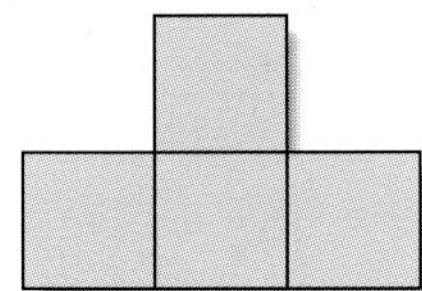

Draw the other four.

2. How many different triominoes are there? Draw them.

3. What determines the name of a polyomino?

4. Draw an example of an octomino.

Mental Math

Calculate.

1. $2 \times 10 \times 6$ **2.** $10 \times 9 \times 4$

3. $8 \times 5 - 7$ **4.** $6 \times 5 + 3$

5. $6 + 4 \div 2$ **6.** $8 \div 2 + 5$

7. $9 - 5 + 4$ **8.** $10 - 2 \times 3$

Evaluate.

9. 4^2 **10.** 8^2 **11.** 5^3

12. 2^5 **13.** 10^3 **14.** 6^2

15. 12^2 **16.** 8^2 **17.** 3^3

Multiply.

18. 0.2×1000 **19.** 4.16×100

20. 3.18×10 **21.** 0.006×100

22. 325×0.1 **23.** 36.83×0.01

24. 4862×0.001 **25.** 0.17×0.1

Simplify.

26. $\frac{5}{6} - \frac{2}{3}$ **27.** $\frac{1}{8} + \frac{1}{4}$

28. $\frac{1}{5} \times \frac{4}{7}$ **29.** $\frac{2}{3} \div \frac{3}{5}$

30. $\frac{1}{3}$ of 27 **31.** $\frac{1}{4}$ of 280

Simplify.

32. $(+3) + (+4)$ **33.** $(-6) - (+2)$

34. $(+8) - (+2)$ **35.** $(-9) + (+8)$

36. $(-3) - (-4)$ **37.** $(+7) - (-3)$

38. $(+11) + (-3)$ **39.** $(-12) + (-2)$

Find n.

40. $n + 8 = 17$ **41.** $n - 3 = 6$

42. $8n = 32$ **43.** $\frac{n}{6} = 2$

44. $4n = 3.6$ **45.** $4.1 + n = 6.2$

46. $3.1 + n = 4.5$ **47.** $\frac{n}{2.4} = 2$

Slides, Flips, and Turns

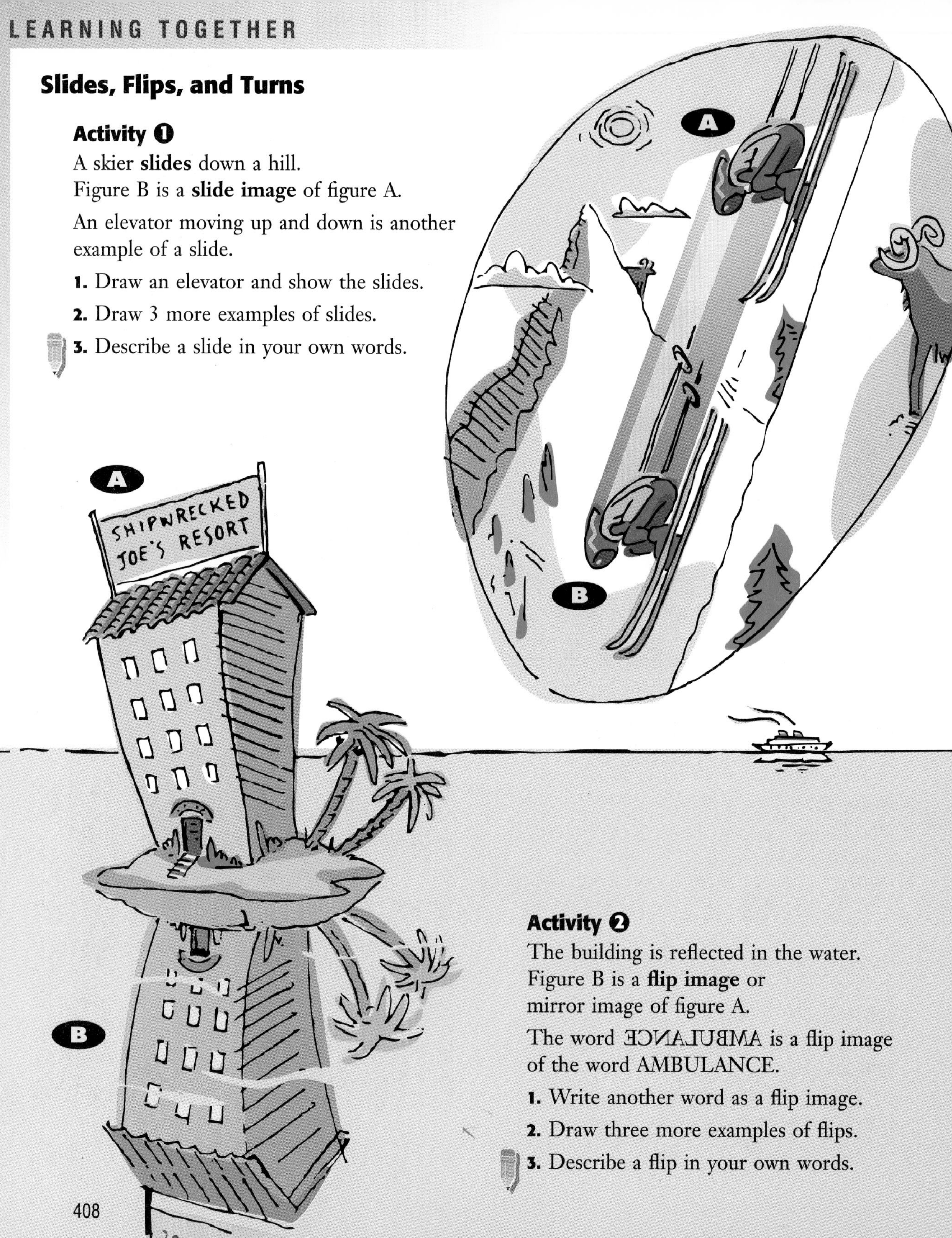

Activity ❶

A skier **slides** down a hill.
Figure B is a **slide image** of figure A.

An elevator moving up and down is another example of a slide.

1. Draw an elevator and show the slides.
2. Draw 3 more examples of slides.
3. Describe a slide in your own words.

Activity ❷

The building is reflected in the water.
Figure B is a **flip image** or mirror image of figure A.

The word ƎƆИA⅃UᗺMA is a flip image of the word AMBULANCE.

1. Write another word as a flip image.
2. Draw three more examples of flips.
3. Describe a flip in your own words.

Activity ❸

A boat ride **turns** about a point.
Figure B is a **turn image** of figure A.

A moving ferris wheel is another example of a turn.

1. Draw a ferris wheel and show the turns.
2. Draw three more examples of turns.
3. Describe a turn in your own words.

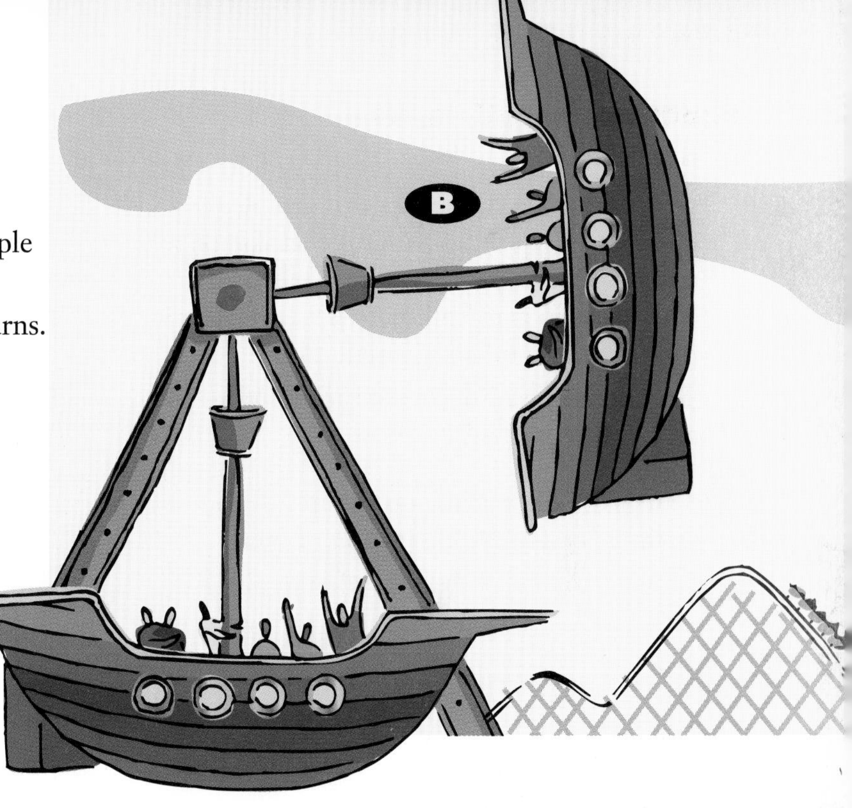

Activity ❹

Patterns can be made by repeating slides, flips, and turns. Which of the following are slides, flips, or turns?

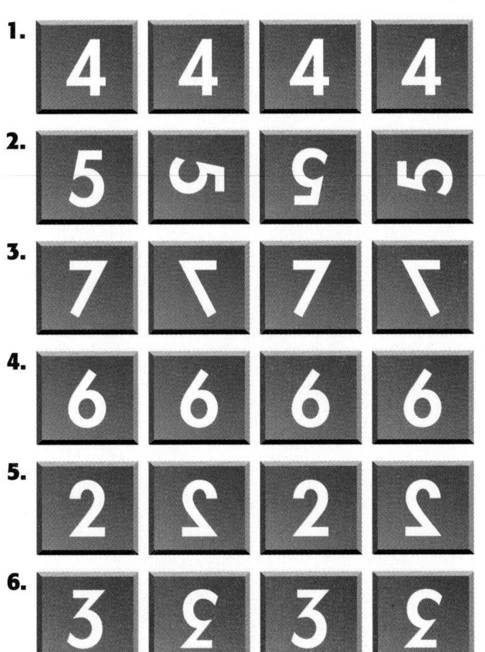

Activity ❺

Identify each of the following as slides, flips, or turns. Copy and continue each pattern by repeating the image 6 more times.

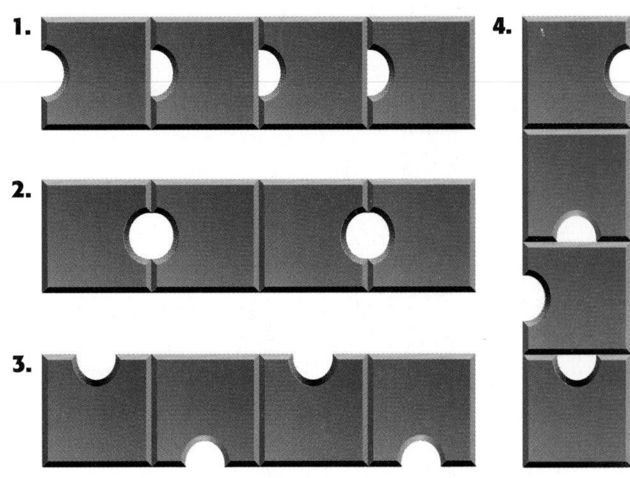

Tessellations

People like patterns. We cover our floors and walls with coloured shapes that are pleasing to the eye. Repeating patterns that completely cover a surface are called **tiling patterns**. There are no gaps and there is no overlapping. A tiling is also called a **tessellation**.

The artist M.C. Escher used tessellations in many of his works.

© 1938 M.C. Escher/Cordon Art Baarn-Holland

Tilings are often made up of flips, or slides, or turns, or some combination of them.

Rectangles and squares can tile the plane.

So can shapes made from rectangles.

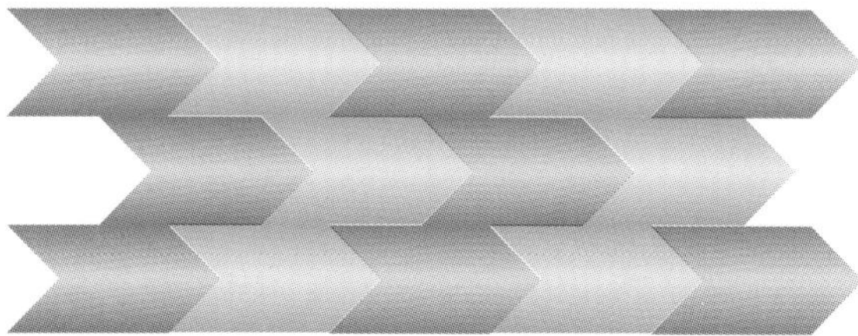

Triangles can tile the plane.
So can shapes made from triangles.

Different shapes can be used together to tile the plane.

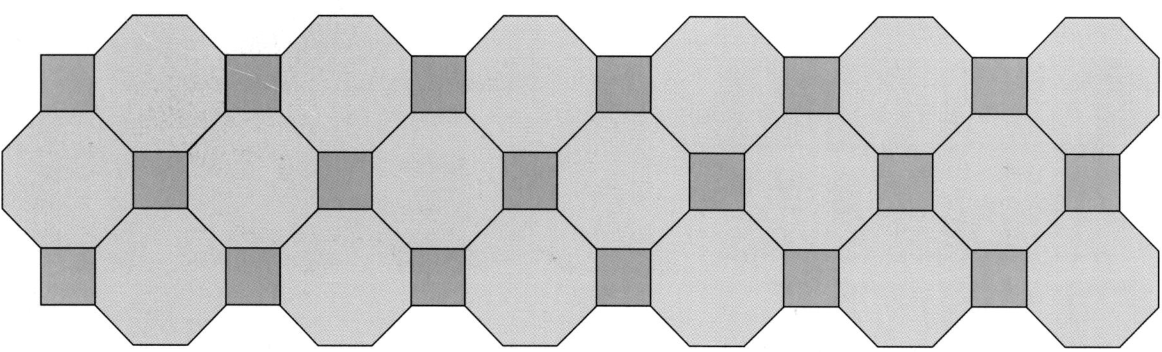

Activity ❶

Create a pattern with one or more of the following shapes.
Colour the pattern to make a pleasing design.

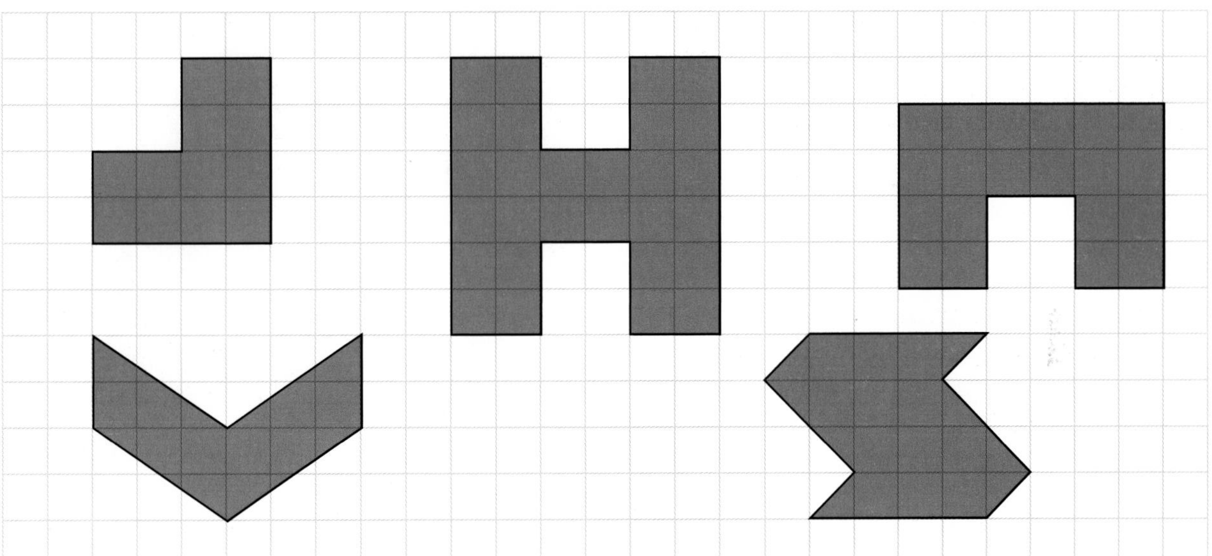

Activity ❷

Create an Escher type drawing.

Start with a figure that will tile the plane, like a square.

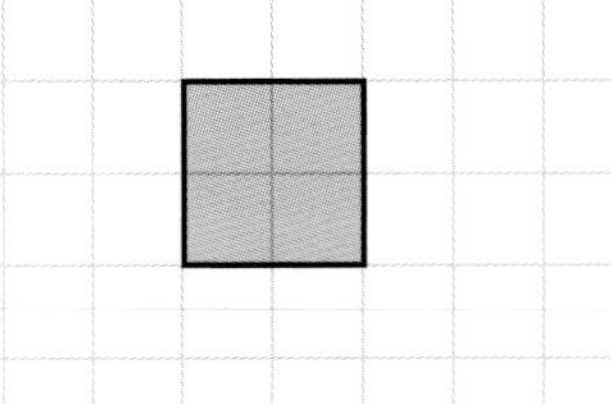

Remove triangles from one side and move them to the bottom.

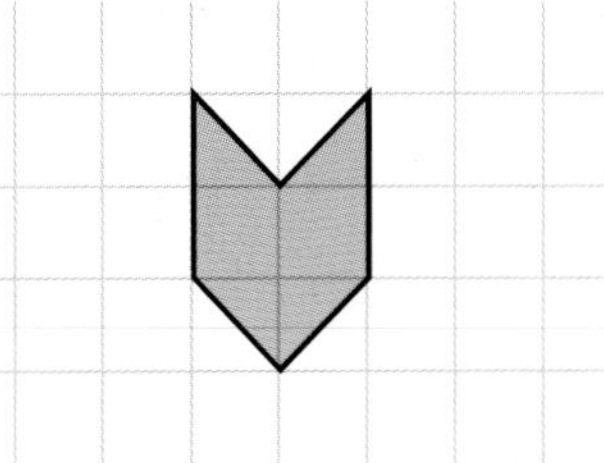

Tile the plane.

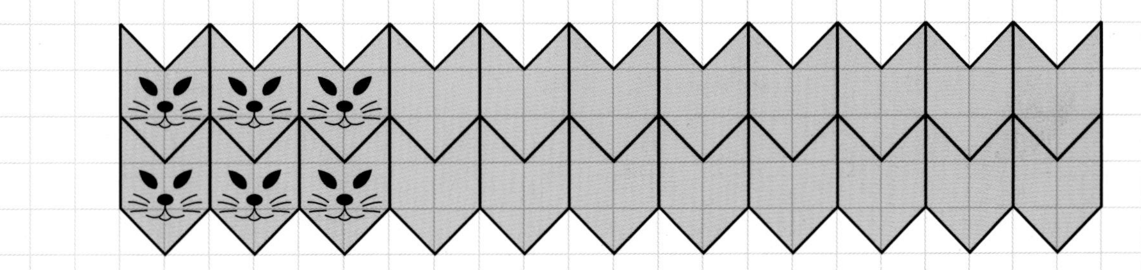

Add your own colours and features.

12.1 Translations

The photo shows a water slide. People riding down the straight part of the slide undergo a **translation**. A translation can be described as a slide in one direction without any turns.

Activity: Study the Diagram

The diagram shows a translation.
An arrow shows both the direction and the length of a translation.

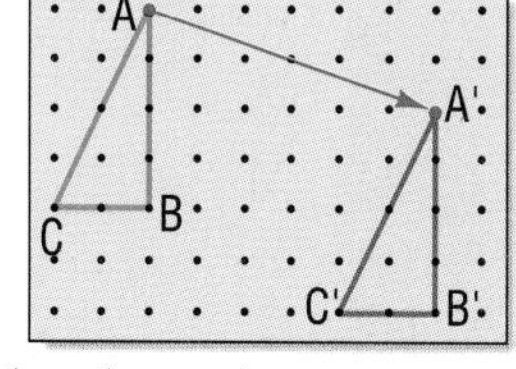

A' is read "A prime."

The translation shown by the red arrow matches △ABC with its **translation image △A′B′C′.**

Inquire

1. How many units is △A′B′C′ to the right of △ABC?

2. How many units is △A′B′C′ below △ABC?

3. How does the shape of △A′B′C′ compare to the shape of △ABC?

4. How does the size of △A′B′C′ compare to the size of △ABC?

A translation is described by the distance and the direction a figure has moved.

Example

Draw the translation image of △DOG six units to the left and four units down.

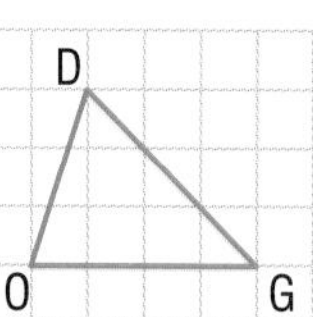

Solution

Draw △DOG.

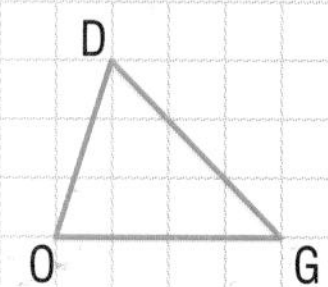

Count 6 units left and 4 units down from D. Mark D′. Repeat for O and G.

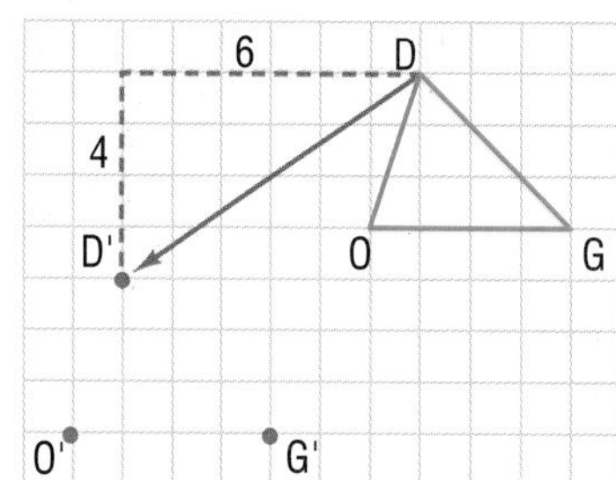

Complete △D′O′G′. △D′O′G′ is the translation image of △DOG.

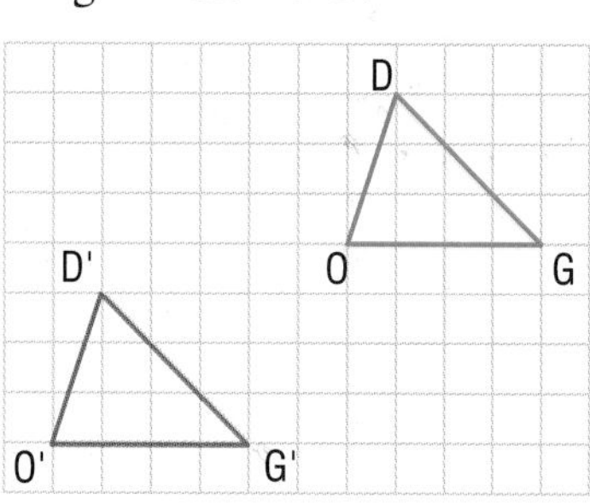

Practice

Describe the following translations.

1. 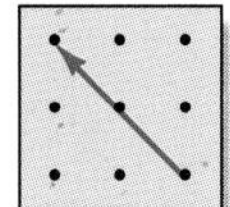 **2.** 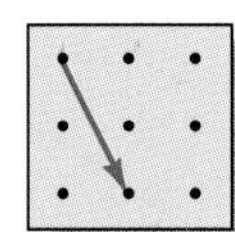 **3.** 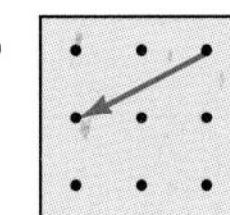

Draw arrows on graph or dot paper to show the following translations.

4. 2 units left, 3 units up

5. 1 unit right, 4 units down

6. 5 units down

7. 3 units left, 2 units down

Problems and Applications

8. Copy the figure. Draw the translation image 4 units right and 3 units up.

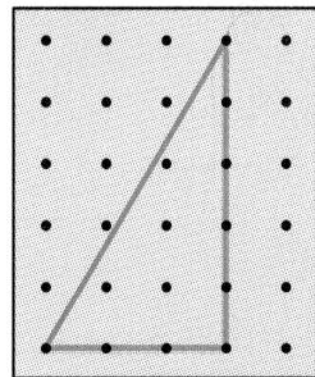

9. Copy the figure. Draw the translation image 5 units left and 3 units down.

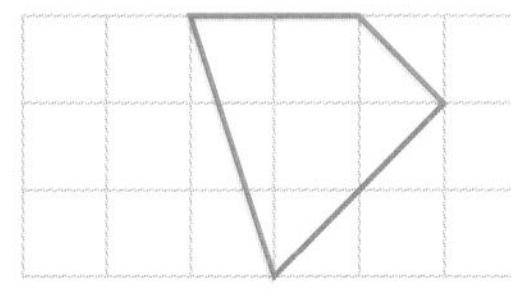

10. Copy the figures shown below. Draw the translation arrow that moves the blue figure onto the red figure. Describe the translation.

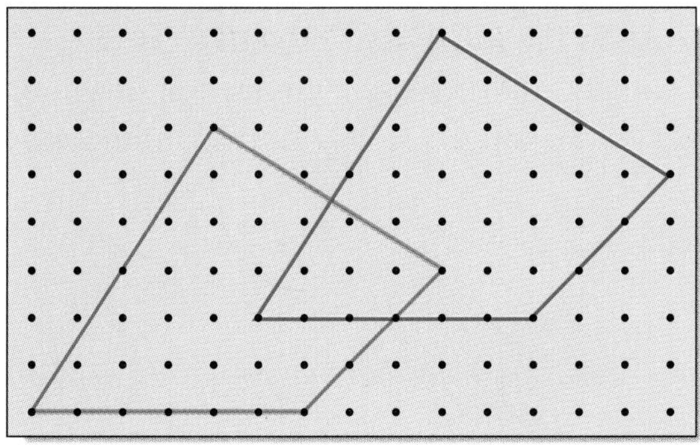

Copy each figure onto grid or dot paper. Draw the translation image of each for the given translation.

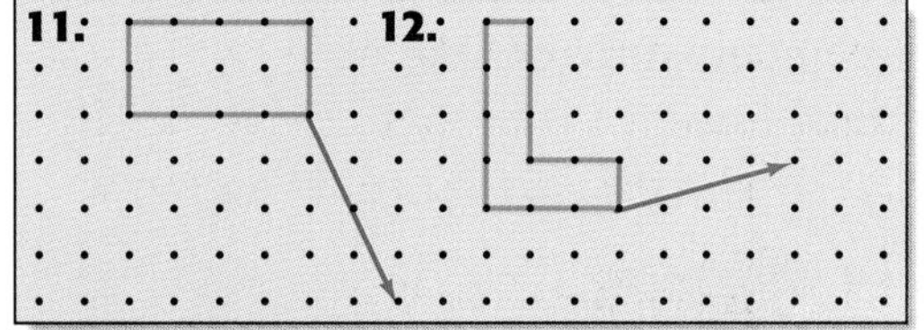

13. a) On grid paper, translate △ABC 4 units to the right and 2 units down.

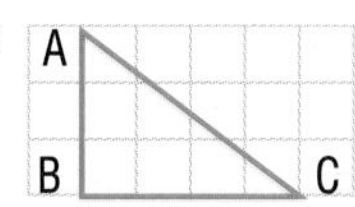

b) Translate the image △A′B′C′ 2 units to the right and 3 units up to give △A″B″C″.

c) What is the one translation that makes △A″B″C″ the image of △ABC?

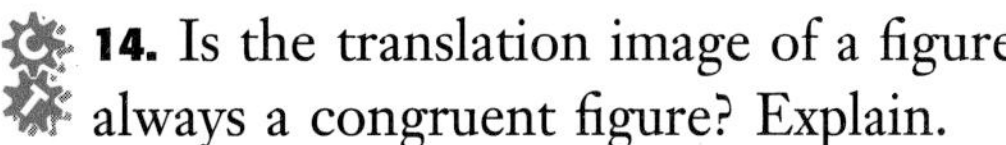

14. Is the translation image of a figure always a congruent figure? Explain.

15. Draw a triangle and its translation image on grid or dot paper. Ask a classmate to describe the translation.

LOGIC POWER

In one move in the game of chess, the knight can go 2 squares in one direction and 1 square in another direction, or 1 square in one direction and 2 squares in another direction.

Start at the top left corner. How many legal moves can you make with the knight so that it does not land on the same square twice?

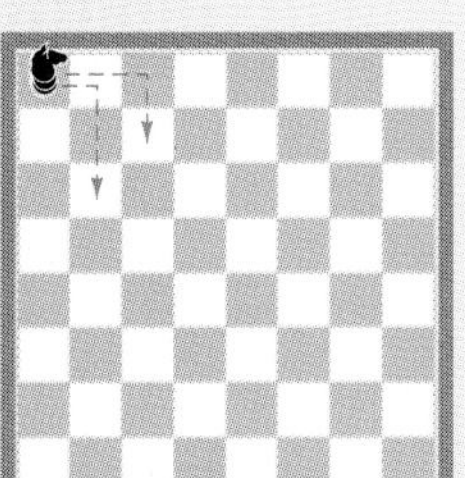

12.2 Reflections

A **reflection** can be described as a flip about a **mirror line** or **reflection line**.

The image of the forest in the lake is a reflection.
The reflection line is the surface of the water.

Activity: Study the Diagram

The diagram shows a reflection. Quadrilateral Q′R′S′T′ is the **reflection image** of quadrilateral QRST.

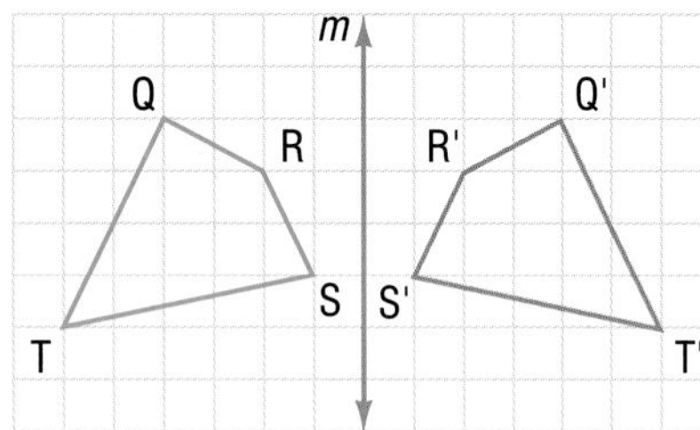

Inquire

1. What is the reflection line?

2. What angle do QQ′, RR′, SS′, and TT′ make with line m?

3. How far are the following pairs of points from the reflection line?
a) Q and Q′ **b)** R and R′
c) S and S′ **d)** T and T′

4. How do the shape and size of Q′R′S′T′ compare with the shape and size of QRST?

Example

Draw the reflection image of △ABC in line m.

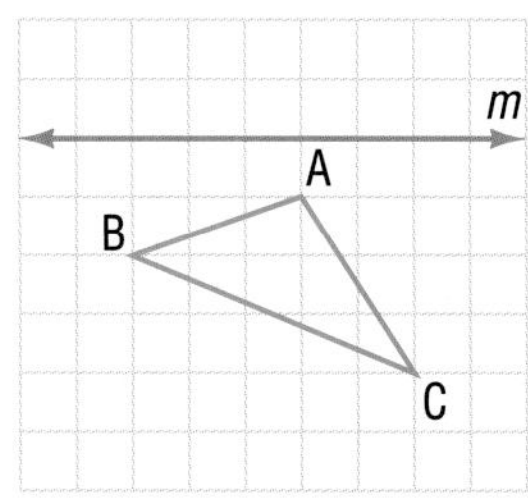

Solution

Draw ABC and line m.

Mark A′ on the other side of m so that AD = DA′. Repeat for B′ and C′.

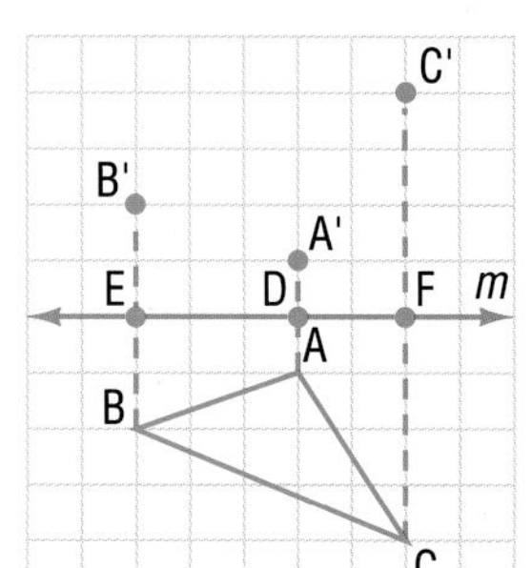

Complete △A′B′C. △A′B′C′ is the reflection image of △ABC in line m.

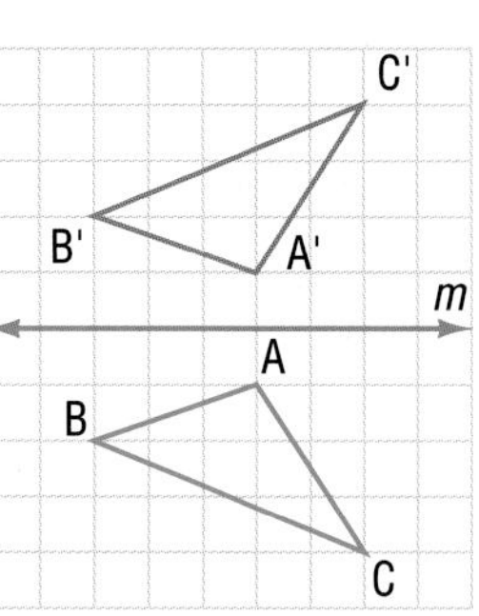

Practice

For the pairs of figures below, name
a) *the points that are the same distance from r.*
b) *the line segments that are perpendicular to r.*

1.

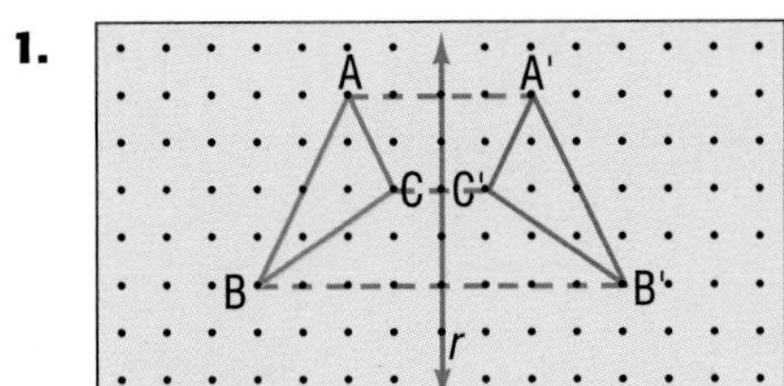

2.

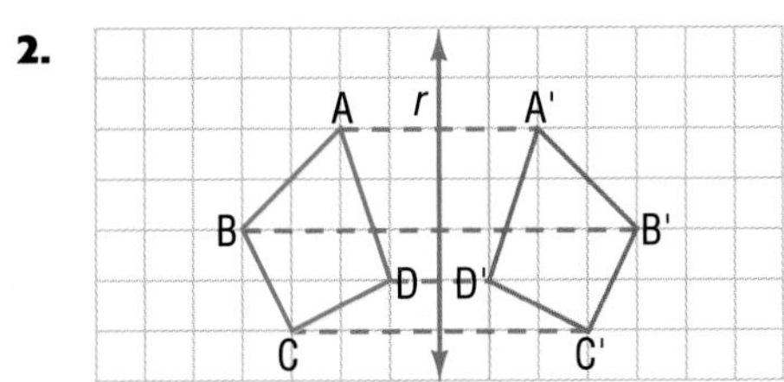

Copy each figure onto grid or dot paper. Draw the reflection image.

3.

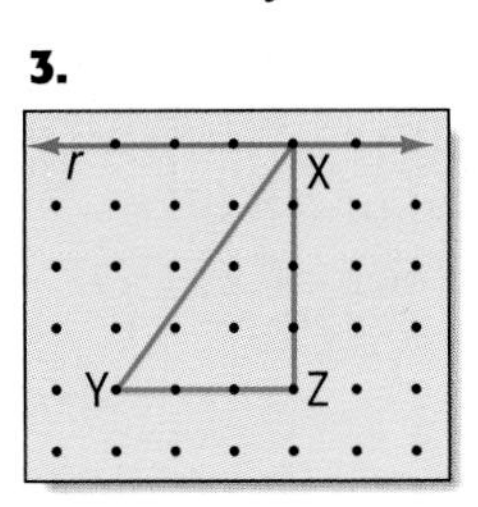

4.

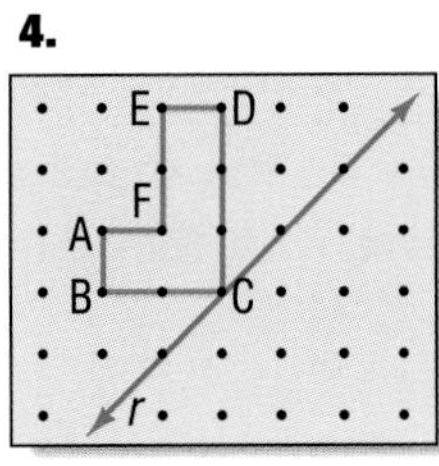

5.

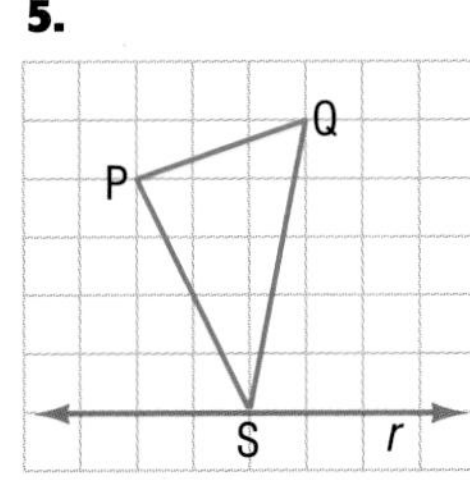

6.

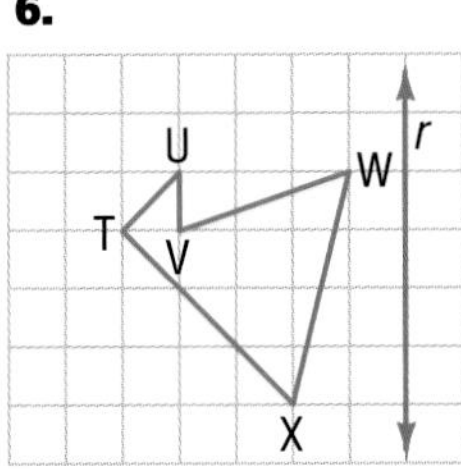

Problems and Applications

Copy the figures and their reflection images. Draw the reflection lines.

7.

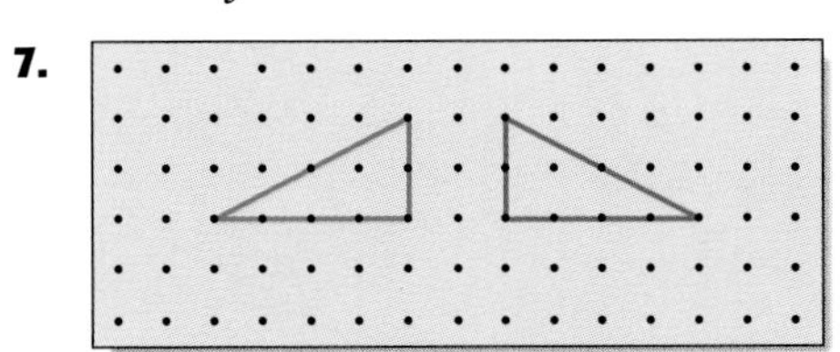

8.

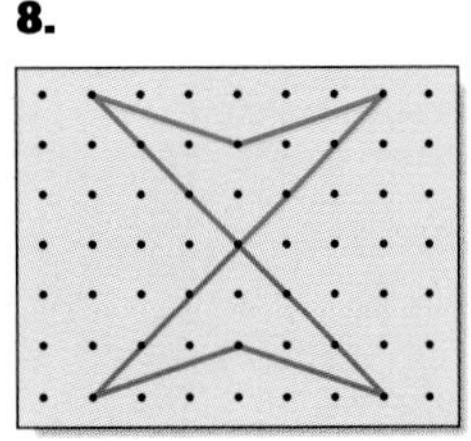

9.

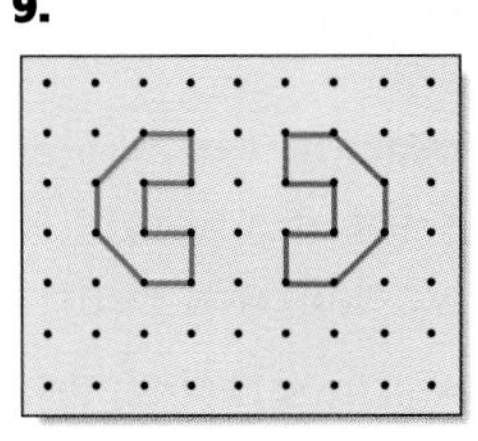

10. a) Copy the design on grid paper. Draw the reflection image.

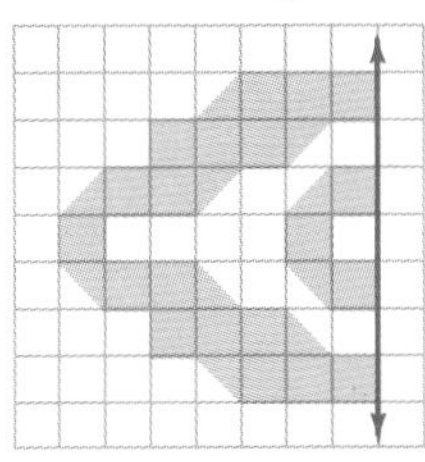

b) Create a design on grid paper. Draw the reflection image.

11. Reflect $\triangle ABC$ in line l to give $\triangle A'B'C'$. Reflect $\triangle A'B'C'$ in line m to give $\triangle A''B''C''$.

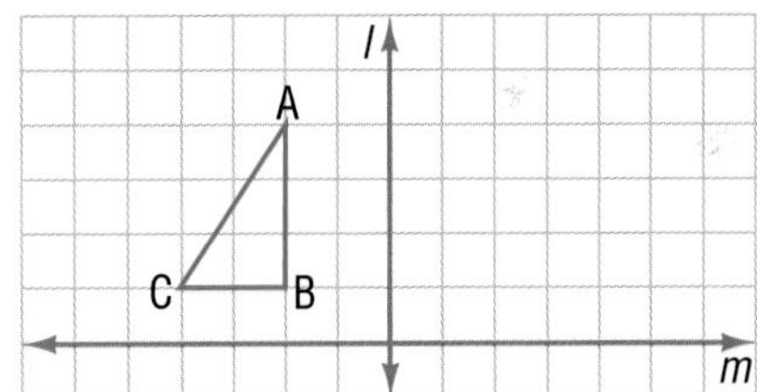

12. Is a figure congruent to its reflection image? Explain.

13. Work with a partner. From the figure, list pairs of triangles and squares that are reflections of each other. For each pair, name a figure, its reflection image, and the reflection line. How many pairs did you find? Compare with your classmates.

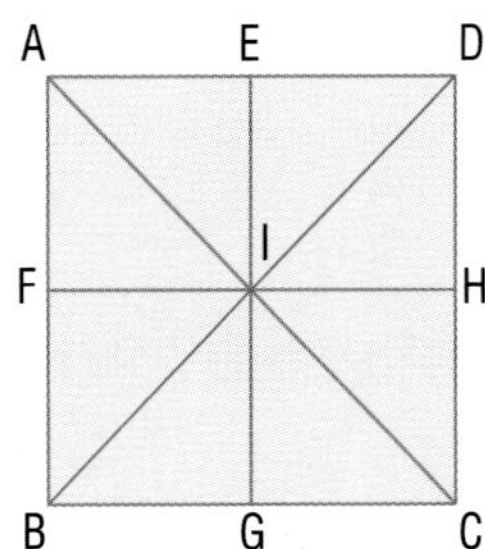

12.3 Rotations

A **rotation** can be described as a turn about a point. This point is called the **turn centre**.

This amusement park ride shows a rotation. The turn centre is the centre of the wheel.

Activity: Study the Diagram

The diagram shows a rotation. Rectangle AB′C′D′is the **rotation image** of rectangle ABCD.

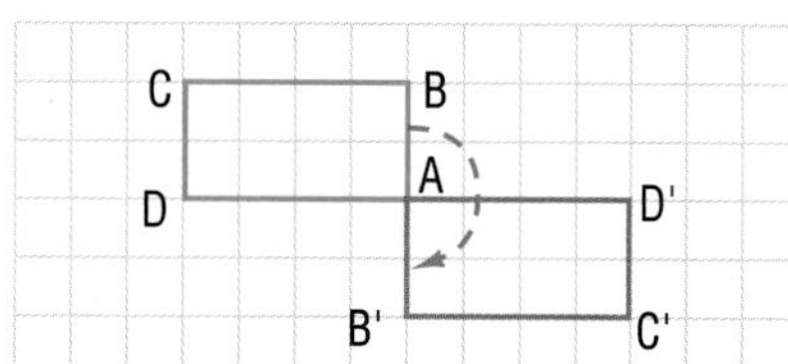

Inquire

1. Where is the turn centre?

2. How many degrees was ABCD rotated?

3. Was the rotation clockwise or counterclockwise about the centre? How do you know?

4. How do the shape and size of AB′C′D′ compare with the shape and size of ABCD?

Rotations can be clockwise or counterclockwise.
A 90° turn is also called a $\frac{1}{4}$ turn.
A 180° turn is a $\frac{1}{2}$ turn and a 270° turn is a $\frac{3}{4}$ turn.

Example

Draw the rotation image of △DEF when it is rotated 90° counterclockwise about A.

Solution

Draw △DEF.

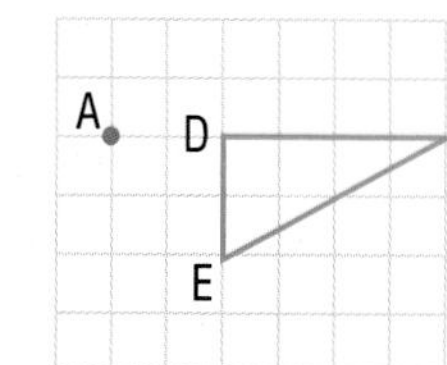

Rotate the tracing 90° counterclockwise about A. Mark D′, E′, and F′.

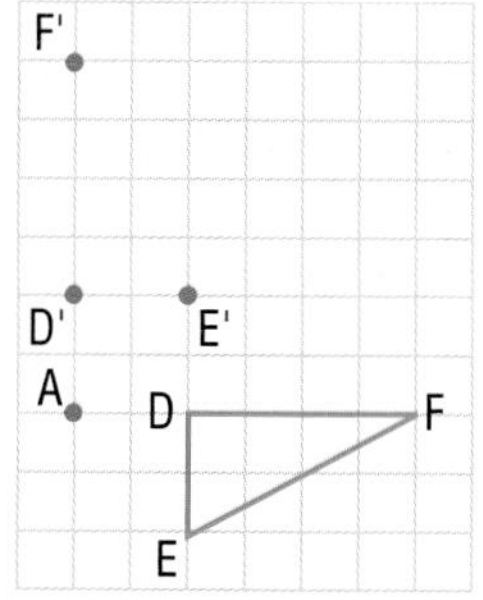

Complete △D′E′F′
△D′E′F′ is the rotation image of △DEF.

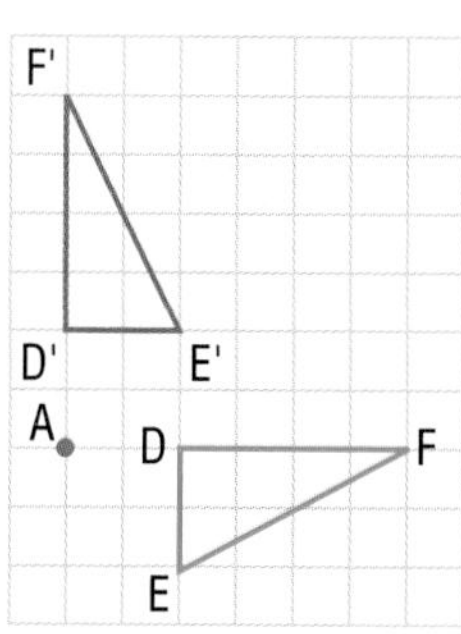

Practice

Describe a clockwise turn and a counterclockwise turn about the given turn centre that moves the blue figure onto the red figure.

1.

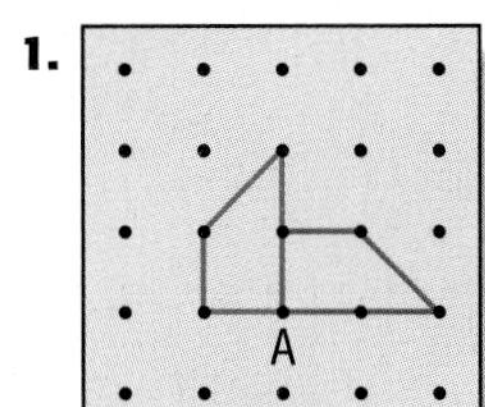

2.

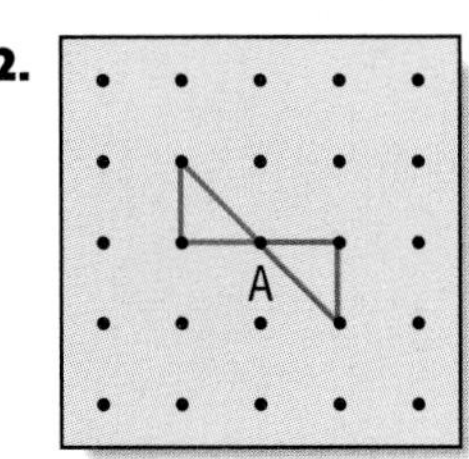

Copy each figure. Draw the rotation image for a 180° turn clockwise about A.

3.

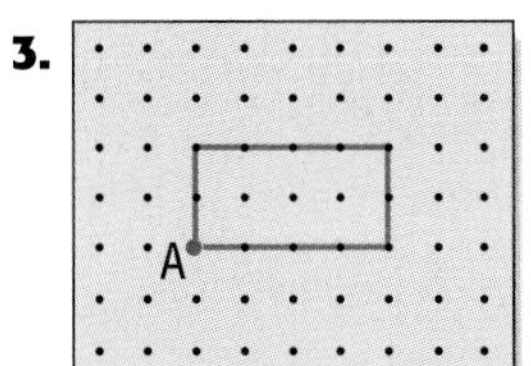

4.

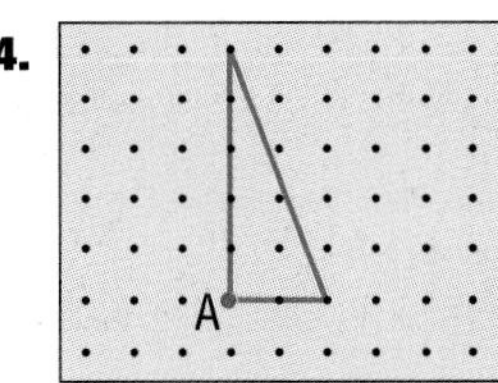

5.

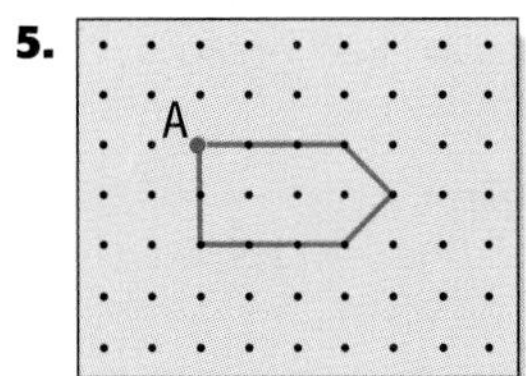

6.

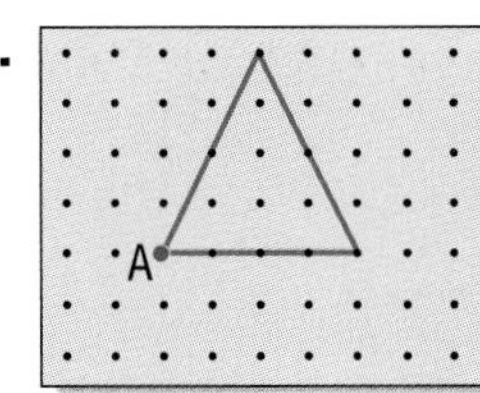

Copy each figure. Draw the rotation image for a 90° turn counterclockwise about A.

7.

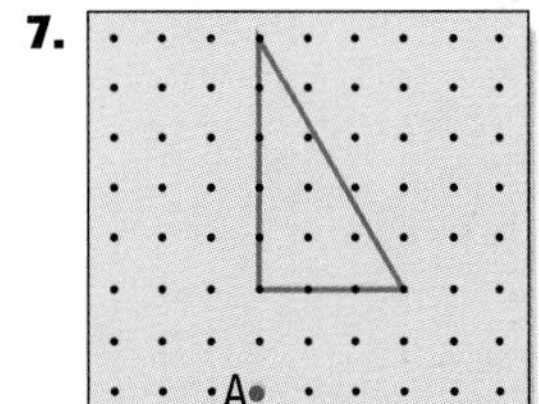

8.

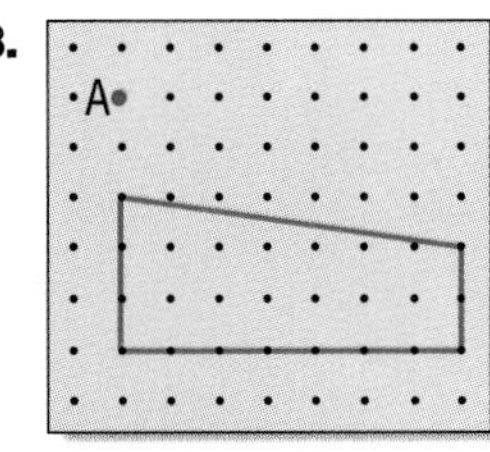

Problems and Applications

Copy each figure. Draw the rotation image for each rotation about A.

a) *180° clockwise*
b) *270° counterclockwise*
c) *270° clockwise*

9.

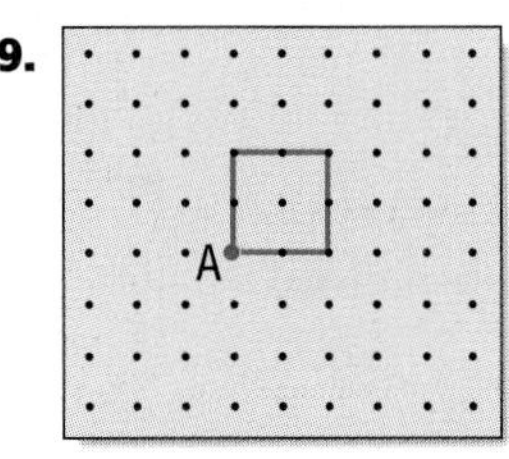

10.

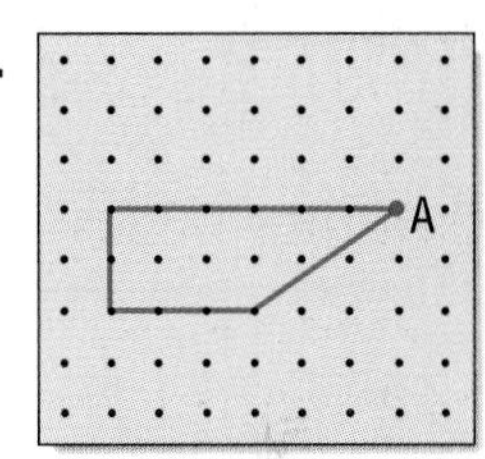

11.

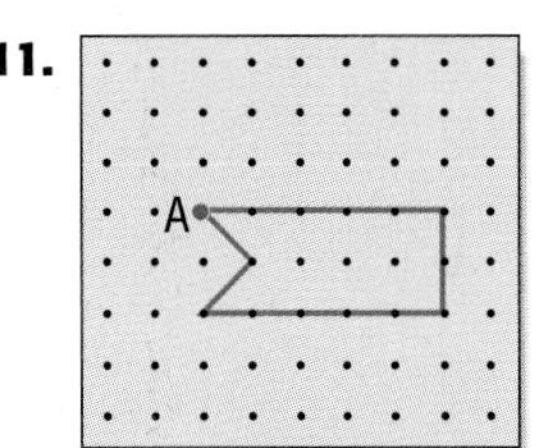

12.

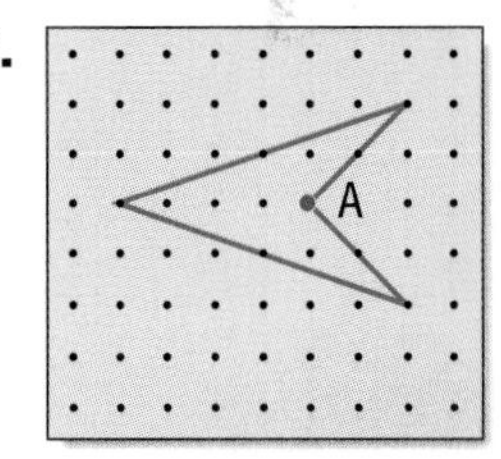

13. Copy the rectangle onto grid paper.

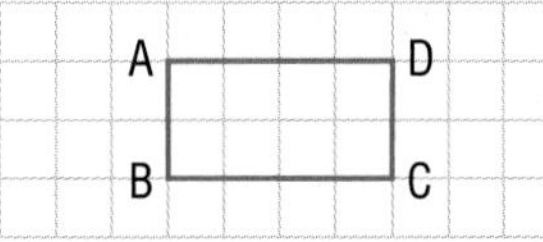

a) Rotate the rectangle 90° clockwise about C.
b) Rotate the image of the rectangle 180° counterclockwise about A′.

14. Copy the figures onto dot paper. Complete the pattern to show three 90° turns clockwise.

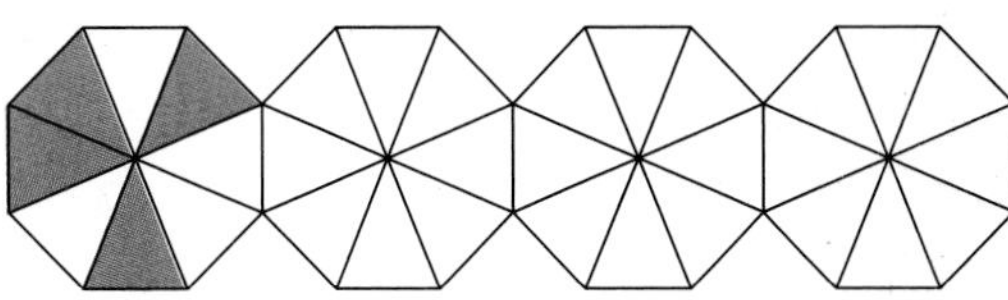

15. Are a figure and its rotation image congruent? Explain.

16. Suppose you rotate a figure 90° clockwise.
a) Name another clockwise rotation that would give the same rotation image.
b) Name a counterclockwise rotation that would give the same rotation image.

Transformations in Computer Graphics

In recent years, computers have become widely used in the fields of art and design.

Many examples of computer graphics make use of transformations.

Activity ❶

Examine the computer graphics shown here.

Describe any translations, rotations, or reflections you see in each picture.

Compare your descriptions with your classmates'.

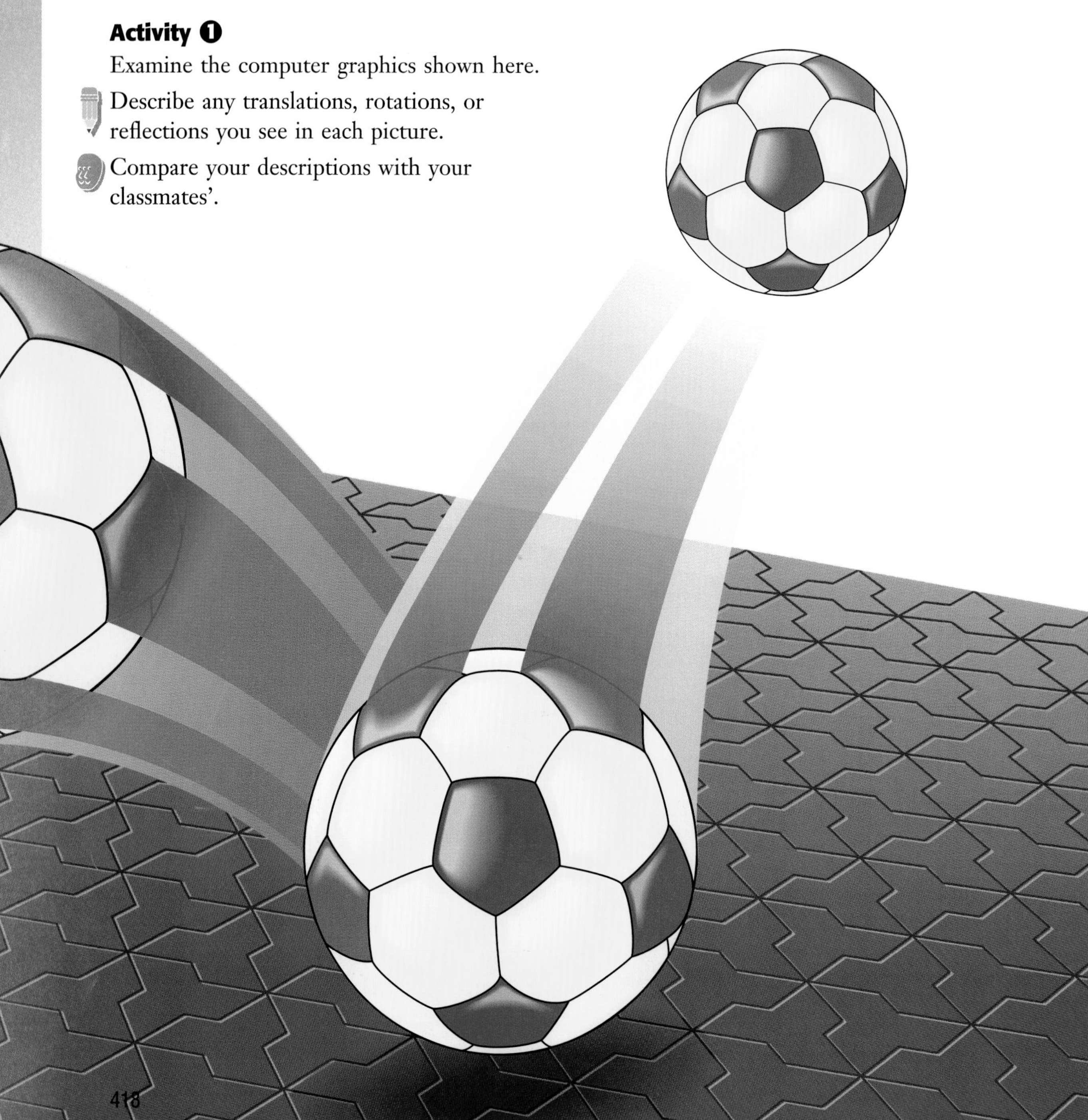

12.4 Lines of Symmetry

A **line of symmetry** divides a figure into two congruent parts.

A baseball diamond has one line of symmetry.

Activity: Do the Experiment

Fold a piece of paper once.
Cut out a shape like the one shown.
Unfold the shape.

Inquire

1. What figure have you made?
2. What does the crease do to the figure?
3. How many lines of symmetry does the figure have?
4. Fold another piece of paper horizontally, then vertically. Cut out a shape like the one shown. Unfold the shape.
5. What do the creases do to your figure?
6. How many lines of symmetry does the figure have?

A hockey rink has 2 lines of symmetry.

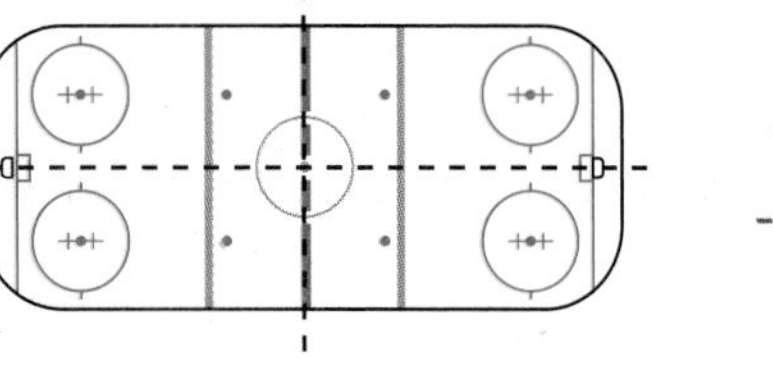

The gameboard for Solitaire has 4 lines of symmetry.

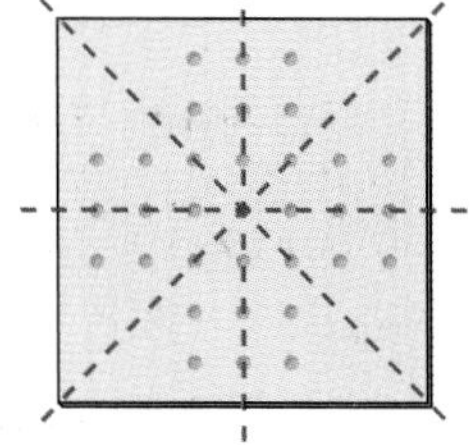

A Snakes and Ladders gameboard has no lines of symmetry.

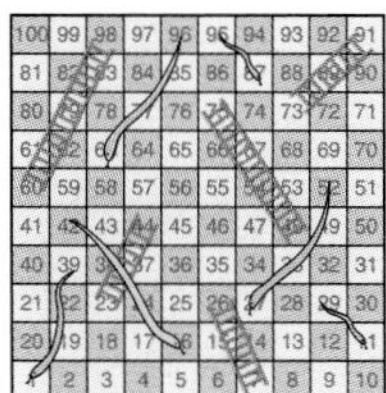

Example

Draw all the lines of symmetry on the hexagram.

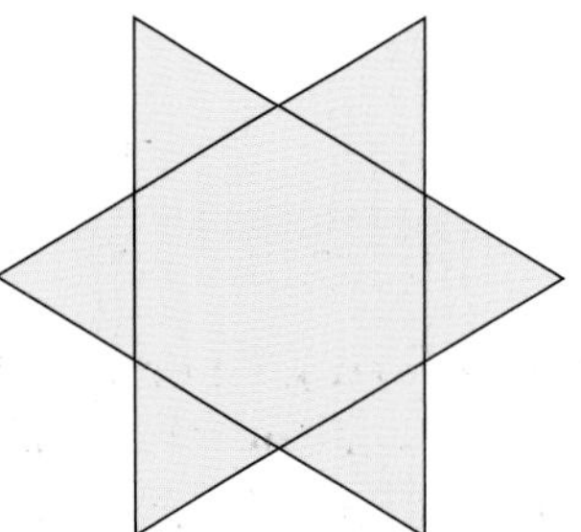

Solution

The hexagram has 6 lines of symmetry.

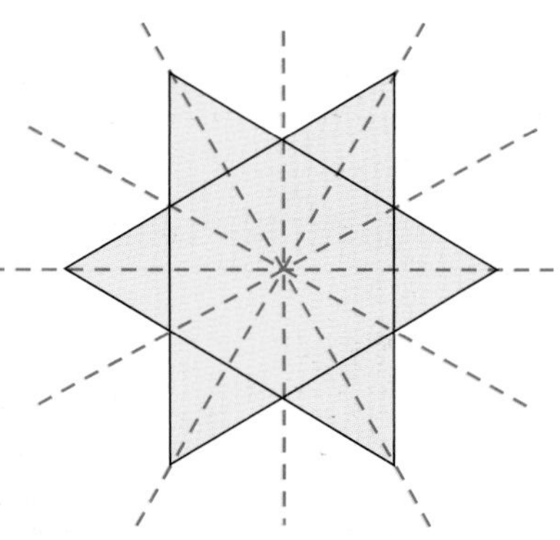

Practice

1. Print your name in block letters.
a) How many of the letters have one line of symmetry?
b) How many of the letters have two lines of symmetry?

Copy each figure and draw all the lines of symmetry.

2.

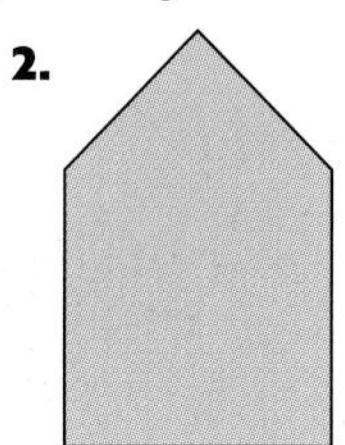

3.

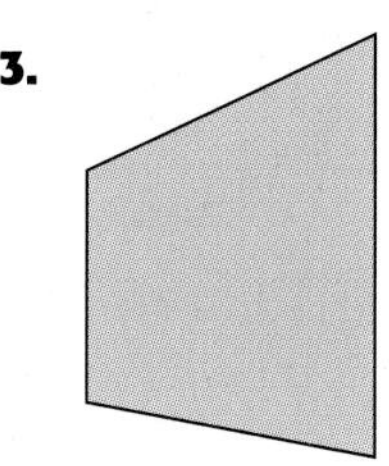

4.

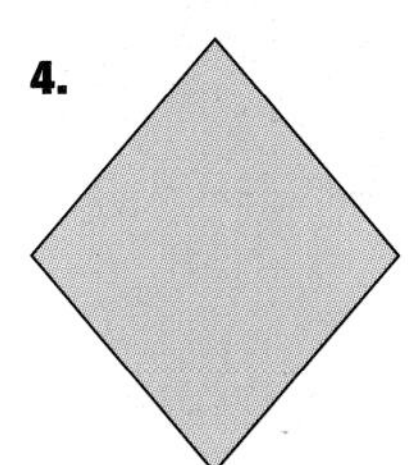

5.

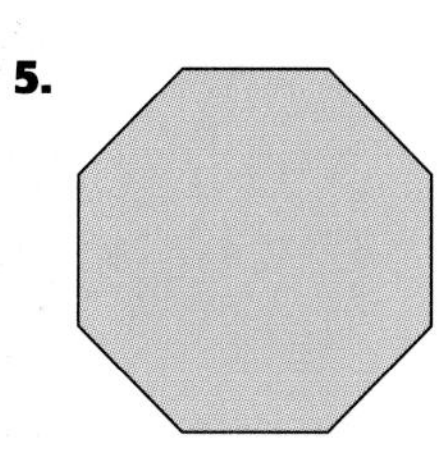

Problems and Applications

Copy the equilateral triangles. Draw all the lines of symmetry for each pattern.

6. **7.** **8.**

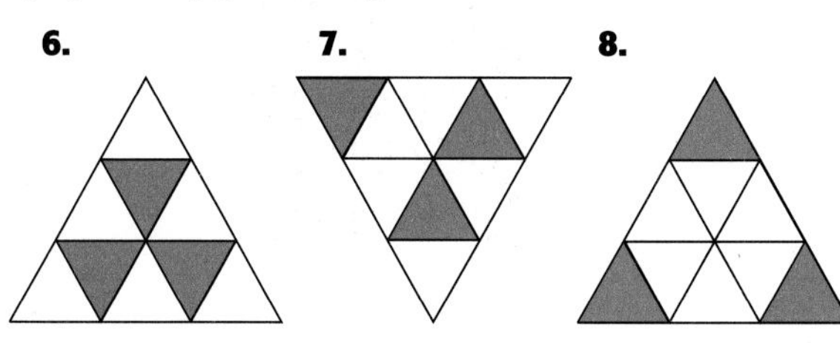

Copy the squares and complete shading the parts so that the patterns have the given number of lines of symmetry.

9.

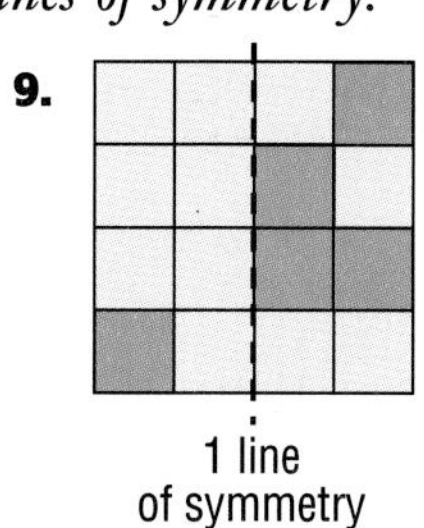

1 line of symmetry

10.

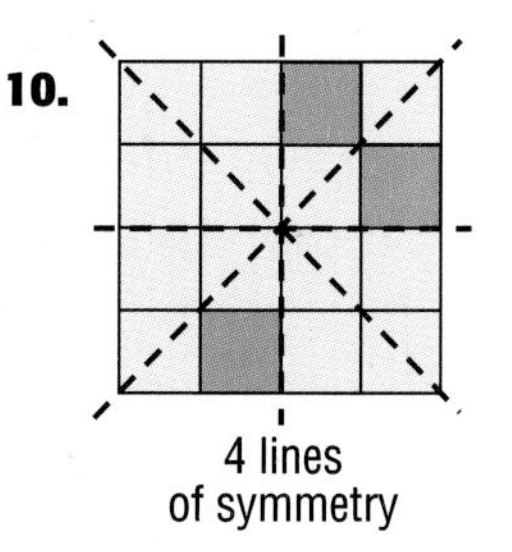

4 lines of symmetry

11. **12.**

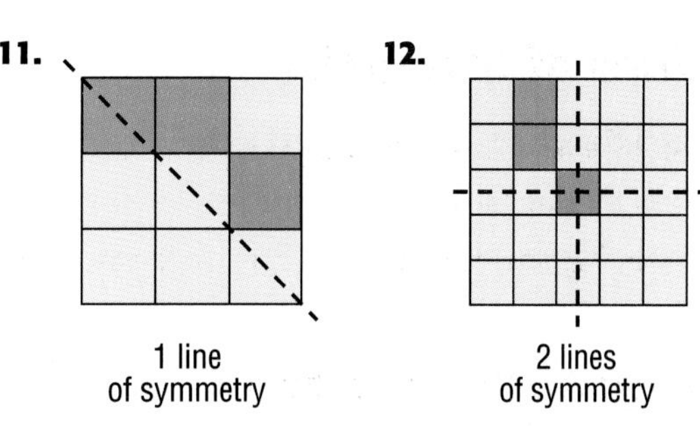

1 line of symmetry

2 lines of symmetry

Copy each flag and show any lines of symmetry.

13.

Canada

14.

Sweden

15.

India

16.

Panama

Each design is drawn on a paper that is folded into four pieces. Draw the shape that will result if the design is cut out and the paper opened.

17.

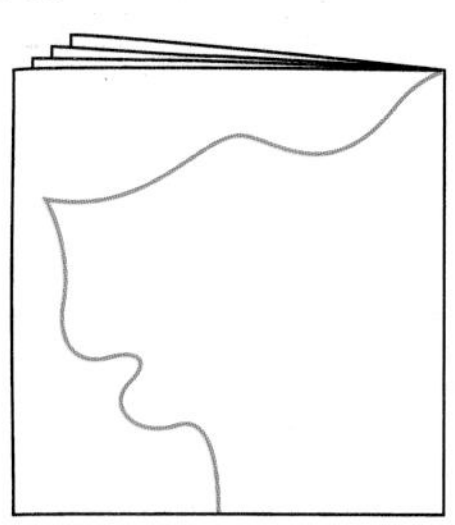

18.

19. Create your own designs like those in questions 17 and 18. Challenge your classmates to predict the shape if the design is cut out and opened.

12.5 Rotational Symmetry

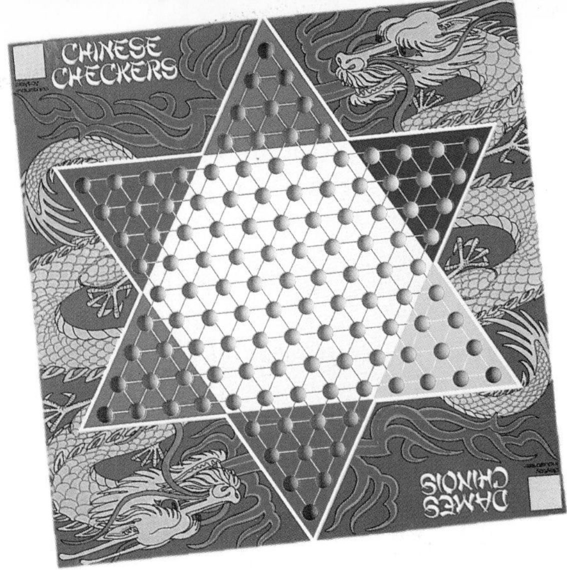

The Chinese Checkers gameboard is designed to look the same shape from the viewpoint of each of the six players.

The star shaped game area can be rotated around its centre and mapped onto itself 6 times in one complete rotation.

A figure that can be mapped onto itself with a turn of less than one complete rotation has **rotational symmetry.**

The game area has rotational symmetry of order 6.

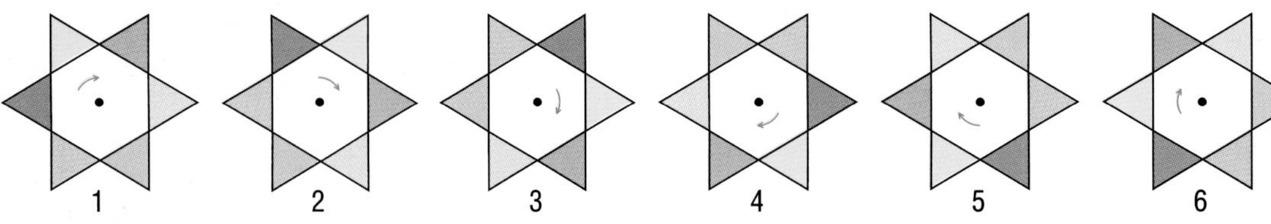

Activity: Do the Experiment

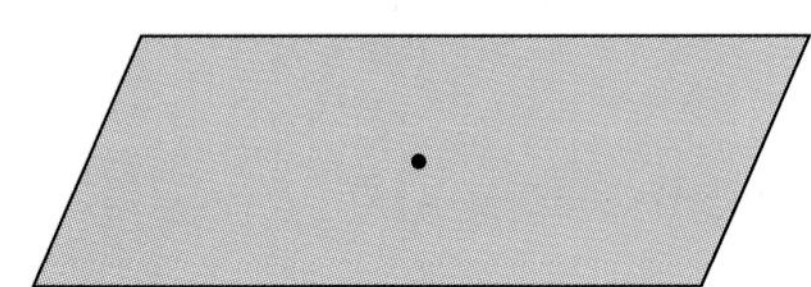

Draw a parallelogram and mark its centre.
Trace the parallelogram.
Hold the tracing at the centre with a pin or thumbtack. Rotate the tracing.

Inquire

1. How many times does the parallelogram fit onto itself during one complete rotation?

2. Perform the same experiment with an equilateral triangle and a square.

3. How many times does the triangle fit onto itself during one complete rotation?

4. How many times does the square fit onto itself during one complete rotation?

A tracing test can be used to test the rotational symmetry of any figure.

Example

Determine the order of rotational symmetry for the figure.

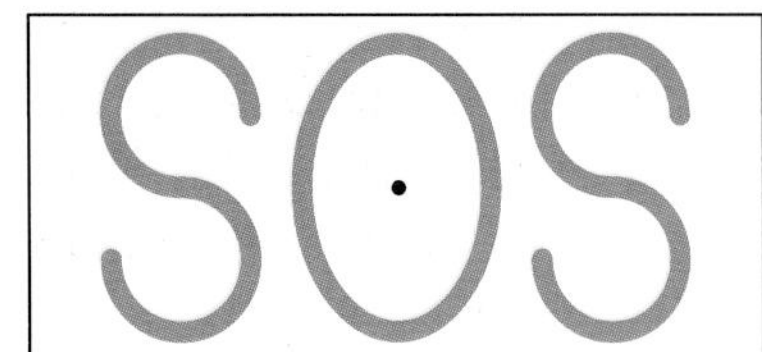

Solution

Make a tracing.
Rotate the tracing to fit it onto the figure as often as possible.
We find that the message maps onto itself twice in one complete rotation.
The message has rotational symmetry of order 2.

Practice

1. A B C D E F G H I
J K L M N O P Q R
S T U V W X Y Z

Write the block letters that have rotational symmetry.

2. The following designs were made by drawing a block letter, then drawing it again after a 180° turn.

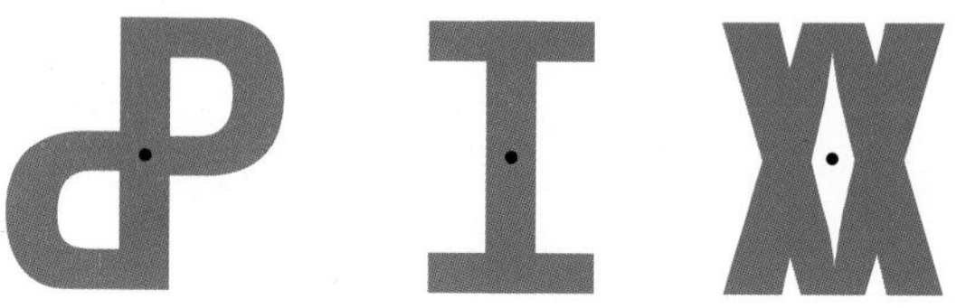

a) What 3 letters were used?

b) Draw the designs that result from rotating each of the following letters 180°.

Z L R Y X

c) Which letters from part b) have rotational symmetry?

Problems and Applications

A wooden toy has holes into which geometric shapes can fit. What order of rotational symmetry does each of the shapes have?

3. 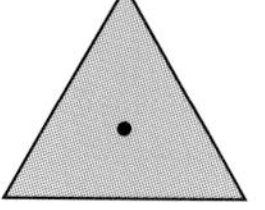

4. 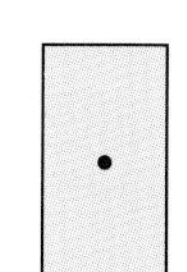

5. 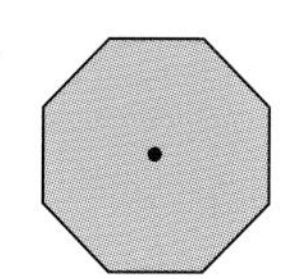

6. 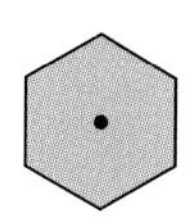

7. 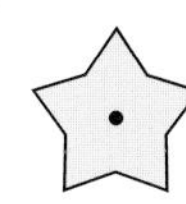

8. 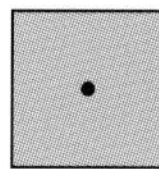

9. 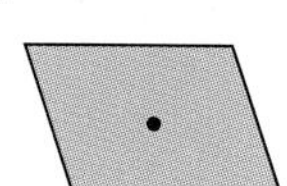

10. 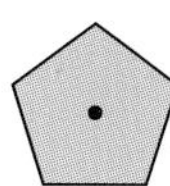

Use the tracing test to determine the rotational symmetry for each of the following.

11. 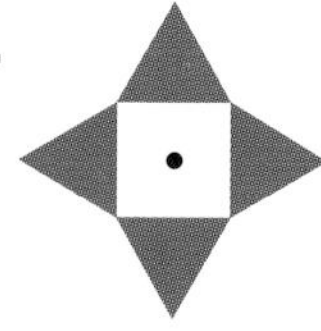

12. 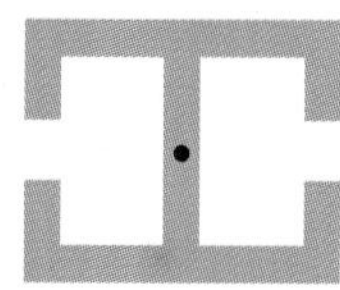

13. 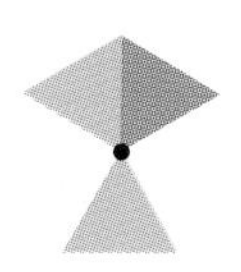

14. 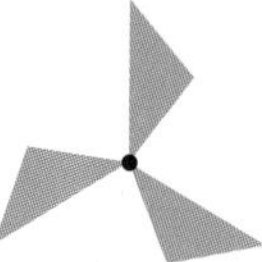

15. 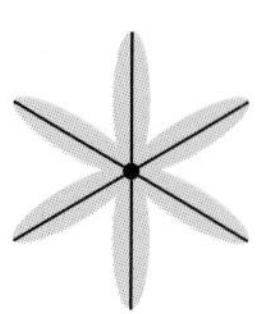

16. 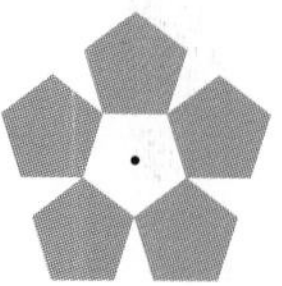

Copy and complete shading each figure so that the designs have the given order of rotational symmetry.

17. 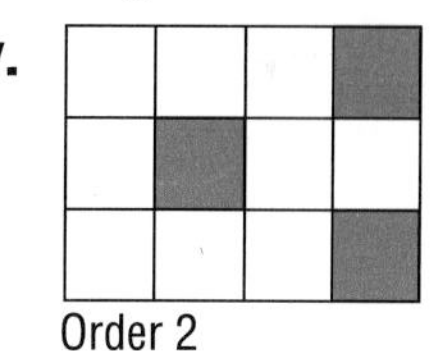

Order 2

18. 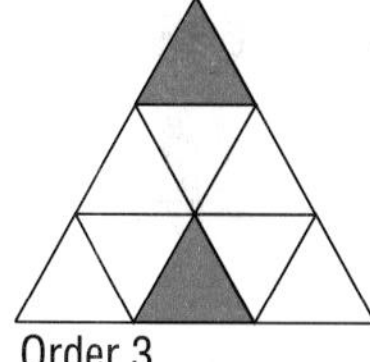

Order 3

19. 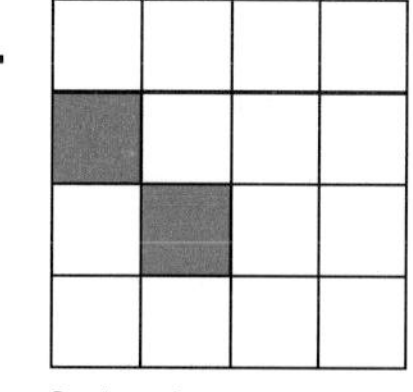

Order 4

20. 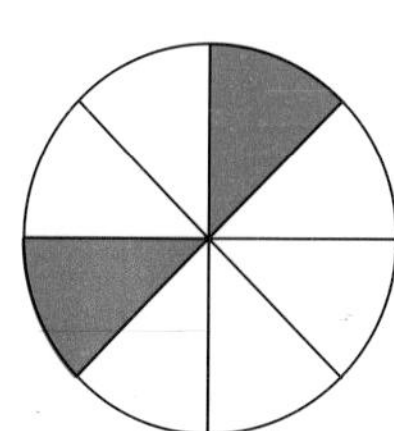

Order 2

21. 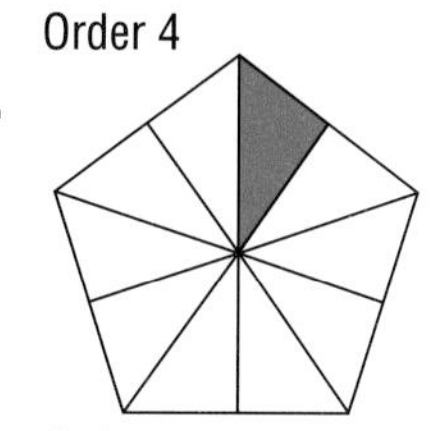

Order 5

22. 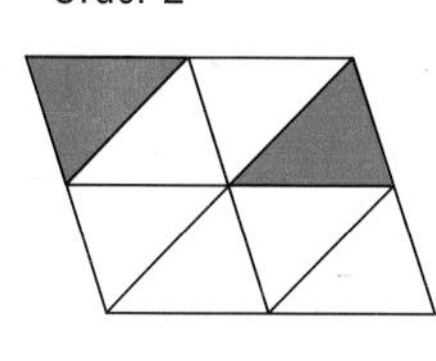

Order 2

23. Work with a classmate. Find logos in magazines and newspapers that have rotational symmetry. Display your logos and label the order of symmetry.

Enlargements and Reductions

Activity ❶

Enlarge the rabbit by using 2 squares for every one square on the diagram.

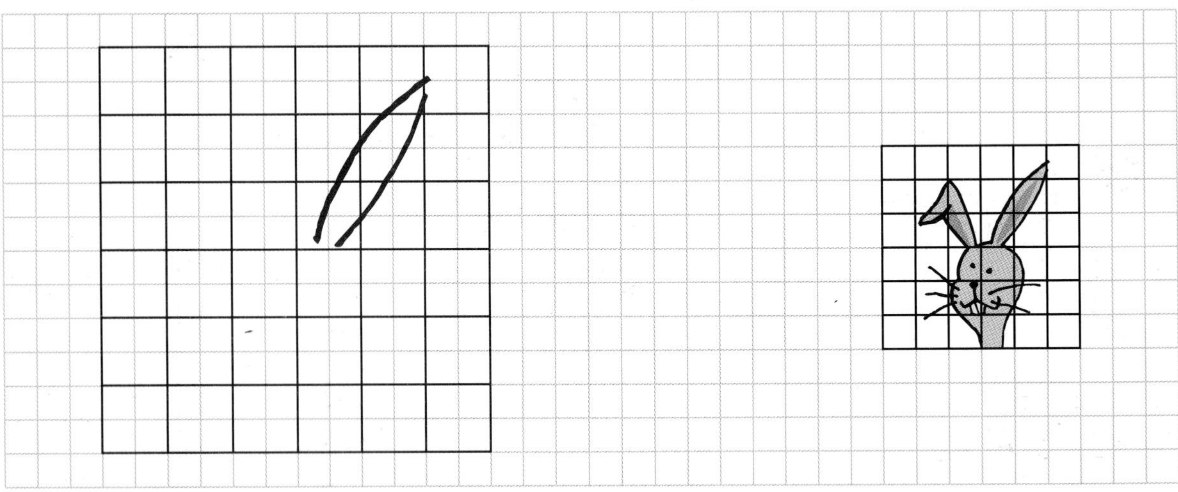

Activity ❷

Reduce the dog by using one square for every 2 squares on the diagram.

Activity ❸

Draw a grid on a picture from a magazine or newspaper. Enlarge and reduce the picture by drawing it on another grid.

Distortions

Activity ❶

Distorted grids can be made up of straight lines.
The second diagram shows a distortion of the clown. Trace the third grid and make another distortion of the clown.

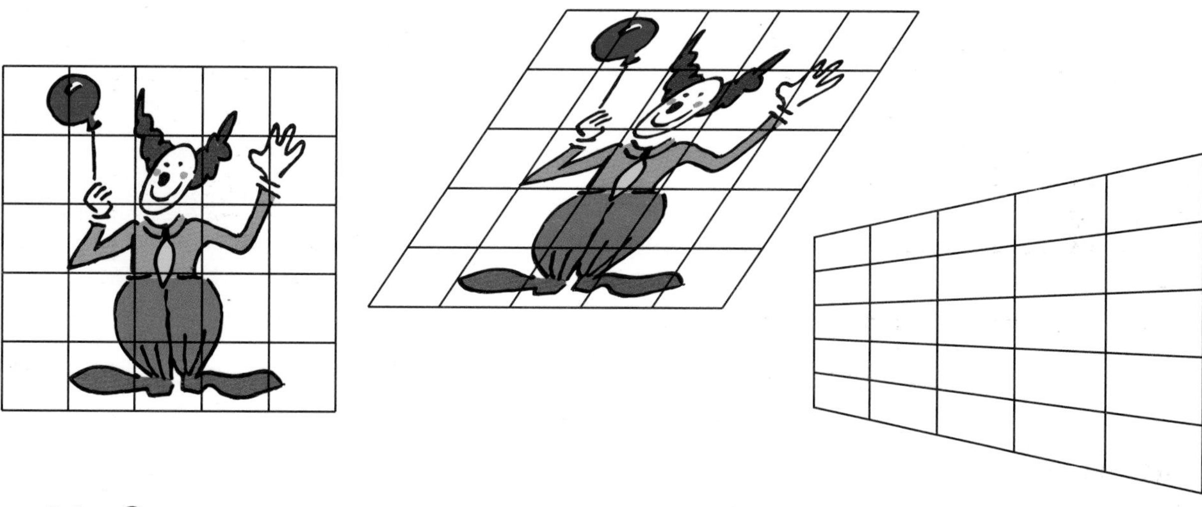

Activity ❷

Distorted grids can be made up of curved lines.
Trace one of the grids and make a distortion of the lion.

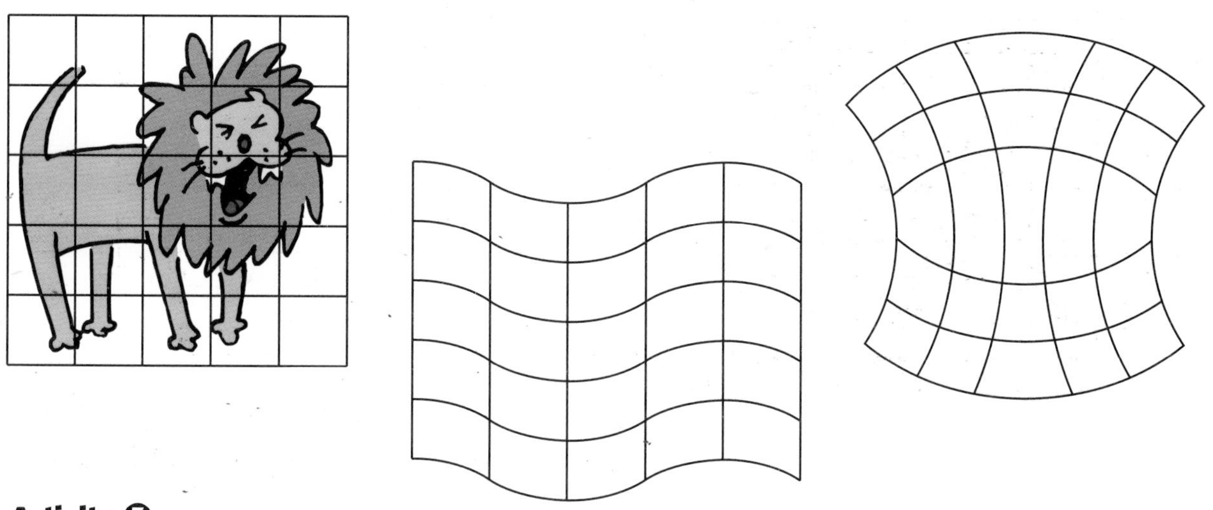

Activity ❸

Draw a grid on a picture from a magazine or newspaper and make a distortion of the picture.

SENDING *MESSAGES* INTO SPACE

Suppose there are intelligent beings living on planets that orbit other stars. Because these stars are so far away, our only hope of contacting them in the near future is through radio signals. For example, the closest star to Earth is Proxima Centauri. It is 40 000 000 000 000 km away. It would take the fastest space ship about 175 000 years to get there. However, radio signals travel at 300 000 km/s. It takes a radio signal only 4 years and 2 months to reach Proxima Centauri.

Since we do not know the language of the beings that might receive our signal, we would probably send pictures instead of words. One way would be to send a series of dots and dashes that could be used to make a picture on a grid. For example, if we let a dot be an O and a dash be an X, then a picture of a dog could be sent as follows.

XXOOOOXOOXOXXXXOXOOX

The being that received this signal would need to break it into 4 groups of 5.

XXOOO OXOOX OXXXX OXOOX

Plotting the result on a 4 by 5 grid would give the picture of a dog.

XXOOO

XXOOO
OXOOX

XXOOO
OXOOX
OXXXX

XXOOO
OXOOX
OXXXX
OXOOX =

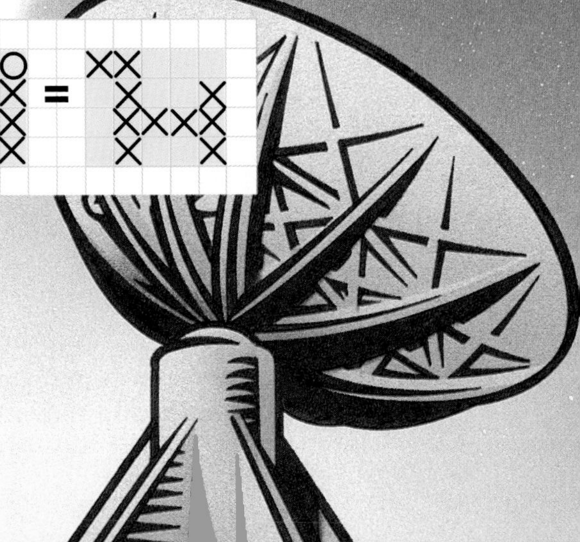

Activity ➊

1. Work with a classmate. Make up a picture to be sent into space on a 4 by 5 grid. Translate the picture into Xs and Os.

2. Have another classmate decode the Xs and Os.

Activity ❷

Suppose that scientists have decided that a good picture to represent us on Earth needs a string of 91 dots and dashes.

OOXXXOOOXXXXXOOOXXXOOOOOXOOOXXXXXXX
XOXXXOXXOXXXOXXOXXXOXXOXXXOXOOXOXOO
OOXOXOOOOXOXOOOOXOXOO

The beings receiving our signal realize that we have sent a picture. Since the only two factors of 91, other than 91 and 1, are 13 and 7, the signal can be divided into 7 rows of 13 or 13 rows of 7.

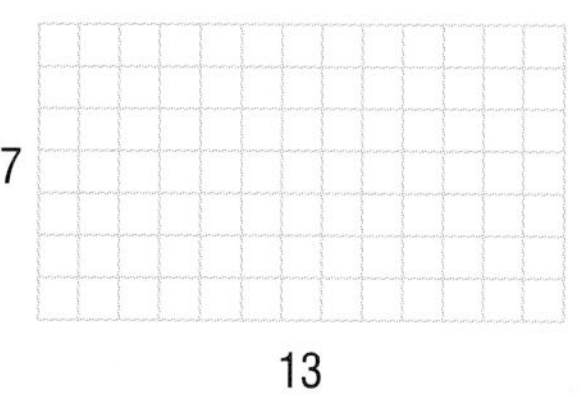

13

7

Suppose the receiver uses 7 rows of 13 and divides the signal up into groups of 13.

OOXXXOOOXXXXX
XOXXOXXXOXXOX
OXOXOOOOXOXOO

OOOXXXOOOOOXO
XXOXXOXXXOXOO

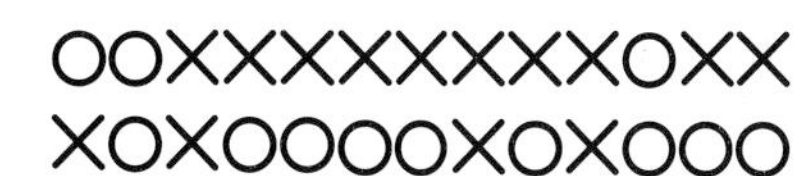

OOXXXXXXXXOXX
XOXOOOOXOXOOO

The picture means nothing.

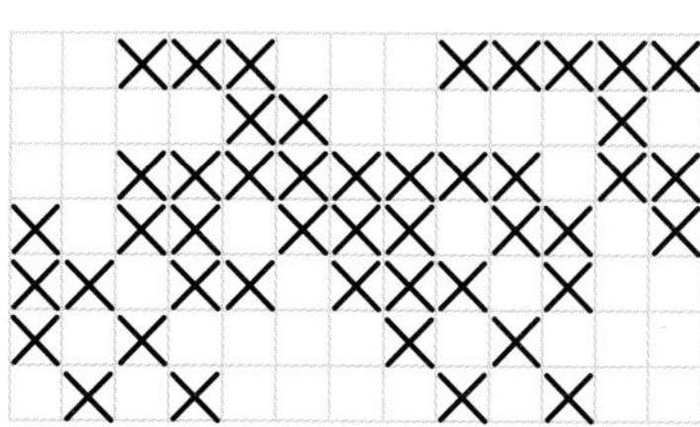

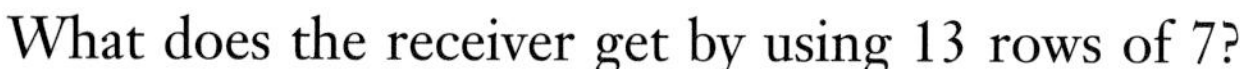

What does the receiver get by using 13 rows of 7?

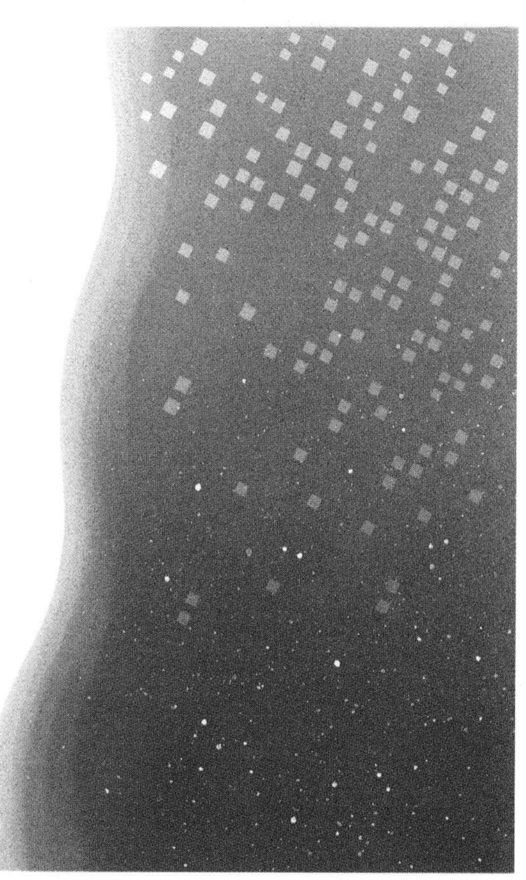

Activity ❸

1. Draw a grid on which the numbers of rows and columns are both prime numbers not less than 5. The product of the number of rows and number of columns will give the total number of Xs and Os in your signal.

2. Devise a signal on your grid to represent

a) the side view of a table

b) the front view of a picture frame

3. Have a classmate interpret the signal and compare the result with the picture you intended.

Review

Copy each figure onto dot paper. Draw the translation image of each for the given translation.

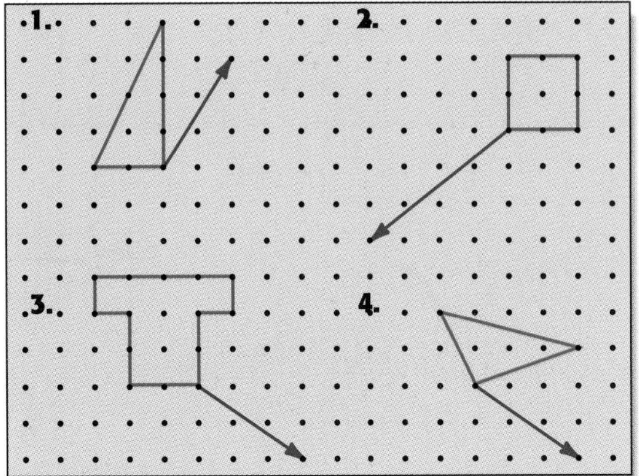

Copy each figure onto dot paper and draw the reflection image.

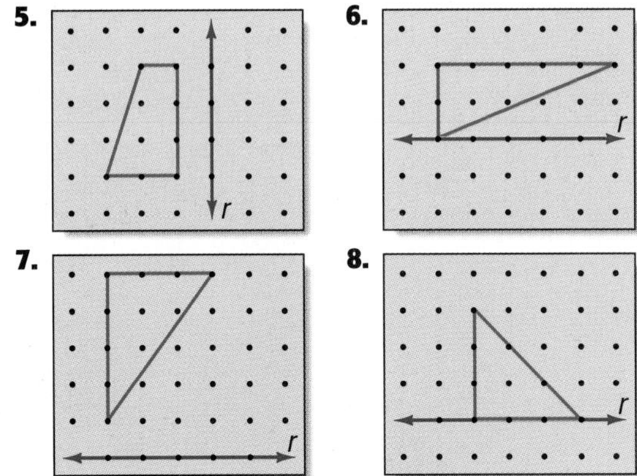

Copy each figure onto dot paper. Draw the rotation image for each rotation about A.

a) *90° counterclockwise*
b) *180° clockwise*
c) *270° counterclockwise*

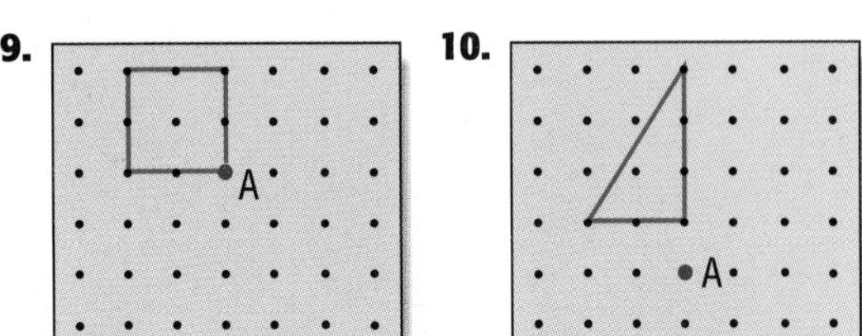

Copy each figure and draw all lines of symmetry.

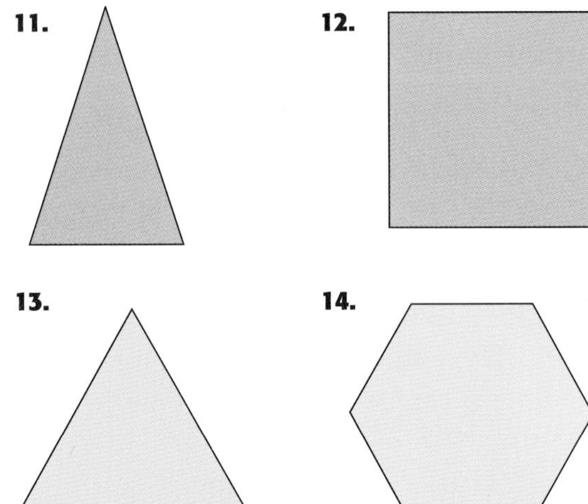

Determine the rotational symmetry for each of the following.

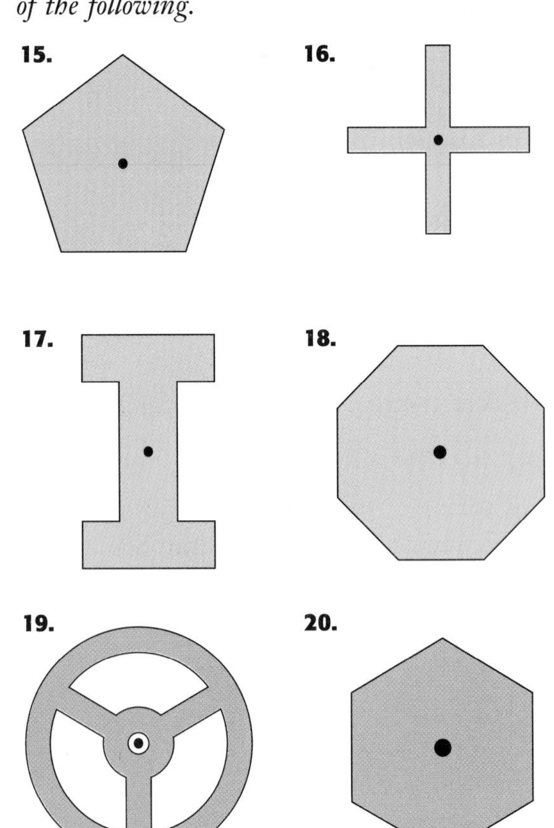

21. Copy the figure onto grid paper.

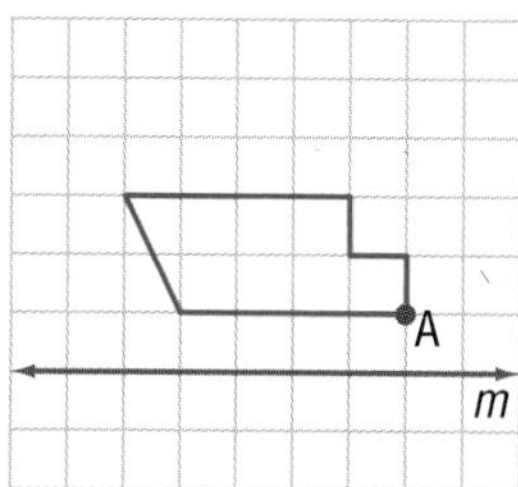

Draw the figure as it would appear after each step.

a) a translation 3 units up and 2 units left, a rotation of 180° clockwise about A, a translation 4 units down and 3 units right

b) a reflection in the line *m*, a translation 4 units up and 2 units right, a reflection in the line *m*

c) a rotation of 90° clockwise about A, a reflection in the line *m*, a rotation of 180° clockwise about A.

22. Copy the figure onto grid paper. Draw each of the following images.

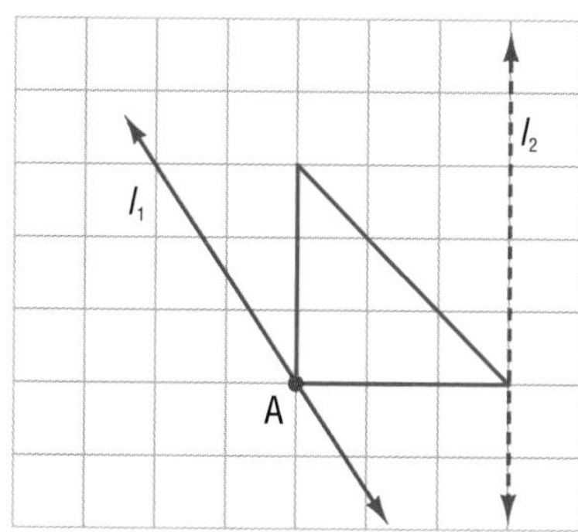

a) a translation 3 units right and 4 units up

b) a reflection in each reflection line

c) a 90° turn counterclockwise about A

23. State whether each of the following transformations results in an image that is congruent to the original figure.

a) a translation

b) a reflection

c) a rotation

Group Decision Making

Saving the Environment

In this activity, you will ask people to respond to the following statement.

Tell me one thing we should start doing, one thing we should stop doing, and one thing we should continue doing in order to save our environment.

1. As a class, brainstorm the groups of people you should survey. The groups could include students, teachers, parents, school support staff, and people living near the school.

2. Decide as a class what group of people each student group will survey.

3. As a group, decide how your part of the survey is to be done and how many people will be surveyed.

4. As a group, conduct the survey.

5. As a group, summarize the responses, ranking the suggestions. Discuss as a group possible reasons for the suggestions you received.

6. Prepare a group report for the class. Include a graph or chart that displays your results.

7. As a class, discuss the reports. Decide what action you recommend as a result of the reports.

8. Evaluate the survey as a class. Suggest other issues for which this simple type of survey could be used.

Chapter Check

Find the translation image of each figure.

1. 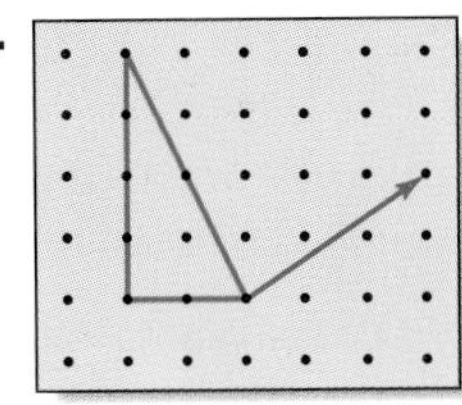

2. 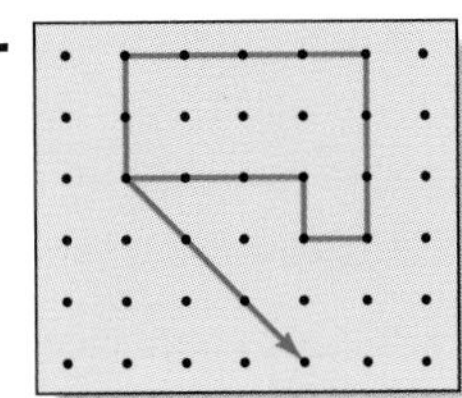

Find the reflection image of each figure.

3. 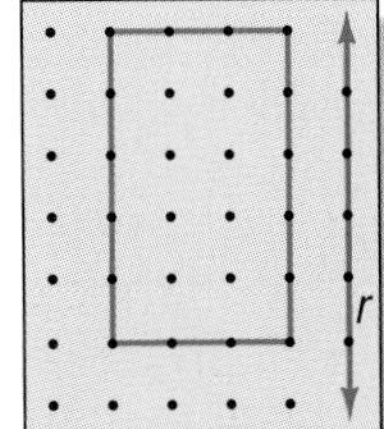

4. 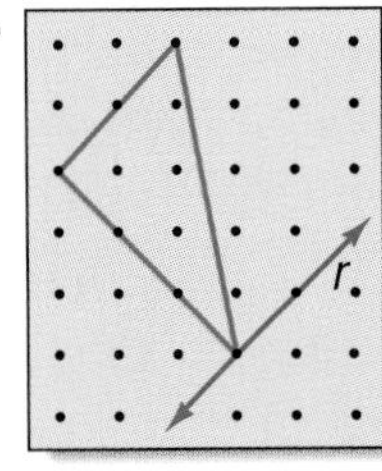

Draw the rotation image for a 90° rotation counterclockwise about A.

5. 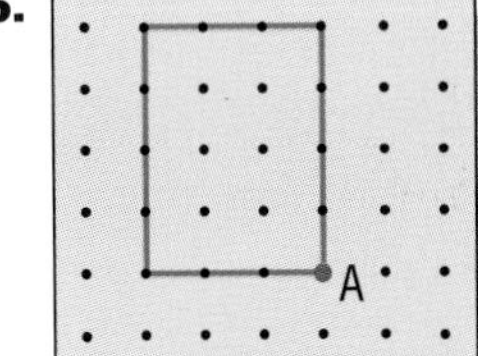

6. 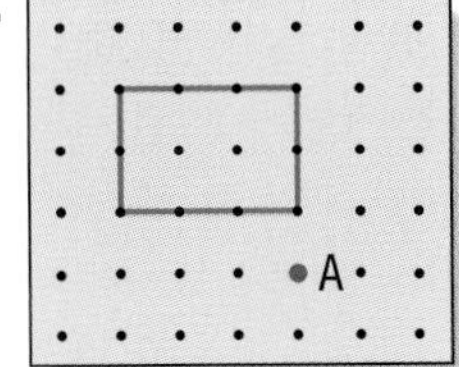

7. Copy the figure onto grid or dot paper.

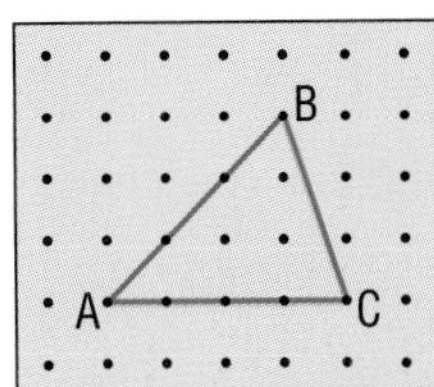

a) Draw the translation image for a translation 3 units up and 4 units right.
b) Draw the rotation image for a turn 270° clockwise about C.

How many lines of symmetry does each figure have?

8. 

9. 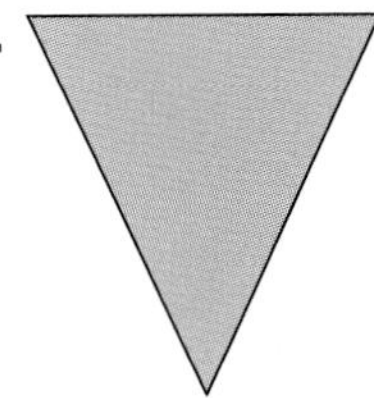

Determine the order of rotational symmetry for each figure.

10. 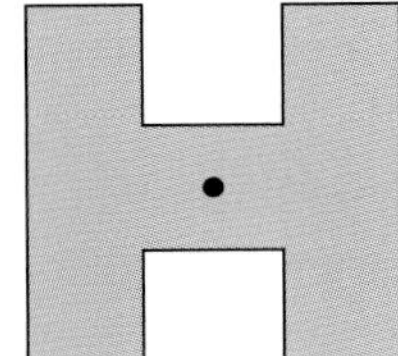

11. 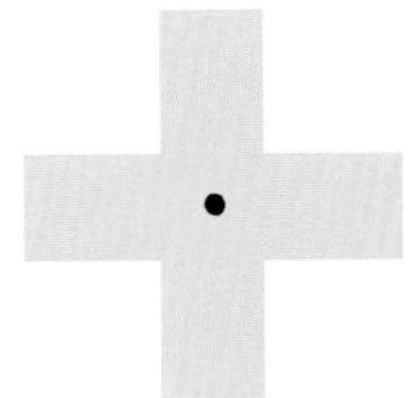

Using the Strategies

1. Marcos received $7.42 change when he bought a model kit. The store clerk gave him 25 coins which included pennies, nickels, dimes, quarters, and dollars. How many of each coin did Marcos receive?

2. Susan has a piece of wood that measures 85 cm by 70 cm. What is the greatest number of 10 cm by 10 cm geoboards that she can cut from the wood? What assumptions have you made?

3. On what day of this year was the year 300 000 min old?

4. The students at a new school must decide on their school colours. There are four colours to choose from: red, blue, yellow, and green. They must choose two colours. How many different colour combinations are there using these colours?

5. Three tennis balls cost $10.75. What is the cost of 10 tennis balls?

6. The shirt and shorts are on display in a store window.

a) Estimate the cost of the shirt and shorts.
b) Calculate the cost of the shirt and shorts, including your provincial sales tax and GST.

7. Theresa and Dave are doing a science project. They counted 118 trees in one hectare of a forest. Estimate the number of trees in the forest if there are 450 ha of forest. What assumption did you make?

8. If you do not stop, it takes about 6 h and 15 min to drive from Quebec City to Fredericton. Chantel left Quebec City for Fredericton at 07:55. If she stopped twice along the way, once for 15 min and once for 35 min, at what time did she arrive in Fredericton?

9. In a 30-min television news broadcast, 13 min are used for local news, 10 min are used for national news and 3 min are used for world news. The rest of the time is used for commercials. How much time is used for commercials?

10. Terri has 3 part-time jobs. One week, she worked 5 h at a doughnut shop, where she earned $6.35/h. She pumped gas for 6 h and earned $5.50/h. She also raked leaves for 4 h and earned $4.00/h. How much did she earn that week?

11. In a magic square the sum of the rows, columns, and diagonals is the same. The following is not a magic square.

5	0	8
7	4	2
1	6	3

Change the positions of 3 pairs of the numbers to make a magic square.

DATA BANK

1. How long was the shortest term of office for a Canadian Prime Minister?

2. Which feels warmer, a temperature of -9°C in a wind of 16 km/h or a temperature of -15°C in a wind of 8 km/h?

Chapter 9

1. The chart gives the scores for 6 teams in a soccer league after 9 games.

Tigers	5	Penguins	3
Lions	2	Bruins	0
Colts	1	Seals	1
Tigers	4	Seals	3
Penguins	2	Lions	2
Bruins	5	Colts	1
Lions	3	Tigers	0
Penguins	4	Colts	2
Seals	3	Bruins	3

Teams get 2 points for a win and 1 point for a tie. Organize the data into a table that shows games won, games tied, games lost, and each team's points. Rank the teams in order from most points to fewest points.

2. The chart shows the numbers of absences for each grade at Memorial School over a period of 5 months.

Grade	Sept.	Oct.	Nov.	Dec.	Jan.
6	9	13	15	7	12
7	4	9	11	3	2
8	8	12	9	1	1

Draw a bar graph showing the total number of absences for each month.

3. Find the range and mean of these test scores.

78, 79, 98, 56, 66, 72, 77, 91

4. Find the median and mode of these test scores.

70, 79, 91, 78, 67, 83, 67

5. What are the following probabilities if you choose one marble without looking?

a) P (red)

b) P (blue)

c) P (green)

d) P (yellow)

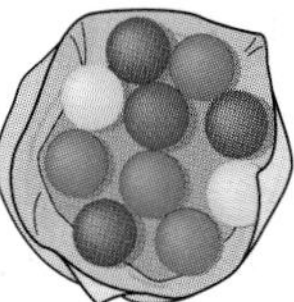

Chapter 10

Write the opposite of each integer.

1. +6 **2.** −2 **3.** +4

4. −8 **5.** +11 **6.** −1

7. Place each integer on an integer line.

−2, −4, +2, −5, −1, +6, 0

8. Which of the following integers are greater than −4 and less than +4?

+5, −3, +2, 0, −2, +3, −9, +8

9. Write the integers in order from smallest to largest.

−3, +2, 0, +5, −4, −1, +1

Add.

10. $(+3) + (+4)$ **11.** $(-2) + (-5)$

12. $(+5) + (-2)$ **13.** $(-6) + (+2)$

Subtract.

14. $(+5) - (+2)$ **15.** $(-7) - (-2)$

16. $(-4) - (+3)$ **17.** $(+3) - (+5)$

Multiply.

18. $(+3) \times (+6)$ **19.** $(+5) \times (-3)$

20. $(-4) \times (-2)$ **21.** $(-5) \times (-6)$

Divide.

22. $(+18) \div (+6)$ **23.** $(-24) \div (+4)$

24. $(+20) \div (-5)$ **25.** $(-30) \div (-6)$

26. $\frac{+12}{-4}$ **27.** $\frac{-20}{+5}$

28. $\frac{+36}{-9}$ **29.** $\frac{-30}{-3}$

Find the missing integer.

30. $(+5) + ■ = (+11)$ **31.** $(-4) + ■ = (+1)$

32. $(-3) - ■ = (+2)$ **33.** $■ - (-4) = (+2)$

34. $■ - (+2) = (-4)$ **35.** $(-2) \times ■ = (+10)$

36. $■ \times (+3) = (-18)$ **37.** $■ \times (-4) = (+16)$

38. $(-24) \div ■ = (+6)$ **39.** $■ \div (-5) = (-2)$

Chapter 11

Evaluate each expression for $x = 6$.

1. $4x$

2. $x + 5$

3. $2x + 1$

4. $3x - 8$

Evaluate each expression for $x = 3$ and $y = 4$.

5. $x + y$

6. $2x - y$

7. $2x + 3y$

8. $x + y$

Solve the following equations.

9. $x + 3 = 7$

10. $y - 4 = 8$

11. $m - 4 = 0$

12. $7 + r = 15$

Write the following using symbols.

13. six is added to y

14. seven less than y

15. t divided by three

16. five times w

Complete the tables.

x	$3x+2$
1	
2	
3	
4	
5	
6	

y	$2y-1$
0	
1	
2	
3	
4	
5	

Find 5 points for each equation and draw a graph.

17. $y = 2x + 1$

18. $x + y = 7$

For each of the following, write an equation and solve.

19. When 7 is added to a number, the result is 23. Find the number.

20. When 8 is subtracted from a number, the result is 11. Find the number.

21. Maria is 5 years older than Colleen. The sum of their ages is 21. Find their ages.

22. Seven more than twice George's age is 33. How old is George?

Chapter 12

1. Copy the figure onto grid paper.

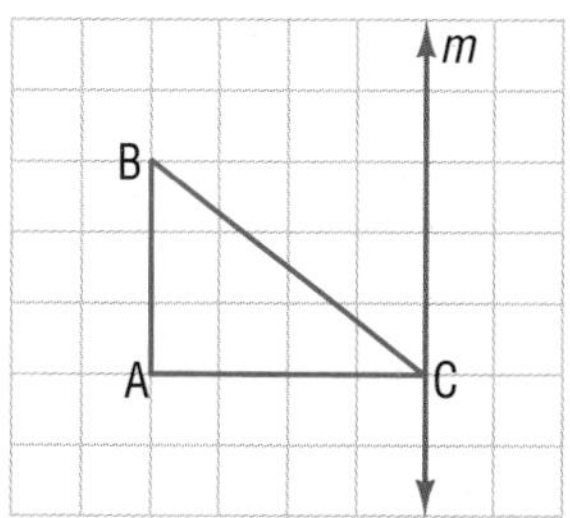

a) Draw the image after a translation of 3 units to the right and 2 units up.
b) Draw the image after a reflection in the reflection line m.
c) Draw the image after a rotation of 90° counterclockwise about A.

2. Copy each figure.

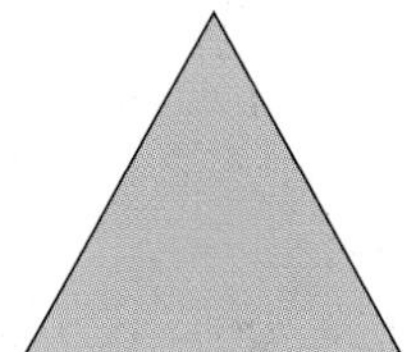

a) Draw any lines of symmetry for each figure.
b) Determine the order of rotational symmetry for each.

3. Copy the figure onto grid paper.

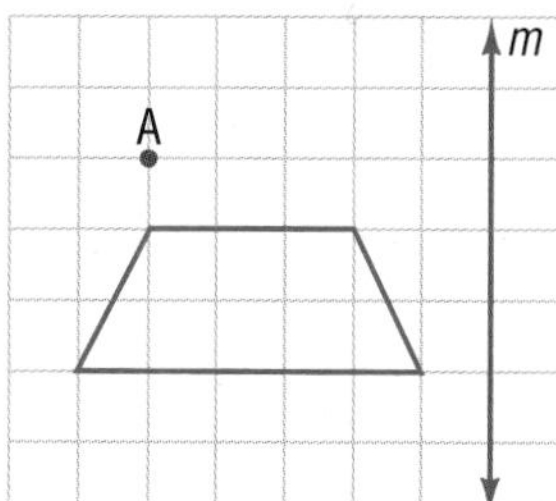

Draw the figure as it would appear after each step of the following series:
a rotation 90° counterclockwise about A,
a translation 3 units down and 4 units right,
and a reflection in the line m.

Geometric Constructions

Set up 12 toothpicks as shown. Move 3 of them to make 3 squares the same size as the one in the middle.

Make the following design with 5 toothpicks. Move 2 of them to make 5 squares the same size as the ones shown.

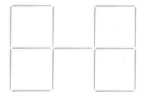

There are 12 toothpicks in the following design. Move 5 of them to make 3 squares that are the same size.

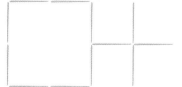

Construction Patterns

Activity ❶

The points on the 10-point circle have been joined using the following multiples of 4.

4, 8, 12, 16, 20

To join multiples greater than 8, think of 12 as 2, then 16 as 6, and 20 as 0.

1. What shape have we constructed?

2. Predict, then construct a figure on the 10-point circle for each of the following. Continue joining points until the figure is closed.

a) multiples of 3 **b)** multiples of 5
c) multiples of 6 **d)** multiples of 8

3. Are any of the figures the same? Why?

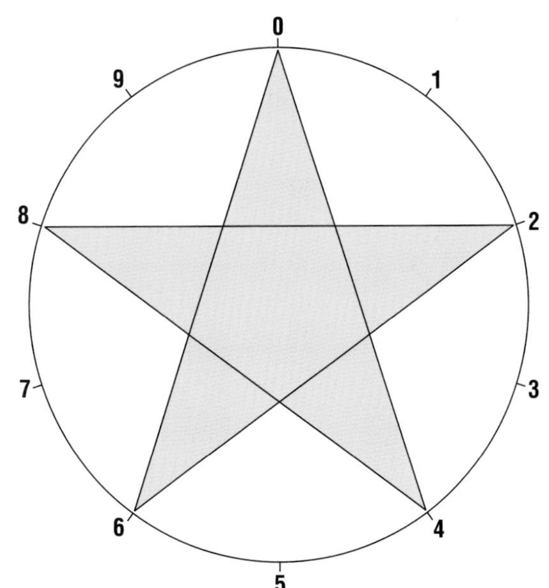

Activity ❷

Many designs are made with circles. Three examples are shown below.

1. Use a ruler and compasses to construct the following designs.

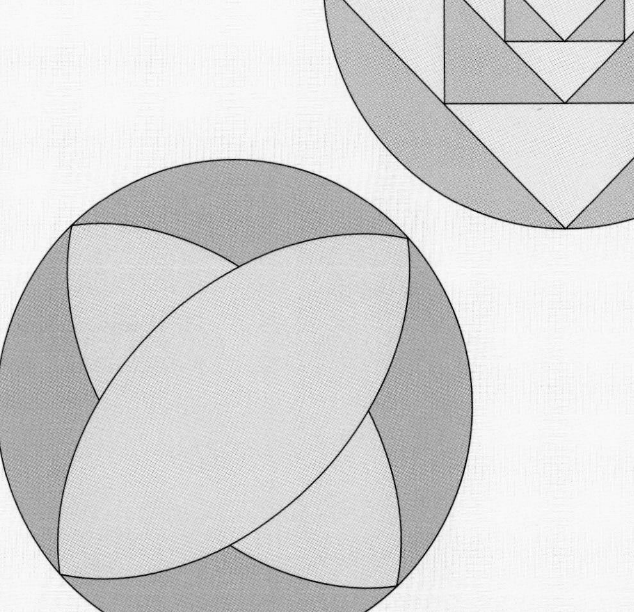

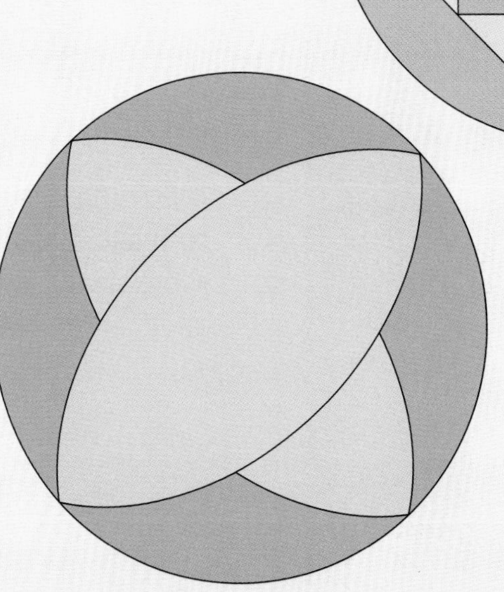

Activity ❸

Some designs are constructed with circles and straight lines. An example is shown below.

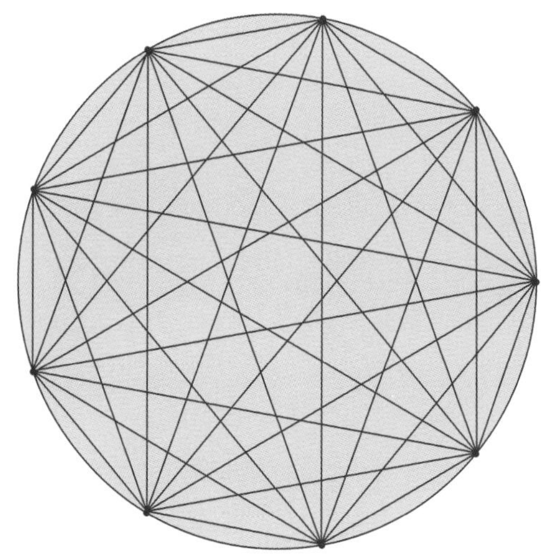

1. Use your ruler and compasses to construct a design with circles and straight lines.

Activity ❹

Construct a design with circles and straight lines on dot paper or squared paper. Two examples are shown.

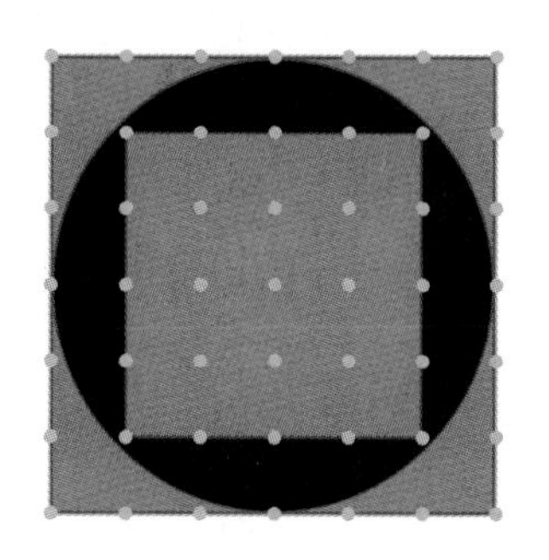

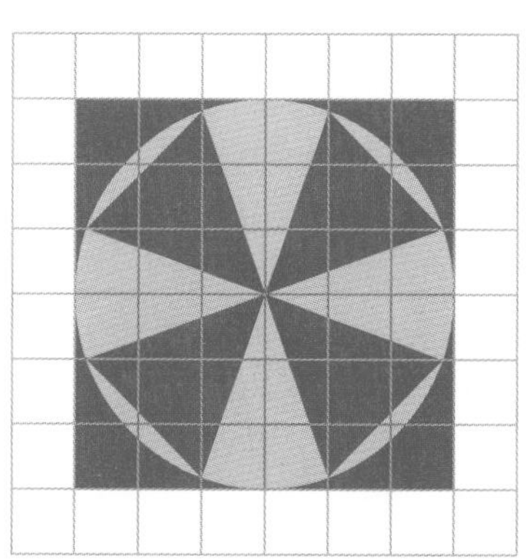

Mental Math

Calculate.

1. \$1.99 + \$2.99 **2.** \$3.99 + \$3.99
3. \$2.99 + \$3.99 **4.** \$4.99 + \$5.99
5. \$10.99 + \$4.99 **6.** \$12.99 + \$10.99
7. \$3.49 + \$5.49 **8.** \$6.49 + \$8.49

Calculate.

9. \$4.95 + \$3.95 **10.** \$6.95 + \$9.95
11. \$10.95 + \$5.95 **12.** \$25.95 + \$15.95
13. \$19.95 + \$9.95 **14.** \$4.95 + \$16.95
15. \$30.95 + \$50.95 **16.** \$39.95 + \$19.95

Calculate.

17. \$2.99 + \$1.95 **18.** \$3.99 + \$4.95
19. \$10.99 + \$3.95 **20.** \$19.99 + \$6.95
21. \$8.99 + \$8.95 **22.** \$11.99 + \$5.95
23. \$25.98 + \$3.95 **24.** \$32.98 + \$5.95

Calculate.

25. \$2.99 + \$1.75 **26.** \$3.99 + \$2.75
27. \$4.99 + \$3.50 **28.** \$1.99 + \$4.25
29. \$6.99 + \$6.50 **30.** \$2.50 + \$3.99
31. \$5.75 + \$4.99 **32.** \$7.50 + \$2.99
33. \$2.49 + \$1.99 **34.** \$3.98 + \$3.99

Calculate.

35. 3 at \$2.99 **36.** 4 at \$4.99
37. 6 at \$3.99 **38.** 5 at \$9.99
39. 4 at \$3.98 **40.** 2 at \$7.98
41. 3 at \$4.95 **42.** 3 at \$19.95
43. 4 at \$3.95 **44.** 3 at \$4.98

13.1 Constructing Congruent Line Segments and Angles

Congruent line segments have the same length.
Congruent angles have the same measure.

Activity: Explore the Method

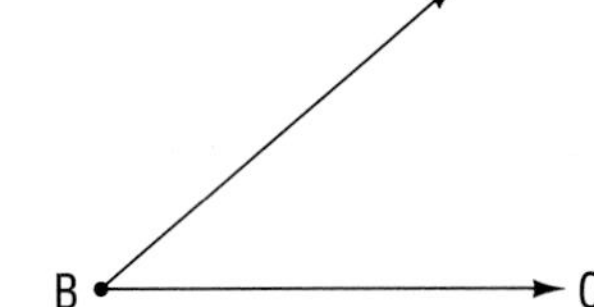

Use each of the following to construct a line segment congruent to line segment AB and an angle congruent to ∠ABC.

a) paper folding **b)** tracing paper **c)** Mira

A • ——— • B

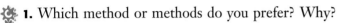

Inquire

1. Which method or methods do you prefer? Why?

2. Describe the steps in your method.

3. Compare your method with your classmates' methods.

Example 1

Use ruler and compasses to construct a line segment congruent to AB shown above.

Solution

Study the steps.

Step 1

Step 2

Step 3

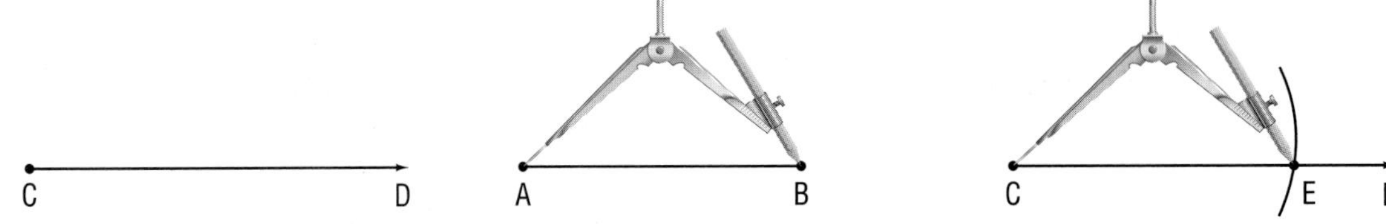

Repeat the construction in your notebook. Then, write a description of each step.

Example 2

Use ruler and compasses to construct an angle congruent to ∠ABC shown above.

Solution

Study the steps.

Step 1 **Step 2** **Step 3**

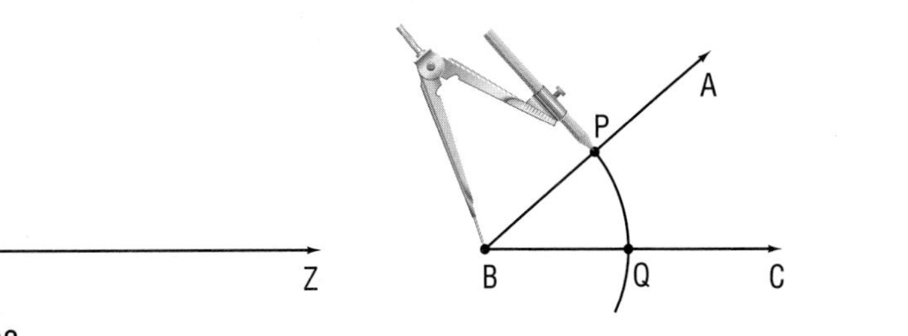

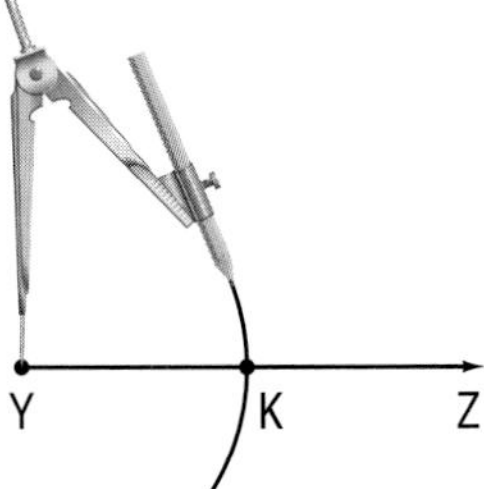

Step 4

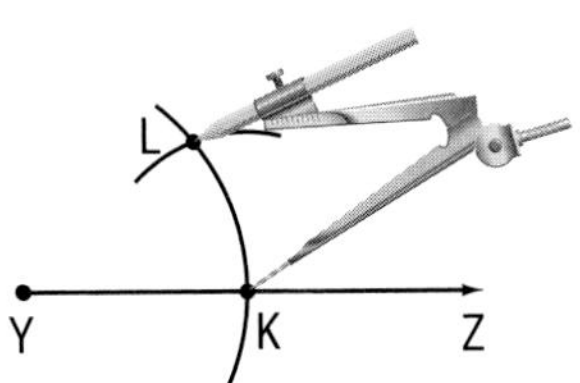

Step 5

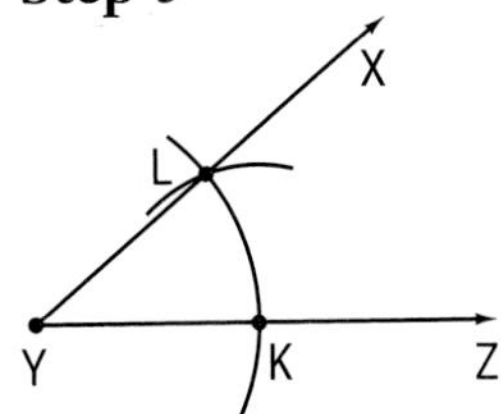

Repeat the construction in your notebook. Then, write a description of each step.

Practice

Draw a line segment of the given length. Use the method of your choice to construct a congruent line segment.

1. 4 cm **2.** 6.2 cm **3.** 55 mm

4. 9 cm **5.** 7.8 cm **6.** 69 mm

Draw each angle with a protractor. Then, use the method of your choice to construct a congruent angle. Check your construction by measurement.

7. 40° **8.** 90° **9.** 60°

10. 75° **11.** 120° **12.** 160°

Problems and Applications

13. Trace ∠WXY. Construct an angle twice the size of ∠WXY.

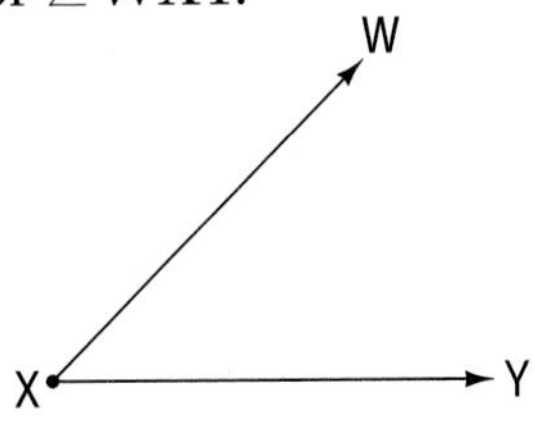

14. Use a ruler and protractor to draw the figure shown. Then, construct a figure congruent to it.

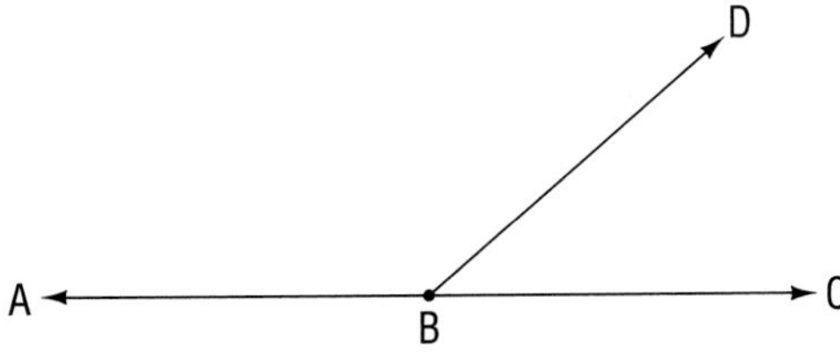

15. Use a protractor to draw a 35° angle. Construct an angle three times larger.

16. Draw a 30° and a 50° angle with a protractor. Construct an angle whose measure is the sum of the two angles.

17. Draw any line segment. Use any method of your choice to construct a triangle whose sides are the same length as your line segment.

LOGIC POWER

Each side of the box is painted a different colour. Predict the number of different ways you can put this block into the box. Check by acting out the problem.

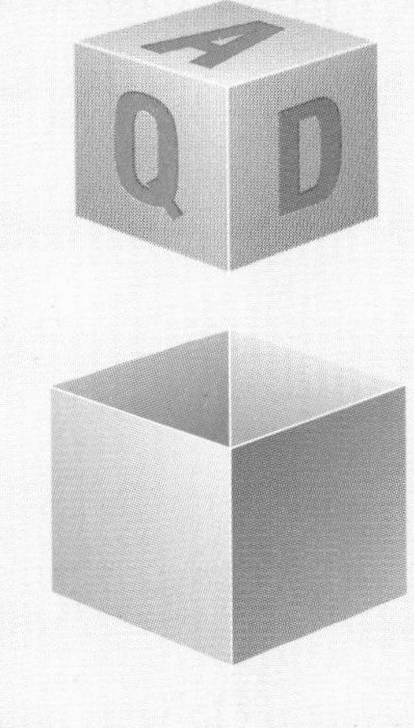

13.2 Constructing Bisectors

A **bisector** divides a figure into 2 equal parts. The **right bisector** of a line segment divides the line into 2 equal parts at right angles.

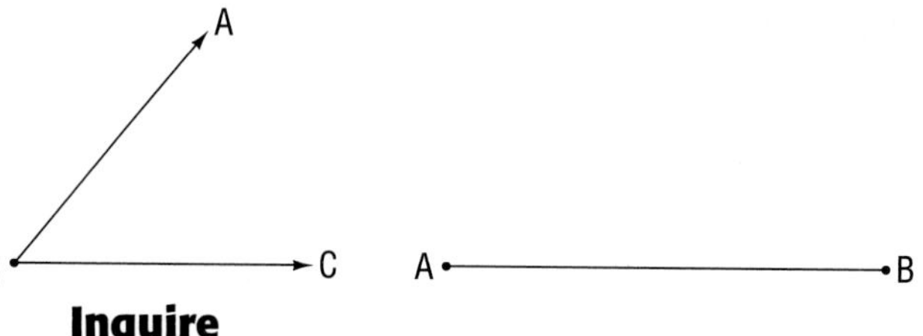

Activity: Explore the Method

Use each of the following to bisect ∠ABC and to construct the right bisector of line segment AB.

a) paper folding **b)** protractor **c)** Mira

Inquire

1. Which method or methods do you prefer? Why?

2. Describe the steps in your method.

3. Compare your method with your classmates' methods.

Example 1

Use ruler and compasses to construct the bisector of ∠ABC shown above.

Solution

Study the steps.

Step 1

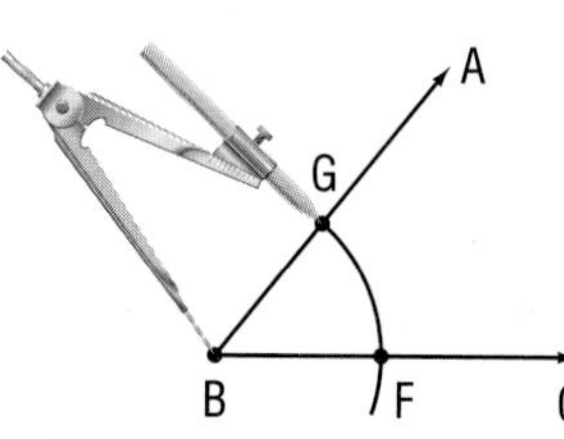

Step 2

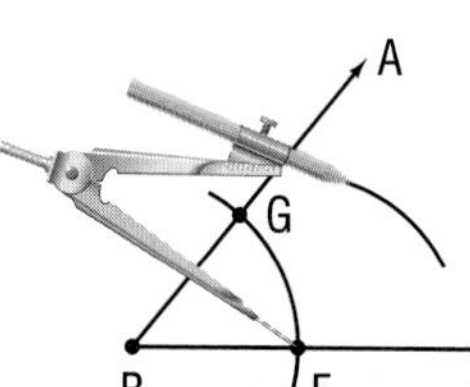

Step 3

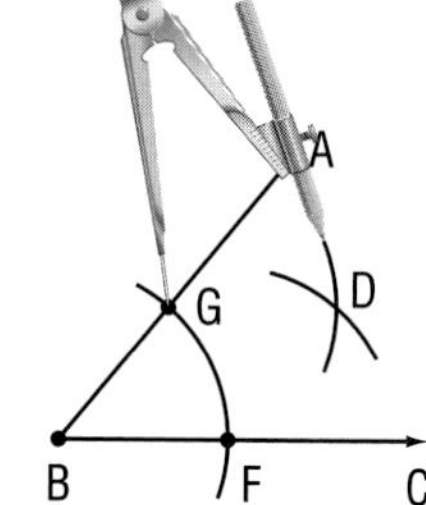

Step 4

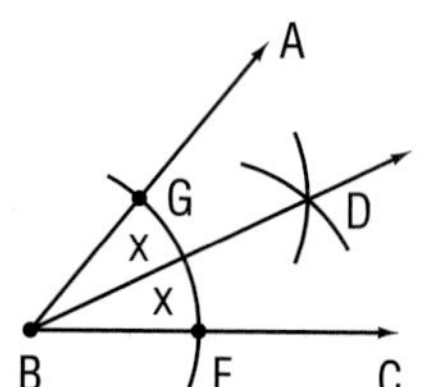

Repeat the construction in your notebook. Then, write a description of each step.

Example 2

Use ruler and compasses to construct the right bisector of AB shown above.

Solution

Study the steps.

Step 1

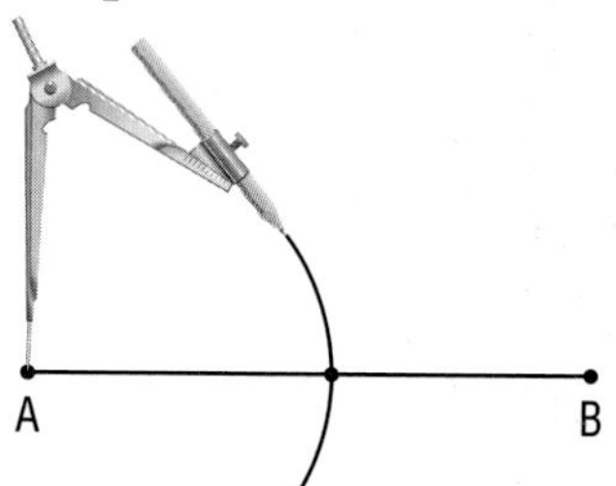

Step 2

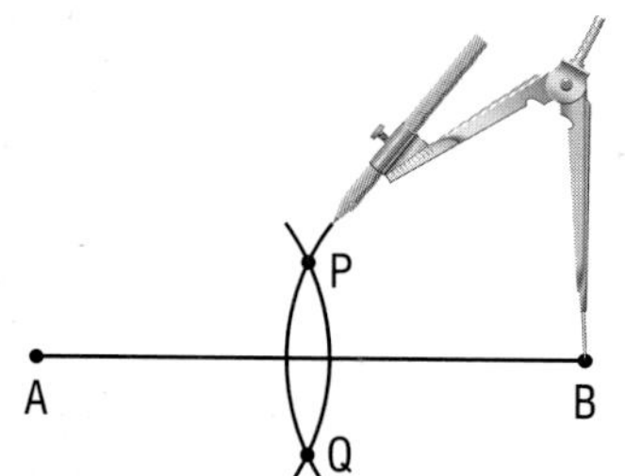

Step 3

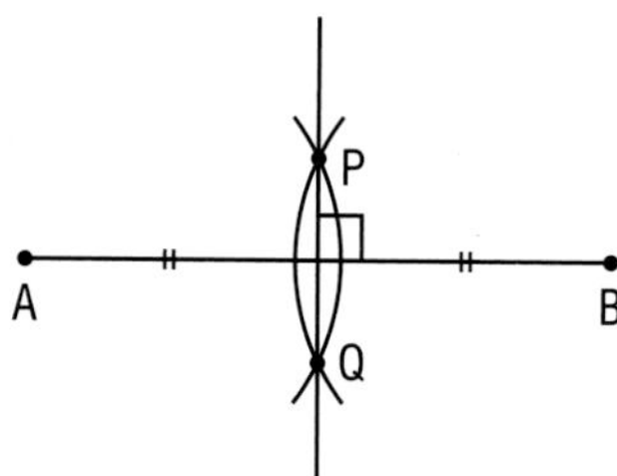

Repeat the construction in your notebook. Then, write a description of each step.

Practice

Draw an angle with each of the following measures. Use the method of your choice to construct the bisector of each angle.

1. 80° **2.** 30° **3.** 50° **4.** 145°

Draw a line segment with each of the following lengths. Use two methods of your choice to construct the right bisector of each line segment.

5. 4 cm **6.** 10 cm **7.** 9 cm

Problems and Applications

8. Draw straight angle ∠RST.

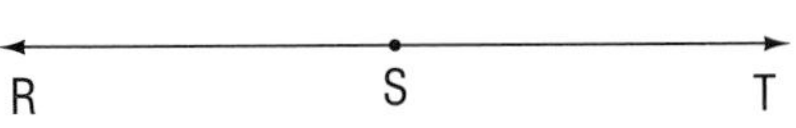

a) Bisect ∠RST.
b) What are the measures of the two new angles?

9. Draw an acute, a right, and an obtuse triangle.

a) Bisect all the angles for each triangle.
b) Extend each bisector to meet another bisector. Describe the result.

10. Draw any △DEF. Construct the right bisector of DE.

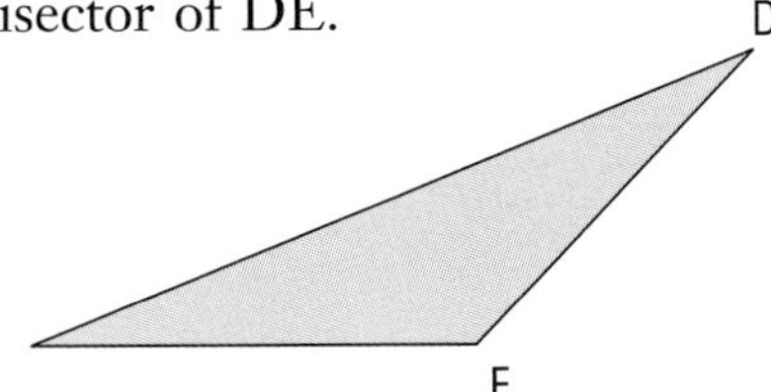

11. a) Draw any △MNO. Construct the right bisector of each side.
b) Extend each right bisector to meet another right bisector. Describe the result.

12. Draw any △PQR.

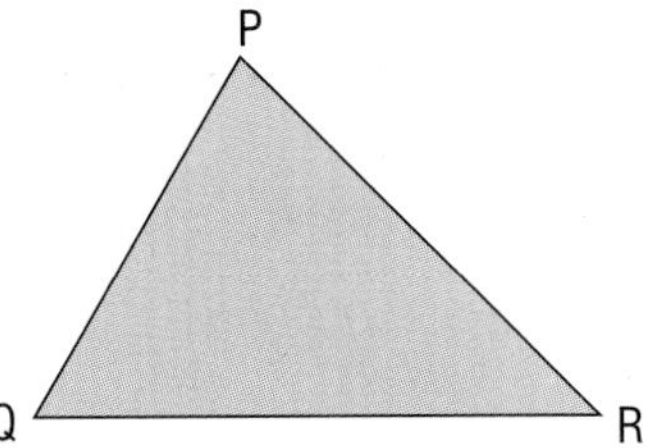

a) Construct the right bisectors of PQ and QR. Label the point where they intersect A.
b) Use compasses to draw a circle with centre A and radius AP. Describe your results.

13. Draw any obtuse △ ABC.

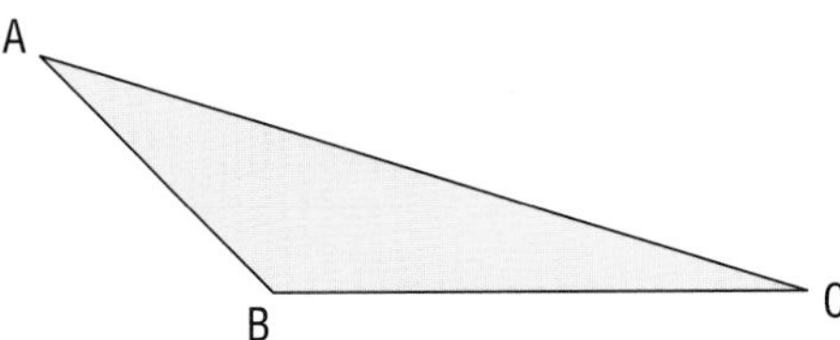

a) Construct the right bisectors of AB and BC and label the point where they meet P.
b) Use compasses to draw a circle with centre P and radius PA. Describe your results.

14. Use your research skills to find out what a *compass card* is and how it is used. Construct a compass card.

NUMBER POWER

How many squares, including the large one, are in the diagram shown below?

13.3 Constructing Perpendiculars

If 2 lines are perpendicular, they meet at a 90° angle.

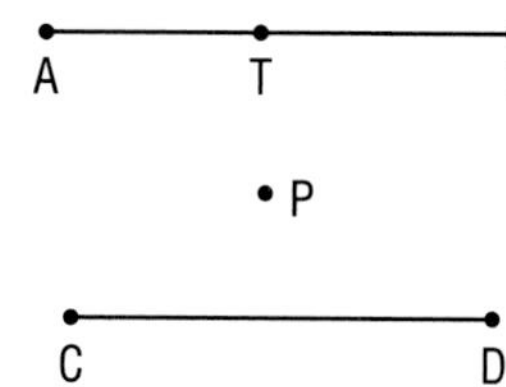

Activity: Explore the Method

Use each of the following to construct a perpendicular to AB at T and from P to CD.

a) paper folding **b)** protractor **c)** Mira

Inquire

1. Which method or methods do you prefer? Explain.

2. Describe the steps in your method.

3. Compare your method with your classmates' methods.

Example 1

Use ruler and compasses to construct a perpendicular to AB at T shown above.

Solution

Study the steps.

Step 1  **Step 2** **Step 3** **Step 4**

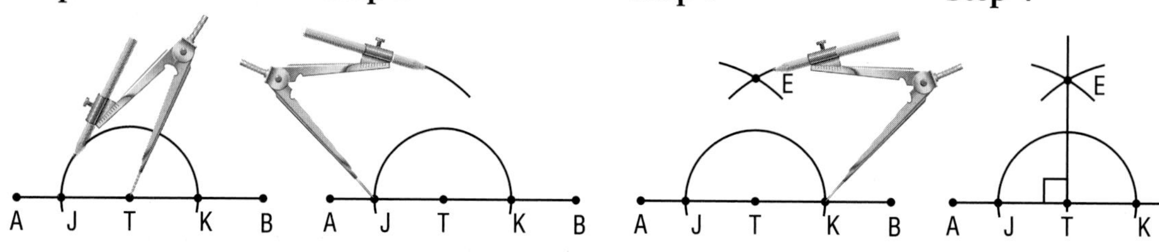

Repeat the construction in your notebook. Then, write a description of each step.

Example 2

Use ruler and compasses to construct the perpendicular from P to CD shown above.

Solution

Study the steps.

Step 1 **Step 2** **Step 3** **Step 4**

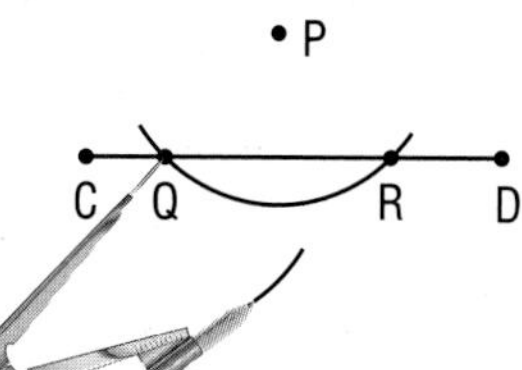

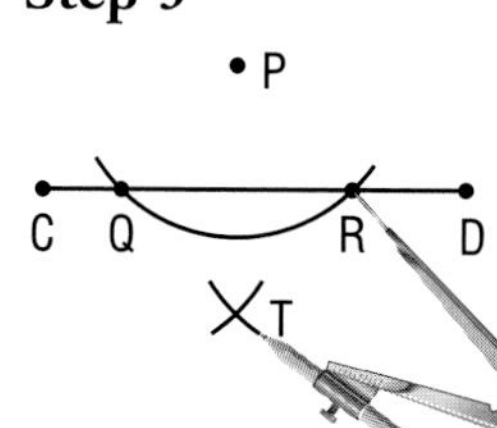

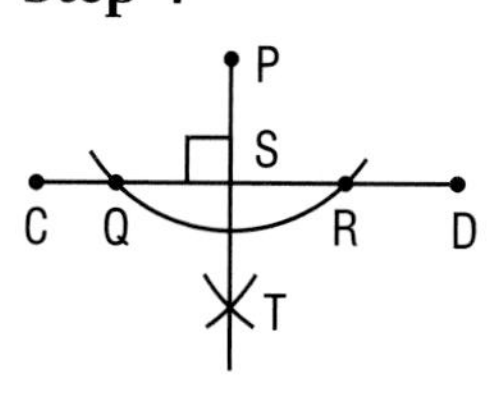

Repeat the construction in your notebook. Then, write a description for each step.

Practice

Draw each diagram. Use the method of your choice to construct a perpendicular at P.

1. **2.**

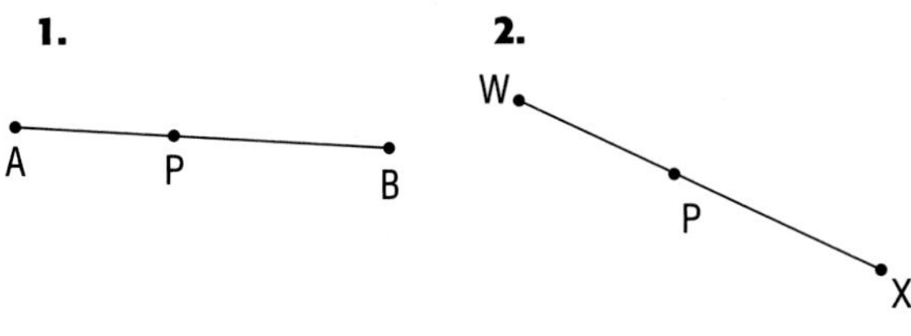

3. **4.**

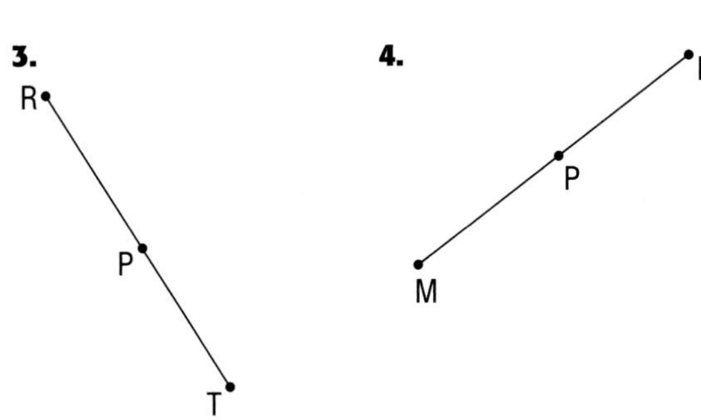

Draw each diagram. Use the method of your choice to construct a perpendicular from P to the line segment.

5. **6.**

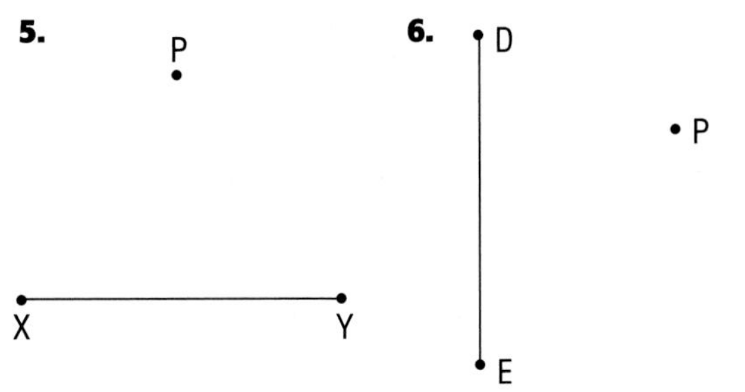

7. **8.**

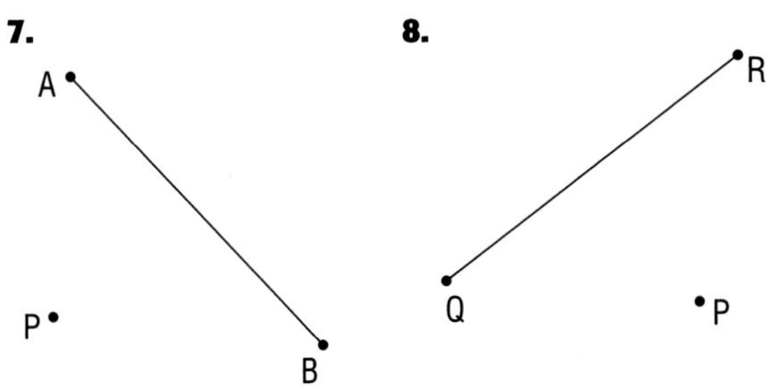

9. Construct a perpendicular to JK at J.

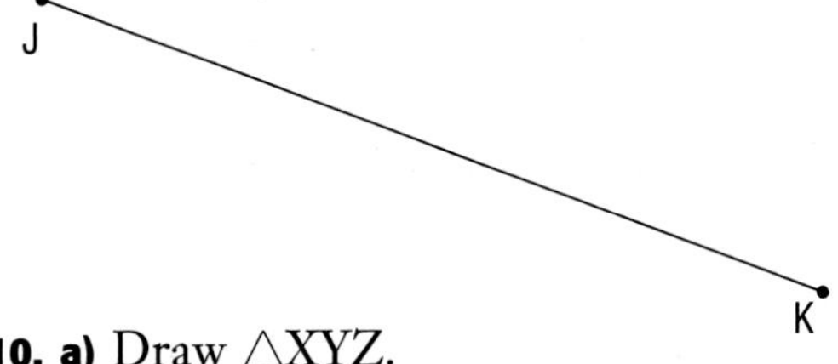

10. a) Draw △XYZ.

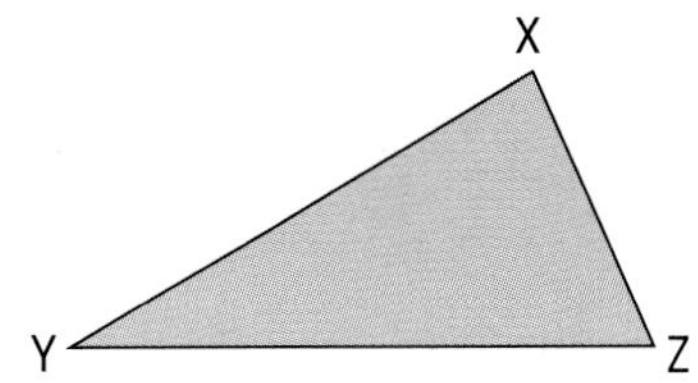

Construct the perpendicular from X to YZ, intersecting YZ at M. XM is called an **altitude** of △XYZ.

b) Draw △PQR.

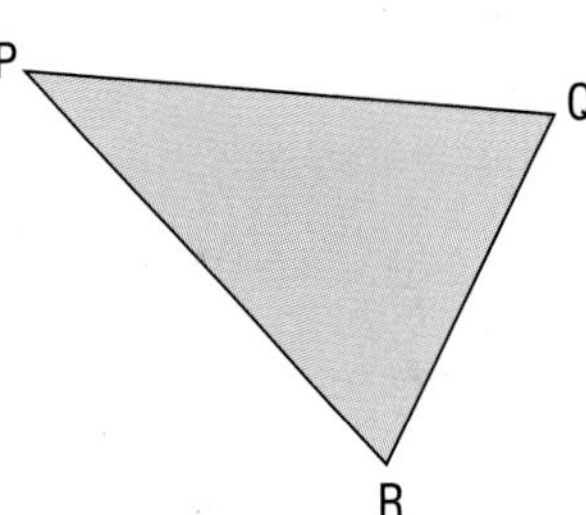

Construct the 3 altitudes for △PQR. Describe your results.

DESIGN POWER

Create designs that include 5 circles of the same size and have the following number of lines of symmetry.

a) 2 **b)** 4 **c)** 3 **d)** 5

Compare your designs with your classmates'.

13.4 Constructing Parallel Lines

By permission of Johnny Hart and Creators Syndicate Inc.

Lines that are in the same plane and do not meet are called **parallel lines.**

Activity: Explore the Method

Given point P and a line AB, use each of the following to construct a line through P parallel to AB.

a) ruler **b)** paper folding **c)** Mira

P

A B

Inquire

1. Which method do you prefer? Explain.

2. Describe the steps in your method.

3. Explain why the line through P is parallel to AB.

Example

Use ruler and compasses to construct a line through P parallel to AB shown above.

Solution

Study the steps.

Step 1

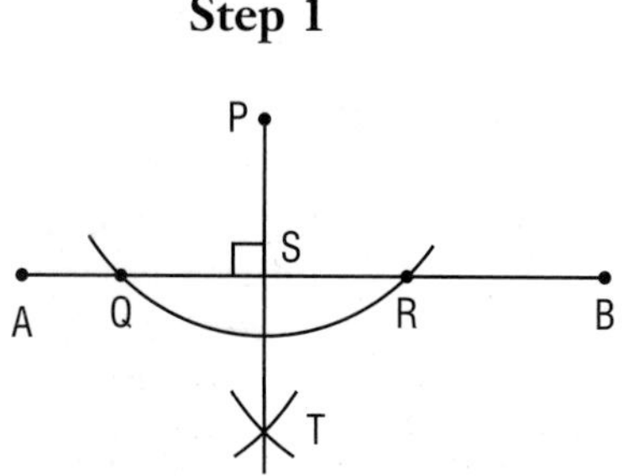

Step 2

D P F C S A Q R B T

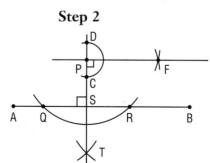

Repeat the construction in your notebook. Then, write a description of each step.

Practice

Copy each diagram. Use the method of your choice to construct a line through P parallel to the line segment.

1.

P

A B

2.

X P

Y

3.

M N

P

4.

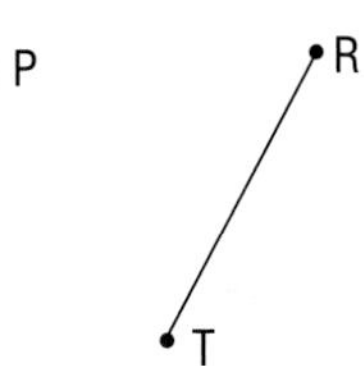

Problems and Applications

5. Trace the figure shown.

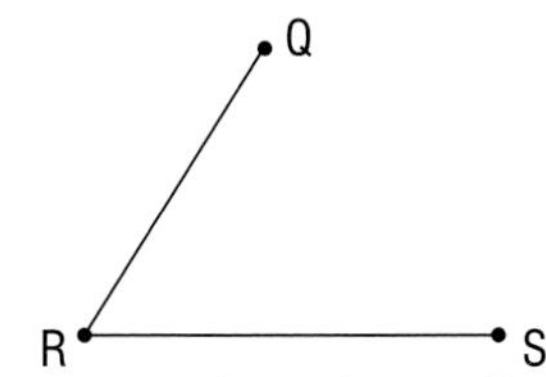

a) Construct a line through Q parallel to RS.
b) Construct a line through S parallel to QR.
c) Name the new figure.

6. Construct a square with 5-cm sides.

7. These diagrams show another way to construct parallel lines. The compasses are set to radius AP.

Step 1

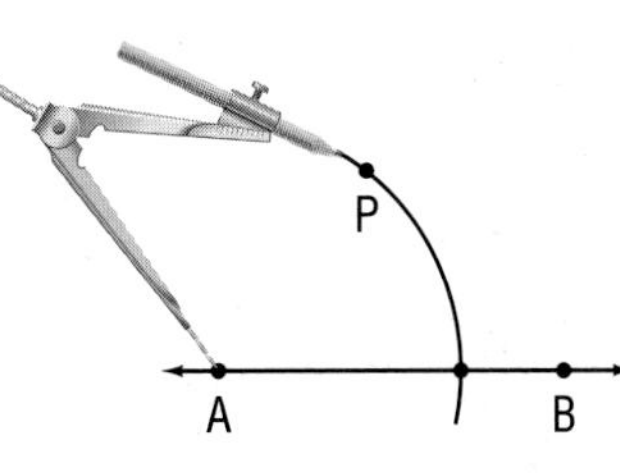

Step 2

P

A B

Step 3

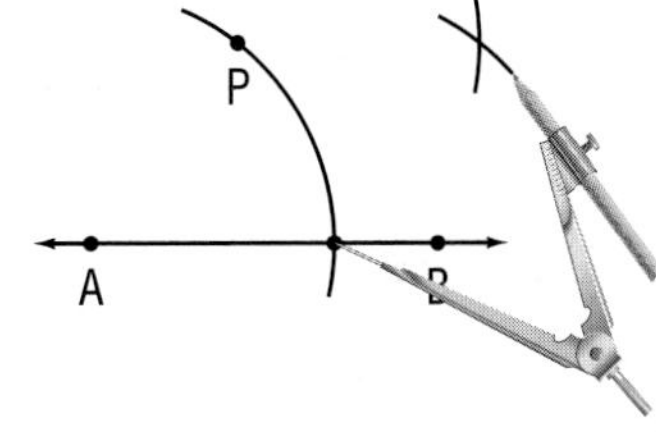

Step 4

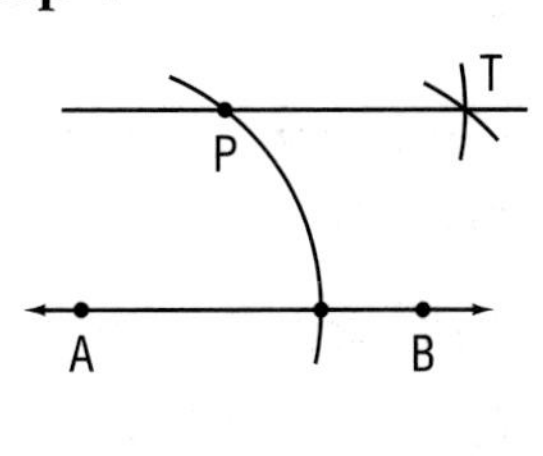

a) Copy the construction and describe the steps.
b) How could you check that PT is parallel to AB?

8. Suppose that the point P is not given. Construct a line parallel to AB and 5 cm from AB.

9. Architects draw parallel lines. Research the methods they use. List other jobs where parallel lines need to be drawn. How are they drawn?

NUMBER POWER

Copy the diagram. Put the numbers from 1 to 9 on the dots so that each side of the triangle adds to 17. The 4 has been placed for you.

4

Computer Assisted Design

The diagram shows a computer-generated design for a simple threaded bolt.

The computer allows us to rotate the design to inspect different views. We can also sketch the design in any direction to observe the effect.

Activity ❶

1. What are the advantages of computer-assisted design over drawing by hand?

2. Describe any advantages that drafting has over computer-assisted design.

3. Compare you opinions with your classmates'.

Activity ❷

1. Research the uses of computer-assisted design.What mathematics does the designer need to know?

2. Describe any uses that you did not expect.

3. Describe your findings to your group.

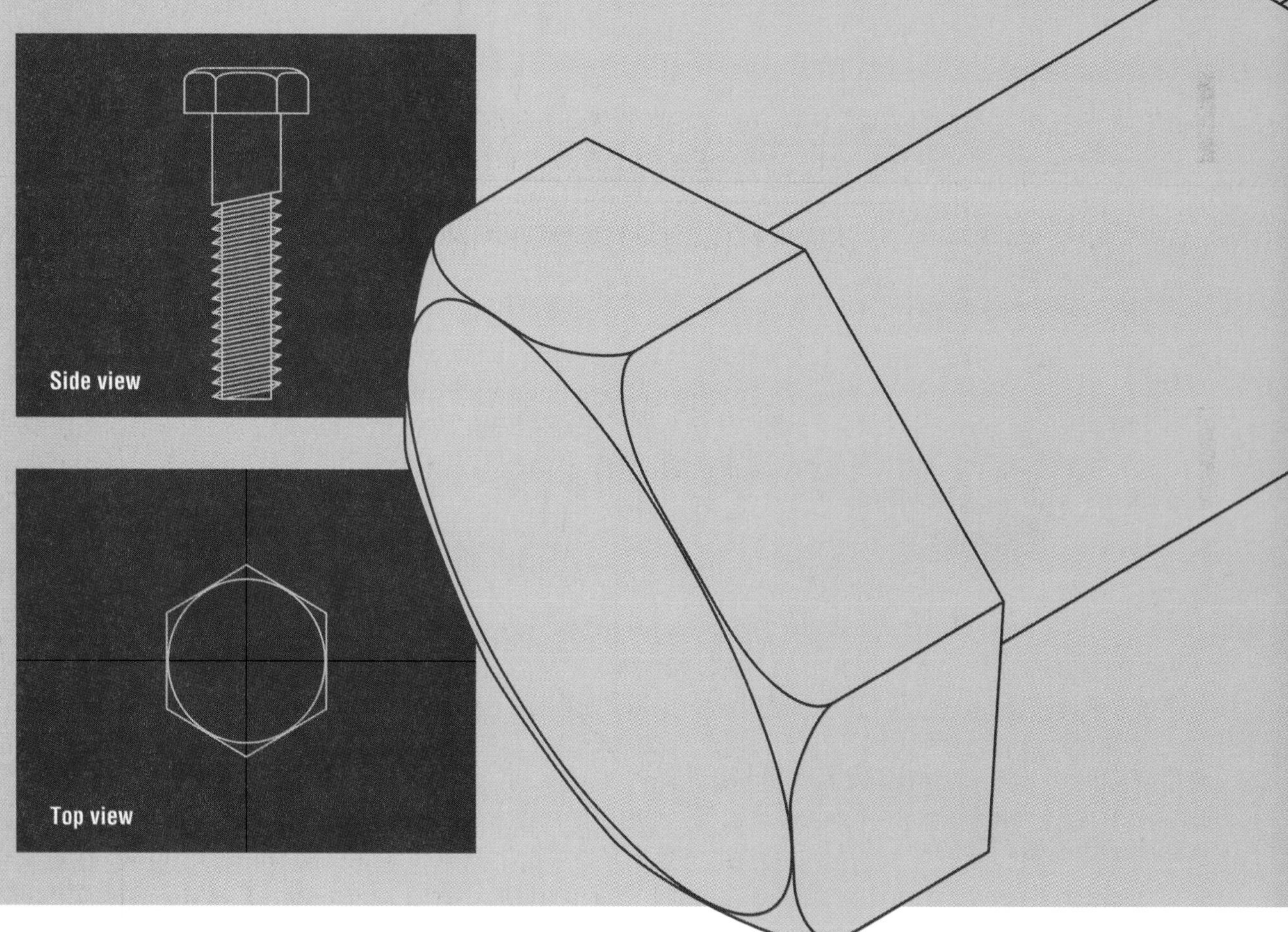

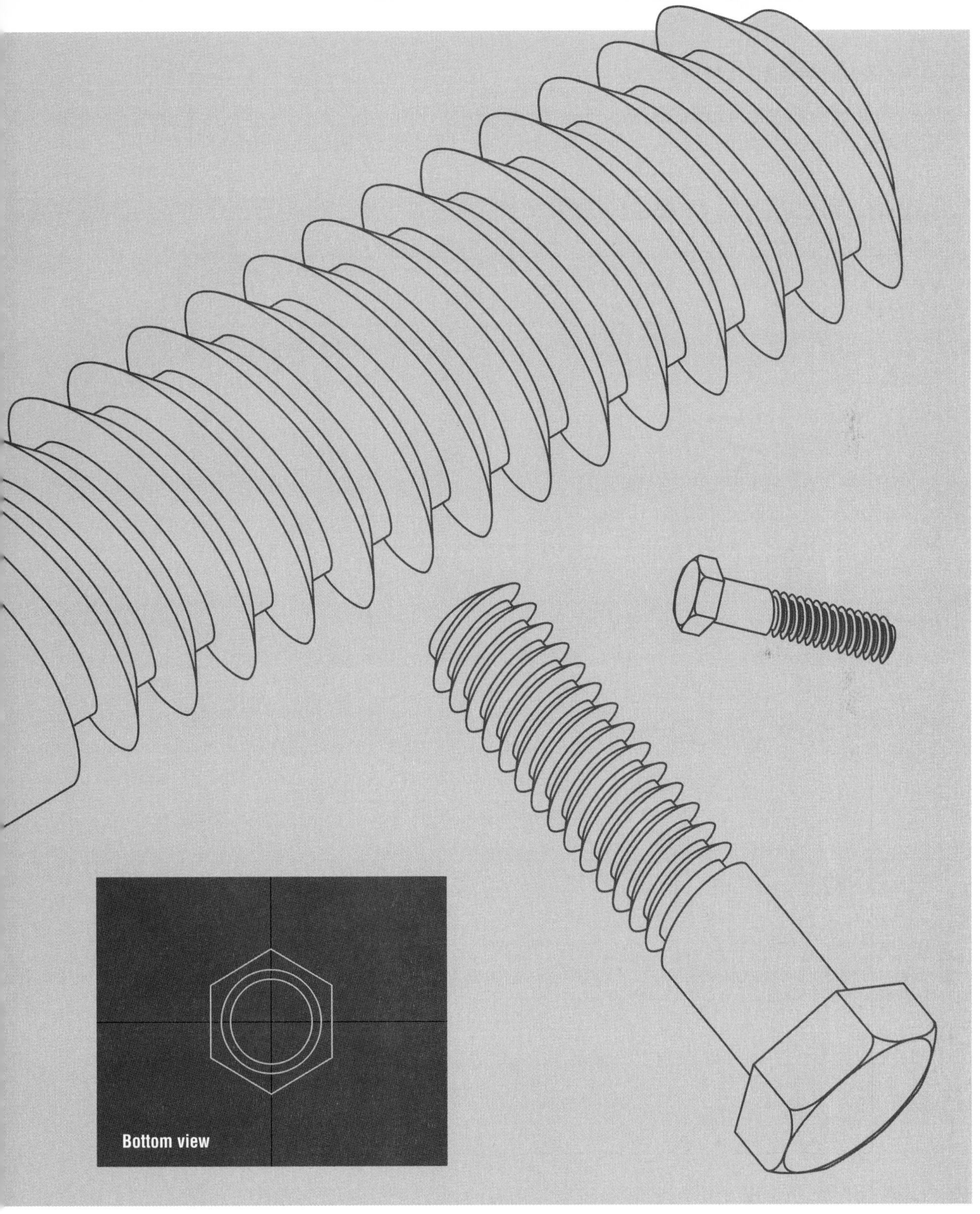
Bottom view

13.5 Constructing Polygons

A variety of polygons can be drawn using different construction methods.

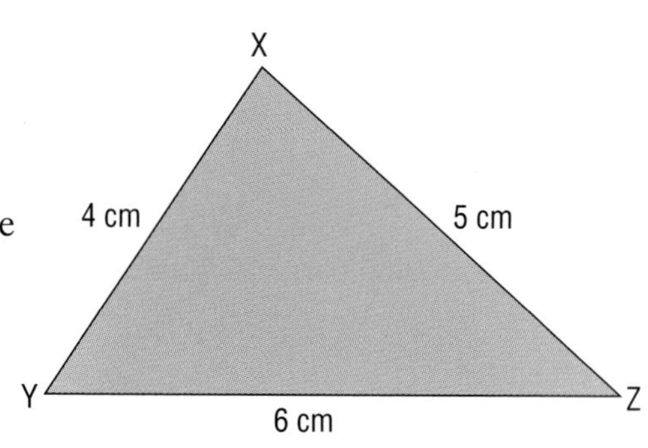

Activity: Explore the Method

Use each of the following to construct △XYZ, where XY = 4 cm, XZ = 5 cm, and YZ = 6 cm.

a) tracing paper
b) ruler and protractor

Inquire

1. Which method do you prefer? Compare your decision with your classmates' decisions.

2. Describe the steps in your method.

3. Use any method to construct these polygons.

a) square **b)** rectangle **c)** parallelogram
d) rhombus **e)** hexagon **f)** triangle

Example

Use ruler and compasses to construct △XYZ shown above, where XY = 4 cm, XZ = 5 cm, and YZ = 6 cm.

Solution

Study the steps.

Step 1

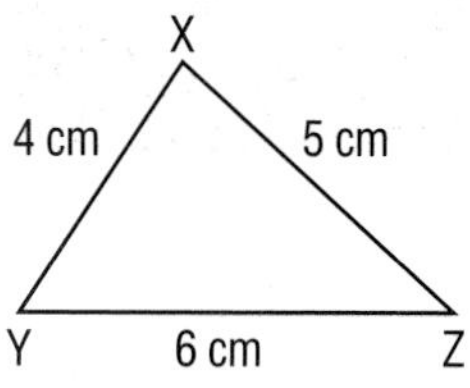

Step 2

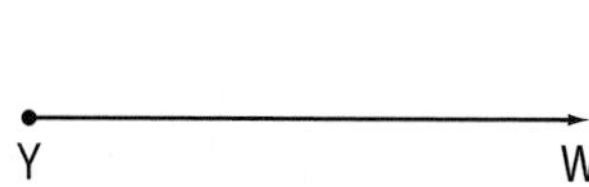

Step 3

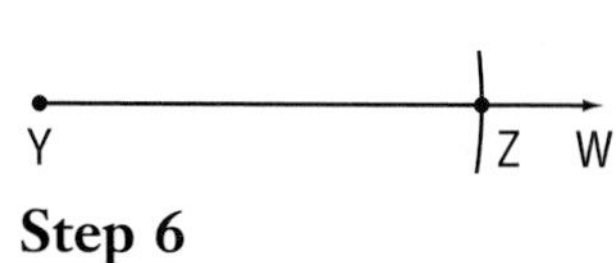

Step 4

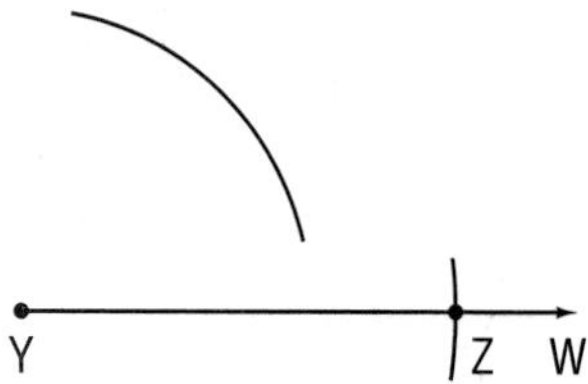

Step 5

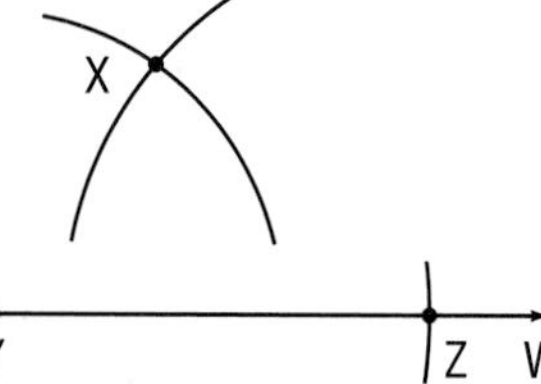

Step 6

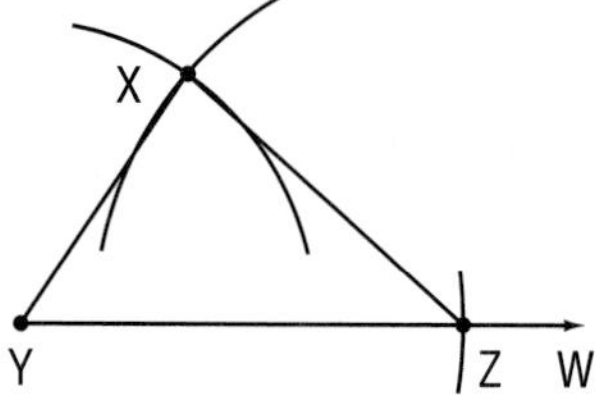

Repeat the construction in your notebook. Then, write a description of each step.

Practice

Use the method of your choice to construct the figure in questions 1–10.

1.

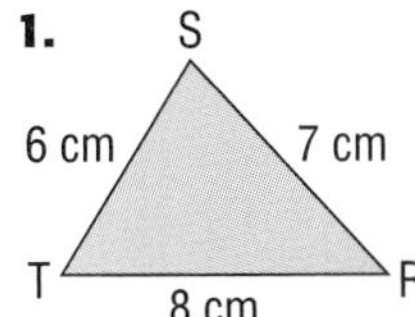

2.

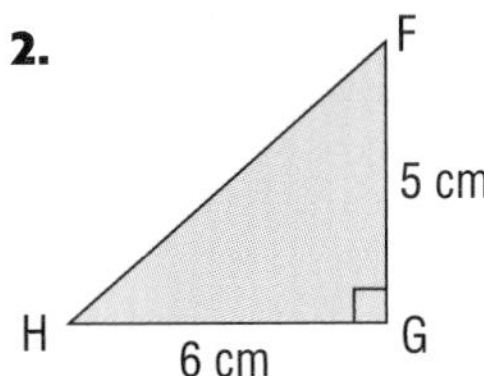

3. △ABC, where AB = 4.5 cm, BC = 6 cm, and AC = 5.5 cm.

4. △DEF, where ∠E = 90°, DE = 6.3 cm, and EF = 6.7 cm.

5. Equilateral triangle RST, where each side is 4.7 cm.

6. Isosceles triangle XYZ, where XY = 4 cm and the other 2 sides are each 5 cm.

7. Square ABCD, where each side is 8 cm.

8.

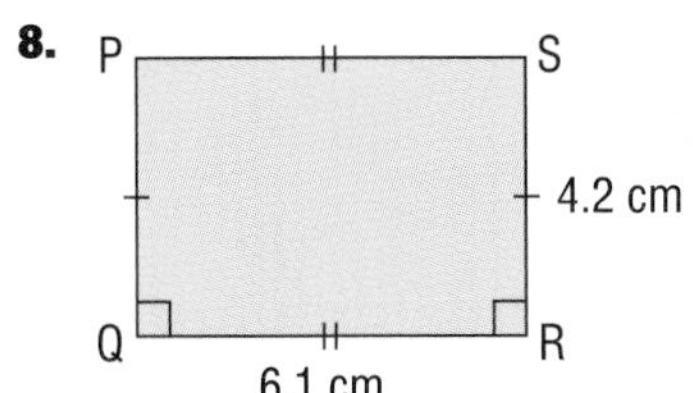

9.

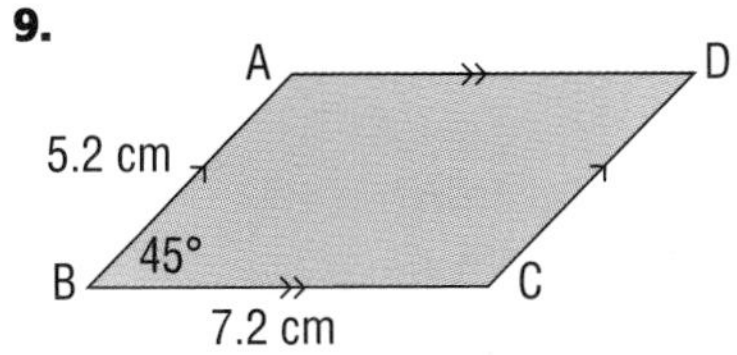

10.

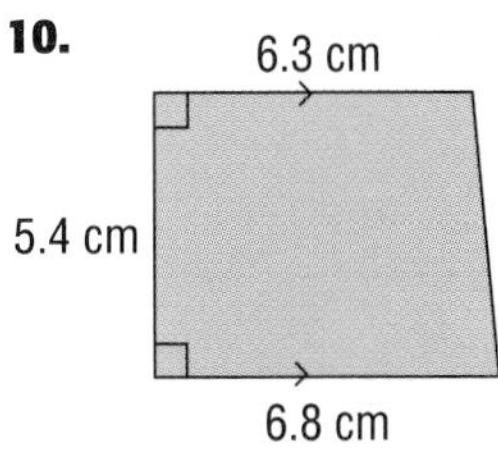

Problems and Applications

Construct the logos by whatever method you choose.

11.

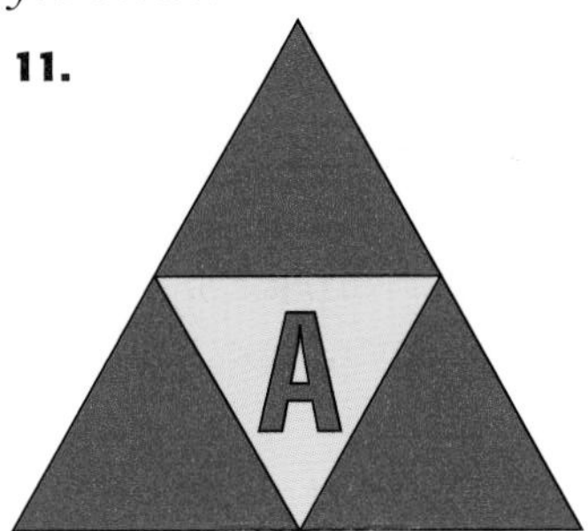

12.

13.

WORD POWER

The words *lion*, *goat*, and *kangaroo* each contain 50% vowels and 50% consonants. List 5 other creatures whose names contain 50% vowels and 50% consonants. Compare your list with a classmate's.

Paper Airplanes

People who design and draw the plans for airplanes use lines, angles, triangles, and symmetry.

Paper airplanes are similar to real airplanes. In fact, the designs for modern planes may have first been tested using paper airplanes. To make a paper airplane, use heavy paper, tape, and scissors.

Activity ❶

1. Build the plane. It is designed to fly long distances.

2. Test how far it will fly.

a) Crease the paper on its centre line.

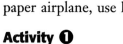

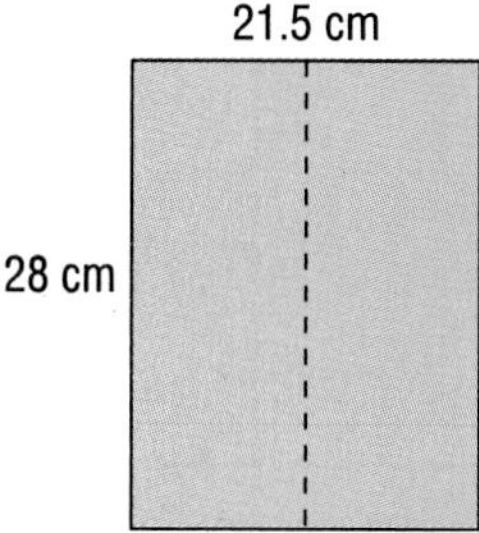

b) Fold the corners in toward the centre.

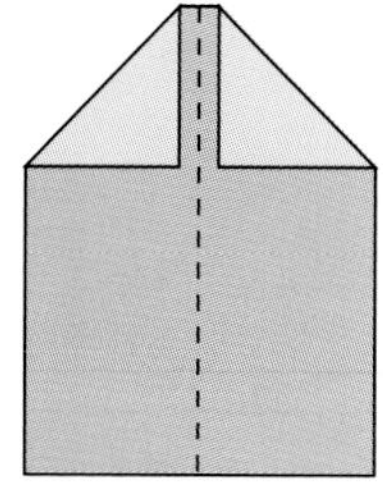

c) Fold the sides in toward the centre on the dotted lines.

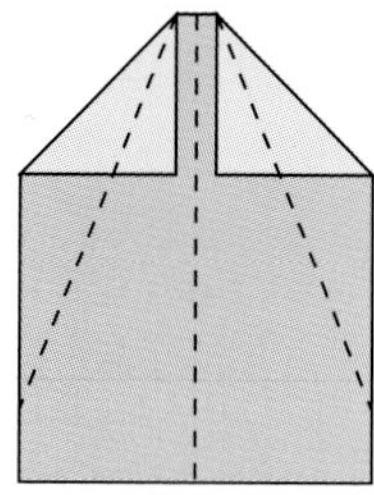

d) Fold the sides away from you along the dotted line.

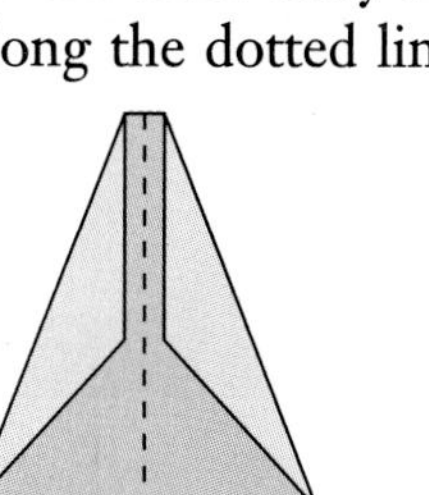

e) Turn the plane sideways.

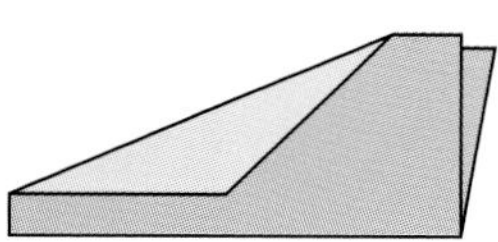

f) Fold each side down on the dotted line.

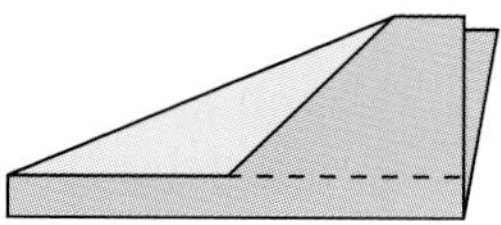

g) The plane looks like this.

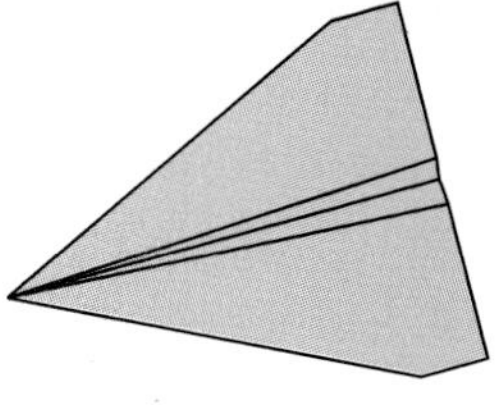

h) Hold the wings with tape.

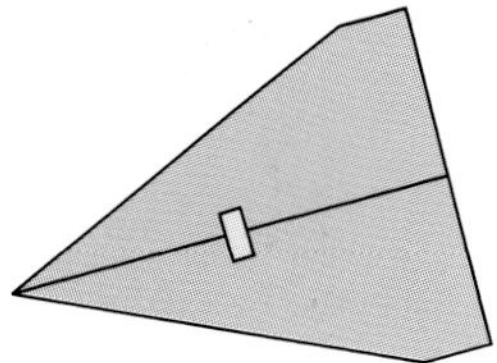

i) Tape the bottom of the plane as shown.

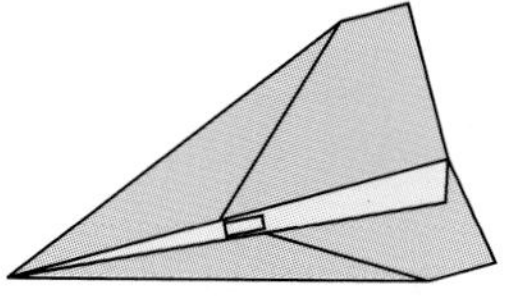

Activity ❷

1. Build the plane. It is designed to perform aerobatics (stunts).

2. Experiment with different ways of launching the plane to see if there is any effect on its performance.

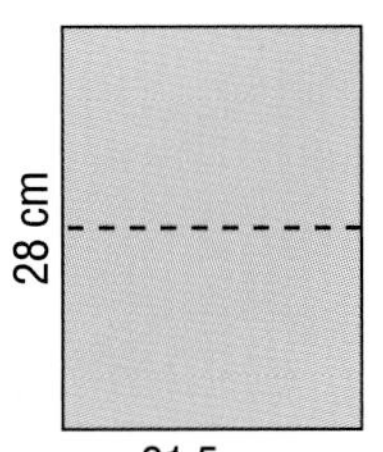

a) Crease the paper across the centre.

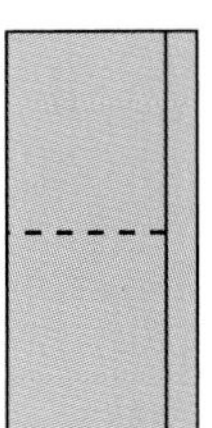

b) Start with a 6-7 mm fold.

c) Continue until there are 11 or 12 cm left.

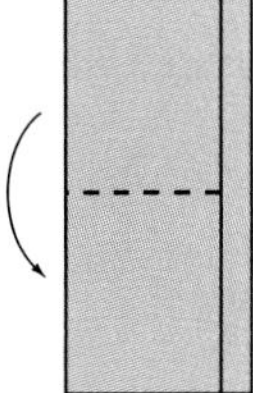

d) Fold in half (top down).

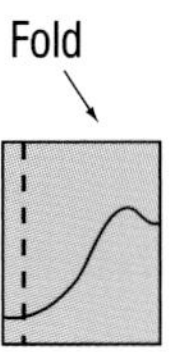

e) Cut as shown.

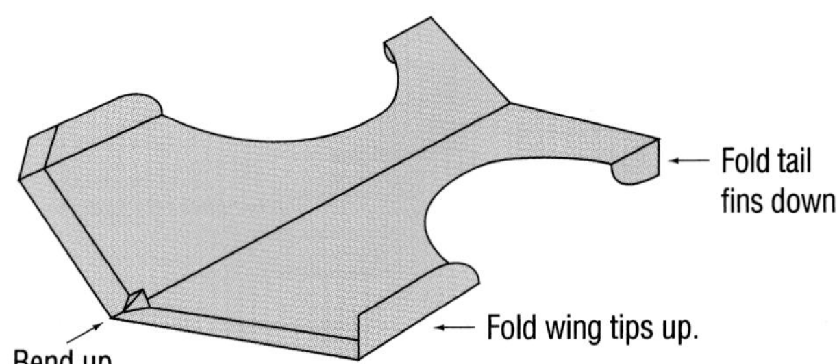

Activity ❸

1. Build the helicopter. It is designed for vertical as well as horizontal flight.

a) Copy the design shown on the right onto a sheet of paper and cut it out.
b) Cut along all solid lines.
c) Fold A forward.
d) Fold B backward.
e) Fold C in.
f) Fold D in.
g) Fold up at E.

2. Experiment with different ways of launching the helicopter. Which seems to be the most effective?

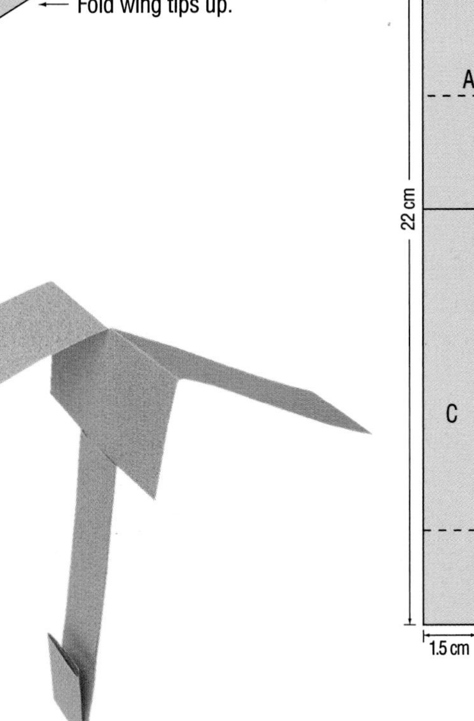

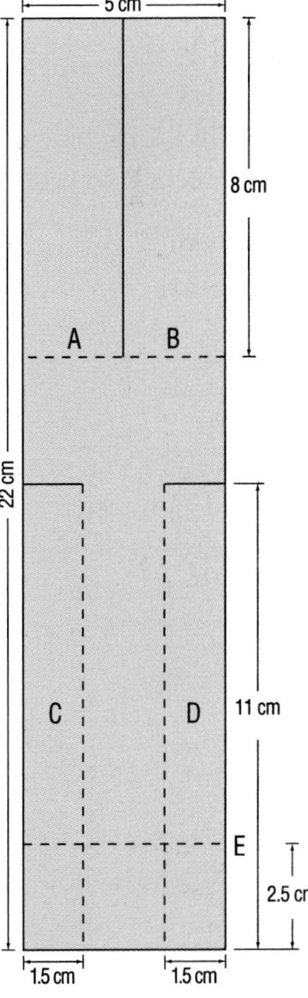

Review

1. Draw and label a line segment AB.

a) Use 2 different methods to construct a line segment equal to AB.

b) Which methods did you use?

c) Which method did you prefer? Why?

Draw line segments with the following lengths. Use the method of your choice to construct a line segment congruent to each.

2. 8 cm 3. 12 cm 4. 15 cm

5. Draw and label an acute angle ABC and an obtuse angle XYZ.

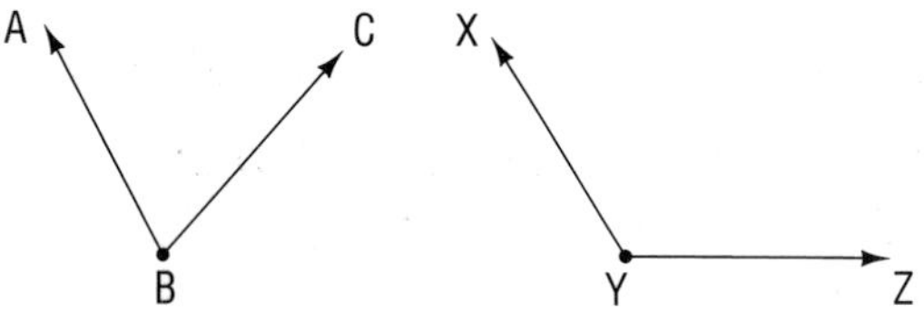

a) Use 2 different methods to construct an angle equal to each of your angles.

b) Which methods did you use?

c) Which method did you prefer? Why?

Draw angles with the following measures. Use the method of your choice to bisect each angle.

6. 70° 7. 110° 8. 45° 9. 94°

10. a) Draw an acute angle, an obtuse angle, and a right angle.

b) Bisect each angle. Check by measuring.

c) Which method did you use? Why?

11. a) Draw line segment AB with point P on the line.

b) Construct a perpendicular to AB at P.

c) Which method did you use? Why?

d) Name another method that you could have used.

12. a) Draw line segment AB with point P not on the line.

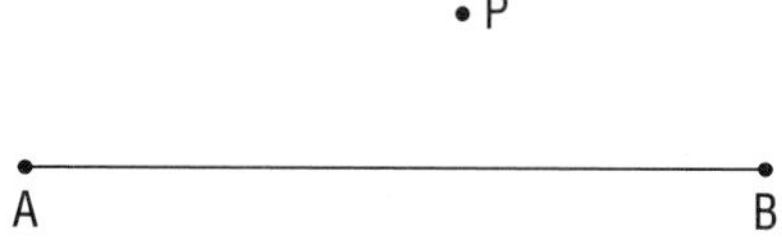

b) Construct a perpendicular from P to AB.

c) Which method did you use? Why?

d) Name another method you could have used.

13. a) Draw a line segment RS. Use 2 different methods to construct the right bisector of RS.

b) Which methods did you use?

c) Which method did you prefer? Why?

14. a) Draw line segment AB with point P not on the line.

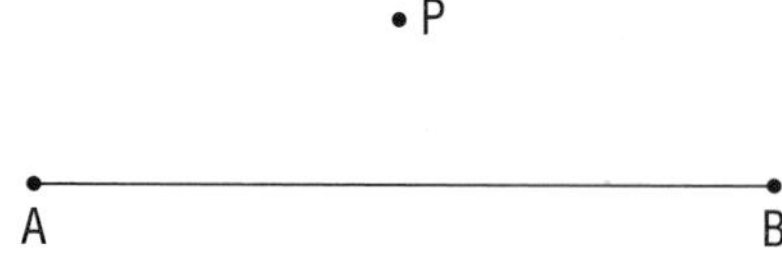

b) Construct a line through P parallel to AB.

c) Compare your method with a classmate's.

d) Explain why you chose the method you did.

15. Draw any △PQR.

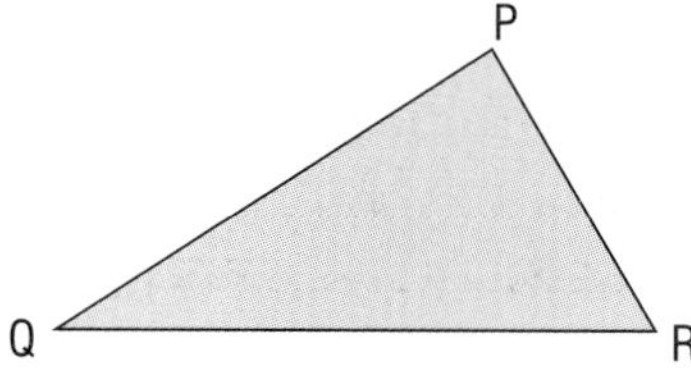

a) Construct a line through R parallel to QP.

b) Construct a line through Q parallel to PR.

c) If the lines through R and Q intersect, what figures have you constructed?

16. Construct square ABCD with each side 4 cm in length.

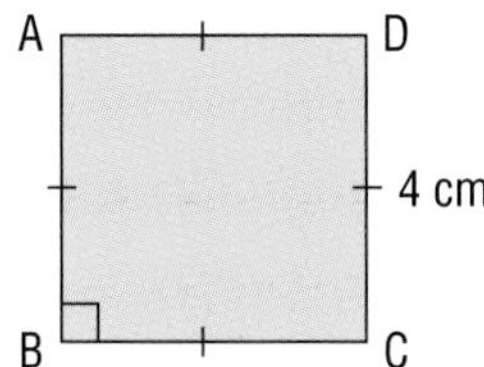

a) Construct the right bisectors of AB, BC, CD, and AD.
b) Extend the right bisectors so that they intersect.
c) Describe the new figures that you have constructed.
d) Join the points where the right bisectors intersect AB, BC, CD, and AD.
e) Describe the new figure.

17. a) Construct △DEF, where DE = 5 cm, EF = 6 cm, and DF = 7 cm.
b) Bisect each angle in the triangle.

18. a) Construct △ABC where AB = 6 cm, BC = 6 cm, and AC = 6 cm.
b) Bisect ∠A.
c) Construct the perpendicular from C to AB.
d) Construct the right bisector of AC.
e) Explain your results.

19. a) Construct any △ABC.

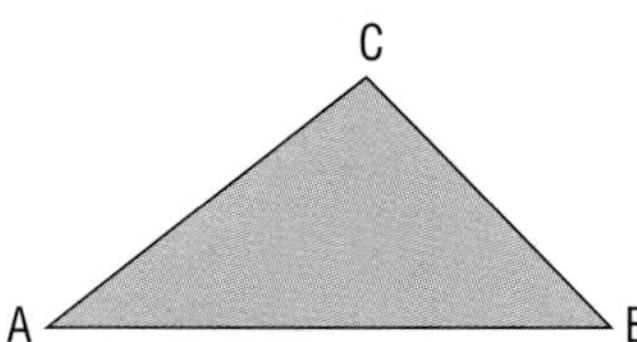

b) Construct the right bisector of AB and label the point on AB, E.
c) Construct the right bisector of AC and label the point on AC, F.
d) Join EF. Measure EF and BC. Explain your results.

Group Decision Making
Organizing a Career Day

The purpose of this activity is to plan a mathematics career day for the students in your school.

1. As a class, brainstorm what will happen on your mathematics career day. Then, decide on a list of tasks. This list might include surveying the students about the type of careers in mathematics that interest them, inviting appropriate speakers, arranging visits to workplaces, obtaining films and videotapes, arranging lunch, rooms, and a schedule of the day's events.

2. As a class, put the tasks in the order that they should be performed. Set the timelines for the tasks to be completed. Decide which groups will take on what tasks.

3. Choose one member from each student group to serve on a class steering committee to co-ordinate the activities.

4. Meet in groups. Decide how your group's tasks will be accomplished.

5. Meet as a class to resolve any problems that the class or individual groups may have.

6. Carry out your group tasks. The steering committee should meet regularly to co-ordinate the activities.

7. Run the career day.

8. Meet in groups first, then as a class, to evaluate the day.

Chapter Check

1. Draw any acute angle ABC. Construct an angle equal to your angle.

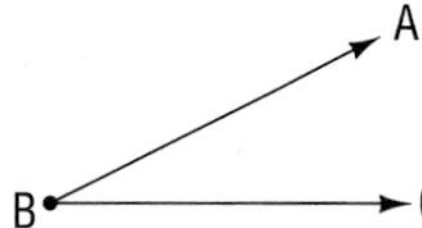

2. Draw a line segment XY with a point P on the line. Construct a perpendicular to XY at P.

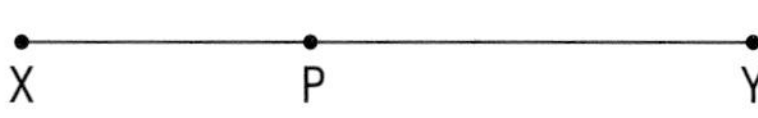

3. Draw a line segment FG with a point P not on the line. Construct a perpendicular from P to FG.

•P

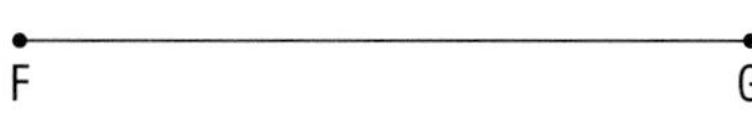

4. Draw any acute angle QRS. Bisect your angle.

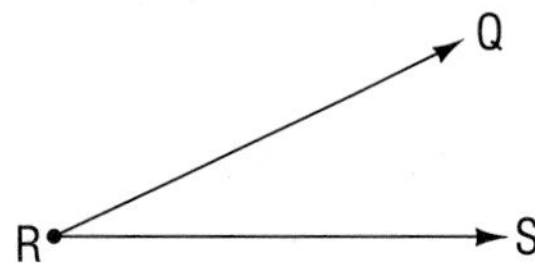

5. Draw a line segment AB. Construct the right bisector of AB.

6. Draw a line WX with a point P not on the line. Construct a line through P parallel to WX.

•P

7. Construct a triangle with sides 3 cm, 4 cm, and 5 cm.

NESTLINGS

chapter one
when dinosaurs ruled the earth.
5-11

dinosaurs used long, long rulers, and could draw lines that stretched on and on forever.

by the time they were through, we had the lines of latitude and longitude, all expertly ruled.

not many people know these things.
you don't say.

Reprinted by permission of Warren Clements

Using the Strategies

1. a) Calculate the volume of the box of tissues.

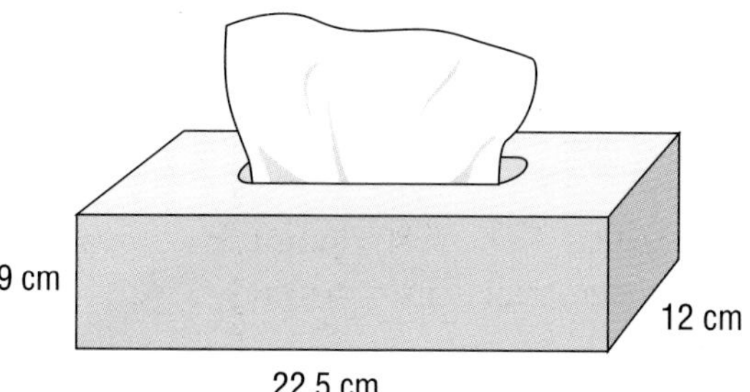

b) Boxes of tissues are packed in cartons with 9 boxes on the bottom (3 boxes by 3 boxes) and 4 layers of boxes. What is the volume of the carton?

2. Charlene works as a guide in a white water rafting park. She has the choice of being paid $43.00 a day or $1.50 per person in her group. How many does she need in a group to make more than $43.00?

3. There are 4 teams in a volleyball tournament. Each team will play each of the other teams twice. How many games will be played in the tournament?

4. Gerry gets up at 06:15. It takes him 55 min to dress and eat breakfast. Then, he drives 1 h and 15 min to arrive at his job in Edmonton. At what time does he arrive in Edmonton?

5. Use the digits 1, 2, 3, 4, and 5 to give the smallest 2-digit answer.

```
  ■ ■ ■
−   ■ ■
―――――――
```

6. A staircase 3 steps high is built with cubes. How many cubes will be needed for a staircase 8 steps high?

7. Use the following information to calculate the cost of these pizzas.

a) a small pizza with bacon, olives, and pepperoni

b) a large pizza with all 6 toppings

c) a medium pizza with green peppers, bacon, pineapple, and anchovies

Special Pizza Month

Small	Medium	Large
$7.25	$10.45	$13.95

Includes 2 Toppings
Extra Toppings 75¢

Toppings

pepperoni, green peppers, olives, pineapple, bacon, anchovies

8. a) Determine the rule used to produce the sequence of numbers.

3, 5, 9, 17, 33, …

b) Write the next three numbers in the sequence.

c) Use the same rule to complete the following.

4, 9, 19, ■, ■, ■
2, ■, 11, ■, ■

9. Canada celebrated its 125th birthday in 1992. The United States celebrated its 200th birthday in 1976. How many years older than Canada is the United States?

DATA BANK

1. How many planets are closer to the sun than the Earth?

2. Use the DATA BANK to create a problem. Have a classmate solve it.

CANADIAN DRIVING DISTANCES BETWEEN CITIES

	Edmonton	Halifax	Montreal	Ottawa	Quebec	Regina	Saint John	St. John's	Saskatoon	Toronto	Vancouver	Victoria	Whitehorse	Winnipeg
Calgary	299	4973	3743	3553	4014	764	4664	6334	620	3434	1057	1162	2385	1336
Edmonton		5013	3764	3574	4035	785	4704	6367	528	3455	1244	1349	2086	1357
Halifax			1249	1439	982	4228	309	1503	4485	1788	6050	6154	7099	3656
Montreal				190	270	2979	940	2602	3236	539	4801	4905	5850	2408
Ottawa					460	2789	1130	2792	3046	399	4611	4715	5660	2218
Quebec						3249	673	2363	3507	809	5071	5176	6120	2678
Regina							3919	5581	257	2670	1822	1926	2871	571
Saint John								1727	4176	1479	5741	5845	6790	3347
St. John's									5839	3141	7403	7775	8452	5010
Saskatoon										2927	1677	1782	2614	829
Toronto											4492	4596	5528	2099
Vancouver												105	2697	2232
Victoria													2802	2337
Whitehorse														3524
Winnipeg														

AREAS OF CANADIAN PROVINCES

Province	Area (km^2)	Province	Area (km^2)
Newfoundland	404 517	Ontario	1 068 582
New Brunswick	73 436	Manitoba	650 087
Nova Scotia	55 491	Saskatchewan	651 900
Prince Edward Island	5 657	Alberta	661 185
Quebec	1 540 680	British Columbia	948 596

CANADIAN FLYING DISTANCES BETWEEN CITIES

From	To	(km)
Calgary	Edmonton	248
	Montreal	3003
	Ottawa	2877
	Regina	661
	Saskatoon	520
	Toronto	2686
	Vancouver	685
	Victoria	725
	Winnipeg	1191
Charlottetown	Ottawa	976
	Toronto	1326
Edmonton	Calgary	248
	Ottawa	2848
	Regina	698
	Saskatoon	484
	Toronto	2687
	Vancouver	826
	Winnipeg	1187
Halifax	Montreal	803
	Ottawa	958
	Saint John	192
	St. John's	880
	Sydney	306
	Toronto	1287
Montreal	Calgary	3003
	Fredericton	562
	Halifax	803
	Moncton	707
	Ottawa	151
	Saint John	614
	St. John's	1618
	Toronto	508
	Vancouver	3679
	Winnipeg	1816

From	To	(km)
Ottawa	Calgary	2877
	Charlottetown	976
	Edmonton	2848
	Halifax	958
	Montreal	151
	Toronto	363
	Vancouver	3550
	Winnipeg	1687
Regina	Calgary	661
	Edmonton	698
	Saskatoon	239
	Toronto	2026
	Vancouver	1330
	Winnipeg	533
St. John's	Halifax	880
	Montreal	1618
	Toronto	2122
Toronto	Calgary	2686
	Charlottetown	1326
	Edmonton	2687
	Halifax	1287
	Montreal	508
	Ottawa	363
	Regina	2026
	St.John's	2122
	Vancouver	3342
	Windsor	314
	Winnipeg	1502
Victoria	Calgary	725
	Vancouver	62
Windsor	Toronto	314
Winnipeg	Calgary	1191
	Edmonton	1187
	Montreal	1816
	Ottawa	1687
	Regina	533
	Saskatoon	707
	Toronto	1502
	Vancouver	1862

PRIME MINISTERS SINCE CONFEDERATION

	Prime Minister	From	To
1	Rt. Hon. Sir John A. Macdonald, (Cons.)	01-07-1867	05-11-1873
2	Hon. Alexander Mackenzie, (Lib.)	07-11-1873	08-10-1878
3	Rt. Hon. Sir John A. Macdonald, (Cons.)	17-10-1878	06-06-1891
4	Hon. Sir John J.C. Abbott, (Cons.)	16-06-1891	24-11-1892
5	Rt. Hon. Sir John S.D. Thompson, (Cons.)	05-12-1892	12-12-1894
6	Rt. Hon. Sir Mackenzie Bowell, (Cons.)	21-12-1894	27-04-1896
7	Rt. Hon. Sir Charles Tupper, (Cons.)	01-05-1896	08-07-1896
8	Rt. Hon. Sir Wilfrid Laurier, (Lib.)	11-07-1896	06-10-1911
9	Rt. Hon. Sir Robert L. Borden, (Cons.)	10-10-1911	12-10-1917
10	Rt. Hon. Sir Robert L. Borden, (Unionist)	12-10-1917	10-07-1920
11	Rt. Hon. Arthur Meighen, (Unionist-Lib. and Cons.)	10-07-1920	09-12-1921
12	Rt. Hon. Wm. Lyon Mackenzie King, C.M.G., (Lib.)	29-12-1921	08-06-1926
13	Rt. Hon. Arthur Meighen, (Cons.)	29-06-1926	25-09-1926
14	Rt. Hon. Wm. Lyon Mackenzie King, C.M.G., (Lib.)	25-09-1926	07-08-1930
15	Rt. Hon. Robert B. Bennett, (Cons.)	07-08-1930	23-10-1935
16	Rt. Hon. Wm. Lyon Mackenzie King, (Lib.)	23-10-1935	15-11-1948
17	Rt. Hon. Louis Stephen St. Laurent, (Lib.)	15-11-1948	21-06-1957
18	Rt. Hon. John G. Diefenbaker, (Cons.)	21-06-1957	22-04-1963
19	Rt. Hon. Lester B. Pearson, (Lib.)	22-04-1963	20-04-1968
20	Rt. Hon. Pierre Elliott Trudeau, (Lib.)	20-04-1968	04-06-1979
21	Rt. Hon. Charles Joseph Clark, (Cons.)	04-06-1979	03-03-1980
22	Rt. Hon. Pierre Elliott Trudeau, (Lib.)	03-03-1980	30-06-1984
23	Rt. Hon. John Napier Turner, (Lib.)	30-06-1984	17-09-1984
24	Rt. Hon. Martin Brian Mulroney, (Cons.)	17-09-1984	

WHALES

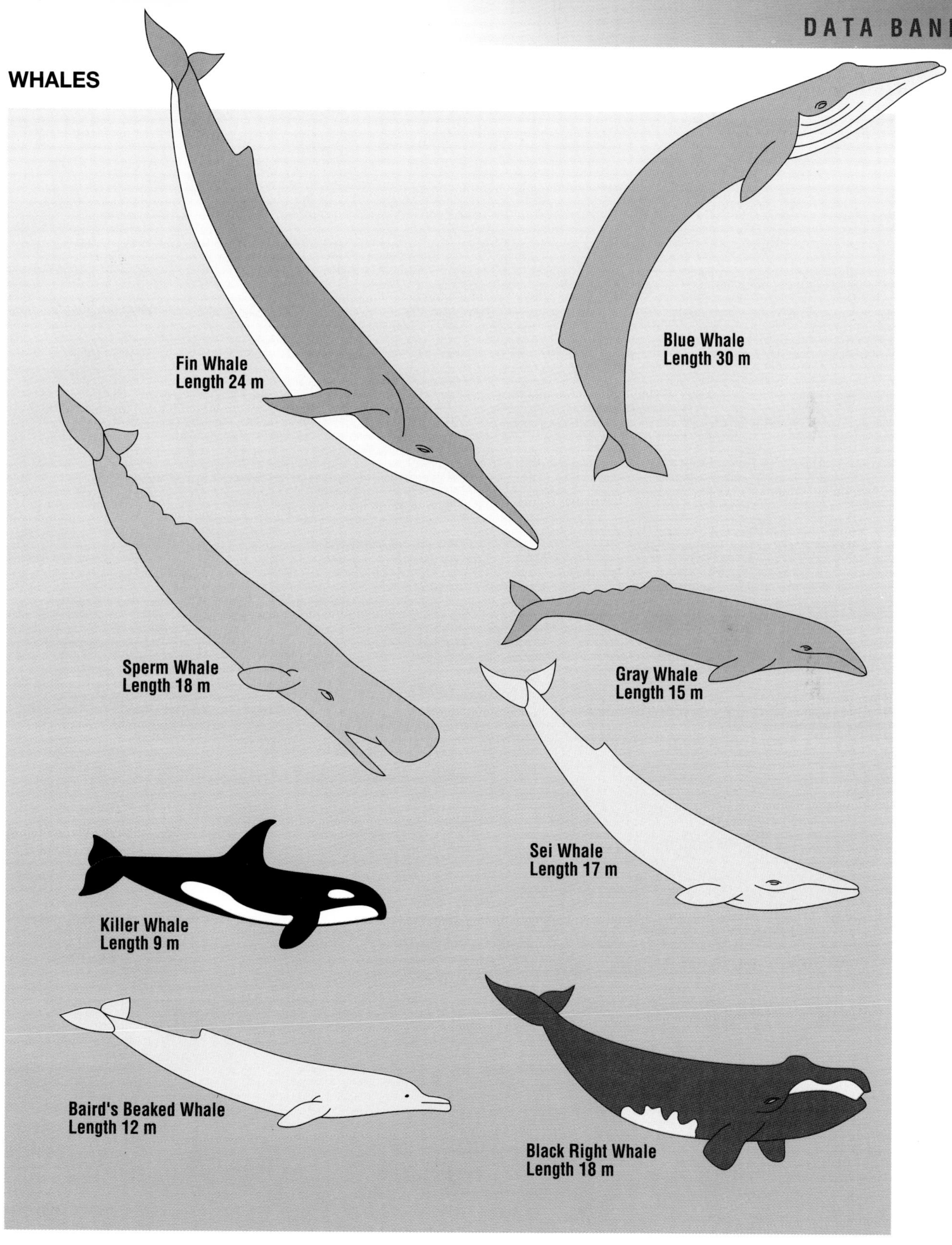
Fin Whale
Length 24 m
Blue Whale
Length 30 m
Sperm Whale
Length 18 m
Gray Whale
Length 15 m
Sei Whale
Length 17 m
Killer Whale
Length 9 m
Baird's Beaked Whale
Length 12 m
Black Right Whale
Length 18 m

TIME ZONES

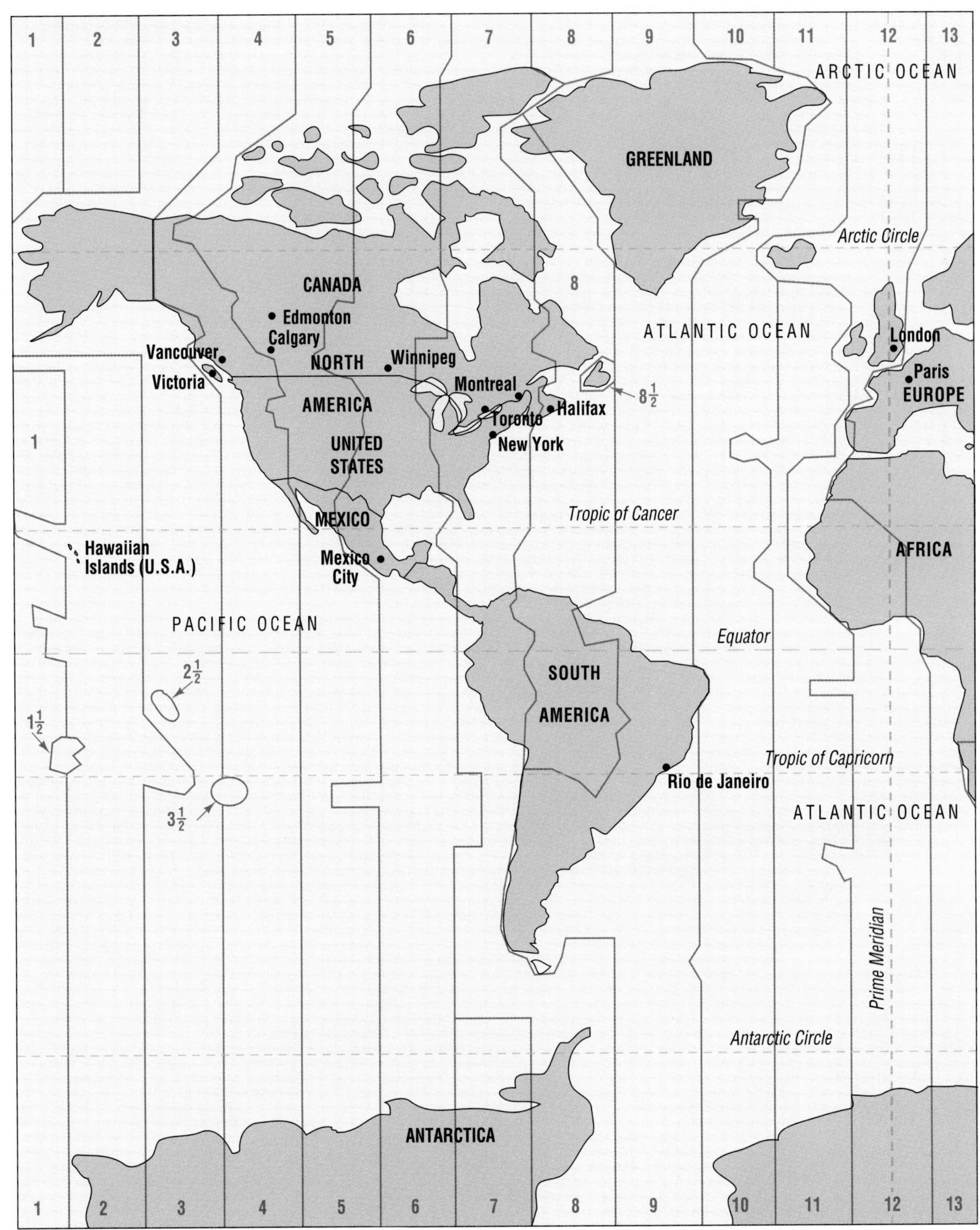
1
2
3
4
5
6
7
8
9
10
11
12
13
ARCTIC OCEAN
GREENLAND
Arctic Circle
CANADA
8
Edmonton
Calgary
ATLANTIC OCEAN
London
Vancouver
NORTH
Winnipeg
Victoria
Montreal
$8\frac{1}{2}$
Paris
EUROPE
AMERICA
Toronto
Halifax
UNITED STATES
New York
1
Tropic of Cancer
MEXICO
Hawaiian Islands (U.S.A.)
AFRICA
Mexico City
PACIFIC OCEAN
Equator
$2\frac{1}{2}$
SOUTH AMERICA
$1\frac{1}{2}$
Tropic of Capricorn
Rio de Janeiro
$3\frac{1}{2}$
ATLANTIC OCEAN
Prime Meridian
Antarctic Circle
ANTARCTICA
1
2
3
4
5
6
7
8
9
10
11
12
13

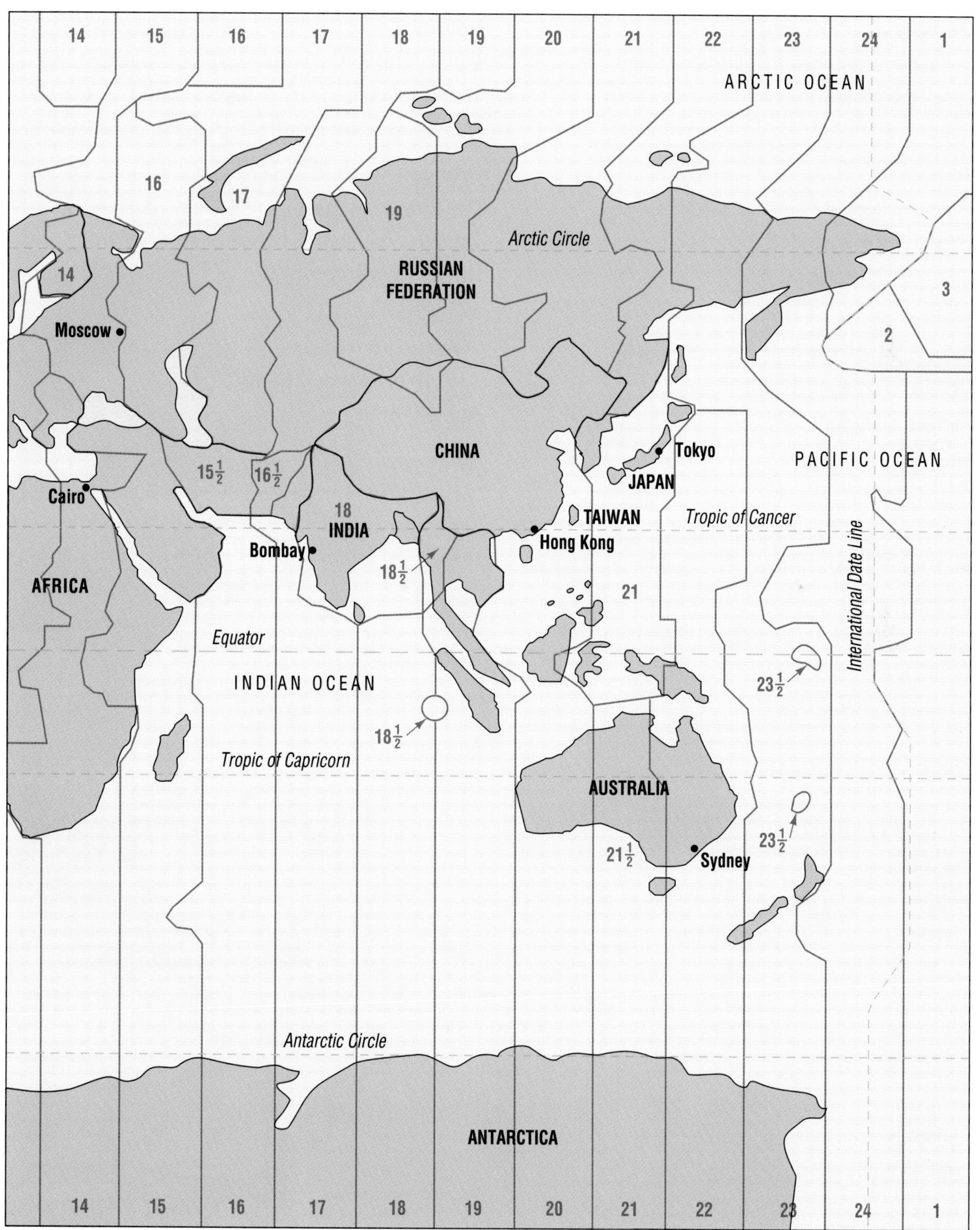
14
15
16
17
18
19
20
21
22
23
24
1
ARCTIC OCEAN
16
17
19
14
Arctic Circle
RUSSIAN
FEDERATION
3
2
Moscow
CHINA
Tokyo
PACIFIC OCEAN
15½
16½
JAPAN
Cairo
18
INDIA
TAIWAN
Tropic of Cancer
Bombay
Hong Kong
International Date Line
AFRICA
18½
21
Equator
INDIAN OCEAN
23½
18½
Tropic of Capricorn
AUSTRALIA
23½
21½
Sydney
Antarctic Circle
ANTARCTICA
14
15
16
17
18
19
20
21
22
23
24
1

PLANETS: DISTANCES, ORBITS, MOONS

Mercury

Distance from the sun: 58 000 000 km

Time to orbit sun: 88 d

Number of moons: 0

Venus

Distance from the sun: 108 000 000 km

Time to orbit sun: 225 d

Number of moons: 0

Earth

Distance from the sun: 150 000 000 km

Time to orbit sun: 1 year

Number of moons: 1

Mars

Distance from the sun: 228 000 000 km

Time to orbit sun: 687 d

Number of moons: 2

Jupiter

Distance from the sun: 779 000 000 km

Time to orbit sun: 12 years

Number of moons: 16

Saturn

Distance from the sun: 1 425 000 000 km

Time to orbit sun: 29.5 years

Number of moons: 18

Uranus

Distance from the sun: 2 870 000 000 km

Time to orbit sun: 84 years

Number of moons: 15

Neptune

Distance from the sun: 4 497 000 000 km

Time to orbit sun: 165 years

Number of moons: 8

Pluto

Distance from the sun: 5 866 000 000 km

Time to orbit sun: 248 years

Number of moons: 1

WIND CHILL CHART

Wind Speed	Thermometer Reading (degrees Celsius) Cold / Very Cold / Bitterly Cold / Extremely Cold														
	4	2	−1	−4	−7	−9	−12	−15	−18	−21	−23	−26	−29	−32	−34
Calm	4	2	−1	−4	−7	−9	−12	−15	−18	−21	−23	−26	−29	−32	−34
8 km/h	3	1	−3	−6	−9	−11	−14	−17	−21	−24	−26	−29	−32	−36	−37
16 km/h	−2	−6	−9	−13	−17	−19	−23	−26	−30	−33	−36	−39	−43	−47	−50
24 km/h	−6	−9	−12	−17	−21	−24	−28	−32	−36	−40	−43	−46	−51	−54	−57
32 km/h	−8	−11	−16	−20	−23	−27	−31	−36	−40	−43	−47	−51	−56	−60	−63
40 km/h	−9	−14	−18	−22	−26	−30	−34	−38	−43	−47	−50	−55	−59	−64	−67
48 km/h	−11	−15	−19	−24	−28	−32	−36	−41	−45	−49	−53	−57	−61	−66	−70
56 km/h	−12	−16	−20	−25	−29	−33	−37	−42	−47	−51	−55	−58	−64	−68	−72
64 km/h	−13	−17	−21	−26	−30	−34	−38	−43	−48	−52	−56	−60	−66	−70	−74

LONGEST RIVERS IN THE WORLD

River	Continent	Length (km)
Nile	Africa	6695
Amazon	S. America	6437
Chang Jiang	Asia	6379
Ob Irtysh	Asia	5410
Huang He	Asia	4672
Congo	Africa	4667
Amur	Asia	4416
Lena	Asia	4400
Mackenzie	N. America	4241
Mekong	Asia	4184
Niger	Africa	4168

HIGHEST MOUNTAIN IN EACH CONTINENT

Mountain	Continent	Height (m)
Everest	Asia	8848
Aconcagua	S. America	6960
McKinley	N. America	6194
Kilimanjaro	Africa	5895
El'brus	Europe	5642
Vinson Massif	Antarctica	5140

DEPTHS AND AREAS OF THE GREAT LAKES

Lake	Depth (m)	Area (km^2)
Superior	405	82 100
Michigan	281	57 600
Huron	229	59 600
Erie	64	25 700
Ontario	244	18 960

Glossary

A

Acute Angle An angle whose measure is less than 90°.

Acute Triangle A triangle with all 3 angles less than 90°.

Altitude of a Triangle A perpendicular line from a vertex to the side opposite that vertex.

Angle The figure formed by 2 rays or 2 line segments with a common endpoint called the vertex.

Angle Bisector A line that divides an angle into 2 equal parts.

Arc A part of the circumference of a circle.

Area The number of square units required to cover a surface.

Average The mean of a set of numbers found by dividing the sum of the numbers by the number of numbers.

Axes The intersecting number lines on a graph. The axes are used for reference in locating points.

B

Bar Graph A graph that uses bars to represent data visually.

Base (of a polygon) Any side may be called the base.

Base (of a power) The number used as the factor for repeated multiplication: 6^3 — Base is 6.

Binary System A number system that consists of the two digits 0 and 1.

Bisector A line that divides a figure into two congruent parts.

Bit The smallest unit of information in a computer.

Broken-Line Graph A graph that represents data, using line segments joined end to end.

Byte A group of 8 bits.

C

Capacity The greatest volume that a container can hold, usually measured in litres or millilitres.

Chord A line segment that joins 2 points on the circumference of a circle.

Circle A closed figure with all of its points the same distance from its centre.

Circle Graph A graph that uses sectors of a circle to show how data is divided into parts by percent.

Circumference The perimeter of a circle: $C = 2 \times \pi \times r$ and $C = \pi \times d$.

Common Denominator A number that is a common multiple of the denominators of a set of fractions: The common denominator of $\frac{1}{2}$ and $\frac{1}{3}$ is 6.

Common Factor A number that is a factor of two or more numbers: 4 and 6 — CF is 2.

Common Multiple A number that is a multiple of two or more numbers: 6, 10 — CMs are 30, 60, 90, ….

Complementary Angles Two angles whose sum is 90°.

Composite Number A number that has more than 2 different factors: $6 = 1 \times 2 \times 3$

Computer Spreadsheet A computer application that stores information in cells and allows a variety of computations to be performed using formulas.

Congruent Figures Figures with the same size and shape.

Coordinate Plane The 2-dimensional or (x, y) plane. Also known as the Cartesian plane.

Coordinates An ordered pair (x, y) that locates a point on a graph.

Corresponding Angles Angles that have the same relative position in geometric figures.

Corresponding Sides Sides that have the same relative position in geometric figures.

Cube A polyhedron with 6 congruent square faces.

Data Facts or information.

Database An organized and sorted list of information, which is usually generated by a computer.

Decagon A polygon with 10 sides.

Decahedron A polyhedron with 10 faces.

Degree (measure of an angle) The unit for measuring angles: $1^\circ = \frac{1}{360}$ of a complete turn.

Denominator The number of equal parts in the whole or the group: $\frac{3}{4}$—The denominator is 4.

Diagonal A line segment joining 2 nonadjacent vertices in a polygon.

Diameter A chord that passes through the centre of a circle.

Discount An amount deducted from the price of an article.

Divisible A number is divisible by another number when the remainder is zero.

Dodecagon A polygon with 12 sides.

Dodecahedron A polyhedron with 12 faces.

Edge The straight line that is formed where 2 faces of a polyhedron meet.

END Statement The last statement in a computer program.

Equation A number sentence that contains the symbol = .

Equilateral Triangle A triangle with all sides equal.

Equivalent Fractions Fractions that represent the same part of a whole or group: $\frac{1}{3}, \frac{2}{6}, \frac{3}{9}, \frac{4}{12}$.

Equivalent Ratios Ratios that represent the same fractional number or amount: 1:3, 2:6, 3:9.

Expanded Form The way in which numbers are written to show the total value of each digit: $235 = 2 \times 100 + 3 \times 10 + 5 \times 1$.

Exponent The raised number used in a power to indicate the number of repeated multiplications of the base: 4^2—The exponent is 2.

Exponential Form A shorthand method for writing numbers expressed as repeated multiplications: $81 = 3 \times 3 \times 3 \times 3 = 3^4$.

Expression A mathematical phrase made up of numbers and variables, connected by operators.

Face A plane surface of a polyhedron.

Factors The numbers that are multiplied to produce a specific product.

Factor Tree A diagram used to factor a number into its prime factors.

Flow Chart An organized diagram that displays the steps in a problem's solution.

Fraction A number that describes part of a whole or part of a group.

Frequency The number of times an item or event occurs.

Frequency Table A table that uses tallies to count data.

Graph A representation of information in pictorial form.

Greatest Common Factor (GCF) The largest factor that two or more numbers have in common:
8, 12, and 24—GCF is 4.

Grid A pattern of dots or lines.

Height The perpendicular distance from a vertex of a polygon to the opposite side.

Heptagon A polygon with 7 sides.

Hexagon A polygon with 6 sides.

Hexahedron A polyhedron with 6 faces.

Hypotenuse The side opposite the right angle in a right triangle.

Image The figure produced by a transformation.

Improper Fraction A fraction whose numerator is greater than its denominator: $\frac{12}{5}$.

Inequality A statement that one expression is greater than, less than, or not equal to another expression.

INPUT Statement A statement that tells the computer a value will be inserted.

Integers Numbers in the sequence ... -3, -2, -1, 0, 1, 2, 3, ...

Intersecting Lines Two lines that cross each other at one point.

Inverse Operations Operations that counteract each other, such as addition and subtraction.

Isosceles Triangle A triangle with 2 equal sides.

LET Statement A statement that assigns a value to a variable in a computer program.

Line A set of points that contains no endpoints.

Line of Symmetry A line that divides a figure into 2 congruent parts.

Line Segment A part of a line. A line segment has 2 endpoints.

Lowest Common Denominator (LCD) The lowest multiple shared by 2 or more denominators: $\frac{1}{8}$, $\frac{1}{6}$—LCD is 24.

Lowest Common Multiple (LCM) The lowest multiple shared by 2 or more numbers: 5, 10, 15—LCM is 30.

Lowest Terms A fraction whose numerator and denominator have no common factors other than 1.

Magnitude Size.

Mapping A correspondence of points between an object and its image.

Mass The amount of matter in an object, usually measured in grams and kilograms.

Mean The sum of the numbers divided by the number of numbers in a set.

Median The middle number in a set of numbers arranged in order. If there is an even number of numbers, the median is the average of the two middle numbers.

Midpoint The point dividing a line segment into 2 equal parts.

Mixed Number A number that is the sum of a whole number and a fraction: $9\frac{5}{8}$.

Mode The number that occurs most frequently in a set of data: 1, 2, 2, 6, 6, 6—Mode is 6.

Multiples Repeated additions within a group: 5, 10, 15, 20 are multiples of 5.

Net A pattern used to construct a polyhedron.

Nonagon A polygon with 9 sides.

Number Line A pictorial representation of a set of numbers.

Numerator The number of equal parts being considered in a whole or group: $\frac{5}{7}$—The numerator is 5.

Obtuse Angle An angle whose measure is more than 90° but less than 180°.

Obtuse Triangle A triangle with 1 angle that measures more than 90°.

Octagon A polygon with 8 sides.

Octahedron A polyhedron with 8 faces.

Opposite Angles The equal angles formed by 2 intersecting lines.

Order of Operations The rules to be followed when simplifying expressions: **1.** brackets **2.** exponents **3.** division and multiplication **4.** addition and subtraction.

Ordered Pair A pair of numbers, (x, y), indicating the x and y coordinates of a point on a graph.

Origin The intersection of the horizontal and vertical axes on a graph. The origin is described by the coordinates (0, 0).

Outcome The result of an experiment.

Parallel Lines Lines in the same plane that never meet.

Parallelogram A quadrilateral with opposite sides parallel and equal in length.

Pentagon A polygon with 5 sides.

Percent A fraction or ratio in which the denominator is 100.

Perfect Number A number whose factors, other than the number itself, add up to the number: 6 = 1 + 2 + 3.

Periods The groups of 3 digits separated by spaces in numbers with more than 4 digits: 123 456 789 contains 3 periods.

Perpendicular Lines Two lines that intersect at a 90° angle.

Perspective The different views of an object: top, bottom, side, front.

Pi (π) The quotient that results when the circumference of a circle is divided by its diameter.

Pictograph A graph that uses pictures or symbols to represent similar data.

Platonic Solids All regular polyhedra.

Polygon A closed figure formed by 3 or more line segments.

Polyhedron A 3-dimensional figure having polygons as faces.

Polyomino A shape made of squares joined along whole edges.

Polyominoid A shape made by joining cubes face to face.

Power A number written in exponential form: 3^4.

Prime Factorization A composite number expressed as a product of prime factors: $42 = 2 \times 3 \times 7$.

Prime Number A number with exactly two different factors, 1 and itself: $3 = 1 \times 3$.

PRINT Statement A line in a computer program. This statement tells the computer what to print.

Prism A polyhedron with two parallel and congruent bases in the shape of polygons. The other faces are parallelograms.

Probability The ratio of the number of ways an outcome can occur to the total number of possible outcomes.

Program A set of instructions that a computer carries out in order.

Proper Fraction A fraction whose numerator is smaller than its denominator: $\frac{2}{3}$.

Proportion An equation which states that 2 ratios are equal: $\frac{3}{4} = \frac{6}{8}$.

Pyramid A polyhedron with one base and the same number of triangular faces as there are sides on the base.

Quadrilateral A polygon with 4 sides.

Quotient A number resulting from division.

Radius The length of the line segment that joins the centre of a circle and a point on the circumference.

Range The difference between the highest and lowest in a set of numbers:
10 to 15 — Range is 5.

Rate A comparison of two measurements with different units: $\frac{9 \text{ m}}{2 \text{ s}}$.

Ratio A comparison of two numbers: 4:5 or $\frac{4}{5}$.

Ray A part of a line. A ray contains one endpoint.

Reciprocals Two numbers whose product is 1.

Rectangle A quadrilateral with opposite sides parallel and equal in length, and four 90° angles.

Rectangular Prism A prism whose bases are congruent rectangles.

Reflection A flip transformation of an object in a mirror or reflection line.

Reflex Angle An angle whose measure is more than 180° but less than 360°.

Regular Polygon A closed figure in which all sides and all angles are equal.

Regular Polyhedron A 3-dimensional figure having identical regular polygons as faces.

Repeating Decimal A decimal where a digit or digits repeat without termination: $\frac{9}{11} = 0.8181818...$ or $0.\overline{18}$.

Rhombus A quadrilateral with opposite sides parallel and all 4 sides equal.

Right Angle An angle whose measure is 90°.

Right Bisector A line that divides another line into 2 congruent segments at a 90° angle.

Right Triangle A triangle with 1 angle that measures 90°.

Rotation A turn transformation of an object about a fixed point or turn centre.

Rotational Symmetry A figure has rotational symmetry if it maps onto itself more than once in a complete turn.

Rounding A process of replacing a number by an approximate number.

RUN Statement The instruction that tells a computer to execute a program.

Sample A selection from the total population available.

Sample Size The number of items selected from the total population.

Scale Drawing An accurate drawing that is either an enlargement or a reduction of an actual object.

Scalene Triangle A triangle with no sides equal.

Set A collection of objects or numbers.

Shell A 3-dimensional object whose interior is empty.

Similar Figures Figures that have the same shape but not always the same size.

Simplest Form The form of a fraction whose numerator and denominator have no common factors other than 1.

Skeleton A representation of the edges of a polyhedron.

Solid A 3-dimensional object whose interior is completely filled.

Square A quadrilateral with 4 equal sides and 4 right angles.

Standard Form The way in which numbers are usually written. The value of each digit is not shown: 453 000.

Stem-and-Leaf Plot Information tabulated so that the last digit is the leaf and the digit or digits in front of it are the stem.

Straight Angle An angle whose measure is 180°.

Substitution The replacement of a variable by a number.

Supplementary Angles Two angles whose sum is 180°.

Surface Area The sum of the areas of the faces of a 3-dimensional figure.

Survey A sampling of information.

Tangram A square cut into 7 shapes: 2 large triangles, 1 medium-sized triangle, 2 small triangles, 1 square, and 1 parallelogram.

Terminating Decimal A decimal whose digits terminate: 3.154.

Tessellation A repeated pattern of geometric figures that will completely cover a surface.

Tetrahedron A polyhedron with 4 triangular faces.

Translation A slide transformation of an object.

Transversal A line that intersects parallel lines.

Trapezoid A quadrilateral with exactly 2 parallel sides.

Triangle A polygon with 3 sides.

Twin Primes A pair of prime numbers that differ by two: 17 and 19.

Unit Fractions Fractions that have 1 as their numerator.

Unit Rate A comparison of two measurements in which the second term is 1: $\frac{3\text{ m}}{1\text{ s}}$ or 3 m/s.

Variable A letter or symbol used to represent a number.

Vertex The common endpoint of 2 rays or line segments.

Volume The number of cubic units contained in a space.

Whole Numbers Numbers in the sequence 0, 1, 2, 3, 4, 5, ...

Index

A

Acropolis, 126
Acute angles, 90
Acute triangle, 98
Addition
- fractions, 176
- integers, 350–351
- mental math, 12
- mixed numbers, 180
- numbers, 18
- order of operations, 72
- solving equations by, 378

Algebra, 367–399
- coordinate plane, 394
- expressions, 370
- number tiles, 368
- ordered pairs, 392–393
- solving equations, 374
  - by addition, 378
  - by division, 379
  - by multiplication, 380
  - by subtraction, 377
  - in two steps, 381
- symbols, 372, 373
- variables, 370
- words, 372

Algebraic logic
- order of operations, 39

Altitude of triangle, 146
Angles, 86, 88
- acute, 90
- bisectors, 440
  - constructing, 440
- complementary, 90
- congruent, 438
  - constructing, 438
- degrees, 88
- interior of triangle, 100
- obtuse, 90
- protractor, 88
- reflex, 90
- right, 90
- straight, 90
- supplementary, 90

Area, 119–155
- estimating, 134
- figures, 140
- measuring, 134
- parallelogram, 142
- perimeter, 136
- rectangle, 138
- square, 138
- surface of polyhedra, 276–277
- triangle, 146
- working with, 150

Average, 322
- range of set, 322

Axis, 394
- *See also* Graphs, axis
- horizontal, 394
- vertical, 394

B

Bar graphs. *See* Graphs, bar
Base
- parallelogram, 142
- triangle, 146

BASIC, 148
- cls, 183
- end, 148
- for, 183
- if … then …, 183
- input, 148
- new, 148
- print, 148
- programming, 149, 183
- run, 148

Binary system, 62
- number theory, 62

Bisectors, 440
- angles, 440
- lines, 440
- right, 440

Brackets in order of operations, 72
Braille, 398
Broken-line graphs. *See* Graphs, broken-line

C

Calculation, 4
- calculator, 4
- choosing a method, 4
- computer, 4
- estimating, 4
- mental math, 4
- paper and pencil, 4

Calculator power, 27
- exponent, 69
- lowest common multiple, 67
- patterns, 397
- repeating decimal fractions, 193
- squares, 331

Calculators
- integers, 360–361
- pattern power, 211, 248
- ratio, 211
- technology, 248

Capacity, 287
- estimating, 287
- mass, 288
- measuring, 287
- volume, 288

Careers
- business, 401
- career day, 453
- community service, 259
- health, 377
- media, 77
- technology, 210
- travel, 157

Carroll, Lewis, 152
Centicube, 282
Circle
- circumference, 128
- diameter, 128

Circle graphs. *See* Graphs, circle; Graphs, pie
Circumference
  circle, 128
  perimeter, 128–129
Codes, 354–355
Commission, 255
  percents, 255
Complementary angles, 90
Composite numbers, 56
Computer calculation, 4
Computer assisted design, 446–447
  technology, 446
Computer databases, 320
  technology, 320
Computer graphics
  technology, 418
  transformations, 418
Computer spreadsheets, 390–391
Computerized home, 31
Congruent figures, 108
  corresponding parts, 108
  geometry, 108
Consumer Price Index, 250
  percents, 250
Coordinate plane, 394–395
  graphs, 396–397
  horizontal axis, 394
  ordered pairs, 394–395
  origin, 394
  vertical axis, 394
  x-axis, 394
  y-axis, 394
Cube, 278
Cyphers, 354–355

D

Data, 302
  collecting, 302, 304–305
  sampling, 302
  statistics, 302, 304–305
Decagon, 104
  regular, 278
Decimal system
  numbers, 8–9
  place value, 8–9
Decimals, 192
  fractions, 192
  percents, 233, 238, 240
  repeating, 192
  terminating, 192
Degrees, 88
  angles, 88
  protractor, 88
Denominator, 170
  fractions, 170
  lowest common, 172
  numerator, 170
  ratio, 206
Design power
  circles and symmetry, 443
  triangles, 103
Diameter of circle, 128
Dinosaur museum, 335
Discount, 232, 252
  percent, 232
  percents, 252
  sale price, 252
Distortions, 425
Divisibility
  factors, 52–53
  rules, 52
  tests, 50–51
Division
  divisibility tests, 50
    factors 52–53
  equations, 379
    solving by 379
  fractions, 187–188
  integers, 358–359
    sign rule 358
  mixed numbers, 190
  numbers, 34–35
  order of operations, 72
  powers of ten, 28–29
  quotients, 28
  reciprocals, 188
  short, 32–33
  zero, by, 33
Dodecahedron, 278
Dodgson, Charles, 152
Dominoes, 406
Doublets, 153

E

Enlargements, 424
Equations, 374
  algebra, 374
  inequalities, 386
  problem solving, 384
  reading, 382
  solving, 374
    by addition, 378
    by division, 379
    by multiplication, 380
    by subtraction, 377
    in two steps, 381
  writing, 382
Equilateral triangle, 98
Escher, M.C., 410
Estimating
  area, 134
  capacity, 287
  fractions
    differences, 174
    sums, 174
  length, 122
  mass, 286–289
  percents, 244
  volume, 282–285
Estimation, 4
  calculation, 4
  differences, 16
  mental math
    products, 24–25
    quotients, 30
  multiplication, 24–25
  quotients, 30
  sums, 16
Exponents, 68–69
  base, 68
  calculator power, 69
  exponential form, 68
  multiplication, 68
  order of operations, 72
  power, 68
Expressions, 370
  algebra, 370

F

Factors, 52
  divisibility, and, 52

greatest common, 64–65
prime, 58–59
Figures
three-dimensional, 266
Flips. *See also* Transformations
reflections, 414
Flow chart, 60
Fox, Terry, 216
Fractions, 163–195
addition, 176
comparing, 172
decimals, 192
denominator, 170
division, 187–188
equivalent, 168
estimating
differences, 174
sums, 174
improper, 170
lowest common denominator, 172
lowest terms, 168
mixed number, 170
multiplication, 182, 184
music, 163
numerator, 170
order of operations, 194
ordering, 172
percents, 232, 238, 240
reciprocals, 186
rounding, 174
simplest form, 168
subtraction, 178
tangram, 165
tick-tack-toe, 166
unit, 177

G

Game show, 334
Geography and geometry, 96
Geometric construction, 435
bisectors, 440
congruent angles, 438
congruent line segments, 438
construction patterns, 436–437
paper airplanes, 450–451
parallel lines, 444–445
perpendiculars, 442–443
polygons, 448–449
Geometry, 81–113
angle, 86
congruent figures, 108
constructions, 435
geography, and, 96
hexagon, 101, 104
illus., 84–85
line, 86
line segment, 86
LOGO, 106
nature, and, 290–291
pentagon, 101, 104
percents, 234
point, 86
polygon, 104
quadrilateral, 101, 104
ray, 86
shapes, 84
tangram, 82–83
three-dimensional. *See* Three-dimensional geometry
triangles, 98–99
Gnomon, 195
Goods and Services Tax, 253
percents, 253
Graphs
bar, 310–311
drawing, 312–313
broken-line, 310–311
drawing, 314–315
circle, 316–317
drawing, 318–319
sector, 318
coordinate plane, 394–397
horizontal axis, 312, 314, 394
ordered pairs, 396–397
picture, 308–309
pie, 316–317
drawing, 318–319
scale of axes, 328–329
stem-and-leaf plots. *See* Stem-and-leaf plots
vertical axis, 312, 314, 394
Greatest common factor (GCF), 64–65
Euclid's method, 65

H

Hectare (ha), 135
Height triangle, 146
Heptagon, 104
Hexagon, 101, 104
regular, 278
vertex, 101
Horizontal axis, 312, 314, 394
Hundred chart, 48–49

I

Icosahedron, 278
Improper fractions, 170
Inequalities, 386
equations, 386
Integers, 341–361
addition, 350–351
calculator, 360–361
comparing, 346
division, 358–359
sign rule, 358
investigating, 349
models, 348
multiplication, 356–357
sign rule, 358
negative numbers, 344
number jigsaw, 342
number line, 346
numbers, 344
ordering, 346
positive numbers, 344
subtraction, 352–353
Interest, 251
loan rate, 251
simple, 251
Interior angles of triangles, 100
Intersecting lines, 94
Isosceles triangle, 98
planes of symmetry, 271

L

Latitude, 195
Length
estimating, 122
measuring, 122
Line segments, 86

congruent, 438
constructing, 438
perpendiculars, 442
Lines, 86
bisectors, 440
constructing, 440
intersecting, 94
parallel, 94
transversal, 94
perpendicular, 94
right bisector, 440
segment, 86
symmetry, 110, 265, 420–421
Lines of symmetry, 110, 265, 420–421
polyhedra, 271
three-dimensional geometry, 265
transformations, 420
Logic power
chess games, 413
clock hands, 87, 89
coin arrangements, 189
coin square, 133
coloured cube in a box, 439
cube stacking, 353
cubes, 35
dropping ball, 223
factors, 151
favourite song, 75
geoboard triangles, 155
geography, 61, 131
gloves, 5
intersecting triangles, 181
map problem, 185
measuring methods, 373
painted cubes, 209
sons and daughters, 307
sports, 281
volume, 285
work relations, 55
LOGO
geometry, 106
rhombus, 272
square, 106, 272
Lowest common denominator (LCD), 172
Lowest common multiple (LCM), 66–67
calculator power, 67

M

Marathon of Hope, 216
maps, 216
Terry Fox, 216
Mass, 286
capacity, 288
estimating, 286–289
measuring, 286–289
volume, 288
Mathematics of a pencil, 2
Mean, 322
range of set, 322
Measuring
area, 134
capacity, 287
length, 122
mass, 286–289
perimeter, 124
volume, 282–285
Median, 324
Mental math, 3, 49, 83, 121, 165, 203, 233, 265, 301, 343, 369, 407, 437
addition, 12
calculation, 4
estimating differences, 16
estimation
products, 24–25
quotients, 30
sums, 16
multiplication, 13
powers of ten, 22
division, 28–29
properties of operations, 13
reciprocals, 186
rounding, 10
subtraction, 12
Mixed numbers, 170
addition, 180
division, 190
fractions, 170
multiplication, 190
subtraction, 180
Mode, 324
Models and integers, 348
Multiplication
equations, 380
solving by, 380
estimation, 24–25
exponential form, 68
exponents, 68
fractions, 182, 184
integers, 356–357
sign rule, 358
mental math, 13
mixed numbers, 190
numbers, 26–27
order of operations, 72
powers of ten, 22
Music and fractions, 163

N

Net, 274
Nets of polyhedra, 274
Nonagon, 104
Number connections, 1–41
Number line, 346
Number power
addition, 313
addition puzzle, 71
binoculars, 25
birthdays, 141
division by zero, 33
factors, 145, 277
fingernail growth, 215
line addition, 247, 357
mean, median, and mode, 325
multiples, 91
number of squares, 441
order of operations, 39, 73
perfect number, 57
sums, 37, 191, 205
triangular addition, 381, 423
unit fractions, 177
Number theory, 47–75
binary system, 62
composite numbers, 56–57
divisibility tests, 50–51
exponents. *See* Exponents
greates common factor. *See* Greatest common factor
hundred chart, 48–49
lowest common multiple. *See* Lowest common multiple
perfect number, 57
prime numbers, 56–57
Number tiles, 368

algebra, 368
Numbers
addition, 18
comparing, 6
composite, 56–57
decimal system, 8–9
division, 34–35
expanded form, 8
integers, 344
line. *See* Number line
mixed, 170
multiplication, 26–27
negative, 344
ordering, 6
percents, 242
perfect, 57
place value, 8–9
positive, 344
prime, 56–57
rounding, 10–11
overestimate, 11
round down, 10
round up, 10
underestimate, 11
standard form, 8
subtraction, 18
theory. *See* Number theory
Numerator, 170
denominator, 170
fractions, 170
ratio, 206

O

Obtuse angles, 90
Obtuse triangle, 98
Octagon, 104
perimeter, 126
regular, 278
Octahedron, 278
Octomino, 407
Order of numbers, 6
Order of operations, 38–39
addition, 72
algebraic logic, 39
brackets, 72
division, 72
exponents, 72
fractions, 194
multiplication, 72
number power, 73
subtraction, 72
Ordered pairs, 392–393
coordinate plane, 394–395
graphs, 396–397
Origin, 394
coordinate plane, 394

P

Paper airplanes, 450–451
Parallel lines, 94
constructing, 444–445
planes, 444
transversal, 94
Parallelogram, 104
area, 142
base, 142
height, 142
Parthenon, 126
Pattern power
calculators, 211, 248
coloured circles, 245
completing equations, 15
dot diagrams, 387
geoboard squares, 105
multiplying decimals, 29
number differences, 179
perimeter, 125
polyhedra, 275
powers, 317
reversed digits, 95
series calculation, 359
technology, 248
Patterns in tables of values, 388
Pentagon, 101, 104
perimeter, 126
regular, 278
vertex, 101
Pentominoes, 119
Percents, 231–257
commission, 255
Consumer Price Index, 250
decimals, 233, 238, 240
designs, 236
discounts, 232, 252
estimating, 244
fractions, 232, 238, 240
geometry, 234
Goods and Services Tax, 253
greater than 100%, 250
numbers, 242
parts of 100, 232
Provincial Sales Tax, 254
simple interest, 251
Perfect number, 57
Perimeter, 119–155
area, 136
circumference, 128–129
measuring, 124
octagon, 126
pentagon, 126
rectangle, 126
square, 126
triangle, 126
working with, 130
Perpendicular lines, 94
Perpendiculars
constructing, 442
geometric constructions, 442–443
line segments, 442
Perpetual calendar, 40
Perspective, 280–281
Pi, 128
Pictograph, 308–309
Picture graph, 308–309
Pie graphs. *See* Graphs, circle; Graphs, pie
Place value
decimal system, 8–9
number, 8–9
Planes and parallel lines, 444
Planes of symmetry
isosceles triangle, 271
polyhedra, 271
Platonic solids, 278–279
Polygon, 104
decagon. *See* Decagon
geometric construction, 448–449
geometry, 104
heptagon. *See* Heptagon
hexagon. *See* Hexagon
nonagon. *See* Nonagon
octagon. *See* Octagon
pentagon. *See* Pentagon
quadrilateral. *See* Quadrilateral

regular, 104
three-dimensional geometry, 265
triangle. *See* Triangles
Polyhedra, 268–269
classifying, 268
cube. *See* Cube
dodecahedron. *See* Dodecahedron
edge, 268
face, 268
icosahedron. *See* Icosahedron
identifying, 268
lines of symmetry, 271
nets of, 274–275
octahedron. *See* Octahedron
planes of symmetry, 271
prism, 268
pyramid. *See* Pyramid
regular, 278
Platonic solids, 278
shell, 270
skeleton, 270
solid, 270
surface area, 276–277
tetrahedron. *See* Tetrahedron
vertex, 268
Polyominoes, 407
Powers of ten
mental math, 22
division, 28–29
multiplication, 22
Prime factors, 58–59
Prime numbers, 56
Prisms, 268
volume, 284
Probability, 330–335
experiment, 330–331, 332
outcome, 330
Problem solving
drawing a diagram, 60
drawing a flow chart, 60
finding missing information, 132
guess and check, 20
identifying extra information, 112
looking for a pattern, 14
making assumptions, 36
sequencing operations, 92
order of operations, 92
solving simpler problem, 74
using a databank, 70
using a formula, 144
using a table, 102
using logical reasoning, 154
work backward, 54
Proportions and ratio, 208
Protractor, 88, 318
angles, 88
degrees, 88
Provincial Sales Tax, 254
percents, 254
Proxima Centauri, 201
Pyramid, 268

Q

Quadrilateral, 101
parallelogram. *See* Parallelogram
polygon, 104
rectangle. *See* Rectangle
regular, 278
rhombus. *See* Rhombus
square. *See* Square
trapezoid. *See* Trapezoid
vertex, 101
Quotients
division, 28
estimation, 30

R

Range of set, 322
Rates, 201–225
unit, 222
unit pricing, 224
Ratio, 201–225
calculators, 211
denominator, 206
equal, 206
equivalent, 206
introduction to, 204
maps, 216
numerator, 206
proportions, 208
scale drawings, 214
scales, 216
technology, 210
triangles, 212
Ray, 86
Reciprocals, 186
division, 188
fractions, 186
mental math, 186
Rectangle, 104
area, 138
perimeter, 126
Reductions, 424
Reflections, 414–415
flips, 414
mirror line, 414
reflection image, 414
reflection line, 414
Reflex angles, 90
Rhombus, 104
LOGO, 272
Right angles, 90
Right bisector of lines, 440
Right triangle, 98
Rotational symmetry, 422
Rotations, 416–417
clockwise, 416
counterclockwise, 416
symmetry, 422
turn centre, 416
turns, 416
Rounding, 10
fractions, 174
mental math, 10
numbers, 10–11
overestimate, 11
underestimate, 11

S

Sample, 306–307
predictions from, 306
Sampling, 302–303
data, 302
Scale drawings, 214
ratio, 214
Scalene triangle, 98
Scales, 216
ratio, 216
Sector of circle, 318

See-saw math, 376
Simple interest, 251
Slides. *See also* Transformations
  translations, 412
Space messages, 426–427
Sphere, 101
Spreadsheets, 390–391
Square, 104
  area, 138
  LOGO, 106, 272
  perimeter, 126
Statistics, 299–335
  average. *See* Average, Mean
  data, 302, 304–305
  graphs. *See* Graphs
  mean. *See* Average, Mean
  median. *See* Median
  mode. *See* Mode
  predictions from samples, 306
  probability. *See* Probability
  range of set, 322
  sampling. *See* Sampling
Stem-and-leaf plots, 326–327
Straight angles, 90
Straight line in a coordinate plane, 394
Subtraction
  equations, 377
    solving by, 377
  fractions, 178
  integers, 352–353
  mental math, 12
  mixed numbers, 180
  numbers, 18
  order of operations, 72
Sundial, 195
  gnomon, 195
Supplementary angles, 90
Surface area, 276
  polyhedra, 276–277
Symbols, 372
  algebra, 372
  words, 372
Symmetry, 110
  lines, 110

T

Tables of values, 388
  patterns, 388
Tangram
  fractions, 165
  geometry, 82–83
  tan, 82
Technology
  calculators, 211, 249, 360
  computer assisted design, 446
  computer calculations, 62
  computer databases, 320
  computer graphics transformations, 418
  computer programs, 148
    BASIC, 148, 149, 183
    LOGO, 106, 271
  computer spreadsheets, 390
  computerized home, 31
  on the job, 210
  spreadsheets, 390–391
  the arts, 248
Tessellations, 410–411
  Escher, M.C., 410
  tiling patterns, 410
Tetrahedron, 278
Tetrominoes, 407
Three-dimensional tick-tack-toe, 63
Three-dimensional geometry, 263–291
  figures, 266
  lines of symmetry, 265
  models, 264
  polygons, 265
Transformations, 405–427
  computer graphics, 418
  distortions, 425
  enlargments, 424
  flips, 408, 414
    image, 408
    tessellation, 410
  lines of symmetry, 420
  reductions, 424
  reflections. *See* Reflections
  rotational symmetry, 422
  rotations. *See* Rotations
  slides, 408, 412
    image, 408
    tessellation, 410
  translations. *See* Translations
  turns, 408, 416
    image, 408
    tessellation, 410
Translations, 412–413
  slides, 412
Transversal, 94
Trapezoid, 104
Triangles, 98
  acute, 98
  altitude, 146
  area, 146
  base, 146
  equilateral, 98
  geometry and, 98–99
  height, 146
  interior angles, 100
    sum of, 100
  isosceles, 98
  obtuse, 98
  perimeter, 126
  polygon, 104
  ratio, 212
  regular, 278
  right, 98
  scalene, 98
  similar, 212
  vertex, 98
Triominoes, 407
Turns. *See also* Transformations
  rotations, 416

U

Unit fractions, 177
Unit pricing, 224
Unit rate, 222

V

Variables, 370
  algebra, 370
Vertex, 98
  hexagon, 101
  pentagon, 101
  polyhedra, 268
  quadrilateral, 101
  triangle, 98
Vertical axis, 312, 314, 394
Volume, 282–285
  capacity, 288

centicube, 282
estimating, 282–285
mass, 288
measuring, 282–285
prisms, 284

Word power
animal names, 449
changing vowels, 241
common letters, 65
country names, 143
creature names, 279
letter changes, 19, 93
prime words, 59
provincial names, 380
reversed words, 371
word changes, 311
word rings, 175, 225
Words, 372
algebra, 372
symbols, 372

x-axis, 394

y-axis, 394

Text Credits

xx top right © 1938 M.C. Escher/Cordon Art Baarn-Holland, **44** Reprinted by permission: Tribune Media Services, **78** Reprinted by permission: Tribune Media Services, **152** "Fit the Fifth: The Beaver's Lesson" by Lewis Carroll which appeared on pages 30–31 of *The Hunting of the Snark* published by Pantheon Books, © 1966 Kelly Oechsli, **198** PEANUTS reprinted by permission of UFS, Inc., **228** Reprinted by permission: Tribune Media Services, **231** Copyright © Ward Lock Educational, U.K., **257** Copyright © 1987, Queen's Printer for Ontario. Reproduced from Wild Furbearer Management in North America, with permission of the Ontario Ministry of Natural Resources., **260** By permission of Johnny Hart and Creators Syndicate Inc., **364** PEANUTS reprinted by permission of UFS, Inc., **402** Reprinted by permission: Tribune Media Services, **410** © 1938 M.C. Escher/Cordon Art Baarn-Holland, **444** By permission of Johnny Hart and Creators Syndicate Inc., **454** Reprinted by permission of Warren Clements

Photo Credits

xiii Ian Crysler, **xiv, xv** Dan Paul, **xviii** Ian Crysler, **xx top left** J.A Kraulis/Masterfile, **xx bottom left** Canapress Photo Service, **xx top centre** Photo courtesy of Royal Bank of Canada, **xx bottom centre** Roland Weber/Masterfile, **xx bottom right** G. Biss/Masterfile, **xxi, xxii** Dan Paul, **xxv** All-Sport UK/Masterfile, **1** NASA, **3** Dan Paul, **7** Canapress Photo Service/Ryan Remiorz, **8** NASA, **13** Ian Crysler, **17** Dan Paul, **22** Ian Crysler, **24 top** National Archives of Canada/Neg. No. PA 61741, **24 bottom** Photo courtesy of Canadian Airlines International, **25** Dan Paul, **26** Masterfile/Barry Blackman, **29** Canapress Photo Service/Roy Antal, **32** Dan Paul, **34** NASA, **35** The Image Bank/David W. Hamilton, **37** UPI/Bettmann, **40** NASA/The Canadian Space Agency, **41 top right** Canapress Photo Service, **41 bottom left** Environment Canada—Parks Service, Alexander Graham Bell National Historic Site, **41 bottom right** Jack Marshall/Canada's Sports Hall of Fame, **41 bottom centre** With the permission of the Department of the Secretary of State of Canada, **46–47** Greg Holman, **50–51, 56** Ian Crysler, **60** Dan Paul, **61** © Bell Canada, 1989. Courtesy Bell Canada Telephone Historical Collection, **64** Stadium Corporation of Ontario, **68** Canada Wide/Mark O'Neill, **71 bottom left** NASA, **71 top right** Masterfile/Wayne Lynch, **72** Ian Crysler, **82** Dan Paul, **84 top right** Reproduced with the permission of Canada Mortgage and Housing Corporation, **84 centre left** Masterfile/David Sailors, **84 centre right** Masterfile/Ben Simmons, **84 bottom left** LEGO ® Brand building bricks are produced by INTERLEGO A.G. Billund, DENMARK, **84 bottom right** Courtesy of Fisher-Price Inc., **85** Imagebank/Marc Romanelli, **85 bottom right** Photo courtesy of the province of British Columbia, **86** Canapress Photo Service, **88** The Bettmann Archive, **90** Photographer Jim Groves. Reproduced courtesy of The Bell Homestead, Brantford, Ont., 1991, **93** Dan Paul **98** Don Ford, **100, 101** Dan Paul, **104** Photo courtesy of the National Gallery of Canada, **108** Dan Paul. With the permission of the Department of the Secretary of State of Canada, **110 top right**, **110 centre left**, **110 bottom right** Dan Paul, **112** The Ontario Ministry of Tourism and Recreation © 1991, **115** Ian Crysler, **122** Dan Paul, **124** Ian Crysler, **126** The Bettmann Archive, **128** Dan Paul, **129** ALLSPORT USA/Russell Cheyne, **134, 135, 136, 137** Dan Paul, **138** Ian Crysler, **142** Dan Paul. Flag of the Federative Republic of Brazil, **148** Dan Paul, **152, 153** The Bettmann Archive, **165, 166** Dan Paul, **168** Ian Crysler, **170** Dan Paul, **172** United Nations Photo, **174** Canapress Photo Service, **178 top right, 178 bottom left** Dan Paul, **183** Ian Crysler, **186, 188** Dan Paul, **193** ALLSPORT USA/Tony Duffy, **195, 206** Dan Paul, **218, 220** Canapress Photo Service, **223** Canadian Pacific Limited, Image no. 1429, **235** Joe Lepiano, **240** Courtesy of the Township of Cumberland, **242** Canapress Photo Service/Hans Deryk, **244** Bob Mummery, Courtesy Edmonton Oilers Hockey Club, **246** Dan Paul, **248** Ian Crysler, **249, 252** Dan Paul, **253** Bianchi Project 7 distributed by Mariah Cycles, Toronto, Canada, **254** Dan Paul, **262–263** Greg Holman, **272–273** Ian Crysler, **276** Courtesy of the Royal Ontario Museum, **282 284, 286, 287** Dan Paul, **290–291** Rafael del Vecchio/Masterfile, **290 left** ZEFA/Masterfile, **290 right** Klaus Hackenberg/Tony Stone Worldwide, **291 top** Freeman Patterson/Masterfile, **291 centre** Gary Black/Masterfile, **291 bottom** Carl Purcell/Masterfile, **300, 304–305, 328, 332** Ian Crysler, **340–341** Joe Lepiano, **360** Dan Paul, **361** Ian Crysler, **368, 372, 382 bottom** Dan Paul, **382 top, 384 top** Ian Crysler, **384 bottom, 386, 390** Dan Paul, **398 top** The Bettmann Archive, **398 bottom** Joe Lepiano, **399** Canine Vision Canada, **406** Dan Paul, **412** All-Sport/Masterfile, **414** Joe Lepiano, **416** Dan McCoy/Masterfile, **420, 422** Dan Paul, **434–435** Greg Holman, **450, 451** Dan Paul

Illustration Credits

xv Pronk&Associates. By permission of Texas Instruments, **xvii** Angela Vaculik, **xix** Andrew Plewes, **xxiii** Kent Smith, **2** Andrée Chevrier, **4** Seth, **5** Michael Herman, **10** Seth, **16** Margo Stahl, **18** James Laish, **20** Andrew Plewes, **24, 28** Kevin Ghiglione, **30** Andrée Chevrier, **31** Margo Davies Leclair/Visual Sense Illustration, **36** Kent Smith, **38** Walt Gunthardt, **39** Pronk&Associates. By permission of Texas Instruments, **45** Michael Herman, **50** Margo Davies Leclair/Visual Sense Illustration, **52** Kent Smith, **53** Margo Davies Leclair/Visual Sense Illustration, **54** Michael Herman, **62, 63** Jun Park, **64** Kevin Ghiglione, **66** Margo Stahl, **70** Margo Davies Leclair/Visual Sense Illustration, **74** Gord

Pronk, **75** James Laish, **80–81** Ted Nasmith, **92** Kevin Ghiglione, **96** James Laish, **102** Andrée Chevrier, **106–107** Jun Park, **118–119** Michael Herman, **120** James Laish, **123** Margo Davies Leclair/Visual Sense Illustration, **132** Jack McMaster, **136** Seth, **137** Michael Herman, **140** Margo Davies Leclair/Visual Sense Illustration, **144** Jack McMaster, **149** Margo Davies Leclair/Visual Sense Illustration, **152, 153** Steven Hutchings, **154** Walt Gunthardt, **162–163** Kent Smith, **166** Margo Davies Leclair/Visual Sense Illustration, **176** Andrée Chevrier, **179** Carl Wiens, **180** Kevin Ghiglione, **181** Carl Wiens, **184** Margo Davies Leclair/Visual Sense Illustration, **187** Jun Park, **190** Michael Herman, **194** Carl Wiens, **200–201** Ted Nasmith, **202** Andrew Plewes, **204** James Laish, **208** Kevin Ghiglione, **209** David Chapman, **210** Kent Smith, **211** Pronk&Associates. By permission of Texas Instruments, **212 top** Margo Davies Leclair/Visual Sense Illustration with the permission of NASA/The Canadian Space Agency, **212 bottom** Margo Davies Leclair/Visual Sense Illustration, **214** Angela Vaculik, **215** David Chapman, **216, 218, 219** James Laish, **220** Seth, **221 bottom** Seth, **221 top right** Walt Gunthardt, **222** Bernadette Lau, **224** Michael Herman, **227** Kevin Ghiglione, **230–231** Kent Smith, **231** Jun Park with permission of Ward Lock Educational, U.K., **232 bottom** Margo Davies Leclair/Visual Sense Illustration, **234** Thach Bui, **236** Andrew Plewes, **238** Margo Davies Leclair/Visual Sense Illustration, **250** David Chapman, **251** Kevin Ghiglione, **255** Angela Vaculik, **256** Tim Halstrom, **266** Jane Whitney, **276** Michael Herman, **278** Angela Vaculik, **286** Seth, **298–299** Tomio Nitto, **300** Michael Herman, **302** Seth, **306** Andrew Plewes, **307** Margo Davies Leclair/Visual Sense Illustration, **310** Steve MacEachern, **312** Angela Vaculik, **314** Michael Herman, **316, 318, 320–321, 322** Kevin Ghiglione, **324** Angela Vaculik, **326, 327** Carl Wiens, **330** Kevin Ghiglione, **334** Walt Gunthardt, **335** David Chapman, **337** Seth, **342** Andrew Plewes, **344** Angela Vaculik, **346** David Chapman, **348** Michael Herman, **354, 355** Paul Zwolak, **358** Michael Herman, **366–367, 370, 374** Michael Herman, **390–391** Margo Davies Leclair/Visual Sense Illustration, **398–399** Pronk&Associates, **401** Michael Herman, **404–405** Ted Nasmith, **408, 409** Steve MacEachern, **418–419** Jun Park, **424, 425** Steve MacEachern, **426, 427** Andrew Plewes, **446–447** Jun Park, **459** Margo Davies Leclair/Visual Sense Illustration

Technical Art by Pronk&Associates.

Additional technical art by: Margo Davies Leclair/Visual Sense Illustration, Jun Park, Jane Whitney